The Great Ideas

THE
GREAT IDEAS
TODAY
1969

WILLIAM BENTON *Publisher*

ENCYCLOPÆDIA BRITANNICA, INC.

Chicago · London · Toronto · Geneva · Sydney · Tokyo · Manila

DISTRIBUTED TO THE TRADE BY:
PRAEGER PUBLISHING, INC., NEW YORK, WASHINGTON

THE GREAT IDEAS TODAY 1969

ROBERT M. HUTCHINS   MORTIMER J. ADLER
Editors in Chief

OTTO BIRD
Executive Editor

Contributors

CLARK KERR	JOHN R. SEELEY	JOHN G. BURKE
EDWARD H. LEVI	JOHN I. GOODLAD	ETIENNE GILSON
NOAM CHOMSKY	HERBERT FEIGL	MARK VAN DOREN

William R. Dell	William Gorman	Frederick Huchting
Managing Editor	*Contributing Editor*	*Assistant Editor*

Will Gallagher	Cynthia Peterson
Art Director	*Associate Art Director*

Donald Rentsch	Geoffrey Ward	Leslie Thompson
Layout Artist	*Senior Picture Editor*	*Picture Editor*

J. Thomas Beatty	Anita Wolff
Production Manager	*Production Coordinator*

Copy Editors

Elizabeth Chastain	Peggy Collins	Mary Reardon

Carol Hanius   *Clerical Assistant*

THE GREAT IDEAS TODAY 1969

A NOTE ON REFERENCE STYLE

In the following pages, passages in *Great Books of the Western World* are referred to by the initials 'GBWW,' followed by volume, page number, and page section. Thus, 'GBWW, Vol. 39, p. 210b' refers to page 210 in Adam Smith's *The Wealth of Nations*, which is Volume 39 in *Great Books of the Western World*. The small letter 'b' indicates the page section. In books printed in single column, 'a' and 'b' refer to the upper and lower halves of the page. In books printed in double column, 'a' and 'b' refer to the upper and lower halves of the left column, 'c' and 'd' to the upper and lower halves of the right column. For example, 'Vol. 53, p. 210b' refers to the lower half of page 210, since Volume 53, James's *Principles of Psychology*, is printed in single column. On the other hand, 'Vol. 7, p. 210b' refers to the lower left quarter of the page, since Volume 7, Plato's *Dialogues*, is printed in double column.

Gateway to the Great Books is referred to by the initials 'GGB,' followed by volume and page number. Thus, 'GGB, Vol. 10, pp. 39-57' refers to pages 39 through 57 of Volume 10 of *Gateway to the Great Books*, which is James's essay, "The Will to Believe."

The Great Ideas Today is referred to by the initials 'GIT,' followed by the year and page number. Thus 'GIT 1968, p. 510' refers to page 510 of the 1968 edition of *The Great Ideas Today*.

PART ONE

The University Today
A Symposium

INTRODUCTION

The university has become front-page news. Usually the occasion is some outburst or commotion on the part of the students. Such activity is the symptom of a deeper-lying malaise. The university has become unsure of itself, and questions are raised regarding its very nature and function and purpose.

The university has become so intimately a part of Western society that its health is integral with that of the whole society. Hence concern with the university reaches outside its own walls to all those concerned with the good life and the good society.

In organizing a symposium on the university we have deliberately restricted our attention to the academic situation in the United States. The crisis of the university is worldwide, and, although some of the problems confronting universities in America and Europe are the same, or at least similar, many are radically different as arising out of very different situations.

We have also deliberately sought out men who not only know the university from within but who also hold different and opposed positions regarding its condition and the remedies needed to improve it. Two of our contributors come from academic administration, but from very different kinds of institutions. Dr. Clark Kerr has long been associated with one of our greatest state universities while Dr. Edward Levi has been identified with one of the foremost private universities. The other two contributors have taken positions often described as "antiadministration." But while they may join in criticism of the existing institution, they differ regarding the special function of the university. Dr. Noam Chomsky defends, as he has illustriously exemplified in his own work in linguistics, the role of the university as a center of research. Dr. John Seeley argues, on the other hand, that the responsibility of the university is primarily if not totally to the student and his personal development.

Much of the criticism directed against the existing university is often more a condemnation of our time and of our society than it is of the university. Hence, we are including as part of our symposium an article by Dr. Mortimer Adler that not only addresses itself to the need for an educational revolution, but also deals directly with the question whether our century is a good time in which to be alive and our country a good place in which to live.

As a contribution to the analysis and discussion of the university we are reprinting three of the basic documents regarding the nature and function of the university: Humboldt's memoir on the organization of institutions of higher learning, the heart of Newman's position as expounded in his *Idea of a University*, and John Stuart Mill's *Inaugural Address* at St. Andrews University.

2

CLARK KERR

Clark Kerr was born in 1911 in Stony Creek, Pennsylvania. He received an A.B. degree from Swarthmore College (1932) and an M.A. from Stanford University (1933). He studied at the London School of Economics and the Institute of International Relations, and was a Traveling Fellow of the American Friends Service Committee (1935–36). After teaching at Antioch College and at the University of California at Berkeley, he returned to the London School of Economics as a Newton Booth Fellow (1938–39). He received his Ph.D. in economics from the University of California, taught at Stanford (1939–40) and at the University of Washington (1940–45), and also served as a public member of the Regional War Labor Board. After the war, he returned to Berkeley to organize the Institute of Industrial Relations at the University and became a Professor of Industrial Relations. In 1952 he was appointed Chancellor of the Berkeley campus. From 1958 until 1967 he was President of the University of California; it nearly doubled in enrollment and was reorganized into nine campuses, three of them new. Since 1967, he has served as chairman and executive director of the Carnegie Commission on Higher Education. Dr. Kerr is a trustee of the Rockefeller Foundation. Widely known as a speaker, he has been the Godkin Lecturer (1963) and Pollak Lecturer (1967) at Harvard, and the Marshall Lecturer (1968) at Cambridge University. His books include The Uses of the University *(1963) and* Labor and Management in Industrial Society *(1964).*

4

The Pluralistic University
in the Pluralistic Society

The university in America is under attack. Much of the attack relates to disagreement over its functions. The attacks come from several directions: from those who look back to former days, from those who want new directions entirely, from those who accept the university of today but want better service from it. A more fundamental reevaluation of the university is going on now than ever before in our history.*

The functions of the university have always been more or less complex and never as simple as some have supposed. The historical tendency has been for university functions to become more complex, and to leave simplicity ever farther behind. Yet there are still those who cry for the simple life, the homogeneous institution.

The university, through its expanding functions, is also ever more central to the life of society; more involved in more of the affairs of more individuals and institutions. Yet there are still those who say the university should stand outside society, or should stand within but serve only one social force—and that social force the one they favor.

The functions of the university have often been controversial and not fully accepted by everyone. Currently the controversy is more intense than in earlier periods. Yet there are those who think that controversy should be foreign to the university.

Complexity, centrality to society, and controversy mark the American university of today. Is this inevitable? Is it to some extent undesirable? And, to the extent it is deemed undesirable, what should be done?

The American university is now almost 100 years of age. The first true university was Johns Hopkins in 1876; Harvard transformed itself from a college into a university during the immediately subsequent period. There were other new beginnings, such as at Chicago and Stanford, and many additional transformations by the time of World War I.

The rise of the university has been the dominant feature of the past century of higher education in the United States. Today there are 200 universities granting the Ph.D. degree. Their enrollments total about

---

* The position in this essay is being developed by the author as "The Function of the University," the Patton Lectures he is delivering at Indiana University in the fall, 1969.

5

2,500,000 students, or roughly 40 percent of all enrollments in higher education; and their expenditures are about 60 percent of all expenditures in that field. These 200 institutions provide much of the direction and the tone for the more than 2,000 campuses of the United States. Their graduates do most of the teaching; their requirements for graduate admission influence the curricula at all levels nearly everywhere; their leaders are the most influential in academic affairs and in national policy toward higher education. Among the 200, 50 universities give 75 percent of the doctoral degrees and carry on most of the research; and these 50 set the pace for the 200.

It is especially these 50 leadership institutions that are today in trouble, and their troubles affect and extend into the 200 and the 2,000, and into all of society. Many of the problems of society are now being fought out at Columbia and Chicago and Madison and Berkeley. The great university is under attack from within and without.

I should like, first, to indicate the nature of the attacks; second, to describe the actual functions, in their multiplicity, now performed by higher education; and, third, to evaluate these functions and propose some reforms from my point of view as a proponent of the pluralistic university in a pluralistic society.

Two points should be made clear in advance of discussing the problems of the American university today.

One point is that the problems of the university assume different but related forms in Rome, Berlin, Paris, London, Tokyo, Calcutta, Madrid, Warsaw, Prague, Moscow, Peking, Buenos Aires; they are found wherever great universities with their concentrations of intellectuals come into contact with the surrounding industrial society, and, of almost equal importance, with their own myriad selves.

The other point is that this is not the first time in history that the functions of the university have been under intense discussion. In England, for example, there were violent discussions when Henry VIII separated Oxford and Cambridge from the Church, when Cromwell separated them from the Crown, when Parliament in the middle of the last century separated them from the Anglican aristocracy; in Germany, at the time of the Thirty Years' War, with the battle over the Reformation that also tore the universities apart, and again when Humboldt started the University of Berlin at the beginning of the nineteenth century; in France, when Napoleon took moribund institutions and sought to turn them into servants of the new state; in the United States, when the newly created modern university began taking over from the classical college a century ago, and later when Lowell and then Hutchins attempted a counterrevolution.

The university in the toils of intense controversy is not limited to this one place—the United States—and this one time—the second half of the twentieth century. The university in many places and at many times

6

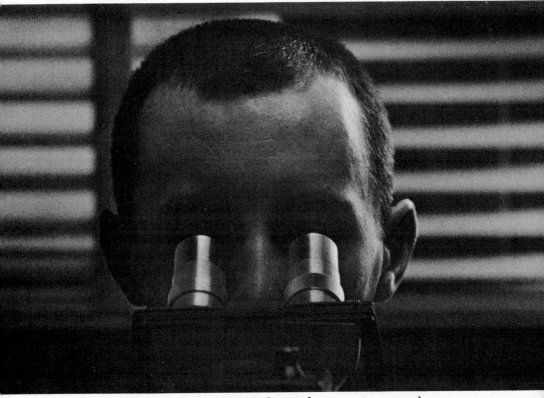

Many in the modern university support this emphasis on pure research, on truth, on new knowledge

has been torn by internal and external conflict; the ivory tower of fond but forgetful memory has often been a bloody battlefield. And the university has always survived, though often changed. It, and the church, are the two most persistent institutions society has known. This has been true in the past. It is true now. It will be true in the future.

RETURNING TO A GOLDEN AGE

There are those who would like the university to return to a Golden Age of purity and harmony. They see in the past their hopes for the future. But which golden age? At least three golden ages now seem attractive to one or another of those concerned with a better vision for higher education. Each of these Golden Ages is quite distinctive; each is essentially incompatible with the others; each has its merits.

1. The "Golden Age of Research" hearkens back to the Johns Hopkins of 1876, and the Humboldt of Berlin in 1809. The emphasis is upon pure research, upon the autonomous scholar, upon "isolation and freedom" and

7

the "pure idea of learning," to quote Humboldt.[1] "It is a further characteristic of higher institutions of learning that they treat all knowledge as a not yet wholly solved problem and are therefore never done with investigation and research." Discovery of truth is the great challenge, the highest aspiration of academic man.

Abraham Flexner,[2] in particular, but many before and since, lamented the fall from grace that came with desertion of the single-minded pursuit of the Holy Grail of Truth. The path down from Humboldt's "summit" led to applied research, to service (the "service station"), to the new professions like business administration, to football stadia, to correspondence courses. This was the "false path" that was followed by all American universities, even Harvard and Johns Hopkins. Rockefeller University alone would have been seen as staying at the "summit."

Many in the modern university support this emphasis on pure research, on truth, on new knowledge. They and their precursors have made enormous contributions to knowledge and, through knowledge, to society, and, in the course of doing so, to the growth and prestige of the university. We know more about physiology, and the health of the people has been improved; about agriculture, and there is more food and fiber; about sources of energy, and there are more material goods; and much else. The pursuit of truth has carried society and the university a very long way forward.

But this Golden Age had its seamy side. It led to the dominance of the full professor in the German university and of the science "star" in the American. It led to ultraspecialization in the curriculum and rigidity in course sequences, as against the broader point of view sought by many students. It led to heavy dependence on the state as the source of research funds in the older Germany and the newer United States alike. It led to a single-minded pursuit of truth in narrow field after narrow field with little or no concern for the broader consequences of the application of piecemeal truth. It led to heavy emphasis on the areas of science where new discoveries could most easily be made, to the neglect of other areas, especially the humanities.

Nor was the purity of the approach easy to defend. How pure is "pure" research? The tendency was always for some scholars to move down the seamless web from the very pure to the wholly applied, with no clear

1 Wilhelm von Humboldt, *Humanist Without Portfolio: An Anthology of the Writings of Wilhelm von Humboldt.* Trans. and intro. by Marianne Cowan. (Detroit: Wayne State University Press, 1963). This memoir is reprinted below, p. 348.

2 Abraham Flexner, *Universities: American, English, German* (New York: Oxford University Press, 1930).

place to draw the line and call a halt. Moreover, it turned out that contact with actual problems to be solved enhanced even the purest of research. World War II was an enormous stimulus to pure research in science, just as the Great Depression was to pure theory in economics. Also, knowledge and service tend to merge. The people with knowledge often have a passion to make it available, and those who can use it want access to it. The transition from knowledge to service, from the laboratory to the "service station," drew inspiration from both the producers and consumers of the new knowledge. The path to this version of sin was downhill all the way; the fall from the "summit" was both inevitable and irreversible. Yet individual summits of pure research have dominant positions in all the great universities.

2. The "Golden Age of the Classics" is a vision that looks back to Cardinal Newman's[3] "idea of a university," to John Stuart Mill's[4] "accumulated treasure of the thoughts of mankind," to Thomas Aquinas, to the Lyceum of Aristotle and the Academy of Plato. The best historical model would perhaps be Oxford as seen by Newman a little over a century ago, before it was changed by Parliament and the scientists. The search was for wisdom as found in the classics, in the "Great Books"; and as refined and applied through dialogue and "free speculation." The "intellectual" and the "moral" were intertwined, as Mill noted in his *Inaugural Address* at St. Andrews in 1867; "knowledge" and "conscience" supported each other. The university should make students "more effective combatants in the great fight which never ceases to rage between Good and Evil." The emphasis was not on the new truth but the old wisdom, on the "liberal knowledge" that Newman thought prepared a man "to fill any post with credit, and to master any subject with facility." The university was for the generalist, not the scientific specialist; it was "a place of teaching universal knowledge"; it was a beautiful ivory tower.

Hutchins and Barzun have led the current laments of those who regret the fading of this great ideal; and Hutchins sought with great courage and some modest effect to resurrect it at Chicago. To Hutchins[5] the uni-

---

3 John Henry Cardinal Newman, *The Idea of a University Defined and Illustrated* (London, 1873). Originally *Discourses on the Scope and Nature of University Education, Addressed to the Catholics of Dublin* (Dublin, 1852), excerpted below, p. 356.

4 John Stuart Mill, "Inaugural Address," delivered to St. Andrews University, Feb. 1, 1867, *Dissertations and Discussions: Political, Philosophical, and Historical,* Vol. IV (Boston, 1867), reprinted below, p. 384.

5 Robert M. Hutchins, *The Learning Society* (New York: Frederick A. Praeger, Inc., 1968; originally "Education: The Learning Society," in *Britannica Perspectives,* ed. Harry S. Ashmore [Chicago: Encyclopædia Britannica, Inc., 1968], Vol. II).

versity has become a "nationalized industry" as a result of the "rise of the nation-state and the beginning of the Industrial Revolution." Hutchins saw as evil influences both the "service" that Flexner hated, and the "research" that Flexner loved, for research leads to specialization and a degradation of the teaching function. The purpose of a university is to have people "think together so that everybody may think better than he would alone," and not to have each go off in his own direction in pursuit of new knowledge or added skills. "Many large American universities appear to be devoted to three unrelated activities: vocational certification, child care, and scientific research." This is a long way from the "ancient ideal" of the "autonomous intellectual community" where "unity and clarity of purpose are fundamental."

To Barzun,[6] "the fabric of the former single-minded, easily defined American university" has been torn apart. Where Hutchins looks all the way back to Aristotle in Athens, Barzun looks back only to Nicholas Murray Butler's rule at Columbia; for the decay Barzun sees has taken place since Butler's retirement at the end of World War II. The university has become "bankrupt in mind and purse" now that it is no longer a "sheltered spot for study only," now that it has entered "the market place." The Manhattan Project, the GI Bill of Rights, the legacy of faculty participation in the New Deal, and of academic advice to a world power, are markers on the road to ruin; and the university has come to cater to "proletarian culture"—even Chicago and Columbia. Only St. John's College, Annapolis, which draws much of its inspiration from Hutchins, remains true to the classics. Barzun is critical of "service," such for example, as helping to meet the needs of urban life. Yet all institutions have rendered service to some segment of society. The service that Barzun favors is service best fitted to the interests of an aristocracy and of the "liberal professions" that draw their members from an aristocracy and cater to it.

This ideal of a perpetual discourse about general ideas today holds the allegiance of many students and a few teachers. It gets resurrected on a grand scale, not as a continuing pursuit but as an *ad hoc* inspiration, when great issues such as civil rights and the war in Vietnam rend the nation. And the university does remain as one of the few places in modern society where fundamental discussions of basic issues can and do take place. In a world of specialists, the university is one of the last hunting grounds for the generalist; and society can be as much aided by better general views as by better specialized research.

Oxford and Cambridge before 1850 and Yale College in 1828 (at the time of the famous faculty report defending the classical curriculum) did

---

6 Jacques M. Barzun, *The American University: How It Runs, Where It Is Going* (New York: Harper & Row, Publishers, 1968).

not appear so golden to their own contemporaries, except to the guilds that ran them. The classical approach looked more to the past than to the present or the future, and thus had a conservative cast. As a result, the campus seemed isolated from the contemporary reality. General discussions lacked the sharpness that comes from attention to actual and specific cases, and often became ideological and sectarian in their nature—it was no accident that many of the teachers were trained in theology. The whole approach either led to or was at least compatible with an *in loco parentis* approach to the students, as insistent concern with a rigid curriculum and the development of "character." Moreover, the approach had greater appeal to the children of an hereditary aristocracy and of a comfortable upper-middle class than to those of workers and farmers; it made a greater contribution to the would-be gentlemen than to the ex-artisans. It was sometimes hostile to science—one of the great and growing streams of human thought. And the contest of Good against Evil came to be fought at least as much by the middle class and the working class, without benefit of a classical education, as by the members of the aristocracy, who were supposed to be the "more effective combatants" by virtue of their education.

The Classical College did not and indeed could not survive as *the* model of the university, nor could it be restored. The spread of democracy meant that opportunity had to be made available to new elements of the population to whom a classical education did not prove so attractive. Industrialization demanded new skills beyond those of a merchant class or a colonial service or the historic professions; it demanded engineers and architects and administrative specialists. No longer could the professions of real value be limited to those that had served the upper classes: the doctors, the lawyers, the ministers. New professions arose and the university came to train for them also. The welfare state brought new demands for teachers, public administrators, and public health personnel. And science could not be ignored. The new culture might be called "proletarian." It was also more democratic, more technological, more oriented toward the general welfare, more scientific. And any university that limited itself to the classics for the aristocracy would have condemned itself to oblivion in the new age—but none chose to do so.

Yet elements of the old Classical College grace any system of higher education, and merit preservation as well as encouragement. In fact, the new leisure class of affluent students is bringing a resurrection, a renewed attention, to "knowledge" and to "conscience."

3. The "Golden Age of the Scholarly Community" looks back to the Middle Ages when small bands of scholars met in face-to-face discussions in a legendary "community of scholars"—with more emphasis on "community" and less on "scholars." One modern version is that of Paul Good-

man,[7] who favors educational communities of a couple of hundred students (150 is suggested as ideal) meeting in free discussion with a few senior persons drawn from practical pursuits in the surrounding society. The historical model cannot be that of the early Bologna, for the students ruled the rebellious professors there; nor of the early Paris, which was under the domination of the church. It may be the early Oxford and Cambridge, before they became highly organized and subject to traditions; or perhaps the religious discussion groups around the monks that congregated at Glendalough in Ireland. In any event, the model, past or proposed, assumes small communities of scholars voluntarily formed, in which everyone participates as equals, but with some having more experience than others. One such community, although rather large in size from this ideal point of view, is the new student-run Rochdale College on the edge of the University of Toronto.

The tutorial and the seminar and the "bull session" may be taken as modern counterparts of the ancient communities of scholars; and each has made and does make a substantial contribution to personal and intellectual development.

The "scholarly community" would seem to fit best those aspects of education which benefit from the oral tradition, the personal example, and the experimental doing of things, like an apprenticeship. It relies less on books and not at all on laboratories—the library is at the center of the Classical College, and the laboratory of the Research University; the small discussion group takes their places in the Scholarly Community. Tests and degrees and formal curricula are not an inherent part of it; in fact, they are rather anathema to it. This approach is better at affecting sensitivity and understanding than at imparting high skills and deep knowledge, or discovering new and complicated relationships.

In a world that also calls for high skills and deep knowledge and new discoveries, the "community of scholars" can at best be an aspect of or an appendage to higher education. It could be the totality of higher learning only when knowledge was more limited and consisted more of beliefs and observations than of intricate theory and complicated facts— only when the world was a simpler place.

And yet this personalized kind of education about the general nature of the world and the individual's place within it holds great and valid attraction for many students in the fragmented and mechanized world of today.

The "golden age" of the Community of Scholars goes back to the days before the printing press, when the oral tradition was supreme; that of the Classical College to an era before the laboratory, when the classical

---

7 Paul Goodman, *The Community of Scholars* (New York: Random House, Inc., 1962).

texts were the greatest source of knowledge; and that of the Research University, to an epoch before egalitarianism and the welfare state became such central features of society and when science was viewed as the great and even the only key to progress. Each "golden age" relates to its own layer of history; each has its great contributions; each has left an important legacy within the higher education of today. Yet no one of these models was as "golden" when it existed as hindsight makes it appear; and none could serve as the sole model for the university of modern times. The earliest of these "golden ages" fitted the religious orders of a more religious era; the next, the aristocracy of a less democratic society; and the last, the scientific elite in a period of rapid industrialization. Why were these earlier models abandoned, and why can they not be re-created readily? Basically the reason is that each one, in turn, became increasingly incompatible with the changed conditions of its society.

FLYING THE FLAG OF DISSENT

O thers view the functions of the university from the perspective not of past models but rather of future possibilities. They emphasize the function of evaluation, criticism, dissent as a central purpose of the university. This function of dissent was a possible activity of each of the "golden age" universities, but it was not a main function. Social change might be a consequence of scientific research; it might be accepted and accommodated effectively by leaders trained in the classical tradition; it might flow from the little communities of scholars. But social change was not the avowed *raison d'etre* of any of them as they actually existed.

Those who see dissent as a central function of the university may be divided into three general groups, with many variations and refinements within each grouping.

1. First, there are those who emphasize the "dissenting professor" and his protection—the professor who individually and of his own free will decides to criticize some aspect of society or society in its totality. The rules governing academic freedom and tenure grow out of the concept of the "dissenting professor." Some believe that the professor, out of his knowledge, has an obligation to provide a free and independent criticism of the surrounding society in his area of specialty. Others view the professor as having a more generalized obligation, as an educated man and a free agent, to comment upon the affairs of society outside as well as inside his specialty. They argue that few other persons are so well stationed and so well equipped to perform this essential service to society. Many of the policies of the American Association of University Professors are aimed at guarantees of this right to dissent. The *Lehrfreiheit* of the German universities was to protect this function. Acceptance of this role,

as *a* role of the professor, is almost universal among the best of the American universities.

2. A more recent development is the call for the "dissenting academy," to use the phrase of Roszak.[8] Here the responsibility of providing dissent is collective, rather than individual: the "central business of the academy is the public examination of man's life with respect to its moral quality"; universities should "cease functioning as the handmaidens of whatever political, military, paramilitary, or economic elite happens to be financing their operations." Galbraith[9] sees this responsibility (or possibility) as extending beyond the universities to the wider circle of the "educational and scientific estate," which, with its increasing numbers and new positions of power, can become a major force for social change. "The responsibility of intellectuals," says Chomsky,[10] is "the creation and analysis of ideology," not just the creation of experts to run society.

The supporters of the "dissenting academy" see the academy, as a collectivity, helping to change society. They seek to have faculties and professional associations as a whole, such as the sociologists, take positions on public issues. Some even seek to have "the University" as a corporate body take positions on the great issues of the day, for "a university that will not speak for man . . . has ceased to be a human enterprise."[11] They do not support violence in these efforts of the academy, on the grounds that violence has no moral validity in an intellectual community and, in any event, is ineffective against the armed power of the state. The reliance is on persuasion and also, perhaps, on passive disobedience. To perform this dissenting function effectively, the academy requires corporate autonomy and freedom from external obligations for its individual members. The campus becomes, in the words of Tussman,[12] "the most crucial of battlefields" where "the essential vitality of society is tested."

3. Beyond the "dissenting academy" lies what may be called the concept of the "partisan camp," the university which serves as a base for guerrilla activity against the surrounding society. This was the successful strategy of Mao in China and of Castro in Cuba, and the unsuccessful effort in 1968 of the student rebels in France. The universities were also one base for violent activity as Hitler conquered Germany. It is argued that the trustees and administrators of the traditional university must be

8 Theodore Roszak, ed., *The Dissenting Academy* (New York: Random House, Inc., 1968).

9 John Kenneth Galbraith, *The New Industrial State* (Boston: Houghton Mifflin Co., 1967).

10 Noam Chomsky, "The Responsibility of Intellectuals," in Roszak, *op. cit.*

11 Richard Lichtman, "The University: Mask for Privilege?" *The Center Magazine*, January 1968.

12 Joseph Tussman, "The Collegiate Rite of Passage," *Experiment and Innovation*, July 1968.

viewed as "occupying powers" and that "terror reigns,"[13] and that the occupying powers should be thrown out and the terror ended. A university, to become "partisan," must have autonomy from control by the police, and internal authority must rest largely in the hands of the students.

Proponents of these latter two views have some things in common. Most are suspicious of the customary service to interest groups outside the university and to the state, as inhibiting the independence for dissent. Generally there is opposition to vocational education, to the training of experts—of "mandarins"—to serve the established order; and to narrowly oriented research unconcerned with its social results. Generally all of them favor broad policy research, an emphasis upon teaching, the encouragement of a moral commitment by students.

Individual dissent is now well accepted within the modern university; the basic battles have been won. It is protected by the rules of the campus and the efforts of the administration. Its costs in public support are generally accepted. It is part of the reality of the pluralistic university as it now exists.

The "dissenting academy" is not accepted. The proponents seek rules or informal actions that discourage or prohibit service and research involving actual or implied commitments to the established order (particularly the "military-industrial complex"), that reward individuals for their contributions to dissenting activities or punish them for "improper" service to the established order, and also, perhaps, that favor the appointment to the faculty of persons with a record of dissent or potentialities for dissent. They may also seek actions by the collective faculty or the collective profession or both, attacking policies of the established order, and appropriate policy statements from the university as a corporate body. For these tasks it is essential to have faculty control of university governance, or at least substantial influence over it, perhaps with student allies. Efforts at such results lead to great internal strains within a faculty, or, if successful, to the development of a faculty or segments of a faculty with a single point of view; to major battles over governing authority with trustees and public bodies; and to public distrust of an institution that is inclined to constant and unified dissent rather than to more or less balanced comments. Some German universities during the Reformation were captured by the Protestants, and others remained under the Catholics, as German society divided. The "dissenting academy" was a divided academy; and this may be the natural tendency at all times and in all places.

The "partisan camp" either helps destroy society or is destroyed by society.

---

13 John R. Seeley, "The Fateful Trumpet, II" (unpublished manuscript, April, 1966).

Even the "partisan university" may have its occasional and temporary place in acting against a clearly oppressive regime

These three views reflect the essential natures of the liberal, the radical, and the revolutionary university. Dissent for the first is an important product; for the second, the main product; and for the last, the sole product.

Dissent, in any of these three forms, has never (with a few temporary exceptions) been the sole or even the central function of actual universities; it has never been the basic organizing principle in the long run.

18

Yet dissent is one function of an academic institution, and a particularly important one if handled effectively, especially now that so many other sources of independent comment, such as the church, the trade union, the independent newspaper editor, have become muted. Even the "partisan university" may have its occasional and temporary place in acting against a clearly oppressive regime (as Harvard and Columbia did before and during the American Revolution, and as Charles University in Prague did in a restrained fashion in the face of the recent Russian invasion). The appropriateness of the nature of dissent is related to time and to place.

Criticisms of the modern university made from the side of dissent sound like many of those from the side of the "golden age." Proponents of each

19

view quote one another in condemnation of the actual university. None, for example, like the "service station" aspect of the modern university; all speak for "free speculation"; and all prefer a simplification of present functions. They vary greatly among themselves, however, in what they would put in place of the university today—the Research University with its laboratories, the traditional College with its classics, the small community of participating scholars and practitioners, the academy dissenting as a collectivity, or the partisan camp. The critics seem united against the modern university, but they stand divided as architects of the new institution that is to take its place. They are comrades in arms as they attack the status quo, but enemies when it comes to putting something in its place.

SERVING THE SPECIAL INTERESTS

C riticism comes also from sources other than from the philosophical positions we have been discussing. It flows from a sense that the university is not providing adequate service for some point of view or some group. These special interests either accept the modern university in general but criticize it specifically, or they are unconcerned with the totality and concentrate only on their own claim for service. The philosophical positions set forth above are more eternal and global in their approach; these special interest positions, more current and particular.

The special interest criticisms spring from many groups:

> From the conservatives, including many parents, who feel that the university is not properly socializing the students in the manners and beliefs of the surrounding community, that the campus is not politically quiet and culturally orthodox, that the campus neglects its duties *in loco parentis.*
>
> From the organized alumni, often conservatives and often parents, who believe that the old campus traditions are not being maintained.
>
> From the employers of the graduates, the consumers of the research, the users of the services, who complain that the work of the university is not practical enough, not useful enough, that industry or agriculture or the trade unions or the elementary and secondary schools or the government are not getting the immediately effective services they want; from all those who say that the graduates should have better vocational skills, research more geared to their immediate needs, services more responsive to their requests.
>
> From students in general, who say that teaching is neglected, that the curriculum is too rigid and too irrelevant, that the routine "grind" goes on endlessly, that even their own parents can no longer perform the *parentis* role; from black students, in particular, who

say the academic life of the white culture is repugnant to them and must be changed.

From neglected areas of the campus such as the humanities, the lesser professions, and the creative arts, which claim more of a place in the sun.

From historically neglected areas in society, such as religious institutions and the newer professions (like real estate), or newly neglected areas, such as the American Legion with its interest in ROTC, which claim their share of attention.

The first four groups want "better" service; the latter two, more service or even some service.

These views about functions demonstrate the variety of expectations that have come to converge on the modern university: that it conserve the past; that it give useful service to the currently powerful forces in society; that it not neglect any group that feels a claim upon its attention. These concerns indicate the myriad groups that feel related to the university, and the extent to which the university is many different things to many different people. A full view of the university requires an appreciation of the claims of these special interests on its functions, an understanding of how potentially useful it has become to how many people.

THE INTRICATE WEB OF FUNCTIONS

It is customary to say that the university has three functions: teaching, research, and service. Actually, as the above discussion has indicated, the pattern of functions is more complicated, and any effort to understand the problem must include a comprehension of the complexities. Neither the actual criticisms of functions nor the possible solutions can be evaluated with the simplified threefold system of categorization.

Higher education may be said to perform a series of services related to production, to consumption, and to citizenship.

1. The functions related to production are all those that potentially add to the output of goods and services in society:

> *The talent hunt.*—the selection, guidance, rating, and placement of students for productive occupations. Higher education acts as a great sorting machine. It rejects as well as selects and grades.

> *The training in vocational, technical, preprofessional, and professional skills.*—This is carried on at three levels: terminal vocational work often included in the junior college program leading to a certificate or an Associate in Arts degree, introductory technical training leading to the Bachelor's and Master's degree, and advanced

professional training leading to the Doctor's degree. Related to this is postgraduate retraining.

Research.

Service.—through formal and informal advice and consultation.

All of these functions are best carried out by specialists and through highly organized programs that proceed in sequence, step by step. They draw support from industry, government, the professions, and the academic world itself. The test of performance is technical competence. The line of authority is from the expert to the novice.

2. The consumption functions are those that relate to current consumption of goods and services by the students or by others in the campus community, or to "durable" consumption through changed tastes, sensitivities, skills, and opportunities that lead to a fuller life for the individual:

General education.—This gives the student a better understanding of his cultural heritage and perhaps of other cultures as well, and assists him to understand more deeply himself and his relationships with others. The classics, with their emphasis on personal character, were once the single chosen instrument for general education. Now there are several approaches available. General education for cultural and recreational purposes is increasingly demanded and is available also at the older adult level.

Provision of community life on campus.—Once this life was highly moral and religious; later it came to be predominantly collegiate—athletics, journalistic activities, fraternities, sororities, and so forth. Currently the emphasis is more on external political activity, on service projects to aid others, on experimental cultures of dress and conduct, on artistic affairs; and increasingly there is the tendency to consider people other than strictly defined members of the campus as part of the "community"—the walls fall down. In the early American colleges, community life was determined by the college itself. Beginning with the movement for student control of extracurricular activities a century ago, the nature of the community life has been more responsive to the changing interests of the students, to the wishes of the peer group.

Custodial.—Students, somehow, must be housed and fed, given medical care and personal counseling, and preferably kept out of trouble during the period between the time they leave the homes of their parents and start their own families.

Holding operation.—Many students, particularly at the lower division, but also at the M.A. level, are uncertain about what they want to do—get a job, get married, get more education, choose a new field of emphasis. The college provides a place for them to be and an excuse for being while they survey their opportunities and make up their minds. The high dropout rate at these levels can also be viewed as a high "drop-in" rate to other activities. The college, by providing a holding pattern for many students, extends their practical range of choices and the time to make these choices, and thus may improve the quality of the choices.

These several functions are best assisted by persons oriented not so much toward subject matter as toward students as individual human beings, and through programs that are flexible and diversified in response to the changing and varied interests of the students. These functions consider the student—not industry, government, the professions, or the academic world—as their main source of orientation. The test of performance is less in technical competence and more in student acceptance. The line of authority is more from the consumer (the student) and less from the teacher and the administrator. Influence over the student relies more on guidance than on control of a technical program. This is the realm for the generalist, not the specialist.

3. The citizenship functions of higher education are those that relate to the performance of students, alumni, and faculty members in relation to their civic responsibilities:

Socialization.—This involves giving the student a basic understanding of the nature of and the rules governing political, economic, and community life. Some would add: indoctrination.

Evaluation.—This calls for critical analysis of the purposes and conduct of established society, and for opportunities to voice objections and make proposals. Some would add: direct social action.

Remedial.—Students drawn from many types of homes, many different communities, many diverse school systems come to the campus with quite different qualities of preparation. Once there, the concept of equality of opportunity requires that provision be made so that deficiencies can be made up and subsequent competition put on a more equal footing.

Returning for a moment to our earlier discussion, the Research University approach ties in most closely to the talent hunt, high level training, and research; the Classical College, to general education; the Community of Scholars, to community life; and the several approaches to dissent, to the function of evaluation.

Higher education over the past few years has seen an enormous shift in the concern attached to these several functions. During and after World War II, with the emphasis upon military and material strength, and going back a century to the rapid industrialization of the United States, the emphasis was upon the functions tied to production. Prolonged prosperity and personal affluence are shifting the emphasis toward the functions tied to consumption, and internal and external political controversies of great intensity, toward functions tied to citizenship. Jobs are more taken for granted, and public policy is less accepted. Higher education is now caught in the turmoil of these historic shifts. The shift is from domination by production considerations toward consumer sovereignty and citizenship participation. Russia, by contrast, still conducts higher education under the domination of production considerations and "socialization" of its own sort. Japan is now shifting violently away from its once predominant emphasis on the functions related to production. In England, the trends are more mixed, partly because the functions related to production were never so heavily emphasized. Other shifts are taking place around the globe in the comparative emphasis upon one function or another. As the emphasis from function to function shifts, the institution is, of course, changed—also the roles and the lives of individuals within it, and they are not passive about these shifts.

THE FUNCTIONING OF THE FUNCTIONS

Toynbee has noted that "there seems to be a worldwide consensus that the traditional system of higher education does not meet, any longer, the educational needs of a more and more rapidly changing society."[14] I should now like to examine how the present functions of higher education relate to a changing society, how adequately they are being performed when viewed one at a time, and how they may best be related to each other in different types of institutions.

1. Higher education is a part of society, not apart from it. It is a partially autonomous subsystem of society. It draws on the material resources of society, and may add to them in the long run as much as or more than it draws out. It reflects the political arrangements of the surrounding society and seldom has much more freedom than is generally provided other institutions and their members, and it almost never has much less freedom. It draws on the accumulated cultural resources of

---

14 Arnold J. Toynbee, "Higher Education in a Time of Accelerating Change," Academy for Educational Development, Paper No. 3, 1968.

its society and, beyond that, of the world, but it can never be far in front of the cultural resources of the world. Thus higher education benefits from rich material resources, a favorable political climate, and cultural growth, and, generally, the more it adds to each, the more in turn it will benefit from each.

Society is changing, and the functions of higher education are changing. The university, like all other human institutions, has always survived by changing, and change always starts from where you are.

The changes now needed in the functions of American higher education related to production, reflecting changes in society, would seem to be these: a search for talent from more elements of society, particularly from low-income groups and disadvantaged minorities; the extension of training into advanced adult levels and newly arising professions and occupations; the development of research into the general consequences of specific research, now that research is increasingly viewed as a potential enemy of mankind rather than as a constant friend; and service to urban life such as the land-grant university has previously provided to rural life.

In the functions related to consumption, the changes encouraged by changes in society include these:

> a great new emphasis on general education, perhaps reoriented around social problems and field service, reflecting the interests of the new generation of affluent students facing a life of greater opportunity beyond work and thus more like the aristocratic clientele of the older Classical College—and this new general education may well include place for more such subjects as the creative arts and religious philosophy;
> much greater stress on the intensity and diversity of community life, reflecting the new vitality and sense of freedom of students, the attraction to them of the view that life is drama, their craving for a variety of personal experiences, their emphasis on peer group culture;
> the rejection of custodial functions by the campus, reflecting the greater maturity of students and the more permissive environments from which they have come—the campus can no longer be a "company town";
> more realization of the importance of the holding-pattern function of some campuses, as access to higher education becomes more nearly universal and is made available to many who may not be fully committed to it.

The first of these directions of change in the functions related to consumption will please Hutchins; the second, Goodman; the third, nearly all students; the fourth, the half of the students who do not go straight through.

The major changes in the functions related to citizenship may well be these: a tendency to count more on the high school for the socialization function; an inevitable increase, at least temporarily, in remedial work; and a new attention to the function of evaluation, both because society is undergoing such great change and because elements on campus are taking such great interest in the direction of these changes.

2. Higher education has fulfilled its individual functions with varying degrees of success.

Generally, the production functions have been well performed. Manpower has been supplied at a high level of skill for an expanding economy, and research has moved well in advance of technology to assist ever higher levels of productivity. However, there are inadequacies aside from lack of full adaptation to the changing nature of the external society as noted already. The talent hunt, according to the best available evidence, has often eliminated the most creative, experimentally minded students. Training facilities have thus far been inadequate to supply the needs for Ph.D's and M.D.'s. Secret research is anathema to the open nature of a campus in that it places students and professors in untenable categories of the "cleared" and the "not cleared"; yet it has been accepted on many campuses.

The consumption functions have been poorly performed. The undergraduate curriculum for the student wanting a liberal education, rather than a vocational preparation, is often a disaster area. It has come under the dictatorship of the graduate program, as Riesman[15] has noted, with its emphasis upon specialization and its downgrading of undergraduate instruction. It serves the research interests of the faculty more than the educational concerns of the students. The guild has been dominant over the interests of the consumers. William Rainey Harper, when founding the University of Chicago, was one of the few who realized how the graduate emphasis of the university might overwhelm the undergraduate concerns of the college, and how they might be incompatible. The development of attractive and inspiring communities for undergraduates has been sadly neglected, with little realization of what a major aspect of their lives is determined by the quality of the communities in which they live. Too little attention has been paid to the possibilities of placing auxiliary enterprises, like residence halls and cafeteria, in the hands of private entrepreneurs or student cooperatives so that consumer tastes and preferences can be reflected more readily than through institutional policies and rules. Additionally, the holding function calls for an affirmative attitude toward the experimental dropout, and not one of condemnation and retribution.

---

15 Christopher Jencks and David Riesman, *The Academic Revolution* (New York: Doubleday & Co., Inc., 1968).

Clark Kerr

The citizenship functions are always more delicate in a society in turmoil than in a society more content with itself. Generally the function of socialization has been handled with balanced description and comment, not with the rigid indoctrination of communist nations. The remedial function has been neglected; it has too often been assumed that all students enter on an equal footing; and too little has been done in working with high schools to improve their performances. The function of evaluation, as noted earlier, is subject to great internal and external debate. To be effective it must be carried out with a reasonable sense of balance so that no important point of view dominates unfairly or is excluded—this approach is in keeping with the morality of academic life that all voices should be heard, and with the need to preserve the credibility of the academic community before the surrounding society; with an emphasis on constructive proposals rather than destructive criticisms alone, for the sake of drawing society toward better solutions; and with reliance on persuasion, since resort to violence is antithetical to devotion to reason and can readily lead to reactions that endanger the essential freedoms of the academic community and even of society. In a volatile political climate tending toward polarization, the academic community should be one of the strongholds of reflection and reason and the arts of persuasion. Generally this has been the approach of the "liberal university" now under such aggressive attack from the more extreme supporters of the "dissenting academy" and all of the supporters of the "partisan camp." The academic community needs to give the most careful consideration to the performance of its evaluative function so that it abides by its own highest principles and helps to meet the needs of the society for better solutions to urgent problems.

Overall, the individual functions more poorly performed are general education and the creation of exciting communities; and the function most in need of clarification is the function of evaluation.

3. Higher education must live with itself as well as with society. Not all functions are equally well performed when combined with others, since some are inherently contradictory. Not all institutions of higher education need be alike; some can specialize in one set of functions and others in another. How best may the several functions be combined?

The two-year community college and the four-year urban college can best serve in the areas of technical training (including related adult education); performance of the holding function (including providing options for advancing into general education and preprofessional work); and remedial work.

The liberal arts college, either as an independent institution, or as a largely independent entity with its own budget and its own curriculum but attached as a "cluster college" to a university, can best perform the functions of general education and the provision of an effective community life, and can help provide general evaluation of society. To perform these functions well, these colleges should glory in their diversity and their flexibility.

The university best supplies advanced technical and professional training (along with the specialized technical school, the state college, and the independent professional school—each in its area of competence and at the appropriate level), research, and service; and its particular contribution to evaluation is in the more technical and specialized areas. General education is less well performed in the monolithic university because of its inherent nature; it is carried on better in a different environment from that of the university, where it has been a notable failure.

It might be said that the community colleges and the urban colleges best serve certain of the citizenship functions; the liberal arts colleges, certain of the consumer functions; and the universities, certain of the production functions. Since the production functions are now particularly well performed, it is the other functions that require the intensified attention that over the past century has been paid to the production functions almost alone.

Each campus must live with itself. Perkins[16] has suggested the goal of "internal coherence": Each activity on the campus should "strengthen the others." The more modest goal suggested above is that the activities be able to coexist effectively with each other, each drawing strength from, and hopefully also adding strength to, the common campus environment; and, thus, that essentially incompatible functions be eliminated—ones that are weakened by others or weaken others. Beyond the compatibility of functions lie the questions of whether they are worthwhile in and of themselves, whether they are suitable to the campus or are more suitably performed elsewhere, and whether they are of a level of quality that matches the general quality of the overall endeavor. The campus does not have a residual function that requires it to fulfill all the otherwise unmet needs of society. It must pick and choose. Internal consistency is one important principle of choice. Thus it has often been neglected.

It deserves a passing note that functions affect other aspects of the university. One is scale. The liberal arts college performs best when small, when it is a community; the junior college when it is moderate in size, when locally oriented; and the university when it is large enough to warrant adequate library and other research facilities, when nationally and internationally oriented. Another aspect is governance. The liberal arts college needs to be particularly responsive to its students, the junior college to its community, and the university to its faculty. A third aspect is financing. The production and citizenship functions have more of a

---

16 James A. Perkins, *The University in Transition* (Princeton, N.J.: Princeton University Press, 1966).

claim on public funds, and the consumption functions on private money.

In summary, five competing views about the proper nature of higher education in the United States now confront the reality of the existing system: the Community of Scholars serving the changing and diverse interests of students, the Classical College serving the generalist, the Research University serving the pursuit of knowledge, the Dissenting Academy serving the reform of society, and the Partisan Camp serving revolutionary change in society. The reality is a pluralistic system in a pluralistic society serving many functions including constant evaluation of society. The single-purpose campus is as unlikely as the single-purpose wife; the nature of both is to serve more than one function. Nor can there easily be a single model for the multipurpose campus, since some functions combine better than others and there are a number of functions in totality to be performed by higher education.

It is relatively easy to attack the current reality from the perspective of a Golden Past that is no longer totally relevant or from that of a Utopian Future that may never be totally realized. It is more difficult to assist higher education as it actually exists, to change as society changes, to improve its individual functions, to preserve its own integrity. This is the greater challenge.

EDWARD H. LEVI

Edward Hirsh Levi was born in Chicago in 1911. He attended the University of Chicago where he received a Ph.B. (1932) and a J.D. (1935), and Yale University where he earned his doctorate as a Sterling Fellow (1935–1938). He was Assistant Professor of Law at the University of Chicago from 1936 until 1940. He then went to Washington as special assistant to the Attorney General. He became first assistant in the War Division (1943), chairman of the interdepartmental committee on monopolies and cartels (1944), and first assistant of the Antitrust Division (1944). After the war, he returned to the University of Chicago as Professor of Law. He became Dean of the Law School in 1950, Provost of the University in 1962, and has served as President of the University since last year. He has acted as: counsel to the subcommittee on monopoly power of the Judiciary Committee of the 81st Congress; member of the research advisory board of the Committee for Economic Development; and member of the board of the Social Science Research Council. He was the Thomas Guest Professor at the University of Colorado in 1960. He is coeditor of Gilbert's Collier on Bankruptcy *(4th ed. 1936) and of* Elements of Law *(1950). His other books are* Introduction to Legal Reasoning *(1949, rev. 1962) and* Four Talks on Legal Education *(1952).*

The University
as Custodian of Reason

I trust I will be forgiven a personal word.* I approach this unlikely moment with many memories. I come to it also with understandable concern. I do not misconceive the importance of this office, which has changed through the years. Rather, the goals, achievement, and tradition of this university are disturbingly impressive. Our university has had a standard of extraordinary leadership, difficult to maintain. I am grateful to Chancellor Hutchins, Chancellor Kimpton, and President Beadle for their presence today. They will understand my anxiety. It is not that we fear mistakes. Perhaps we should fear not to make them. President Hutchins in his address—given forty years ago—spoke of the university's experimental attitude, its willingness to try out ideas, to undertake new ventures, to pioneer. In some cases, he said, the contribution was to show other universities what not to do. Let me say, with rueful pride, since that time we have made many similar contributions. I hope we always will.

It is natural for this university to believe it believes in pioneering. After all, this university came into being as a pioneering first modern university, borrowing ideas from Germany and England, building upon the New England college, joining undergraduate instruction and a panoply of graduate research in what, some said, surely would be a monstrosity—all this done with middle western enthusiasm and a confidence that the best could be obtained here if only it could be paid for. Much has been written of the financial arrangements of those days, the creative use of material resources generously given. But the basic faith was not in material resources. The faith was in the intellectual powers of the mind. It was considered important, more important than anything else in the world, to uncover and understand the cultures of the past, to appreciate the works of the mind, to penetrate the mysteries of the universe, to know more about the environment, the societies, and the nature of man. The university's seriousness of purpose was proven from the first by its insistence

---

* Text of the Inaugural Convocation Address given at the University of Chicago, November 14, 1968.

31

The conditions of public discussion have changed.

upon freedom of inquiry and discussion. Intellectual tests for truth made other standards irrelevant. Schools for the propagation of special points of view might exist, William Rainey Harper wrote, but they could not be called universities. The emphasis on the need to question and reexamine, as part of both the inquiry of research and the inquiry of teaching, established a basic unity for all of the university. The basis of that unity underscored the relationship between teaching and research. That unity encouraged discussion among disciplines. It supported the individual scholar as he crossed accepted boundaries of knowledge. It made possible—even compelled—continuing debate concerning the place of professional, specialized, general, and liberal education within the university. It made the university self-critical.

"On an occasion such as this," as Mr. Kimpton stated on a similar occasion, "the important roles are not played by those who are present. . . . Our efforts are given importance by the opportunities and responsibilities . . . we inherit." So I have stressed those virtues that from the beginning and until now have characterized our institution: a willingness to experiment, a commitment to the intellectual search for truth, a freedom of inquiry, and a concern for the educational process as though the freedom of man depended upon it. This is our inheritance. It is an inheritance preserved and strengthened, indeed made possible, by the action and faith of many who are present today.

We meet in a time of great difficulty. The society is divided. The conditions of public discussion have changed. More people can take part and react because they can be reached. Both the numbers involved and the means of communication increase the likelihood—and certainly the powers—of distortion. The problems are complex; the limits of knowledge are agonizingly apparent in matters of public policy. Meanwhile the investigations of the social sciences have made clearer the nonrational components of human behavior. The relevance and integrity of reason are questioned at the same time as impatience emphasizes the manipulative aspects of concepts and institutions.

The outrage of this war continues.

The view of the world as it is or could be is conditioned for many by the protective walls or barriers of higher education. Formal education at both the college and graduate level is highly regarded as the gateway to success. More than 45 percent of our young people in the applicable age group are in college—an extraordinary change and, with some qualifications, an extraordinary achievement. But the joyous news that the bank of knowledge is overstuffed, and can be drawn upon only with the assistance of the latest generation of computers, adds to the impression of a technical, industrialized society in which individual thought and concern are powerless—in which basic decisions appear to have been made in other times or by other people in other places. The very idea that centers of education are for thoughtful, and therefore personal, consideration of values, and for increased understanding, is lost by those who insist that universities are mechanisms of service to be used in a variety of ways for the interests of the larger community.

There are many institutions for service in our society. Centers of learning and instruction have considerable difficulty in performing their central tasks; one may question the wisdom of assigning to them additional duties. In any event, among colleges, schools, and universities there are important differences. Our history, capacity, and objectives are not all the same. Each institution must find its own mission.

The mission of the University of Chicago is primarily the intellectual search for truth and the transmission of intellectual values. The emphasis must be on the achievement of that understanding that can be called discovery. President Beadle has spoken, as is his special right to do, of "the incomparable thrill of original discovery." He has referred to the importance of having students participate in the process through which knowl-

Centers of education are for thoughtful, and therefore personal, considera-tion of values, and for increased understanding.

edge is reaffirmed and additions to knowledge are made. This, of course, is the process of education—whatever the means used—and it applies to the dialogue as well as to the experiment. We should reaffirm the close connection between the creativity of teaching and the creativity of research. And we should reaffirm also our commitment to the way of reason, without which a university becomes a menace and a caricature.

It is of course easy to be in favor of reason. But the commitment is somewhat more demanding and difficult. President Harper in his decennial report took occasion to emphasize "that the principle of complete freedom of speech on all subjects has from the beginning been regarded as fundamental to The University of Chicago." At the same time he repeated the policy that "The University, as such, does not appear as a disputant on either side upon any public question and . . . utterances which any professor may make in public are to be regarded as representing his opinion only." Academic freedom is stronger now than it was then. But the propriety of the corporate neutrality of the university on public policy issues having moral aspects has been seriously challenged. The position questions the power or persuasiveness of ideas in themselves, recognizes the superior authority of official certification, or places reliance on other forms of power. Perhaps the position reflects the kind of frustration described by Louis Wirth in 1936. Professor Wirth wrote:

> At a time in human history like our own, when all over the world people are not merely ill at ease but are questioning the bases of social existence, the validity of their truths, and the tenability of their norms, it should become clear that there is no value apart from interest and no objectivity apart from agreement. Under such circumstances it is difficult to hold tenaciously to what one believes to be the truth in the face of dissent, and one is inclined to question the very possibility of an intellectual life. Despite the fact that the Western world has been nourished by a tradition of hard-won intellectual freedom and integrity for over two thousand years, men are beginning to ask whether the struggle to achieve these was worth the cost if so many today accept complacently the threat to exterminate what rationality and objectivity have been won in human affairs. The widespread depreciation of the value of thought, on the one hand, and its repression, on the other, are ominous signs of the deepening twilight of modern culture.

The issue raised is central to what a university should be and what it should stand for. It is of course quite true that the ideas of individual scholars in universities are not likely to immediately sway the world, although some have had considerable effect. The tasks which university faculty have undertaken, sometimes within, sometimes without the universities, should not obscure the fact that universities exist for the long run.

They are the custodians not only of the many cultures of man but of the rational process itself. Universities are not neutral. They *do* exist for the propagation of a special point of view; namely, the worthwhileness of the intellectual pursuit of truth—using man's highest powers, struggling against the irrelevancies that corrupt thought, and now standing against the impatience of those who have lost faith in reason. This view does not remove universities from the problems of society. It does not diminish, indeed it increases, the pressure for the creation and exchange of ideas, popular or unpopular, which remake the world. It does suggest that the greatest contribution of universities will be in that liberation of the mind which makes possible what Kenneth Clark has called the strategy of truth. "For," as he says, "the search for truth, while impotent without implementation in action, undergirds every other strategy in behalf of constructive social change." One would hope that this liberation of the mind would result from a liberal education at Chicago at both the undergraduate and graduate levels.

One can well understand the impatience of those who prefer a different relevance of practical action. In some areas, implementation, leading to a more basic examination of consequences and meaning, has been made an appropriate part of training and research. But this may be insufficient to satisfy those who, for the time being at least, and for laudable and understandable reasons, would prefer a different way of life. Nevertheless, they stay within the educational system, caught by its pretense and rigidity. They feel they must stay a long time. Not only has the number of years required for formal education steadily increased as college and graduate work are treated as necessities, but the model presses for the total absorption of the student's interest either in the curriculum or in ancillary activities. We are set on a course that suggests that every young person up to the age of twenty-five, every young family really, should have an educational institution as a surrogate for the world.

Quite apart from the fact that institutions of higher learning should not be surrogates for the world, the satisfaction with which this development is greeted should be tempered. This development in part is a response to distortions caused by the Selective Service System. Much of the education at the graduate level—in some areas, not all—is unnecessary, or even worse is disqualifying, for professional work, as for example the undergraduate teaching for which it is required. I do not expect agreement on that, and I am probably wrong. For some areas I doubt whether the extended time can be justified as a reflection of the increase in knowledge. Rather, it appears as an unimaginative response on the part of the educational system to the existence of increased leisure time within the economy. And if the goal of a college education for everyone is to be met in a way to do the most good, the purposes and ways of that education, even the period of time involved, should be reexamined. I realize this has been done before, but perhaps it will not hurt too much to take another look.

What I am trying to suggest is that for those who are interested in pioneering, there is much to think about. The university is a member of many communities. We cherish the relationship with other universities. We are a member of their world community. We are also an urban university on the South Side of Chicago. In many ways through many activities various members of the university faculties and students are working within the community. We seek to be a good neighbor. Most of us are in fact neighbors. The community has much to offer us. The fact that most of our faculty live here has helped to maintain the oneness and interdisciplinary character of this institution. It has made it possible to measure the effect of new enterprises and responsibilities upon the institution as a whole. This guideline enforces self-restraint. It is, I think, of benefit both to the community and to the university. New models for pediatric care, for counseling and psychiatric assistance, and new approaches to the major problems of urban education should emerge from the endeavors which have been planned and developed with representatives of the community. These are not the only scholarly-service-training activities in which members of the faculty are engaged within the community that have significance far beyond the problems of one neighborhood, and that over time may well determine the quality of life in world urban centers. The work in the complex problems of communities within the city is an encouraging continuation of historic research begun fifty years ago by the Chicago School of Sociology.

In 1902 President Harper referred to the firmly established policy of the trustees "that to the faculties belong to the fullest extent the care of educational administration." "The responsibility," he said, "for the settlement of educational questions rests with the faculty." On this policy the initial greatness of the university was built. The trustees, whether they agreed or not with particular decisions, have been the strongest advocates of this policy. And the faculty have fulfilled this responsibility, protecting on the one hand the freedom of the individual scholar, and shepherding at the same time, although not without some pain, some of the most interesting programs for both undergraduate and graduate instruction attempted in this country. I stress the position of the faculty because obviously the quality of this university rests upon them and is created by them. And the burdens upon them have increased because the conditions of education have changed. Sir Eric Ashby in a notable address at the University of Witwatersrand quoted from an essay on "The Open Universities of South Africa" as follows: "There is no substitute for the clash of mind between colleague and colleague, between teacher and student, between student and student. . . . It is here the half-formed idea may take shape, the groundless belief be shattered, the developing theory be tested. . . . It is here the controversy develops, and out of controversy, deeper understanding." Today when there is doubt and skepticism concerning the very tradition of intellectual freedom and integrity upon which the intellectual pursuit of knowledge is based, it is important that the university through its faculty meet these questions head on.

This university has indeed been fortunate in the dedication which throughout the years it has evoked. It has been surrounded by a circle of friends, who by their aspirations for the university and their own self-sacrifice have assured its pursuit of quality and its inner integrity.

I am proud to be in this place, and I shall do my best.

NOAM CHOMSKY

Noam Chomsky was born in Philadelphia in 1928, and took his bachelor's degree (1949), master's degree (1951), and doctorate (1955) from the University of Pennsylvania. He left Harvard's Society of Fellows, where he had been a Junior Fellow since 1951, to join the faculty of Massachusetts Institute of Technology in 1955. He became a Professor of Modern Languages in 1961, and the Ferrari P. Ward Professor of Modern Languages and Linguistics in 1966. He also teaches undergraduate courses in political and social change. In 1965 Dr. Chomsky became a national sponsor of a citizens' committee to publicize tax refusal as protest against the war in Vietnam. He is a member of the American Academy of Arts and Sciences, the Linguistic Society of America, the American Philosophical Association, the Association for Symbolic Logic, the American Academy of Political and Social Science, and the Aristotelian Society. He is a founder and member of RESIST, and a council member of the International Confederation for Disarmament and Peace. He is the author of Syntactic Structures *(1957),* Current Issues in Linguistic Theory *(1964),* Aspects of the Theory of Syntax *(1965),* Cartesian Linguistics *(1966),* Topics in the Theory of Generative Grammar *(1966), and* Language and Mind *(1968); and coauthor of* The Sound Pattern of English *(1968). A collection of his periodical essays on social issues,* American Power and the New Mandarins, *appeared this year.*

The Function of the
University in a Time of Crisis

Writing 150 years ago, the great liberal reformer and humanist Wilhelm von Humboldt defined the university as "nothing other than the spiritual life of those human beings who are moved by external leisure or internal pressures toward learning and research." At every stage of his life, a free man will be driven, to a greater or lesser extent, by these "internal pressures." The society in which he lives may or may not provide him with the "external leisure" and the institutional forms in which to realize this human need to discover and create, to explore and evaluate and come to understand, to refine and exercise his talents, to contemplate, to make his own individual contribution to contemporary culture, to analyze and criticize and transform this culture and the social structure in which it is rooted. Even if the university did not exist formally, Humboldt observes, "one person would privately reflect and collect, another join with men of his own age, a third find a circle of disciples. Such is the picture to which the state must remain faithful if it wishes to give an institutional form to such indefinite and even accidental activities."[1]

The extent to which existing institutional forms permit these human needs to be satisfied provides one measure of the level of civilization that a society has achieved. One element in the unending struggle to achieve a more just and humane social order will be the effort to remove the barriers —whether they be economic, ideological, or political—that stand in the way of the particular forms of individual self-fulfillment and collective action that the university should make possible.

It is the great merit of the student movement of the 1960's to have helped shatter the complacency that had settled over much of American intellectual life, both with regard to American society and to the role of the universities within it. The renewed concern with university reform is in large measure a consequence of student activism. A great deal of energy has been directed to problems of "restructuring the university": democratizing it, redistributing "power" in it, reducing constraints on student freedom as well as the dependence of the university on outside institutions. I suspect that little can be achieved of real substance along these lines. Formal changes in university structure will have little effect

---

1 "On the Inner and Outer Organization of the Higher Institutions of Learning in Berlin," translated in part in Marianne Cowan, *Humanist Without Portfolio* (Detroit: Wayne State University Press, 1963), reprinted below, p. 348.

on what a student does with his life, or on the relation of the university to society. To the extent that reform does not reach the heart of the university—the content of the curriculum, the interaction between student and teacher, the nature of research, and, in some fields, the practice that relates to theory—it will remain superficial. But it is doubtful that these matters will be significantly affected by the kinds of structural reforms that are now being actively debated on many campuses.

It is pointless to discuss "the function of the university" in abstraction from concrete historical circumstances, as it would be a waste of effort to study any other social institution in this way. In a different society entirely different questions might arise as to the function of the university and the problems that are pressing. To one who believes, as I do, that our society must undergo drastic changes if civilization is to advance—perhaps even to survive—university reform will appear an insignificant matter except insofar as it contributes to social change. Apart from this question, improvements in the university can no doubt take place within the framework of the presently existing "institutional forms," and drastic revision of these forms will contribute little to it.

It is never an easy matter to determine to what extent deficiencies of a particular institution can actually be overcome through internal reform, and to what extent they reflect characteristics of society at large, or matters of individual psychology that are relatively independent of social forms. Consider, for example, the competitiveness fostered in the university, in fact, in the school system as a whole. It is difficult to convince oneself that this serves an educational purpose. Certainly it does not prepare the student for the life of a scholar or scientist. It would be absurd to demand of the working scientist that he keep his work secret so that his colleagues will not know of his achievements and not be helped by his discoveries in pursuing their own studies and research. Yet this demand is often made of the student in the classroom. In later life, collective effort with sharing of discovery and mutual assistance is the ideal; if it is not the norm, we rightly interpret this as an inadequacy of those who cannot rise above personal aggrandizement, and to this extent are incompetent as scholars, scientists, and teachers. Yet even at the most advanced level of graduate education, the student is discouraged by university regulation from working as any reasonable man would certainly choose to do: individually, where his interests lead him; collectively, when he can learn from and give aid to his fellows. Course projects and examinations are individual and competitive. The doctoral dissertation not only is required to be a purely individual contribution; beyond this questionable requirement, there is a built-in bias toward insignificance in the requirement that a finished piece of work be completed in a fixed time span. The student is obliged to set himself a limited goal, and to avoid adventuresome, speculative investigation that may challenge the conventional framework of scholarship, and, correspondingly, runs a high risk of failure. In this respect, the institutional forms of the university encourage mediocrity.

Perhaps this limitation is one reason why it is so common for a scholar to devote his career to trivial modifications of what he has already done. The patterns of thinking imposed in his early work, the poverty of conception that is fostered by too rigid institutional forms, may limit his imagination and distort his vision. That many escape these limitations is a tribute to the human ability to resist pressures that tend to restrict the variety and creativity of life and thought. What is true even at the most advanced levels of graduate education is far more significant at earlier stages, as many critics have eloquently demonstrated. Still, it is not evident, even in this case, to what extent the fault is one of the universities and to what extent it is inherent in the role assigned them in a competitive society, where pursuit of self-interest is elevated to the highest goal.

Some of the pressures that impoverish the educational experience and distort the natural relation of student and teacher clearly have their origin in demands that are imposed on the school. Consider, for example, the sociological problem defined by Daniel Bell: "Higher education has been burdened with the task of becoming a gatekeeper—perhaps the only gatekeeper to significant place and privilege in society; . . . it means that the education system is no longer geared to teaching but to judging."[2] Jencks and Riesman make a similar point: "College is a kind of protracted aptitude test for measuring certain aspects of intelligence and character." The result: "Reliance on colleges to preselect the upper-middle class obviously eliminates most youngsters born into lower-strata families, since they have 'the wrong attitudes' for academic success."[3] The effect is that the university serves as an instrument for ensuring the perpetuation of social privilege.

The same, incidentally, holds for later life. To achieve the Humboldtian ideal, a university should be open to any man, at any stage of life, who wishes to avail himself of this institutional form for enhancing his "spiritual life." In fact, there are programs for bringing corporate executives or engineers from industry to the university for specialized training or simply for broadening their cultural background, but none, to my knowledge, for shoemakers or industrial workers, who could, in principle, profit no less from these opportunities. Evidently, it would be misleading to describe these inequities merely as defects of the university.

In general, there is little if any educational function to the requirement that the university be concerned with certification as well as with education and research. On the contrary, this requirement interferes with its

---

2 Daniel Bell, "The Scholar Cornered," *American Scholar*, XXXVII, No. 3 (Summer, 1968), 401–6.

3 Christopher Jencks and David Riesman, *The Academic Revolution* (New York: Doubleday & Co., Inc., 1968), pp. 104, 100.

proper function. It is a demand imposed by a society that ensures, in many ways, the preservation of certain forms of privilege and elitism.

Or consider the often-voiced demand that the universities serve the needs of the outside society—that its activities be "relevant" to general social concerns. Put in a very general way, this demand is justifiable. Translated into practice, however, it generally means that the universities provide a service to those existing social institutions that are in a position to articulate their needs and to subsidize the effort to meet these needs. It is not difficult for members of the university community to delude themselves into believing that they are maintaining a "neutral, value-free" position when they simply respond to demands set elsewhere. In fact, to do so is to make a political decision, namely, to ratify the existing distribution of power, authority, and privilege in the society at large, and to take on a commitment to reinforce it. The Pentagon and the great corporations can formulate their needs and subsidize the kind of work that will answer to them. The peasants of Guatemala or the unemployed in Harlem are in no position to do so, obviously. A free society should encourage the development of a university that escapes the not-too-subtle compulsion to be "relevant" in this sense. The university will be able to make its contribution to a free society only to the extent that it overcomes the temptation to conform unthinkingly to the prevailing ideology and to the existing patterns of power and privilege.

In its relation to society, a free university should be expected to be, in a sense, "subversive." We take for granted that creative work in any field will challenge prevailing orthodoxy. A physicist who refines yesterday's experiment, an engineer who merely seeks to improve existing devices, an artist who limits himself to styles and techniques that have been thoroughly explored, is rightly regarded as deficient in creative imagination. Exciting work in science, technology, scholarship, or the arts will probe the frontiers of understanding and try to create alternatives to the conventional assumptions. If, in some field of inquiry, this is no longer true, then the field will be abandoned by those who seek intellectual adventure.

These observations are clichés that few will question—except in the study of man and society. The social critic who seeks to formulate a vision of a more just and humane social order, and is concerned with the discrepancy—more often, the chasm—that separates this vision from the reality that confronts him, is a frightening creature who must "overcome his alienation" and become "responsible," "realistic," and "pragmatic." To decode these expressions: he must stop questioning our values and threatening our privilege. He may be concerned with technical modifications of

the university is a legitimate target for protest

existing society that improve its efficiency and blur its inequities, but he must not try to design a radically different alternative and involve himself in an attempt to bring about social change. He must, therefore, abandon the path of creative inquiry as it is conceived in other domains. It is hardly necessary to stress that this prejudice is even more rigidly institutionalized in the state socialist societies.

Obviously, a free mind may fall into error; the social critic is no less immune to this possibility than the inventive scientist or artist. It may be that at a given stage of technology, the most important activity is to improve the internal combustion engine, and that at a given stage of social evolution, primary attention should be given to the study of fiscal measures that will improve the operation of the state capitalism of the Western democracies. This is possible, but hardly obvious, in either case. The universities offer freedom and encouragement to those who question the first of these assumptions, but more rarely to those who question the second. The reasons are fairly clear. Since the dominant voice in any society is that of the beneficiaries of the *status quo*, the "alienated intellectual," who tries to pursue the normal path of honest inquiry—perhaps falling into error on the way—and thus often finds himself challenging the conventional wisdom, tends to be a lonely figure. The degree of protection and support afforded to him by the university is, again, a measure of its success in fulfilling its proper function in a free society. It is, furthermore, a measure of the willingness of the society to submit its ideology and structure to critical analysis and evaluation, and a measure of the willingness to overcome inequities and defects that will be revealed by such critique.

Such problems as these—which will never cease to exist, so long as human society continues—have become somewhat more critical in the last few years for a number of reasons. In an advanced industrial society, the linkage between the university and external social institutions tends to become more tight and intricate, because of the utility of the "knowledge that is produced" (to use a vulgar idiom) and the training that is provided. This is a familiar insight. Half a century ago, Randolph Bourne noted that the World War had brought to leadership a liberal, technical intelligentsia, "immensely ready for the executive ordering of events, pitifully unprepared for the intellectual interpretation or the idealistic focussing of ends"; pragmatic intellectuals who "have absorbed the secret of scientific method as applied to political administration" and who readily "lined up in the service of the war technique." Turning to the university, and taking Columbia University as the prototype, he described it as "a financial corporation, strictly analogous, in its motives and responses, to the corporation which is concerned in the production of industrial commodities . . . The university produces learning instead of steel or rubber, but the nature of the academic commodity has become less and less potent in insuring for the academic workman a status materially different from that of any other kind of employee." The trustees, he claimed, define their obligation in this way: "to see that the quality of the commodity which the university produces is such as to seem reputable to the class which they represent." "Under trustee control," Bourne went on, "the American university has been degraded from its old, noble ideal of a community of scholarship to a private commercial corporation."[4]

Bourne's characterization of the university can be questioned in many respects, but it nevertheless has an unpleasant ring of authenticity, today even more than at the time when he wrote. It will not escape the reader that the student movement of the past few years has—quite independently —developed a very similar critique, often with the same rhetoric. Again, one can point to exaggerations and even flights of fancy, but it would be a mistake to overlook the kernel of truth within it.

A further reason why the problems of the universities have become a more urgent concern than heretofore is that the universities have, on an unprecedented scale, come to be *the* center of intellectual life. Not only scientists and scholars but also writers and artists are drawn to the academic community. To the extent that this is true, to the extent that other independent intellectual communities disappear, the demands on the university increase. Probably this is a factor in the university crises of the past few years. With the depoliticization of American society in the 1950's and the narrowing of the range of social thought, the university seems to have become, for many students, almost the only center of intellectual stimulation. Lionel Trilling, in a recent interview, pointed out that he cannot draw on his own experience as a student to help him comprehend the motivation of the "militant students" at Columbia: "Like all my friends at college, I hadn't the slightest interest in the university as an institution: I thought of it, when I thought of it at all, as the inevitable philistine condition of one's being given leisure, a few interesting teachers, and a library. I find it hard to believe that this isn't the natural attitude . . ."[5] This is an apt comment. In the past, it was for the most part the football and fraternity crowd who had an interest in the university as such. But in this respect there have been substantial changes. Now, it is generally the most serious and thoughtful students who are concerned with the nature of the universities, and who feel hurt and deprived by its failings. Twenty years ago, these students—in an urban university at least—would have looked elsewhere for the intellectual and social life that they now expect the university to provide.

Personally, I feel that the sharp challenges that have been raised by the student movement are among the few hopeful developments of these troubled years. It would be superficial, and even rather childish, to be so

---

4 *The World of Randolph Bourne*, ed. Lillian Schlissel (New York: E. P. Dutton & Co., Inc., 1965).

5 *Partisan Review*, Summer, 1968.

*In the past, it was for the most part the football and fraternity
crowd who had an interest in the university as such*

mesmerized by occasional absurdities of formulation or offensive acts as to
fail to see the great significance of the issues that have been raised and
that lie beneath the tumult. Only one totally lacking in judgment could
find himself offended by "student extremism" and not, to an immensely
greater extent, by the events and situations that motivate it. A person who
can write such words as the following has, to put it as kindly as possible,
lost his grasp of reality: "Quite a few of our universities have already
decided that the only way to avoid on-campus riots is to give students
academic credit for off-campus rioting ('field work' in the ghettos, among
migrant workers, etc.)."[6] Consider the assumptions that would lead one to
describe work in the ghettos or among migrant workers as a form of
"rioting," or, for that matter, to regard work of this sort as necessarily
inappropriate to a college program—as distinct, say, from work on biological warfare or counterinsurgency, which is not described in these terms.
Less extreme, but still seriously distorted, is the perception of the student
movement expressed by George Kennan, who is concerned with what he
sees as "the extremely disturbed and excited state of mind of a good portion of our student youth, floundering around as it is in its own terrifying
wilderness of drugs, pornography, and political hysteria."[7] Again, it is
striking that he is so much less concerned with the "extremely disturbed
and excited state of mind" of those responsible for the fact that the tonnage
of bombs dropped on South Vietnam exceeds the total expended by the
U.S. Air Force in all theatres of World War II, or with those responsible
for the anti-Communist "political hysteria" of the 1950's, or, for that
matter, with that great mass of students who are still "floundering around"
in the traditional atmosphere of conformism and passivity of the colleges,
and whose rioting is occasioned by football victories.

The irrationality which has been all too characteristic of the response

---

6 Irving Kristol, "A Different Way to Restructure the University," *New York Times
Magazine*, December 8, 1968. No less revealing is his next sentence: "And at
Harvard—of all places!—there is now a course (Social Relations 148) which en-
rolls several hundred students and is given for credit, whose curriculum is devised
by the SDS, whose classes are taught by SDS sympathizers, and whose avowed
aim is 'radicalization' of the students." Why, in fact, is it so scandalous that
Harvard ("of all places!") should have a student-initiated course offering a radical
critique of American society and its international behavior?

7 Speech to the International Association for Cultural Freedom on Dec. 2, 1968, at
Princeton, N.J.; *New York Times*, Dec. 4, 1968. Cf. *Democracy and the Student
Left* (Boston: Little, Brown & Co., 1968). Zbigniew Brzezinski, who interprets
the student movement as basically "Luddite," describes Kennan as "in a mood
of rage at the young."

to the student movement is itself a remarkable phenomenon, worthy of analysis. More important, however, is the effort to take the challenge presented by the student movement as a stimulus to critical thinking and social action, perhaps of a quite radical nature—a necessity in a society as troubled as ours, and as dangerous. Since World War II we have spent over a trillion dollars on "defense," and are now expending billions on an infantile competition to place a man on the moon. Our scientists and technologists are preparing to construct an antiballistic missile system at an ultimate cost of many billions of dollars though they know that it will contribute nothing to defense, that in fact it will raise a potentially suicidal arms race to new heights. At the same time, our cities crumble, and millions suffer hunger and want, while those who try to publicize these conditions are investigated by the FBI. It is intolerable that our society should continue to arrogate to itself—in part for consumption, in part for unconscionable waste—half of the far from limitless material resources of the world. There are simply no words to describe our willingness to destroy, on a scale without parallel in the contemporary world, when our leaders detect a threat to the "national goals" that they formulate, and that a passive and docile citizenry accepts. It may appear to be an extreme judgment when a social scientist, a native of Pakistan, asserts that "America has institutionalized even its genocide," referring to the fact that the extermination of the Indians "has become the object of public entertainment and children's games."[8] A look at school texts confirms his assessment, however. Consider the following description in a fourth-grade reader of the extermination of the Pequot tribe by Captain John Mason:

> His little army attacked in the morning before it was light and took the Pequots by surprise. The soldiers broke down the stockade with their axes, rushed inside, and set fire to the wigwams. They killed nearly all the braves, squaws, and children, and burned their corn and other food. There were no Pequots left to make more trouble. When the other Indian tribes saw what good fighters the white men were, they kept the peace for many years.
> "I wish I were a man and had been there," thought Robert.[9]

A child who acquires such attitudes in the schools will become the man who can behave in the way described by a British eyewitness:

> I asked one American who had just ordered a strike on some huts and some sampans (blowing the latter to bits with parts of the boat and the bodies flying in all directions) if air attacks like that did not

---

8 Eqbal Ahmad, in *No More Vietnams?*, ed. Richard M. Pfeffer (New York: Harper & Row, Publishers, 1968).

9 Harold B. Clifford, *Exploring New England*, New Unified Social Studies (Chicago: Follett Publishing Co., 1961).

people shouldn't continue to live here

kill many harmless civilians. "But people shouldn't continue to live here," he said.[10]

It is hardly necessary to add that attitudes created in the schools are supported by the mass media, not only directly, but by their encouragement of a general passivity. There is much truth in the observation of Paul Lazarsfeld and Robert Merton that:

> . . . these media not only continue to affirm the *status quo* but, in the same measure, they fail to raise essential questions about the structure of society. Hence by leading toward conformism and by providing little basis for a critical appraisal of society, the com-

10 Richard West, *Sketches from Vietnam* (London: Jonathan Cape, Ltd., 1968).

*forces that seek to reconstruct social life on a more human
scale on the basis of "participation" and popular control*

mercially sponsored mass media indirectly but effectively restrain the cogent development of a genuinely critical outlook.[11]

This is not the place for an extended discussion; it is enough to point out that, for reasons suggested by these few remarks, it is a matter of great urgency, for ourselves and for world society, that our institutions and ideology be subjected to serious critical analysis. The universities must be a primary object of such analysis and, at the same time, must provide the "institutional form" within which it can be freely conducted. In these specific historical circumstances, it is useful to recall a remark of Bertrand Russell:

> Without rebellion, mankind would stagnate, and injustice would be irremediable. The man who refuses to obey authority has, therefore, in certain circumstances, a legitimate function, provided his disobedience has motives which are social rather than personal.[12]

It is these historical circumstances that define the context for a study of the function of the university and the current challenge to the university.

Reactions to the recent wave of student unrest throughout the world have varied widely. Nathan Glazer asks "whether the student radicals fundamentally represent a better world that can come into being, or whether they are not committed to outdated and romantic visions that cannot be realized, that contradict fundamentally other desires and hopes they themselves possess, and that contradict even more the desires of most other people." He tends toward the latter view; the student radicals remind him "more of the Luddite machine smashers than the Socialist trade unionists who achieved citizenship and power for workers."[13] Consider, in contrast, the reaction of Paul Ricoeur to the massive rebellion of French students in May, 1968:

---

11 "Mass Communication, Popular Taste, and Organized Social Action," in W. L. Schramm, ed., *Mass Communications* (Urbana: University of Illinois Press, 1949); quoted by D. W. Smythe and H. H. Wilson in a study of "Cold War-Mindedness and the Mass Media," in which they conclude that "the principal *function* of the commercially supported mass media in the United States is to market the output of the consumer goods industries and to train the population for loyalty to the American economic-political system"; in *Struggle Against History*, ed. N. D. Houghton (New York: Washington Square Press, 1968).

12 *Power* (New York: W. W. Norton & Co., Inc., 1938), p. 252. He concludes his essay with these words (p. 305): ". . . just as we teach children to avoid being destroyed by motor cars if they can, so we should teach them to avoid being destroyed by cruel fanatics, and to preserve, as far as possible, the instinctive joy of life that is natural to healthy children. This is the task of a liberal education: to give a sense of the value of things other than domination, to help to create wise citizens of a free community, and through the combination of citizenship with liberty in individual creativeness to enable men to give to human life that splendor which some few men have shown that it can achieve."

13 " 'Student Power' in Berkeley," *The Public Interest*, No. 13 (Fall, 1968).

The signs are now eloquent. The West has entered into a cultural revolution which is distinctively its own, the revolution of the advanced industrial societies, even if it echoes or borrows from the Chinese revolution. It is a cultural revolution because it questions the world-vision, the conception of life, that underlie the economic and political structures and the totality of human relations. This revolution attacks capitalism not only because it fails to bring about social justice but also because it succeeds too well in deluding men by its own inhuman commitment to quantitative well-being. It attacks bureaucracy not only because it is burdensome and ineffectual, but because it places men in the role of slaves in relation to the totality of powers, of structures and hierarchical relations from which they have become estranged. Finally, it attacks the nihilism of a society which, like a cancerous tissue, has no purpose beyond its own growth. Confronted with a senseless society, this cultural revolution tries to find the way to the creation of goods, of ideas, of values, in relation to their ends. The enterprise is gigantic; it will take years, decades, a century. . . .[14]

Glazer (like Brzezinski—*see* note 7) sees the student rebels as Luddites, displaced and unable to find their role in the new society of advanced technology and complex social management. They "come from the fields that have a restricted and ambiguous place in a contemporary society."[15] Ricoeur, on the other hand, expresses a very different perception: in the advanced industrial societies in the coming years there will be a sharp conflict between the centralizing force of a technical bureaucracy, managing society for dubious ends, and the forces that seek to reconstruct social life on a more human scale on the basis of "participation" and popular control. Both interpretations sense that a major historical process is underway. They differ in their judgment as to where they expect (and no doubt hope) it will end, and correspondingly, in the interpretation they give of student dissidence and rebellion. Both expect the university to be at the center of the conflict. Optimists may hope that it will be in the eye of the hurricane—but it is more realistic to expect that it will continue to be caught up in controversy and turmoil.

It is hardly in doubt that we are in the midst of a historical process of centralization and bureaucratization not only in the economy but also in politics and social organization. The crisis of parliamentary institutions is a worldwide phenomenon.[16] Reactions can be seen not only in the university rebellions but also in the search for forms of community organization and control—which have forced their way onto the front pages in recent

---

14 *Le Monde*, June 9–10, 1968.

15 Glazer, *op. cit.*

16 For some illuminating discussion, *see* Michael Kidron, *Western Capitalism Since the War* (London: George Weidenfeld & Nicholson, Ltd., 1968).

(ABOVE) MEXICO; (BELOW) GERMANY

ENGLAND

CANADA

JAPAN

*the crisis is a worldwide
phenomenon*

months—and even, it seems, in tentative gropings toward more direct worker's control, often in opposition to the highly bureaucratized trade unions that are increasingly more remote from the day-to-day concerns of those whom the leadership claims to represent.[17] In Eastern Europe there are somewhat analogous developments. The student movement must, I believe, be understood in this more general context. The universities will not be able to isolate themselves from the profound social conflict that appears likely, though its course can hardly be guessed. The linkage of the universities to other social institutions, noted earlier, guarantees this. In fact, there may be very serious questioning, in coming years, of the basic assumption of modern society that development of technology is inherently a desirable, inevitable process; and with it, a critique of the role of the university in advancing knowledge and technique and putting it to use. When students in Western Europe take as their war cry the chant "Ho, Ho, Ho Chi Minh," they are not merely protesting the Vietnam war and the crushing of the poor by the rich that it symbolizes; they are also reacting against the values of industrial society, protesting the role assigned to them as managers of this society, and rejecting the kind of rationality uninformed by any sense of justice, which—as they see it with considerable accuracy—translates into practice as the knowledge how to preserve privilege and order but not how to meet human needs. The American student movement is also animated in part by such concerns.

In many respects, the university is a legitimate target for protest. The unflattering portrait given by such critics as James Ridgeway[18] may be overdrawn, but it is basically realistic, and quite properly disturbing to the concerned student. Recognition of these characteristics of the university leads to revulsion and often militancy. Nevertheless, the problems brought to the surface may be irresoluble within the framework of the university itself. Consider, for example, the matter of government contracts for research. It is a classical liberal ideal, echoed also by Marx, that "Government and church should . . . be equally excluded from any influence on the school."[19] On the other hand, there is little doubt that government research contracts provide a hidden subsidy to the academic budget, by supporting faculty research which would otherwise have to be subsidized by the university. Furthermore, it is quite probable that the choice of research topics, in the sciences at least, is influenced very little by the source of funds, at least in the major universities. It is doubtful that scientific education can continue at a reasonable level without this kind of support. Furthermore, radical students will certainly ask themselves why support from the Defense Department is more objectionable than support from capitalist institutions—ultimately, from profits derived

17 *Ibid.*
18 *The Closed Corporation* (New York: Random House, Inc., 1968).
19 Karl Marx, *Critique of the Gotha Programme* (1875).

by exploitation—or support by tax-free gifts that in effect constitute a levy on the poor to support the education of the privileged.[20] It is impossible to escape the fact that the university is ultimately a parasitic institution, from an economic point of view. It cannot free itself from the inequities of the society in which it exists. At the same time, it is dependent for its existence as a relatively free institution on values that are upheld in the society at large. When, for example, a Senator Fulbright criticizes the universities for having "betrayed a public trust" by associating themselves with the military-industrial complex instead of acting as an independent critical institution, he is expressing the values that permit the university to function as a free institution to the extent that it does. It is not impossible that these values will be a casualty of the domestic turmoil that is itself in part a consequence of American militarism. It would be foolish to remain blind to these dangers.

One legacy of classical liberalism that we must fight to uphold with unending vigilance, in the universities and without, is the commitment to a free marketplace of ideas. To a certain extent, this commitment is merely verbal. The task, however, is to extend, not to limit, such freedom as exists—and it is not inconsiderable. Students are right to ask why faculty members should be permitted to contribute to the weapons cult or to work on counterinsurgency. They also point out, with much justice, that it is unreasonable to claim that this is simply a freely undertaken commitment. Access to funds, power, and influence is open to those who undertake this work, but not, say, to those who would prefer to study ways in which poorly armed guerrillas might combat an enemy with overwhelming technological superiority. Were the university truly "neutral" and "value-free," one kind of work would—as noted earlier—be as well supported as the other. The argument is valid, but does not change the fact that the commitment is nevertheless undertaken with eagerness and a belief that it is right. Only coercion could eliminate the freedom to undertake such work. Once the principle is established that coercion is legitimate, in this domain, it is rather clear against whom it will be used. And the principle of legitimacy of coercion would destroy the university as a serious institution; it would destroy its value to a free society. This must be recognized even in the light of the undeniable fact that the freedom falls far short of ideal.

Those who believe that radical social change is imperative in our society are faced with a dilemma when they consider university reform. They want the university to be a free institution, and they want the individuals in it to use this freedom in a civilized way. They observe that the university—or to be more precise, many of its members—are "lined up in

---

20 Cf. Marx, *op. cit.*, "If in some states of [the United States] the higher educational institutions are also 'free,' that only means in fact defraying the cost of the education of the upper classes from the general tax receipts."

the service of the war technique" and that it often functions in such a way as to entrench privilege and support repression. Given this largely correct observation, it is easy to move to some serious misconceptions. It is simply false to claim—as many now do—that the university exists only to provide manpower for the corporate system, or that the university (and the society) permit no meaningful work, or that the university merely serves to coerce and "channel" the student into a socially accepted life style and ideology; even though it is true that the temptation to make choices that will lead in these directions is very great. To an overwhelming extent, the features of university life that rightly are offensive to many concerned students result not from trustee control, not from defense contracts, not from administrative decisions, but from the relatively free choices of faculty and students. Hence the dilemma noted above. "Restructuring of the university" is unlikely to be effective in eliminating the features of the institution that have sparked student criticism. In fact, many of the concrete proposals that I have seen are, I suspect, likely to have the opposite effect; namely, they may lead toward a system of enforceable regulations that may appear democratic on paper but will limit the individual freedom that exists in an institution that is highly decentralized and rather loose in its structure of decision-making and administration, hence fairly responsive to the wishes of its members.

It is possible to imagine useful reforms; I suspect however that they will have at best a small effect on the way the university functions. The real problem is a much deeper one: to change the choices and personal commitment of the individuals who make up the university. This is much harder than modification of formal structures and is not likely to be effected by such restructuring in any very serious way.

More to the point, I believe, is the view expressed in the Port Huron statement of 1962, more or less the "founding document" of SDS:

> The university is located in a permanent position of social influence. Its educational function makes it indispensable and automatically makes it a crucial institution in the formation of social attitudes. In an unbelievably complicated world, it is the central institution for organizing, evaluating, and transmitting knowledge . . . Social relevance, the accessibility to knowledge, and internal openness—these together make the university a potential base and agency in the movement of social change.
>
> Any new left in America must be, in large measure, a left with real intellectual skills, committed to deliberativeness, honesty, and reflection as working tools. The university permits the political life to be an adjunct to the academic one, and action to be informed by reason.[21]

---

21 Reprinted in Mitchell Cohen and Dennis Hale, eds., *The New Student Left* (Boston: Beacon Press, Inc.; rev. ed., 1967).

University reform, in my opinion, should be directed toward such goals as these: not toward imposing constraints, but rather toward lessening them; not toward enjoining the work that now is often dominant—much of which I personally find detestable—but toward opening up alternatives. This can be done, I think, though it will require a degree of intellectual commitment that has, by and large, been lacking on the part of those concerned with university reform.

The university should compensate for the distorting factors introduced by external demands, which necessarily reflect the distribution of power in extra-university society, and by the dynamics of professionalization which, though not objectionable in itself, often tends to orient study toward problems that can be dealt with by existing techniques and away from those that require new understanding. The university should be a center for radical social inquiry, as it is already a center for what might be called "radical inquiry" in the pure sciences. For example, it should loosen its "institutional forms" even further, to permit a richer variety of work and study and experimentation, and it should provide a home for the free intellectual, for the social critic, for the irreverent and radical thinking that is desperately needed if we are to escape from the dismal reality that threatens to overwhelm us. The primary barrier to such a development will not be the unwillingness of administrators or the stubbornness of trustees. It will be the unwillingness of students to do the difficult and serious work required and the fear of the faculty that its security and authority, its guild structure, will be threatened.

These, I think, are the real barriers to serious reform and innovation in the universities, as matters now stand, though new barriers may arise if these are successfully overcome. These are the primary problems that should motivate and direct efforts to change the university. In general, I think that the so-called new left has a task of historic importance; and I think that this task was formulated quite fittingly in the Port Huron statement, when it spoke of the necessity for "a left with real intellectual skills, committed to deliberativeness, honesty, and reflection as working tools," committed to a political life in which "action is informed by reason."

These are goals that can easily be forgotten in the heat of conflict, but they remain valid ones, and one can only hope that they will be continually resurrected as a guide to positive action.

JOHN R. SEELEY

John R. Seeley, born in 1913 in London, came to the United States in 1940 and received an A.B. degree in Sociology from the University of Chicago in 1942. During the next three years in the Canadian Army, Captain Seeley wrote his first book, The Pulhems Dictionary: A Manual for Manpower Classification (1944). *After the war, he returned to Chicago for postgraduate work and an instructorship in the Social Sciences. In 1947 he became executive officer of the Canadian Mental Health Association, and the following year he joined the faculty of the University of Toronto. In 1953 he went to Indianapolis as executive director of Community Surveys, Inc. He returned to Toronto in 1957 to serve as research director of the Alcoholism Research Foundation, and in 1960 he became Professor of Sociology and then head of the department at York University. From 1963 until 1966 he was connected both with the Massachusetts Institute of Technology, as sociologist in their medical department, and with Brandeis University, as Professor of Sociology and department chairman. Since 1966 he has been Dean and program director of the Center for the Study of Democratic Institutions in Santa Barbara, California. He is co-author of* Crestwood Heights: A Study of the Culture of Suburban Life (1956), Community Chest: A Case Study in Philanthropy (1957), The Alcohol Language (1958), *and* Liver Cirrhosis Mortality as a Means to Measure the Prevalence of Alcoholism (1960). *A selection of his numerous articles appeared in 1967 as* The Americanization of the Unconscious: Collected Essays in Social Psychiatry.

The University
as Slaughterhouse

At a teach-in at the University of California at Berkeley, designed to save the "Berkeley Eleven," two years ago, I referred to that great institution as "The Minimum Security Wing of the California Correctional System." That figure may have been apt for that faraway time, two years ago. But events have moved so rapidly and analysis has revealed so much more that the analogy is evidently inept and belatedly liberal. What I had in mind then was only the fact that if the students, the "trusties," did not properly show appreciation of the liberties generously granted them by "their" Administration in Berkeley, which works hand-in-glove with a "manpower channeling" Administration in Washington, they had the nice alternatives of forced servitude in the medium-security penitentiary, openly so labeled, or the other penitentiary called "The Services." The second choice would add the forced risks of kill or be killed, or both, to the open principle of coerced and uncritical obedience.

The figure of speech, so far as it went, was in the nostalgic days when the University's Graduate School could still grant its 2-S deferment, amounting to virtual exemption from open forced servitude to the State, to those it decided to protect: the obedient and malleable and already advantaged. The university's apparent principal role was to decide in general who was to get the most of what there was to get of Mr. Lasswell's famous trinity: income, deference, and safety. What made the allocation poignant beyond Mr. Lasswell's dreaming was that safety referred not only to physical safety, but to moral safety as well; or, for believers, perhaps even to the question of salvation. Those few not chosen from the many called, or those fewer still *ejected* from the few chosen, were thus cast, if they had not the heroism for prison nor the craft to simulate homosexuality or mental disorder, for the last violation of conscience: the killing, contrary to deepest conviction, of their brothers, at home or abroad, on no warrant that could satisfy even moderately fastidious consciences. Indeed the "bind" the university offered had a diabolical perfection of its own. Those driven by conscience to protest minor injustices and crimes in the university itself in disapproved ways were driven by the university out of its parentally protecting arms and into legally coerced participation in the major crime of direct personal involvement in the more evident and organized slaughter of the disadvantaged. In form and in fact, it was as though those who protested—with less than the expected good manners—against corporal punishment in prisons were given the choice of becoming inmates of those same prisons or paid hangmen in the prison service.

When I say that the figure will no longer serve, I mean that it is now evident that the posture and policy then obtaining was merely a surface manifestation of a deeper and more malignant malady. The university's action and talk on this matter is like a revelatory Freudian slip. It is not that the university erred in its judgment, or was momentarily wicked in expelling and throwing into the waiting maw of Selective Service, its best, most rightly protesting, and dissident students (its veriest own children, under its own devised doctrine of *in loco parentis*). It is rather that that policy and posture dramatized precisely some small part of what the university is and has become. The university stands at the end of and thus "de-termines," a long process of spiritual slaughter, of procured spiritual abortion that begins at the kindergarten or nursery school door and ends at the graduate school gate, and we cannot understand the university's part without seeing the single functional "educational system" whole. The doctoral degree it awards is the mark of success, the significa- tion that "society" has triumphed, in that, so far as possible, a once-upon- a-time potential human being has been machined into a machine part— or, if he, in turn, becomes a professor, has been made into a machine tool to stamp out more machine-parts and more machine-tools. (Of course, there are exceptions, and accidents and failures of "quality control" in all manufacturing processes.) The basic business of the school *from be- ginning to end* is "the corruption of the young," in a sense opposite to that charged against Socrates. And the university crowns, perfects, and completes that process. It also provides, through its Schools of Education especially, the cadres to prepare in the lower educational echelons its future fodder.

The university cannot thus be understood if discussed in isolation from "the college," or the preceding high school, junior high, or grade school. And it cannot be ameliorated or mitigated if it is not understood. Not only does the university, through its assimilated Graduate Schools of Educa- tion, now provide the inferior educational theory by which the guides of the very young guide themselves in self-conception and learn how to act out that conception in practice, but it also trains the key trainers and then accredits, "matriculates," the products of their processing. Thus by omis- sion or commission the university determines or permits what these *eviscerata* shall be. To save the appearances, it goes through a form of complaint against this "input"—as does the high school against the junior high, and in fact every grade-teacher against the next-preceding, and all prior grades. But, that *pro forma* protest entered, the university does not refuse entry, as, I suppose, it hardly *can* morally reject what are, in effect, already its foster-children, fostered by its own graduates, on principles principally taught in its own enterprise. It is all one family. Indeed, despite much rhetoric and a little token action to the contrary, it most gladly accepts the school's most characteristic product: the "docile," in the now-perverted use of that term. The docile in this debased modern usage, are those who have successfully incorporated the basic game of "learning well while remaining responsibly critical." "Responsibly critical," means having a capacity, a trained capacity, to miss the mark of what matters, while making footnote critiques on what doesn't. The apt analogy for this school output is that of "free slaves," encouraged to comment, within limits, on the weight of fetters or the number of ounces of fatback or hog jowl provided or on the proper weight of the lash. On the best school-plantations, there is a great air of highly praised independence, but woe betide these free critics if they make in speech, let alone in act, a critique of the slave system. *That* is labeled extremism; and even a third-grade kid, encouraged by nearly all teachers and taught by the very atmosphere of the school, knows enough to join his class in the laughter or pained silence that follows that kind of well-understood, though never-spoken-of, misbehavior.

I am not telling secrets. Everyone knows the facts. Those that are not on film or in fiction are in well-attested print. It is indeed now a proud claim that the school—meaning the entire kit and caboodle from Grade 0 in kindergarten to Grade 19 at Ph.D. or Grade 22 after post-doctoral training—is the society's "principal instrument of socialization." The very word is university-born, as well as university-borne, and so are the subtler techniques in the exercise thereof. Socialization is the "value-free" word for what the kids call "co-optation," and what in a more old-fashioned vocabulary was called corruption. Its essence lies in the "internalization," to be achieved as cunningly, covertly, and smoothly as possible, of "the society's norms." The two missing terms of reference—the Self, and the achievement of its fullness and integrity, and the Good against which "the society's norms" are to be tested and criticized, to be reformed, made over, or overthrown—have simply disappeared from thought and polite discourse. More precisely, "socialization" theory and practice—standing high reason and even common sense on their heads—make the historic and happenstance and parochial "social norms," so far as they can, the *test* of the Good, and "adjustment" to these becomes the measure of the wholeness of the Self. "Deviance" is the new "value-free," problem-posing but pejorative and insidious characterization of those who do not wholly succumb. Deviance, as defined, is, presumably, what Jesus, Socrates, and the Buddha had or manifested, or, in the gentler version, suffered from. But what they suffered from is, on the socialization test, the mark of the bad, or at least of the defective: the sign that somehow process or person has failed.

There is absolutely no known reason to believe for an instant that these things must needs be: that the school, let alone the university, must "reflect" the surrounding society. In the first place, the society is not, like the snowcapped Sierras, something that is just there. It is nothing more than persons in their structured interaction. The structure is what they set up to steady or order their interaction. Indeed, they recreate it daily by interacting in that fashion and can de-create it—and do—whenever they begin to act otherwise. But those men so acting and reflecting are not just data either. They are yesterday's *educational output;* and the most influential are yesterday's university output! To insist that the school must reflect society, therefore, would be to say that the school can do no more than mirror its own prior mistakes. If so, we are all damned and doomed. But it is not so. For the umpteen grades of school are in their totality a *differentiated* "part" of society—that part that is mandated to make the society in some most sensible sense *other*, by *not* repeating its previous maiming mistakes. The school moreover is precisely that part that does have some freedom to do so, and that could, with any courage or conviction, seize irresistibly a great deal more. It could do so, if it knew how to teach its present or former pupils, because in a world of competitive societies, failing a worldwide fascist conspiracy of the right or left, the society that does *not* yield this freedom to its schools is extinction-bound at a reasonably rapid rate. That the educational system is likely to fall into the same errors and go a-whoring after the same strange gods as the society-in-general, is quite another matter and altogether likely, just as a bad doctor might be taken in by and treat the complaints of his patient rather than what they suffer from. But, that is just exactly what scholar and physician are set up, both by a higher code and by some explicit social sanctions, *not* to do. The fundamental mandate, moral and social, is to correct, not to echo. We already have a vast social institution of trained liars, advertising experts, and such, to "mirror," create, "image," embellish, and institute systematic error and irrelevance. The university and the school system that it crowns and culminates exist to civilize, and this is their moral mandate in the world, regardless of what "power groups" demand. This mandate or mission means precisely to take a given society, always fundamentally relatively barbarian, out into the light and onto the height. The voice of the school in society, like that of enlightened conscience in the person, is a still, small, barely audible one. It speaks of what is latent as possibility but barely functional in actuality. And its call will not be heard without a strong, highly audible, and exemplary institution to represent, defend, advance, and define it, and demand effective action upon its promptings. The conscience whispers feebly of love, truth, wisdom, peace, order, justice, the humane; the rest shouts raucously of interest, shrewdness, calculation, the reduction of men from ends to means, the always imminent collapse of the thin and

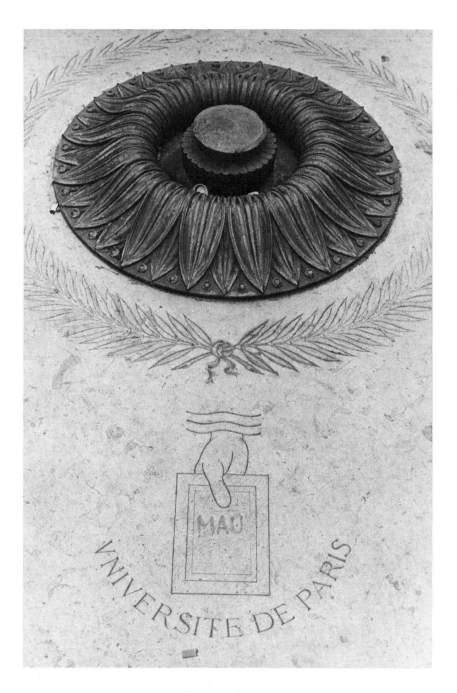

the always imminent collapse of the thin and vulnerable skin of civilization

vulnerable skin of civilization into the solid, chunky, almost involuntary beef of barbarity. The school is mandated to tip and keep tipped that always precarious balance. Between the society that mirrors the concentration camps and the one that reflects the sacred academy lies a mere micro-membrane, on whose preservation the evasion of possibly permanent hell-on-earth depends.

When it is asked therefore what would be lost if the university, the present university, were shut down, the successive answers might well be: very little; the total confusion in the society generally that the university engenders rather than dissipates; the principal support and necessary condition of the society's present headlong rush to destruction; and the destructive hegemony that the university has over the rest of the educational process, which might, just *might*, break back loose into some rough-hewn compatibility with what its students continuously, explicitly or implicitly, cry for. What they cry for with one voice, though in many manners, is a chance to become human and political, as inseparable joint conditions of their becoming good and effective human beings, in a society that has place for such men.

The closely connected question, "What ought to be the university's function and peculiar and proper contribution to today's world?" can hardly be answered without reference to the next question, "Ought the two main functions of the university to be the advancement of knowledge, and its dissemination?"

The only proper answer to the second question is "Neither!" But, since these, especially the first, *are* the principal admissible functions of the university today, their acceptance blocks the proper answer to the prior question.

The inadmissible actual major functions of the university are, of course, the provision of exculpatory or mildly admonitory advice to the going order; the processing of the young for "slots" in a society so ordered and conceived; boondoggling waste of such real resources as there are to put off, by endless research, action on problems to which we already know with sufficient clarity the answers; and the bundling together of such a variety of disparate aims and functions that the institution cannot be consistently attacked. It thus has all the strength, stability, and meaninglessness of the modern "conglomerate corporation," which, in fact, is what it is, and almost all it is. If it produces better baby food, and improved personnel-shredding grenades, and develops the one out of research on the other, how attack it? It acquires the inviolability of the modern state, which also produces and bundles welfare programs and social security together with the monopoly of all massive crime that

the processing of the young

68

matters from Hiroshima to Dresden to Maidanek to Vietnam to institutionalized anti-Semitism to the rape of Czechoslovakia's soul. The object of the conglomerate is stability and unassailability. How assail the man who uses castor oil to convince dissidents but makes the trains run on time and "restores national pride"?

To return to the admissible aims: "the advancement and dissemination of knowledge." More likely crucial for the collapse of the university as a truly respectable institution, and its becoming a virtual tool of the special interests and the state, is the view, the Faustian myth now institutionally incarnate, that its functions are, may be, or ought to be the advancement *or* the dissemination of knowledge. The belief is on one view as madness, on another, willful heresy. The myth is taken over from the civilization, refined and heightened in the university, and fed back into the civilization which it threatens thereby to collapse. For "knowledge," in this context, means essentially and almost wholly, "knowledge about," "neutral knowledge," knowledge capable of any use from the total enslavement of the psyche from within, to the building of the Doomsday Machine that could already blow up the world, and will shortly catch at the cosmos. To discover, for instance, the existence and effects of more and more virulent and undetectable poisons, and then actively to disseminate such knowledge to all who have enough income and leisure to read, is—other activities absent—to promote murder while mindlessly maintaining moral and legal immunity. It is not what we do with regard either to discovery or to dissemination when we are guided by wisdom and practical philosophy. It is only what we preach and practise when we talk the arrant nonsense called philosophy of education.

For as long as any approximation of common sense held sway, and any sense obtained of evident good and evil, better or worse, the seeking of such knowledge could hardly have been deemed a good in itself. And, once discovered, if discovery came about, such intelligence would so far as possible have been *restricted* to two *protective* professions: physicians (as they were once supposed to be) and perhaps police (as they were once supposed to be). The physician to whom any such existing knowledge was to be entrusted was under sacred oath: a promise in an order transcending "the society," or indeed any temporal order. But more: he was *formed* in one single process with the acquisition of such knowledge to be of such character as to share in that true paternity which in its perfection was taken to be the very image of the Absolute. The physician, so far as he was true father to all men, even if only in respect to the health of their minds and bodies, participated necessarily in degree in the Fatherhood of All. And on that condition, and that alone, and only insofar as it held, could his increase of knowledge, his participation in science and competence (tending toward omniscience and omnicompetence) be justified at all, or even considered harmless. In effect, knowledge and love in its active mode were rendered, so far as humanly possible, indivisible. The knowledge and love formed and informed the art of medicine, so that it tended to the increase of such goods as health for the body and comfort for the mind, and hence to health, meaning whole-ness and wholesomeness, and hence to participation in the Good.

Outside of this context, both "knowledge" (in the sense the university intends), and its indiscriminate dissemination appear to be anything but useless; they are harmful, if not positively evil. "Knowledge," in education, as in society, as in psychotherapy, can and usually will—apart from valid need, and apart from capacity to "integrate"—be damaging in one way or another, sometimes to the point of destroying the capacity of the per-son, such as it then is, to operate as a personality at all or to operate to any good purpose in reference to himself or others. If "integration" is to be had, the "knowledge" must be at least emotionally manageable and, if possible, emotionally developmental. It must be at least unlikely to throw the person into an unmanageable moral crisis. It must be readily relatable, "sense-makingly," to knowledge already in hand. And it must be capable of being understood, in every sense, in reference to its im-plications for action, whether that action goes to the self or others.

The least evil that can come out of knowledge "advanced" and "dis-seminated" under less rigorous criteria is increasing confusion and loss of education and the very capacity for education. The most that can come out of such abandoned and irresponsible practice, even in a mod-erately stable person, is suicide, psychological or physical or both. And indeed this is widely the result of education thus universally pursued. The "intellectual apathy" so often alluded to is itself partial psychic suicide; and the anti-intellectualism so often alleged is the defense against the standard attempted intellectual murder. (Perhaps homicide is the better figure; it is unlikely that teachers consciously intend the destruc-tion of mind and person that they actually produce in most who come under their ministrations.) And as for the person, so for the society. Knowledge so defined destroys society and culture; and rampant knowl-edge so set loose destroys absolutely. "Like a God self-slain on his own strange altar," Western civilization lies all but dead under its own learnéd knife.

Nor is relief to be had from mere restructuring. In a sense it does not matter much whether the university is defined as including the college but not coextensive with it, or as R. M. Hutchins has urged timelessly, as something separate and distinct from it. For separation would only at-tenuate slightly the capacity of the separated university to undermine what might be good in a college, and would not—unless students and faculty were willing to pay prohibitive social and spiritual prices—disrupt its baleful control. Under separation, it would still be true that the uni-versity's entrance requirements would edge all education into the univer-

Teaching is a sacred calling

sity's fainter image, and that the university's products, systematically incapacitated for wisdom, would be the men of eminence generally dominating Boards of Regents, and the higher administrative and faculty reaches in the colleges. Moreover, and more important, I would argue that in any place of education, *a fortiori* in a university, the strictures previously enumerated upon what is proper and permissible learning must apply. Operations free of these constraints are not education, but the securing of "intelligence," in a commercial or military sense—which is to say preparation for war, hot or cold, armed or economic. (Economic war is what happens when people do not need a gun held over them to ensure they hold still while their pockets are picked, in part, if not clean.)

The university, on this view, *must* be the crown and throne of education, the pinnacle of the *magisterium* secular. Its alternative is, in its "value-freedom," to become the servant and adjunct, and indeed, in the end, the bastion of mere power. Should the latter course continue to be followed, a new institution following a quite different course must arise if anything worthy of the name of civilization is to survive or come into being.

The business of the university then is to finish the education of students, in the sense that when they leave it, permanently or temporarily, they are fitted to continue and test their education in greater independence of it. But "finish" must then, of course, mean bring to some climactic point, rather than, as at present, finish off. The climactic point is not to be taken as suggesting that there will not be further and higher climaxes, but only that, until the whole society becomes, in effect, an educational system of worth, there will be here a peak in the process of controlled and formal attempts to educate: at least, a pause, *pro tempore*.

In one sense education inevitably begins with fertilization of the ovum and ends with the extinction of consciousness. The greater part of it does not even pass consciously through the conscious mind, and the more important part of it, conscious or unconscious, the early "imprinting," occurs, for the most part, before any formal educational institution directly enters the picture. But it is not this education, certainly not in its totality, that is the concern of the school. The concern of the school is nevertheless with pupils, *élèves*, those to be elevated. Its art is the art of elevating. And as with all arts this presupposes a clear vision of ends, an understanding, bordering upon an entry into, the "material" upon which the art works, appropriate "tools," and knowledge of their use and effect. The figure fits perhaps more than ordinarily ill, for the images evoked suggest far too much passivity in the material, constancy or invariance in the tool, specificity in the end envisioned, and designingness or cunning in the artist.

Teaching is a sacred calling that is difficult enough to follow—even harder to describe. It has little to do with what is currently called instruction. It, legitimately, demands docility of the learner only insofar as the teacher is himself caught up in a special and transcendent obedience. His client is not or not only the child before him, or the children he happens to have, or their parents, or the school or school system or society—still less the nation-state which may well be the enemy of all of them. It is none of these that "employs" him; indeed, he cannot be employed. His task may well be stated as the heightening of "the unity and community of minds," but only if every key word is taken in a special sense.

The special cast given to the meaning of "mind" since about the seventeenth century makes it serve but ill in its modern meaning. Not only is it, in one of its uses, set over against the body, but, so isolated, it has come to mean the cognitive, if not the calculative, function or faculty. Flowing out of and contributing to this view, a division of labor accompanied by appropriate specialization quite naturally ensues. In this division of labor, persons called teachers and institutions called educational are appointed to tend to the cultivation of this supposed cognitive function, and to see to some characteristics of the resultant cognitive content of the mind thus defined. On this theory, the Trinity of knowing-loving-being is to be split like the atom. The "being" is presumably left to society, the "loving" to the family or the church or happenstance. The result of the split, insofar as it succeeds, is an isolated being, a surgically truncated loving, and a knowing that is of its very essence alienating and, therefore, self- and other-destructive. The greater the "unity" of the mind, thus heretically and idolatrously defined, the more powerfully it hovers, like the hydrogen bomb, over both self and society. It is an open question whether there *can* be a community of such minds; but if it were possible it would have all the properties of a sort of satanic church.

There is no more appropriate aim for teaching—itself a part of parenting, in its specific and universal senses—than the fostering of the unity of the *person* in a high community of *persons.* Since George Herbert Mead conclusively and philosophically showed mind, self, and society as co-emergents, and since Freud and his successors conclusively and empirically exposed in greatest detail the how of this co-emergence in any particular case, one might have thought the point sufficiently made.

What should differentiate home for the preschooler, from school for the pupil, and college and university for the student, is not a gradual separation of cognitive functions from all others, and increasing complexity and narrowing of the cognitive material to be "studied," but the assisted evolution of the co-emergent unities of person and community, becoming ever less particular and parochial and tending at the limit to freedom from the constraints of time and space. The "educated" baby is the one who can sufficiently enter into and appreciate the role of his mother so that he can become at least a primitive self to himself, a baby, a particular baby—even while simultaneously she is *constituted* a mother in virtue of her entry into that dyad-community. Being, knowing, and loving are here clearly co-emergents—or, more exactly, trinitarian in their essence. The task of the university is not, must not be, in discontinuity with that process, but is to be, must be, the crowning and culmination of it. The culmination must therefore also lie in the realm of intimacy and at-homeness: the co-emergent intimacies and at-homeness, again, with reference to the self and the other. But "the other" is now, so far as possible, the cosmos and all men, everywhere, past, present, and to come; and "the self" is the enlarged, enhanced, and infinitely complex self that can stand in that relation to all that was and is and may yet be.

Any answer to the questions as to who "owns" the university and who should, and what, if any, should be the role of trustees, must be closely connected with these views. It is clear that the present university *is* owned by a riffraff of special interests, economic, political, administrative, and intellectual. It is owned in the sense that coercive, alien, and destructive decisions can be and are made by these or their representatives over the conditions and nature of the university's life. It is not so much the nature of this riffraff—though that *is* an additional problem—but the fact that anyone can assert ownership of, or conceive of himself as capable of owning, an unownable good, that is, in the current jargon, "mind-blowing." Who owns a baby's soul? Who owns the cosmos? Who owns the historical process—or the civilization itself? Not even the existent society—perhaps especially not the existent society—can *own* the interaction among various grades of scholars, the fostering-cherishing-enhancing process that the university *is*. As to how such a process is to be ordered and governed, the question barely arises if the process is itself on a proper footing. The question is not whether a community of learning should be self-governing, because the one notion is implied in the other: a community of its nature governs itself; that which truly governs itself is a community. The trustees are therefore the members of the community, the community actual and virtual, visible and invisible. And the degree of their trusteeship is from day to day, moment to moment, the degree of their participation in that community. Trusteeship is a moral, not a legal, status. For trustees or regents as now conceived, there is no place whatever. Their very existence rests on a wholly different theory not reconcilable with the nature of education or the university's tasks: that the university is somehow to be made "responsible" to the state or to the public or, in practice, to the interests of the giant corporations. The university can only be responsible as institution to itself as process. If it corrupts itself, it corrupts itself, and hopefully no one will then go to it. It can only be helped to corrupt itself—not prevented from doing so—by lodging any part of the responsibility for its purity outside of itself. If to help it keep itself pure, it feels called upon to consult from time to time with

*the "troubles on campus"
derive from the failure . . .
of what is called the university*

the wise and good who are not in its immediate community, it is free to do so, but it is not free to delegate any "decision making" to anyone else.

The relation of the university and its members to political and social action is implicit in the views already set forth. As far as the members in their severalty are concerned, they obviously have the duties of exemplary citizens in as well as educators of the society. These are not disjointed roles, the one underpinned by the general role of all citizens, the other by the special task of teacher. If the university is, as it should be, that community formally enjoined to see specially to the enhancement of person and society, then for both educational and moral reasons, it is the responsibility of the university's members to instruct, criticize, admonish, and, if necessary, act to enlighten and redeem the society generally. The educational reasons cut both ways: it is often impossible to educate the society except by action; it is generally impossible to educate oneself except in action—indeed there is a sense in which one does not know what

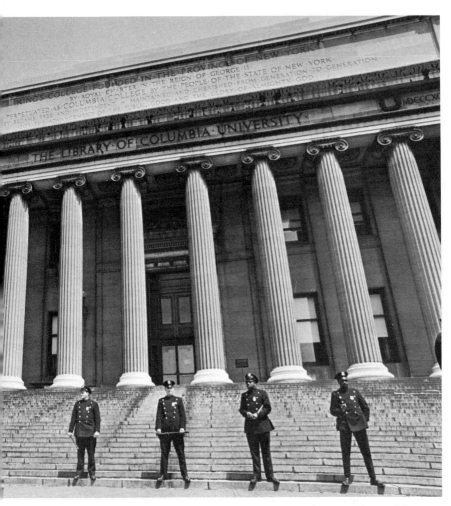

one knows until he starts to act on his knowledge in the face of human adversity.

What is true for the members of the institution in their severalty is true—but perhaps at a different level of particularity—for the institution *qua* institution. One would not expect, and one should not demand, that the university as such take a stand upon or act with reference to every puny partisan division among men. But on all those great questions that touch intimately the very quality and character, the moral value, of the civilization itself, the university is not simply free to take a stand, in word and even in action, but morally bound to do so. If it is a reproach to the church that she took so little action against Mussolini or Hitler and the ideas they stood for, it is at least equally scandalous that universities as such have taken no stand, have failed to lay their institutional lives upon the line, in the face of the great evils and degradations—verging upon bestializations—of our time. If the university as such cannot take such stands and accompany them by appropriate action, then it cannot perform even its narrower role of educating its students; for education, as conceived here, depends on a credible authority, an authority inherent in a paternity. And a credible authority has both moral grandeur and the influence and special kind of power that flows from it. The power is not the power of numbers—how many legions has the Pope?—but the power of legitimation, the power to bind and loose, upon which all other power ultimately rests. If the university saw itself in its proper role and charged with its proper responsibility, its powers of interdict could no less make powerful modern states tremble than the corresponding powers of the church once did with respect to recalcitrant princes. The power is always there; it belongs to whoever has moral ascendancy. If the university does not have such ascendancy it is by neglect, default, or abdication.

It should be evident that nearly everywhere the "troubles on campus" derive directly or indirectly from the failure, the malversation, in exactly these respects, of what is called the university. No matter what the "triggering" causes—crowded classrooms in Paris or the disputed strip before the Sather gate at Berkeley—and no matter which side of the alleged iron curtain, what the university is finally taxed with and attacked for is just its incapacity or unwillingness to educate in the sense defined, that is to foster, or even permit, the emergence of an integral and authentic community of persons of integrity and authenticity. The very peculiar but modern idea of knowing which justifies the reference to the university as a "knowledge factory" lies alike at the bottom of the sickness of a technology-ridden civilization, and of the troubles of the university conceived of as a part of such a society. The protesting students very often know only—but with moral certainty—out of their direct experience that the "knowledge industry" is the primary locus for the destruction of men and the dehumanization of the social order. It is, as it stands, the velvet-gloved butcher of the spirit.

A Catechism
For Our Times

MORTIMER J. ADLER

Here are seven questions to which all of us, young and old, should have answers. The answers we give should not be matters of faith, but conclusions of reason, supported by fact. When we differ in the answers we give, our differences of opinion should be amenable to discussion, should be susceptible to the weight of argument and evidence, and should be settled by efforts at persuasion.

I have placed the questions in an order that enables each answer to throw light on the answers to follow.

1. By what standard can we judge the relative merits of different centuries, societies, and cultures?
2. What should government do, in shaping the political, economic, and social institutes of a society, to safeguard and facilitate the pursuit of happiness by all its people?
3. In what ways does the culture of a society—especially the value system that underlies its *mores*—encourage or discourage the individual in his efforts to make a good life for himself?
4. Is this—our century—a good time to be alive?
5. Is the United States today in the forefront of the twentieth-century revolution?
6. Is ours a sick society? Curably or incurably sick?
7. Do we need a moral and an educational revolution?

1. *By What Standard Can We Judge the Relative Merits of Different Centuries, Societies, and Cultures?*

One century, society, or culture is better than another in proportion as its technological conditions, its political, economic, and social institutions, and its actual value system promote or facilitate a really good life for a *larger proportion* of its human beings.

One century or culture is worse than another in proportion as its various components work in the opposite way—to deprive a *larger proportion* of its members of the external conditions they need in order to make good lives for themselves, or to impede, interfere with, or even discourage their efforts in this direction.

The ideal, of course, is a society and culture that provides *all* its members—all *without exception*—with the external conditions they need, and at the same time encourages them in their pursuit of the good life.

By "ideal" I do not mean a state of affairs that is perfect in every way. That is utopian and unattainable. I mean no more than normal or healthy. Thus, for example, if the purpose of men in associating is to enjoy the good of communal life, which is peace, then war in any form represents a pathological social condition, one that defeats the very purpose for which men associate. A society rent by civil strife or one that is engaged in external war is malfunctioning; and, in this medical sense of the term, it is pathological or abnormal. If I speak of war as an instance of social pathology or abnormality in this sense, I am obviously not using the word "abnormal" to mean unusual in a statistical sense; for, either through civil strife or external conflicts, almost all societies since the beginning of history have been abnormal or pathological.

Another example may help to reinforce what I have just said. The purpose of men in associating, in families, tribes, or states, is not only to enjoy the blessings of peace, but also to achieve other goods that the isolated individual could not achieve for himself. Among these are wealth, a decent supply of the means of subsistence, and sufficient free time for the goods that can be achieved through play and leisure. Hence when the technological conditions of a society are such that widespread poverty or destitution cannot be eliminated, and the lives of most men are consumed in back-breaking toil from dawn to dusk, working in a state of chattel slavery or abject servitude, the society is pathological or abnormal in the sense indicated. It is not functioning as a society should; i.e., it is not serving the purpose for which men form associations. Once again it must be said that, from the beginning of history to the present time, most, if not all, societies have been pathological or abnormal.

war in any form represents a pathological social condition

2. *What Should Government Do, in Shaping the Political, Economic, and Social Institutions of a Society, to Safeguard and Facilitate the Pursuit of Happiness by All Its People?*

O n the conceptual plane, there can hardly be a better statement of the objectives of government than the one made in the Preamble to the Constitution of the United States. These objectives are:

> "[To] establish justice, insure domestic tranquillity, provide for the common defence, promote the general welfare, and secure the blessings of liberty. . . ."

Taken together with the proposition in the Declaration of Independence, that all men, being by nature equal, are equal in all their natural rights, rights that a just government must attempt to secure equally for all, the objectives set forth in the Preamble provide a standard for measuring the goodness of any government, including our own at various stages in its history from the beginning to the present day.

Let us now consider these objectives in relation to the parts of a good life—the means that the individual must employ in his effort to make a good life for himself. The means consist of the following seven classes of goods:

1. *Goods of the body,* such as health, vigor, and the pleasures of sense.
2. *Goods of the mind,* such as knowledge, understanding, prudence, and even a modicum of wisdom; together with such goods of the mind's activity as skills of inquiry and of critical judgment, and the arts of creative production.
3. *Goods of character,* such as the moral virtues of temperance, fortitude, and justice in relation to the rights of others and the good of the community.
4. *Goods of personal association,* such as family relationships, friendships, and loves.
5. *Political goods,* such as domestic tranquillity—both civil and external peace—and political liberty, together with the protection of individual freedom by the prevention of violence, aggression, coercion, or intimidation.
6. *Economic goods,* such as a decent supply of the means of subsistence; living and working conditions conducive to health; medical care; opportunities for access to the pleasures of sense and to aesthetic pleasures as well; opportunities for access to the goods of the mind through educational facilities in youth and in adult life; and enough free time from subsistence work, both in youth and in adult life, to take full advantage of these opportunities.
7. *Social goods,* such as equality of status, of opportunity, and of treatment in all matters affecting the dignity of the human person.

Of these seven classes of goods, the first four belong to the inner or private life of the individual. They are acquired and preserved by him as a result of the way in which he conducts himself, employs his faculties, and husbands his personal resources. Whether or not he acquires and accumulates these goods in the course of his life depends mainly on him. This is particularly true of the goods of character and of personal association. These are the least dependent on the good fortune of beneficent external circumstances. With regard to his acquirement of the goods of the body and the goods of the mind, the individual is more dependent on favorable external conditions—on conditions conducive to health and provisions for medical care, in the case of bodily goods; on opportunities for schooling, learning, and creative work, and on having enough free time to take advantage of these opportunities, in the case of the goods of the mind. Hence, with regard to all the goods subsumed under the first four categories, the actions of government can do no more than *indirectly* abet the pursuit of happiness by the actions it takes.

The last three classes of goods are environmental or external in the sense that the individual's possession of them is mainly dependent on the outer or public conditions of his life. Thus, for example, unless he is fortunate enough to live in a republic—under constitutional government or a government of laws—and unless he is among those who are enfranchised as citizens with suffrage under that constitution, he will be deprived of political liberty. Unless he either has income-producing property or has what I am going to call the "economic equivalents of property," he will not have, through forms of wealth and the things that wealth can provide, the economic goods that he needs for the pursuit of happiness— things that are good not only because they maintain his life and health, but also because they facilitate his acquirement of other goods, especially the goods of the mind or the goods of leisure. Unless he enjoys equality of status, opportunity, and treatment, he will, in varying degrees, be deprived of access to the goods he needs for his personal development and for the enhancement of his dignity as a person.

Hence, so far as government can shape and control the political, economic, and social institutions of the community, it secures the individual's right to make a good life for himself largely through measures that *directly* affect his possession of political, economic, and social goods and, indirectly, through them, other goods that are not wholly within the power of the individual, as, perhaps, only the goods of his own character are.

Thus, for example, it may be practicable now, though it was not always practicable in the past, for a government to see that no individual starves or is undernourished; but no government, now or ever, can see to it that he is temperate and does not ruin his health by gluttony. Similarly, it may be practicable now for a government to provide adequate educational facilities for every child and even for every adult; but no government can prevent an individual from neglecting these opportunities, or compel him to acquire and use the goods of the mind. A government can give every man suffrage and, therewith, political liberty, but it cannot give him the civic virtue whereby he uses that freedom well; just as it cannot make him just in his use of other forms of freedom that it grants him and safeguards.

3. *In What Ways Does the Culture of a Society—Especially the Value System That Underlies Its Mores—Encourage or Discourage the Individual in His Efforts to Make a Good Life for Himself?*

Let me now briefly summarize the criteria for judging one culture as better than another by reference to its favorable or adverse effects on the pursuit of happiness. One culture is better than another in proportion as

(1) it regards wealth always as a means and never as an end, and so does not look upon the continual expansion of the economy, beyond the production of useful wealth, as an end in itself, to which everything else should be sacrificed or subordinated;

(2) it subordinates business to the pursuits of leisure, the production and consumption of wealth to the goods of the mind;

(3) it provides ample means for the mind to refresh itself from business, through the pleasures of play, through the enjoyment of the arts, through the advancement of the sciences, and through all forms of learning and of creative work;

(4) it subordinates the goods of the body to the goods of the mind, and places its disapproval upon unlimited indulgence in sensual pleasures or even upon excessive preoccupation with amusements and recreations that do not contribute to the growth of the mind or to the improvement of the individual as a person;

(5) it cultivates the refinements of life and even a modest degree of elegance, but at the same time censures extravagance and the lust for luxuries, or even creature comforts and conveniences beyond all reasonable need;

(6) it honors the man of private and civic virtue above the man who succeeds, by foul means or fair, in the rat race for power, fame, or wealth;

(7) it esteems intrinsic human excellence above any and every form of merely external or worldly success.

How does a society honor the things that should be cultivated there if its members are to be aided and abetted in their pursuit of happiness?

One part of the answer lies in the cultural institutions that it creates, maintains, and develops at the public expense—its libraries, its museums of art and science, its theaters, its public parks, and so on. But the heart of the answer lies in that one of its cultural institutions which most directly affects every individual: its educational system—not only its schools, colleges, and universities but also the educational facilities it provides for continued learning in adult life.

I am not concerned here with equality of educational opportunity, but rather with the quality of the schooling and other educational opportunities that is afforded both young and old. If, for example, all children were given an equal number of years of schooling, from kindergarten through college or university; and if, in addition, they enjoyed equal educational facilities during these years, but the schooling they received were directed mainly toward technological and economic advances rather than to the pursuits of leisure and the development of human excellence, the educational system would operate against rather than for the individual's making a good life for himself.

To know whether the culture of a society is or is not favorable to the pursuit of happiness, one need look no further than the scale of values embodied in its educational system—the objectives it is designed to serve. Only if an educational system subordinates all forms of specialized, technical, professional, or vocational training to discipline in the liberal arts and to all forms of humanistic learning for their own sake—only if it places truly liberal education first, and relegates all merely utilitarian programs of education to second place—does it reflect a scale of values that accords with the order of real goods in the pursuit of happiness. Then and only then do we have a persuasive sign that the culture of a society is beneficent because it honors the things that should be cultivated there for the sake of a good human life.

4. *Is This—Our Century—a Good Time to Be Alive?*

The answer is unqualifiedly yes. It is better than any earlier period of human life—better in that it provides the external conditions of a good human life to a greater extent and for more human beings than ever before on earth.

For the first million years of human life on earth, members of the hominid family led bestial, not characteristically human, lives—that is, they lived mainly, if not exclusively, on the bare subsistence level.

Beginning 35,000 years ago, technological progress began to be made which brought man to the verge of civilization: the domestication of animals; the transition from stone to iron implements; the establishment of permanent settlements, etc.

But not until 6,000 years ago, with the emergence of civilized societies, with superior agricultural technology, with political or quasi-political institutions, with an increased division of labor, and almost always with human slave labor—not until then were the external conditions of a good human life provided for a fortunate and privileged few.

. . . *means for the mind to refresh itself from business, through the pleasures of play, through the enjoyment of the arts, through the advancement of the sciences, and through all forms of learning and creative work*

In short, from the beginning until 6,000 years ago, the external conditions for leading a good human life were available *to no one.* Beginning 6,000 years ago, with the rise of cities and civilized societies (which are one and the same), and from then until now—or rather until the end of the nineteenth century—we have had all over the world what I am going to call the parochial civilizations of privilege, based on an inequality of conditions for their human members.

In all of these historic, parochial civilizations of privilege, the external conditions of a good human life were provided only for the few, at the expense of misery for all the rest. And it seems fair to say that, under the circumstances of the time, especially the poor technology of the time, these inequalities of condition could not have been rectified—except, perhaps, by going backward to a state of affairs in which no one could lead a good human life.

The second great revolution in human affairs began yesterday—with the opening of this century. The twentieth-century revolution, which began first in the United States and Western Europe, is now sweeping the world. Please note that I said "began"; for the twentieth-century revolution has only just started even in the countries where it first began. It may take anywhere from 100 to 500 years, maybe even 1,000, before this revolution yields its full results on a worldwide basis, with the emergence, for the first time, of a world civilization that is based on universal conditions of equality for every human being on earth—*all* men with *no* exceptions.

What is this twentieth-century revolution? It involves, *first of all,* extraordinary advances in science and technology, resulting in vastly increased power to produce wealth, in the elimination of inhuman forms of subsistence work at the level of sheer drudgery, the reduction in the amount of time that must be spent in producing wealth, etc. All these changes indicate that it may at last be possible to eliminate slavery, poverty, unequal educational opportunities, unequal conditions of health, etc.

Second, the twentieth-century revolution involves a commitment, in varying degrees, to the democratic and socialistic principles that all men, being by nature equal, are entitled to an equality of social, economic, and political conditions. It calls for the elimination of all class divisions, especially the division between the economic *haves* and *have-nots.* It calls for political equality—the equality of citizenship, with political rights, liberties, and privileges for all. It is not only democratic but socialistic in that it accepts the ruling principle of the welfare state: that the state should make every effort to promote the general economic welfare, in which all citizens shall participate up to at least the minimum level of a decent and secure standard of living. Hence this is not only the first century in which men can project the elimination of war by the constitution of a world federal government; it is also the first century in which men can project the advent of a truly classless society, pervaded by a universal equality of conditions. For the first time in history, it seems practicable to eliminate the twin evils of class and war that, as Toynbee points out, have beset civilized life from its beginning.

Though these great advances in the conditions of mankind may take centuries more to bring to their full fruition, even now, in this century, many more men than ever before on earth *can* think about their lives as a whole because external conditions are now such that it has at last become *possible* for them to make good lives for themselves.

5. Is the United States Today in the Forefront of the Twentieth-Century Revolution?

Let us list and compare the states or countries in which the twentieth-century revolution has begun and taken hold, limiting our attention for the moment to political, economic, and social conditions.

In varying degrees, all these states are characterized by political democracy, economic welfare programs, the broadening of public education, public health programs, reduction in the hours of human labor, improvement in the types and conditions of subsistence work, increase in recreational facilities, participation in the enjoyment of the arts, increases in longevity, advances in communication and public information, etc.

Let me designate this type of state as the technologically advanced, democratic, welfare state, moving toward—approximating but not yet fully achieving—the ideal of the classless society, with a universal equality of conditions and with ample free time for all.

In the world as it is today, we find this type of state realized in varying degrees:

(1) In the highest degree, by the United States, Sweden, Japan, and a few states of the British Commonwealth.

(2) In the next rank, by Great Britain, the states of Western Europe (with the exception of Spain and Portugal), and by the Soviet Union and the smaller socialist republics, such as Yugoslavia, Czechoslovakia, and perhaps Poland and Rumania.

(3) Far below this are most if not all of the states of Central and South America.

(4) The twentieth-century revolution may have begun, but it has not yet taken hold to any appreciable degree in the Middle East, in Africa, in China, and Southeast Asia. The two possible exceptions in Asia are North Vietnam and South Korea.

All of the states in which the twentieth-century revolution is now underway, and especially those in which it has made substantial progress, are vastly superior to any societies that ever existed on earth before, so far as their political, economic, and social conditions are concerned; vastly superior to the best of ancient societies—to the Athens of Plato, which unfortunately did not live up to the encomiums heaped upon it by Pericles 50 years earlier; to the Rome of Cicero and to the China of Confucius; in all of which the conditions of a good life were accessible only to the *very few*, and then at the cost of misery to the great mass of men whose lives were either ruined by slavery or consumed by stultifying toil.

How does the United States compare with other leading states of the same type—states that are technologically advanced and that have begun to approximate an equality of conditions, political, economic, and social?

The comparison is difficult to make, because it is multi-dimensional. Thus, for example, the United States is much less class-structured than England, has a higher median income than Sweden, has achieved a greater equality of educational opportunity than most European countries, though not more than Australia or Canada, and so on. It also has more political equality and liberty than the U.S.S.R. and its satellites. On the other hand, economic equality may be more fully achieved in Sweden and in New Zealand; public health may be better cared for in any number of European countries; political democracy may work more responsibly in England; and so on.

With all such considerations in mind, I still think it is fair to say that, from the point of view of *providing* the external conditions of a good human life for a larger proportion of its citizens, the United States is, *on balance*, as good as, if not better than, any other country in the world today, and vastly better than any state that ever existed in the past. It fails most of the tests enumerated in the answer to Question 3. But it fails them no more—and probably less—than any other nation in the world today.

The twentieth-century revolution has just begun and it still has a long way to go before it reaches its full fruition—the full realization of the sound principles that have motivated it, the reaping of all the advantages that advanced technology has the power to confer while at the same time overcoming the serious threats that are the avoidable, not inevitable, consequences of these advances.

The war on poverty has just begun; so has the struggle against racism in all its forms. These efforts must be carried forward; and it will take many years to see them through to complete success.

No country is free from the evils of war or the chicanery of foreign policy; and none can be, as long as the jungle or anarchy of sovereign states exists. Foreign affairs is the domain of power politics, and will always remain so until we have advanced to world peace secured in the only way it can be secured—*by world government*. That, by the way, is the next revolution that lies ahead: the step forward from our parochial societies, always in a state of war with one another, and with an irremediable inequality of conditions as between the *have* and the *have-not* nations

—forward to a world society, under world government, with an equality of conditions for all men everywhere.

Until that happens, all sovereign states, vis-à-vis one another, are about equally bad; and the United States is no better but also no worse than the rest. And until that happens, the evils of poverty and racism cannot be eradicated on a worldwide basis—perhaps not completely even at home.

With all its past and present imperfections, the United States has shown itself more susceptible to social improvement than any other country. Its history, as has been well said, has been the history of a continuing revolution prosecuted mainly by legal and peaceful means. More radical institutional changes have been made in a relatively short time in American history and, for the most part, with less violence, than in the history of most other countries—with the possible exception of England. This holds out a great promise for further positive developments by peaceful means.

6. *Is Ours a Sick Society? Curably or Incurably Sick?*

Ideal conditions have never existed in the past and do not yet exist anywhere on earth. All existing countries, including the United States, are socially defective or *pathological*. If the word "pathological" means "sick," it also raises the question whether the pathology is remediable, whether the sickness is curable. It seems to me perfectly clear that the existing social pathologies are all remediable. If that were not the case, the twentieth-century revolution could go no further, as it must and will.

Hence those who call the United States a sick society, and mean by that one that is mortally or incurably ill, are willfully shutting their eyes to all the available facts and refusing to acknowledge obvious trends of change that support reasonably optimistic predictions.

There is a middle ground between the perfection of blooming health and mortal or incurable disease. And that is where we are—a relatively healthy society with some spots of pathology, some curable defects or deficiencies. The importance of recognizing the soundness of the middle ground in criticizing the United States can be illustrated by the difference between two questions that one can ask about a house that one is thinking of buying because one wants to live on the site where it exists. One can ask, "Is it so bad a house that the only thing to do with it is to tear it down or gut it, and start from the ground up?" Or one can ask, "With all its defects, is it nevertheless good enough to remodel, improve, and redecorate?"

The present state of the U.S.A. should inspire us to ask the second of these questions. And we should answer it by saying that the United States, with all its defects, is good enough to deserve our trying to improve it by carrying forward the peaceful revolution, reform by due process of law, that has been the course—more than that, the genius—of our development from the beginning. Recourse to violence is justified only when civil or legal measures are not available.

While saying this, we should also recognize the justifiable impatience of all those who are still oppressed by injustices that are not yet rectified and may not even be rectifiable with sufficient speed to satisfy them. The deep unrest that exists among those who are still oppressed, even the revolutionary violence that the wrongs they have long suffered now impel them to incite, is itself a sign that the time is at last ripe for the needed reforms. The politically, economically, and socially oppressed have always spearheaded the revolutionary changes needed to right the wrongs that they have suffered and can no longer tolerate. Sometimes the time is not ripe for the changes demanded in justice, and revolution is then bloody and abortive. But today we are confronted with oppressed groups, all over the world as well as in our own country, whose revolutionary impulses are fired by rising expectations—by the great progress that has already been made, which promises the possibility of further progress, and by the possibility, now as never before, of institutional reforms that will make the twentieth-century revolution, when completed, the first revolution in the history of mankind that will have really meant "all"—*all without exceptions*—as it moves towards its ultimate goal of an equality of political, economic, and social conditions for every human being on earth.

7. *Do We Need a Moral and an Educational Revolution?*

The things that are most prized and honored in America are the expanding production of wealth, whether the wealth produced satisfies real needs or only artificially induced wants; technological advances either for their own sake or for the sake of creature comforts and conveniences that are in excess of genuine need; external or worldly success as measured by the acquisition of money, fame, or power rather than the development of the inner man and the growth of the human being as a person; the expansion of the sensate life rather than the intensification of the life of the mind.

The high value set upon these things represents a fundamental disorder of goods, a perverse scale of values, placing lower over higher goods, mistaking merely apparent for real goods, and even erecting goods that are only means into ends to be sought for their own sake as if they constituted the good life as a whole. Whereas the favorable political, economic, and social conditions that have been achieved in our type of society make it possible for a large proportion of our population to make good lives for themselves, this unfavorable moral atmosphere or climate militates against the possibility of their succeeding; it disinclines them

*We should also recognize the justifiable impatience of all
those who are still oppressed*

to make the effort; it turns their lives in one or another wrong direction.

The unfavorable moral atmosphere and cultural influences that are here being criticized exist, in varying degrees, in all technologically advanced industrial societies. The perverse scale of values that sets up cultural obstacles to leading a good life in the United States today prevails in the *mores* of every other country of the same general type. "Materialism"—a preference for external goods over the goods of the human spirit—is as prevalent in Europe as in the United States, and in Eastern as well as Western Europe. The cult of sensuality, addiction to a life of play and frivolity, the existentialist cop-out which consists in living from day to day with no accounts carried forward and with no thought of a good life as a whole—these things flourish everywhere, not just in America; and it is to these things that too many of the young, unfortunately, tend to turn when they are disaffected with the materialism of their elders, not only in the United States but in Europe as well.

What all this calls for is a moral revolution, but a moral revolution that can begin only after the moral problem is itself understood and the solution of that problem is envisaged in all its details. That, in turn, calls for an educational revolution; but these two revolutions would seem to be so interdependent that, in fact, neither may be possible unless both come into being simultaneously.

I would like to say a few words about the educational revolution that is needed in the United States—one that will reverse the so-called academic revolution that Professors Jencks and Reisman have so accurately described in their recent book. I confine my attention to the United States not because the educational revolution is most needed here, but because it is here that all the externals of equal educational opportunity have been more fully achieved than anywhere else. This makes the misdirection of our educational system to the wrong ends so great a travesty on our success in the externals.

The rebellion of the students in our colleges and universities is thoroughly justified by wrongs that they are suffering at the hands of their institutions, but wrongs of which most of them are only dimly and, at best, inchoately aware. They are being cheated and defrauded by an educational system that has displaced genuinely liberal and humanistic training by all forms of specialized, technical, and vocational training that is intended to fit the young for their places in the industrial machine rather than to fit them for a good life by preparing them to make a good use of their free time in the pursuits of leisure. As I pointed out earlier, the reform of abuses is usually spearheaded by those who suffer under them. Today the young feel abused, but many of them project their complaints against the wrong objects—the political, economic, and social institutions of our society. The root cause of their malaise is rather the cultural disorder of a society that is devoted mainly to technological advances and industrial development, and is reflected in the misdirection of the educational system to the wrong ends.

The young complain again and again of the inadequacy and irrelevance of the education they are receiving. They are right. They have suffered, and the generations to come will suffer even more, unless the university system is radically reformed, unless colleges are emancipated from the heavy and deadening hand of graduate and professional schools, and unless the universities themselves become once more communities of scholars and cease to be service stations for the industrial state, R & D agencies for government and private industry, or even havens for professors to pursue their special interests without regard to the best interests of the students whom they should be serving.

It is particularly in the classrooms of our colleges that the young are suffering the worst abuses. To correct these abuses, not only must curriculums be revised, but faculties must once again consist of teachers not professors—men interested in liberal and humanistic learning for themselves as well as for others, more than in research or in the advancement of knowledge in some specialized or technical field. Unfortunately, most of the young, precisely because they are so poorly educated, do not and cannot know the kind of education that they so sorely need—the kind that would have maximum relevance not to business or worldly success, but to the business of making good lives for themselves and to success in that effort. What they need is genuinely liberal and humanistic learning as a means to the good life, the dullest among them as well as the brightest. But the brightest among them do not now want the kind of education that they most need, as is indicated by the types of courses that they themselves arrange for when they set up their own Free Universities. They do not want the kind of education that they need, because they have not been taught the basic moral lessons about the shape of a good human life, about its constituent parts and the means they must employ to achieve it.

❖ ❖ ❖ ❖ ❖ ❖ ❖ ❖ ❖ ❖ ❖ ❖ ❖ ❖ ❖ ❖ ❖ ❖

The foregoing answers to the seven questions that we must all consider and attempt to answer are "catechistic" in the sense that they merely provide a framework within which evidence and reasons can be assembled and marshaled. When that is done, the answers indicated above can, in my judgment, be supported to a degree that is little short of being demonstrative. *In view of this, what should be said of and to the critics of our century and our society?*

Many of them, old as well as young, direct their complaints at the wrong objects. One of the most regrettable features of our century and of our society is not the fact that it has a large number of highly vocal critics who complain about it, but rather the often mistaken, unreasonable, and off-the-beam ways in which they voice their complaints.

On the one hand, the dissident young, frequently under the influence of their professors, together with the leaders of the New Left and others who are full of disaffection for our century and our society, do not hesitate to make moral pronouncements about social evils that they think must be immediately eliminated—and they make these pronouncements with a dogmatic certitude that is inappropriate to such matters, and with an emotional conviction that is unaccompanied by a commitment of their minds to the moral principles and moral reasoning that underlie their charges of injustice and iniquity.

It is perfectly clear that they do not know or understand the moral principles that would give support to their charges, and that they have not engaged in the moral reasoning that could make their criticisms tenable. Exactly the same principles that might support criticism of the war in Vietnam, of racism, and of poverty, should also lead them to criticize a society that exaggerates the importance of sensual pleasures, that engages in the overproduction of superfluous commodities, and that does not draw a line between the frivolous and the serious use of free time. Exactly the same principles and reasoning would also help them to understand what is wrong with being a beatnik, a hippie, a self-alienated refugee from reason, or an existentialist cop-out—wrong in a way that can ruin a human life; or what is wrong with overindulgence in sex; what is wrong with psychedelic escapism, with attempts to expand the sensate life but not the life of the mind; what is wrong with pure emotionalism and the rejection of reason; and so on.

On the other hand, the self-appointed guardians of the morals and patriotism of our society are no less dogmatic in their pronouncements, or in their suggested cures for the evils that they profess to see. They propose, for example, the re-injection of morality in the schools in the form of simple homilies that are as irrelevant today as they were in the past, when they abounded; and they propose, too, that patriotism be taught by distortions of history to emphasize the contributions of persons they think were "patriots," while ignoring those of persons of whom they disapprove. But morality cannot be taught by homilies, nor patriotism by the example of men who were often foolhardy and sometimes not patriots at all.

It is true of these critics, too, that they do not know or understand the principles that would give moral support to their charges. Exactly the same principles that might support their criticisms of the educational system, or of the young, or of corruption in government, should also lead them to criticize a society that exaggerates the importance of wealth and wealth-getting, and an economy that depends too much on defense contracts. Exactly the same principles would help them to understand what is wrong with being a businessman (when business is considered as an end in itself)—wrong in a way that can ruin a human life; what is wrong with overindulgence in alcohol or sports or television; what is wrong with intellectual escapism, combined with ignorance of and contempt for the life of the mind; what is wrong with cruelty and the excessive use of force and the rejection of compromise; and so forth.

Most important of all, these critics—all of them—fail to recognize that many of their criticisms, leveled against America and Americans, apply to all societies and to the human race generally.

In the course of the centuries, human institutions have been greatly improved, and they might be further improved without limit, as William Graham Sumner has remarked, *were it not for folly and vice.* Folly and vice are human defects, not American defects. Twentieth-century America has no monopoly on folly and vice; nor do the critics of the twentieth century have a monopoly on conscience-stricken reactions to human folly and vice. Plato charged the Athenians who condemned Socrates with folly and vice. The dialogues of Plato are a more penetrating critique of the false values of Athens, at the time when it was the glory of antiquity, than anything now being said about America, because Plato had a true scale of values on which to base his criticisms. That is clearly not the case with the most vociferous and emotional critics of American society today.

These things being so, let me suggest three considerations that must be borne in mind when one examines the current attacks on our society and our century. *First*, one should ask whether or not the objects of attack are simply human folly and vice. *Second*, to put these attacks or criticisms into historical perspective, it is necessary to consider the facts in terms of which the twentieth century must be compared with all earlier centuries, and the United States with all other countries in the world today. Many of the critics of our country seem to be totally oblivious of these facts or emotionally unwilling to acknowledge their obvious significance when they are presented. *Third*, one should ask whether those who criticize their country and their fellow countrymen have the moral wisdom—a correct understanding of the good life and a reasonably sound plan for achieving it—that would commit them to a really good life for themselves and direct them in its pursuit. One should also ask whether their own scale of values, the end they aim at and the means they employ, betokens their possession of the moral virtues and of prudence. The evidence—too often, I regret to say—suggests that they do not. They are as much subject to folly and vice as are the objects of their criticism. And the only salvation for them, as for all the rest of us, is the moral wisdom that must be learned to correct the folly, and the moral discipline that must be cultivated to correct the vice.*

* This article is based on the conclusion of the University of Chicago's 1968 Encyclopædia Britannica Lectures, *The Time of Our Lives*, which will soon be published in their entirety by Holt, Rinehart & Winston.

PART TWO

The Year's Developments
in the
Arts and Sciences

JOHN I.
GOODLAD

*John I. Goodlad was born in North Vancouver, British Columbia,
in 1920. He received his teaching certificate from Vancouver Normal School in 1939 and taught in a one-room, eight-grade school
before becoming principal of Surrey Schools. He served as educational director of the Provincial Industrial School for (Delin-
quent) Boys (twelve grades), and earned his master's degree
from the University of British Columbia in 1946. After receiving
his doctorate from the University of Chicago in 1949, he joined
the faculty of Emory University and Agnes Scott College as Associate Professor of Education. The following year he became
Professor and director of their teacher-education program. In
1956 he returned to the University of Chicago as head of the
Center for Teacher Education. He joined the University of California at Los Angeles in 1960 as Professor and director of the
University Elementary School, and in 1967 he became Dean of
the university's Graduate School of Education. He now also
serves as director of the Research and Development Division, Institute for Development of Educational Activities, Inc. He has
been an editorial advisor to periodicals including* Child's World,
Journal of Teacher Education, *and* Progressive Education. *A list
of his writings, ranging from professional articles to encyclopedia
contributions, runs to hundreds of items. Among his books are:*
Educational Leadership and the Elementary School Principal
(*coauthor, 1956*), The Nongraded Elementary School (*coauthor,
1959; rev. ed., 1963*), Computers and Information Systems in Education (*coauthor, 1966*), *and* School, Curriculum, and the Individual (*1966*).

Schooling and Education

For the United States the years from 1957 to 1967 constituted the Education Decade. There may be education decades again, but it is unlikely that there will be another quite like this one. It began with Sputnik and the charge to education to win the Cold War. It ended with a hot war and the growing realization that education is a long-term answer to mankind's problems and must not be confused with social engineering. The danger now is that we are becoming disillusioned with education, without realizing that we are only beginning to try it.

The years 1957–67 could be described more accurately, perhaps, as the Decade of Schooling. The school years were extended upward and downward; the school curriculum was revised from top to bottom; the school was poked and probed at all levels and from every possible perspective; the Elementary and Secondary Education Act of 1965 brought the federal government into schooling as never before; dropout and alienation from school became prime topics for social science research; the schools became both a focal point for social protest and a vehicle for social reform; schooling joined politics and world affairs as leading topics of social discourse. "Innovation" and "revolution" were used interchangeably and indiscriminately in discussing the changes proposed for or taking place in the schools.

The past two years have witnessed a settling down from the ferment of the 1957–67 period. War has drained off funds needed to finance early educational commitments of the Great Society and denied funds to the later commitments. The educational problems of the cities have never been so glaringly apparent nor seemed so far from solution. In 1968 the New York City school system was torn apart by a crippling teacher strike. More important for tomorrow, the city became sharply divided over a proposal to decentralize control to local communities, an issue likely to confront every major school system during the next few years. Meanwhile, there is a desperate need for better schools everywhere, but particularly in the cities. The bubbling, innovative ideas of the Education Decade have not yet transformed our schools in any general way.

But perhaps the most disquieting element of all in 1969 is uncertainty about the place of education and the role of the schools in a society that can put man behind the moon but cannot put poverty, pollution, and war behind man. In launching his administration, President Johnson pointed out that, if one probes deeply enough, one finds education at the heart of every problem. In a sense, he was right. For the long run, no doubt, education is the answer to mankind's problems. For the short haul, however, social engineering is the more likely answer to overpopulation, hunger, joblessness, and human misery. This is especially true in times of revolution—and we are in a great revolution of the human spirit. Enlightened social engineering is the answer to men's problems; the times demand it. Enlightened education is the answer to mankind's problems; the future depends on it.

Education is a never ending process of developing characteristic ways of thinking and behaving on the part of individuals, nations, and, in fact, mankind. Each generation has access to a long heritage from which to derive perspective. Its thinking is shaped by current books, magazines, and newspapers; by movies and television; and by a kaleidoscopic array of events and stimuli which are part of everyday life. Schooling—elementary, secondary, and higher—constitutes the most planned and ordered but not necessarily the most influential part of this process.

In the discussion that follows I will never stray far from schooling. The difference between education and schooling and the relationship between the two will take on increased significance as the essay progresses. Neither education nor schooling has been reviewed as a special topic in the preceding editions of *The Great Ideas Today*. It seemed unwise, therefore, to confine myself narrowly to the past year, especially when the previous decade was so rich educationally.

I begin by comparing certain emphases of the 1950's and 1960's with emphases of the preceding era—the school curriculum serving as a useful point of entry—and conclude with a look into the future. In between, I roam over changes currently taking place in the schools, the advance of educational science, and some of our most pressing educational problems and issues. Regretfully, I write almost exclusively of education and schooling in the United States, with a Western perspective, at the very time in history when a world perspective—no, a mankind perspective—is imperative. But such an all-encompassing view would require both a larger canvas and more collaborators. I write as one who has been close to the day-to-day practices of schooling. An educational philosopher, economist, or learning theorist would view quite differently the ground I cover but, more likely, would choose to cover other ground.

References are handled in two ways. Those which are used only to support or elaborate a specific point are placed as footnotes on the page where they are used. Those which are discussed at greater length, provide basic data or viewpoints, or would be useful for the reader's further reading are listed as a Bibliography at the end. Some of these are not included specifically in the text, but they nonetheless influenced the ideas which follow.

John I. Goodlad

THE EDUCATION DECADE: A BRIEF OVERVIEW

W orld War II and its aftermath brought visible disillusionment with the two preceding decades of American schooling. During the 1920's and 1930's the leaders of so-called Progressive Education proposed a much broader role for the schools than the teaching of reading, writing, and arithmetic. They decried narrow formalism, proposing that the schools "teach the whole child" and that the pressing social issues of the time become the subject matter of instruction. Two books probably represent the characteristic progressive statements of the period. The first (1928) emphasized self-expression;[1] the second (1933) called for a school close to life, a school program which has "definite reference to the needs and issues which mark and divide our domestic, economic, and political life in the generation of which we are a part."[2]

But, as Lawrence Cremin so insightfully points out in his *Transformation of the School,* "there are [in these books] pitifully few specific leads regarding curriculum, methods, and organization, the day-by-day concerns that so condition the life of any school." The teachers, imbued with heady ideas of the power of education, somehow were to reform the schools. There were no new intensive pedagogical retraining programs for these teachers, no packages of new teaching materials, only a handful of experimental schools to provide models, and precious little educational science. Progressive education was more of the mind than of the classroom.

Reading, writing, and arithmetic went on in the schools, much as they had gone on traditionally. This was part of the trouble. Their content and their teaching needed to be updated, and other subjects needed fresh attention. By the beginning of World War II the teaching of foreign languages had virtually disappeared from most schools. Military testing programs revealed widespread academic deficiencies among high-school graduates, particularly in mathematics and the sciences. By the early 1950's the varied voices of criticism were in full cry: Schools are neglecting the fundamentals; life adjustment education has been too long in the saddle; Johnny can't read; and—aging progressivists must have squirmed— the schools repress creativity and individuality.

The period from 1949 to 1955 marks the ending of one era and the beginning of another. Telling criticisms of contemporary American education by Bernard Iddings Bell[3] and Mortimer Smith[4] in 1949 were followed

---

1 Harold O. Rugg and Ann Shumaker, *The Child-Centered School* (Chicago: World Book Co., 1928).

2 William H. Kilpatrick (ed.), *The Educational Frontier* (New York: Century Co., 1933), p. 71.

3 Bernard Iddings Bell, *Crisis in Education* (New York: Whittlesey House, 1949).

4 Mortimer B. Smith, *And Madly Teach* (Chicago: Henry Regnery Co., 1949).

by those of Albert Lynd,[5] Arthur Bestor,[6] Robert Hutchins,[7] and Paul Woodring[8] in 1953. All were penetratingly critical of progressive education. In 1955 Rudolf Flesch[9] blistered the reading approach that had predominated in the schools for three decades. Quietly, in 1955, the Progressive Education Association closed its doors.

If I were to pick just one pivotal year to mark the close of what had been and the emergence of what was to be, this year would be 1951. In 1951 the widely respected progressive school superintendent Willard Goslin was forced out of Pasadena, a showplace of modern pedagogy, by a coalition of citizens opposed to school taxes and progressive education.[10] In 1951 the First Commission on Life Adjustment Education for Youth reiterated most of the well-worn phrases of the progressive education movement in its report and brought down a torrent of criticism.[11] In 1951 the University of Illinois Committee on School Mathematics launched the first of what were to be several nationwide projects in "the new math," a restructuring of school mathematics which seems to have had its genesis at the University of Chicago in the mid-1940's.[12] The subject disciplines were soon to return to center stage in a sweeping reform of the school curriculum.

Change, by definition, moves away from what exists. The conservative period in American education following World War II was *against* what was perceived to have existed before. It was largely *for* what progressive education eschewed. But this conservatism was not very relevant to the 1950's; nor was it very understandable or salient to a mobile generation of young, ambitious parents looking to a new future. The world had changed—changed profoundly.

Sputnik was symbolic and catalytic. It was symbolic of the fact that an explosion of knowledge was rivaled only by an explosion of the human spirit. It was catalytic because the instant orgy of condemnation of the schools and of self-condemnation by educators was followed quickly by plans for action and a broken front of educational reform. Education and the schools became linked with integration of the races, the eradication of crime and poverty, health, prosperity, and peace for all mankind. We

---

5 Albert Lynd, *Quackery in the Public Schools* (Boston: Little, Brown & Co., 1953).

6 Arthur E. Bestor, *Educational Wastelands* (Urbana: University of Illinois Press, 1953).

7 Robert M. Hutchins, *The Conflict in Education in a Democratic Society* (New York: Harper & Brothers, 1953).

8 Paul Woodring, *Let's Talk Sense About Our Schools* (New York: McGraw-Hill Book Co., Inc., 1953).

9 Rudolf F. Flesch, *Why Johnny Can't Read* (New York: Harper & Brothers, 1955).

10 David Hulburd, *This Happened in Pasadena* (New York: The Macmillan Co., 1951).

11 First Commission on Life Adjustment Education for Youth, *Vitalizing Secondary Education* (Washington, D.C.: U.S. Office of Education, 1951).

12 John I. Goodlad, *School Curriculum Reform in the United States* (New York: The Fund for the Advancement of Education, 1964).

narrowed our educational expectations for a few years, back there in the early 1950's. But in the Education Decade that followed the demise of progressive education, we outdid that optimistic movement in our expectations for what education—and by that we meant the schools—could and, indeed, should do.

Because Sputnik was so catalytic—and its impact must not be underestimated—this awesome triumph of man often is viewed as marking the death of progressive education and the birth of a new educational era. Preceding paragraphs reveal, however, that progressive education already had been laid to rest and that fresh educational thrusts already were well begun. The orbiting, man-made satellite vastly accelerated these thrusts. Education became a national and a federal concern. The National Science Foundation (created in 1950) served as the agency for financing large-scale curricular revisions in mathematics and the natural sciences, beginning in the high schools and soon extending down into the elementary schools. Education in the nation's interests became the name of the game.

And the guiding slogan became, "Education is too important to be left to the educators." But this is misleading. Power merely shifted from one group of educators to another. Scientists, especially physicists, suddenly were revered. A physicist at Massachusetts Institute of Technology, Jerrold Zacharias, brought together scientists and selected classroom teachers in a new pattern of curriculum building. Other scientists, generously financed by the National Science Foundation, followed the pattern, adding their own variations. Soon, there was a new alphabet soup of American schooling and versions for export: the products of the Physical Sciences Study Committee (PSSC), the School Mathematics Study Group (SMSG), the Biological Sciences Curriculum Study (BSCS), the Chemical Bond Approach Project (CBA), the Chemical Education Materials Study (CHEM), and more.

This first round of school curriculum reform in the Education Decade, extending from the late 1950's into the 1960's was a middle- and upper-middle-class affair, embracing primarily college-bound students. The anticipated economic collapse, predicted ominously and frequently, had not materialized. An expanding, prosperous middle class of ambitious young men and women saw education as the means to even better things for their children. They turned to their schools—often new schools in new communities, with young teachers and young administrators—with great expectations. These educators responded, reaching out eagerly to become co-workers in the trial use of materials prepared or backed by illustrious scholars in prestigious universities, an association that was not lost on college-conscious parents. The cry of the disadvantaged was as yet only a whisper.

While new communities were springing up, old values were crumbling. Job opportunities took young couples away from familiar haunts to challenges they had not faced before. A new kind of unemployment appeared: unemployment in the midst of plenty because of job obsolescence. Very little was "for sure." People were beginning to realize that a fast-changing culture demanded both adaptability and a rational approach to new problems. The old ways of keeping school would not suffice.

Meanwhile, knowledge was piling up at an intimidating rate. But sheer accumulation presented only part of the problem. All knowledge is subject to revision following new insights into the nature of phenomena. A fact is a fact from some but not all perspectives—and then only temporarily. This notion is stimulating to some people but devastating to others. To cope with the explosion of knowledge, the curriculum needed fresh infusions of content and a comprehensive reorganization.

Federal leadership in Washington viewed rapid advances in mathematics, science, and foreign-language teaching as essential to the nation's ultimate strength and status in *world* affairs. The National Science Foundation became the prime grantor of funds for school projects in these fields. The publication of James B. Conant's *Slums and Suburbs* in 1961 focused attention on what we should have realized all along: Our inner cities were in dire trouble. Goodness knows, the data had been with us long enough! To cope with our *domestic* problems through education, the United States Office of Education came more vigorously into the picture, adding the social sciences and English to the curriculum-reform movement, and laying plans for across-the-board federal involvement in educational change.

The effort for curriculum change in elementary and secondary schools received its momentum from forces and interests lying largely outside the state and local school systems charged legally with responsibility for determining what to teach. The pervasive nature of these forces and interests, as well as their financial support, makes it easy to see why this movement frequently has been labeled "national" and why it was accompanied by the fear of a national curriculum. The total curriculum has been influenced by federal government sources in that funds have been made available more generously for some subjects than for others, resulting in a curricular imbalance. But federal grantors have been careful to maintain a "hands off" policy when it comes to the production of learning materials. Curriculum makers are free to follow their predilections, and they have been producing curricular alternatives at a bewildering rate. If there are similarities in approach from project to project, they result from imitation and lack of imagination rather than the imposition of restrictions by funding agencies.

But the course of curricular change—and, in fact, educational change in general—was vigorously directed from within, too, by new ideas and research into knowledge, learning, teaching, and the individual. The book which most influenced the new breed of curriculum reformers was

The Process of Education, by the psychologist Jerome Bruner, published in 1960. "Structure" (of the disciplines) and "intuition" (in learning) became as central to the jargon of the new era as "the whole child" and "life-adjustment" had been to the progressive era. Bruner's phrase, ". . . any subject can be taught effectively in some intellectually honest form to any child at any stage of development" (p. 33), came to be quoted often to justify "solid fare" in the curriculum, extending downward to the early years.

Bruner's ideas of "spiraling" in the curriculum go back to Whitehead, who spoke of enriched repetition in successively new contexts, as do his ideas on structure and discovery. But Bruner links up with Dewey, too, in his concern for humanizing knowledge to make it popular. Cremin, in his little book *The Genius of American Education,* reminds us, however, that Bruner did not take us back to first questions and that it is time to ask Spencerian questions more insistently than ever: What knowledge is of most worth? What priorities in education? (p. 56).

What my colleagues and I wrote about the current curriculum scene in 1966 (*The Changing School Curriculum*) is equally relevant in 1969. A generation of American youth is now growing up with a diet of the new alphabet soup: BSCS, CBA, ESS, PSSC, SMSG . . . . From the beginning the movement has been directed at teachers and students in the classroom. It has not sought to change the basic structure of American education or the thinking of administrators, although the present curriculum-reform wave has profound implications for both. Thousands of teachers have attended yearlong or summer institutes designed to update their understanding and teaching of academic disciplines. Millions of children and youths are bringing home assignments in mathematics, for example, that are incomprehensible to their parents. High-school students approach biology, chemistry, and physics in ways and with assumptions that appear different from our own experiences as we recall them. The degree and kind of change vary from subject to subject, from school system to school system, and even from school to school within a single system. Although the movement is nationwide, it is by no means national in the sense of being uniformly prescribed from state to state or from school district to school district.

In virtually every field the focal point for teachers and students alike is an instructional materials package: invariably a textbook or series of textbooks (often paperback) and frequently supplementary books, workbooks, teachers' manuals, filmstrips, films, programmed materials, and laboratory experiments. Students often learn about subject matter through audiovisual media of instruction and whenever possible by directly observing phenomena and the methods of dealing with these phenomena.

If previous eras of curriculum development can be described as child centered or society centered, this one can be designated as subject or discipline centered. The ends and means of schooling are derived from organized bodies of knowledge. Further, the curriculum is planned by physicists, mathematicians, and historians, and students are encouraged to think like these scholars.

Many curriculum builders seek to organize their fields around the primary structural elements of each discipline: the concepts, key ideas, principles, and modes of inquiry. It is assumed that understanding these elements (rather than merely possessing the facts) gives the student the intellectual power to attack unfamiliar problems and enables him to grasp intuitively the relationship of new phenomena not previously encountered to phenomena already experienced. Ability to think inductively becomes a built-in goal, and teachers are encouraged to let students discover meanings for themselves.

The current curriculum-reform movement is marked by an updating of content, a reorganization of subject matter, and some fresh approaches to methodology in fields traditionally taught in the schools. It is not simply a return to the Three R's. Grandpa would never recognize today's Three R's. Many of the central concerns of progressive education—emphasis on principles rather than facts, on learning through problem-solving rather than by precept, and on individual differences—are stressed and extended by some of today's curriculum builders. But the stress, until recently, has been almost exclusively on the discipline as a separate entity in the curriculum: not science but biology, chemistry, or physics; not social studies but history, geography, or economics; not English but literature, composition, or grammar.

The separate-subject approach creates few immediately apparent problems for the secondary school. Traditionally, high-school teachers have been prepared in a major field and supporting disciplines. Teaching that field in the high school permits a smooth transition from their own studies. Fusing two or more subjects, on the other hand, adds a curriculum-planning burden to teaching demands and often calls for collaborative effort with colleagues. Perhaps this is why curriculum innovations such as the core curriculum (usually combining English and social studies) never achieved more than very modest success.

But teaching each field as a discrete entity raises some questions about whether the subject matter is meaningful to the adolescent or whether his school day and the rest of his life remain worlds apart. From a more academic point of view, one wonders too about the subjects left out of the curriculum, simply for lack of time. Some fields of study are now more deeply entrenched in the high school than ever before, mostly because large sums of money have been available for their updating. As a consequence, some relatively new subjects representing exciting advances in human knowledge have been left at the curriculum periphery—and will remain there unless a deliberate effort is made to include them in the curriculum design. It would seem that there are decisions of curriculum planning that are too far-reaching to be left to subject-matter specialists alone.

The separate-subject approach, however, creates some immediately apparent problems for the elementary school. First, elementary-school teachers in most states are prepared as generalists rather than as specialists in subject fields. Second, there is a limit to the number of disciplines that can be taught within the time available, and some difficult choices must therefore be made. There simply is no room in the curriculum for thirty or more separate subjects. Third, if the basic structures and concepts of the academic disciplines form the curriculum design of secondary education, what is to be the approach for elementary education? Is there something of a more basic nature than what has been conceived for the high school?

Problems such as these have caused curriculum planners to wonder whether it is wise to build the curriculum revision at the elementary-school level on assumptions that were valid for the secondary school. Some reexamination was called for, and new ideas are beginning to emerge. For example, although four major efforts to reorganize the elementary-school science curriculum differ markedly in their emphases, not one of them is committed to developing each science field separately. All see the need either to combine the disciplines at the outset, or to begin separately but then to effect syntheses and integrations. The prevailing mood is one of experimentation, of trying a variety of approaches to see what will happen.

It must be remembered that the impetus, planning, and financial support for the type of subject-centered curriculum revision now taking place do not come from the state and local school districts legally responsible for precollegiate public education in the United States. The curriculum products of the Physical Sciences Study Committee, the School Mathematics Study Group, the Chemical Bond Approach Project, etc., provide both ends and means of schooling for the classroom. It would be reassuring to believe that school districts use the products of one curriculum study group in preference to another because they have carefully examined them and found them better suited to those aims of education to which the districts are committed. But this is rarely the case. Few state departments of education, and even fewer school districts, have seriously tried to determine the precise purpose of their schools and the objectives to be achieved. And yet Americans cling stubbornly to the idea of local control of education while permitting, through sheer neglect, many of the most important decisions to be made by remote curriculum planners. To develop an increased awareness of what these decisions are, and to whom we are leaving the responsibility for making them, is a curricular agenda item for tomorrow.

Another agenda item concerns the problem of fitting the various curricular pieces together. The curriculum and the students of tomorrow may be better served by subjects and subject combinations other than those deemed important today. But curriculum planning takes place in such a piecemeal fashion that across-the-board examination of the total school experience of children and youth is not likely to occur. In all probability, new accretions and formulations will occur in the traditional school subjects if the curriculum revision procedures of the past decade continue. But ongoing inquiry in fields not now firmly established in the curriculum is likely to go unnoticed unless we concentrate on the aims of schooling rather than on the organization of specific subjects.

A third item for tomorrow's agenda pertains to curriculum experimentation. Since local school leaders are directly responsible to local patrons and taxpayers, they either cannot experiment or do not consider themselves free to do so; and state educational leaders generally do not control or have access to schools that might be used for experimental purposes. Approaches to change, therefore, are almost necessarily cautious; and the changes that are instituted are "safe." Such innovations as are introduced, furthermore, are given an aura of success, achieved most often through an association with a prestigious institution of higher learning. "Experiments" are rarely experiments but are rather the trial-and-error refinement of assumptions that are seldom questioned.

Some of the needed experimentation must be in recasting knowledge for purposes of teaching. Some of it must be in pedagogy and in the education of teachers who understand both what they teach and why they teach it as they do. Some of this experimentation must be the testing and combining of curricular alternatives in a variety of educational settings.

But if we are at all alert to the signs of the times, two other kinds of experimentation are needed immediately. School curricula at all levels must become more relevant to the lives of the students. The activism recently characteristic of some college students is now extending downward into the secondary schools. A vigorous group of educational critics is insisting that schools everywhere—not just the schools of harsh environment ghettos—are largely irrelevant and in desperate need of new purposes. The experimentation now needed must redefine the ends and means of education and the role of what we formally know as school.

The second kind of experimentation is likely to bring teachers and learners at all levels into much more active participation in planning and conducting educational programs. Teachers, too, are becoming activists. Opportunities for self-directed learning are likely to be vastly expanded. Educational guidance increasingly will transcend the vocational in seeking to come to grips with "the person." School will become less visible as a physical entity in the educational scheme of things. And more of us

School curricula at all levels must become more relevant to the lives of the students

will be teaching one another, and more of us will be studying as a way of life.

It is impossible even to sketch the panorama of recent educational developments. The school curriculum, more than other aspects of formal education, tends to reflect at least some of the larger social, political, and economic concerns of the times. The rest of schooling, on the other hand, is more likely to respond to pressures from within, to research findings in the field, and to salient innovative practice. The words "innovative" and "revolutionary" frequently have been applied to the schools in recent years. But we are beginning to conclude that there has been more talk than action.

I review briefly, then, four areas of schooling which have been the focus of much recent attention. These are: (1) the organization of the school as an environment for learning; (2) the means and processes of learning and teaching; (3) early schooling; and (4) the provision of equal educational opportunity for the environmentally disadvantaged.

The organization of schools.—School structure has been going through what might be described as a loosening up, an unshackling. Some of this has been in response to a growing body of data about individual differences among human beings. The instructional theme of providing for individual differences has brought with it attacks on the traditional lockstep, egg-crate school, especially at the elementary-school level. The lockstep is represented by grade levels which lock side-by-side pupils of the same age and advance them together through identical, graded subject matter. The egg-crate school places in separate, side-by-side cells some thirty pupils and a teacher who attends to all or nearly all of their daily teaching. Nongrading, to replace the lockstep, and team teaching to replace the egg-crate, have been proposed as alternatives to the compartmentalized school most of us knew in our childhood. They are described and discussed in such works as *The Nongraded Elementary School* (1959, revised 1963), by Goodlad and Anderson; *Planning and Organizing for Teaching* (1963), a publication of the Project on Instruction of the National Education Association; *Team Teaching* (1964), edited by Shaplin and Olds; and *The Changing American School* (1966), a portion of the yearbook of the National Society for the Study of Education.

Nongrading, in concept, sweeps away the graded superstructure, graded content, graded textbooks, graded normative standards, graded children, graded teachers, graded expectations, and the graded nomenclature to which we have long been accustomed. These accouterments of graded schools are so familiar that we resist their departure. For graded schools, nongrading theoretically substitutes continuous pupil progress uninhibited by grade barriers; subject matter organized sequentially around fundamental concepts, principles, and ways of thinking; instructional materials gathered from a variety of sources to meet the varying abilities and interests of the pupils for whom they are intended; and performance standards inherent in the demands of the task rather than the norms of a class or grade; and still other provisions.

Team teaching casts aside the traditional, monolithic deployment of teacher resources. Instead of 30 pupils in a self-contained classroom with one teacher for all subjects or in a departmentalized plan with one teacher for each subject, visualize 75, 100, or 150 students supervised by a team of teachers and teacher aides, deployed into instructional groups of various sizes and space provisions appropriate to these group sizes. The teaching team functions under a leader—rarely the same person for long—and delineates staff functions according to the needs of students, the abilities of teachers, and the demands of the tasks. A considerable portion of time goes to pupil diagnosis, counseling, and remediation of learning difficulties.

Nongrading and team teaching are well enough established in theory and in practice to have spawned a sizable body of publications. Many schools in the United States carry the nongraded or team-taught label or both. But none has fully achieved what has been envisioned for nongrading and team teaching. Visions of what might be intoxicate the mind, while practice lags far behind. The gulf is due in part to the fact that successful introduction of these reforms depends not only on radically different ways of *thinking about* the conduct of schooling but also on sophisticated *engineering* skill. More flexible approaches to school organization must be fitted with equally flexible patterns of curriculum and teaching. The variables to be accounted for are many and complex. Clearly, the computer promises not only to individualize instruction but also to manage the factors to be manipulated in the environment where both individual and group instruction are to take place.

Already, school buildings are being redesigned to accommodate nongrading and team teaching and the computer cables which facilitate individualized instruction in these schools. The prisonlike structures of generations past are gradually being replaced by colorful, airy buildings, some of which feature large, open spaces under domed roofs, and what Harold Gores of the Ford Foundation's Educational Facilities Laboratories refers to as snap-on walls. Increasingly, too, such schools have at their core an instructional materials center with books, records, films, filmstrips, and assorted pamphlets. The schoolhouse, perhaps more than the instruction in it, is changing, providing us with public buildings which are both functional and pleasing to the eye. But even here, progress is slow, and many schools on the drawing boards still resemble their predecessors more than they do the forward-looking learning centers that we might have—which, incidentally, cost no more to build. We continue to cling to some of our Puritan traditions, favoring austere school buildings, not because they cost less, but because "learning should hurt a little."

Media and process.—Progressive educators eschewed textbooks. But they provided no practicable alternative. The textbook became and is today the dominant medium of instruction in the schools and colleges.[13] Even most of the new curriculum projects, in mathematics, biology, chemistry, and so on, set as their goal the production of a textbook, although some richly supplement the book with films, experiments, and supplementary readings. In fact, the current breed of curriculum reformers seems to be acutely aware of the need to place in the hands of teachers a familiar and easily used instructional tool. This awareness no doubt stems in part from recent research in the behavioral sciences, suggesting that human behavior is not easily changed and that the acquisition of specific skills and knowledge requires the careful prearranging of what is to be learned. This careful prearrangement finds its most refined expression in what has become known as programmed instruction.

In 1960 A. A. Lumsdaine and Robert Glaser brought together a massive compendium of what they considered to be the most significant body

---

13 A 1962 study revealed that the textbook not only kept its preeminence from 1956 to 1961 but gained slightly in importance. See *The Principals Look at the Schools* (Washington, D.C.: National Education Association [Project on the Instructional Program of the Public Schools], 1962), p. 24.

The prisonlike structures of generations past are gradually being replaced by colorful, airy buildings, some of which feature large, open spaces under domed roofs, and what Harold Gores of the Ford Foundation's Educational Facilities Laboratories refers to as snap-on walls.

of material on programmed instruction. In the 1930's Sydney Pressey, the psychologist and the "father of the teaching machine," designed a device for pacing the student through programmed material at his own rate, preventing him from repeating errors, and reinforcing his learning by repeatedly rewarding success for its own sake. Much of the theoretical and empirical underpinning of this approach has been developed by B. F. Skinner in the training of pigeons and rather engagingly applied to humans in his fictitious, scientifically shaped Utopia.[14] Programming involves, first, precise definitions of the learning outcome intended, and then the sequential, step-by-step delineation of learning "sets," each set being contributory to the acquisition of some larger unit of learning. Theoretically, precision in the determination and arrangement of these sets supports Bruner's dictum that "any subject can be taught effectively in some intellectually honest form to any child at any stage of development."

Pressey's teaching machine was rediscovered in the Education Decade and broke in upon the scene in the early 1960's as part of the great educational revolution. Brave, new, entrepreneuring companies based on the machine appeared and quickly disappeared. Even a few relatively conservative publishing houses were badly burned. The teaching machine did not take over. Part of the problem lay with the gadgetry; the greater part lay with the need to program large quantities of palatable learning fare. But the pioneers in programming were far more interested in exploring learning theory than in the comparatively dull business of producing material. Somehow, the producers and the theorists never quite got together.

But the school and the teacher were not ready anyway. The school's lockstep is not conducive to the individuality of programmed instruction. Teachers are not accustomed to their students being at thirty different places in their work—even though this is really where a class is at any given moment. Further, only a few teachers have managed to include more than talking and the printed page in their instructional arsenal. School radio, introduced in the late 1930's, succeeded in becoming little more than a tack-on, a break from the real business of the day. Educational television, introduced in the 1950's, fared little better. And, in both media, most programs intended for classrooms have been dreadful. Strangely, teachers have not taken to films and filmstrips, either, in spite of the quantity of material available and the quality of much of it. To use any of these media requires good planning and considerable managerial skill. Neither the school day nor the school setting has been particularly conducive to either.

A new instructional medium, the computer, now looms on the horizon. It is proving to be virtually hypnotic for that small army of social scientists

---

14 B. F. Skinner, *Walden Two* (New York: The Macmillan Co., 1948).

interested in information processing but has entered only a little into formal educational processes.[15] The uses for storing and retrieving vast quantities of data on students, teachers, institutions, and costs, and for scheduling various congeries for the same place and time, are reasonably clear. But the more sophisticated uses for human learning are far from clear; so-called computer-assisted instruction is still in a primitive, experimental stage. Interesting and rather expensive research and development proceed apace at such universities as Illinois, Massachusetts Institute of Technology, Pittsburgh, Texas, and Stanford, and in the laboratories of those technologically oriented companies increasingly moving into the education and information industries. Already, however, it is unmistakably clear that the computer is a superb device for reconstructing at least a part of human brain functioning; that it will become exceedingly important in learning and teaching; and that it is an avaricious devourer of human-made instructional programs.

The current thrust toward individualized instruction carries with it an implicit directive: The learner should become self-propelling. Producers of materials, especially those involved in the new curriculum projects, often are so imbued with this idea that they have striven for "teacher-proof" materials to be used by students with little or no teacher intervention. Interestingly, the more teacher-proof these materials have become, the less latitude has been left for the student to deviate from the prescribed programs. A remote teacher has been substituted for one close at hand. Associated with this notion of self-propulsion is the idea that students should work out basic principles inductively; that is, by building from specific observations and experiments as scientists do. They are to come to think like physicists, historians, and linguists. Programmed texts, programmed workbooks, and programmed machines would appear to allow little opportunity for self-propelled intuitive leaps into the speculative, as well as the hard-nosed empirical, world of the scientist. Conant,[16] and Dewey[17] before him, wisely remind us that thinking is of two modes, with the scientist sometimes employing the theoretical-deductive mode of thought, sometimes the empirical-inductive, sometimes both, and almost always believing in some working hypothesis as a point of departure. Modern educational thought is a mixed bag. It is unlikely that a reasonably consistent rhetoric will emerge soon.

Early education.—It is difficult, if not impossible, to synthesize in any

---

15 *See* John I. Goodlad, John F. O'Toole, Jr., and Louise L. Tyler, *Computers and Information Systems in Education* (New York: Harcourt, Brace & World, Inc., 1966); Donald D. Bushnell and Dwight W. Allen (eds.), *The Computer in American Education* (New York: John Wiley & Sons, Inc., 1967).

16 James B. Conant, *Two Modes of Thought* (New York: Trident Press, 1964).

17 John Dewey, *The Sources of a Science of Education* (New York: Liveright Publishing Corp., 1929).

meaningful way all of the forces from outside the formal educational enterprise and all of the drives from within that combined to create an enormous interest in stimulating the cognitive development of the young child through deliberate effort. One of the most significant factors, however, has been the growing body of research in the behavioral sciences pertaining to the nature and nurturing of intelligence. Not long ago, we believed that I.Q., a measure of the relationship between age and intellectual functioning, was fixed and immutable. But careful observation of retarded three-year-olds during subsequent years of special nursery-school training reveals a shift toward normal intellectual functioning. The possibilities of enhancing cognitive development through intervention at birth has stimulated both promising research and disturbing quackery. "Teach your child to read in the cradle" and "prepare your kindergartner for Harvard" are common prototype titles of articles in some women's magazines.

Perhaps the most timely book in the field was *Stability and Change in Human Characteristics*, by Benjamin S. Bloom, in 1964. After reviewing approximately one thousand longitudinal studies of child development, Bloom set forth the intriguing thesis that, in most areas of development, some 50 to 80 percent of the behavior characteristic of late adolescence already is structured between the ages of five and eight. In other words, the child is father to the man. Reactions to the book have ranged from bizarre proposals for early schooling to expressions of hopelessness over the human condition. The solid implication is, however, that the early years of life are highly formative ones. Damage and deprivation experienced before entrance to school are difficult to overcome, even under the most intensely positive school conditions.

Studies into early human behavior at long last are vying in status among psychologists with studies into animal behavior. The infant human has come into his own as a subject for scientific investigation. It is becoming increasingly clear that human awareness comes earlier in life than we once believed; that various responses to stimuli can be speeded up through intervention; that lack of stimulation and mental sluggishness go hand in hand; that mental development often is impeded and impaired long before the child embarks on the school road. Most psycholo-

gists in the cognitive field believe that attainment of full adult potential depends on rich, appropriate, early intellectual stimulation.

We know much less about the kind and quality of stimulation that is most conducive to the attainment of full potential. We do not know when or whether to remove the young child for at least part of the time from what appears to be a rich, rewarding home environment. And there is long-standing controversy about whether the early school environment should emphasize play and social interaction, or whether the child should experience a regimen of carefully programmed lessons. Ironically, it is the parent from the "cognitive home" who is most likely to seek and get early schooling for his child. And it is the underprivileged community that is least able and least likely to provide nursery school and kindergarten for the children from its homes.

The literature of early learning is voluminous; we are just beginning to get a literature of early education.[18] The trouble is that there has been precious little *study* of the educative process at any level, but especially in the years before regular schooling begins. In 1966 the United States Office of Education charged a committee, under my chairmanship, with the responsibility of setting up an interlocking network of university centers for purposes of studying childhood education, planning programs for children on the basis of pooled findings and insights, training teachers, and disseminating information. This national laboratory is now in existence, with several university centers, but it is virtually starving for resources because of escalating war costs. Meanwhile, our efforts to increase and improve early education are closely associated with education of the disadvantaged.

Education of the disadvantaged.—The facts regarding both the pitifully inadequate school provisions for and the correspondingly low academic attainments of an environmentally deprived segment of our population have been with us for some time. We had plenty of data decades ago. But it took a decision of the Supreme Court of the United States (1954), the march of time, political events, social upheavals, and a host of additional factors and events to bring them startlingly to our attention. And then the urgently needed social engineering became obfuscated by well-intentioned, unrealistic, and oversold expectations for education. A non-utilitarian, long-term commitment to education is the hope of mankind. But to confuse education and social engineering is to court annihilation.

Poverty prevails in two out of three families whose head has completed

---

18 *See,* for example, Maya Pines, *Revolution in Learning* (New York: Harper & Row, Publishers, Inc., 1967); Susan W. Gray and associates, *Before First Grade* (New York: Teacher College Press [Columbia University], 1966); Fred M. Hechinger (ed.), *Pre-School Education Today* (New York: Doubleday & Co., Inc., 1966); Robert D. Hess and Roberta M. Baer (eds.), *Early Education: Current Theory, Research, and Action* (Chicago: Aldine Publishing Co., 1968).

less than nine years of formal schooling; a child growing up in a family of $12,000 income, as contrasted with one in a family of $3,000 income, has four times the chance of attending college; every year 100,000 of our brightest high-school graduates cannot contemplate a college education; in the last decade, jobs for high-school graduates rose by 40 percent while jobs for those who failed to complete high school dropped by 10 percent. And the homes in which poverty prevails, and in which college attendance is out of the question, are predominantly the inner-city homes of Negroes. Conant, in *Slums and Suburbs*, put the matter bluntly: "This republic was born with a congenital defect—Negro slavery." The combined forces of urbanization, advances in technology, inequality in educational opportunity, and racial discrimination have so concentrated a disproportionately large Negro population in the nation's urban centers that problems of urban renewal, civil rights, and education of the disadvantaged have become almost inseparably intertwined.

During the 1960's these and more in an assorted potpourri of vital social issues and problems have been caught up in governmental policies and programs at the federal level. Through the Equal Educational Program of the Civil Rights Act of 1964, the 88th Congress of the United States provided special assistance to public schools seeking to effect desegregation and instructed the Commissioner of Education to report on "the lack of availability of equal educational opportunities for individuals by reason of race, color, religion, or national origin in public educational institutions at all levels." Through the Economic Opportunity Act of 1964, this Congress also provided assistance to students of low-income families in their pursuit of higher education through promoting work-study programs; opportunities for persons over the age of eighteen to assume their adult responsibilities by initiating for them basic programs of instruction in reading and writing; and encouragement to school systems to provide early educational opportunities for the disadvantaged to offset the disabling effects of their respective environments. Then, in the astonishing and precedent-setting Elementary and Secondary Education Act of 1965, the 89th Congress allocated the lion's share—$1.1 billion—to assist school districts with their momentous tasks of keeping children from low-income families in school and giving them the kind of education they need (Title I). But these tasks remain momentous—second only to the attainment of world peace in their critical significance for the United States and, more important, for mankind.

Growing interest in early education and concern for improving the educational status of disadvantaged children have gone hand in hand. Bloom's data (*Stability and Change in Human Characteristics*) were timely, implying grave difficulties in overcoming through schooling the effects of deprivation brought to school by the disadvantaged child. At the time these difficulties were gaining attention in the United States,

121

Head Start has been an amazing demonstration in human engineering

leading educators in Israel were putting together a program of compensatory education for the so-called Oriental Jew.[19] Immigrant children brought to school an environmental disadvantage which subsequent schooling did not overcome. An initial disparity in academic attainment grew progressively worse. The Israeli experiment in early education was designed to expand steadily each year until it embraced all four-year-olds. Enthusiasm in that country sobered somewhat as it was realized that initially positive effects, with respect to academic attainment, tended to subside when the compensatory program was discontinued on children's entry into regular school.

The closest parallel to the Israeli experience in the United States has been Head Start, operated under the aegis of the Office of Economic Opportunity. Head Start has been an amazing demonstration in human engineering in that, in its first year of operation, a few months of frenetic organizing resulted in summer educational programs for tens of thousands of underprivileged preschool children. The word *preschool* is significant here because these short-term summer efforts were designed to prepare children for the academic demands of first grade. The appropriateness of a middle-class system of primary schooling for the common problems and unique needs of the group for whom Head Start was intended became a later agenda item.

The beneficial effects of Head Start have been widely acclaimed and equally widely disputed. Hard data are lacking. Some school superintendents, in districts where Head Start was planned closely with local school authorities, have been rhapsodic in their testimonials regarding the subsequent readiness of the children involved for first grade. Sociologists and psychologists, acutely aware of the difficulties involved in short-term approaches to the modifications of human behavior, have been skeptical. Almost everyone agrees that the brevity of the summer sessions, the uncertainties about how best to intervene in the developing behavior of young children, the paucity of trained workers, and the persistence of environmental deprivation following entry into school are formidable limitations.

In 1969 two critical and closely related themes pertaining to the education of disadvantaged children and youth stand out. The first: how to overcome invidious, continuing, environmental deprivation and its effects not only on intellectual stimulation but also on self-image and personal expectations. Inquiry here is revealing and suggestive, but the full story of human withering and unfulfilled potential remains to be written. The second: how to increase the intensity and improve the quality of the

---

19 Moshe and S. Smilansky, "Bases for Intellectual Advancement of Culturally Disadvantaged Children," a paper presented at the 7th Annual Research Roundup of Children and Youth at the University of California, Los Angeles, July, 1965.

school. General discussion of this problem follows in a later section. Both of these themes were brought into sharp and unified focus with publication late in 1966 of the controversial Coleman report, *Equality of Educational Opportunity*, and the subsequent discussion of it which remained intense during subsequent years.[20]

Undoubtedly, criticisms of the report for its design, statistical treatment, size and kind of sample, tests, and so on, will stimulate more and better studies in due course of time. Meanwhile, the problems will not wait and the implications—set forth more tentatively and speculatively by James Coleman and his associates, I think, than is generally recognized by the critics—stir the fires of controversy. The first and perhaps most disputed finding is that schools are remarkably similar in the way they relate to the achievement of their pupils. When socioeconomic factors are controlled, it appears that differences among schools account for only a small fraction of differences in pupil achievement. Even though Coleman reports that the achievement of minority pupils depends more on the schools they attend than does the achievement of majority pupils, he brings into the spotlight the question of how much can be accomplished by upgrading curricula and facilities. The second major finding suggests that a pupil's achievement is strongly related to the educational backgrounds and aspirations of the other students in the school. The implication here is that a minority pupil from a home lacking in educational strength, placed with schoolmates who have strong educational backgrounds, is likely to improve in academic achievement. But *de facto* segregation tends to congregate in one school setting those students who bring limited educational background from their homes and who, therefore, encounter little among their classmates, and, in another setting, those who both bring and encounter richness in such background.

The Coleman report is used to support advocates of bussing students from one community to another and of educational parks. The argument from the Coleman report for school bussing is self-evident: the mix of students is enriched. If bussing were a two-way rather than a one-way proposition, however, we could be more confident that our present minority group schools are, indeed, equal to majority group schools with respect to the formal educational effort put into them.

The educational park—a more complex, long-term solution to equality of educational opportunity—takes several forms.[21] One of these is appropriate to the densely populated metropolitan area where children and youth of widely divergent socioeconomic status live relatively close to

---

20 *See*, for example, *Harvard Educational Review*, Vol. XXXVIII, No. 1 (Winter, 1968).

21 United States Commission on Civil Rights, *Education Parks* (Washington, D.C.: The Commission, 1967).

each other. The local segregated school is replaced by a much larger integrated unit which encompasses the varied populations of several schools. Another plan proposed in 1967 for Chicago and Pittsburgh would bring students from all segments of the metropolitan area into several large school units. The basis of assigning students would assure a balanced mix. In both instances, but especially in the first, the educational park would serve as a cultural and continuing education center for people of all ages.

These plans and many more are but palliatives, contrived adaptations designed to place on the schools responsibility for remedying the cancerous illness of the larger social context. And this cancer is racial prejudice and all the human injustices that go with it. Education in the broadest sense and in the long run probably is the answer to preventing cancer in all its forms. Present instrumental expectations for the schools are an extension of self-loving philanthropic traditions and tendencies. Charity has never been and never will be adequate. Enlightened social engineering is our central responsibility. Participation in this social engineering—including the development of better schools—by those who are now disadvantaged, offers these persons good work, self-respect, and some hope of viewing education as a way of life.

EDUCATIONAL SCIENCE

The Education Decade was a period of searching for better ways to conduct the formal educational enterprise. It was a time of innovation. The programs of local parent-teacher associations featured topics such as nongrading, team teaching, and individualizing instruction. Primary-age children talked glibly of "sets" and "the commutative law." Parents became uneasy when structural English began to replace the age-old grammar they had known. High-school students in Nevada followed a weekly timetable determined by a computer in Palo Alto, California. Elementary-school pupils in Mississippi spent part of their mathematics lesson responding to computer terminals controlled by a computer and instructional staff at Stanford. The egg-crate school, in at least a few places, began to yield to the concept of malleable, flexible space which could be adapted to the needs of teachers and students.

As we shall see, these changes were not general. But they were and are relatively well known and discussed by both educators and well-informed laymen. Today, it is fair to say, every major city in the United States and most of the outlying schools are trying nongrading, team teaching, flexible scheduling, programmed or computerized instruction, and interesting first departures in school building design. And, of course, new instructional materials are carrying the so-called curriculum-reform movement into most of the schools of the nation. Unfortunately, limited understanding and clumsy implementation often have blunted the thrust of recent educational reform.

Meanwhile, a long-neglected side of educational advancement has been making a modest showing. This is the search for principles, for an educational science, on which to base action and from which to predict consequences. The corps of well-trained individuals committed to educational research is desperately small; there has been a reluctance to break new ground in the search for methods appropriate to the study of educational problems; and the financial resources available have been puny. Nonetheless, a field is being staked out—one that should prove attractive to scholars and, ultimately, to foundations and government funding agencies.

Inquiry into educational phenomena cuts across such established disciplines as philosophy, history, biology, psychology, political science, economics, anthropology, sociology, and more. Whether or not there is a discipline of education is frequently and inconclusively argued.[22] Nonetheless, phenomena which are classified best under the rubric "education" are being systematically studied from a variety of perspectives, with results that are affecting and increasingly will affect educational practice. An embryonic science of education is beginning to emerge.

Reviewing the substance and methods of this budding science is far too comprehensive a task to be undertaken here. The study of education is nothing more than a study of man from still another perspective, and so work in the field falls into classic categories: the nature of knowledge and knowing, the individual and groups, learning and teaching, man and society, and so on. Clearly, then, it is virtually impossible to differentiate sharply the study of education from the study of human behavior in general. To give the flavor, let me touch upon the kinds of inquiries which support and advance educational developments discussed on preceding pages.

As my colleagues and I point out in *The Changing School Curriculum* (1966), current curriculum revision in the schools reflects recent thinking about knowledge, how to organize it, and how one knows. Today's scientists view knowledge as what man perceives. Therefore, knowledge does not merely accumulate but is recast again and again within fresh theoretical constructs. Facts become facts only within the perspective of the viewer. Robert Karplus, a physicist at the University of California, Berkeley, believes this kind of thinking to be so important that he wants it taught to children when they are very young, before their thinking is distorted by the view that knowledge is immutable. Using a mobile viewer,

---

22 *See*, for example, John Walton and James L. Kuethe (eds.), *The Discipline of Education* (Madison: The University of Wisconsin Press, 1963); Marc Belth, *Education as a Discipline* (Boston: Allyn and Bacon, Inc., 1965).

Mr. O., in his Science Curriculum Improvement Study, Karplus teaches young children to observe carefully from every possible perspective, to cast and then recast hypotheses on the basis of changing observations.

The word *intuition* had little scientific status until Bruner brought it to the fore again in his *Process of Education.* He joined it with the concept of "structure," proposing that knowing involves a grasp of the structural elements of a discipline—principles, concepts, modes of thinking. Understanding this structure provides a base from which to take intuitive, speculative leaps along the road toward new insights. The student discovers for himself. This "discovery method" became central to curriculum projects which entered the schools: the University of Illinois Arithmetic Project, the Greater Cleveland Mathematics Program, Science—A Process Approach, and many more.

Very little of this curriculum building has involved systematic testing of the fundamental assumptions underlying it. Rather, it has been a process of engineering, of refining in practice curricula based on principles believed to be sound. At times, scientists in the various disciplines have seemed overly certain with respect to these principles. Mathematicians and physicists often have been willing to take firm positions regarding how people learn and how knowledge should be organized, while remaining very cautious about their own fields in reminding us that knowledge is tentative, that the scientific view is one of never being sure.

Uncertainty about how humans learn is the guiding motivation among educational researchers inquiring into what Robert Glaser defines as the design of instruction (in a chapter of that title in *The Changing American School,* 1966). Such inquiry gets to the very heart of formal educational processes: analyzing what is involved in subject-matter competence, diagnosing the student's present level of attainment, creating conditions for acquiring increased competence, and measuring learning outcomes. This is demanding, significant, scientific work of a kind likely to contribute to a solid, professional base for teaching. It provides the bridge between basic laboratory studies in brain functioning and the practice of education in the field: planning curricula, programming instruction, preparing tests, organizing classrooms, and all the rest. Just a very few years ago, psychologists could not have cared less about contributing to the building of such a bridge, but it is becoming increasingly respectable. E. R. Hilgard, a first-rate psychologist, concluded a recent educational yearbook on theories of learning with the following observation: "We believe that scientific psychology of learning has the obligation to go all the way from theory to practice, using criticized data in every step."

Understanding the nature of learning and designing instruction are enormously complicated by the uniqueness of each individual and the differences in readiness, response, and accomplishment among individuals. The study of human variability is not a new field of inquiry. But, as

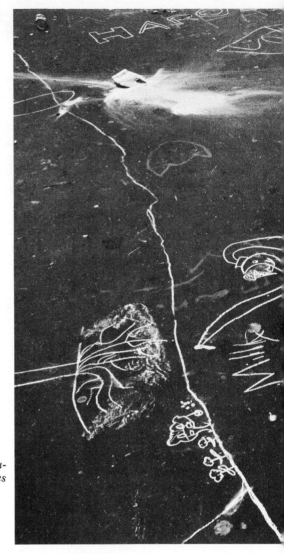

Some relish in the opportunity to respond to classmates

Suppes[23] points out, this line of scholarly activity has been strangely neglected in the educational realm. There has not been gathered a body of evidence on the educational dimensions to match the data on human variability as, for example, a biological phenomenon. But this condition probably will not prevail for long. The educational aspects and implications of individual human differences are now central to much educational inquiry. There have been, this past year, dozens of conferences on individual differences, ranging from those concerned almost exclusively with progress on research to those concerned exclusively with educational practice. In contrast, just a few years ago the literature on individual

23 Patrick Suppes, "Modern Learning Theory and the Elementary School Curriculum," *American Educational Research Journal*, Vol. I (March, 1964), 79–93.

differences as they pertain to education and schooling was thin; now a varied body of material is available.

Out of these attempts to understand individual differences have come insights which are compelling for schooling. Children of like age are markedly different in their readiness to take advantage of school. Some are reading before they enter; others are as yet unable to perceive the shapes of letters and words. Some relish in the opportunity to respond to classmates; others draw back into themselves. Each of these children must be diagnosed as an individual, and programs must be provided in the light of such diagnosis. But, too often, the die seems already cast. Children from intellectually stimulating homes tend to fall readily into school patterns; school and home reinforce each other. The deprived child is disadvantaged at the outset. Schools and teachers are poorly equipped to rectify perceptual difficulties and severe emotional disturbances. The gap between the "haves" and "have-nots" grows steadily greater as children progress through school.

Research shows that there is about a five-grade spread in achievement within a class of thirty pupils by the time this class reaches the fifth grade. Further, each child ranges in his own achievement over several grade levels. Thus, Billy may be achieving at the eighth grade in spelling, at the sixth in reading, and at the fourth in mathematics. In recognition of these individual differences, scientists inquiring into the design of instruction are seeking to devise ways whereby pupils may proceed at their own rates of speed. At the heart of this work are the principles of programming set forth for his teaching machines by Pressey[24] three decades ago and subsequently refined by Skinner.[25] The material to be learned is analyzed for its difficulty and then broken down into short, hierarchical steps usually referred to as "sets." Advancement to the next set depends on mastery of those leading to it. The student is rewarded not only by self-evident knowledge that he is progressing successfully but also by words of praise built into the progression of material to be learned. Careful programming of sets presumably assures that all students, given sufficient time, will be able to master the learning sequences.

The advent of computers has led to development of sophisticated instructional systems combining sight, sound, and touch. In learning spelling, for example, students listen to recorded words controlled by the computer, write the words on a terminal resembling a television screen, and correct errors by observing the same words flashed on the terminal. Similarly, in mathematics, students respond to exercises on terminals remote from the generating computer and, subsequently, receive computerized printouts analyzing the nature of their errors.

Interesting as these applications may be, the educational scientist is much more interested in the new possibilities for detailed research into subject-matter learning. The computer permits a complete analysis of the responses of all students, identification of persistent errors, and the systematic redesign of instruction. Many of the variables which have so confounded the study of human learning can now be controlled and their effect isolated. As in other fields, the computer is now facilitating studies never before possible—studies which ultimately will lead to a science of education.

An accelerating development in educational science is the direct study

---

24 Sidney L. Pressey, "A Simple Apparatus Which Gives Tests and Scores—and Teaches," *Teaching Machines and Programmed Learning: A Source Book*, ed. by A. A. Lumsdaine and Robert Glaser (Washington, D.C.: Dept. of Audio-Visual Instruction, National Education Association, 1960), pp. 35–41.

25 B. F. Skinner, "Teaching Machines," *Science*, Vol. CXXVIII (October 24, 1958), 969–77.

of educational practices as "natural" phenomena. Until recently, what teachers and pupils did in classrooms, for example, was considered to be "too messy" for respectable social science research. Three of the pioneers in this work, each pursuing different lines of inquiry, are Hughes,[26] Smith,[27] and Flanders.[28]

Hughes observed in classrooms, quantifying her observations of how teachers and students used their time. She concluded that, even in classes judged by supervisors to be good, a disproportionately large amount of time was spent in routine, "controlling" activities, with substantially less than half the time going to productive learning. From tapes of lessons, Smith developed a classification scheme for analyzing teaching techniques. He discovered, for example, that few teachers are able to determine when a problem lends itself to deductive analysis rather than to the mustering of hard data and, therefore, are unable to guide class discussions along productive lines. Flanders developed a comprehensive scheme for classifying classroom interaction patterns both quantitatively and qualitatively. Observers are trained to use the system so that generalizations can be made rather easily with respect to teacher domination, pupil-to-teacher interaction, pupil-to-pupil interaction, and so on. The nature of various classroom patterns can then be compared to other variables, such as pupil achievement or attitudes.

More recently, Jackson[29] spent hundreds of hours observing life in the classroom and concluded that it does not seem to be a very intense learning environment. He raises searching questions about the impact on boys and girls of approximately a thousand hours spent each year in a school classroom, and he wonders whether school can be an exciting, provocative place, given our present, largely unquestioned assumptions about how it should be organized and conducted.

Clearly, studies of this kind have profound implications for teacher education, which has often proceeded insufficiently aware of what teachers actually do. Education courses are made up, by and large, of material

---

26 Marie M. Hughes and associates, *Assessment of the Quality of Teaching in Elementary Schools: A Research Report*, U.S. Department of Health, Education, and Welfare, Office of Education, Cooperative Research Project No. 353 (Salt Lake City: University of Utah, 1959).

27 B. Othanel Smith, *A Study of the Logic of Teaching*, U.S. Department of Health, Education, and Welfare, Office of Education, Cooperative Research Project No. 258 (Urbana: Bureau of Educational Research, College of Education, University of Illinois, 1960); B. Othanel Smith and associates, *A Study of the Strategies of Teaching*, U.S. Department of Health, Education, and Welfare, Office of Education, Cooperative Research Project No. 1640 (Urbana: Bureau of Educational Research, College of Education, University of Illinois, 1967).

28 Ned A. Flanders, *Teacher Influence, Pupil Attitudes, and Achievement*, Cooperative Research Monograph No. 12 (Washington, D.C.: U.S. Department of Health, Education, and Welfare, Office of Education, 1965).

29 Philip W. Jackson, *Life in Classrooms* (New York: Holt, Rinehart & Winston, Inc., 1968).

extracted from history, philosophy, and psychology, but the relevance and usefulness of this material has not been systematically tested against the rigorous demands of teaching.

The trouble, to date, with direct studies of educational practice is that they have not been cumulative. Each researcher has been interested in a particular segment of the whole and, consequently, has neither used similar instruments nor replicated another researcher's work. The ultimate solution is to have a much larger array of researchers swarming over the phenomena of education, probing away at the whole.

Education is a process of producing change in individuals. Schooling usually seeks rather specific changes. Perhaps the most significant contribution to be made by a science of education would be the discovery of the relative weights to be placed upon various factors contributing to educational change. It is here that both the complexity of education and the primitive character of educational science show up. Educators have tended to reflect a curious singleness with respect to their explanations of pupil learning or non-learning. Intelligence probably is cited most frequently as the prime causal factor. But other explanations include teachers, administrators, the curriculum, the dollars spent on schooling, teaching techniques, and environmental factors.

To recognize that all of these factors and more play a part would be a good beginning, but debate has tended to languish within the categories. Thus there are competing schools of thought within a single contributing category, such as "teaching techniques." The teaching of reading affords a good example, with the "whole-word" approach usually being pitted against some form of word-analysis, usually phonetic. We are now coming to see that the differences among methods often are so slight that they are cancelled out by other contributing factors, such as class composition, teacher personality, supplementary materials, and so on. The child frequently learns nearly as well by one technique as by another, if sufficient time is provided. But he may not learn by any technique if his perceptual abilities are impaired or if his home environment is stultifying.

The Coleman Report, *Equality of Educational Opportunity* (1966), mentioned earlier, has served to shake many educators out of their singleness of view regarding the causes of learning or non-learning. Coleman's controversial findings suggest that what the school puts in by way of teachers and program, for example, may be less influential than what each child brings from his home and encounters there from other homes. In other words, students in certain select suburban schools do well because of the achievement orientation of virtually all of the homes represented in the school. By contrast, students in the urban ghetto bring little from their homes and encounter little from other homes bearing on success in school. Following Coleman, then, instead of debating this or that teaching technique for the ghetto school, perhaps we should be devising ways of achieving a more heterogeneous mix of students.

Coleman's findings and conclusions will be debated until there is a substantial body of corroborating or negating evidence. Whatever the outcome, he has served to remind us that the study of education is much more than the testing of alternative teaching strategies. We must build models that include the supposed major causal factors and then seek to determine the relative influence of each. This is an exceedingly complex research enterprise, but at least it does not suffer from the naïve, simplistic notions prevalent just a few years ago.

One recent development in the advance of educational science promises to move this enterprise along. This is the collaboration of more than a dozen nations in cross-national studies of educational achievement. The first of these studies has now been reported in *International Study of Achievement in Mathematics* (1967), edited by Thorsten Husén. Comparative studies of fields in addition to mathematics are now proceeding.

The potential usefulness of these comparative studies for advancing educational science is partially revealed by this first study. Three countries regarded as advanced educationally—Japan, Sweden, and the United States—differed markedly in their relative standings, Japan heading the list of countries in mathematical achievement, and Sweden and the United States ranking near the bottom. The *simple* answer to the question *Why?* is that mathematics is poorly taught or inadequately emphasized in the schools of Sweden and the United States. This could be the correct answer but many alternative explanations come to mind. The answer could lie in the educational aspirations of Japanese boys and girls, or in the cultural orientation of Japanese families, or elsewhere. The virtue of cross-national studies in building an exploratory science of education is that they permit the comparative analysis of cultural factors which differ from country to country but which cannot be adequately differentiated within any one country. For example, we are likely to get far more insight into the role of sex differences in learning by comparing countries which differ in their treatment of the sexes. Similarly, with each of the factors contributing to learning, we are likely to get a clearer picture of its contribution when sharply contrasting cultural practices are compared.

Unfortunately, we do not as yet even know the major components of a model of causal factors in the learning process, let alone the respective contribution of each component of the model. How much of the whole do we assign to family context—10 or 20 or 30 percent? To teacher factors, such as age, sex, and education? To pedagogy? To the curriculum? To the total dollars spent and how they are distributed? The answers will be a long time in coming. But at least educators are becoming aware of the fact that learning is dependent on much more than how hard pupils work and how zealously teachers teach. They are becoming aware, too, that educational science, if it is to emerge at all, will be forged from the stuff of educational practice by scholars from many disciplines willing and able to adapt their research methods to the unique demands of educational phenomena.

SCHOOLING AND EDUCATION: TODAY AND TOMORROW

O n preceding pages I have sought to describe and analyze a period of intense educational ferment, specifically as it has influenced and involved the elementary and secondary schools of the United States. Viewed from one perspective, this ferment appears to have been a series of vigorous reflex actions spurred by devastating criticisms of the schools, internal malaise, and external events. Viewed from another, it appears to have been a natural, predictable expression of an almost unquestioning faith in schools by a nation that pioneered in mass education. Put on one pair of glasses, and the schools appear to be moving posthaste toward becoming centers of intense, exciting learning, marked by concern for and attention to the individual. Put on another, and our schools appear to be, in general, mired in tradition, insensitive to pressing social problems, and inadequate to the demands of learning.

Where are the schools today? How widespread have been the changes described on preceding pages? What must be done in the 1970's, and what lies ahead for the balance of the twentieth century? There are many answers to such questions. What follows is a highly personal response to them, focused on learning, teaching, and the role of schools.

While conducting studies of new approaches to school curricula (reports published in 1964 and 1966) and participating in James B. Conant's study of the education of American teachers (published in 1963), I visited many schools and classrooms. Although the Education Decade was well under way, the reforms it espoused were not conspicuously present in the schools visited. Was the sample inadequate, or were proposed changes losing their momentum before reaching their target? Several colleagues joined me in an effort to probe more deeply, visiting some 260 classrooms in approximately one hundred schools clustered in or around the major cities of thirteen states. Our report, as yet unpublished, seeks to compare certain expectations for schooling with what we observed. It must be remembered that our observations were confined almost exclusively to the first four years, kindergarten through the third grade, of the precollege educational system.

If the most frequently discussed and recommended educational practices, such as those described in this essay, were already implemented, what would constitute a checklist of reasonable expectations? First, teaching would be characterized by efforts to determine where the student is at the *outset* of instruction, to diagnose his attainments and problems, and to base subsequent instruction on the results of this diagnosis. Second,

*one would expect classrooms to be characterized by a wide
variety of learning materials*

learning would be directed toward "learning how to learn," toward self-sustaining inquiry rather than the memorization and regurgitation of facts. Third, this inquiry would carry the student out of confining classrooms and into direct observation of physical and human phenomena. Fourth, one would expect classrooms to be characterized by a wide variety of learning materials—records, tapes, models, programmed materials, filmstrips, pamphlets, and television—and not dominated by textbooks. Fifth, attention to and concern for the individual and individual differences would be clearly revealed in assignments, class discussions, use of materials, grouping practices, and evaluation. Sixth, teachers would understand and use such learning principles as reinforcement, motivation, transfer of training, and so on. Seventh, visitors might reasonably expect

135

to see vigorous, often heated, small and large group discussions, with the teacher in the background rather than the forefront of discourse. Eighth, one might well expect to find rather flexible school environments marked by little attention to grade levels and extensive use of team teaching activities involving groups of teachers, older pupils, parents, and other persons in the teaching-learning process. And, certainly, it would be reasonable to expect to find innovative ways of dealing with special educational problems such as those presented by environmentally handicapped children.

"Reasonable" though these expectations may have been for us at the outset of our visits to schools, they do not constitute an accurate description of what we found. We were unable to discern much attention to pupil needs, attainments, or problems as a basis for beginning instruction, nor widespread provision for individual opportunities to learn. Most classes were taught as a group, covering essentially the same ground for all at approximately the same rate of speed. Teaching was predominantly telling and questioning by the teacher, with children responding one-by-one or occasionally in chorus. In all of this, the textbook was the most highly visible instrument of learning and teaching. If records, tapes, films, filmstrips, supplementary materials, and other aids to learning were available in the schools we visited, we could not attest to their presence by what we observed in the vast majority of classrooms. When small groups of students worked together, the activities engaged in by each group member were similar and bore the mark of the teacher's assignment and expectations. Rarely did we find small groups intensely in pursuit of knowledge; rarely did we find individual pupils at work in self-sustaining inquiry. Popular innovations of the decade—nongrading, team teaching, "discovery" learning, and programmed instruction—were talked about by teachers and principals alike but were rarely in evidence.

On a more general and impressionistic level, teachers and students appeared not to be intensely involved in their work. Only occasionally did we encounter a classroom aura of excitement, anticipation, and spontaneity; when we did, it was almost invariably a kindergarten class. This is not to say that classroom inhabitants were uninvolved but, rather, to suggest that it may be erroneous to assume that teaching and learning in the schools, more than other human enterprises, are characterized by excitement and enthusiasm. On the positive side, however, the teachers we observed were warm and supportive, not the sadists some polemicists have pictured them to be.

From our data we were unable to differentiate practices in schools enrolling a high proportion of disadvantaged or minority group children from practices in other schools. Our descriptions of classrooms enrolling predominantly Mexican-American children, for example, were not distinguishable from our descriptions in general. Nor were there marked differences in our respective descriptions of classrooms in the inner city, on the fringe of the urban environment, and in suburbia.

It is dangerous to generalize about something so large, complex, and presumably diverse as schooling in the United States, or even about the first four years of it. So far as our sample of schools is concerned, however, we are forced to conclude that much of the so-called educational-reform movement has been blunted on the classroom door.

Before the reader blames schoolteachers and principals, some additional observations are in order. The elementary schools we visited were anything but the "palaces" of an affluent society. In fact, they looked more like the artifacts of a society that did not really care about its schools—a society that expressed its disregard by creating schools less suited to human habitation than its prisons. These artifacts reflect the strange notion that learning proceeds best in groups of thirty, that teachers are not to converse with each other, that learning should be conducted under rather uncomfortable circumstances, and that schools proceed best with their tasks when there is little or no traffic with the outside world.

We had hoped to conduct sustained interviews with the teachers we observed. But there were rarely quiet, attractive places to confer; we held our interviews on the run or, more favorably, when we were able to have breakfast or dinner together. These teachers wanted to talk about education: what "good" things had we observed elsewhere; would we comment on the virtues of current innovations; did we have suggestions for improving the teaching we had just observed; and on and on. Interestingly, those with whom we talked had a rather favorable image of what they were doing in the classroom: they thought they were individualizing instruction, teaching inductively, encouraging self-propelled learning, and so on. Neither principals nor teachers were able to articulate clearly just what they thought to be most important for their schools to accomplish. And neither group was very clear on the changes that should be effected in the near future.

As one thinks about both our observations and our conversations with teachers, several disquieting observations come to mind. Public schooling probably is the only large-scale enterprise in this country that does not provide for systematic updating of the skills and abilities of its employees and for payment of the costs involved. Teachers are on their own so far as their in-service education is concerned, in an environment designed for "telling" others that is grossly ill-suited to intellectual pursuits with peers. Teachers, we assume, can readily cast aside their old, inappropriate ways and acquire markedly different ones through some process of osmosis.

We might well expect sixteen or more years of schooling to educate teachers and others for self-renewal—and this frequently is the case. But general failure to do so for large numbers of its products constitutes the greatest failure of our educational system. In the colleges as well as in

the lower schools, the processes and fruits of human experience are so cut up in the curriculum and so obfuscated by detail that cohesiveness, relationships, and relevance are obscured.

Turning to another aspect of our educational malaise, an enormous amount of energy goes into merely maintaining the system. Studies have shown that administrators favor teachers who maintain orderly classrooms, keep accurate records, and maintain stable relations with parents and the community. Other studies reveal that middle managers in the educational system, such as principals and supervisors, tend to be recruited from among teachers who demonstrate these orderly qualities. Thus rewarded for maintaining the system, they are not likely either to challenge it or to reward subordinates who do.

they looked more like artifacts of a society that did not really care about its schools

Just as teachers and principals appear to be uncertain about what their schools are for, the communities they serve provide no clear sense of direction or guidelines. There is some evidence to suggest that parents are somewhat more favorably disposed toward educational change than are those who administer the schools or teach in them, but legions of educators who push at the forefront of innovative practice stand ready to show their community-inflicted scars.[30] Many parents are more interested in changes in the abstract or for someone else than in changes involving their own

---

30 *See,* for example, parental reactions to recently proposed changes for the schools as reported by George Gallup, *The Gallup Polls on Innovation* (Melbourne, Fla.: Institute for Development of Educational Activities, Inc., 1968).

children. Social change is a formidable enterprise under the best of circumstances. Schooling too often presents only the worst of circumstances, with resistance being built into both the setting and the internal structure.

It should come as no surprise, then, that comprehensive experiments in schooling are the rarest of all educational phenomena. Small wonder that teachers practise little individualizing instruction, inductive teaching, nongrading, team teaching, or other recently recommended practices. They have not seen them. If teachers are to change, they must see models of what they are to change to; they must practise under guidance the new behaviors called for in the exemplar models. If teachers are to change, the occupation itself must have built into it the necessary provisions for self-renewal. The creation of these conditions is an important agenda item for the decade ahead.

To contemplate the computerized education we will undoubtedly have some day is heady stuff. But the 1970's present less glamorous challenges. Seers of bygone decades occasionally asked whether our schools had outlived their usefulness—and we laughed. The question is no longer funny. The schools are conspicuously ill-suited to the needs of at least 30 percent of their present clientele: large numbers of children and youth from minority groups in harsh environments; those tens of thousands who suffer from crippling mental, physical, and emotional handicaps; and a few whose rare giftedness separates them sharply from their peers. But the lack of fit between school and client extends into other realms until one is forced to ask whether our educational system serves even 50 percent of its clientele in reasonably satisfying ways. Learning disabilities evidenced in the primary grades often go undiagnosed, persist throughout life, and seriously limit human participation. Talents in music, art, and creative writing lie largely outside of the school's scope and usually are brought to fruition in the home, when parents can afford to, or not at all, when parents cannot. The human models in these fields, so necessary to refinement of childhood talent, are inaccessible to the school because of teacher certification restrictions or sheer failure to recognize their powerful role in educating the young.

We even wonder whether those students who appear to be adjusting well are acquiring desirable traits and repressing undesirable ones. Success in school seems to assure further success in school; good grades predict good grades. But neither assures nor predicts much else: good work habits, good citizenship, happiness, compassion, nor other human virtues. The incidence of dropouts, nonpromotion, alienation, and minimal learning reinforce our apprehension that schools have become or are fast becoming obsolete. They appear to have been designed for a different culture, a different conception of learning and teaching, and a different clientele.

The tasks of rehabilitating the schools, then, are formidable, indeed.

We dare not ask whether we *should* rehabilitate our schools, although this is a good question. Impotent and irrelevant though much schooling may be, the schools are at present the only educational institution deliberately created and maintained for inculcating something of man's heritage, for developing the basic tools of literacy, and for instilling some powers of rational thought and criticism. Although our civilization abounds in educational institutions and media, from scuba-diving lessons to television, none is centrally committed to this basic, cultural role. By seeking to rehabilitate the *educational* role of the school, rather than its various residual functions (baby-sitting, social stratification, economic investment, etc.), perhaps we will keep the meaning of education before us, experiment with improved means, and ultimately transfer the process to new and better institutions should the schools fail us and we them.

A brief analysis of television serves both to illustrate what I mean by rehabilitating the *educational* role of the school and to project us into the varied possibilities of an electronic educational future. Some of us still remember those wonderful evenings of intellectual discourse with friends before that "glass-faced bastard" (of *The One Hundred Dollar Misunderstanding* fame) took over. At first, exposure to the glass face meant only a few hours' diversion each week, watching the favorite programs we had only heard before. But now there are "hot" and "cold" stimuli, Marshall McLuhan's nonlinear communication, and a television generation. From birth to graduation from high school, today's young man or woman spends an average of fifteen thousand hours before television sets and just over twelve thousand hours (one thousand hours each year) in school. I do not believe that these hours of schooling provide anything like an antidote for the formidable array of violence, cruelty, dishonesty, prejudice, and inhumanity to man provided by newspapers, magazines, movies, and television.

Our schools did not adopt television; nor did television adopt the schools. An occasional educational television program became a "tack-on" to the curriculum. During the Education Decade a national network occasionally found it mildly profitable to feature a "special" on the schools. Meanwhile, however, television went about its business, and the schools went about theirs. Television has not yet taken on the essentially educational function of humanizing the content of experience for teaching and learning. It seeks only to entertain, to hold the viewer. But neither have the schools been markedly successful in producing an intensely human environment in which children and youth are caught up in man's adventure, whether in the arts, politics, the sea, or outer space.

Herein lies our dilemma. On one hand, a powerful medium has caught the attention—indeed, the very lives—of our children and youth. But it lacks significant substance to nurture a civilization and appears to care not, despite its protestations, whether it uplifts or debases. On the other

141

hand, the only institution charged specifically with the performance of educational functions fails to "grip" a significant portion of its clientele. Unfulfilled educational promise lies between.

Even in schools run by humans, we have not succeeded in developing intensely humanistic learning environments—not in process, not in content, and not in perspective. They do not, in general, foster man's most creative traits, nor grapple with his great ideas, nor relate these ideas and talents to the contemporary environment where man's dramas are continuously reenacted. The schools are bogged down with routine, trivialities, and the lesser literacies. In the rat race to cover what is in the textbook, schooling has lost sight of education as an end in itself and has become instrumental to the next textbook, the next grade, higher education, and the Gross National Product. And now into this human-based environment at a critical time in the history of schools, education, and man comes an electronic teacher of great power, the computer. The instructional era now on the horizon is one of man–machine interaction. Will the computer dehumanize learning and teaching even more? The choice is ours.

On an experimental basis, computers are demonstrating their usefulness in teaching spelling, mathematics, reading, and a host of cognitive skills. Tapes, video screens, records, and other devices are combined with computer memory to produce a unique instructional system of sight, sound, and touch. Current writings on computer-aided instruction present a picture of instructional efficiency and the freeing of human teachers to do those truly *human* educational things. But what are these things? . . . and have teachers been prepared to engage in them?

Already it is clear that computers, unlike television, are more efficient by far than humans in performing routine instructional tasks and in assuring error-free performance on the part of learners in those basic skills to which teachers devote so much time. It is clear, then, that computers have a viable, albeit threatening, role in the schools. The critical problem is how computers and people are to live together productively in the school environment. If educators continue to confuse instruction in the basic skills with education, then teachers will merely monitor the computer and, in time, become its servant. Under such circumstances, there eventually would be no need for schools as other than custodial agencies, since computer terminals might more readily and profitably be placed in homes. State and local budgets, together with some transportation problems, would be substantially relieved.

A happier alternative, however, is that there will be a separation of those instructional tasks most appropriate for electronic teachers from those educational activities most appropriate for human teachers. Efficiently taught in the basic tools of their culture, young people would have much more time than is now the case to pursue education as a way of life. With the processes of providing these tools freed from the restraints of human time and energy for teaching them, they would become readily accessible to all. But this alternative, too, destroys or drastically changes the school as we have known it.

The tireless computer is fully capable of working twenty-four hours a day every day. It can recall the same material and teach the same lesson over and over. It can be made as accessible to the three-year-old as to the sixty-year-old. And it can provide subject matters singly or in various combinations and sequences. No need, then, to confine teaching to the hours between nine in the morning and three in the afternoon; nor to withhold schooling until the age of five or six; nor to delay certain subjects until high school or college; nor to complete sixteen units of work in four years. Suddenly, we come to realize that schools as we know them are largely the product of limitations and conventions in the use of human energy. Introduce a new source of instructional energy, and learning is unshackled.

But still to be accounted for in schooling are "those educational activities most appropriate for *human* teachers." Their human character demands libraries, seminar rooms, museums, studios, art galleries, courts of law, government offices, airports, housing developments, fields, ponds, counseling centers, hospitals, quiet study corners, work experiences, visits with exemplary models of accomplishment, and on and on. Take the educational environment beyond school and classroom, and learning can be humanized.

With fundamental learning effectively taken care of, perhaps we will look up from our myopic equating of education with schooling and our instrumental views of both to the urgent need to value education for its own sake, to grapple with education's first question: What kinds of human beings do we seek? But even before looking toward where we want to be, perhaps we should ask basic questions about where we are. To what extent is each individual being provided with opportunities to develop his unique potentialities? To what extent is each individual developing a deep sense of personal worth—the kind of selfhood that is prerequisite to self-transcendence? To what extent are our young people coming into critical possession of their culture?

143

BIBLIOGRAPHY

BLOOM, BENJAMIN S. *Stability and Change in Human Characteristics.* New York: John Wiley & Sons, Inc., 1964.

BRICKMAN, WILLIAM W., and LEHRER, STANLEY (eds.). *Automation, Education, and Human Values.* New York: School and Society Books, 1966.

BROWN, GEORGE W., MILLER, JAMES G., and KEENAN, THOMAS A. *Edunet.* Report of the Educom Summer Study on Information Networks. New York: John Wiley & Sons, Inc., 1967.

BRUNER, JEROME S. *The Process of Education.* Cambridge, Mass.: Harvard University Press, 1960.

COLEMAN, JAMES S. *Equality of Educational Opportunity.* Washington, D.C.: Office of Education, United States Department of Health, Education, and Welfare, 1966.

Committee for Economic Development. *Innovation in Education: New Directions for the American School.* New York: The Committee, 1968.

CONANT, JAMES B. *Slums and Suburbs.* New York: McGraw-Hill Book Co., Inc., 1961.

CREMIN, LAWRENCE A. *The Genius of American Education.* (Horace Mann Lecture.) Pittsburgh: University of Pittsburgh Press, 1965.

———. *The Transformation of the School.* New York: Alfred A. Knopf, Inc., 1961.

Department of Education and Science. *Children and Their Primary Schools.* A Report of the Central Advisory Council for Education (England). London: Her Majesty's Stationery Office, 1967. 2 Vols.

———. *Primary Education in Wales.* A Report of the Central Advisory Council for Education (Wales). London: Her Majesty's Stationery Office, 1967.

Designing Education for the Future: An Eight-State Project. *Prospective Changes in Society by 1980.* Reports Prepared for the First Area Conference, Denver, Colo., July, 1966. New York: Citation Press, 1967.

———. *Implications for Education of Prospective Changes in Society.* Reports Prepared for the Second Area Conference, Denver, Colo. January, 1967. New York: Citation Press, 1967.

———. *Planning and Effecting Needed Changes in Education.* Reports Prepared for the Third Area Conference, Denver, Colo., June, 1967. New York: Citation Press, 1967.

———. *Cooperative Planning for Education in 1980.* Report No. 4. New York: Citation Press, 1968.

———. *Emerging Designs for Education.* Reports Prepared for an Area Conference, Denver, Colo., May, 1968.

GAGNÉ, ROBERT M. (ed.). *Learning and Individual Differences.* Columbus, Ohio: Charles E. Merrill Books, Inc., 1967.

GARDNER, JOHN W. *No Easy Victories.* New York: Harper & Row, Publishers, Inc., 1968.

GERARD, RALPH W., and MILLER, JAMES G. (eds.). *Computers and Education.* New York: McGraw-Hill Book Co., Inc., 1967.

GLASER, ROBERT (ed.). *Teaching Machines and Programmed Learning, II: Data and Directions.* Washington, D.C.: Department of Audiovisual Instruction, National Education Association, 1965.

GOODLAD, JOHN I. (with Renata von Stœphasius and M. Frances Klein). *The Changing School Curriculum.* New York: The Fund for the Advancement of Education, 1966.

GOODLAD, JOHN I., and ANDERSON, ROBERT H. *The Nongraded Elementary School.* New York: Harcourt, Brace & World, Inc., 1959 (revised 1963).

HUSÉN, TORSTEN (ed.). *International Study of Achievement in Mathematics,* Vols. I and II. New York: John Wiley & Sons, Inc., 1967.

HUTCHINS, ROBERT M. *The Learning Society.* New York: Frederick A. Praeger, Inc., 1968. (Originally published as "Education: The Learning Society," in *Britannica Perspectives,* ed. Harry S. Ashmore; Chicago: Encyclopædia Britannica, Inc., 1968.)

KEPPEL, FRANCIS. *The Necessary Revolution in American Education.* New York: Harper & Row, Publishers, Inc. 1966.

LUMSDAINE, ARTHUR A., and LINDSLEY, DONALD B. (eds.). *Brain Function and Learning.* (Brain Function, Volume 4; UCLA Forum in Medical Sciences, Number 6.) Berkeley: University of California Press, 1968.

McLUHAN, HERBERT MARSHALL. *Understanding Media: The Extensions of Man.* New York: McGraw-Hill Book Co., Inc., 1965.

MILES, MATTHEW B. (ed.). *Innovation in Education.* New York: Teachers College, Bureau of Publications, Columbia University, 1964.

National Society for the Study of Education. *The Changing American School.* Sixty-fifth Yearbook, Part II. Chicago: The University of Chicago Press, 1966.

———. *The Educationally Retarded and Disadvantaged.* Sixty-sixth Yearbook, Part I.

Chicago: The University of Chicago Press, 1967.

———. *Metropolitanism: Its Challenge to Education.* Sixty-seventh Yearbook, Part I. Chicago: The University of Chicago Press, 1968.

———. *Theories of Learning and Instruction.* Sixty-third Yearbook, Part I. Chicago: University of Chicago Press, 1964.

Project on the Instructional Program of the Public Schools. *Planning and Organizing for Teaching.* Washington, D.C.: National Education Association, 1963.

———. *Schools for the Sixties.* Washington, D.C.: National Education Association, 1963.

Report of the National Advisory Commission on Civil Disorders. New York: Bantam Books, Inc., 1968.

SHAPLIN, JUDSON T., and OLDS, HENRY F., JR. (eds.). *Team Teaching.* New York: Harper & Row, Publishers, Inc., 1964.

NOTE TO THE READER

Dean Goodlad's essay is concerned with schooling, a subject on which it might seem at first that *Great Books of the Western World* has little to say. Of the 443 works contained in the set, only Montaigne's essay *Of the Education of Children* is by title directly on the subject. But as Dr. Goodlad notes, schooling can never be kept completely separated from the study of education, which is "nothing more than a study of man from still another perspective," and on this subject *Great Books* has much to say.

EDUCATION is itself one of the 102 ideas into which the *Syntopicon* is divided, and the chapter devoted to it provides the reader an introduction to the discussion of the idea in *Great Books of the Western World.*

The books assembled in this set offer a means to a liberal education. The reader also should not forget that *Gateway to the Great Books* has been designed to provide materials for the junior as well as the senior high school level.

145

HERBERT
FEIGL

Herbert Feigl was born in 1902 in Reichenberg, in what was then Austria-Hungary. He attended the University of Munich, and received his doctorate in 1927 from the University of Vienna. From 1925 to 1930 he took part in the "Vienna Circle" of Logical Positivists that included Rudolf Carnap and Ludwig Wittgenstein. Feigl lectured on astronomy and philosophy of science at the Vienna People's Institute in the late 1920's. His first book, Theory and Experience in Physics *(1929) won favorable recognition from Einstein. Feigl received a Rockefeller award in 1930 for research on the logical foundation of physics at Harvard University. He joined the philosophy department of the University of Iowa in 1931, and became an American citizen in 1937. The University of Minnesota appointed him Professor of Philosophy in 1940, Director of the Minnesota Center for the Philosophy of Science in 1953, and Regents' Professor of Philosophy in 1967. He has lectured at many universities and professional meetings in this country and abroad. He has been president of the American Philosophical Association (Western Division), and vice-president of the American Association for the Advancement of Science. Feigl's bibliography runs to fourscore articles on philosophy of science, philosophical analysis, and the scientific outlook. He is coeditor of the journal* Philosophical Studies *and of* Minnesota Studies in the Philosophy of Science; *and he serves on the governing board of* Philosophy of Science *and the advisory board of the* Library of Living Philosophers.*

146

The Philosophy of Science

The most incomprehensible thing about the world is that it is comprehensible.—Albert Einstein

Einstein's epigram is profoundly significant. That our universe is comprehensible was for Einstein a conviction somewhat akin to religious faith. It is expressed in some of his other oft-quoted—though often misunderstood—sayings: "God is subtle, but He is not malicious" and "God does not play dice with the world." As those who were acquainted with him knew, and as is clear from several of his published essays, Einstein used religious language metaphorically only. Einstein was not theologically inclined and conceived of God much as Spinoza did. He very likely meant by "God" the order of nature. One can perhaps interpret his sayings as expressing the metaphysical belief that the ground of all existence is humanly incomprehensible but manifests itself in a beautifully harmonious and lawful structure of the universe. Thus Einstein's conception of God had no connection with the moral norms of the Judeo-Christian tradition. What he himself said about mystical experience clearly indicates that he meant by it the rapture and awe with which men of science contemplate the order of the cosmos. He expressed a very similar view in regard to the great works of art and music.

EXPLANATION AND UNDERSTANDING

It is perhaps hazardous to attempt an overall characterization or definition of the aims, and especially the criteria, of the factual sciences. Some claim that such an enterprise is bound to fail because of the radical changes that have occurred again and again in the long history of the scientific quest. Although the "mutations" or "revolutions" in the outlook and the methods of science must, of course, be recognized, I think a definition of science can be given that is not too abstract or superficial. For our purposes it will be best to limit this definition to the scientific enterprise of modern times, that is to science as it has been generally understood since the Renaissance, and especially since the days of Galileo and Newton. It appears that the major aims of the pure factual sciences are description and explanation of the facts of nature, man, and society. Prediction, which is often listed as a major aim is, of course, vitally important for the testing of the correctness of explanations; prediction is also essential in all the applications of the sciences for the achievement of desired ends. But since, as I shall argue, prediction (as well as retrodiction, or the reconstruction of the past) is logically so closely related to description and explanation, it need not be listed separately as a major aim of pure science.

What is meant by "description" is the giving of an account of what there is, or rather of those parts or aspects of existence upon which a given cognitive interest is focused. By an "explanation," we shall mean the accounting for facts or regularities. In many cases, especially in the sort of explanations given in everyday life, and also on the more commonsense levels of technology and medicine, pointing out the cause or causes of a phenomenon is clearly the essential step. It is one thing, for example, to describe the occurrence, intensity, etc., of a thunderstorm and quite another to explain it in terms of the temperatures, humidities, and electric charges of colliding masses of air.

In general, there is a fair measure of agreement on the line of demarcation between scientific and extrascientific (or nonscientific) explanatory endeavors. The methods used for ascertaining the truth of answers to scientific questions (or, if you will, a high degree of confirmation) are inapplicable in the quest for "ultimate" or "absolute" truths concerning transempirical reality. Questions such as are asked by some existentialist philosophers, e.g., "Why is there something rather than nothing?"; or theological questions such as the problem of evil, or as to why God created a world at all, are admittedly not susceptible of solution by the scientific method. Some traditional metaphysical questions, such as those regarding the nature of the Absolute—Substance, Reality, Value, etc.—are similarly nonscientific if they are understood as radically transempirical. It should be clear that the term "nonscientific" need not carry the opprobrium that we associate with the term "unscientific." Astrology, alchemy, phrenology, and other superstitions are generally repudiated as pseudosciences, or as unscientific, precisely because their failure has been amply demonstrated by empirical procedures. Of course, there are frequent borderline cases of endeavors which share the aims of science but in which a responsible decision has not yet been reached. In these cases, as in Psychical Research (ESP), and also in the cases of bold new (or even old) theories, controversy rages. But it is generally understood that only further empirical—observational, experimental, statistical—evidence can decide the issues concerned. In the meantime it seems advisable to keep an open mind—in other words, to maintain the critical, rational approach that, more than anything else, characterizes the basic spirit and attitude of modern science.

The positivist prejudice against the idea—and even the word—*explanation* is understandable in view of the difference between scientific and nonscientific endeavors. The older positivists regarded the search for Absolute Truths or Ultimate Explanations as a wish for knowledge "gone wild." And the later "logical" positivists considered this search as not merely hopeless or fruitless; they repudiated it as cognitively meaningless. No matter whether one agrees with this radically "negativistic" position, modern philosophy of science has made it abundantly clear that a useful distinction can be drawn between description and explanation and that all genuinely scientific explanations are relative and cannot possibly be "absolute." According to the widely accepted current view, explanations are inevitably relative because they always require premises which in the context of a given explanation are not themselves explained but assumed. It still remains true that, at least in most explanations of classical science, the fact or regularity explained is shown to be necessary. But this necessity is no longer located either in the principles which form the premises (*explanantia*) of an explanation, nor in the conclusion which describes what is to be explained (the *explanandum*). Earlier rationalistically oriented philosophies insisted on principles or premises whose truth was conceived as *a priori;* that is, they were supposed to be indubitable, self-evident deliverances of Pure Reason. The current climate of philosophical and scientific opinion (with notable exceptions to be discussed later) is opposed to rationalism inasmuch as *empirical* evidence is considered indispensable for answering factual questions. The very premises of scientific explanation must be justifiable on empirical grounds. This is not to say that explanatory premises can be established by simple inductive inference. This is certainly not the case for the assumptions that constitute the postulates of scientific theories. As Einstein has emphatically said, there is no straight logical path leading from the data of observation to scientific theories. It is by creative imagination that scientific theories are engendered. They are essentially conjectures, admittedly guided by a great deal of background knowledge and the data of observation, that are to be subjected to severe scrutiny by experiment and logical reasoning. Only if the theory in question survives such critical scrutiny, and if its explanatory power encompasses more facts (or regularities) than those that suggested the conjecture, will the theory be accepted as "corroborated" or "confirmed."[1]* Such acceptance is understood to be "only until further notice" in current science and philosophy of science. In other words, scientific laws, hypotheses, and theories are in principle always open to revision. New evidence may well emerge that could refute a widely held theory, or, at least, force the scientists to modify it more or less incisively.

The modern temper of science just briefly described is thus radically different from that of ancient and medieval science. The paradigms of Euclidean geometry and of Aristotelian physics and biology involved "necessity" or "necessary truths" in the premises of scientific explana-

---

* Numbered footnotes appear at the end of the essay.

tion.° This traditional view used to be plausible enough and still exerts a seductive influence in some quarters. If "proof" in the sciences consists in the derivation of conclusions from premises, should there not be ultimate premises ("first principles") which are neither capable of proof nor in need of proof? They would not be provable for the simple reason that all proofs must begin with some unproved premises; an infinite regress is, of course, ruled out here not only as impossible but because it would lead nowhere. The model of classical geometry also inspired the belief that the premises (axioms) must be self-evident, and thus not in need of any proof or justification. As is well known, all these views have been completely abandoned in modern mathematics. A similar development took place in modern empirical science. Formulating it psychologically, we might say that in one respect the level of our aspirations has been lowered. We no longer demand reductions of the unfamiliar to the familiar or self-evident; we renounce direct insight into natural necessities. Our wish for explanation is satisfied if we can find suitable premises (confirmed on other grounds) that allow us to derive the facts or regularities to be explained. Many of the ancient and traditional thought patterns have been abandoned. The first to go was the animistic one, that is, the attempt to explain natural phenomena in terms of the familiar patterns of human emotion, intention, and volition. This was replaced by the mechanistic type of explanation, a conceptual pattern which was triumphantly successful—up to a certain point! Its limitations, always suspected in connection with chemical, biological, and mental phenomena, first clearly became apparent in the last century. The vast range and variety of electric and magnetic phenomena simply did not yield to explanations in terms of Newtonian mechanics. One must wonder how Kant would have responded to the revolutions in mathematics and physics of the nineteenth century. During Kant's lifetime Newtonian mechanics still reigned supreme. In his *Metaphysical Foundations of Natural Science* (1786), Kant had even attempted to elevate Newton's laws of motion to the rank of truths of pure reason—a "synthetic *a priori* proposition."†

Obviously the "comprehensibility" of the world of which Einstein spoke is to be understood in a very different manner. Einstein, and with him the majority of twentieth-century scientists, defines the aim of scientific explanation as the derivation of a maximum of observable facts from a minimum of suitable principles (premises) and concepts. Neither self-evidence nor familiarity are demanded for the acceptance of the premises. This then is the predominant view according to which at least one form of "understanding" or "comprehending" the world can be achieved.

° Euclid's *Elements* is in *GBWW*, Vol. 11; Aristotle's physical works in Vol. 8 and his biological works in Vol. 9.

† Newton's work is in *GBWW*, Vol. 34; Kant's in Vol. 42.

Herbert Feigl

CAUSALITY, REGULARITY, AND NECESSITY

The very meaning of the concept of causality has been, and continues to be, a matter of philosophical controversy. In this, as in many other philosophical disputes, two opposed tendencies have led to apparently irreconcilable positions. There are the "tough-minded" scientists and the radically empiricist philosophers who espouse a "nothing but" point of view. According to this view, causality is nothing but the regularity in the sequence of antecedent and subsequent events; or, even more abstractly, it is a lawful relation of any sort, whether between events (either in temporal succession or even simultaneous), or aspects of events, or measurable magnitudes in their functional relationships.

The traditional and opposite point of view maintains that regularity alone is not enough, and that over and above it there must be some sort of "necessity" or a "bond" connecting causes and effects. Many defenders of this view insist that the meaning of "causality" include the idea of the cause as producing the effect. There are other philosophers who stress the notion that a cause is that which makes a difference in the ensuing events —and belittle, or even deny, that regularity is at all essential for a definition of the "true meaning" of "causality." Along these lines it has occasionally been maintained that there can be causality without repeatability, as in historical events. This contention clearly demands critical scrutiny.

It was David Hume, the great empiricist philosopher of the eighteenth century, whose "reductive" analysis of causality in terms of "constant conjunctions" (i.e., regularity) has been one of the most influential, but also one of the most disputed, philosophical doctrines.* Hume's critique of causality was epistemologically oriented. He asked what there is about the cause-effect relation which can be asserted on the basis of experience. Since all experience, according to Hume, ultimately consists of "impressions," he asked whether the alleged necessity of the causal relation can be evident in our impressions of the events we perceive. His answer was crushingly negative. He traced the "false" doctrines of necessity to either one of two mistakes. Either we project some of our subjective feelings of compulsion into the objective world of events, or we confuse causal regularity with logical necessity. Hume and the positivists who followed him— Comte, Mill, Mach, *et al.*—rejected the first interpretation as superstition or "fetishism." Experience, Hume claimed, discloses nothing more than some uniformities in the course of observable events. The projection of a "bond" or "tie" onto the regular sequences is akin to the animistic explanations that impute a humanlike will to the realities "behind" the observable events, even those of inorganic nature. Hume maintained that there is no reason to believe any such thing. In fact he even adumbrated

---

* For Hume's discussion in *GBWW*, see Vol. 35, pp. 457c–485a.

some of the critique later formulated more aggressively by the logical positivists (especially M. Schlick), who maintained that whatever "surplus meaning" is attributed to the causal relation is not factual (cognitive-empirical) but pictorial and/or emotional. There is no difference that makes a testable difference between the assertion that "A (a certain type of event) is always followed by B (another type of event)" and the assertion that "A is always necessarily followed by B." Hence, the positivists denied any sort of informative significance to the alleged necessity in causality.

Furthermore, again in accord with Hume's views, the logical positivists repudiated as a serious mistake the confusion of causal regularity with logical necessity. This can very easily be understood by comparing and contrasting the following two statements:

(1) Every effect has a cause.
(2) Every event has a cause.

It is clear that sentence (1) is true by virtue of its meaning—in the same way as, for example, "every mother has at least one child" or "all squares have four sides." We simply *mean* by an "effect" an event—change, situation, state of affairs, etc.—which is *due* to a cause. Hence, it would be inconsistent or self-contradictory to speak of an effect that had no cause. The logical character of sentence (2), "Every event has a cause," is such that it could be denied without self-contradiction. If it is suggested that an event by definition implies its having a cause, we should reply that in that case the sentence (2) would be no more informative about the world of facts than any tautology or analytic statement, such as "All uncles are of the male sex." Not even the existence or occurrence of events is implied by (2) *if* thus interpreted.

All contemporary empiricist philosophers admit—even emphasize—that there is logical necessity in the inference from causal laws, conjoined with a description of a state of affairs (initial and boundary conditions) to another state of affairs (the *explanandum*). Although this has already been pointed out in the first section of this essay, it may be useful here to illustrate the point by a very simple example: [2]

(1) Causal law: Friction produces heat.
(2) Antecedent condition: I am rubbing my hands.
(3) Definitional truth: My rubbing hands is a case of friction.
∴ (4) Conclusion (*Explanandum*): My hands get warmer.

The acceptance of (1), (2), (3) as true necessitates logically the acceptance of (4) as true. The necessity of the inference hinges on the necessity of the implication: $[(1) \& (2) \& (3)] \rightarrow 4$.

Despite these considerations, a good many thinkers have defended the view that the principle of causality is a necessary truth of pure reason concerning a basic and pervasive feature of the world of facts. This is the doctrine formulated by such rationalistic philosophers as Leibniz, and, in a somewhat different and highly ingenious way, by Kant. The common-sense core of those highly sophisticated philosophical doctrines can perhaps be understood in terms of two closely related (but not necessarily equivalent) principles: The "Principle of Sufficient Reason," according to which nothing exists or occurs without sufficient reason; and the principle, "Same Causes, Same Effects." Even the man in the street may well consider these statements as self-evident, perhaps even trivial and hardly worth formulating. To the philosophical mind, however, the question arises as to how to account for the self-evidence of these principles. Here the paths of rationalist and empiricist thinkers diverge. Rationalists consider them "eternal verities," "necessary truths" (Leibniz), or conceptual forms or categories imposed on the raw material of sense experience by "Pure Reason"—Kant in one version of his theory of knowledge—or indispensable conditions (presuppositions) for the very possibility of knowledge.*

Empiricists, at least since Hume, explain our belief in the causal order or uniformity of nature as the result of learning and generalizing from multifarious experiences. Having often observed that an event of type A has always been followed by an event of type B,[3] we came to expect that whenever A occurs it will be followed by B. In the older empiricist psychology, this explanation was stated in terms of the association of ideas. In twentieth-century behavioristic psychology, it was "objectified" and stated in terms of conditioned responses in animals and man. Philosophers like George Santayana spoke of "animal faith"; and in one of his discussions of the same phenomenon, Bertrand Russell called it "physiological induction."

These views are obviously opposed to, or at least highly skeptical of, the notion of necessity in causality. We are told that we learn about the uniformities of nature through "trial and error" in our expectations. Beliefs of this sort can, of course, be "extinguished" by repeated disappointment of our expectations. The empiricist logician simply speaks of "refutations" of lawlike statements by genuinely contrary instances. A strict law of nature has always been understood to hold without exception. In the actual practice of scientific research, and even in common experience, there can always be a question as to whether the "exceptions" (contrary instances) are "genuine," or "real" as contrasted with "apparent" exceptions. To give a simple example: Since Newton the law of gravitation has been considered one of the basic laws of nature.[4] As is well known, this law states that the force of attraction between two masses is proportional to the product of the numerical values of those two masses and inversely proportional to the square of the distance between their centers of

---

* To locate Kant's discussion in *GBWW*, see the *Syntopicon* under CAUSE 1.

gravity.* Now, gravitational forces are much weaker than, for example, electrical ones, and it is possible that electrostatic attraction or repulsion may far exceed the gravitational attraction. Hence, if we find from the accelerations or other types of evidence that the attraction between two bodies differs noticeably from "what it should be" according to Newton's law, this need not disconfirm Newton's law. Even in everyday life we use "auxiliary" hypotheses in the explanation of unexpected events. Auxiliary hypotheses are justifiable on the basis of independently ascertainable evidence. In the example just mentioned, we can find out about electric charges or magnetization independently of the evidence that confirms the gravitational attraction. To illustrate by an example the reader may remember from high school physics: "All bodies fall equally fast" is not refuted by the case of the feather and the piece of lead. The frictional resistance of the air is demonstrably different for the feather and the piece of lead. Nor is the physics teacher giving an alibi when he says, "This experiment in electrostatics won't work because the air is too humid today." It can be shown that moist air conducts electricity much better than dry air.

In most cases of causal explanation we are confronted with highly complex phenomena. Hence, a great number of conditions are said "jointly to bring about" a certain effect. We may say that the conjunction of those conditions is sufficient for the occurrence of the effect. Possibly none of them is necessary—in the sense that alternative sets of conditions might be equally sufficient. For example, an increase in the temperature of a room can be achieved by a variety of means: electric heating, oil burner, gas heat, steam heat, forced hot air, etc. Often the word *cause* is used for the differential or "triggering" condition that occurs in a context of "standing" conditions. Thus the explosion of a bomb may be triggered by a switch, or a fuse, or a spark, etc., but a great many other conditions must be fulfilled if the bomb is to go off.

Considerations such as those concerning auxiliary hypotheses about some of the relevant conditions (in addition to the differential or triggering ones) suggest that perhaps the principle of causality is best understood as a regulative norm or maxim of the search for causes, and hence of the scientific enterprise in general. As such, it would not be a statement about the nature of things; it would not be an ontological assertion. As a regulative maxim the principle of causality would rather be an injunction: "If at first you don't succeed—in discovering the cause(s), or the law(s)—try, and try again!"

Construed in this way, the principle would be neither true nor false. It would be neither a premise nor a presupposition of scientific knowledge, but rather a principle of procedure that may or may not be useful or fruit-

---

* Newton's formulation of the law will be found in GBWW, Vol. 34, p. 134a. To locate other places in which he discusses gravitation, consult MECHANICS, 6d(1) in the *Syntopicon*.

MONUMENT TO SIR ISAAC NEWTON, WESTMINSTER ABBEY

ful. Since an essential part of the modern conception of scientific inquiry is that it should disclose any sort of lawful relation, the principle would simply be a corollary of the very definition of science. Some philosophers understand by "presupposition" just this sort of regulative norm. But the majority of philosophers mean by "presupposition" a basic (and possibly indispensable) assumption. It is easy to see, for example, that the statement that scientific inquiry can succeed only if there is an order of nature is an *a priori* and analytic truth; even the most superficial analysis of the meaning of "science" shows that science is possible only if there is some order of nature.

The rationalist philosophers, especially Kant, held a different view. At least in one strand of his critical philosophy, Kant maintained that it is human reason that imposes the causal order upon the raw data of experience; hence the world could not possibly fail to exhibit some sort of lawfulness. This doctrine is, however, fairly generally discredited nowadays. If held in some diluted form, it is usually formulated in the "presuppositional" manner. Nevertheless there is a related doctrine, usually labeled "conventionalism," which is close, if not to the original Kantian, then to the neo-Kantian point of view. According to this new doctrine, we introduce causal order in the world of experience by constructing appropriate concepts—and theories containing these concepts. One way of stating, and at the same time criticizing, this view is to say that it imposes no limitations upon the introduction of auxiliary hypotheses. But scientists have traditionally drawn an important distinction between *auxiliary* and *ad hoc* hypotheses. The latter are looked at with great suspicion, because they are, as the designation indicates, invented for the special purpose of explaining the as yet unexplained phenomenon (or regularity), without having any other justification by independent evidence in their favor. To be sure, at a given stage of scientific investigation some hypotheses may be introduced in the manner of "promissory notes." And at that stage it is usually impossible to say whether it is an auxiliary or an *ad hoc* hypothesis.

The history of science is replete with examples of assumptions of this preliminary sort. The important point is to remain vigilant; the "promise" has to be fulfilled sooner or later. Otherwise the hypothesis remains a piece of idling verbalism or, worse yet, a verbal sedative that stifles scientific curiosity. Scientists know very well the risks involved in issuing promissory notes. But they also know that genuine "cash value" may well accrue from further experimental investigation. Thus, the atomic hypothesis of the ancient Greek philosophers Leucippus, Democritus, Epicurus, was only a first sketch of a theory that was to become one of the most fruitful and best confirmed in all of science.* It is true, the very concept

---

* The fullest extant account of the ancient theory is contained in the work of Lucretius, *GBWW*, Vol. 12.

of the atom underwent (and is still undergoing) a great many incisive alterations and modifications. In our century there are several examples of originally quite daring hypotheses that were only later borne out by new experimental findings. To mention only a few examples from sub-atomic physics: the neutrino as theoretically postulated by Wolfgang Pauli in 1931 was a highly controversial idea at first but was convincingly confirmed some thirty years later; Dirac's hypothesis of the positron or Yukawa's of the meson are equally impressive examples of a similar kind. Turning to biology, we may point to Mendel's original hypothesis of factors (or units) of heredity—later much amplified and fully confirmed through the discovery and identification of the genes. Similarly, the concept of "memory trace"—an assumption of long standing in psychology—is currently being identified neurophysiologically. In all these, and many similar cases, there was at first an *"ad hoc* flavor" that motivated some positivistically oriented scientists to reject such hypotheses.

There is, however, also a different view of the status of causality. As we shall see later, highly responsible scientists have in recent decades been convinced that the principle of causal determinism has been seriously called into question, if it has not been strikingly refuted. In this interpretation the principle of causality is more than an "epistemic" maxim; it is also an "ontological" assertion concerning reality or the basic structure of our universe. If an ontological assertion is to be open to scientific scrutiny, it must be confirmable or disconfirmable by empirical evidence. In order to understand the sense in which recent physics has cast doubt on, or perhaps even refuted, the assumption of strict causality, we must examine more closely the specific form in which the principle of causal determinism was assumed in the sciences of the seventeenth, eighteenth, and nineteenth centuries; and we must at least sketch the new problems that were faced especially by atomic physics in our century. But before we enter into these exciting developments, a brief discussion of some current conceptual analyses of causality and lawfulness will prove useful.

CONDITIONALS, DISPOSITIONS, AND
LEVELS OF EXPLANATION

M any contemporary philosophers hold that there is one way of over-coming or emending the barren Humean conception of causality. In common language we are quite generally disposed to use subjunctive or contrary-to-fact conditionals in formulating causal or lawlike relationships. Thus we might say, "If a strong northwest wind were to prevail, lower temperatures and drier air would result." Or, "If I were to jump out of the window of the second floor of my house, I would fall to the ground." The obvious difference between the subjunctive and the counter-factual conditional is that in the former the truth of the antecedent is left undecided; whereas in the latter, it is assumed that the antecedent is false and that there is a possibility that it is (or was, or will be) unfulfilled. This is clear also from such negative phrasings as, "If it had not been for the prolonged drought, better crops would have come about." Here we simply assert in effect the counterfactual, "If there had been a good measure of rain, the crops would have been better."

Similarly, in common language—certainly in most of the modern Western languages—dispositional ("iffy") properties of various objects, or persons, are expressed in the subjunctive or counterfactual mode. Thus when we ascribe "flammability" to gasoline; or "electric conductivity" to various metals such as copper, silver, iron, etc.; or "irritability" or a choleric character to a person; what we are saying could be explicated in causal if-then statements. These if-then statements formulate empirical or experimental laws. Inasmuch as these laws are confirmable or disconfirmable by empirical evidence, they can be construed as "test-condition→test-result" conditionals. Thus, any sort of disposition, ability, capacity, or propensity may be considered as a property that "manifests" itself if and when appropriate test conditions are applied. When, for example, we say of a person that he knows algebra, or Latin, etc., we do not assert that he is doing algebraic problems all the time; or that he is speaking, writing, or thinking in Latin perpetually; we rather mean to ascribe certain abilities or capacities to that person, and we have a fairly clear notion how to find out—by what kind of testing, probing, or examining.

At the beginning of modern science and philosophy, some thinkers were opposed to the introduction of "occult qualities." But we realize today that such objections apply only to certain misuses of dispositional concepts in scientific explanation. A few decades ago a number of psychologists and sociologists were up in arms against the concept of instinct. Some of their criticisms were directed against the assumption that some abilities of animals, or even of man, were innate, that is, products of inherited constitution, when all the evidence seemed to show that they were acquired through learning from experience. These criticisms are of no particular relevance in the present context, although they are important and still controversial in biology and in developmental psychology. What interests us here are the criticisms that exposed and opposed pseudo explanations that utilize dispositional concepts.

If, for example, we ask for an explanation of why birds build nests, it is almost completely unilluminating to answer: "It is because they have nest-building instincts." All that is achieved by this sort of an explanation is to say that these abilities are inborn—"part of the wiring diagram," as

the current vernacular regarding electronic computers would have it—
and not due to learning. But the question presumably was to account for
this ability of the birds. This would indeed call for more than a sketchy
"promissory note" description of the "wiring diagram" and its functioning. In other words, what is required is neuroanatomical, neurophysio-
logical, endocrinological, etc., information that would, together with
certain environmental conditions, account for the behavior of the birds.

Nevertheless, a word needs to be said about the comparatively slight
explanatory power of dispositional concepts. It is certainly a modest sort
of explanation if we say that a particular bird—say an individual one that
we happen to watch—is building a nest because he belongs to that particular class of birds, that the mating season is on, etc. Even on the first
level of generalization we might say that all starlings build nests because
the starlings are a subclass of a much more extensive class of nest-building
birds. Similarly, if we wish to explain why one iron bar does, and another
does not, attract little steel objects like pins or needles, then we may well
answer that the first is magnetized, while the other is not. If this explanation is to be more than an empty tautology, we must have at least an idea
about the conditions under which magnetization occurs, and perhaps also
under what conditions it disappears. (This, by the way, shows that we
must distinguish different orders or levels of dispositional properties:
"magnetizable" would be a disposition of the first order in this context;
"magnetized," one of the second order—presupposing the first order disposition, or the capacity for being magnetized, possessed by iron, nickel,
cobalt and a few alloys, but not by carbon, silicon, lead, etc.)

As the examples just discussed clearly suggest, we must distinguish
various strata of explanation. On the "lowest" and least enlightening
level we find such explanations as these: Wire conducts electricity because it is made of copper, and copper has a high degree of electric conductivity. But the question "Why is copper a good conductor of electricity?" leads us to a higher level of explanation. Here we may turn to the
atomic structure of copper, and to the theory of electrons, and to the
quantum mechanics of the "electron-gas." Similarly, in the explanation
of biological facts, such as the great similarities between "identical twins,"
we may first refer to Mendel's laws of heredity. But these laws in turn
are derivable from the modern theory of genes; and the mechanisms of
mitosis and meiosis (cell division, etc.) are now becoming much better
understood in molecular biology, especially as a result of the recent discoveries regarding the structures and roles of DNA and RNA.

In a sense, then, the ascription of a dispositional property is (a) at
least a sort of shorthand formulation of an empirical law; and (b) at
most a "promissory note" by which the disposition in question becomes a
placeholder for a concept that is to be introduced on a higher level of
explanation.

The Philosophy of Science

After the foregoing brief survey of the conceptual connections between causality, conditionals, dispositions, and explanations, let us return once more to the idea of causal necessity. The subjunctive and the counterfactual conditionals provide a clue to what is perhaps a small step that can legitimately be taken beyond Hume's empiricist and skeptical (I am tempted to say "ascetic" and "aseptic") explication of the meaning of causality.

To begin with, it can easily be seen that some emendation is needed: the if-then relation between two propositions p and q means no more than what is written in modern symbolic logic by $p \supset q$. The "horseshoe" ($\supset$) between the two propositions is given a definite but very broad generic significance. Its precise meaning can be rendered by saying that $p \supset q$ synonymous (or equivalent) with $\sim p \vee q$, that is, with not-p and/or q. From this it follows that the relation $\supset$ (called "material implication," or "conditional") holds between any propositions p and q provided that it is not the case that p is true and q is false. [Symbolically again: $(p \supset q) \equiv \sim(p \& \sim q)$.] Thus *any* two true propositions "materially imply" each other; similarly any two false propositions, no matter what their meaning is. Also, any false proposition implies any true one. Clearly, this is too wide a meaning for either logically necessary implication (also called "entailment") or for causal implication. Many thinkers have tried to find some middle ground between strictly logical implications and causal ones. Mere universality of implication, as in "for any x, if it has the feature f, then it also has the feature g," will not do either—for several reasons. First, an implication in this generalized form would be true if the antecedent is false. Secondly, even if throughout the whole history of the universe such a generalization were true, as for example, that all animals die before reaching the age of a thousand years, this might well be so only because of accidental circumstances. Perhaps if the world, at least in one of its parts, were to become remarkably free of microbes and viruses, some animals might live longer than a thousand years; or else, some biochemical agent or procedure may yet be discovered that would be, at least to some degree, an "elixir of life." Or, to choose yet a different example, if the temperature in our universe were never in any place to go below a certain point, then—with corresponding assumptions about pressures—hydrogen and helium would always be in the gaseous state and would never be encountered in liquid or solid form. But we might nevertheless have good theoretical reasons to assume with a high degree of confidence that, if the temperature were to fall below a certain point— and the pressure to rise above a certain correspondingly critical point— then hydrogen as well as helium could take on liquid or even solid form.

In fact, the liquefaction of these two gases was achieved under laboratory conditions quite some years ago.

These reflections suggest the question: Can we ever be sure that some laws of nature, as formulated, for example, in physics, are not merely accidentally though universally true but are basic truths independent of special conditions (such as the values of parameters and the location of the pertinent events in space and time)? Great theoretical physicists, notably Newton, Maxwell, Einstein, and Planck, were convinced that there are fundamental laws of nature. It is to these laws, so they thought, that we must turn ultimately for complete and definitive explanation of the observable phenomena. Newton's laws of motion and gravitation, Maxwell's laws of electromagnetism, Planck's quantum law ($E = h\nu$), and Einstein's principles of special and general relativity are perhaps the most typical examples of such fundamental laws (or "basic nomolog-icals"). It was already clear in the time of Newton that his law of gravita-tion, $F = G \dfrac{M_1 M_2}{r^2}$ was more basic than Galileo's law of free fall $S = g \dfrac{t^2}{2}$, in that g is a parameter that varies with the distance from the center of gravity of the earth (or analogously of some other "celestial" body); whereas Newton's G, i.e., the constant of gravitation, was regarded as a "universal" constant.* Similarly, once ample experimental evidence had been accumulated that there are constant ratios in the transformations of the various forms of energy (e.g., mechanical, thermal, electric, radia-tional, etc.), the conversion constants, such as between meterkilograms of mechanical energy and calories of thermal energy, etc., were regarded as fundamental constants of nature. In the same vein some of the constants of recent physics, such as h (Planck's constant of the quantum of action), c, the speed of light (and of electromagnetic waves generally), e, the charge of the electron, have been considered basic invariants. Admittedly, no one can be sure about this. Physicists and astronomers have for some time talked about "secular variations" of c, the speed of light, and it is clear from Einstein's general theory of relativity that c is indeed de-pendent on the strength of the gravitational field, or, as Einstein's theory puts it, on the "curvature of space."

We may conclude that as far as human knowledge is concerned, there can be no guarantee, no certainty, that a given law is basic, even if we have inductive reasons for assuming that it holds universally, that is, throughout all space and all time. Nevertheless, as the examples cited indicate, we can distinguish basic laws from derivative, structure-dependent, or otherwise parameter-dependent, regularities.

As long as the scientists have no reasons—such as might be presented by discordant evidence—to call these more fundamental laws into ques-

---

* The source formulation of these laws in the work of Galileo and Newton can be found by consulting the *Syntopicon* under MECHANICS 1*b* and 6*d*(1).

tion, it is a good and generally accepted scientific practice to consider these laws as pertaining to the "rock bottom" of nature (until further notice!); that it *is* rock bottom, we can never decide conclusively. We cannot even know whether there *is* a rock bottom to nature.

In any case the laws that have "proved their mettle" are the ones that we are inclined to regard as "necessary." It should by now be amply clear that such "necessity" must not be confused with the necessity of logical entailments. Logical necessity as we encounter it in the deducibility of a conclusion from a set of premises obtains, as already indicated, between the conjunction of statements that make up the *explanantia,* and the statement that formulates the *explanandum.* Modern empiricists tend to acknowledge only this logical necessity. But empiricists, and especially the positivists, while reluctant, if not completely opposed, to locutions like "natural" or "causal" necessity, are much more prone to speak of "impossibilities." (This illustrates their rather negativistic philosophical posture.) A *perpetuum mobile* of the "first kind" is ruled out as "naturally impossible," and any would-be "inventors" of such machines, whose energy output exceeds the input, are considered "crackpots" or charlatans, of the same sort as astrologers, alchemists, or phrenologists. Any alleged fact or regularity that is incompatible with well-confirmed "basic" laws is rejected with such a phrase as: "It cannot be done because it is excluded by a basic natural law."

From the point of view of logic, however, the concepts of impossibility, possibility, and necessity are related to one another in a simple way. Whatever is not impossible is, of course, possible. And if a state of affairs is such that its nonoccurrence is impossible, then this simply means that that state of affairs is necessary. So, these three terms, "possible," "necessary," "impossible," allow us quite plainly to interdefine them "ring around the rosy." These interdefinable terms are known as *"modalities."* Although there are still some disputes among logicians in regard to technical aspects, there is fairly general agreement as to the legitimacy and usefulness of the logic of modalities. But, according to the currently prevailing opinion, the *logical* modalities of possibility, necessity, and impossibility are relatively unproblematic as compared with the *causal* modalities. A great deal of work is still needed in order to clarify the precise structure of the causal modalities. A few points, however, are relatively well established by now. There is first of all the condition emphasized by the great nineteenth-century English theoretical physicist Clerk Maxwell: the irrelevance of the spatial and temporal position of an event to its causal efficacy. This simply means that there is nothing "absolute" about space and time. Space and time, as Leibniz clearly realized, are relational structures. The coordinates that indicate where and when events occur do not enter "explicitly" into the equations that formulate the scientific laws.

Herbert Feigl

Regarding the explication of causal necessity, it would seem appropriate to add at least one more defining feature to the Maxwell condition. I am thinking here of *"basic* law" as such an additional point. Essentially this has already been adumbrated in the preceding section. Structure-dependent regularities are clearly not basic. For example, the regularities of the functioning of machines (automats, vending machines, self-regulating systems, such as the servomechanisms) and also of natural phenomena (such as Old Faithful Geyser) and, most interestingly, of organisms, are clearly dependent on the "intactness" of the structure in question. In many cases other conditions, especially environmental ones, also have to be fulfilled.

A full explanation of the regularities of processes in such "systems" therefore requires a knowledge of the basic laws in addition to a description of the structures involved. Strictly speaking, we should not even designate the formulation of structure-dependent regularities as "laws." If the word *rule* were not so ambiguous as to cover both *prescriptive* and *descriptive* meanings, it would be more appropriate to speak of the "rules" according to which such structure-dependent processes occur. This would also allow for the familiar phrase "exception to the rule." And if this terminology is adopted, we can then conceive of laws ("basic laws") as holding without exception. Any genuine, bona fide contrary instance would disconfirm or, strictly speaking, refute a putative law; whereas the idiomatic phrase "no rule without exception" expresses a perfectly legitimate contention. (The phrase "the exception proves the rule" had better be avoided, except in somewhat ironical contexts.)

Summing up in a somewhat different way, we may say that the fundamental laws (or "basic nomologicals") of the universe define a class (or "family") of worlds that is characterized by a set of such laws. The different members of that class differ from one another only in what the physicists call the "initial and boundary conditions," that is, the states of affairs at a given moment of time within a given region of space, and the conditions that obtain at the boundary of that region. Hence, counterfactual conditionals tamper with the actual initial and boundary conditions. They invite a thought-experiment concerning what would occur if these conditions were different from what they actually are. Such considerations are of great significance for a better understanding of the contingent features of our universe. Analogously, it can be illuminating to contemplate universes with basic laws different from those of our universe. In this sense we may speak of "counternomological conditionals." The following examples illustrate counternomologicals: Hoyle, Bondi, and Gold's (now apparently abandoned) hypothesis of the "Steady-State Theory" * in cosmology concerning "continuous creation," or, better,

---

* Bondi's own discussion of this theory may be found in *GIT 1966*, pp. 273 ff.

163

"accretion," of matter, is certainly incompatible with the classical and prevalent conservation principles; or, for a less complex case, consider changing the exponent from 2 to 3 in the inverse square laws of Newton (gravitational force) or of Coulomb (electrostatic, magnetostatic forces). The consequences for derivative laws, such as Kepler's in astronomy, would be quite remarkable.

As Leibniz put it, the laws of logic—such as those of identity, noncontradiction, and of the excluded middle—are valid in all conceivable worlds. The laws of nature, the basic nomologicals of our world, also hold in all those conceivable worlds which differ from ours only in initial and boundary conditions. But we can conceive of universes with differing laws. Whether this manner of speaking is genuinely enlightening may be questioned. But as a picturesque mode of formulation it has perhaps some didactic value.

CONFIRMATION, INDUCTION, AND PROBABILITY

It is not within the scope of the present essay to survey the thorny and still controversial issues of inductive logic, probability theory, and the logic of corroboration or evidential support. A few remarks will suffice for our major purpose—the analysis of the concepts of cause, chance, and explanation. In agreement with common sense, most inductive logicians, at least from John Stuart Mill to Rudolf Carnap, assess the weight of evidence in terms of its quantity and quality. The quantity is essential in the elimination of error due to chance coincidences. This explains why the repetition of experiments, especially in highly complex contexts, is indispensable. It is always possible that some accidental factor (or "nuisance variable") is interfering, but such interference becomes the less likely the more often the experiment is repeated. Still more important is what I just called the "quality of the evidence." This has to do with the manner in which, even in a single experiment, a putative law is tested. Extremely intelligent designs of experimental or statistical tests are needed in order to make the test as "crucial" as possible.

Other considerations may also be relevant in ascertaining the degree of confirmation of an hypothesis of causal connection. Sometimes analogies or models are helpful guides and fruitful heuristic devices. As long as it is remembered that analogies may be limited only to certain features, and, hence, that analogical reasoning may often mislead, there is no harm in utilizing it. Analogical inferences thus may be as highly probable as they are in the anatomy or morphology of plants or animals or as problematic as in inferring the existence of organic life on other planets of our solar system. Some causal explanations, as in the kinetic theory of heat, use analogical models drawn from the mechanics of bodies in translatory motion and collision. This analogy proved—notwithstanding some later modifications—extremely fruitful. But the explanation, attempted by Lesage, of gravitational forces on the basis of particles in motion proved hopelessly sterile. The explanation of the phenomena of light in terms of the corpuscle theory was thought definitively refuted when the facts of diffraction, interference, and polarization seemed to confirm the rival theory of the wave character of light so impressively. But the particle theory of light was, in a highly modified form, reinstated in quantum mechanics and even reconciled with what remains correct in the wave theory. These few examples show that analogies do play an important role in the estimation of the likelihood of a theory, and also that an extremely critical attitude is advisable in employing this sort of reasoning for the validation of scientific hypotheses.

Sir Karl Popper, in many publications, has completely repudiated inductive or analogical justifications of any sort. According to his view, scientific laws can only be refuted or disconfirmed, but never confirmed, let alone verified. The basic logic of his reasoning is simply that universal propositions can never be conclusively verified by any finite amount of evidence. On the other hand, universal propositions can be conclusively "falsified" (i.e., refuted) by a genuine instance to the contrary. We have touched on these matters above. The point at issue between Popper and his opponents (especially Carnap) then amounts to this: Cannot massive evidence *confirm* to a high degree a lawlike proposition? Common sense and scientific procedures certainly answer in the affirmative. Since Carnap, as a consistent empiricist, never claims 100 percent certainty for any inductive inference and acknowledges, indeed insists upon, the basic difference between deduction and induction, he admits, of course, that there is nothing like a *definitive* verification of any lawlike hypothesis. In the analysis of probability he disagrees with the limit-of-relative-frequency concept espoused by J. Venn, C. S. Peirce, R. von Mises, and H. Reichenbach, and yet he does agree with these "frequentists" that all inductive inference is fallible. In the particular form in which Carnap has defined his concept of *degree of confirmation* or logical probability, universal propositions as such always obtain probability zero on the basis of empirical evidence, no matter how extensive that evidence may be. This is, however, a feature only of Carnap's special definition. Carnap's system of inductive logic contains, moreover, a concept of "qualified instance confirmation" which, in a way, does the expected job of providing for the evidential support of laws. Others have offered other definitions that may correspond more closely to the "intuitive" appraisal scientists are wont to give to their hypotheses.

Since these problems are in any case tangential to our main topic, and far too technical for presentation in this essay, I shall venture to indicate briefly what I think is a sensible general approach to a clarification of the inductive procedure in the ascertainment and justification of lawlike hypotheses. A major aim of factual knowledge is the discovery of uniformities, formulated either in causal (deterministic) laws or else in statistical (probabilistic) laws. Scientific observations, experiments, and statistical research are designed to disclose and confirm these all-important uniformities. Admittedly, there is no guarantee of success, nor could there be such assurance for finite human beings. Nevertheless, there is something we can do along the lines of a rationally defensible method. Observations and experiments may be regarded as procedures for "sampling" systematically the indefinitely many "facts of nature" as they are "spread out" in space and time. Since we wish to find whatever regularities there are, it will be best to generalize in the simplest manner possible from samples that are not too small. And, "if at first you don't succeed, try, try again"—which is to say, proceed tenaciously, parsimoniously, but cautiously, with an open mind. What is the rationale of employing the "simplest manner of generalization"? I think it is tantamount to considering the observed sample ("until further notice") as representative of the much larger, even infinite, population of which it is a part. This is rational or reasonable because any other assumption would make the sample nonrepresentative and thus open the floodgate to limitless possibilities. Hence, the simplest generalization has a uniqueness about it. This does not in the least guarantee its truth, but it lends at least a measure of definiteness to the method of induction.

Of course all this is a "rational reconstruction" of inductive inference. It is not an account of the actual procedures of science, certainly not of the way in which theories are constructed and tested. But, as H. Reichenbach has forcefully pointed out, it is one thing to examine scientific theories in the context of discovery—the process of their historico-sociological-psychological development—and it is quite another thing to analyze, explicate, and clarify them in the context of justification. As I have pointed out,[5] even Popper has to face the problem of induction. In his great book *The Logic of Scientific Discovery*, he designates as "corroborated" a theory that has withstood incisive attempts at refutation. But in putting his trust in theories that are highly corroborated, Popper uses inductive generalization. For, on what grounds does he believe that a theory that is up to now well corroborated will stay corroborated forever? And how could he know that a theory that has been refuted, and thus "knocked out," might not "stand up" tomorrow and, in the light of all future evidence, remain correct, even if it had been false up to now?

We cannot get along with only disconfirmation or the lack of it; we must have, and we do have, positive grounds also for the acceptance of laws and theories. Just in what precise form the inductive and hypothetico-deductive procedures should be reconstructed, or how precisely the concept of degree of confirmation is best defined, is one of the major concerns of current work in the logic and methodology of science and in the analysis of the foundations of probability and statistics.

CAUSE AND CHANCE IN "CLASSICAL" SCIENCE: "DETERMINISM"

In this section, an analysis of the "classical," i.e., the deterministic notion of causality, will be undertaken. We shall concentrate on the major features of this notion as they have been conceived especially in physics from Newton to Einstein.

It may be helpful to start with the commonsense notions of cause, effect, and chance, and to trace their affinities, or lack of such, with the scientific concepts of causality as they have developed in the seventeenth, eighteenth, and nineteenth centuries. The concepts of cause and effect, along with the concepts of space, time, and matter, are certainly of fundamental importance even in prescientific thinking. Naturally, commonsense notions are apt to change from one period to another in the history of thought. Scientific discoveries, laws, and theories gradually infiltrate into the world view of the man in the street.

It is perhaps fair to say that the notion of cause in common life is, at least in one important aspect, captured in the Aristotelian and medieval concept of "efficient cause." Causes are said to "bring about" or to "produce" their effects. Thus, we maintain that it is the hot flame under the pot of water that brings about the boiling of the water. Or that it is the severe cold wave that makes the lake water freeze. It is the tapping of the knee that triggers the well-known patellar reflex. It is the mixing of blue and yellow paint that produces a mixture of green color. It is the drinking of several glasses of whiskey that gets you intoxicated and that results in a hangover. It is the steady propaganda that influences the voters. It is the intolerable attitude of the government that gives rise to massive protests. It is the increased demand that engenders an increase in prices. It is his intense desire that impels him to drastic action. Thousands of examples from common speech (whether or not influenced by scientific enlightenment) could be cited, all of them illustrating the "productivity" element in the common conception of causality.

Bertrand Russell[6] urged that the concepts of cause and effect, being "relics of a bygone age," ought to be abandoned and replaced by scientific laws. These laws, he contended, formulate functional relations among variables of many kinds. The variables, and their individual values, represent scientifically measurable or inferable magnitudes. Thus, Russell would presumably replace the commonsense statement "the more you compress a gas, the higher the pressure (and/or the temperature) that will be brought about," by the well-known physical law $p \cdot v = R \cdot T$; where R is a constant and T, p, and v stand respectively for the temperature, the pressure, and the volume of the gas. It is generally thought today that Russell was somewhat too eager to replace the ordinary language of causation by the mathematical formulation of quantitative relationships. For the purposes of everyday life—and, I would add, even for the purposes of the lower levels of accuracy, precision, and explanation in the sciences—the traditional concepts of cause and effect are legitimate and useful. If carefully employed, they will not lead to confusions or fallacies. Moreover, the common cause-effect concepts reflect certain factual features of our world, which could not be covered by the functional representation without much logico-mathematical apparatus. Consider, for example, the asymmetry between cause and effect. The order of temporal succession that is usually, but not always, associated with these concepts could be represented easily enough in mathematical symbolism. But the idea of the unilateral dependency of the effect upon the cause cannot readily be reflected in the mathematical formulation. For, to every mathematical function—in the simplest case, $y = f(x)$—there is its *inverse* function $x = f'(y)$, and the function and its inverse are logically and mathematically completely equivalent. If, for example, $y = x^2$, then $x = \sqrt{y}$. The two formulae say exactly the same thing. Now it is customary, even in pure mathematics, to distinguish between "independent" and "dependent" variables. But there the difference hinges merely upon the focus of attention.

In the realm of matters of fact, there are often other features than just the focus of interest. Common sense is convinced that the temperature of the air, as it varies on a summer's day from early morning to early afternoon to early evening, depends, at least in part, upon the angle of the incidence of the sun's rays. The direction of the causal relation is "one way." The height of the sun above the horizon does not causally depend upon the temperature of the air. But the mathematical function that represents the relation is, of course, reversible. Thus the question arises of how to express the asymmetry. What needs to be explicated is the commonsense truth that changing the temperature of the atmosphere by human intervention, as by heating it with the help of nuclear energy, will not affect the position of the sun above the horizon. Similarly, pressing down, or raising up, a hydrometer—the instrument that measures the density of a liquid—in the liquid in which it is floating will not change the density of the liquid. But a change in the density of the liquid, brought about by adding some soluble substance, will result in a changed position of the hydrometer, that is, in the extent to which it is "sticking out" above the surface of the liquid. It seems, then, that accessibility to practical intervention is in many cases a defining feature of the "independent," as distinguished from the "dependent," variable in causal relations.

Another simple example in which the temporal sequence of cause and effect is of no concern, but where we nevertheless distinguish between determining and determined features or variables, is the relation of the period of oscillation of a simple pendulum (call it *t*) to its length (*l*). The law is formulated by the simple formula: $t = 2\pi\sqrt{\dfrac{l}{g}}$, where π is the well-known mathematical constant of the ratio of the circumference to the diameter of a (Euclidean) circle and *g* is the "constant" of acceleration at a given place on the surface of the earth. By manipulating, that is, by increasing or decreasing the length of the pendulum, we can "affect" or change its period of oscillation. But, to mention what is ridiculously obvious, by taking the pendulum bob and swinging it by hand faster or more slowly than it would swing "naturally," we do not affect its length (or at least not at all in accordance with the inverse function). Again, it seems that the asymmetry depends on which variable is accessible to active intervention.[7]

All this is perhaps only part of what is meant by saying "the cause produces the effect" and not vice versa. When we say that the warp and woof in the weaving loom "produce" the fabric, a piece of cloth, we refer to what Aristotle called the "material cause." The act of weaving would be the efficient cause. The fabric that is produced would be the "final cause."

A great deal has been written about these matters, as well as about the question of the temporal asymmetry or irreversibility of the causal relation. Before we discuss these matters it will be well to characterize the idea—one could be tempted to call it an "ideology"—of classical determinism. Picturesquely, we might first say that it assumes the unlimited "reign of strict law." Less metaphorically, this means that all events instantiate some law or, more usually, a set or conjunction of laws. As we have already hinted, determinism is not to be equated with predictability. Nevertheless, the formulation that Laplace gave—understood as a subjunctive conditional, if not as a counterfactual conditional—is helpful and instructive: If a superhuman mind had complete and accurate knowledge of (a) the total state of the universe at a given time, (b) of all basic laws of nature, and (c) if it had unlimited capacities for mathematical calculation, then such a mind could predict the future development, as well retrodict the entire history, of the universe with certainty and full precision. There can be little doubt that this however fanciful and utopian conception was the ideal model of causal thinking of most scientists in physics and astronomy from Newton to Einstein. The remarkable successes of the deterministic approach during those 250 years in the "exact" sciences encouraged many biologists, psychologists, and even social scientists to think along similar lines.

In retrospect we realize, of course, that the assertion of determinism, especially as an ontological doctrine, was a vast and highly problematic generalization. Precise long-range predictions in the astronomy of our planetary system, the reliability of predictions of the outcome of well-controlled experiments, especially in elementary "classical" physics and chemistry—these, together with at least some moderate successes in discovering laws in biology, psychology, and perhaps in economics, may account for the confidence with which the doctrine of determinism was held. Moreover, philosophically unsophisticated scientists somehow believed, confusedly, that "Same causes, same effects" was somehow a logical truth. Even an outstanding French philosopher of science of the recent past, Emile Meyerson, attempted in vain to reduce the principle of causality to the principle of identity (cf. especially his book *Identité et Réalité*). We have already dealt critically with the fallacious reasoning by which causal relations are reduced to logical truths.

It is important to notice that even in classical physics, especially before roughly the middle of the nineteenth century, not all basic laws conformed to the ideal of determinism. The temporal asymmetry or irreversibility of most processes in nature actually points to a many–one relationship of causes (antecedent conditions) to effects (consequent conditions). For example, a certain final temperature of your bath water can be achieved in a limitless number of ways by mixing hot and cold water of various amounts and temperatures. But once thermal equilibrium has come about, you cannot, even by extremely accurate measurements of the resultant temperature, retrodict the "initial conditions." Similarly, after the big waves of a large lake such as sometimes occur during tempestuous weather have calmed down to a mirror-smooth surface, you cannot reconstruct the preceding wave profiles from even the most precise measurements of the condition of the "calm" water. Examples like these involve what is known as the second law of thermodynamics, the dissipation of energy, or entropy law. In classical, so-called phenomenological, thermodynamics this law was considered basic. Hence, according to the best available view of the world at that time, even the "Laplacean demon," (that superhuman intelligence) could uniquely predict the events of the future but never uniquely retrodict the events of the past on the basis of a knowledge of the "initial conditions" *now*, together with the (then) basic laws of nature. Since physical scientists, unlike historians, are more interested in prediction than in retrodiction, that "one-way" asymmetrical character of the basic laws did not disturb them too much.

Assuming that we represent natural laws in terms of mathematical functions, the question arises whether any function that "fits" the observed facts is to be regarded as a genuine scientific law. For the simple case of the functional relation of a "dependent" variable to an "independent" variable, this can be graphically illustrated by a curve in a two-dimensional coordinate system. The x-axis (abscissa) may then be chosen to represent the independent variable, and the ordinate to represent the dependent variable. Thus a curve may be drawn through the points that represent the numerical values of the function $y = f(x)$. If these values are ascertained by successive, distinct, and separate measurements, the result is a set of points, finite, and discontinuous. Inductive generalization, here in the sense of interpolation and extrapolation, is applied and thus points "in between," as well as "outside" the range of the experimentally given points are added. For interpolation, the customary procedure in "curve fitting" is to draw the "smoothest" curve between the given points. Leaving aside as inessential for our present purposes the problems involved in the correction for errors of measurement, and in the degree of approximation to the "true" functional relationship, the smoothest curve for interpolation can be characterized as the curve for which the integral of curvature for a given interval is a minimum. This can be determined by the techniques of the variation calculus. A simple mechanical model representing the "smoothest" curve can be provided by an elastic metal band, such as is used in the springs of watches; this band would assume the shape of the "simplest" in the above sense of "smoothest" curve, if it is put between closely placed pairs of nails representing the data points in the x,y-plane.[8] As far as I know, no equally obvious mathematical definition of the simplicity of extrapolation has yet been proposed.

Considerations of simplicity are indispensable for a clarification of the concept of law in the sciences. This is easily seen once one realizes that a mathematical function can always be found or constructed that fits to any desired degree of approximation a given set of data-points. No matter how "disorderly" the array of points, an ingenious mathematician can always formulate a function that will be the formally simplest one, in the sense defined above, which will "cover" these points. To be sure, the basic laws of classical and even of modern physics, though many of them are expressed in highly abstract mathematical form, are "simple" compared with what they might be from a purely logical point of view. No doubt, this is at least part of what Einstein meant with his dramatic statement about the comprehensibility of the world.

From the point of view of the logic of inductive inference, there is the following plausible relation between simplicity and the inductive probability of degree of evidential support: Let us consider the ascertainment of the data-points as a kind of "sampling" from the inexhaustible supply of nature; then, repeated success of the simplest interpolations and extrapolations of the formally simplest functions that cover the extant points indicates with a high degree of probability that we have got hold of a "genuine law of nature." This becomes clear if we consider a negative case, for example, the curve resulting on graph paper when the temperature, say, at a certain point in Minneapolis, is registered continuously for a few months or years. No doubt some general trends or features will have a certain degree of statistical regularity, such as the fluctuations between day and night, summer and winter, etc. But surely no scientist would be tempted to look for a strict deterministic law in this case. A strict law, or for that matter a significant statistical law, will be assumed only if the simplest interpolations and extrapolations are successful in predicting or inferring further data-points to be ascertained. The underlying reasoning here is essentially the same as the one discussed above in connection with induction in general: If there are relatively simple laws of nature, then repeated careful and varied sampling will reveal them. That there are simple laws of nature can, of course, never be guaranteed on either logical or empirical grounds. But it is not necessary to assert the order of nature categorically or dogmatically. We can explicate the rationality of scientific method in a manner not essentially different from the justification of human action in general. If, for example, a prospector is out to find gold, he does not know with certainty, and he may not even know with any appreciable probability, that "there is gold in them thar hills." But if he were not even looking (digging, etc.) for gold, how could he ever find it?[9]

Without entering into the intricate issues of inductive logic, it can be seen clearly, I trust, that often-repeated success of the interpolative and extrapolative inferences would be extremely improbable if they were the result of mere chance coincidences. Although it must, of course, be admitted that some scientists can be "fooled" some of the time by fortuitous circumstances, it seems quite implausible that all of them could be misled all of the time. On the other hand, it must also be admitted that radical skepticism, or pessimism, in regard to the efficacy of scientific method can never be conclusively refuted. But, as with pessimism in general, such "philosophical skepticism" could only lead to the complete abandonment of all cognitive endeavors. A cautious optimism, often called a "realistic" attitude, is clearly required for any sort of human activity.

In the deterministically conceived universe there is, of course, only *relative* chance. *Absolute* chance characterizes indeterministically conceived worlds. "Relative chance" actually includes two components of meaning: (1) What appears as chance ("fortuitous," "accidental," "coincidental," etc.) in a deterministic world is relative to our knowledge and ignorance, especially the latter. A collision of two automobiles at a road intersection would not be called an "accident" if it could have been foreseen or predicted (by those concerned) hours before it occurred. (2) A chance coincidence (*relative* chance, again) is considered as "in principle" predictable on the basis of antecedent conditions. But these antecedent conditions may be simultaneous, distant, and mutually (causally) independent events. Consider a simple, but none-too-realistic example from astronomy: Two stars, originally at a very great distance from each other, "happen" to move in such a way that they will come so close to one another that their mutual gravitational attraction—negligibly small at first—will finally bring about a catastrophic collision. Such a crossing or intersecting of independent causal chains is, of course, highly characteristic of our own universe.

Indeed, our universe, as we know it from common life, and as we have come to know it much more fully and precisely through scientific investigations, is not a "block universe." This quixotic idea of a block universe has often been used as a straw man to be knocked over in order to refute the doctrine of determinism. But the conception of determinism in classical science always allowed for the independencies involved in relative chance. It is questionable whether the very idea of a block universe is coherent.[10] In such a universe, the Laplacean demon would have to know with full precision only a tiny part—say a grain of sand—in order to infer the content of the rest of the universe infallibly. No scientifically oriented determinist has ever proposed this sort of extreme ultra-determinism!

Correctly conceived, the determinism of classical science—that is, of mechanics, thermodynamics, optics, and electromagnetism, as well as chemistry, up to at least 1900—asserts both a strict order or lawfulness of nature in its temporal dimension and a large amount of causal independence, certainly of simultaneous but distant events in the "cross sections" of the spatiotemporal world.

We are now prepared to deal with the significance of relative chance in the sciences of the nineteenth century. Let us begin with the simple paradigm of games of chance. Even common sense, influenced probably by at least 250 years of deterministic ideology in science, holds that the appearance of indeterminism is due only to our ignorance of the extremely complex, intricate, and delicate features of the "initial conditions." For example, in spinning a coin, the friction it encounters on the tabletop and in the air, in addition to the amount of spin we give it to start with, etc., etc., together with the laws of mechanics, and a great deal of difficult mathematical calculation, should enable us (or rather the Laplacean demon!) to predict with full certainty and accuracy the outcome: "heads or tails." Analogous considerations apply to roulette, dice, lottery, shuffling cards, etc., etc. The idea has often been put thus: If we could construct a machine that spins coins, or casts dice, etc., under precisely repeated conditions, the outcome should always be the same. (Once more: "Same causes, same effects" is taken for granted.) There is, however, a feature worth noting: In the games of chance just mentioned, as well as in important physical processes to be discussed in a moment, there are discontinuous changes in the outcome—"heads" or "tails," the "ace" or the "deuce," etc.—corresponding to continuous changes in the relevant variables of the initial conditions. A similar situation prevails in the simple mechanism of the Galton Board: small metal balls are released through a funnel onto an array of nails, so that each nail upon which the metal balls impinge represents a "choice point," that is, each ball comes down very nearly vertically upon each nail, and thus, somewhat as in the case of the coin, it will, with about equal probability, go down right or left after rebounding from each nail it hits. It turns out that the balls, when accumulating in appropriate sections at the bottom of the board, will form a "normal" or bell-shaped curve of distribution. Students often ask: But what happens when the little ball comes down exactly vertically and centrally upon a nail? Well, classical physics has the answer to that too: it will bounce back vertically, and with ever diminishing bouncings finally come to rest, precariously poised, on top of the nail! This, however, is a conclusion drawn from highly idealized premises. The slightest irregularities, such as even only a tiny deviation from the vertical direction, or a minimal geometrical or physical asymmetry, would upset the unstable equilibrium. Moreover, the very fact of the random vibrations of the constituent molecules of the ball and the nails would make such an equilibrium "in principle" impossible. "In principle" here means in the light of the molecular and atomic theory of matter and the closely related kinetic theory of heat.

In the kinetic theory of heat and the nineteenth-century theories of statistical mechanics of Maxwell, Gibbs, and Boltzmann, it becomes clear how the ideas of relative chance and of probability help explain the patent temporal irreversibility of most natural processes. This is one of the important asymmetries of causality about which we remarked earlier. The philosophically interesting point here is that this unidirectionality of the processes is actually explainable on the basis of temporally symmetrical basic physical laws. This becomes possible with suitable and perfectly plausible assumptions about the statistical distributions on the micro-molecular level. In Boltzmann's terms, the assumption of "elementary disorder" of molecular motions, as in gases, enables us to derive the laws of diffusion, of heat equalization, and, as was shown later by Einstein and Smoluchowski (1905), the peculiarities of the "Brownian movement" of colloid particles dispersed in liquids or gases. To illustrate this by a simple example, consider two different gases—say pure oxygen and pure nitrogen —separated by a partition in one large container. Pull out the partition, and the two gases begin to mix or "diffuse" into one another. Considering the tremendous number of molecules (under normal temperature and pressure conditions, 27 trillions, i.e., "European trillions"—27×10^{18} per cubic centimeter!) it is overwhelmingly probable that the diffusion will occur. And, although the reverse process (unmixing, the opposite of diffusion) is physically possible, it is so colossally improbable that, to all intents and purposes, such reversions can be disregarded as if they were downright impossible. The interesting thing, however, is that they are theoretically possible, and their actuality has been confirmed by the experimental study of fluctuation phenomena. Such empirical evidence, especially in cases where only small numbers of molecules are concerned, buttressed one of the great revolutionary ideas in nineteenth-century science and foreshadowed a new era of *indeterminism* that was to begin at the turn of the century.

As we have already noted, it is the statistical character of some physical laws, or what we called their "internal" probability, that constitutes the break with the determinism of "classical" science. Such a break occurred with only one law that until at least the middle of the last century was considered to be absolutely fundamental and deterministic. That was the law of the dissipation of energy (or the second law of thermodynamics, or the entropy law). According to this law, in every transformation of energy of one kind into another—thermal into mechanical, or electrical into mechanical or chemical, etc.—there always occurs an increase in entropy or, roughly, waste heat. The "probabilistic" revolution in the physics of the nineteenth century deprived the entropy law of its basic role among the fundamental premises of scientific explanation. This is so, notwithstanding the fact that it is still immensely useful for most problems of macrophysics, and hence for all the older branches of engineering (mechanical, thermal, electrical, chemical . . .). What is philosophically significant is its removal from basic theory. This is thought to involve also some radical consequences in regard to our conception of the direction of time—or as the late A. S. Eddington picturesquely styled it: "time's arrow." Since the processes that were thought to be strictly and absolutely irreversible are now recognized as "in principle," or theoretically, reversible, we can no longer base the unidirectional ("anisotropic") order of events in time on the criterion of increasing entropy. If, though most improbably, the majority of natural processes were to occur in reverse order (as easily visualized by running a cinema film backward) then would we have to say that in such a system time itself was running backward? While some of these questions are still controversial, possibly because still not sufficiently clarified, one thing does seem to be clear: if all processes of the universe, including also the biopsychological processes in human observers and scientists, were strictly reversed, that is, if they were the exact temporal mirror image of what we customarily consider the processes in our universe, then we (not being outside "Godlike" observers) would not be able to tell the difference.

Returning from this speculative excursion to the question of causal determinism, it is important to notice that the "probabilification" of the entropy laws was by no means conceived (in the nineteenth century) as an intrusion of "absolute chance" into the scheme of physical events or their theoretical explanation. While there was perhaps an occasional passing thought in the direction of radical indeterminism, as, for example, on the part of Boltzmann's most brilliant disciple, the Viennese theoretical physicist Franz Exner, Boltzmann himself, and similarly Maxwell and Gibbs, believed in an underlying determinism in the micro-world of atoms and molecules. All three of these great theoretical physicists assumed the strict validity of the laws of classical or Newtonian mechanics for the motions and collisions occurring on the level of molecules or atoms. The statistical element came in only in connection with the "initial conditions," the random distribution of positions and momenta of the molecules in a gas. From this assumption, together with the principles of mechanics, Maxwell derived his famous law of the distribution of velocities of the gas molecules. Roughly, very few have very large or very small velocities, while the vast majority of molecules is ranged around a certain "medium" velocity. Determinism was retained because of the "Newtonian" form of the micro-laws.

It was perhaps for this reason that the physicists during the second half of the last century did not think that the "bottom" of their world had "dropped out"–a feeling that many physicists did have when the quantum theories in our century involved a radical break with classical determinism.

Summing up, and rounding out, our account of the classical causality concept, we may say that it was characterized by the following features or criteria:

1. *Strict determinism*, that is, the admission of relative chance, but the repudiation of absolute chance.

2. *The homogeneity and isotropy of space and time.* This is the "Maxwell criterion," according to which any "absolute" space or time coordinates are irrelevant for what happens in a given spatiotemporal region. Space and time are purely relational structures. Only what's "in time" by way of events is causally relevant.

3. *The temporal symmetry of the basic laws*–especially after the notably asymmetrical entropy law had been "dethroned."

4. *The mathematical form of the basic laws*–expressing functional relationships by a variety of mathematical devices, such as simple unique functions of two or more variables, often symbolized by differential equations or by formulae of the variation calculus. An important example of the latter is the Principle of Least Action–also called "Hamilton's Principle."

5. The mathematical forms just mentioned involved *continuous functions* of the relevant variables and thus represent nature itself as continuous. Strictly speaking, there is nothing conclusively confirmable about this assumption. A large but finite subset of rational numbers would suffice for the quantitative formulation of the values of all variables, no matter whether directly measured or inferred on the basis of measurements.

6. *The idea of "productivity,"* along with the medieval notion of *"causa aequat effectum"* can perhaps be explicated in terms of the distinction of independent and dependent variables in causal relations, together with the conservation principles of mass and energy (considered valid in classical science).

7. *The spatial contiguity* of causal relations–the denial of action-at-a-

distance. This feature became essential only in the *field* physics of the nineteenth century and in Einstein's general theory of relativity (1915). In contrast to these rather recent developments, "action-at-a-distance" was characteristic of Newton's law of gravitation.* Critical scrutiny has revealed that the only testable features of contiguity ("nearby action," *fields* of force) are (a) a finite upper limit (e.g., the speed of light) of the velocities of the propagation of causal influence and (b) "no gaps," that is, no intermediate spatial region is "jumped" by causal influences with spatial distance—as, for example, in the cases of the Newton and Coulomb forces, as well as in the case of light and sound waves in open space.

8. *The temporal contiguity* of the causal relations. This is analogous to the spatial contiguity just discussed. It assumes that there is no action-at-a-distance in time; the supposition is that there are always intermediary "links" between events causally related but separated by a finite interval of time. Both points 7. and 8. could be formulated as the *spatiotemporal contiguity of causal relations.*

Beautiful and obvious as this list of criteria may have appeared to scientists reared in the classical tradition, it is worth noting that each one of these criteria has been called into question at one time, or in one context, or another.

INDETERMINISM OR ABSOLUTE CHANCE IN TWENTIETH-CENTURY SCIENCE

In the present section I shall deal with the philosophical impact of the revolution in the physical sciences brought about by the theory of quanta and quantum mechanics. The philosophical significance of the development of the quantum theory, especially the work of Max Planck, Albert Einstein, and Niels Bohr, from 1900 to 1925, is to be seen in the introduction of *discontinuity* and the first serious, though reluctant, suggestion of *indeterminism*. The subsequent dramatic developments were mainly those of quantum mechanics and wave mechanics with their ideas of "uncertainty" relations (Werner Heisenberg), the statistical interpretation of the De Broglie-Schrödinger wave functions (Max Born), and of "duality" and "complementarity" (Bohr and his disciples), and the highly abstract operator calculus, Hilbert spaces, etc. (P. A. M. Dirac). It was here that physics underwent its most radical transformation—much more "revolutionary" than the comparatively mild and "conservative" innovations involved in Einstein's special and general theories of relativity.

On first superficial reflection the indeterminism of quantum mechanics

---

* Discussions of action-at-a-distance in *GBWW* may be found by consulting ME-CHANICS 6d(2) in the *Syntopicon*.

does not seem to involve an essentially greater measure of unpredictability than does classical deterministic physics—classical mechanics, for example. As Born has pointed out,[11] and as already noted in the preceding section, in regard to practically all natural processes, even the slightest discrepancy between the "true" values of the initial conditions and the values ascertained, or ascertainable, by measurement and inference leads in the long run, and often even in the very short run, to gross inaccuracies in predictions. To illustrate in terms of a simple example given by Born: Assume that a perfectly elastic ball is rolling on a perfectly smooth floor, bouncing back and forth between two vertical walls. In order to predict the precise position of the ball at a precise future time, we would have to know with absolutely perfect exactitude the position and velocity of the ball at a given "moment" of time. The mathematical physicist can very easily write down such initial and boundary conditions. As a German saying has it: *"Papier ist geduldig,"* i.e., "Paper is quite patient"! But speaking in terms of pure and exact mathematics, the specific values of those relevant variables would have to be specific in terms of real numbers. Now, as is well known from set theory, there is (to put it briefly, but loosely) a non-denumerable infinity of real numbers in even the "smallest" finite interval in the continuum of real numbers (e.g., between 1.999999999 and 2.000 . . .). Thus, even if we could neglect interfering factors such as friction, imperfect elasticity, etc., and even if our predictions were highly accurate for a short span of time, we would require an unlimited exactitude in the measurement of the initial and boundary conditions for predictions extended over increasingly longer spans of time.

A similar conclusion seems plausible in regard to an argument advanced by Sir Karl Popper.[12] In order to achieve perfect and complete predictions —even in a "classically" conceived world—it would be necessary to know the precise initial conditions of the measuring instruments by means of which the initial and boundary conditions of the system itself are ascertained, and whose future states are to be predicted. But since observing or measuring these initial conditions would involve further instruments, and so on, this leads to an infinite regress. Alternatively, it is logically impossible for a measuring instrument to record or register its own state completely by "mapping" it on one of its parts. This is, indeed, a very incisive argument against precise and complete predictability. Of course it is not denied that predictions regarding the motions of planets, satellites (natural as well as artificial), and of the outcome of many laboratory experiments are amazingly reliable and precise. What we are concerned with here are fundamental theoretical considerations of vital importance for the philosophical understanding of the world.

There are still other important considerations, among them particularly one arising from Einstein's special theory of relativity, that quite definitely limit predictability "in principle." If the speed of propagation of any and

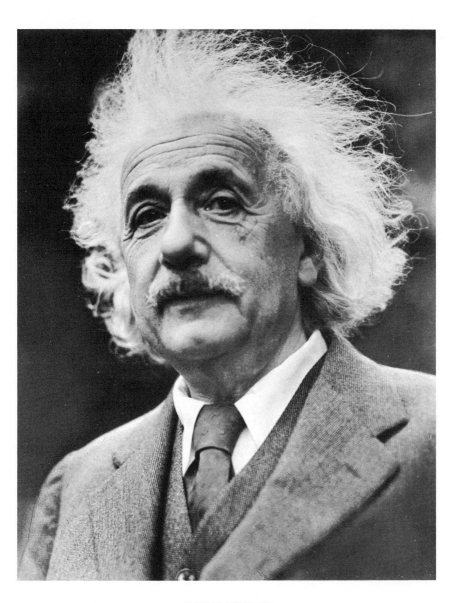

ALBERT EINSTEIN

all causal influences has an upper limit such as c, the speed of light and of electromagnetic waves generally, then whatever influences enter into a given physical system from the outside could not be known before they "arrive" if they travel with the velocity of light. But as regards the idea of determinism, it is still true that if there were observers—"sentinels," or rather, observing instruments—distributed all over the surface of a three-dimensional volume, then the initial conditions together with the information gathered by the "sentinels" about the boundary conditions and their changes during the time interval concerned would "in principle" be sufficient for the prediction of the entire sequence of events in the interior —for that span of time. All this, of course, presupposes the applicability of strictly deterministic laws. It should be obvious that the lack of "advance information" about incoming influences, while involving an essential limitation of predictability, does not in the least establish a refutation of determinism as an ontological hypothesis.[13]

Genuine and serious doubts about ontological determinism, however, did arise with the development of the theory of quanta during the first half of our century. The story is long, involved, and fraught with highly technical and controversial problems. The quantum hypothesis of Planck (1900), later developed and generalized by Einstein (1905), radically transformed classical statistical thermodynamics and the theory of electromagnetic radiations. Planck's formula $E = h\nu$ dramatically symbolizes the break with the continuity assumed in the classical field theories. The symbol h represents the "elementary quantum of action," ν the frequency of the radiation concerned, and E the energy of the radiation. With the help of this new and basic assumption of the "atomistic" character of electromagnetic radiation, Planck was able to replace by his quantum theory the older thermodynamic and electromagnetic theories. Those older theories, though powerful enough within certain domains and certain ranges of the relevant variables, were hopelessly incompatible with well-established experimental facts and regularities. The fruitfulness and explanatory power of the new theory emerged rapidly, especially through the work of Planck himself, soon to be followed by outstanding brilliant contributions by Einstein, Bohr, Arnold Sommerfeld, and others.

Along with the abandonment of continuity came the first inklings of statistical laws to supplant some of the strictly deterministic ones of classical physics. In particular it was the processes of the emission and absorption of electromagnetic radiation by atoms and molecules that were conceived as involving an element of "absolute chance." Similar suspicions soon emerged in regard to the processes of radioactivity in the "spontaneous" disintegration of the nuclei in the atoms of radioactive substances such as radium, thorium, and the isotopes of many other well-known chemical elements, (e.g., carbon, cesium, cobalt, etc., etc.). Highly reliable statistical laws were known for the disintegration of larger amounts of such substances, but it seemed hopeless to find strict laws for the disintegration of individual atomic nuclei.

The great question, of course, was, and still is, whether science here, at what seems to be the "rock bottom" of nature, confronts merely relative or genuinely absolute chance. It is interesting to note that both Planck and Einstein, the originators of quantum theory, retained to the end of their lives (1947, and 1955, respectively) a firm belief in strict determinism. This is generally attributed to their education and the initial success of the "classical" style of physics. In the case of Einstein, it has been said that he contributed the crowning conclusion to classical physics with his special and general theories of relativity. It was indeed the "geometrical method" that guided him in the construction of those theories. Despite the fact that they represent tremendous conceptual revolutions, despite the fact that Einstein went far beyond Newton and Maxwell, his greatest predecessors in the history of theoretical physics, the four-dimensional Minkowski geometry of the special theory and the Riemannian geometry of the general theory are not only compatible with a strict determinism but were really conceived in such a manner as to provide a basic framework for a deterministic physics. Moreover, for about the last thirty years of his life Einstein endeavored to construct a Unified Field Theory. These fascinating, but unfortunately unsuccessful, attempts aimed not only at restoring determinism to our view of the physical universe, but Einstein also hoped to provide a unified theory of gravitation and electromagnetism, and even beyond that a derivation of the characteristics of the basic particles of modern physics—protons, neutrons, electrons, the various types of mesons as well as the particles of "antimatter"! Similar goals have been pursued in a variety of very different ways by David Bohm, J. Vigier, and others.

However, even if the universe is of only finite depth, it might vary from layer to layer by being alternately deterministic or indeterministic. Present-day quantum mechanics, in the form accepted by the majority of physicists, is decidedly indeterministic, in that several but not all of its basic laws are statistical laws. The quantum theorists have conceived and formulated this indeterminism in two ways. First there is Heisenberg's original formulation of the "Uncertainty" or "Indeterminacy" Principle. It maintains that the two sorts of variables which jointly would have to be known with precision in order to make precise predictions as in classical mechanics cannot be so known. We are told that the product of the uncertainties of the location of a micro-particle, such as an electron, and of its momentum is constant. Qualitatively expressed, this means, roughly, that you can't have both a "sharp" position and a "sharp" velocity simultaneously by any sort of measurement in any sort of experimental setup. You can have the value of either of these variables precisely measured, but then the value of the other one becomes quite indefinite. Or, you can strike a compromise and obtain rather "blurred" values for each of the two variables. A similar principle holds for the determinations of energy and time in atomic contexts.

Heisenberg actually derived these "Uncertainty Principles" from the postulates of his so-called matrix mechanics, a highly abstract but equally fruitful theoretical scheme. Nevertheless, in his early book on *The Physical Principles of the Quantum Theory* (1930), he gave an explanation of the Uncertainty Relations that has been predominantly fashionable in elementary expositions of the theory. To paraphrase the popular formulation contained in A. S. Eddington's *The Nature of the Physical World* (1928), we might say: "It does not hurt the Moon to look at it; but the electron gets a kick from being looked at." What is meant is, of course, that in order to ascertain the position and the velocity of an electron it has to be "illuminated" by some sort of radiation. If the position is to be very precisely determined, "light" (electromagnetic radiation) of very small wavelength, and hence of very high frequency, must be used. But according to Planck's basic formula $E = h\nu$, such a radiation—X rays, or rays of radioactive substances—delivers quite a "kick" to the electron and hence makes its velocity extremely uncertain and inexact. And, vice versa, in order to determine the velocity very precisely, radiation of very long wavelength is required; this gives it only a minimal "kick" but blurs exceedingly its position in space. This can be formulated (for the sake of simplicity, I venture a slightly incorrect formulation): "$\Delta x \cdot \Delta v \approx \dfrac{h}{m}$," where Δx symbolizes the inaccuracy ("leeway") in the position of a particle of mass m along the x-axis of a chosen coordinate system; Δv the inaccuracy ("leeway") in the velocity of that particle; h is the Planck constant of "elementary action" again. As is readily seen, the greater the mass m of the particle under consideration, the smaller is the product of the two "uncertainties." These x's and v's may well be considered as intervals roughly corresponding to what in statistics is customarily called the "standard deviation," or, perhaps better, the "probable error."

Heisenberg himself has repeatedly stressed that these Uncertainty Relations are an inevitable result of the interference of the act of measurement with the measured situation. This was often also formulated as an "interaction of the observer with the observed object (or system)." It has led to what in the opinion of many physicists and philosophers is an extremely misleading interpretation; namely, that the subjective states of consciousness of the observer and the observed situation form an indivisible or inseparable "whole." This intrusion of subjectivism in modern physics has maintained itself stubbornly despite the many criticisms offered by such authorities as Einstein, Landé, Born, Schrödinger, Reichenbach, and Popper.

The basic difference of quantum mechanics from classical physics has been formulated in a variety of ways. The most important and influential views are those of Born and Bohr. One of Born's most outstanding achievements was the statistical interpretation of the Schrödinger equations. Schrödinger, the great Austrian theoretical physicist, building on the earlier work of De Broglie, established the so-called wave mechanics. It was soon shown by Schrödinger and Eckart that, despite differences in the mathematical expressions, wave mechanics is equivalent to or "translatable" into Heisenberg's matrix mechanics. Wave mechanics proved heuristically more fruitful; it was also more appealing because some sort of visual imagery could be associated with it. As De Broglie showed, some of the discontinuities in quantum theory, as in the "permissible" energy levels of atoms in Bohr's earlier theories, could be explained by the superposition or "interference" of waves; the "in-between" states do not occur because they are "annihilated" by interference. What was not clear until 1926 was the "nature" of those waves. Schrödinger had held the view that they are a mathematical representation of the "electric density" in the electron shells of the atoms. But Born showed in 1926 that this interpretation led to serious discrepancies with the experimental facts. Born's genius hit upon the statistical interpretation of the amplitude $/\psi/^2$ of the De Broglie-Schrödinger waves. This is to say that, according to Born, $/\psi/^2$ represents a probability, and probability ascriptions are testable by observing the relative frequencies of the relevant events.

The fact that nature is "good enough" to manifest itself in statistical regularities is then a "rock bottom feature of nature," at least according to present-day physics. It is a strikingly new facet of this modern outlook that the magnitude has wave character, and, to put it somewhat picturesquely, though crudely, that these waves and their interferences by superposition are (until further notice!) "ultimate" realities of the physical universe. If this pivotal feature of quantum physics is to be overcome, then a return to determinism could be achieved only by going on to a deeper substratum of nature, such as the "hidden variables." This is an open question at the moment.

From a philosophical point of view, it should be noted that quantum mechanics as a theory, together with its striking confirmatory experimental evidence, is considered by most contemporary physicists to be a conclusive refutation of determinism. Along with the introduction of discontinuities and basic statistical laws, an entirely new conception of matter has come to the fore. It looks very much as though the old and traditional idea of substance as something permanent and indestructible underlying all changes in the universe has to be entirely abandoned. If I may put it crudely, the current theories conceive the elementary particles of matter as something that "pops in and out of existence" according to the "laws of chance"!

It is perhaps premature to speculate about the larger metaphysical im-

183

plications of the new physics. Nevertheless, it seems that an ontology of events (rather than of substance) is clearly indicated. But as to whether the special form of B. Russell's or A. N. Whitehead's event-ontologies will be most appropriate remains to be seen. Quite possibly the bold ideas of J. A. Wheeler on geometricodynamics and superspace present a further alternative.[14]

Although we cannot enter into the details of the current controversies of the interpretations, reinterpretations, or modifications of the extant quantum theories, we shall now return to the closely related issue of prime interest to the main topic of the present essay: Determinism vs. Indeterminism. In the early days of quantum mechanics it seemed plausible to many physicists and philosophers that the new indeterminism of Heisenberg-Bohr-Jordan-Born could not be the "ultimate truth," because it conflicted with the time-honored Principle of Sufficient Reason. Even today there are some scholars who find the very idea of "Absolute Chance" absolutely irrational. But these scholars, who constitute a small minority, do not seem to realize how many of the erstwhile "eternal" and "*a priori*" truths have been shown to be superstitions, sanctified only by a long tradition of philosophical doctrine. The "*a priori* truths" regarding space, time, and matter were definitively refuted by Einstein's theory of relativity. Competent philosophers of science have spoken of a "disintegration of the *a priori*" under the onslaught of modern science.[15] Now, even among those thinkers who have adapted their philosophical views to the modern conceptions of space, time, and matter, we find some who are quite unwilling to abandon their belief in strict causality or 100 percent determinism. A few have tried to accommodate themselves to the situation in quantum mechanics by a change in the definition of "physical state." Indeed if we take the ψ of the Schrödinger equation as a state-variable, it is obvious that ψ, functioning as it does in a differential equation, can be viewed as a variable that fulfills the requirements for initial and boundary conditions within a deterministic scheme. We have seen, however, that ψ is physically significant only in that $/\psi/^2$ represents a probability. Hence, unless the "hidden variable"-theoreticians penetrate to a deterministic substratum, quantum mechanics is, and will remain, essentially statistical and hence indeterministic.[16]

Another way of reconciling quantum mechanics with determinism was suggested by the great English theoretical physicist C. G. Darwin, in his book *The New Conceptions of Matter* (New York: The Macmillan Co., 1931; cf. especially p. 119). Following the lines of thinking in classical statistical mechanics, Darwin, and many others since, thought that the "absolute chance" events on the micro-level are bound to produce practically deterministic effects *en masse* on the macro-level of the phenomena of everyday life. The "law of large numbers," as it has been somewhat questionably labeled, accounts for the "leveling off" or "smoothing out" of all the individual micro-events, and the emergence of a strongly deterministic "surface." True enough, in the majority of natural as well as of technological processes, this is exactly what does take place. The "leveling off" is here due to the same mechanisms at work in the processes of diffusion or of temperature equalization as explained in statistical thermodynamics. But just as in the case of the Brownian movement it is possible to catch hold of effects of individual fluctuations, so it is possible to produce "absolutely" unpredictable and, according to the best available theory, genuinely indeterministic effects on the basis of quantal micro-events.

For a simple example I suggest the Compton effect. This is essentially the collision of a quantum of light—a photon, say in X rays—with an electron. One result of this interaction is that the electron is "bouncing off" in a direction that even the best measurements of the antecedent conditions do not enable us to predict. Suppose, then, we distribute Geiger counters all over the region in which a special case of the Compton effect occurs. Geiger counters are highly sensitive electrical devices that can be "tripped off" by the impact of even a single electron. The Geiger counters could be wired to electrical amplifying devices in such ways that one Geiger counter will trigger the ringing of a bell, another the flashing of a light bulb, another will open a door, and yet another will make a bomb explode. According to the best established current theories, it is absolutely impossible to say with complete certainty which of these diverse events will happen. The most we have is a distribution function for the directions in which the electron can go off in the Compton effect; that is to say, we know only the probabilities, with corresponding relative frequencies "in the long run," of the various directions in which the electron may "fly off." This feature of what is currently considered "absolute" chance may, of course, I repeat, be supplanted by a deterministic account, perhaps in terms of the dynamics of the "deeper" substratum. For the time being philosophers had better be patient and willing to live with an "unfinished" view of the world. And, as pointed out before, there can never be conclusive reasons for saying we have a complete theory. The last word, then, is that there is no last word in the endless quest of science.

Having put Einstein's epigram at the beginning of this essay, I believe there is no better way to conclude it than by quoting Einstein's greatest predecessor in the history of scientific thought, Isaac Newton:

". . . I do not know what I may appear to the world, but, to myself, I seem to have been only like a boy playing on the seashore, and diverting myself in now and then finding a smoother pebble or prettier shell than ordinary whilst the great ocean of truth lay all undiscovered before me . . ."

whilst the great ocean of truth lay all undiscovered before me

The Philosophy of Science

FOOTNOTES

1 "Corroborated" is a term used by Sir Karl Popper in his important and influential *Logic of Scientific Discovery*. "Confirmed" is the term used by R. Carnap in his inductive logic. There are significant differences between Carnap's and Popper's views in this respect.

2 I omit, for simplicity's sake, requisite obvious definitions.

3 For example, friction→heat; lightning→thunder; electric current→magnetic field, etc., etc.

4 I deliberately disregard here the developments in twentieth-century physics that have modified the explanation and formulation of gravitational phenomena.

5 In my essay "What Hume Might Have Said to Kant," in M. Bunge (ed.), *The Critical Approach to Science and Philosophy* (New York: The Free Press, 1964), pp. 45–51.

6 In "On the Notion of Cause" in *Mysticism and Logic* (New York: W. W. Norton & Co., 1929).

7 This is, however, not the whole story of this asymmetry. For a recent, very incisive—but rather technical—analysis, cf. H. A. Simon and N. Rescher, "Cause and Counterfactual," in *Philosophy of Science*, XXXIII, No. 4 (December, 1966), 323–40.

8 I owe these ideas largely to Kurt Gödel, who, in an appendix to the unpublished doctoral dissertation of my late friend Marcel Natkin (University of Vienna, 1928), gave this sort of mathematical formulation of the formal simplicity of interpolation. Aside from the primarily statistical "method of least squares" and Newton's formulae for approximation, I don't know of any other attempts toward a definition of this kind of "simplicity." I dealt briefly with these matters in my first book: *Theorie und Erfahrung in der Physik* (Karlsruhe: G. Braun, 1929), pp. 22–29.

9 It is in this sense that one may speak of a rational justification of inductive inference. Cf. H. Reichenbach, *Experience and Prediction* (University of Chicago Press, 1938). (Also, the more technical, but remarkable, last chapter of his *Theory of Probability* [University of California Press, 1949].) *See also* my "De Principiis non disputandum," in M. Black (ed.) *Philosophical Analysis* (Cornell University Press, 1950; reprinted by Prentice-Hall, Inc., Englewood Cliffs, N.J., 1963).

10 *See*, for example, the discussion by William James in "The Dilemma of Determinism" in his book *The Will to Believe* (New York: Longmans, Green & Co., 1897). Following him, Corliss Lamont, in his recent lively and interesting book *Freedom of Choice Affirmed* (New York: Horizon Press, 1967), confuses scientific determinism with block universe idea and thus has no difficulty in refuting determinism.

Herbert Feigl

11 "Statistical Interpretation of Quantum Mechanics," *Science*, October, 1955, p. 678.

12 In his remarkable article "Indeterminism in Quantum Physics and in Classical Physics, I and II," in *British Journal for the Philosophy of Science*, I (1950), No. 2, 117–33, and No. 3, 173–95.

13 Some otherwise highly competent and brilliant thinkers have attempted—contrariwise—to *demonstrate* ontological determinism on the basis of the special theory of relativity in its geometrical (Minkowski) representation. For an incisive critique of these fallacious arguments, cf. Howard Stein, "On Einstein-Minkowski Space-Time," in *Journal of Philosophy*, LXV, No. 1 (1968), 5–23.

14 Cf. his recent article "Our Universe: The Known and the Unknown," in *American Scientist*, LVI, No. 1 (1968), 1–20.

15 Cf. H. Reichenbach, *The Rise of Scientific Philosophy* (Berkeley: University of California Press, 1951) and *Modern Philosophy of Science* (New York: Humanities Press, 1959).

16 I cannot discuss here the highly sophisticated proof given by J. von Neumann many years ago. This proof convinced quite a few physicists and philosophers that the indeterminism of quantum mechanics cannot possibly be overcome, and that a theory of "hidden variables" is impossible. But J. von Neumann's proof relies on a premise which is tantamount to the assertion of the correctness and completeness of the Heisenberg-Born-Dirac quantum mechanics. And it is just this premise which has come under attack from various sides during the last two decades.

NOTE TO THE READER

The principal sources of the classical conception of SCIENCE are contained in *GBWW* in the works of Galileo, Kepler, and Newton. Discussions of the "revolt" against this view may be found in the works of Einstein, Eddington, and Jeans published in *GGB*, Vol. 8.

GBWW also provides a wealth of material on the main subjects of Professor Feigl's concern. In many cases these subjects are ideas to which whole chapters of the *Syntopicon* are devoted. Thus Chapter 8 is on CAUSE, Chapter 9 on CHANCE, Chapter 61 on NECESSITY; and in them the reader will find references to discussions of these ideas in *GBWW*.

Background material on the nature and methods of science may be found by consulting the chapters devoted to HYPOTHESIS, INDUCTION, and SCIENCE.

JOHN G.
BURKE

John G. Burke was born in Boston in 1917, and received classical schooling at the Boston Latin School before going to the Massachusetts Institute of Technology, where he majored in physical metallurgy and took his B.S. degree in 1938. He joined Bethlehem Steel as a metallurgical assistant in Johnstown, Pennsylvania, and then became a field engineer in Tulsa and Houston, dealing with the technology of petroleum production and refining. In 1941 he was called to active service in the Army and served as chief of the heat treating section of the Watertown (Mass.) Arsenal for one year before he transferred to the Air Force. The pilot of a B-17, he was shot down over Brunswick, Germany, in 1944 and was imprisoned for the remainder of the war in Stalag Luft I, Pomerania. In 1945 he joined Cummins Diesel Engines, Inc., and became vice president and general manager in the following year. In 1948 he established his own engineering firm in Tulsa, specializing in the design and manufacture of high-pressure vessels. He retired from business in 1958 to become a graduate student in the history department of Stanford University, where he received an M.A. (1960) and Ph.D. (1962). He then accepted an assistant professorship at the University of California in Los Angeles, teaching the history of science and the history of technology. He became associate professor in 1967, and also is currently vice chairman of the department. The author of Origins of the Science of Crystals *(1966) and the editor of another book,* The New Technology and Human Values *(1966), he has contributed articles to encyclopedias and professional journals.*

Technology and Values

Recently, the commandant of a military airfield in California, harassed by complaints concerning the scheduling of training missions, the flight patterns, and the continual roar and whine of the jet aircraft, posted signs around the perimeter of the field, which read: "Pardon our noise; it's the Sound of Freedom." The number and the acerbity of complaints, he reported, dropped sharply, but he was unwilling to predict that the inhabitants of the surrounding areas would remain mollified when newer and noisier jets arrived.

This incident portrays in miniature the larger problems faced by our society with respect to our advancing science and technology. In this instance, the sleep or the repose of many individuals was either suddenly broken or constantly disturbed by the piercing and persistent sound. Their right of privacy had been invaded, and, in complaining, they sought to retain this right. But when the signs reminded them that the aircraft symbolized a free society, few continued to protest. Values came into conflict, and, for the time being at least, freedom outweighed personal comfort and privacy.

In the larger sense, technology has been criticized as promoting a materialistic attitude and as threatening man's spiritual values. It has been condemned as contributing to more frequent and more devastating wars, because scientists and engineers have been able to devise and produce increasingly more lethal and more destructive weapons. It is asserted that technological advances in perfecting automated work processes will, in time, create massive unemployment in many levels of the labor force, which will undermine or shatter the human satisfaction in personal achievement. We also now have the capability of constructing a central government computer which, through national networks, could reproduce in seconds a complete dossier of any citizen. This possibility, of course, raises the specter of a secret police force and a fascist-type dictatorship, controlling our lives and depriving us of our freedom. Though aware of these warnings and presumptions, it is difficult for most of us to take them very seriously. Rather, the advance of scientific knowledge and our increasing technological capabilities appear to point to a marvelous future for all mankind. We are as awed by the successes of heart transplantation and of cancer therapy by laser beams as we are delighted by the conquest of space by our astronauts. Though some of our values may suffer because of novel technology, other and higher values, it appears, will be greatly enhanced.

Value conflicts in human affairs are, of course, not new. One conflict gave rise to the Protestant Reformation, and another was in large measure responsible for the American Civil War. But in these cases, the threat of certain practices or institutions to specific values was direct, evident, and immediate. In contrast, the relation between science, as a method of increasing knowledge, or technology, as the application of knowledge for the production of goods and services, and such values as morality or individuality, is, in most instances, obscure and indistinct. The American people, being for the most part optimistic, are confident that any discomforts experienced in advancing to their "manifest destiny" will shortly be corrected, either through scientific and engineering advances or through the normal political process. There are voices, however, like that of the French sociologist Jacques Ellul, who assert that technology is now completely out of human control, and that because of this condition we are proceeding rapidly to disaster.

Because of these diverse conclusions, and because the question of technology and values came under increased scrutiny during 1968, it seemed to me highly appropriate to discuss the issues in the following essay. Further, I have approached the subject largely from a historical point of view, in an attempt to shed new light on some of the major problems involved in the inquiry.

TECHNOLOGICAL INNOVATION AND SOCIAL CHANGE

Examples of technological innovation that have wrought massive long-range social change are numerous. The compass, gunpowder, and printing with movable type were innovations that, in different ways, transformed the structure of western European society and the habits, values, and beliefs of its members. Inasmuch as the history of technology has emerged as a scholarly discipline relatively recently, only a few thorough analyses have been made of the social changes resulting from a single technological innovation. One comprehensive study, however, is that by Lynn White on the social effects of the introduction of the stirrup into western Europe in the eighth century, A.D.[1] Another dramatic illustration involves the introduction and expansion of the railroads in America in the nineteenth century.[2]

From these analyses and others, we can advance several conclusions concerning technological innovation with which many, though certainly not all, historians would agree. First, the mere presence of an innovation, or of knowledge that makes innovation possible, does not necessarily

---

1 Lynn White, Jr., *Medieval Technology and Social Change* (Oxford: The Clarendon Press, 1962).

2 Bruce Mazlish (ed.), *The Railroad and the Space Program* (Cambridge, Mass.: M.I.T. Press, 1965), in particular the essay by Thomas C. Cochran, "The Social Impact of the Railroad."

mean that it will be adopted or utilized. Second, innovation does not occur because of the operation of some pervasive and obscure "force," but because of the action or actions of individual men, who make decisions and operate ordinarily through some type of institution. Third, in the past, innovation appears to have been relatively unpredictable, and, with certain qualifications, it seems likely to remain so, with the result that we cannot predict with any certainty what the nature and structure of future society will be. I should like to present the rationale of each of these conclusions in some detail.

In no respect is technological innovation inevitable. In White's words, "a new device merely opens a door; it does not compel one to enter." Thus, many patents have never been commercially exploited, because either financial resources, the proper type of entrepreneurial skill, or a market was lacking. Similarly, conditions may be more propitious for the exploitation of knowledge at one time than another. For example, given the meager knowledge concerning nuclear fission available in 1939, it is doubtful that the massive effort to develop an atom bomb would have been mounted, had not war with a scientifically capable enemy appeared imminent.

There are many instances in which social mores, values, or conditions prevented innovation. Laws in many localities during the Middle Ages prevented the mining and smelting of metallic ores in order to prevent the devastation of fertile agricultural areas or the destruction of forests.[3] The landscape and the products of agriculture were more highly valued than the debris of the mine; presumably the necessary minerals, mined elsewhere, could be purchased.

During the Elizabethan period, certain types of machines were prohibited in textile establishments, particularly those which fabricated articles in "a deceitful manner," for example gig mills for raising the nap of the fibers of cloth. An amusing instance of restriction involves a certain Hans Spaichl, whose name appears in the archives of the council of the city of Nuremberg no less than twenty-five times between the years 1559 and 1581. Spaichl was a worker who produced lathe-turned articles of copper and brass. He was obviously of an inventive turn of mind, since he continually made improvements for his lathes which workers in other metals wished to adopt. The council took recognition of his skills by refusing him permission to leave the city, by attempting to prevent him from manufacturing and selling the improved lathes, and finally, in desperation, by reimbursing him for lathes secretly manufactured and then destroying them.[4] In both of the above examples, guilds or corporations

---

3 Rolf Sprandel, *Das Eisengewerbe im Mittelalter* (Stuttgart, 1968), p. 325.

4 Friedrich Klemm, *A History of Western Technology* (Cambridge, Mass.: M.I.T. Press, 1964), pp. 153-59.

restricted the dissemination of innovations to ensure the economic well-being of their members. Values, then, can also influence the introduction or pace of novel technologies.

Again, the Turks employed huge siege guns in their assault on Constantinople in 1453, which were partially responsible for the eventual fall of the city and the disappearance of the eastern Roman Empire. Later, however, the Turks failed to recognize the importance of western European artillery innovations. They continued to build massive siege guns and completely neglected mobile field artillery. As a result, they were thoroughly defeated in the Battle of St. Gotthard in 1664, when these weapons were used against them. The feudal structure of the Turkish army contributed to this myopia, but social and economic conditions in the Ottoman Empire during the sixteenth and seventeenth centuries also militated against change.[5]

Somewhat later, the Chinese came under the domination of the technologically more advanced peoples of western Europe. Chinese civilization was essentially humanistic; it had always been successful in absorbing invaders into its culture; it revered tradition. Chinese bureaucracy was composed of scholars who were unsympathetic with the materialistic aspects of commerce, with the unrefined soldiery, and with military affairs in general. With such a cultural background, the exploitation of China by energetic and aggressive Europeans was relatively simple.[6] Carlo Cipolla documents the following quotation from the writings of a nineteenth-century Chinese scholar, Feng Kuei-fen:

> The most unparalleled anger which has ever existed since the creation of heaven and earth is exciting all who are conscious in their minds and have spirit in their blood; their hats are raised by their hair standing on end. This is because the largest country on the globe today, with a vast area of ten thousand *li*, is yet controlled by small barbarians. . . . Why are they small and yet strong? Why are we large and yet weak? . . . What we have to learn from the barbarians is only one thing, solid ships and effective guns.[7]

This is a belated recognition not only of the facts and implications of technological innovation but also of the refusal of Feng Kuei-fen's predecessors to deal with it.

Technological innovation, then, can be accepted or rejected by a society, because men, acting either individually or through institutions, are responsible for it. We are often led to believe through loose rhetoric that there exist economic "forces" or technological "forces" apart from man

---

5 Carlo M. Cipolla, *Guns, Sails, and Empires* (New York: Pantheon Books, Inc., 1965), pp. 90–99.
6 *Ibid.*, pp. 116–26.
7 *Ibid.*, p. 126.

and not fully comprehended. Such expressions are at the least sheer nonsense and at the most pernicious. When Henry Adams, for example, stated that he "found himself at the Great Exposition of 1900, his historical neck broken by the sudden irruption of forces totally new," he was merely revealing that for the past forty years he either had not cared or had failed to look around and see what his contemporaries were about. While Adams was preoccupied with the unquestionably grand art and architecture of the Middle Ages, Bessemer and Emile Martin were perfecting their processes for the manufacture of inexpensive steel; Werner Siemens and Gramme were improving electric generating equipment; Bell was inventing the telephone and Edison the phonograph. Though Adams was unaware of the rapid pace of technological innovation, others were not. Samuel Butler, in his *Erewhon*, and others condemned the intensification of this type of human activity, while such enthusiasts as Carroll D. Wright in *The Industrial Evolution of the United States* approved of it in laudatory terms. Both Butler and Wright, however, were agreed that man and men, not impersonal forces, were responsible for inventions and innovations.

One circumstance surrounding technological innovation that lends credibility to the notion of a "force" in operation is the fact that two or more people, sometimes widely separated geographically, have often invented the same device practically simultaneously. Perhaps the most striking example is that of the incandescent filament lamp, which was successfully produced by Joseph Swan in England in 1878 and by Thomas Edison in the United States in 1879. Even more intriguing is the fact that both used a carbonized cotton thread as the filament, although Edison in his early lamps employed carbonized bamboo. We should not be misled by appearances, however. The possibility of developing an electric light or lamp came into existence very early in the nineteenth century, when the development of the electric storage battery made possible the production of a continuous electric current. In 1809 Sir Humphry Davy noticed the brilliance of the light emitted by an electric spark struck between two carbon electrodes, and his comments were translated into carbon arc lamps within a few decades. At the same time it was recognized that the passage of an electric current through a conductor, for example a metal wire, caused it to become heated to incandescence and emit light. Two problems prevented the immediate exploitation of this knowledge. First, not any conducting substance could serve as a filament; it had to be one that did not melt when incandescent. Second, at high temperatures substances combine rapidly with oxygen and subsequently deteriorate; the lamp, then, had to be devoid of air; that is, it was necessary to produce a high vacuum within the lamp.

Experimentation to solve these problems began in earnest during the 1840's. In England, W. E. Staite, who had contributed to the develop-

CROWDS ATTENDING THE PARIS EXHIBITION, 1900; (BELOW) HENRY ADAMS

[Henry Adams] found himself at the Great Exposition of 1900, his historical neck broken by the sudden irruption of forces totally new.

ment of the carbon arc lamp, produced a lamp in 1847 employing a filament composed of an alloy of platinum and iridium, which had a high melting point but a short life because of the residual air remaining within the bulb. J. W. Starr patented a carbon filament lamp in the United States in 1845, which came to the attention of Joseph Swan in England, who attempted to perfect a carbon filament lamp beginning in 1848. These and dozens of other efforts failed because the inventors could not produce a sufficiently high vacuum within the bulb. The invention of a mercury pump by Hermann Sprengel in 1865 made it possible to obtain a satisfactory vacuum, and subsequent improvements on it led to Swan's and Edison's ultimate success in producing incandescent filament lamps within a short period of time.

The dramatic announcement of an innovation in the press or its sudden appearance on the market masks the long period of development which is present in all cases, as the example of the electric light illustrates. The fundamental principles of mechanical television were known in 1884, but satisfactory commercial transmission did not occur until the late 1930's. In the interim, inventors discovered that the inherent features of mechanical television made it impractical. Further advance required the development and application of electronic pickup and reproducing tubes. Similarly, the invention of the transistor, which made its spectacular debut in 1947, can be traced back to the introduction of the X-ray diffraction of crystals by Max von Laue in 1912 and the beginnings of quantum theory at about the same time.

Innovation, then, is the product of the creative and imaginative utilization of accumulated knowledge and existing techniques. It is a fact, of course, that the growth of scientific knowledge, as well as the empirical and scientific improvement of existing technology, has been peculiarly a product of western European civilization. This problem will be explored later in this essay. In passing, though, it is important to stress that technological innovation has been in no way uniquely determinative of the vast social change that has occurred during the past three centuries in western European civilization and in the cultures emanating from it. Technology is only one factor, though an important one, among others political, economic, environmental, religious, and intellectual in nature. It is, however, only recently that the importance of technological innovation has been appreciated. Leo Marx notes that despite Thomas Jefferson's "passion for utilitarian improvement, gadgets, and labor-saving devices of all kinds," he failed to recognize technological innovation as an agent of change.[8] In fact, the word *technology* was the creation of Professor Jacob Bigelow of Harvard, whose *Elements of Technology* in 1829 brought the word into the English language.

---

8 Leo Marx, *The Machine in the Garden* (Oxford: The Clarendon Press, 1964), p. 147.

Our third conclusion concerned the predictability of past and future innovation. It is easy after the fact, as in the case of the incandescent filament lamp, to determine at what point in time key knowledge became available, and when techniques or instrumentation had advanced to such a state that the preconditions for invention were fulfilled. It was impossible in the early nineteenth century, however, for a person working to perfect the filament lamp to know when the preconditions would be met. Joseph Swan, for example, discontinued his inventive efforts in this direction after his initial failures and only attacked the problem again when he learned that a high vacuum pump was being used by Sir William Crookes in scientific experiments. Given the uncertainty of innovation and the fact that innovation is only one factor contributing to social change, it follows that the prediction of what social changes will take place and what the social structure of the future will be is, to say the least, highly uncertain.

Probably one of the more notable examples of the fallibility of prediction is contained in "Available Energy," an address made by the late eminent scientist Robert A. Millikan in 1928, four years before Chadwick discovered the neutron. Millikan declared:

> The energy available to him [man] through the *disintegration* of radioactive, or any other, atoms may be perhaps sufficient to keep the corner peanut and popcorn man going, on a few street corners in our larger towns, for a long time yet to come, but that is all.[9]

It may be argued that Millikan lacked foresight and imagination, but there were few people in a better position than he was at the time to predict the innovations that might occur from accumulating scientific knowledge.

Here we should distinguish between innovation and what I shall arbitrarily term "novelty." I wish to restrict the word *innovation* to a product or technique that has massive long-range social consequences. Although the transistor may be viewed as a miniature solid-state equivalent of a vacuum tube amplifier, without it many of the computers being produced at present would not have been feasible, and we are only beginning to feel the social effects of their use. Thus, I would argue that the transistor is an innovation. Similarly, cheap cotton underwear was an innovation in the nineteenth century because it had important effects in raising the standards of body cleanliness and in the prevention of disease. The development of new styles of underwear at the present time, however, or the introduction of improved fabrics, I think, constitutes a novelty, because the social effect is limited. I do not mean to infer that in economic terms novelties are unimportant; in this respect they may be much more

---

9 Robert A. Millikan, *Science and the New Civilization* (New York: Charles Scribner's Sons, 1930), p. 111.

important than the original innovation. I merely wish to point out that they have far less influence on the scope of social change.

Now, the outlines of the material environment of the future may be drawn with reasonable accuracy with respect to the extension of today's technological possibilities, that is the introduction of novelties. We can, for example, visualize the existence of super superhighways possessing automatic electronic control devices, which will permit us to travel on them in perfect safety at several hundred miles per hour. Whether these will receive the necessary construction priority is another matter. But, not knowing what innovations the future will bring, we cannot predict the nature and structure of society a hundred years hence.

Several changes have occurred in the nature of scientific and technological activity since the mid-nineteenth century which make prophecy even more risky. First, we have witnessed the professionalization of the scientific and engineering communities and also increasing specialization in both areas, which has enlarged not only the probability of innovation but also the range. Second, commencing in the area of chemistry and extending gradually to all other areas of scientific activity, there has been a continually growing merger of science and technology, or research and development, which is systematic and goal-directed in nature. This condition has had the effect of drastically reducing the period of time taken to translate new knowledge into innovation. Third, there has been an increasing emphasis on a systems approach, wherein all of the parameters or variables surrounding a problem are taken into consideration in its solution: where rationality, economy, and efficiency are simultaneously applied. In addition to these internal changes in the nature of technological activity, there is the presence of massive funds for research and development not only from private but also from governmental sources. As a result, our scientific and engineering schools, both large and small, are now committed to a program of teaching the scientific, economic, and managerial techniques of promoting innovation.

With these factors providing important stimuli to innovation, the changes occurring in our recent past become less surprising. A quarter-century ago television, jet travel, and the computer were infant innovations. These industries presently add almost fifteen billion dollars to the gross national product; they employ almost one million persons; and, what is more significant, they affect society in very important ways. Bell & Howell estimated in 1964 that more than 80 percent of its current sales were in products that did not exist in 1959, and DuPont reported that more than 50 percent of its sales were in products developed since the end of the second World War. Given such conditions, it remains hazardous to predict, especially in the face of other important factors conducive to change, just what the society of the future will resemble. With the pace of technological innovation becoming more rapid and the range of new possibilities wider, society will more likely remain in a constant state of flux with few if any stable aspects.

Thus far, our discussion has centered on technology and social change. Progress has not been mentioned. On December 6, 1852, President Millard Fillmore, in his third annual address, stated: "It is not strange . . . that such an exuberance of enterprise should cause some individuals to mistake change for progress." Indeed, now, as in Fillmore's time, innovation and the extended spectrum of choices made available to man through scientifically based technology is considered by many to constitute true progress. It may be profitable to explore this belief.

PROGRESS

A mong the diverse values held by Americans, the idea of progress is uniquely important; first, because it can be viewed not only as an individual, but also as an institutional, and even a national value; and second, because other values are subordinate to it. Specific types of activity and work result in what may be termed progress; achievement and success may be used to measure progress; freedom seems necessary for progress; and the advance of scientific knowledge and the accomplishments of technology appear to be the hallmarks of progress. Businesses and industries advertise continued profits as evidence of progress, and those that suffer losses must offer careful explanation to retain the confidence of investors. A steady increase in the amount of the gross national product coupled with a low unemployment rate are taken to be the twin indicators of national progress.

Progress, then, connotes optimism, affirmative advance, and directed energy. There is, however, another side to the coin. Accompanying our ebullience is the conviction that progress is only gained at a price; that progress must spell failure, distress, poverty, and even death to some. Noncompetitive businesses or those insufficiently modernized have to fall by the wayside; inefficient or unskilled labor must be jobless or go on relief; death necessarily accompanies the construction of such massive engineering projects as bridges, dams, and skyscrapers. Progress is a curious, janus-faced value, one that requires closer inspection.

The vision of progress is modern in conception. It had no roots in the classical world, and it developed only in western European civilization.[10] The Copernican revolution in astronomy, which occurred during the late sixteenth and seventeenth centuries, was in large measure responsible for its introduction and acceptance. Although the new astronomy removed

---

10 The most authoritative works on this subject are J. B. Bury's *The Idea of Progress* (New York: The Macmillan Co., 1932) and Charles Van Doren's recent and more comprehensive *The Idea of Progress* (New York: Frederick A. Praeger, Inc., 1967).

man and his planet, Earth, from the center of the universe to a position as merely another satellite of the sun, the work of Sir Isaac Newton advanced evidence that the universe was governed by immutable laws that had been in operation since creation and would continue to operate into the unforeseeable future. There was the prospect of an immense and indefinite amount of time stretching into the future, during which the human race, on a plenteous and stable earth, could work out its destiny.

During the period when the idea of progress was gaining credibility, there was as yet no notion of evolution, and the possible degeneration of the human race was not even considered. Men believed that the human species was stable in form and structure throughout time but yet perfectible. The elements composing the idea of progress had both religious and idealistic philosophical roots: that work produces a strong moral character and results in material rewards and happiness; that human reason and rationality are the only valid guides to action; that individuals make up society and must be free; that a good society cares for all of the human beings composing it; and that the central purpose of society is to seek the unity of mankind.

Almost from the inception of the idea, however, visible technological advances rather than claims of man's moral and ethical improvement became the bulwark of the belief in the idea. Thus, in 1577, Louis Le Roy cited the invention of the compass, of gunpowder, and of printing as evidence to prove his argument that progress had been achieved since classical antiquity. During the next few years, Jerome Cardan, Sir Francis Bacon, and Tommaso Campanella employed the identical line of reasoning.

In his *Sketch of a Historical Picture of the Progress of the Human Mind*, written in 1793, the Marquis de Condorcet stressed technological innovation not only as evidence of progress but also as a major factor contributing to it. He predicted that the range, precision, and rapidity of mental operations would be vastly increased in the future by the invention of new instruments and methods. The future, he believed, would be characterized by equality among the social classes of a nation and among nations themselves, and by the progressive improvement of individuals, morally, intellectually, and physically.

During the nineteenth century, progress came to be equated more and more with the advance of technology and economic prosperity. Unlike Jefferson, Alexander Hamilton comprehended fully the relationship between industrial and technological advance and material progress. In his *Report on Manufactures,* prepared for Congress in 1791, Hamilton asserted that not only the wealth but also the independence and the security of the country depended upon the affluence and success of manufacturers. Industrial advance, he stated, was necessary for the perfection of our political institutions and to the safety and welfare of society.

To a large extent, the gradually accumulating wealth of America, and its emergence as the most powerful nation in the world, has been because the course which Hamilton advocated was followed. While in the past, savings, investment, and increases in labor productivity were regarded as the primary factors influencing economic growth, at the present time technological innovation takes the palm. The Council of Economic Advisers estimates that 50 percent of our total economic growth in any year is owing to technological innovation, and some independent economists have raised this estimate to 67 percent. If we think of progress in terms of economic growth, then, existing statistics appear to provide a measure of progress and to demonstrate that technological innovation is largely responsible for it. From this point of view, to assure continued progress it is necessary to have suitably educated or trained people, the natural resources, the capital to exploit new technology, and a developing market to consume the plethora of new products pouring out of this modern cornucopia. It should be noted in passing that the cost of producing some modern innovations demands international markets. A case in point is the supersonic transport plane.

Further, the vast range of goods available to consumers that has been made possible by technological innovation lends massive support to the idea of our progress. Recently, Nevin S. Scrimshaw described the sensational advances accomplished through the application of genetics to the production of fruits, vegetables, and meats. Disease-resisting strains of beans, potatoes, watermelons, and strawberries are now available. Cereal grains contain high-quality protein; cows give richer milk; hens lay more eggs; and broilers are so efficiently raised that they are ready for the market in three weeks.[11] With such evidence, progress in material terms cannot be denied. It is the same with textiles. The no-wrinkle linens, the bonderized materials, now used for clothing are inexpensive, smart looking, and easy to maintain. They are indeed a boon to the housewife. But to cite further examples of our material progress would be tedious and is unnecessary.

We can view the many ways in which living has become more easy and convenient as proof of progress. The modern supermarket symbolizes this fact. But it would appear that in this respect we are presently only in a preliminary stage. David Sarnoff, for example, in noting that the number of computers had increased from one thousand in 1956 to thirty thousand in 1966, and in estimating that one hundred thousand would be in use in 1976, predicted that they would result in a vast increase in personalized services, such as banking, travel, library research, medical care, and personal education.[12] Others forecast that in the near future there will be

---

11 Nevin S. Scrimshaw, "Food," *Scientific American*, CCIX (September, 1963), 75.
12 *Saturday Review*, July 23, 1966, p. 22.

small computers in the form of household robots to relieve the housewife of the last vestiges of her former drudgery. In the computer we seem to have the materialization of Condorcet's dream.

In this same vein we can measure progress by the decline in the number of people engaged in exhausting manual labor. During the period 1940 to 1960 the number of farmers was reduced by 50 percent, while agricultural output rose by 50 percent. In the same two decades labor in coal-mining dropped 60 percent owing partially to a shift to other fuels but also because of an 80 percent increase in productivity from technological innovation. Those formerly required to work by the sweat of their brows have been channeled into trade, services, and government, in which areas the number employed has increased some 400 percent since 1900.

There are other evidences of progress besides economic growth, material abundance, conveniences of life, and the decline of manual labor. Because science and medicine have learned to prevent and cure many diseases, we live longer and are healthier during our lives. In fact, the tremendous accumulation of scientific knowledge would alone appear to be ample proof of human progress. Derek Price has demonstrated that from the mid-seventeenth century to the present the number of working scientists has doubled every fifteen years, with the result that about 90 percent of all scientists that have ever lived are alive today.[13] The same rate of growth has characterized the number of scientific articles published and the number of scientific journals publishing them. Although one might argue that Price has analyzed the accumulation of scientific knowledge from a quantitative rather than a qualitative point of view, his statistics are nevertheless impressive. Still more impressive is his prediction that this rate of growth must of necessity decline, because, as he whimsically puts it, if it did not "we should have two scientists for every man, woman, child, and dog in the population."

In the face of Price's stricture, if we are to ensure continued economic and material progress, it follows from the very nature of things that we must become even more wise. Recently, therefore, the necessity of the continued financial support of science by the federal government has been stressed. This message was elaborated in an address by the new president of the National Academy of Sciences, Philip Handler, to the Council of the American Association for the Advancement of Science:

> For most of us gathered here, it is an article of faith that the attainment of an ever more complete and penetrating understanding of man and the universe in which he finds himself is, of itself, one of mankind's highest goals. Even though this sometimes is disparaged

---

13 Derek J. de Solla Price, *Little Science, Big Science* (New York: Columbia University Press, 1963).

as "science for its own sake," the intellectual edifice thus constructed may well be the most enduring expression of our civilization, fully comparable, in this sense, to the cathedrals of the Middle Ages or the art of the Renaissance. As such, this endeavor fully warrants ample public support. Moreover, it is a second article of faith among us that some of the knowledge so gained will be translated into the technology which, tomorrow, will serve as the means by which man will raise himself from his animal estate, loosen him from his inherent biological limitations, and thus free him for whatever spiritual goals may lie ahead.[14]

It is clear that Handler believes that science should serve the cause of humanity, and also that he urges that the pursuit and accumulation of scientific knowledge is, or at least should be, one of man's most precious values. Like Condorcet, Handler believes in the perfectibility of man, not through moral suasion or feelings of love, faith, and kindness, but through science and scientific education. In fact, if we take Handler's words at face value, it would appear that science will in time produce a new kind of man, a mutation, who will no longer have any animal instincts or emotions. This circumstance would, presumably, constitute true progress, and we may well ponder as to the spiritual goals this new man will seek.

Skepticism of the optimistic theory of the progress of humanity and civilization appeared simultaneously with the expressions of belief in the idea. In fact, it was the quarrel throughout the seventeenth century between the Ancients and the Moderns, primarily concerned with literature and poetry, that brought the idea of progress into clear focus. In the eighteenth century Jean Jacques Rousseau, appalled by the patent inequality between the rich and poor, proposed that civilization was actually a regress, that mankind had been and would be far happier in a more natural and primitive condition.* One consequence of Rousseau's thought was the attempt to alleviate inequality through more democratic educational programs or to annihilate it altogether through revolution. Another result was the romantic movement, whose adherents sought to idealize the past and the glories of a life close to nature.

A new dimension of disbelief was added, however, when the Industrial Revolution brought in its wake human degradation and exploitation. In the 1830's the Sadler Reports to Parliament documented many of the inhumane practices associated with advancing technology and industrialism and created a demand for reforms, some of which were effected. The wretched condition of the poor led some critics to advocate the destruction of the capitalist system and the adoption of socialism as the means

---

14 *Science*, March 3, 1967, p. 1064.

* Rousseau's *Discourse on the Origin of Inequality* is in GBWW, Vol. 38, pp. 323–66.

of ensuring not only the quality of human life but also progress with the novel technological means at hand. Others, however, viewed technology, symbolized by the Machine, as the culprit that was dehumanizing man. Samuel Butler, in his *Erewhon*, wrote that machines have "preyed upon man's grovelling preference for his material over his spiritual interests," and described a Utopian society wherein all machines had been destroyed.

It was, perhaps, Dostoevsky who best delineated the moral and ethical implications of the scientific and technological progress, which became obvious to all by the mid-nineteenth century. In *Crime and Punishment*, Raskolnikov asserts:

> I maintain that if the discoveries of Kepler and Newton could not have been made known except by sacrificing the lives of one, a dozen, a hundred, or more men, Newton would have had the right, would indeed have been in duty bound . . . to *eliminate* the dozen or hundred men for the sake of making his discoveries known to the whole of humanity.[15]

Part of humanity, it seems, has to suffer or die as the price of the progress of science and technology.

In 1859, seven years before *Crime and Punishment* appeared, Charles Darwin published *On the Origin of Species*. The little-known subtitle of Darwin's work was "Or the Preservation of Favoured Races in the Struggle for Life." In the hands of Herbert Spencer this idea was applied not only to the races of mankind but also to social classes. In America, William Graham Sumner of Yale and Andrew Carnegie preached the cause of social Darwinism, which seemed to provide a sound theoretical basis for laissez-faire capitalism. But more than that, social Darwinism supplied the rationale for the statement that Dostoevsky had Raskolnikov utter; it explained why suffering and death must accompany progress. The renowned German scientist and engineer Werner Siemens wrote in 1886 that "it is a very hard but at the same time an unalterable social law, that all transitions to other, even if they be better, conditions, are connected with suffering." It was, he continued, "hopeless to try to stop the stream of this development, or to turn it back," since "it must necessarily follow its predestined course."[16] When such thinking became entrenched, almost every social evil resulting from technological innovation could be rationalized and justified. This type of apology has been employed from Siemens' time to our own. Robert B. Lindsay provided a recent example:

> It is true that thousands . . . manage to kill themselves and others and still more thousands get injured on the roads of the world every

---

15 F. Dostoevsky, *Crime and Punishment* (New York: The Modern Library, Inc., 1944), pp. 254–55.

16 Werner Siemens, "The Scientific Age," *The Popular Science Monthly*, XXX (1886), 814.

year. This is lamentable, and every effort by reasonable control should be made to cut the number down. But a judicial statistical examination of the figures in the light of the enormous increase in traffic should arouse not so much horror that the damage is so great but rather wonder that it is no greater. Perhaps the reasonable view is that mankind has to pay a price for the joy of the more exciting if more dangerous life provided by technology. It is up to society, presumably in the shape of the state, to institute whatever controls the people as a whole can agree to.[17]

Such a statement, of course, provides no answer to the problem of human waste associated with advancing technology. It merely salves the consciences of those in positions of power, whose drive to achievement and success permits them to disregard the human implications of their decisions.

By the end of the nineteenth century many intellectuals had turned their backs on the idea of progress. Leo Tolstoy viewed the direction in which science and technology were proceeding as inimical to man's true interests. Henry Adams believed that industrial society was throttling the creative power of man—that his imagination, love, and aesthetic sensibilities, which were responsible for the creation of such masterpieces as the cathedrals of Mont St. Michel and Chartres, were being destroyed. Oswald Spengler voiced a similar pessimistic message of decline and degeneration. Despite these warnings and despite the waste of life and the destruction occasioned by the technologically advanced weaponry in two world wars, the faith of the majority of the citizens of America, vocalized by the managerial and professional communities, in the idea of progress remains unshaken, as does the belief that true progress can only be achieved by larger dosages of science and technology.

More recently, however, there has been growing disaffection and disillusionment, not only among humanist intellectuals, with our science-centered culture. No one denies the achievements of science and technology, but there is considerable doubt whether these advances constitute progress in any meaningful sense. One of the original goals incorporated in the concept envisioned the unity of mankind. The development of nuclear arsenals by several nations has, instead, transformed the world into an armed camp, fearful of a nuclear holocaust. Many scientists are devoting their careers to weapons projects; the results of their research are classified, so that their work contributes little to the mainstream of science. A case in point is the development by the Department of Defense of chemical and biological weapons. Little is known about these weapons except that the armed forces are learning how to use them effectively and that surveys are being conducted to determine public reaction to

---

17 R. B. Lindsay, *The Role of Science in Civilization* (New York: Harper & Row, Publishers, 1963), p. 232.

their use. Moreover, science has become a cat's-paw in the struggle for national prestige. Many scientists are dubious about the scientific value of the manned lunar project; the space race between the United States and Russia has been compared to the potlatch ceremony of the Kwakiutl Indians, in which two clans gathered around a fire and their chiefs vied with each other in throwing the clan's most valuable property into the fire.[18]

Further, it is obvious that the fruits of scientific and technological advance are denied to a sizeable segment of the American people despite the material abundance of the United States. An adequate diet is still beyond the reach of many Americans, not to speak of modern plumbing, electricity, or telephones. Those men, such as Bacon and Condorcet, who forged the ideal of progress envisioned a society which would benefit all of its members. Instead, the gap between the very rich and the poor, between the highly educated and the illiterate, is just as wide as it ever was in the past. Material progress has blessed a portion of our society, and the values of that portion dictate the decisions concerning priorities.

Aside from the growing recognition of the discrepancy between ideals and realities, there has been criticism of the validity of the current measures of progress. Planned obsolescence, for example, is a widespread practice befuddling the notion and measure of progress. The notion of style changes, we believe, originated with Colbert, the great minister of Louis XIV. In the seventeenth century Colbert persuaded his sovereign to change his wardrobe each summer and winter. The court nobility, of necessity, had to follow the fashions, and this practice benefited French textile manufacturers and tailors. Planned obsolescence became a major factor on the industrial scene in the United States after the depression of 1921, when the problem of used car competition arose. Thereafter most automobile manufacturers began to introduce new models yearly or biyearly with just enough changes to make the secondhand cars out of style and vastly depreciated in value. Yet such waste is neglected in statistics that show our economic progress.

More recently, increased technical knowledge permitted engineers to design equipment or component parts to last only a specified number of years. For example, some radio manufacturers design portable models for a three-year life. An engineer defended this practice for the following reasons: first, that a longer life-span would saturate the market, reduce competition, and thus cause prices to rise; and second, that the consumer

18 Edwin Diamond, "The Rites of Spring," *Bulletin of the Atomic Scientists*, XIX (May, 1963), 26–29. At the annual meeting of the American Association for the Advancement of Science in December, 1968, the president-elect, Dr. Athelstan Spilhaus, criticized spending large sums of money on space ventures like the Apollo 8 moon mission and asserted that the United States should instead spend billions to rebuild its cities and solve the urban crisis.

would be denied the benefits of progress in science if long life was made a product characteristic.[19] Apart from the ethical questions surrounding such conduct, it is doubtful that the illusion of continued economic progress and national prosperity can be maintained in the face of wasteful and widespread practices that create rapid depreciation and force the early scrapping of consumer products.

Progress, then, is an elusive value. Science and technology have contributed to material abundance, but even in quantitative terms the belief that we are an affluent society can be challenged. The notion that science and technology can create a society characterized by health, wealth, and leisure is questionable on historical grounds, since we know that under our present system of distribution these benefits have not accrued to all members of society. Our current unrest, riots, and violent civil disobedience prove this contention. It is therefore extremely doubtful that scientific knowledge and technological capability can solve all of our complex social problems, as some of the more vocal champions of a systems approach promise. In a qualitative sense, moreover, our preoccupation with progress has blinded us to the seriousness of the situation we now face. Our natural resources have been and are presently being consumed in such a profligate manner that some may be exhausted in the not too distant future. But more important, the human environment has suffered a grave deterioration, and this condition is worsening rapidly. These problems warrant discussion.

THE HUMAN ENVIRONMENT

Curiously, the idea of progress, which embodies concern for future generations of mankind, who will presumably have attained a state of near-perfection owing to scientific and technological advance, gives attention in only one respect to the environment in which these descendants of ours will live. It assumes that man will have achieved a supremacy over nature by the creation of an artificial environment, or, in modern technical jargon, an independent life-support system. This concept of progress does not take into consideration the effects of human activity on the natural environment or on other life supported by it. Nor does it inquire concerning the physiological or psychological reactions of man in the artificial environment. Advancing technology has by now interfered with our natural environment to such a deleterious extent that it has become imperative to take action not only to retard but also to reverse this process. The future of man is threatened as well as other forms of life. Further, man's gradual estrangement from nature, his retreat into teeming urban metropolises, and his preoccupation with a scientific-technological

---

19 *Design News*, November 24, 1958, p. 3.

LUDGATE HILL, LONDON, 1872; ENGRAVING BY GUSTAVE DORÉ

retreat into teeming, urban metropolises

culture have resulted in an impairment of the quality of human life, despite increased longevity and material abundance. In the long-range view, these problems are the most pressing of our time.

Man, of course, has been influencing his environment since prehistoric times. Early nomadic communities hunted by setting forests on fire, which drove the animals into the open where they could be more easily tracked and killed. The ancient agricultural civilizations of Mesopotamia and Egypt depended upon the waters of the Tigris and Euphrates rivers and the Nile, respectively. They dredged canals and constructed dams to divert the water and irrigate the fields efficiently. Overfishing of the Baltic and North seas during the medieval period resulted in the near-extinction of herring in those areas, just as certain species of whale are threatened today. Prior to the successful utilization of coal in metallurgical processes in the eighteenth century, the forests of England were almost depleted because of the demand for charcoal. Complaints about the noxious and nauseous fumes from inefficiently burned sulfur-bearing coal in London appear about 1285.

That mining methods had generated vociferous criticism by the mid-sixteenth century is attested to by a passage from Agricola's *De Re Metallica*:

> . . . the strongest argument of the detractors is that the fields are devastated by mining operations, . . . Also they argue that the woods and groves are cut down, for there is need of an endless amount of wood for timbers, machines, and the smelting of metals. And when the woods and groves are felled, then are exterminated the beasts and birds, very many of which furnish a pleasant and agreeable food for man. Further, when the ores are washed, the water which has been used poisons the brooks and streams, and either destroys the fish or drives them away.[20]

A modern conservationist could hardly raise more cogent objections to unrestrained mining operations. Agricola, as an advocate of technological progress, brushes aside these objections by demonstrating that metals are necessary for the advance of civilization, and by asserting that mining operations, in fact, result in either very slight damage or none at all. His statements also have their modern counterparts.

Real environmental pollution, however, commenced during the Industrial Revolution in the nineteenth century. Hydrogen chloride gas, for example, was a by-product of the Leblanc process for producing inexpensive alkali. The pioneer manufacturers, finding no use for it, passed it up tall chimneys to the atmosphere. Its fallout caused such widespread destruction to vegetation, and property damage, that manufacturers were

---

20 Herbert C. and Lou Henry Hoover (trans.), Georgius Agricola's *De Re Metallica* (New York: Dover Publications, 1950), p. 8.

arraigned for creating a public nuisance. The development of techniques for absorbing the hydrogen chloride, and the later recognition of its economic value, prevented even greater environmental pollution.[21]

Rapidly advancing technology from that time to the present, however, has resulted in our air, land, and water being increasingly polluted by industrial and radioactive wastes, pesticides, herbicides, detergents, and fumes. Analyses of the catches of fish show the rapid spread of agricultural pesticides into the oceans. Effluents from nuclear reactors, which concentrate in various organisms, are accumulating at the mouths of rivers. Water pollution from industrial wastes is harmfully affecting marine life on the shores of all major industrial nations. Indeed, Lake Erie has become such an open sewer that limnologists agree that it is unlikely that anyone will ever again see it clean and clear.

In August, 1968, sixty members of the medical faculty of the University of California, Los Angeles, asserted that air pollution had become a major health hazard to most of Los Angeles County during much of the year. Almost all pollution experts agree that automobile exhaust fumes are the chief source of noxious pollutants in the atmosphere, but as yet the automobile industry has been unwilling to mount the necessary effort to reduce materially these dangerous by-products of the internal combustion engine. Neither the industry nor the federal government has moved to institute a program of scientific research required to solve this problem. Nor will the government subsidize research on steam-powered or battery-operated vehicles, which offer a possible alternative. Tons of carbon, sulfur, and nitrogen compounds, as well as oil, soot, and dust, are dumped into the air in the United States every year. The phosphate companies of western America lay down a screen of choking smoke where the skies were formerly clear. From the pulp mills of Idaho and Oregon and from the processing and rendering plants of the eastern seaboard there is emitted an ever increasing stench of nauseating or highly offensive odors.

The ecological balance is delicate and at present only imperfectly understood. Nature, conquered in one respect, retaliates in another. Thus, the technological efficiency of intensive agriculture resulting in single-crop farms also creates favorable conditions for the spread of a particular pest. The boll weevil diffused rapidly over the southern cotton fields when it migrated from Mexico in the late nineteenth century. Similarly, San José scale attacked the bark, leaves, and fruit of most deciduous fruit trees in California, and phylloxera, the plant louse, infected grapevines. Specific pesticides alleviate these infestations, but the long-range effects of the chemical components after use and breakdown are unknown.

Yet we continue to act with surprising temerity. The United States

---

21 Charles Singer *et al.* (eds.), *A History of Technology* (Oxford: The Clarendon Press, 1958), IV, 241.

armed forces are using herbicidal chemicals in a widespread attempt to destroy deliberately the crops and forest vegetation of certain areas of Vietnam. After protests concerning the wisdom of this decision, the Department of Defense finally produced the ecological studies which were used as a basis for the decision. The majority of the members of a committee of the American Association for the Advancement of Science, which reviewed these reports, considered them scientifically insufficient.[22]

But even if we were to eliminate the most flagrant abuses, continued progress at our present rate will pose new environmental problems. The seriousness of overpopulation has been emphasized so widely that it will not be mentioned here. But a continued population rise together with an increase in the per capita use of energy means that the growth rate of the electric power industry, presently about 6 percent per year, will continue unchanged for years to come. Should the use of nuclear power become more extensive, as is commonly expected, there will be a major problem in the disposal of dangerous radioactive wastes. In addition, power plants must get rid of large quantities of heat, which pollutes the cooling water and adversely affects marine life. Nearby residents of Lake Cayuga in northern New York are now questioning the siting of an electric power plant at the lake because of the danger of thermal pollution. Such controversies will undoubtedly become more common in the future.

Leaving aside future problems for present realities, why is it that man continues heedlessly to pollute the environment in the face of clear danger signals? We may condemn the ubiquitous littering of beaches, parks, and playgrounds, or the careless use of fire in forest preserves, as acts of thoughtlessness, but an increase in the number or proximity of trash barrels or the posting of entreaties to preserve the beauties of nature have little effect. Similarly, we may blame the more serious pollution damage on industrialists who tolerate the visible effects or are insensible to forecasts of a deteriorating environment because of short-term monetary profits. Such attitudes are not new.

It is probable that the exploitation and consequent despoliation of nature is not a superficial problem but, rather, has deep psychological or religious roots. If one views nature as antithetical to human purposes and goals, one may consciously or subconsciously attempt to control and overcome the forces of nature, regardless of the ensuing costs to the environment. On the other hand, if one regards nature as neutral, or as beautiful and beneficent, one would be less likely to destroy its beauty for sheer material benefit but rather attempt to work with nature as a partner. The recent controversies between lumber barons and conservationists concerning the centuries-old redwood forests in California may be cited as an example of this basic difference in psychological outlook.

---

22 *Science*, July 19, 1968, pp. 253–56.

John G. Burke

There is a technological bond as well as an aesthetic one between man and nature. Man must exploit nature in order to survive. But must the exploitation be so savage and the despoliation so irreparable? Was this the relationship in all ages and places?

Lynn White has answered the latter question in the negative.[23] "What people do about their ecology," White states, "depends on what they think about themselves in relation to things around them. Human ecology is deeply conditioned by beliefs about our nature and destiny—that is, by religion." Christianity, White believes, is responsible in no small measure for our ecologic crisis, because Christian teaching emphasized that God created the earth for man's enjoyment and use. Some Christians, as St. Francis of Assisi, venerated all of the objects of God's creation, but many became activists and exploited nature mercilessly with religious sanction. This creed was novel, and it was diametrically opposed to the beliefs of ancient paganism and of nearly every Asiatic religion concerning the environment. White's analysis appears to be substantiated by later historical developments. The vision of continual and unlimited progress, instituted by Sir Francis Bacon* and his contemporaries, omitted consideration of the natural environment because the Christian tradition had already made it subservient to man and merely the object of his exploitative activities.

The natural environment, then, has suffered grievously for our increasing technological assault, and we cannot afford to pursue this reckless course much longer. But equally serious is man's progressive estrangement from nature and his retreat into a technological culture. Lewis Mumford has pointed out that the symbol of our artificial civilization is the clock. From earliest childhood the clock conditions our lives; it regulates our every action. Mumford states that "in terms of the human organism itself, mechanical time is . . . foreign; while human life has regularities of its own, the beat of the pulse, the breathing of the lungs, these change from hour to hour with mood and action, and in the longer span of days, time is measured not by the calendar but by the events that occupy it." [24] Unquestionably, civilization gained in efficiency by the introduction of the clock. At the same time, however, the clock marked the beginning of the progressive regimentation of Western man, of the inroads of technology into his way of life, and of the apparent necessity for him to adapt to the imperatives of a technological culture.

There is now a persistent, erosive invasion of privacy. Not only are law enforcement agencies devoted to the use of the polygraph or lie detector, but it is also widely employed in personnel screening by private indus-

---

23 *Science*, March 10, 1967, pp. 1203–7.
* See *Novum Organum*,ʼI. 83–100 in *GBWW*, Vol. 30, pp. 121b–127c.
24 Lewis Mumford, *Technics and Civilization* (New York: Harcourt, Brace & World, Inc., 1963), p. 15.

tries and governmental agencies on a local, state, and federal level. It is impossible to determine the extent of damage to the mental health or the reputation of persons who "fail" such tests. Yet, in the face of attacks on the scientific validity of the polygraph and on the ability of many of the operators of these machines, this practice continues to thrive. Similarly, there is invasion of privacy through wiretapping and eavesdropping by the use of sophisticated electronic equipment. Businessmen use tiny transmitters concealed in wastebaskets or in washrooms for internal plant security and to monitor the content of employees' conversations. Credit information is now placed on computer tapes and relayed on demand across the country, so that a prior bad rating, whether justified or not, stigmatizes an individual for the rest of his life.

In modern civilization we face a gradually increasing level of noise, from automobile traffic, riveters, electronically amplified rock-and-roll music in restaurants, and jet aircraft. In the environs of our airports, the decibel level approaches a deafening 90 inside of buildings and an earsplitting 120 in the open air. When land surrounding the Los Angeles airport was condemned to provide for expansion, a group of property owners filed suit, contending that the prices offered by the airport authority were based on values of land that had been depressed by the noise. Despite evidence that the decibel level exceeded that permitted industrial workers, the suit was thrown out of court. The judge ruled that the noise was "not of a substantial nature," and he added that people "must bear a certain amount of inconvenience" in modern civilization.

It is now known that sonic booms are responsible for rock falls that have occurred in several national parks. Some have irreparably damaged prehistoric Indian dwellings. But beyond this, if supersonic transports are permitted to make night transcontinental flights across the United States, it is estimated that more than ten million persons will have their sleep violently disturbed. Yet the Federal Aviation Agency, without prolonged consideration, made the decision to fund the supersonic transport, brushing aside opposition with vague assurances that there would be no noise problem. Leading the opposition to a noise abatement bill in Congress were senators who had a clear political stake in the advancement of the supersonic transport program.

Our cities which supposedly exist to create and nurture civilization present an entirely different aspect. They contain miles of grease-stained concrete and asphalt, forests of electric power lines and smokestacks, tawdry gasoline stations, unsightly junkyards, and massive advertising billboards. They are not only unsafe but aesthetically repulsive. Buckminster Fuller states that "the almost totally anarchistic piecemeal development and remodification of cities exclusively for the benefit of the prime investors and without comprehensive consideration of the total welfare of all mankind for all future time is getting us into ever greater trouble."[25] The flight to the suburbs is an escape from the ugliness of the artificial environment, and the spirits of those left behind in the ghettos fester in the squalor of their surroundings.

Man, having become only a unit in mass housing, mass transportation, mass education, mass consumption, and mass communication, has been subjected to an increasing blandness and insensitivity concerning his individuality and his fate. The prefrontal lobotomy, which was in vogue during the 1940's and early 1950's, was supposedly employed as a therapeutic device to reduce the trauma of schizophrenia. It was, however, also definitely used to increase scientific knowledge concerning the localization of brain functions. For the Veterans Administration, it seemed to offer an opportunity to eliminate the overcrowded condition of government hospitals. More than eighteen thousand persons had prefrontal lobotomies in the fifteen-year period beginning in 1936. The postoperative "age" of most patients undergoing surgery was judged to be approximately three and one-half years, and these patients became lazy, irritable, untidy, and careless. Significantly, this operation was banned in the Soviet Union, the Russian doctors asserting that it violated the principles of humanity.

Physicians do not always inform patients of all the risks of an operation, and some surgeons have extended an operation into a new area of the body without the patient's consent. Heart transplantation appeared abruptly on the scene without any prior discussion of the legal or ethical rights of the donor or of what criterion should be used to determine death. We should not be at all surprised in the light of the startling progress being made in biology—in particular, genetics—that eugenics programs are being advanced which will presumably perfect the human race. The late Hermann Muller proposed three criteria on the basis of which people would be allowed to procreate: health, intelligence, and social cooperation.[26] Granted that biologists can determine genetic defects, that is, give a definition of health, it is still a grave moral issue whether it is desirable, for example, to eliminate myopics from the population. But on what basis can "intelligence" be judged, when there is little consensus on what constitutes this faculty even among psychologists? The ambiguity of the term "social cooperation" is manifest. Far from being an idealistic goal of humanity, such thinking betrays a total rejection of the individual human life.

The increase in the numbers of persons hospitalized for mental disease or seeking psychiatric help, and the statistics indicating that a sizeable

---

25 *Joint House-Senate Colloquium to Discuss a National Policy for the Environment,* 90th Congress, 2nd Session, July 17, 1968, p. 198.

26 Hermann J. Muller, "The Prospects of Genetic Change," *The American Scientist,* XLVII (1959), 551–61.

THE AMERICAN ENVIRONMENT

And let us be clear at the outset that we will find neither national purpose nor personal satisfaction in a mere continuation of technical progress, in an endless amassing of worldly goods. We cannot measure national spirit by the Dow-Jones average or national achievement by the gross national product.

For the gross national product includes our pollution and advertising for cigarettes, and ambulances to clear our highways of carnage. It counts special locks for our doors and jails for people who break them. The gross national product includes the destruction of the redwoods, and the death of Lake [Erie]. It grows with the production of napalm and missiles and nuclear warheads, and it even includes research on the improved dissemination of bubonic plague. The gross national product swells with equipment for the police to put down riots in our cities; and though it is not diminished by the damage these riots do, still it goes up as slums are rebuilt on their ashes. It includes Whitman's rifle and Speck's knife, and the broadcasting of television programs which glorify violence to sell goods to our children.

Robert Kennedy, 1967

percentage of the population of the United States will spend at least a part of their lives in mental institutions, should give us pause for thought. Not having comparable statistics for the past, we cannot state with certainty that there has been an absolute increase in the occurrence of mental illness, or whether we have just devised new methods of coping with the problem of the mentally ill. But we do know that mental illness is associated with rapid social change. René Dubos writes that "psychotic disorders . . . occur wherever and whenever social changes are too rapid to allow for gradual successful adaptation. If psychiatric illnesses are truly increasing in the Western world, the reason is . . . in the accelerated rate at which old habits and conventions disappear and new ones appear."[27] And, if madness does not result, the monotonous and mechanical efficiency of modern industrial society leads to boredom.

The Apollo spacecraft exemplifies in microcosm the status of man vis-à-vis the technological society in which he exists. Apollo is one of the most complicated and sophisticated machines ever designed and built. It generates its own electricity; it transmits television; it sends eighty billion bits of information back to earth daily. It navigates by the stars with great precision, and, despite its tremendous velocity, its speed and location can be detected with incredible accuracy at the distance of the moon. Yet it contains no civilized toilet; frequent chlorination makes the taste of the drinking water abominable; and the astronauts must sleep in their seats. The food is freeze-dried in vacuum-packaged plastic bags. It is reconstituted by injecting water into and kneading the bag for several minutes, after which the food is squeezed into the mouth. The contrast between the perfection of the mechanical and electronic components of the Apollo system and the crudeness of the devices for sustaining life is sharp. In the same manner, the increasing perfection of the technological means of modern society is becoming markedly incongruous with the culture in which the technology operates.

Industrialists, scientists, and engineers constantly inform us that we must adjust and adapt ourselves and our institutions to the new state of affairs in which technological innovation and social change will be continuous. Malcolm P. Ferguson, former president of Bendix Corporation, announces that "resistance to change is a normal human reaction. But if anything is to be learned from the past it is that we are powerless to resist change and that our energies are much better spent adapting to it."[28]

Ferguson's statement is typical of the thinking of those who misunderstand the thrust of arguments against permitting the continuation of present scientific-technological trends in our society. Mere social change is not at issue, but rather constant and blind change that has no purpose.

---

27 René Dubos, *Mirage of Health* (New York: Harper & Brothers, 1959), p. 175.
28 *Dun's Review and Modern Industry*, May, 1962, p. 43.

There is the further question whether it is not possible to reap the benefits of scientific and technological progress and yet prevent the destruction of our natural environment and the deterioration of the quality of human life. Can we not monitor the direction of technological advance and ensure that our descendants will *have* a future by focusing, in our decisions, on the individual man and his environment?

VALUES AND DECISIONS

We may encapsulate the complex problem posed by technology in a few sentences. We are in a period of rapid and largely uncontrolled technological change, and from this activity we are deriving many material and economic benefits. Many current technological processes, however, are depleting our natural resources wastefully and inefficiently and are causing a deterioration of our environment. Further, technological change is contributing to a feeling of insecurity and hopelessness among a large segment of the population, to the invasion of traditional human rights, and to the impairment of the quality of human life.

There are three prerequisites which are essential to the solution of this problem: (1) widespread public understanding of the problem and a desire that some legislative action be taken to solve it; (2) exhaustive studies by experts of the causes of the problem and recommendations for its solution; (3) willingness on the part of the President and Congress to take massive corrective action, if necessary breaking with tradition and establishing a precedent.

A century and a half ago, Americans confronted an analogous, if less complicated, situation: the continued threat of marine boiler explosions. In the years between 1817 and 1852, thousands of people were killed or maimed when steam boilers aboard coastal or river steamboats exploded. Gradually the three preconditions mentioned above were met. Through newspaper accounts, the public became aware of the growing menace, and, beginning in 1840, memorials from chambers of commerce, boards of trade, and other organizations poured into Congress, exhorting senators and representatives to pass drastic remedial measures. As early as 1830, knowledgeable members of the scientific and engineering community began to investigate the problem, and in 1836 the Franklin Institute of Philadelphia presented a comprehensive report on the explosions to Congress, appending a list of detailed recommendations as to what provisions a corrective law should incorporate. Successive Congresses, believing that the enlightened self-interest of manufacturers of boilers and owners of steamboats would alleviate the situation, vacillated. A toothless, ineffectual law was placed on the books in 1838, but it was not until 1852 that stringent and restrictive legislation was passed, regulating all aspects of boiler manufacture and use. This was the first instance in

which Congress established and empowered a federal agency to prescribe in detail the conduct of a privately owned business, and the
legislation became a precedent for the creation of such regulatory agencies
of the federal government as the Interstate Commerce Commission, the
Food and Drug Administration, and the Civil Aeronautics Board. A
sorry chapter in United States history ended, with the curbing of technology in the public interest.[29]

We are in much the same position today with respect to the ability of
the various governmental departments and agencies to cope with the
problem of technological change as Americans were a hundred and
fifty years ago in approaching the problem of boiler explosions. Present
governmental units were established to treat problems in rather sharply
defined areas; consequently, none has the broad powers or experience
to deal with the wide scope of the problem presently facing us. A dozen
or more departments and agencies are involved with different aspects of
technological innovation. Bureaus within the Interior, and Health, Education, and Welfare departments, for example, handle environmental problems; and various features of the human environment concern Labor,
Housing and Urban Development, Justice, and Health, Education, and
Welfare. At the same time, some governmental agencies and departments
aggravate environmental problems. The Atomic Energy Commission continues to license nuclear power plants without having adequately solved
the problem of radioactive waste disposal. The Federal Aviation Agency
encourages the development of a supersonic transport plane without
facing squarely the problem of excessive noise. The Department of Defense permits the deployment of herbicidal chemicals without studying
completely the effects of this action upon the ecological balance. The
Executive Department and Congress have not as yet considered the
necessity of a well-planned coordinated approach.

The first element necessary for the solution of the boiler explosion
problem is also lacking at present. The public is, to a large extent, unaware of the implications of the technological change now occurring.
Lulled into complacence by the abundance and variety of the new
products of the new technology, by the unceasing message of progress,
and by the promises of new "breakthroughs" by scientists and engineers,
the majority of people view the future in terms of the science fiction they
see on television.

To be sure, there is an awareness at times that all is not right in our
technological society. The widespread power failure in the northeastern
states in November, 1965, which could not be explained for days, demonstrated the utter dependence of our society on machines. Complaints

---

29 John G. Burke, "Bursting Boilers and the Federal Power," *Technology and Culture*,
VII (1966), 1–20.

of air pollution are increasing in urban areas. Riots and violence in ghettos call attention to the fact that many citizens do not share in the abundance of the "affluent" society. A few resolute communities have even enacted ordinances to prosecute those responsible for sonic booms overhead. Sporadically, there are accounts in newspapers of the causes of environmental pollution.

These unconnected incidents, however, have not resulted in any general comprehension of the central problems emanating from and associated with technological change, nor is there any widespread public demand that something be done. The public appears satisfied with a piecemeal approach—job retraining, slum clearance, smog control devices, and countless "task force" reports. To create public understanding, it would appear necessary to employ the same methods used to sell soap, cigarettes, expensive cars, or to elect governors and presidents. Over the years, public relations firms and advertising agencies have perfected techniques to merchandize almost any product, idea, or man by catering to or trading on specific individual or social values. A widespread campaign of environmental education may be the only way to enlighten the general public concerning the character and implications of technological change, and thereby to elicit demands for governmental action.

The prospect of the development by experts of exhaustive studies of the problems associated with technological change, with recommendations for an overall solution—that is, the second element of the boiler explosion problem—is more promising. Committees of scientists and concerned citizens have been successful in instituting programs which served to impede some projects which threatened the environment. The studies of the St. Louis Committee on Nuclear Information publicized the dangerous effects of radioactive fallout from atmospheric nuclear tests and should certainly be given partial credit for the nuclear atmospheric test ban agreement. Renamed the Committee on Environmental Information, this group of scientists is currently discussing many aspects of environmental pollution in its publication: *Scientist and Citizen.* Its work has stimulated the formation of a dozen similar groups across the nation. Similarly, the Scenic Hudson Preservation Conference has been involved in a lengthy legal battle to prevent the despoliation of Storm King Mountain on the Hudson River by the construction of a Consolidated Edison power plant. Resources for the Future, Inc., of Washington, D.C., has published numerous studies concerned with overpopulation, natural resources, and the systematic management of wastes produced by society. Scientists in a number of universities have developed research and educational programs directed at seeking more knowledge about the environment and training more people in the principles of ecology. The efforts of such groups and individuals have, in many instances, resulted in retarding the progressive deterioration of the environment and have contributed fundamental knowledge to a sound environmental program.

In like manner, psychiatrists, psychologists, and sociologists, as individuals or in *ad hoc* groups, have studied our technological culture either from the point of view of the stresses, tensions, or boredom produced in individuals or from the standpoint of such widespread behavioral symptoms as incivility, cynicism, amorality, and violence. For the most part, the remedies proposed in this area have been palliative rather than radical. Education to acculturate racial minorities, job training, prettification, and rehabilitation of slum areas are offered as solutions. In only a few cases are more fundamental corrective measures suggested, such as relocating industries in less congested areas in order to aid population redistribution and alleviate urban concentrations, and insisting upon laws that will sharply reduce noise levels, invasions of privacy, and other assaults upon the individual. Further, social scientists are still far from a solution to other immediate problems arising from novel technology such as the most suitable working environment for humans and the creative use of free time both before and after retirement.

The third element necessary for the solution of the boiler explosion problem was the willingness on the part of the federal government, in particular the Congress, to pass unprecedented corrective legislation. At present there are indications that some laws will be passed in the not too distant future concerned with solving these varied yet intimately connected problems. Whether the initial effort, as in the case of the boiler legislation, will be so heavily excised or amended as to make it practically worthless, is still in question. One encouraging sign was the assembling, in July, 1968, of a joint Senate-House colloquium to discuss a national policy for the environment. In attendance were officials of the executive branch, members of the Senate and the House, and prominent scientists, who discussed the possibility of a concerted approach to the problem.

A month earlier, a group of Congressmen, led by Richard J. Ottinger of New York, sponsored a resolution to amend the Constitution to define the rights of citizens with respect to the natural environment and the employment and conservation of natural resources. The amendment would guarantee that "the right of the people to clean air, pure water, freedom from excessive and unnecessary noise, and the natural, scenic, historic, and esthetic qualities of their environment" shall not be abridged.[30] Further, the amendment would require periodic surveys and would restrict activities that would adversely affect these resource values on public lands. At the joint colloquium, Representative Ottinger also suggested the creation of a special agency to exercise a supervisory function over the environment, to act as an intervener, to review the plans and projects of the various governmental departments and agencies with the power

---

30 *Joint House-Senate Colloquium, op. cit.,* p. 124.

to delay for critical attention at the least or at most to stop completely those that appeared to threaten environmental values.[31]

Among other efforts by the 90th Congress to prevent environmental deterioration and to cope with technological change, the notion of "technology assessment" stands out. To give substance to this idea, a resolution was offered by Senator Muskie to establish a Select Senate Committee on Technology and Human Environment, and a bill was introduced in the House by Representative Daddario of Connecticut to create a five-member Technology Assessment Board, whose members would be appointed by the President. In Daddario's view, technology assessment is a systematic method of identifying, assessing, and dealing with the implications and effects of technological innovation. On the one hand, assessment would ascertain the potentials of technological innovation and stimulate it if desirable; on the other, it would seek to determine undesirable by-products and side effects and to inform the public in order that appropriate means might be taken to minimize or to eliminate them.

There are also proposals to create a "fourth branch" in the government. One plan visualizes the branch as an independent entity, on a par with the executive, legislative, and judicial branches, and assuming an equal role in the traditional system of checks and balances. It would employ social scientists for the most part but also include natural scientists, who would enjoy economic and career stability. Ideally, the branch would seek to be neutral in a political sense. Its mission would be primarily evaluative; collecting data concerning the nation's economic, environmental, and social well-being; defining potential problems; and developing alternative plans for their solution. Its purpose would be to present the most desirable public policies vis-à-vis technology and in this manner ensure the wisest planning decisions for society. Its only power, however, would derive from the public, who, presumably fully informed of the agency's conclusions, would press for their adoption through the usual political process.

In contrast to this approach stressing assessment or evaluation, another proposal for a fourth branch envisages one entitled the National Science Policy Agency. It would be composed of the present Office of Science and Technology, the National Science Foundation, and the national research laboratories, such as Oak Ridge and Argonne. The branch's purpose would be to support the nation's basic scientific research and provide the necessary facilities. It would accumulate information on the basis of which the executive and legislative branches would authorize major technological programs. It would nurture and support the development of new technologies until such time as the projects were large enough to warrant independent financial support from the government. Under

---

31 *Ibid.*, pp. 60–61.

this plan, it appears that the branch would have no influence whatever on the technological decisions of other departments of the government, nor do its proponents seem concerned about any unforeseen or undesirable effects of technological innovation.

As auspicious as some of these programs might appear, there is no cause for optimism that any would accomplish the desired results in preventing the continued deterioration of the natural environment and the quality of human life. Three existing conditions would militate against success: first, the unswerving belief in the power of science and technology; second, faith in private enterprise as the keystone of democracy; and third, the firmly entrenched near-autonomy of the Department of Defense. Let us consider each of these separately.

The proponents of massive governmental support for subsidizing scientific research, for underwriting scientific education, and for developing scientific knowledge into new technologies, have over the past twenty years promoted and instilled the belief that such a program is not only a contributing factor but also a necessary condition of economic and social progress. Lloyd Berkner, for example, asserted in 1963:

> We are witnessing a technological revolution derived from the powerful science of our time, leading to vastly improving productivity and greater wealth of our population . . . In a sense, at mid-century, we moved almost abruptly from the traditional economy of scarcity which had plagued mankind from the beginning of history, into an economy of plenty. For the first time in history, man has acquired, out of science and technology, the power to produce adequately to supply all his needs, with a significant excess remaining.[32]

We shall not dwell on the fact that a theory which ascribes economic and social progress solely to the acquisition and use of scientific knowledge is, philosophically speaking, a new type of economic determinism of the Marxian variety, with productive scientists and engineers cast in the role of the outmoded "forces of production." In any event, the end result has been that a number of scientists are now not only in powerful administrative positions in the federal government but have also assumed policy-making situations. They compose what Don K. Price has termed the "scientific estate," and they are uniformly committed to the belief that if science is supported in ever increasing increments and scientists are left free to pursue the truths of science, the nation will continue to prosper. Price calls attention to the dangers of this approach:

> The main philosophical threat to our freedom is not that science will

---

32 Portion of a statement by Lloyd Berkner, *Select Committee on Government Research, House of Representatives*, 88th Congress, 1st Session.

tempt us to invent a new materialistic dialectic, or establish a "1984" style dictatorship. It is rather that if we rely on science alone we will be left with no sense of the purpose of existence, and thus no basis for determining our political goals to guide the blind forces of technology.[33]

Any proposed legislation, then, seeking to prevent the dangerous by-products of technological innovation must deal ultimately with the science which spawns and nurtures the new technology. It must either control the direction of science or somehow infuse a sense of social purpose into the scientific estate. Neither course, I suggest, is practically possible. The present diffused power, the influence of the scientific estate, and the awe in which this group is held by our elected representatives are obstacles too formidable to overcome.

Let us turn to the second condition, the free enterprise system. Americans have long mistakenly identified the free enterprise system as an end of democracy rather than as an effective means of attaining the benefits of democracy. Faith in the enlightened self-interest of manufacturers and businessmen to act in the public welfare was partially dispelled, as we have seen, in the boiler explosion peril. Continued disillusionment was, in fact, responsible for the creation of the varied federal regulatory agencies. But though tarnished, the reputation of private enterprise and public faith in its owners and managers and in their public pronouncements remain secure. Given this situation, any legislation that would *compel* private enterprise to plan for the prevention of environmental blight in its productive or distributive schemes is doomed to failure. Can one visualize, for example, the passage of legislation forcing aluminum producers, aluminum can manufacturers, or brewers and bottlers to retrieve from garbage dumps or to pay for the recovery of the billions and billions of aluminum cans discarded each year? Yet the cans are virtually indestructible, and, in addition to their unsightly appearance along the roadsides, they represent the waste of a precious natural resource. Similarly, manufacturers could certainly produce automobiles to last fifteen years or more, and methods could be devised to recover all parts when a car is scrapped. In view of powerful auto manufacturers' lobbies in Washington, however, it is highly unlikely that laws can be enacted to accomplish these ends.

Dr. Philip Lee of the Department of Health, Education, and Welfare pointed out the nature of this problem:

> Thus far the so-called natural resource policies have been designed not to work toward enhancement or protection of these resources, but to indicate the maximum level of exploitation which we will

33 Don K. Price, *The Scientific Estate* (Cambridge, Mass.: Harvard University Press, 1965), p. 107.

permit . . . When we get down to the point, somebody is going to
have to say that no longer will we permit a continuing degradation
of these resources.[34]

At issue here is not capitalism vs. socialism, a competitive market system
vs. a planned economy. Rather, it is the choice between leaving our
future to the vagaries of a system wherein the only criterion of value is
the profit motive or to one wherein the long-range effects of technology
in terms of social and environmental values is of paramount importance.
The executive and legislative branches of the federal government have
had little inclination heretofore to penalize private enterprise harshly
for polluting the environment. An effective system of technology assessment would require a system of unprecedented control over private enterprise which, in the present atmosphere, appears out of the question.

But even should the scientific estate suddenly develop a social conscience and private enterprise submit to widespread controls for future
social benefits, there would still remain the problem of dealing with the
near-autonomous and almost sacrosanct Department of Defense. Its research programs are secret, and all decisions purport to be in the national
interest, so that any intensive questioning of them is suspect in terms of
patriotism. The program to produce chemical and biological weapons
for offensive purposes, for example, is justified by statements that it serves
as a deterrent. The question as to why the United States would deem
it necessary to retaliate in kind while our nuclear arsenal is filled to over-
flowing remains unanswered. About one hundred industrial firms in the
United States obtain the lion's share of Defense Department contracts,
and it is only when conflicts arise between the services or the contractors,
as in the TFX plane controversy, that the rationale of these contracts is
aired. At present, the nation is suddenly apprised of the necessity of the
installation of what will undoubtedly prove to be a tremendously expensive anti-ballistic missile system—peculiarly enough, just as the costly
and unpopular war in Vietnam appears to be coming to an end. Unless
Congress can extend the umbrella of technology assessment over the
entire federal establishment, it is patent that the perils to the environment
will remain, and efforts to improve the human condition will be unavailing.

I am convinced that a system of compulsory technology assessment
would be successful. If assessment boards were established, composed of
natural and social scientists, humanists, businessmen, and industrialists,
men whose joint wisdom could weigh short-term advantages of innovation
against long-range social values, and the decisions of which would bind
private enterprise and governmental agencies alike, the nation would
benefit in terms of its natural resources, its environment, and in the quality
of the life of its present and future citizens. A system of assessment boards

---

34 *Joint House-Senate Colloquium, op. cit.,* p. 44.

John G. Burke

might function in the same way as does the present federal judiciary, wherein local problems could be decided on a local level with right of appeal to a supreme board. I believe, however, that the introduction of such a system, or any other deemed to be less cumbersome and more effective, will only be effected when, as in the case of bursting boilers, a series of calamities has occurred. As our history demonstrates, the nation does not act to confront the future with vision and foresight; rather, it reacts to disaster.

NOTE TO THE READER

The problem discussed by Dr. Burke is a peculiarly modern one, and the urgency of facing it is only now becoming generally recognized. Yet there is much material for thinking about the various issues that are involved in it to be found in *Great Books of the Western World*.

As Dr. Burke points out, the idea of progress is closely connected with all our thinking about technology and values. This idea is one of the 102 Great Ideas used for indexing the *Great Books*, and in Chapter 71 of the *Syntopicon* the reader will be able to locate the discussions of this idea in his set of *Great Books*.

The topic most directly relevant to Dr. Burke's discussion is SCIENCE 1b(2): The effects of science on human life: the economic and social implications of technology.

The underlying and basic issue in the whole discussion is our conception of the good human life, and on this subject the *Great Books* have much to offer. Chapter 33 of the *Syntopicon* provides a guide to this material, especially HAPPINESS 2a on the quality of a happy life and 2b on the content of a happy life.

235

PART THREE

The Contemporary
Status
of a Great Idea

ETIENNE
GILSON

Etienne Gilson, one of the most eminent scholars of the twentieth century, was professor of the Collège de France from 1932 until 1951, founder of the Pontifical Institute of Mediaeval Studies at the University of Toronto in 1929 and its director until 1968, member of the French delegation to the San Francisco Conference on the United Nations in 1945, senator of the Fourth French Republic from 1947 to 1948, and is, as a member of the Académie Française since 1946, one of "the forty immortals" of France. Born in Paris on June 13, 1884, Gilson took his baccalaureate at the Sorbonne in 1907 and his doctorate in 1913. He served as a French Army officer during World War I, spending two years as a prisoner of war. In 1919 he became professor at Strasbourg, and in 1921 at the University of Paris. His career of productive scholarship results thus far in a bibliography of books and articles covering seventy pages. During the past academic year Professor Gilson gave a series of lectures on Thomism at the University of California at Berkeley. Some of his best-known books came out of famous lectureships he has held at European and American universities. Among them are The Spirit of Mediaeval Philosophy *(Gifford Lectures at Aberdeen, 1930–31),* The Unity of Philosophical Experience *(William James Lectures at Harvard, 1938),* Being and Some Philosophers *(Powell Lectures at Indiana, 1940),* Painting and Reality *(Mellon Lectures at Washington, 1955). His many studies of mediaeval thinkers have contributed decisively to the contemporary reassessment and reinterpretation of the achievements of the Middle Ages. Master of an elegant and lucid style, in English as well as French, he has written extensively on literature as well as on philosophy and theology. Yet while he is a scholar and an author, Gilson prides himself most on being a Christian philosopher.*

The Idea of God
and the Difficulties
of Atheism

I have often been asked for a demonstration of the existence of God. Let me confess that I have never been able to develop a passionate interest in the question. I am certain that there is a God, but that certainty does not rest on any demonstration of his existence. It seems to me so absolutely certain that a reality transcending both myself and the world actually exists that the prospect of looking for proofs of something I feel so sure of appears to me a waste of time. My certainty, in fact, makes me curious about the reasons atheists have for believing there is no God. To me, the inexistence, or nonexistence, of God is the question. Therefore, I wish to test some of the reasons invoked in favor of atheism. Dogmatic and positive atheism is what I am speaking of—the doctrine which, after mature reflection and serious consideration of the problem, concludes as a rational certainty that nothing answering the word "God" exists in reality. By "nothing" I mean no "being."

I shall begin by defining the notion of which the affirmation will be considered an affirmation of God, and the negation a negation of God. The constituent elements of that notion, its *essentialia* as Christian Wolff would say, are three in number: (1) God must be a transcendent being, that is, a being that exists apart from both myself and the world; (2) he likewise must be a necessary being; (3) he must be the cause of whatever else exists.[1] The reason for setting up these precise requirements is that affirming the existence of anything called God is not necessarily the same as affirming God.

For instance, *New World and Word of God* recently observed that "the first attribute of that God [of the Christians] is not being, it is not all-powerfulness, but rather it is love." The God of the Christians certainly is Love, but for him to be love, he first has to *be*. That is true even of

---

1 M. J. Adler, "God, Religion and Modern Man," a lecture delivered at the Aspen Institute for Humanistic Studies, August 9, 1966. I am indebted to Dr. Adler for his kindness in sending me a copy of that remarkable lecture, the more so as there is nothing in it to which I cannot unreservedly subscribe. Philosophical agreement is too scarce a commodity not to heartily welcome whenever one is lucky enough to find it. For the ensuing remarks, see *Esprit* (October, 1967), pp. 482 and 486.

Christ: if he *is* not, he cannot possibly *be* God. One cannot rightly define Him as the "communication of Himself," as "the gift of oneself," nor define his allpowerfulness as the "communication of being," without first acknowledging that He has some being to communicate, that in short, he *is* being.

It has rightly been observed that there are all sorts of atheism. If there is not exactly a "scientific" atheism—science is not qualified to deal with the notion of God—there is at least an atheism born in the minds of those who are exclusively devoted to scientific problems handled by scientific methods. A purely personal attitude, such positivist atheism is neither demonstrable nor refutable; we are not concerned with it. There is also a practical atheism, perhaps its most widely represented form, inasmuch as religion considers it the most insidious threat within the consciences of the believers themselves—impiety, living as though there were no God. We are not concerned with that form of atheism either. There is also a social and political form of atheism, such as the Marxist atheism of the modern Russian state. We would like to put it aside, for it is neither philosophical nor theological in essence, but we cannot since it constantly intrudes upon the very questions with which we are now concerned.

Thus only one form of atheism is relevant to our discussion, philosophical atheism. It can also be called theological in the sense that the metaphysical notion of God, which is at stake, is the crowning piece of what is called "natural theology"; we shall not concern ourselves with the self-revealed God of religion. To the extent that it claims to be taken seriously, the new "religious atheism" does not make sense. Neither can I find any sense in the notion of a "Christian atheism," in which the notion of Christ would act as a substitute for that of God, for indeed the God of Christ is the Christian God. Should our reflections lead us to the conclusion that atheism does not exist, it should be understood as meaning that atheism does not exist as a philosophical conclusion.

Is God Dead?

The words of Nietzsche, "God is dead," have become a cliché. Yet, when he wrote them in *Thus Spoke Zarathustra*, those words represented only the first half of his message. The other half was: "I am teaching you the superman." To Nietzsche, the first half did not make sense without the second. Zarathustra, leaving the forest where he had visited an old hermit, summed up the interview to himself: "That old saint has not yet learned that God is dead." For Nietzsche, that was only the first of the required conditions under which the reign of man, the lawful successor of God, was about to begin.

The meaning of those words, however, is not quite clear. Literally understood, they signify that a certain being, named God, has finally ceased to exist. Thus understood, the proposition is meaningless,[2] for even the pagan Greeks used to identify the notion of "God" with "immortal being." To say "the immortals," or "the gods," was to say the same thing, just as for us to say "a mortal," or "a man," is still to use two practically synonymous terms. The bond between the notions of divinity and of immortality has become so tight that even to us, the notion that a God should die is absurd. If there ever was a God, there must still be one, for if that being died, he was no God. There is no point in belaboring that truism, except that too many people content themselves with repeating certain slogans without realizing that, in fact, they are devoid of meaning. However, let us admit that Zarathustra was not announcing the final demise of some mortal being wrongly believed to be immortal. His formula then could mean that the belief—widely accepted until recently—that there is a God has finally ceased to be accepted as true. But if that is all it means, the celebrated formula is little more than a banality. What did it really mean to Nietzsche?

ETHICAL ATHEISM

To Nietzsche himself, the notion of the death of God was an essentially ethical notion. In leaving the forest and its hermits, Zarathustra leaves behind saints who, living in solitude as he himself has done, spend their lives in the praise of God. The hermits symbolize the race of those men who renounce the world, abdicate the autonomy of their wills, and submit their minds to the recognition of transcendent values, imposed upon them from on high. Such values are known to us under the names of *good* and *evil*, and codified in what we call ethics. To go beyond good and bad is to overcome those conventional notions of good and bad conduct, as well as of right and wrong ways of thinking.

Generally speaking, the reformation which Nietzsche seeks is the elimination of the Judeo-Christian ideal of humility and its exaltation of meekness, in order to substitute for it a glorification of power, of force, in short an exaltation of all the powers of man at their highest level. What is truly dead, therefore, is the Christian God of traditional ethics. Why does Nietzsche say of that God that he is dead? Because it has become impos-

---

2 In "God, Religion and Modern Man," quoted above, Dr. Adler defines what he calls the existential meaning as simply: "God does not exist." Hence he concludes that "all of our new theologians—our death-of-God theologians—are atheists . . . . They indulge in the most outrageous double-talk in order to try to persuade their readers that, with the death of God, a new theology has come into existence; or what is more absurd, a new era in man's religious life . . . The 'death of God' movement should be described as the death, not of God, but of theology and religion." This perfectly clear-cut statement of the problem is unassailable; one can only wonder if it is not made with an intellectual precision foreign to that class of so-called theologians.

sible even to blaspheme him, since no longer is there anyone to hear our blasphemies. "Formerly, the greatest of all blasphemies was the blasphemy against God, but God is dead and that blasphemy died along with him." From now on, the truly grievous blasphemy is against man; it consists in attributing to the earth less importance than to heaven, in giving less importance to man than to God.

The volcanic thought of Nietzsche defies summary. What he omits is not necessarily foreign to his mind; in this case, however, it can be observed that Nietzsche's negation of God does not apply, explicitly at least, to the physical and metaphysical notion of God as creator of the world and man. Were I asked what he thought of the question, I would not know what to answer. It is even harder for me to imagine what would have become of that notion if Nietzsche had subjected it to his own criticism and replaced it with a new one. He would have objected to the God of the Jews and of the Christians in any case, but what about the gods of the Greeks? Did not their worshipers conceive them as so many supermen, or superworkers, like the Demiurge of the *Timaeus*, a divine author of nature and a quasi creator of the world? For indeed, Plato says, everything is becoming, nothing really is, and everything that becomes must of necessity be produced by some cause, for "without a cause nothing can be produced."

Nietzsche himself was conscious of not having answered that part of the problem, for he was a moralist rather than a metaphysician, and he knew it. Careless readers may fail to observe this important limitation of his point of view, but Nietzsche himself was aware of it. In his own words, "It is theology that has stifled God, just as morality has stifled ethics," but God himself is not putrefying after the manner of a corpse, but he is rather, "like a snake shedding its old skin and putting on a new one. God is shedding his *moral* skin, and you soon will see him back, beyond good and evil." In one of his notes, headed *The refutation of God*, Nietzsche wrote: "In reality, only the *moral* God is refuted."[3]

There thus remains a whole theological field which Nietzsche knew he

---

3 Nietzsche, *Also sprach Zarathustra*, French transl. by G. Bianquis (Paris: Gallimard, 23 ed., 1950), Appendix, § 62, p. 310. By turning Nietzsche's words into a slogan, the mass media have obliterated that important distinction, but Jean Paul Sartre has clearly perceived and vividly illustrated it in his play *The Flies*. In the central scene of the drama Zeus urges Orestes to recognize him as the supreme power that rules the world; Orestes answers that nature indeed stands on the side of God, but if there is a God for nature, there is no God for man because man, unlike nature, is endowed with a will and therefore is free. Aristotle had not foreseen this unexpected application of his own principle that everything caused is caused either by a nature or by a will. To him, even the will is a sort of nature. Not so in the doctrine of Nietzsche; for this reason his ethics does not consist in accepting the values found by reason in nature, but, rather, in overthrowing them. Sartre has correctly understood Nietzsche's brand of atheism: God and nature on one side; man and his will on the other.

had not covered. To most of those who repeat after him that God is dead, the God they have in mind is precisely the metaphysical God, creator of the heaven and earth, preserver of the universe, and, to man, a Providence. Of course, the metaphysical atheists are well aware of some of the consequences of atheism on the level of practical morality, but it is remarkable that a "libertine" used to be considered both an atheist and a rake. "If there is no God," the father of *The Brothers Karamazov* says, "all is permitted!" This explains why the name of libertine used to be given to "one who professed free opinions, especially in religion," and to "one who professed a licentious life."

Nietzsche, however, believed that "unless we ourselves make the death of God a grandiose act of renunciation and a continuous victory over ourselves, we shall have to bear the loss."[4] Once it is agreed that there is no God above man, man himself will have to be God. But man as he now is, rather, as he must now become: the Superman. Along with the new God, Nietzsche intends to retain some religion, to the extent that religion essentially is "a doctrine of the hierarchy," as he says, "of a cosmic scale of power." He continues: "In this century of populism, a noble and well born mind should begin each day *by thinking of the hierarchy*, for that is where his duties lie, along with the subtlest of his misdecisions."[5]

I am not attempting to turn Nietzsche into a defender of the belief in the existence of God. His moral atheism is absolute, violent to the point of being pathological, as it was in fact to become at the end of his life, in his *Ecce Homo;* but his atheism is actually an antichristianism (including an antisemitism); it is a violent denunciation of the Jew Christ, the man of sorrows, and the preacher of an ideal based on the refusal to serve this world, the only world there is. The *non serviam* of Nietzsche is a revindication, to the benefit of man, of the privileges usurped by the God of the Jews and of the Christians. His Superman is man such as he is about to become after having liberated himself from the fetters of conventional religion and morality.

This is going to be an uphill fight for which few men are fit. Nietzsche probably would despise most of those who now pretend to be his disciples. "They overthrow images and statues," Nietzsche says, "and they say there is nothing holy and deserving to be worshipped, because they themselves are incapable of forming for their own use the image of a God, and of creating him."[6] What does the authentic thought of Nietzsche have in

---

4 *Ibid.*, § 61, p. 310. This point has been stressed by Jean Paul Sartre in his book *Existentialism Is a Humanism.* Atheism is the heroic effort of a free will resolved to liberate itself from the fetters of both nature and God.
5 *Ibid.*, § 63, p. 310, and § 72, p. 311.
6 *Ibid.*, § 110, p. 317.

common with the cheap brand of atheism now associated with his name? As he once said: "It has always seemed to me impossible to teach the truth there where a vile way of thinking obtains."[7]

By what sign, you may well ask, will it be known that God is really dead? To this I would answer: by the complete silence and oblivion into which his very name will have sunk. When something is truly dead, nobody will waste his time demonstrating that it has really deceased. Jupiter and Neptune are dead; we would not dream of proving that these myths have lost all conceivable reality, except for their poetic existence in imagination. The dead are soon forgotten. If there really were no God left, nobody would speak of him; such great writers as Nietzsche would not drive themselves crazy fighting the illusion of his existence. People do not simply say: everybody knows there is no God; his nonexistence is not considered a matter settled once and for all, so much so that we now can quietly dismiss it from our minds. But, that is undoubtedly what will happen when God is really dead; his very notion will then become merely an archaeological curiosity.

This has already happened to many now antiquated notions, and the founder of French Positivism, Auguste Comte, thought that all metaphysical notions—that is, all notions that cannot be justified scientifically— would meet the same fate. In his *Discourse on the Positive Spirit*, Comte suggested that all opinions on insoluble problems should be neither refuted nor even denied, but simply neglected, overlooked; they should be allowed by "sound philosophy" to fall into disuse. By sound philosophy, Comte meant a refusal to deal with notions that are pure products of the imagination bearing on objects inaccessible to direct observation. Such notions, Comte would say, are susceptible neither of affirmation nor of negation. "No doubt, nobody has ever logically established the non-existence of Apollo, of Minerva etc.; nor has the nonexistence of the fairies of the East and of other similar poetic creations ever been demonstrated, but that has not prevented the human mind from irrevocably

---

7 *Ibid.*, § 105, p. 317. I am not denying the atheism of Nietzsche; I only wish to define its nature. If he ever said: "I am the first atheist," which I doubt he did, it was in the same sense that he said: "I am the first immoralist" (*Ecce Homo*, French transl. by Alexandre Vialatte [Paris: Gallimard, 1942], p. 99). In his own language, the "Infamous" is neither religion nor God, it is Christianity, Jesus Christ, and his notion of moral life. For Nietzsche, his cosmic mission was to reveal to the world the pestilential character of Christian ethics, with its deification of weakness and of renunciation. In doing that, Nietzsche has "cut in two the history of mankind" (p. 175); he is "Dionysus in front of the Crucified" (p. 177). Christianity has dethroned the values of life and enthroned the values of death. The result is a "morale," which Nietzsche calls: "an idiosyncrasy of decadents guided by the secret intention, often successful, to revenge himself on life" (p. 174). Immoralism is the very essence of Nietzsche's atheism (p. 172). Plain atheism is only a "natural instinct" with him (p. 42); for him atheism is the natural rebellion against everything that pretends to transcend—except, of course, man himself.

giving up such ancient beliefs, as soon as they ceased to agree with the situation then obtaining."

Comte was quite right. However, even if it would be ridiculous to demonstrate that Napoleon I is dead—a proposition, by the way, that cannot be demonstrated scientifically—it is far from ridiculous to undertake the demonstration of the proposition that there is no God. The mere fact that men still go to the trouble of declaring themselves atheists, and of justifying their disbelief by means of such arguments as the existence of evil, clearly shows that the issue is still a living one. If the death of God means his final death in the minds of men, the persistent vitality of atheism constitutes for atheism its most serious difficulty. God will really be dead when no one will still think of denying his existence. Until then, the death of God remains an unconfirmed rumor.

CASUAL ATHEISM

It is often said, and deplored, that the modern churches have lost the support of the working classes, and it may well be true, but nobody exactly knows the extent or depth of the loss. Looking at facts from without, it rather seems that atheism is invading all social groups.

Cicero asserted, as something self-evident, that philosophers do not believe in the existence of gods. He probably was right, for indeed the gods of the Roman pantheon, which itself included all the other pantheons of the Empire, offered an easy target for philosophical criticism in Cicero's lifetime. No doubt that was the meaning of his remark: philosophers could not be expected to believe in the legends of the Greco-Roman gods. At any rate, if the ancient philosophers were atheists, the cause of the phenomenon was not that they were poor and formed an exploited proletariat.

There were many poor artisans and peasants in the cities and villages of sixteenth- and seventeenth-century Europe; yet the churches were full, and nothing authorizes the supposition that atheism prospered among those needy populations. On the contrary, it was the wealthy classes that were the hotbeds of immorality and incredulity. The French and Italian libertines of the time, the rakes of the English Restoration, the incredibly dissolute life at the court of the Most Christian King of France Louis XIV, clearly show that atheism and immorality prosper in wealth as much as in poverty. But agnosticism and licentiousness are not atheism. The dukes of Vendôme and Nevers, as Saint-Simon describes them in his *Mèmoires*, seem to have been moral wrecks, but whether they died as confirmed atheists is very difficult to say.

La Bruyère, who personally knew the libertines of the royal court, made a remark that is universally applicable when he said that straight atheism, solidly grounded on philosophical reasons, is hard to find. "I would be exceedingly curious to find a man really convinced that there is no God; he at least would be able to tell me the invincible reason that has convinced him of it." Finding none, he added: "The impossibility in which I find myself of proving that there is no God unveils to me his existence."[8]

La Bruyère does not say, "*proves* to me his existence," he only says *unveils*. The absence of any proofs of the nonexistence of God does not amount to a proof of his existence, but that absence invites us to think that some fact or reason—the nature of which remains to be determined —must account for it. Those who say that God does not exist find themselves in exactly the same situation into which they put their opponents. I do not pretend that there are no arguments in favor of their position; I only observe that they do not seem to care to employ any such arguments —if they do, none of them has ever been able to find a conclusive answer to the question.

This is what La Bruyère seems to have had in mind in that passage, perhaps a little flippant in tone but so pertinent, where, after saying that "atheism does not exist," he specifies that atheism does not exist at least as a philosophically justified position; he declares: "The noblemen, more suspect of atheism than the rank and file, are too lazy to make up their minds that God does not exist. Their indolence leaves them cold and indifferent on that capital point, as well as on the nature of their soul and on the importance of a true religion; they neither deny nor concede such things; they do not think of them at all."[9]

This is exactly it: they do not think of such things; let us only add that this atheism, so to speak of inadvertence, is not more proper to the nobility than to the rank and file, since we find it in Friedrich Nietzsche, who did not belong in either class. Let us read more of the *Ecce Homo* passage already quoted: "God, immortality of the soul, redemption, deliverance, so many ideas to which I never devoted any attention or time, not even in my early youth. Perhaps I have never been enough of a child for that? I could not see atheism as a conclusion, or a consequence; with me it is a natural instinct." To Nietzsche a more important question than that of salvation, so dear to the theologians, was that of food, or let us say, of diet. What should one eat in order to be well and strong? After relating a few culinary experiments, some of them unfortunate, Nietzsche dogmatically concludes: "The best all around cooking is that of Piedmont." Food is surely important, but cooking is not a problem comparable in importance to that of the existence of God. That Nietzsche thinks it is, or pretends that it is, shows what little interest he has in the question. He

---

8 La Bruyère, *Les Caractères ou les mœurs de ce siècle*, ed. G. Servois and Alf. Rébelliau (Paris: Hachette, 1901), "Des Esprits forts," p. 480.
9 *Ibid.*, p. 481.

himself admits it: "I am too inquisitive a mind, too sceptical, and too proud to satisfy myself with one of those gross answers that are an insult to a thinker, something like a final and brutal prohibition against proceeding—a positively no thinking."[10]

If such is the spontaneous reaction of a mind like Nietzsche's to the mere mention of the word "God," one can easily imagine how philosophically superficial the atheism of most atheists is. I do not pretend to know the inner thoughts of the majority of those who consider themselves atheists; it only seems to me that La Bruyère's description of atheists tallies remarkably with Nietzsche's own atheistic attitude. An agreement between such different men and mentalities suggests that the type is a fairly common one. Some do not think of the question; others feel indignant at the mere mention of it. By and large, La Bruyère was right; whether or not it be possible to prove that there is no God, no atheists go to the trouble to prove it. If that is insufficient proof of God's existence, it at least suggests that there are no invincible reasons to deny it.

WHAT THE ATHEISTS CALL GOD

O f all the branches of theology, that of atheism has recently become the most confused one. At the same time it has become a major concern not only with the various churches but with the world of journalism as well. Once successfully launched by its author as a kind of challenge, the formula of Nietzsche has become a sort of slogan. The weekly *Time* has given the best proof it could that the question is a live one. For the first time in forty-three years, on April 8, 1966, its cover carried no portrait of any man of the week, no image or picture of any sort, nothing but these three words: *Is God dead?* After vainly searching for months, the editors had given up their quest for "a work of art suggesting a contemporary idea of God," and "came to the conclusion that no appropriate representation could be found." For the first time, the problem of the death of God has filled the space usually devoted to political, business, or entertainment personalities.

One readily believes *Time* when it speaks of the enormous effort required for the preparation of the five pages entitled "Toward a Hidden God." Some readers will regret not being given the complete results of their extensive inquiry, but that would have far exceeded the space available. At any rate, the documents retained by the editors already provide ample matter for reflection.

Let us first observe the survival of the spiritual family already described by La Bruyère, that of the atheists by inattentiveness, or oversight. Some of them are very distinguished persons. For instance Claude Lévy-Strauss,

---

10 Nietzsche, *Ecce Homo*, p. 42.

Professor of Social Anthropology at the Collège de France, calmly declared that he personally has never found himself confronted with the notion of God. A truly astonishing statement, one might think, for an ethnologist who has endured many and severe hardships to observe *in vivo* what little is left of some tribes barely surviving in the forests of the Amazon. Lévy-Strauss considers it perfectly possible that he should spend his whole life in the knowledge that he shall never account for the universe, but since he professes to know nothing of God, not even that he is dead, we cannot expect from him any information on the problem. But there are many other things for which Professor Lévy-Strauss will never account in that very same universe, for instance, the cause of the existence of the very same Amazonian tribes so lovingly studied by him; yet his indifference to the question did not prevent them from existing while he was studying them. From the fact that an eminent professor of ethnology is not interested in the problem of God's existence, it would be a *non sequitur* to conclude that God does not exist. Inattentiveness accounts for such naïve forms of atheism and makes itself felt in the very vagueness of its expression.[11]

This type of atheism has a second characteristic. When it chooses to invoke positive reasons, it starts from a previously given notion of God and, finding it unsatisfactory upon later examination, it then infers that since *that* God is not satisfactory, there can be no God of any kind. In other words, we had formed a certain notion of God; that notion accounted for a number of things, but when we realize that the explanation raises bigger difficulties than those which it explains, we drop it.

That is what happened to Simone de Beauvoir on the day she realized that it was easier for her to think of a creatorless world than of a creator responsible for all the contradictions of the world.[12] The argument would be conclusive if the problem of the existence of a creator of the world depended for its solution on the personal notion that Mme de Beauvoir entertains of his nature. She belongs to a school of thought that forcibly stresses the meaninglessness of reality. No philosopher, of course, has invoked the notion of a creator in order to account for that kind of a universe but, rather, to account for the surprising intelligibility of the one we live in. Leibniz thought that he had found an answer to the question. Thomas Aquinas probably would explain to us why the problem is both unavoidable and insoluble, but that is not our problem. One only asks

---

11 *Time* (April 8, 1966), p. 60, col. 3. Similar to the atheism of inattention is the atheism of distraction, that of the people John Courtney Murray described as being "too damn busy" to find the time to worry about God. All that was already familiar to Moses Maimonides, followed by Thomas Aquinas and renovated by Pascal in his famous notion of "divertissement" (hunting, games, anything that can help man to forget both himself and God).

12 *Ibid.*, p. 60, col. 3.

what weight the personal decision of such and such a professor of philosophy should carry in the discussion of the question. One even wonders what unit of weight the professor can use in deciding that the arguments in favor of a godless universe are more weighty than those against it. The reasons of Leibniz for engaging in the maze of his *Theodicy* are known. He preferred to risk it rather than to admit that there are no intelligible reasons why there should be something rather than nothing. Renouvier preferred to resort to the hypothesis of a finite God rather than to leave that fundamental question unanswered. Still others prefer to leave it at that, which nobody can prevent them from doing, but one hardly needs a Gallup Poll among professors of philosophy in order to determine the correct answer, the more so inasmuch as the professors of philosophy might happen not to be the best possible judges of the question.

Many priests and ministers seem to identify atheism with the abstention from religious practice, which they call an absence of religion. When it is reported that in 1965, 97 percent of the U.S. population has answered that they believed in God, that impressive figure probably means that being asked: *Do you think there is a God?*, 97 percent have put a cross in the *yes* column, and only 3 percent answered *no*. There is no ambiguity in those replies, for although there be many individual differences in the way of affirming God, and of denying him, all those who have answered *yes*, for whatever reason and in whatever sense, certainly intended to distinguish themselves from those who answered *no*. The case is different when it comes to the quality of that belief in God and the inquirer observes that of the 97 percent who said they did believe in God, only 27 percent declared themselves deeply religious.[13] At that point, the inquiry is moving to a different ground. Religion is a moral virtue, and all those who believe in God do not necessarily possess that virtue. Of those who possess it, how many, who do not consider themselves deeply religious, nevertheless are so after the manner of the publican? At any rate, to know whether or not one is deeply religious and to know whether or not one believes there is a God, are two different questions. No religious man, however slightly religious he may be, is an atheist. To Nietzsche, such a man remains one of the many "who do not know that God is dead."

Still another shift takes place when the inquiry gauges the depth of the religious feeling by the frequency of the church attendance. Over 120 million Americans today belong to some particular church, and a recent Gallup Poll reveals that only 44 percent of them attend religious services every week. Many consider themselves as religiously lukewarm because they are seldom seen in a church. But that is something else again. To

---

13 *Ibid.*, p. 61, col. 1.

believe there is a God is not necessarily to profess a particular religion, and to profess a certain particular religion is not necessarily to practise its cult with the assiduity which recommends itself. A wide gulf separates the proposition that there is a God from the decision to worship him, in a particular way, at certain times, and in certain places. The belief in the existence of God is common to different religions, although they may have different modes of worship. The usual ways to pay homage to God are contingent and human; liturgy can seem to some of us too flashy and theatrical, while others find it rather mean; in both cases it may be resented as unbearable. That is the moment when the American girl says, in the anguish of her heart: "I love God, but I hate the church."[14] For a believer, that surely is an uncomfortable feeling, but it is not the same as believing that God is dead.

Professor Novak, of Stanford University, is one of those who complain about their inability to "understand God, and the way in which he works. If, occasionally, I raise my heart in prayer," this witness continues, "it is to no God I can see, or hear, or feel. It is to a God in as cold and obscure a polar night as any unbeliever has ever known." Some churchmen actually betray a similar uncertainty. For instance, the Episcopal Dean of the National Cathedral of Washington, Francis B. Sayre, confesses himself to be "confused as to what God is" too, but, he adds, "so is the rest of America."[15]

Rather than indicating atheism, such remarks are confessions of ignorance about the essence of God, and they reveal a soul far advanced on the path to the only knowledge of God accessible to us in this life. When the Episcopal Dean of the National Cathedral of Washington modestly confesses: "I am confused as to what God is," he uses the very words of Thomas Aquinas in the passage of his question on the *Sentences*, where he describes the condition of one who, progressing from negation to negation toward a purer notion of God, ultimately finds himself "in a certain confusion."[16] In other words, the Dean and the rest of America should not worry too much about their failure to reach, beyond analogies, a clear notion of the essence of God. Their "learned ignorance" (*docta*

---

14 *Ibid.*, p. 61, col. 2.
15 *Ibid.*, p. 61, col. 1–2.
16 *Ibid.*, p. 61, col. 2. (Cf. Thomas Aquinas, *In I Sent.*, dist. 8, art. 1, ad 4, ed. Mandonnet, vol. I, p. 196.) The classical theme of *docta ignorantia* can be misunderstood; for instance, as when the Roman seminarian says: "God is all that which I cannot understand." The categories of the "hard to understand," even of the "incomprehensible," do not suffice to situate God among objects of thought. Naturally, the fact that painters naïvely represent God as a human being is irrelevant to our problem (*loc. cit.*, p. 61, col. 2 and 3). What the article calls "the anthropomorphic God of Raphael" is only that of the paintings of Raphael. Strictly speaking, God cannot be painted at all.

ignorantia) represents for Aquinas the apex of the knowledge of God accessible to us by purely natural means.

SCIENTIFIC ATHEISM

It has been said that the more active agent of the secularization of modern minds is "science."[17] There is some truth in that statement, but in what sense?

We must first eliminate from the discussion the well-known clashes between religious beliefs and scientific ideas of the world. The conflicts are only too real, but they take place only between science and mythology, and not between science and religion. Mythologies are an inevitable phenomenon. Man does not think without images; even if he thinks of some object whose very nature escapes imagination, he will form some image of it. The Greek and Roman pantheons had to be opposed by the early Christians because they were a worship of "false gods" and prevented the recognition of the "true God," yet even the first Christians never pretended that the false gods of the pagans did not exist; on the contrary, they identified those gods with what they themselves called the devils. At our present distance from the quarrel, we need not take sides. In fact, we could not, even if we wanted to. This much at least can be said, that an element of genuine piety must have been present in the pagan worship of the idols, just as a genuinely religious feeling expressed itself in many of the pagan fables. The Greek philosophers did not wait for Christianity in order to denounce the immorality of the stories which the pagans were telling about their gods, but there still is, and there always will be, a mythological element in our way of imagining a being that by virtue of its very essence is beyond nature and therefore escapes imagination. To substitute science for mythology in our representations of God and of the divine, is to substitute a new mythology for a former one. It's up to the theologians to settle the thorny problem of "the names of God," but the very existence of the problem shows that some mythology is unavoidable, because we cannot name God without imagining him, and we cannot imagine him without more or less mythologizing him.

All that science can do in this respect is to update our mythologies; true religious faith is not concerned with such operations. Whether the created world is that of Homer and of the Babylonian myths, or that of Aristotle, of Galileo, of Descartes, of Newton, of Darwin, or of Einstein, is not a problem for religious belief. Religions have now learned not to tie their own truths to scientific systems, which succeed one another in the

---

17 *Ibid.*, p. 62, col. 3.

world at ever increasing speed. Whatever science says the world is, any believer is willing to accept as the best notion the human mind can now form about the work of God. But God himself remains for us the hidden God, the invisible cause of the visible world, of whom we only know *that* he is, *what* he is not, and *how* the world he has made is related to him.

Much more to the point is the remark, attributed to the Anglican theologian David Jenkins, that the growing prestige of science is obscuring every other mode of knowledge, including even that of religious faith.[18]

For such a devaluation of the spontaneous belief in the existence of God to have taken place, a confusion must have occurred between the very notion of God and the so-called proofs of his existence, for indeed, neither Descartes, nor Leibniz, nor Pascal, nor Kant, nor Bergson has ever found in science any reason to doubt the existence of God. So the true problem must be a different one, and we shall now attempt to define it.

The True Problem

All the questions so far discussed concern our knowledge of God, our way to conceive of him, the theological speculations about his nature, as well as the personal feelings his notion raises in us, but none

---

18 *Ibid.*, p. 62, col. 3–p. 63, col. 1. This remark is true in itself, and it summarizes an immense historical experience. The development of science since the end of the Middle Ages has favored the spreading of what can be called the "scientific spirit," that is to say, a generalized desire to know everything in a scientific way and a general rejection of all problems and solutions incapable of scientific treatment. Such a positivist, or scientific, mentality is a fact. Science is a fecund source of improvements for the material side of human life; metaphysics and theology are not. More important still, science and its methods are chiefly intent on the knowledge of nature and of man only to the extent that he can be handled as one more being of nature. Hence the progressive decay of the classical humanities at the same time as that of metaphysics and theology. Science needs no ontology since it presupposes the very givenness of being. The most dangerous aspect of the present crisis in the churches is that the scientific mentality has now invaded countless minds wholly innocent of scientific knowledge and formation. When those are the minds of churchmen, as often happens, the peril gets worse, and it is at its worst when such churchmen, prompted by a misdirected religious zeal, seek in scientism itself for a remedy to the destructive effects it works on humanism, theology, and religion. This problem has been clearly seen and discussed in *Gaudium et spes*, the Vatican II Pastoral Constitution on the Church in the World of Today, *Foreword*, 3, 5, 7; on the roots and forms of contemporary atheism, 19, especially § 2. Concerning the remedies for atheism, it is remarkable that (21, § 5) the Council mentions only four remedies, none of which is borrowed from philosophy: (1) an adequate presentation of the doctrine (in which, however, metaphysics probably has a part to play); (2) the purity of life of the Church and its members; (3) the testimony of a living and adult faith trained to acknowledge the obstacles and able to overcome them; (4) lastly, "that which most contributes to reveal the presence of God, is the brotherly love of the faithful working together, with a unanimous heart, for the faith of the Gospel and exhibiting themselves as a sign of unity."

of them directly concerns the objective reasons for holding that God is still alive or that he is already dead.

I can think of no better way to deal with the problem than to attempt a philosophical reexamination of what is called, rather improperly, proof by the universal consensus. It is a fact, not that all men agree that there is a God, but that in all countries and, as it seems, at all times, however low their level of culture, all men have heard of some higher being, or power, on which man depends for his safety and prosperity, in short, for his life. Whether they call it God or something else is another question. The ethnologists are right in denouncing the illusion of civilized observers, most of them missionaries, who indiscriminately attribute a notion of God to all populations, civilized or not, with which they establish contact. The Gods of Aristotle, Descartes, and Kant are certainly not known to all peoples. The philosophical notion of a divinity is too highly abstract for minds not yet initiated to logical and scientific modes of thinking; but even the most primitive of populations betray an awareness of the kind of realities (beings, or forces) which they call supernatural. By that word, I merely mean an awareness that what we can see and touch is not the whole of reality, and that the unseen part of reality is more important for us than the one we see. Even in our own days, animism, or "spiritualism" as they say, is a widespread form of worship in some primitive tribes of Africa and the Amazon. At any rate, the peoples of the Western world are more easily observable; and no matter how far back we dig into the past we find some divinities—even, as in the case of Jehovah, that of one (true) God fighting for the complete elimination of the other (false) gods.

THE IDEA OF GOD

Saint Augustine distinguished three different sources of the notion of God: the poets, the City, and the philosophers. Before him, Aristotle had distinguished two such sources, the starry sky and the self-awareness of the soul, thus prefiguring the well-known saying of Kant: the starry sky above me, the moral law within. Self-observation shows the situation in a still simpler light. Western man lives in a society where the notion of God comes to him through family and school; religion is imbedded in the various literatures, and in the many locutions of his language. Why should so many men take pleasure in swearing by a God and a hell in the existence of which they profess not to believe? To know if a human being born and bred in total solitude would form such ideas is a meaningless question, for indeed such a man does not exist, and, if he did, how could we communicate with him? It is certain that as a social animal, man finds the notion of some divine being, and power, present in the society in which he lives, as soon as he is conscious of belonging to it. This seed, this germ, even if it is an exceedingly confused feeling, is the origin and substance of the future notion of God in the minds of philosophers as well as of plain believers. Born of rational reflection or of revelation, all further information about the divinity will apply itself to that elementary religious feeling.

These remarks do not imply any particular answer to the question: how do men come by that elementary feeling, or notion, of the divinity? Some of them *assure us* they have seen God, be it only in a cloud, as Moses saw Yahweh; others say that God unexpectedly raised them up to himself, thus revealing to them things they cannot describe and telling them words they are unable to repeat; but most of them simply find in the sight of the universe, as well as within their own souls, visible marks of his existence. It was a trite teaching of the Fathers of the Church and of the scholastic theologians, all of them following the tradition of the Old and New Testaments, that God has left on his work the visible mark of his crafts-manship so that it is inexcusable for us to pretend not to know of his existence. The clearest of those marks is man himself, especially his intellect and will, made by God in his own image and likeness.

Each of these answers is valid in its own way, but all of them raise some difficulties. In the case of the privileged men who claim to have seen God, all we can do is to believe them; but our belief in their revela-tion is very different from our having been granted that revelation. As to the classical answer, inspired by the Apostle, that men have known God from seeing his creation, it may be true, but it leaves unanswered the main question for a philosopher: How, without some preexisting notion, or feeling, of the divinity, did men form the concept of a cause so utterly different in nature from its observable effects? Euhemerism tells us that the first gods were men divinized by other men, but the difficulty remains. The question indeed is: How do men come by that notion of God, so utterly different from that of man? If I have an idea of God, I understand the proposition of Euhemerus—I can conceive the gods as so many supermen. But the question actually is how and why should I think of a God who is as far from divinity as man is?

We are here reaching a point that I cannot help finding mysterious. A certain notion is found in the minds of many men for which there is no known model in experience. That all peoples have a certain notion of the sun, of the moon, of the earth with its mountains, rivers, forests, and all the animals that live on it, is not mysterious. A notion of the sun is found everywhere because the sun exists for all men to see. The first problem raised by the presence of the notion of God in the mind of man is to know where it comes from, since no man alive has ever seen God, nor even a god. We don't even know what he should be like in order to look like him.

From this point of view the remark of La Bruyère becomes fully intelli-gible. It was neither a paradox nor an artifice to get rid of a problem. It is a simple truth. The question was: Does that being—of which we have a notion, if not an idea—actually have existence or not? Naturally, when we think of such a being, we conceive him as real. At any rate, we are not aware of making up the notion; we find it there, and though its presence does not prove that an actual being answers the notion in reality the *onus probandi* lies with him who denies it rather than with him who affirms it. The problem of the inexistence of God comes first. How could man have formed the notion of a being not given in sense experience, and not of his own conscious making, if that being does not exist?

The primacy of the notion with respect to the proof is seen in several of the traditional ways of presenting the problem of the existence of God. It almost looks as though no way of posing the problem could successfully avoid inscribing the notion among its data.

First is the concrete meaning of the celebrated doctrine of the innateness of the idea of God. If it is innate, its presence in human minds is thereby accounted for and, by the same token, the actual existence of its object becomes practically certain. In fact, all the defenders of the innateness of the idea of God infer from it that God actually is, or exists. That seems to be the only thing the innateness of the notion of God means to them, for if asked how they understand it, they give very different answers. It may be a kind of reminiscence in the manner of Plato; or it can mean that every man at some time in his life discovers he has a certain notion of God, as if it had always been there. Or else it can mean that since that notion cannot have come to the mind from outside it must have come from within in a way that remains to be defined. The point is that even the demonstrations of the existence of God taken from the physical world presuppose in the mind the presence of a confused notion of divinity. Each one of the five ways of Thomas Aquinas starts from a nominal definition of God; without such a conditional concept of God, the mind would not know what it has found at the end of its demonstration.

Here I would like to add parenthetically that the famous *quinque viae* of St. Thomas[19] are in themselves purely rational and philosophical demonstrations. I mean by that that they could be extracted from the *Summa* and introduced, just as they are, in a treatise of philosophy; but even a philosopher could not ask the question of whether God exists without first having in mind some notion of what he is looking for. Each one of the five ways leads to the existence of a first being in a certain order of reality: motion, efficient causality, possibility and necessity, etc. After concluding that such a prime being exists, Aquinas simply adds: "And all understand that it is God." In other words, all understand at once that the prime immovable mover is the being that they are already used to calling God even before proving his existence. There is therefore a

---

19 Aquinas, *Summa Theologica*, Pt. I, q. 2, art. 3; *GBWW*, Vol. 19, p. 12c.

precognition of God anterior to the proofs. The same is true of the second way: "One must therefore posit a prime efficient cause, which all call God: *quam omnes Deum nominant.*" What can be the origin of that prenotion—from the first education of the child, from the universal consensus in consequence of which practically nobody can spend his life without having heard the word "god"? In his treatise *On Separate Substances*, chapter I, Aquinas goes so far as to speak of an innate knowledge of God, at least in this sense that whenever men have reached the notion of a first principle of all things it was innate in them to call it God. That spontaneous anticipation is not a proof, yet it still plays its part in the interpretation of the proof. Were it not for that anticipation, we would not know that the Prime Being, Mover, Cause, etc., is the very same being which all men agree in calling "God."

From the very outset Aquinas knows that what he is looking for is God, and indeed nothing is more fitting in a Sum of Theology. In his own *Metaphysics*, the philosopher Avicenna never says "God," but always *Primus*, and that too is most fitting, because "God" is a religious rather than a philosophical notion. As soon as we say that the Prime Being is God, we cease talking philosophy and begin to talk theology in the religious sense of the word. To Aquinas the origin of the notion of God was well known; it was God himself revealing to man his own existence. But there can be other sources of our knowledge of God, and the common, spontaneous belief of men in the existence of supernatural beings resembles the revealed knowledge of God in that it is not abstractly speculative, not "philosophical" or "metaphysical." It is not obtained by proceeding one step beyond physics in the scientific investigation of reality and its causes. Just as faith is a revelation from on high, the plain, common notion of God is a reaction of the whole man to the confusedly perceived presence of God in nature and in himself. That is the truth hidden in the well-known notion of an *anima naturaliter Christiana* of Tertullian. One cannot be a Christian by nature, only by Christ, but had Tertullian spoken of an *anima naturaliter religiosa*, he would have been right.

No particular notion of God is here at stake. Even what is considered the most formidable objection to the existence of God, namely, the presence of evil in the world, in no way affects what has just been said about the presence of the idea of God in us. On the contrary, it rather strengthens the significance of that fact. If it is absurd that there should be evil in a God-created universe, the omnipresence of evil, since it is felt and experienced by all men with an overwhelming evidence, should make it impossible for human minds to form a notion of God. Now they do not think of God despite evil, but quite particularly when suffering evil and especially when in fear of death. As Spinoza puts it at the very beginning of his *Tractatus theologico-politicus*, if men always knew with certainty how to run their business, or if they always were favored by fortune, superstition would find no place in their minds. This, Spinoza adds, is the true cause of superstition, despite the claim of others that it arises from the presence of a certain confused notion of the Divinity in the minds of men. Ever since the time of Lucretius, the notion that fear is the very root of religious feeling has been a familiar one, but it certainly looks paradoxical to claim, at one and the same time, the fear of evil as the chief source of man's belief in the existence of God and as an argument against it.

A detailed survey of the history of the problem would, I believe, support that conclusion. One cannot understand otherwise how such a scientific genius as Descartes can have imagined that the presence in us of the notion of God constitutes a solid basis for a proof of his existence. As is well known, Descartes considered that notion an innate idea.[20] Some think, with John Locke, that his position can be refuted simply by establishing that there are no innate ideas.[21] But even if his opponents are right, Descartes still could ask them: if my idea of God is not innate in me, how did I form it? For that is the true meaning of the Cartesian notion of the innateness of the idea of God. The innateness of the notion cannot be distinguished from the power of forming it. Since I find the model of such a notion neither in me nor outside of me, it must have been "put in me by some substance itself actually infinite." Hence the conclusion of the third *Metaphysical Meditation:* "consequently it follows of necessity that God exists." The objection of Locke and the empiricists that the elements of the notion are provided by sense experience does not alter the fact that the notion itself has no model in interior or exterior reality. No infinite object is given in any kind of experience. To say that the elements of the concept of God are so given does not explain the presence in us of the pattern according to which the elements are associated in the mind so as to constitute such a concept. In fact, many successors of Descartes, from Malebranche up to the later school of the so-called ontologists, draw the natural inference: if I think of a being called God, then that being exists. This was what I meant by saying that what stands in need of rational justification is atheism, much more than the spontaneous belief that there is a God.

PROLETARIAN ATHEISM

Karl Marx did not content himself with observing that God does not exist, which is the proper position of speculative, or theoretical, atheism. He decided to suppress God—to eradicate the very notion from

---

20 Descartes, *Meditation III; GBWW,* Vol. 31, pp. 81d–89a.
21 Locke, *Essay I.* iii, 8–16; *GBWW,* Vol. 35, pp. 114–117a.

men's minds. The poet Heinrich Heine said that Kant was the Robespierre of natural theology. (Robespierre publicly said of King Louis XVI: "We are not here to judge him, but to kill him.") What Heine said of Kant is much more true of Marx—his first intention was indeed to kill God. Because Marx was essentially a revolutionist, his whole doctrine was dominated by the notion of praxis. As with some theologians, thought for him was only legitimate as a means of action. In trying to understand Marx, his justly famous saying should be recalled: "Until now the philosophers have contented themselves with interpreting the world in several different ways. It is now a question of transforming it."[22]

It could therefore be said that the atheism of Marx is no concern of philosophy nor the philosophers. His decision, that there is no God, lies outside, in an order where the philosopher is powerless. One can persecute believers, close the churches, and kill the priests, just as in past centuries one could burn atheists at the stake, but one fails to see what "philosophical" meaning can be attributed to such acts. The very decision to turn philosophy into a praxis is not—if taken in itself—a philosophical decision. If the belief that there is a God is truly necessary for salvation, then it is the duty of the theologians to make men believe there is a God; if it is necessary for the success of the proletarian revolution to suppress the belief of men in the existence of God, then men should be made to disbelieve it. In neither case are philosophers as such concerned with the proceeding.

Why then are we, as philosophers, talking about it? We are talking about Marx for the same reason we are talking about Aquinas. Aquinas says that we should believe there is a God, and having said so he at once proceeds rationally to demonstrate it in five different philosophical ways; so also, having decided to kill God, Marx proceeds at once to the task of proving that, in fact, God has never existed except as a harmful illusion in the minds of men. Thus Marxist atheism is the speculative justification of a politico-practical decision.

The project of examining such a doctrine with a view to refuting it, therefore, does not make sense. One does not dialectically refute a decision of the will. A dialogue, as they call it today, between any form of theism and Marxian atheism is doomed to failure beforehand because the two positions belong to two specifically different orders. In the words of one of its recent exponents, Marxist philosophy is "before everything else a guide for action, an instrument in the hands of the proletariat."[23] Armed

---

22 Marx, "Thèses sur Feuerbach," XI, in *F. Engels et la fin de la philosophie classique* (Paris: Les Revues), p. 145. In view of what follows, note Thesis X: "The basis of ancient materialism was bourgeois society. The basis of the new materialism is human society, or socialized humanity" (p. 145).

23 G. Yakhot, *Qu'est-ce que le matérialisme dialectique?*, translated into French from the Russian (Moscow: Editions du Progrès), p. 46.

with that revolutionary theory, the proletariat becomes a fearless fighter for the realization of Marxist ideals, that is, for the whole of Marxist mankind. "For that reason a momentous historical task devolved upon Marxism from its first appearance—to establish an alliance between Marxist socialist theory and the proletarian movement—an alliance between the spiritual weapon of theory and the material power capable of using that weapon, that is to say, the proletariat, the 'people'."

One sees at once under what conditions that declaration of principles becomes intelligible. First, we are asked to concede their right to speak of spiritual forces in a materialistic doctrine; but that is nothing. The real difficulty is to conceive *theory* as a *weapon;* in other words, to accept as an objective view of reality as it is any doctrine that is expressly conceived in order to transform it. The proper philosophical order would be: first, to see reality as it is, and then, as scientists do with the physical world, to imagine possible and desirable transformations of it by means of engineering. The radical error of Marxism is to justify revolutionary social changes by an erroneous view of the social reality.

For the same reason, I can see no point in attempting to refute the Marxist conception of the history of philosophy that reduces it to a never ending fight between materialism and idealism. That notion is the more surprising since Marxism, which professes to be a straightforward materialism, sees itself as a reinterpretation of Hegelianism, which is the clearest case of idealism one could quote.[24] But perhaps the notion of the opposition between idealism and materialism is not perfectly clear in the minds of our own Marxist contemporaries.

How does contemporary Marxism understand the opposition of materialism and idealism? It is the fundamental problem in philosophy, G. Yakhot says, and it can be asked, with Engels, in the following terms: "Has the world been created by God, or does it exist from all eternity? To this question, the materialists and the idealists give mutually exclusive answers."[25]

Aquinas saw no contradiction between the notion of a world created by God and that of an eternally existing world.[26] Moreover, the question of the eternity of the world has nothing to do with that of its materiality.

---

24 "Hegel founded objective idealism. For him, the absolute Idea, the universal Spirit, was the basis of nature and of society . . . The absolute idea is the Demiurge, the creator of reality, the latter being but the external manifestation of the Idea. You certainly have noticed that, in saying this, Hegel simply restates, under a veiled expression, the religious notion of the creation of the world by God." (Yakhot, *op. cit.*, pp. 35–36.) The author shows (p. 37) how the dialectical method of Hegel, having finally "betrayed itself in favour of his metaphysical system" and thus begotten German imperialism, "nevertheless became one of the speculative sources of Marxism."

25 *Op. cit.*, p. 14.

26 Aquinas, *op. cit.*, Pt. I, q. 46, art. 1–2; *GBWW*, Vol. 19, pp. 250a–255a.

God could have created a universe of pure immaterial substances, or spirits, like that of Berkeley, and could have created it from all eternity. Or else there might be both matter and spirit in an uncreated and eternal universe like that of Aristotle. There is obviously a great deal of confusion on this point in contemporary Marxism.

The reason for it is that, in the mind of the Marxists, unless matter is eternal, one cannot be sure that there is not a God to create it, and since they are reluctant to think of a material God—a notion familiar to the Stoics, the Epicureans, and even to the Christian Tertullian—the mere notion of God seems to them to entail some sort of idealism, the possibility, that is, of some actually existing immaterial being. "Idealism," Lenin used to say, "has been invented in favor of religion and to defend it."[27] Obstinately confusing the two notions of materialism and of the eternity of the world, Yakhot insists that according to materialism, "matter, nature, have always existed." Aristotle also believed that matter and nature were eternal, but he was no materialist. If nobody has created matter, Yakhot goes on to say, "the evolution of the world does not stand in need of a supreme and divine force. God is superfluous, the world eternally evolves without his intervention. Thus and in this way does materialism lead to the negation of God. It is unavoidably tied up with atheism. The materialist is at the same time an atheist." This obviously is a warring and fighting atheism. Yakhot asks: who profits by the theses of theism and idealism, who "if not the capitalists and the profiteers! By doing so, idealism supports all that which is reactionary and out-of-date, from the profiteers up to religion."[28] Summing up his whole doctrine in a terse formula, Yakhot concludes: "All philosophy expresses the interests of a well-determined class."[29]

Nothing is harder to refute than an evidently false statement. It is a well-known fact that Christianity was originally and for a long time thereafter a religion of a poor and small people. As to the notion that each and every philosophy answers a determined social and economic class, it is so amazingly false that one does not know what to answer. In what sense is the philosophy of Parmenides the expression of a class? For what class did it cease to be true between his own time and that of Hegel? How could one explain that the philosophy of Aristotle, true for him in the Macedonian empire in the fourth century B.C., still was true for a Persian

---

27 Yakhot, *loc. cit.*

28 *Op. cit.*, p. 15. To the ensuing remarks a Marxist would answer that, from the point of view of their influence on speculation, all non-Marxist economic systems are practically identical. All idealisms "invite in some way or other the workers to give up their fight against capitalism and misery." (*Ibid.*) In that sense, one could say that St. Francis of Assisi has served the interests of the capitalists and exploiters of the people. Here too, "Who is not with me is against me."

29 *Op. cit.*, p. 17.

Muslim, Avicenna, in the tenth century, for the Spanish Muslim Averroës in the twelfth century, for the Christian monk Thomas Aquinas in the thirteenth century, and, to make a long story short—even supposing we could put all those men into the same social and economic class—how are we to add to the collection a twentieth-century French philosopher who is as little partial to the capitalist class as Jacques Maritain? Even reducing all the systems to two classes, idealism and materialism, what relation is there between the materialism of the Greek Epicurus—according to whom, the wise man with a little bread, water, and a few friends, is the equal of Jupiter himself—or of the slave Epictetus, on the one side, and that materialism, on the other, of such a modern Jew as Marx, himself living under conditions just as bourgeois as the Russian Lenin?

To sum up, in saying that there is a God, you work for capitalism, whereas in saying that there is no God, you work for the proletariat; the proletariat is the truth, consequently there is no God. The position is perfectly consistent; only it is a position, as they used to say in the old philosophical schools, *extranea philosophiae*—innocent of all philosophical meaning. Until the proletariat becomes the whole of mankind, even for Marxism the death of God remains a mere hope; to non-Marxists, it means nothing.[30]

THE CORE OF THE PROBLEM

The experiment of the Marxist state to eradicate from minds the notion of God—and its failure—is doubly significant. On the one hand, it suggests that belief in the existence of some divine being is a fact of nature—mankind does not seem to be able to subsist without it. Let us repeat that this does not prove the existence of an object answering that spontaneous and natural belief. It may be that man cannot live, and that mankind cannot endure, so to speak biologically, without some belief of that sort, but that still would not prove that the notion of God is more than a necessary illusion. My point is that, even as an illusion, its generality,

---

30 There would be no point in discussing the arguments of the Marxists in favor of their own position. They presuppose an ignorance of the history of philosophy encyclopædic in its dimensions. They regularly mistake the notion that the world is eternal for the different one, that the world is uncreated: "The scientific thesis that the world is eternal definitively overthrows the religious belief in the creation of the world." (Yakhot, *op. cit.* p. 62.) Now Aquinas sees no impossibility in the notion of an eternally created universe. As to the discovery, attributed by the Communist Party to the great Russian scientist Lomonosov, that "in nature nothing is born of nothing, and nothing vanishes without leaving traces of itself" (p. 63), it is at least as old as the verse of the Roman poet Persius, *"gigni de nihilo nihilum, in nihilum nil posse reverti"* (*Sat.* III, 34). The Church, Marxists say, is incapable of refuting these arguments (p. 64). Now it is precisely because nothing can come from nothing that the Church requires an uncreated God as the cause of a created world.

its persistence, its apparent ineradicability are remarkable. No other notion presents the same characteristics; as a simple fact alone that notion is a problem. Philosophical reflection is required in order to solve it.

It is noteworthy, on the other hand, that the spontaneous belief in the existence of God, far from dissolving at once under the scrutiny of reason, offers a remarkable resistance to all efforts to destroy it. A striking confirmation of that truth is found in a letter from Benjamin Constant dated Hardenberg, 11 October, 1811, to his friend Claude Hochet:

> In a few days, hopefully, I shall see written completely my History of Polytheism. The whole plan has been recast as well as more than three quarters of the chapters. I had to do so in order to obtain the order I had in mind, an order which, I think, I have now attained. Another reason was that, as you know, I am no longer that intrepid philosopher, certain that there is nothing after this world, and so well pleased with it that he rejoiced in the thought that there is no other one.
>
> My work is a singular proof of the truth of Bacon's saying, that a little science leads to atheism and more science to religion. It was positively by scrutinizing the facts, by collecting them from all sides, and by stumbling on the countless difficulties they oppose to incredulity, that I finally saw myself forced to regress into religious ideas. I certainly did so in perfect good faith, for each and every backward step cost me a great deal. Even at present all my habits, all my memories still are those of a philosopher, and I am fighting to defend, one after the other, all the positions which religion is reconquering from me. There even is a sacrifice of self-love involved in the process, for I believe it would be hard to find a stricter logic than the one I had used in attacking all the opinions of that kind.
>
> My book had absolutely no other defect than to run counter to all that which, at present, I consider good and true. I certainly would have had a political success. I even could have had still another kind of success, for at the price of a few very slight pushes, I could have made of the book what people now prefer, to wit, a system of atheism for gentlemen, a manifesto against the priests, the whole being combined with the admission that there should be certain fables for the rank and file, an admission that gives satisfaction to political authority as well as to personal vanity.

Up to a point, such personal experiences may well account for the durability of the widespread belief in the actual existence of an object answering the notion of God. Even under heavy social and political pressure some men refuse to give up that notion, sometimes for no reason at all, but also sometimes because reason finds it most acceptable and rationally justified.

From this second point of view—that of its intrinsic rationality—the notion of God constitutes a still more remarkable fact. To state it as succinctly as possible, the mind finds the strange characteristic about the notion of God that its object cannot be thought of as nonexistent. There is only one other notion of which the same thing can be said, namely, being. That similarity, incidentally, accounts for the fact that all the proofs of the existence of God ultimately consist in establishing the necessity of a certain being and its primacy in the various orders of reality. Being is the very name of God when the spontaneous notion is translated into the language of philosophical reflection. At any rate, it looks as absurd to think of a nonexisting God as it is to speak of a nonexisting being. All the rest, including the universe and our very selves, we can imagine as not existing, but the only way to do the same with God is to refuse to take his idea into account. "If God is God," St. Bonaventure says, "God exists." This necessary quality of the relationship between the notion of God and that of actual existence is another fact to be taken into account.

The whole history of the so-called ontological argument, plus that of ontologism, could be quoted in support of this assertion, but since I am here dealing with the notion of God and its intrinsic necessity as an empirical fact, I shall content myself with recalling the testimony of the one or two authorized philosophers and theologians.

To quote St. Anselm in relation to this problem is superfluous, but even though Aquinas does not consider valid the proof of the *Proslogion*,[31] he too upholds the view that, speaking of God as taken in himself, his existence is evident: *"Nam simpliciter quidem Deum esse per se notum est; cum hoc ipsum quod Deus est, sit suum esse."* ("Absolutely speaking, that God exists is self-evident, since what God is is His own being." *Contra Gentiles* I, 11, 1.)

The Fifth *Metaphysical Meditation* of Descartes contains a perfect formulation of that inseparability of the two notions of God and of actual existence. Confronted with the objection that there is nothing to prevent us from attributing actual existence to God, even though God does not exist, Descartes answers by stressing the uniqueness of the existential implication of the notion of God. From the fact that there can be no mountain without a valley, it does not follow that there are mountains and valleys, whereas, "from the sole fact that I cannot conceive God without existence, it follows that existence is inseparable from Him and, consequently, that He exists." The argument of St. Anselm is justified by Descartes as follows: "While from the fact I cannot conceive God without existence, it follows that existence is inseparable from Him, and hence that He really exists; not that my thought can bring this to pass, or impose any necessity on things, but, on the contrary, because the necessity which lies in the thing itself, i.e. the necessity of the existence of God, determines

---

31 St. Anselm's *Proslogion* is reprinted below in Part Four, p. 316.

me to think in this way."[32] In other words, it may not be necessary that I should ever think of God, but, if I do, I cannot think of him otherwise than as existing in reality. For, Descartes goes on to say, "is there anything more clear and manifest than to think that there is a God, that is to say, a sovereign and perfect being, in whose notion alone necessary or eternal existence is comprised and, consequently, who exists?" The consequence, I repeat, may not be valid, but the fact itself that the notion of God is such, and is the only one to be such, can hardly be denied.

Read in the light of that fact, the long history of the ontological argument ceases to be that of a sophism. However we interpret it, that puzzling notion is there. In short, Ariste says to Theodore in Malebranche's second *Entretien métaphysique:* "You define God as God has defined himself when he said to Moses: *God is He Who Is* (Ex. III, 14)." One can think of this and that being without its existing, one can see its essence without seeing its existence, one can see its idea without seeing it, but "if one thinks of God, he must needs be." Even in the doctrines of such "atheists" as Spinoza and Hegel, the very notion of what they still call God entails that of its existence. Volumes could be written on the history of that notion. They would not be useless, but we are interested here in the notion of God as a given observable fact only.

We will now examine the part played by that notion in the affirmation of the existence of its object, or more what precisely is the fundamental obstacle to its negation.

Is the Nonexistence of God Truly Thinkable?

The preceding considerations invite us to wonder if the nonexistence of God can really be conceived, that is, other than in words only. It is both satisfying and distressing to observe that we are, in a quite unpremeditated way, rediscovering the old tracks left by our great predecessors in similar inquiries. In fact, not seeing how the existence of God can be denied, or at least why it should be denied—and yet that it is denied—we can think of only two explanations. First, those who do so are fools (*insipientes*); second, they deny it in words only without fully realizing the import of their words. The first answer is too blunt for our modern notion of a philosophical discussion, but we still can ask the atheists if they truly realize the meaning of the words they use. When they deny the existence of God, do they really mean it?

THE CAUSE OF THE IDEA

From whatever angle we consider the problem, we are led back to the same question. What is the cause of the idea of God in us and of its exceptional, not to say unique, existential connotations?

---

32 Descartes, *Meditation V; GBWW*, Vol. 31, p. 94b–c.

This question, let us repeat, is quite distinct from that of the nature of a possible demonstration of the existence of God. The so-called physical proofs seem to evade it. They say that our intellect forms that idea on the basis of the data of sense experience, and that we conceive the notion of God *a creatura mundi*. No doubt this is true, but what secret light leads the mind from the sight of the material universe to the notion of an eternal, immaterial, and self-subsisting cause? I look at things, Augustine says, and I ask them: Are you my God? They answer me: We are not thy God; look for him above us. Tell me at least something about him, Augustine insists, and all of them, heaven, sun, moon, stars, answer with a loud voice: He is He Who made us.[33] Well and good, but who or what suggested to Augustine his own questions? Why was he asking for a God, for *his* God?

All the so-called physical proofs of the existence of God will develop from that starting point, but they all raise the same question: How do you know what you are looking for? The real message of Augustine is precisely his acute feeling of the inevitability of the question. However we look at it, the origin of the proof lies in the mind from which the question arises. Where in the mind does it come from if not from some cognition which, while perhaps not a cognition of God himself, is at least a cognition of an object so different from those of sense perception, with characteristics that transcend everything else, an object that can be none other than what we call God? The doctrine of the divine illumination is too well known to need repeating. We also know how the epistemology of Augustine differs from that of Aquinas,[34] and how that difference affects the very structure of their respective proofs of the existence of God. What often escapes notice is how deeply the two epistemologies and two natural theologies agree in spite of their differences; and it is worthwhile observing because their meeting point lies in the most secret mystery of our knowledge of God.

The five ways of Aquinas, precisely because they start from sense experience, constitute five inductive arguments. Now there is something mysterious about all induction. There is nothing mysterious in deduction because its conclusions are already contained in the premises. Incidentally, this accounts for the frequent attempts of theologians, even within the so-called Thomist school, to turn each of the five inductions of the *Summa Theologica* into deductions starting from first principles, such as those of causality, identity, and finally, noncontradiction. Now, of course, all demonstrations must take place in accordance with principles and under their control; however, the last term of these inductions is not a prin-

---

33 Augustine, *Confessions*, X. vi. 9; *GBWW*, Vol. 18, p. 73c–d.
34 *See* my study on *The Christian Philosophy of Saint Augustine* (New York: Random House, 1960), Introduction, chap. ii.

ciple of knowledge but is rather a cause of reality; not a thought, but a being—the Prime Mover, the Necessary One, the Prime Cause, the Prime Being, and the Supreme End. In no one of these cases is the conclusion already given in the premises; on the contrary, it transcends them infinitely. The operation, of course, is the work of the intellect, but the question remains: How, in virtue of what power, does the intellect, starting from sense cognition, reach those lofty conclusions so different from its starting point? This is not a question for Aquinas alone, it was already a question for Aristotle, and it still is a question for all philosophers. Let us call it the mystery of induction. In the many works contained in his *Organon*, Aristotle has said precious little on the subject. Always both glib and scientifically precise in dealing with the deductive operations of the intellect, Aristotle has devoted only twenty lines to the problem of induction—more precisely, to the problem of the inductive process by which, starting from sense perception, we rise from it to the cognition of principles.

Twenty lines are not much on the question of knowing how the intellect reaches the first principles in the light of which it knows all the rest. But there are good reasons for Aristotle's surprising discretion, and we can appreciate them by reading with due care what he says on the question in the *Posterior Analytics*. The first sentence alone would deserve a long, attentive meditation: "It is therefore evident that induction is what makes us know principles, for it is by means of it that sensation causes the universal in us." So the instantaneous operation whereby, given a sense perception, the intellect forms in itself a concept, is already an induction. According to Aristotle, the formation of principles by the intellect is of the same nature. Here is the most mysterious and, to my mind, the most important passage in the whole *Organon:*

> Since, with the exception of intuition, no kind of cognition is more exact than science, it must needs be an intuition that grasps the principles. This follows, not only from the preceding considerations, but also from the fact that the principle of demonstration is not itself a demonstration. So there can be no science of science. If therefore we possess some kind of true knowledge other than science, it is intuition alone that is the principle of the principle itself, and science is to the whole of reality as intuition is to the principle.[35]

The difficulty of the passage is due to its density and also to the fact that, instead of appealing to reason, as does the theory of syllogistic deduction, it appeals to the intuitive power of the intellect. What Aristotle

---

35 Aristotle, *Posterior Analytics II.* xix, 100^b 12–17; *GBWW*, Vol. 8, p. 137.

says here is hard to put into more explicit words, because what he is trying to say is found at the coming together of three converging, yet distinct, philosophical problems: the origin of general ideas or universals, the origin of principles, and the origin of the idea of God.

The problem of universals is, or should be, the *crux philosophorum*. Personally, I confess that it remains a mystery to me despite all that I have read on universals. We all repeat the mediaeval formula: *sensus est particularium, intellectus universalium* (sense knows particulars, the intellect universals). The wise thing to do is to accept it and keep out of trouble. But I find it difficult to believe without adding many qualifications. The objects of sense cognition are particulars, but I do not perceive particulars as such; I only perceive sensible qualities, color for sight, sounds for hearing, etc. It is also true that the objects of intellection are universals, but I cannot think without images, so that sensations leave their mark of origin on every concept. What really happens is that intellectual cognition and sense experience are inextricably blended together. For instance, I say I see a dog, but *dog* is an abstract concept; it represents or signifies a species. Now I do not see or touch any species, whether it is a dog or a man or anything else. I see patches of colors, at most colored patterns, and I *know* that what I see or touch is a certain sort of animal or a man. Perception is intellectual as much as, if not more than, it is sensible. The traditional theory of abstraction invoked in order to account for the fact that the intellect separates, in the particular, the intelligible from the sensible does not go beyond the mere formulation of a fact. Neither Aristotle nor any Aristotelians have said how that metaphysical chemistry operates, or, let us say, how sense and intellect operate in that metaphysical chemistry. If the intelligible that is present in the sensible is not a concept, then what is it? Aristotle boldly declares that it is sensed. I see a dog because, by a sort of rapid induction, I know that the particular sense pattern that I see is caused by an individual belonging to the species of what my intellect knows to be what I call a dog. Not nominalism, not realism, not even the curious hybrid called "moderate realism" has fully been able to account for the mysterious induction that ends with what sensation gives to the intellect—not a mere sensible quality, but the pattern of sensible qualities we call a thing.

What about principles? Aquinas says principles are not innate, but that they are known in the natural light of the intellect in connection with sense knowledge. Again, what the principles say is given in the material objects that make up the substance of reality, yet the principles themselves are immaterial and exist as such only in knowing minds. I perceive beings, not being. I observe agents and patients, and I call the former causes and the latter effects, but I do not observe causality itself. By a bold induction, I can infer that there are no effects without causes—but this is simply to explicate the definition of either *cause* or *effect*. It was Hume, as I seem to remember, who said that this is just about the same thing as saying that there are no husbands without wives. If you corner a metaphysician, he will finally agree that there is something mysterious in our cognition of any principle. No wonder, since we know them in the light of the agent intellect, which, Aquinas says, is the light of which it is said in Scripture *Signatum est super nos lumen vultus tui Domine* (*Psalms*, 4: 6–7), as if to say: "It is by the imprint of the divine light that everything is shown to us."[36] Therefore, even in the natural light of the intellect, there is some trace of the mystery that surrounds the divinity.

I also mentioned the notion of God in the human mind, and, on that point, it should suffice to recall some of our preceding remarks on the distinction between the Prime Being whose existence philosophy proves, on the one hand, and the God of sacred theology, on the other. But let us bypass that incidental difficulty in order to consider the very operation by which, in philosophy, the intellect affirms the existence of a first cause of the universe. It is of exactly the same nature as that by which it forms the notion of its own principles of knowledge, particularly of its own first principle—being, which is but another name for God. That operation again is an induction, and there is a marked tendency among philosophers to reduce the terms or steps of that induction to the smallest possible number, so that it becomes in the final analysis a kind of immediate inference. The relative implies the absolute: motion implies immobility; finitude implies infinity; caused causality implies uncaused causality; etc. All the five ways end with that sort of "passing to the limit" under the form of an "impossibility to go on to infinity." But is that impossibility owing to the nature of the intellect or to the nature of reality? Its intervention in the proof led Kant to say that all the proofs of the existence of God imply some hidden recourse to the ontological argument. The remark is correct in the sense that even in the concluding phase of the so-called physical proofs, there is no difference between affirming the necessity of positing an absolute and of affirming its existence. There always is something not quite satisfactory in an induction when its last term can only be inferred without actually being perceived. Behind all the demonstrations of the existence of God, there lurks old man Parmenides. For being is, and if God is being, God is. That is something we feel sure of prior to any demonstration of any sort, and is not that certitude the moving force that drives us on in our quest till we reach an absolutely first term which, as such, necessarily is and—since its being is necessary—is God? To put it even more simply, since we ask *Utrum Deus sit* (whether God exists), the notion of God is already here, and the notion of him is that of a necessary being.

---

36 Aquinas, *op. cit.*, Pt. I, q. 84, art. 5; *GBWW*, Vol. 19, p. 447b.

Etienne Gilson

Atheists like to denounce the shortcomings of the proofs of God's existence, and many of the proofs are inadequate, but some of them appear convincing to trained metaphysical minds, while there has never been a convincing metaphysical proof that there is no God.

I am not claiming that there are no professed atheists—men who remain persuaded, after mature reflection, that no reality answers the word "God." My point is, first, that anybody can quote half a dozen or more classical proofs of the existence of God even if he does not subscribe to them; on the other hand, proofs of the nonexistence of God are scarce. My next point is that such proofs consist in showing that the proofs of the existence of God are not conclusive—a different proposition than the nonexistence of God. Third, the very fact that the nonexistence of God requires proof is corroboration of the reality of what I have called the spontaneous and naïve belief in the existence of God. The violent campaigns conducted by the atheistic governments against religion would not be necessary were it not so certain that the people, left to themselves, would go on believing that there is a God and in worshiping him. Besides, why look at governments when the case of private individuals is so clear? Men never consider what they significantly call "losing their faith" a happy event. There is no apparent reason why this should be so. To have rid oneself of what one has come to consider an error, or a mere prejudice, should be a cause instead for celebration. Literature, however, abounds in depressing descriptions of how thinkers and writers have lost their faith. A case little known outside the circle of specialists in French literature is that of the poet Stéphane Mallarmé. Though chary of confidences on such questions, Mallarmé wrote to his friend Henry Cazalis that he was just emerging from an exhausting crisis in the course of which he had finally overcome—not without tremendous efforts—"that old plumage," God. Why should there be such resistance to an idea of something that does not exist?

To us philosophers, perhaps the most instructive of such cases is that of Immanuel Kant. For Kant remains an outstanding example of what he himself considered the first virtue in a philosopher—seriousness, the habit of never playing with ideas but of treating them seriously. Kant could not stand cheating in philosophy, and this makes the more remarkable his attitude toward our problem. Having asked in the *Critique of Pure Reason* if speculative reason is qualified to establish the existence of a being, which is doubly impossible for sense experience, Kant answered his own question in the negative, but he did so with regret and not without adding qualifications to his answer.

The modern successors to Kant have stressed the negative part of his doctrine, stated in the conclusion of his *Critique of Pure Reason*, that no metaphysical knowledge is possible. Accordingly, the existence of God is among the many propositions that must be considered indemonstrable, but it is only one of them. What is truly remarkable in Kant's case is that after reaching that conclusion he continued to feel absolutely certain of the existence of God. Indeed, in his *Critique of Practical Reason* Kant went out of his way to demonstrate that that indemonstrable conclusion remained a truth nonetheless. It is true, one remembers, as a postulate, because otherwise the necessary character of moral duty, which to Kant is a fact, would be impossible.

I do not think that Kant was contradicting himself. On the contrary, I wish to stress the obstinacy with which he insists that the conclusions of the second *Critique* leave intact the conclusions of the first one. Why should Kant still feel sure that there is a God after demonstrating that it is impossible for speculative reason to prove it? From this point of view, the central chapter of the *Critique of Practical Reason* is I,2,7: "How is it possible to conceive an extension of pure reason from the point of view of practice without, at the same time, extending its knowledge from the point of view of speculation?" Indeed, how can such a trick be performed successfully? However I arrive at it, the certitude acquired by practical reason is, by definition, a rational certitude. Rational faith, as Kant calls it, cannot extend our knowledge in the speculative order even though reason —as is the case with moral duty—is bound to bow to it. In short, the certitude that there is a God both precedes and survives intact the demonstration that it cannot be demonstrated. More brilliant homage was never paid to the rational indestructibility of a notion whose intrinsic certitude remains unaffected by the demonstration of its indemonstrability.[37] That indestructibility of the notion of God in the human mind is the heaviest stumbling block in the path to atheism. It should help us to realize that logic, dialectic, and physics cannot have the last word, because they do not have the first one. It is natural that man should look for a rational justification of his spontaneous belief that there is a God, but because belief comes first, that belief is independent of such justifications; it is their cause rather than their effect.

THE FIRST WORD

It might seem to follow that there can be no atheists, but I do not mean that. I mean that even when atheism is real, it is a negation implying the presence in the mind of the very notion it denies, a negation fighting, more or less successfully, against a natural tendency of reason to affirm it.

To reject that affirmation as metaphysical is a great naïveté. Of course it is metaphysical to say there is a God, but it is equally metaphysical to say there is no God. "To believe that there is a God," Charles Péguy wrote,

---

37 Kant, *Critique of Practical Reason*; GBWW, Vol. 42, p. 349b–353a.

"is a metaphysical, a religious operation; to believe that there are several gods implies as many such operations as there are gods, and to believe that there is neither one God nor several is to perform as many negative operations, both metaphysical and religious, as it would require positive operations to affirm them." Péguy concludes in the language of the School-men "that atheism is a philosophy, a metaphysics; that it perhaps is a religion, even a superstition; and that it can become what is the most wretched thing in the world, a system or, rather, and to speak more exactly, that there can be several atheisms and many of those things at one and the same time; nay, that atheism is indeed all those things by the same title and neither more nor less than so many theisms and so many deisms, so many monotheisms and so many polytheisms, and mythologies, and pantheisms; that it too is a mythology, like the others and, like the others, is a language; and that, if it comes down to the fact that there must needs be languages, there are more intelligent ones."[38]

In short, an inverted metaphysical position remains metaphysical. Neither would it help atheism to object, in the manner of Kant, that we know the notion of God for what it is, namely a transcendental "illusion" of reason. Even if that were true, one still would ask why, once de-nounced as an illusion, that ancient notion should not at once vanish from human minds? For millennia it was believed that the sun moved around the earth; it still looks that way to our eyes, but we know it is not so, and we have ceased to believe it. It also was believed that the universe consisted of solid concentric spheres; but since Galileo demon-strated that that is not true, the notion of heavenly spheres has vanished from our minds. The other notion, that those spheres are animated, or at least moved, by movers of their own, is now nothing more than a histori-cal curiosity for us. Perhaps some of us still have a poetic hankering for it, but that is all; we may wish it were true, we no longer believe that it is. One of the convictions most solidly implanted in people's minds used to be that the animal species had always been such as we see them. When Boucher de Perthes exhibited fossils for the first time, he was cruelly ridi-culed, yet it was the French Academy of Sciences that was making itself ridiculous; the old belief in the immutability of the animal kingdom is now dead, and we feel no temptation to revive it. Why then should not the old belief in God also be likewise dead, now that we know that it is an illu-sion? Indeed, why did Professor Kant continue to believe in it, even to the

---

38 Charles Péguy, "De la situation faite au parti intellectuel," in *Œuvres en prose* (*1898–1908*) (Paris: La Pléiade), pp. 1072–73. In the preceding pages (1071–72) Péguy had insisted that "metaphysical negations are metaphysical operations by the same title as metaphysical affirmations." The "negative affirmations," as he aptly calls them, are "inverted metaphysical affirmations," often more precarious than are pure metaphysical affirmations. Péguy remarks in the same vein con-cerning the belief in an eternal life: to refuse to believe it is just as metaphysical an operation as to believe it (p. 1073).

point of demonstrating its necessity in a new way after he himself had established it was an illusion?

The difference of the notion of God from the others is that, in all the other cases, what was at stake was some illusion of imagination, while what is at stake in the case of the notion of God is, in Kant's own words, an illusion of reason. An amazing notion indeed, but one which we should nevertheless subscribe to if the illusory character of the belief in God were really demonstrated. As a matter of fact, Kant did not even attempt to demonstrate it. All he did was to ask himself: Is the certitude of that notion of the same nature as that of the scientific notions that constitute the science of Newton? The answer, of course, has to be negative; but this simply means that as soon as you stop asking metaphysical questions, you cease getting metaphysical answers. If it is asked why we should go on asking metaphysical questions, the answer is because thought is by its very essence metaphysical. To think is to think being and about being. If being is an illusion, transcendental or not, then thinking itself is an illusion; at least knowing is an illusion and we should quit worrying about all problems related to it. Science would then remain possible, but the very notion of science itself would lose its intelligibility.

This takes us back to the remark that all proofs of the existence of God are essentially metaphysical, and that the proofs are all related to the essentially metaphysical notion of being, conceived as transcending species, genus, and any conceivable particular determinations, but as including them at the same time as it transcends them. The considerable task of analyzing the metaphysical notion of being is not my concern now. My present point is that anyone losing sight of that notion, because he substitutes physical being for it, by the same token loses sight of the idea of God. As he ceases to see the notion, it is no wonder that its object ceases to exist for him.

By a strange coincidence, that very peripety marked the personal evolution of Kant himself. When one says that Kant proved that the notion of God is a transcendental illusion, we should ask, which Kant, and at what time of his life? In 1764, answering a question asked by the Academy of Berlin, Kant wrote his *Inquiry Into the Distinctness of the Principles of Natural Theology and Morals.* He then found himself at grips with the problem of what it is possible to know about God. Realizing the immensity of the task to examine all that all philosophers had said on the question, Kant contented himself with observing that "the capital notion that presents itself to the metaphysician here is the absolute necessity that there actually be some being." In addition, he said, "To grasp it, one first should ask *whether it is possible that there should be absolutely nothing?* For he who asks the question is bound to realize that where no *existence* is given, there remains nothing to be *thought* nor, generally speaking, any possibility of any kind, so that he must only look for what is to be found at the origin of all possibility. That reflection will broaden itself and thus establish the determined concept of the absolutely necessary being."

It is to be regretted that Kant reached that point but then seemed to lose courage and did not proceed along that metaphysical way. It is true that that was the Wolffian way of possibility, which ultimately proves to be a metaphysical blind alley. In a realistic epistemology, the question: *Could there be nothing?* does not arise, because in fact there is something, and if it were possible that nothing should be, there would be nothing. Not only would there be no thought, as Kant says, but Kant himself would not be there to ask the question. Because something is, then, there is necessary being, for actual reality is necessary by right. The only question still to be asked about it is: In all that necessary being, what has a right to be called God? A thought that moves within being also moves within actual existence from the very first moment of its inquiry; similarly, it moves within necessity, proceeding as it does from conditioned necessities to absolute necessity. The question then cannot possibly be whether or not there is a God, for that is beyond doubt; the question is what, or who, is our God?

The idea that the contemporary position on the question is new is an illusion. There is nothing new about materialism. Augustine himself had first been a materialist, and today he might well be a Marxist; but if he were, he would again ask matter, along with all the goods it contains—including the social and economic—Are you my God? And with a loud voice they still would answer: We are not thy God. Augustine then would perhaps ask Kant: Is the voice of duty my God? But moral conscience too would answer with a loud voice: I am not thy God; for indeed in what light do I see what is right and just, and how is it that every man, consulting his own reason, spontaneously agrees with other men as to what is true and false, morally right and wrong? If there is anything above man, Augustine asked, shall not we agree that it is God? Yes, Comte says, and that is Humanity; and yes again, Nietzsche agrees, the Superman is God. But humanity and superman do not take us far beyond man, and so our end is in our beginning. If God is a strictly transcendent being, even the false gods we are being offered are witness to the true one. True atheists are not scarce; they do not exist, because true atheism—that is, a complete and final absence of the notion of God—is not only difficult, it is impossible. What indeed exists is an immense crowd of people who do not think of God, and perhaps a still larger crowd of worshipers of false gods, but that is something different from consciously accepting the world and man, without any further explanation, as self-sufficient cause and end. There is indeed ample justification for doubt, hesitations, and uncertainties in man's seeking for the true God, but the very possibility of such a quest presupposes—no, it implies—that the problem of the existence of God remains for the human mind a philosophical inevitability.

The Idea of God

RECENT BOOKS AND
ARTICLES

BADO, WALTER, S. J. "What Is God? An Essay on Learned Ignorance," in *The Modern Schoolman*, XLII (November, 1964), 3–32.

BARTH, KARL. *Anselm: Fides Quaerens Intellectum. (Faith in Search of Understanding.)* English Translation by I. W. ROBERTSON. New York: Meridian Books, 1962 (paperback).

BORNE, E. *Atheism*. New York: Hawthorn Books, 1961.

CHRISTIAN, W. A. *Meaning and Truth in Religion*. Princeton: Princeton University Press, 1964.

COLLINS, JAMES. *God in Modern Philosophy*. Chicago: Henry Regnery Co., 1959.

———. "Philosophy and Religion," in *The Great Ideas Today 1962*, ed. by ROBERT M. HUTCHINS and MORTIMER J. ADLER. Chicago: Encyclopædia Britannica, Inc., 1962, pp. 314–72.

Commonweal. "God: Commonweal Papers (1)." LXXXV (February 10, 1967).

Continuum. Issue devoted to the contemporary experience of God. V (Winter, 1967).

DANIÉLOU, J. *God and the Ways of Knowing*. New York: Meridian Books, 1957.

DIRSCHERL, D. (ed.). *Speaking of God*. Milwaukee: Bruce Publishing Co., 1967.

FABRO, CORNELIO. *God in Exile: A Study of the Internal Dynamic of Modern Atheism from Its Roots in the Cartesian Cogito to the Present Day*. Westminster, Md.: Newman Press, 1968.

FERRÉ, FREDERICK. *Basic Modern Philosophy of Religion*. New York: Charles Scribner's Sons, 1967 (paperback).

FLEW, ANTONY. *God and Philosophy*. New York: Harcourt, Brace and World, 1966.

FLEW, ANTONY, and MACINTYRE, ALASDAIR (eds.). *New Essays in Philosophical Theology*. New York: The Macmillan Co., 1955, 1964 (paperback).

GILSON, ETIENNE. *A Gilson Reader*. Selected Writings of Etienne Gilson, ed. by ANTON C. PEGIS. Chapter 12, "God and Christian Philosophy," pp. 192–209. Garden City: Hanover House, 1957.

HARTSHORNE, C. *Anselm's Discovery: A Reexamination of the Ontological Proof for God's Existence*. LaSalle, Ill.: Open Court Publishing Co., 1966 (paperback).

———. *A Natural Theology for Our Time*. LaSalle, Ill.: Open Court Publishing Co., 1967.

HICK, J. H., and McGILL, A. C. (eds.). *The Many-faced Argument: Recent Studies on the Ontological Argument for the Existence of God*. New York: The Macmillan Co., 1967 (paperback).

JOHNSON, O. A. "God and St. Anselm," in *The Journal of Religion*, XLV (October, 1965), 326–34.

LACROIX, J. *The Meaning of Modern Atheism*. New York: The Macmillan Co., 1965.

LEFEVRE, PERRY. *Philosophical Resources for Christian Thought*. New York: Abingdon Press, 1968.

LUBAC, H. DE. *Discovery of God*. New York: P. J. Kenedy and Sons, 1960.

MATSON, W. I. *The Existence of God*. Ithaca: Cornell University Press, 1965.

MURRAY, J. C. *The Problem of God*. New Haven: Yale University Press, 1964.

NEVILLE, ROBERT C. *God the Creator: On the Transcendence and Presence of God*. Chicago: University of Chicago Press, 1968.

NOGAR, RAYMOND J., O. P. "The God of Disorder," in *Continuum*, IV (Spring, 1966), 102–13.

PHILLIPS, D. Z. (ed.). *Religion and Understanding*. New York: The Macmillan Co., 1967.

PLANTINGA, A. *God and Other Minds: A Study of the Rational Justification of Belief in God*. Ithaca: Cornell University Press, 1967.

———. (ed.). *The Ontological Argument: From St. Anselm to Contemporary Philosophers*. Garden City: Doubleday Anchor Books, 1965 (paperback).

SIX, J. E. *L'athéisme dans la vie et la culture contemporaines*. 2 vols. Paris: Desles, 1967–68.

SMART, N. *Philosophers and Religious Truth*. London: SCM Press, Ltd., 1964 (paperback).

SMITH, JOHN E. *Experience and God*. New York: Oxford University Press, 1968.

———. *Reason and God: Encounters of Philosophy and Religion*. New Haven: Yale University Press, 1967 (paperback).

STEARNS, J. BRENTON. "On the Impossibility of God's Knowing That He Does Not Exist," in *The Journal of Religion*, XLVI (January, 1966), 1–8.

VALECKY, L. C. "Flew on Aquinas," in *Philosophy*, XLIII (July, 1968), 213–30.

PART FOUR

THE GREAT BOOKS LIBRARY

MARK
VAN DOREN

*Mark Van Doren was born in Hope, Illinois, in 1894. He received
his M.A. from the University of Illinois in 1915; his first critical
work,* Thoreau, *appeared the following year. He took his Ph.D. at
Columbia University in 1920, and began his distinguished, thirty-
nine-year career as Professor of English there. Simultaneously, he
was literary editor of* The Nation *(1924–28) and its film critic
(1935–38). He is one of the founders of the Great Books movement, having helped to originate the famous Humanities course
at Columbia in the 1920's, and acting for many years as a sup-
porter of and lecturer at St. John's College; his views on* Liberal
Education *were published in 1943. His first book of poems,* Spring
Thunder, *appeared in 1924; a collection culled from numerous
volumes won the Pulitzer Prize for Poetry in 1939. Subsequent
volumes of verse included* Selected Poems *(1954),* Collected and
New Poems *(1963),* The Narrative Poems of Mark Van Doren
(1964), and the latest of some sixty books, That Shining Place
*(1969). He has written novels—*The Transients *(1935) and* Wind-
less Cabins *(1940)—and a large number of short stories; many of
these were gathered in* Collected Stories *(1962),* Collected Stories
Volume II *(1965), and* Collected Stories Volume III *(1968). He is
also a playwright:* The Last Days of Lincoln *was published in
1962, and* Three Plays *appeared in 1966. He has written studies
of* The Poetry of John Dryden *(1920),* Shakespeare *(1939),* Haw-
thorne *(1949), and a critique of ten great poems,* The Noble
Voice *(1946). Occasional criticism was collected in* The Private
Reader *(1942) and* The Happy Critic *(1961). He served on the
advisory board of editors of* Great Books of the Western World.

Great Books of the Twentieth Century in Literature

The latest work of literature in *Great Books of the Western World* was Dostoevsky's *The Brothers Karamazov* (1880). On the assumption that a modern *Great Books* may some day exist, and if so that it will embrace the period, roughly a hundred years, between 1880 and whatever date at which the twentieth century shall by that time have arrived, what works of literature should be included in it? I have been asked to speculate concerning this, and in the following pages I shall do so in the spirit of one who guesses rather than knows. For there is no science of the future, and it is with the future reputations of modern authors that I shall be concerned. Nothing whatever can be known about such things. The mortality of reputations, literary or otherwise, is notoriously high; many a book considered by its contemporaries to be a classic has been ruthlessly beached upon the shores of time. And so it could be with some, or even many, of the books that I shall name. All I can do is use the judgment available to me.

The word *literature*, I must furthermore confess, embarrasses me at the very beginning. How does it happen that the word has come to mean only one kind of book out of the many kinds there are? And worse yet, how does it happen that this kind has been distinguished by the qualifying term *imaginative?* History, philosophy, and science are imaginative too; or if not, they are nothing. The best word would be *poetry;* but that too has lost most of its traditional content. In essence it meant *story:* the lives of invented individuals; or if not wholly invented, then individuals reshaped to suit the poet's purpose. Story is not history, though the two are related; it is not philosophy, though if philosophy is totally absent from it we cannot believe it; it is not science or mathematics, though if the elegances of those are missing in it we shall yawn. Story, then, is story; or as Aristotle put it, poetry is poetry. And Aristotle's three kinds of poetry are still the only kinds there are: epic, dramatic, and lyric. Modern epic poetry is represented by the novel; dramatic poetry by the drama; and lyric poetry by the song and the short story. Even lyric poetry, when it is powerful, has epic and drama at its roots: as song, it implies story; as short story, it implies still more story than it states. I trust it is clear that I have accepted Aristotle's refusal to identify poetry with verse.* When either verse or prose is powerful, poetry is present. It is the power that matters.

---

* *On Poetics*, 1451b4; *GBWW*, Vol. 9, p. 686a.

For practical purposes I shall assume that the modern *Great Books* which may some day exist will have room for as many as ten volumes of literature—I return to the term, again with the desire to be practical, and with the certainty that I shall be understood. And I shall assume that the ten volumes will be generous in size, for I intend to pack a great deal into each one. If in some cases this is too much, the editor can decide what must be trimmed; I shall not be the editor, God forbid. I am not deciding, I am suggesting. I am guessing what books of recent or present time will live. Or perhaps I am only saying what books I hope will live for the simple reason that I especially like and respect them. Here then are the ten volumes.

I. MARK TWAIN AND SHOLOM ALEICHEM

I put these men together, as others have, because they are both masters of humor, and also because each of them masterfully renders a place and its people. In Mark Twain's case the place is Middle America, and the people speak a special English proper to that place. In Sholom Aleichem's case the place is the Pale of Settlement in Eastern Europe, and the people speak Yiddish. It is perhaps only a coincidence that each author's name is a pseudonym: Mark Twain for Samuel Langhorne Clemens (1835–1910) and Sholom Aleichem for Solomon Rabinowitz (1859–1916). The pseudonyms, as a matter of fact, in both cases are pertinent to the material with which the authors deal. "Mark Twain" was a term used by Mississippi River pilots, and "Sholom Aleichem" is still the most familiar Hebrew greeting—so familiar, so casual, that instead of meaning "Peace be unto you," it can mean on occasion simply "hello." Mark Twain was born on the Mississippi River but wrote about it years after he had moved away; he died in New York. Sholom Aleichem was born near Kiev (Yehupetz in his stories); lived in Russian cities before he emigrated, toward the end of his life, to the United States; and died in New York (the Bronx). The imagination of each man, wherever he lived and wrote, was most richly at home in a region he knew to the bottom and deeply loved. Mark Twain never forgot the Mississippi; and Sholom Aleichem, who for decades had entertained and moved the entire Yiddish-speaking world, asked that only these words be put on his tombstone: "Let me be buried among the poor, that their graves may shine on mine, and mine on theirs." The resemblances are innumerable. A further one is that the regions rendered, the places immortalized, have now ceased to be. Mark Twain's Middle America, lazy and remote, mysteriously out of the world, is not there any more; and the Kasrilevkas of Sholom Aleichem, the villages into which his poor beloved Jews were huddled, have been utterly depopulated by Hitler.

Not that the successful rendering of a place is in itself sufficient proof of literary greatness. We must be on guard against the tendency, everywhere noticeable in our time, to assume that the sole duty of a novel, or of any story, is to be true to life as it is lived somewhere outside the story. Its first and last duty is to be true to itself and to human life as every human being knows it; so that the final test of any fiction is its power to convince and move those readers who have no firsthand knowledge of the place where its action is set. Such readers may end up by adopting the place as their very own, and even by feeling homesick because they cannot be literally there. But that is not the same thing as recognizing a patch of earth with which one is already familiar. Poetry, in other words, is not identical with history, as Aristotle explained centuries ago.* Whereas, to our loss, we now tend, as I have said, to identify the two. And yet, as I have also suggested, there is a connection between them. A story has to take place somewhere, and this had better be a place of whose reality we are convinced. Stories without roots in the known earth have little or no chance to survive; the penalty they pay is a thinness, a meaningless abstraction. Whereas the London of Dickens, the Moscow of Tolstoy, the Spain of Cervantes—well, how could we do without those, even though what happens in them is ultimately more important than they are in themselves? To be universal we must begin by being local, and the locality, as I have said, had better be one of whose existence we have no doubt. So poetry must have history in it, as for that matter history must have story in it: must move, must be narrative, must have a beginning, middle, and end as the raw material of the past perhaps has not. But this merely reminds us that the writing of history is an art; so is the writing of fiction, but it cannot do without reference to recognizable reality.

The reality of Mark Twain's two masterpieces, *Life on the Mississippi* (1883) and *The Adventures of Huckleberry Finn* (1884), is a dream reality, I grant; but I do not doubt the reality of such dreams as these. I would include in Volume I the first twenty chapters of *Life on the Mississippi*, written nearly a decade before the huge book to which they serve as introduction, and of course *Huckleberry Finn* entire. The earlier work, someone may object, is autobiography rather than fiction, but I choose to call it fiction, since the river becomes alive in it as only things created do. The fact that Mark Twain was a river pilot in his youth has nothing to do with the final effect, which is of a river, vast and wild beyond imagination, that winds with tortuous force between banks it cuts away, then builds again, as the ocean does its shores. Beyond these banks people live, but not as the river lives, nor as the men who navigate it. Mr. Bixby, the veteran pilot who initiates Mark Twain into the mysteries of points and shoals, is a hero worthy of Homer, except that he is absolutely American too, and his vernacular authenticates itself with every amazing revelation

---

* *Ibid.*

he makes: of the size of the river, of its Protean character, and of the unlikely objects—trees, barns, houses—that float down it like chips in a gutter. The revelations are both magnificent and amusing, for on its grand scale this is a very funny book; the fun, however, being always subdued to the overarching wonder of the element whose vagaries the youthful pilot has set himself to learn. There is a glory in all this that only poetry can achieve; and so I call it poetry, or fiction if you prefer.

Huckleberry Finn is no less centered on this same river, which slides through its pages as if nothing on either shore—no village, no house, no person—counts in eternity as it surely does. There are plenty of people off there, and a goodly number of them have roles in the story before it is finished; but the river is the chief person of the book, unless Huck is— Huck, who lies in the bottom of his little boat and looks at the sky and congratulates himself because at last he has escaped from the respectable world where he will never be at home. He is Mark Twain, if you please, remembering his youth and getting even with the Establishment that wants him to forget it. For he was never wholly comfortable in the world he spent the second half of his life in. Indeed, this is understatement, for he never left off castigating that world, even though the fame and riches it bestowed upon him pleased him. Doubtless he was never more happy than he was as he wrote this book and listened to the priceless dialogues between Huck Finn and black Jim who went with him most of the way. Not only was the river out of this world as any river, independent of its banks, knows how to be, but Huckleberry Finn, thumbing his nose at authority, was also out of any world whose problems are too numerous to endure.

Sholom Aleichem's body of work came into being by the accident that a few sketches he contributed to a newspaper in Kiev were immediately and widely successful; more were called for; and the rest of his life was spent in trying to meet the demand, not merely in Russia but around the world. His fame in 1916, when he died still working, was something not to be measured. More than 150,000 persons lined the streets of New York on the day of his funeral, to which deputations came from both nearby and distant cities and towns. The reason was that his stories—hundreds of them—had spoken for an entire people, and the characters in them had become household possessions, as they still are and will continue to be. He himself had started life in a Kasrilevka; and though the rest of his days were to pass elsewhere, he never forgot his origins. He never lost the accent of the "little people," the obscure, put-upon people whose life was saved from being miserable by the fact of their living it together, with laughter, with shouting, with whispering, with prayers, with curses, with love, with tears. The world he renders is everywhere warm, is frequently ridiculous, is frank in expressing itself, is schooled in the disciplines of want and courage, of no hope and of hope. All that the people of the

Pale really had was themselves and their Bible, plus a deep sense of their ancient beginnings in a world far away from here.

Of these people Sholom Aleichem was a faultless historian. Yet he was more than that, too. He was their poet, their secular psalmist; he was somebody who understood them even better than they understood themselves. And it is here that he emerges as a universal figure. For it is not necessary to be a Jew in order to feel the force of his tales. Doubtless Jews feel it most directly and keenly, but he reaches everyone who has a heart and mind. His Tevye the dairyman is one of the finest creations in modern fiction; and then there are dozens of others who are not the least like Tevye. They may be found in the following stories that I would include in Volume I:

> *The Town of the Little People*
> *The Inheritors*
> *Tevye Wins a Fortune*
> *A Page from the Song of Songs*
> *Two Dead Men*
> *The Clock That Struck Thirteen*
> *Home for Passover*
> *The Enchanted Tailor*
> *A Yom Kippur Scandal*
> *In Haste*
> *Eternal Life*
> *Hannukah Money*
> *Tit for Tat*
> *Modern Children*
> *The Convoy*
> *The Fiddle*
> *The Day Before Yom Kippur*
> *Three Little Heads*
> *A Country Passover*
> *The Lottery Ticket*
> *Hodel*

II. IBSEN, SHAW, AND CHEKHOV

It would be unthinkable, for me at any rate, to begin this volume of plays with any others than Ibsen's. The only question is, which ones? For this dour, embattled Norwegian (1828–1906) tried his hand at many types of drama: tried, and nearly always succeeded. In verse, in prose, in tragedy, in comedy, he had done massive work; and by the time of his death he was acknowledged master of the European theater. Playfulness, perhaps, was the only thing his genius lacked. In retrospect he seems a grim figure, even a scowling one, with eyes set firmly in search of significant themes. And that is the only figure which many see when they hear his name. But this, I am confident, is only because they have not been reading him: have not been in contact with his unparalleled intensity. For he is unfailingly intense; and since he is a highly skillful playwright, he therefore is unfailingly effective. There is a darkness in his plays, indicative of the cold country where he was born and died—though he lived in voluntary exile from it for twenty-seven years. But the intensity is never absent, nor the attention to dramatic detail which distinguishes him among the playwrights of the world.

I have selected *A Doll's House* (1879), *Hedda Gabler* (1890), and *John Gabriel Borkman* (1896). It has been painful to leave certain of the others out, but of these I am sure. *A Doll's House* is well-nigh perfect in its rendering of the young wife Nora who leaves her husband and shuts the door behind her—a famous door that nobody forgets. Nora's husband, Torvald Helmer, is perfect too in his less admirable way; he has thought to make a child of Nora, and he thinks he has succeeded until the dramatic moment when she tells him she must go forth into the real world and find out for herself what it is like. *Hedda Gabler* is no less successful in the handling of its heroine, but she is far from being another Nora, with sweetness in her as well as strength. In Hedda there is nothing but a cold, contemptuous strength, an unexplainable unrest, a cruelty of heart which makes us fear her at the same time that it fascinates us. She is a Medea of the North, with no children to kill but with two men to hurt—her husband and the author whose manuscript she burns— before she ends the play by shooting herself: good riddance to all-but-divine rubbish. *John Gabriel Borkman*, whose hero, a disgraced banker, at first is only heard, not seen, as he walks overhead and broods upon the good he had intended to do with the money he embezzled, is powerful not only because of him but also because of his wife Gunhild and her twin sister, whose mutual loathing at the start is like something out of Greek tragedy. A Greek tragedy the whole play is: dark and bitter, yet beautiful too in the way it works itself out.

It has been equally difficult to choose among the fifty-odd plays of Bernard Shaw (1856–1950), that inexhaustible fountain of comedy who when he stopped bubbling at the age of ninety-four had established a reputation quite as firm as Ibsen's. If he had any hero among his contemporaries it was Ibsen; not that he was anything like Ibsen save in his insistence upon candor as he anatomized the society of his time. He always met resistance and always overcame it—in his case, as he once modestly remarked, by being "unbearably brilliant." His high spirits, his impudence on occasion, his absolute fearlessness, and his genius for dialectic—his complete understanding of whatever it is that makes good talk—these were his comic weapons, and they never failed him. He is the master of comedy in modern times, and that alone would explain his presence here. As for his dialectic, the distinction of it lies in his power to comprehend those persons in his plays who think differently from him; he gives them ample chance to refute him and even to ridicule him, though he never abandons the position he assigns to some character who more or less represents his own thinking. He had stout convictions, but so do all of his people, every one of whom he seems to like at the same time that he finds him—or her—absurd. His plays have sometimes been dismissed as nothing but talk—the essence, as it happens, of the comic spirit. Tragedy is action, comedy is talk. And there is always something more to say.

It has been difficult to choose, but here are my choices:

> *Caesar and Cleopatra*
> *Man and Superman*
> *Major Barbara*
> *Heartbreak House*
> *Saint Joan*

Caesar and Cleopatra (1898) conveys among other things the conviction of Shaw that Julius Caesar was one of the great men of all time, and therefore superior, Shaw thought, to the figure Shakespeare gave him to cut in the great play that bears his name. Shaw's Caesar is witty—of course—and strong-willed: two qualities with which he endows all of his heroes. The story is of how Caesar came to Egypt before Antony did and found another Cleopatra than Shakespeare's. *Man and Superman* (1903) has in John Tanner a man who preaches, somewhat in Ibsen's vein, a doctrine of the "life force"—Ibsen, in his gloomy vein, was forever praising life and light—but John Tanner is Shaw's own man: opinionated, headstrong, eloquent, yet wittily aware of his own absurdity if someone like Ann, whom he loves in spite of his resolution never to yield his freedom to any woman, has the audacity to point it out. This may still be Shaw's masterpiece, despite all the fine work that followed it. It is endlessly engaging. *Major Barbara* (1905) contains in Andrew Undershaft a further vehicle for Shaw's conviction that strength of intellect and will is everything. Undershaft, a munitions-maker, justifies his trade on the ground that it may help men to shoot and kill such abominations as poverty, which he thinks the Salvation Army, in the person of Barbara, sentimentally encourages rather than cures. The dialectic is between these two, and again the adversaries are generously matched. *Heartbreak House* (1919), written in the shadow cast by World War I, is subtitled by Shaw "A Fantasia in the Russian Manner on English Themes." The reference is surely to Chekhov (1860–1904), of whom more later; but Chekhov nowhere has a character as positive in force as Captain Shotover, another of Shaw's frank heroes whose conversation is perpetually salted with surprises. But the fabric of the play symbolically expresses a society which has seen its own fabric shattered by falling bombs. *Saint Joan*

(1923) is Shaw's only tragedy, if indeed it is a tragedy; and doubtless it is, since the death of Joan at the end is truly painful. But even here the razors of Shaw's dialectic go on flashing, for the heart of the play is the series of conversations between Joan of Arc and the authorities—religious, secular—who either try to tell her how she can be saved or else explain to her why she has to die. Once more we have a conflict of wills, and once more the balance is even; for the death of Joan does not absolve those who burned her, even though they had the best of reasons. They represented authority, and authority makes sense, as over and over Joan is told. So, however, does a conscience like this girl's: there is the irreducible difference.

Of Chekhov's plays it would be a temptation to say, as many have done, that their chief value is as a record, or perhaps a revelation, of the decay into which Russian society had fallen by the close of the nineteenth century. And it is true that the prevailing mood in these plays is despair, or if not precisely that, then a sort of witless wonderment as to what life has come to mean. The people are restless; they feel that they are caged; no prospect is satisfactory; they want to be somewhere else; they remember better times than these, and they dream of better times to come; they are absentminded; they are bored. So the temptation is to say: Ah, that is how it was then and there; now we know what Russia was like before the Revolution. Once more we are faced by the question of poetry and history, of the root and the flower. And we cannot dismiss the reality that surrounds Chekhov's scenes. But we must remember that if the only merit of these scenes is their truth to a perishable moment in time, then the chances of their surviving into future ages are bound to be slight, since that moment will surely be forgotten. Was Falstaff, a decayed knight, true to his type in fourteenth-century England? The absurdity of the question is its own answer.

If I did not believe that Chekhov's plays would survive, these three would not be included here:

> *Uncle Vanya*
> *The Three Sisters*
> *The Cherry Orchard*

Sonia and her Uncle Vanya (1897), left at the end in the same predicament that they were in before the pompous Professor Serebryakoff came to muddle their existence, see only monotony ahead of them, only a dreary round of days. "What can we do?" asks Sonia. "We must live out our lives. . . . You have never known what it is to be happy, but wait, Uncle Vanya, wait! We shall rest. We shall rest. We shall rest." This is not the speech of a woman who typifies something; it is the speech of a woman indeed, and she could have existed in any play at any time. The delicate compassion of Chekhov transcends time and place. So does it in *The Three Sisters* (1901), whose heroines are stifled in the atmosphere they must breathe; they dream of Moscow, where they fancy life would be perfect, but they will never get there. Which does not mean at all that the only aim of Chekhov is to expose the limitations of provincial towns. It is, I think, to give us Olga, Masha, and Irina, along with their brother Andrei, exactly as they are: alike, yet different, and all of them unhappy as people anywhere, given the present situation, might reasonably be. *The Cherry Orchard* (1903) could seem to be the best case for proving, if proof was desired, the documentary nature of Chekhov's dramas. The irresponsible Liuboff Andreievna and her still more irresponsible brother Gaieff, who imagines he is playing billiards when he is supposed to be thinking seriously about the future of the estate—his mind is never where *he* is—are so vivid before us that we can have the illusion of being on-lookers at a certain moment when the history of Russia opens itself for our inspection. Yet the vividness is the answer. These people are not copied from anything. They hold their places in the long line—but not too long—of persons that drama has managed to make live and keep on living.

III. LYRIC POETRY

G *reat Books of the Western World* made no attempt to represent the lyric poetry of Europe. The reason is that lyric poetry suffers more than any other kind from translation. The language of lyric is a highly specialized thing, so fine in its effects that only a comparable genius in another tongue can be trusted to carry it over without fatal loss. Rilke's German, Mallarmé's French, Lorca's and Neruda's Spanish, to cite no further instances, have so far failed to find the comparable English, so that readers of existing translations, some of which are of course better than others, still have to believe rather than know how good the originals are. We are left, then, with six poets of England, Ireland, and the United States who in my opinion cannot be ignored. The lyric poetry of the period under review has substance and beauty, and I cannot imagine a corpus of modern literature that would leave it out.

Emily Dickinson.—She was at her best during the American Civil War, but Emily Dickinson (1830–1886) became known only at the end of her century, and it was not until the present century that she came to be recognized as one of the world's great poets. It was in this century too that publication of her work became complete. Only a handful of poems escaped into print while she lived as a recluse in Amherst, Massachusetts; when she died she asked that all her manuscripts be burned; this was not done, but their publication was gradual, volume by volume, until now the total number of her poems in print is 1,775—an astonishing number, and it suggests that she had no other life than poetry, plus of course the precious things—friends, animals, the weather, love, death, God—that the poetry was about. In brief, it was about nothing less than the whole world, which she knew as only genius knows it. Her style is terse to the limit; she lights landscapes, actual or imagined, temporal or eternal, as lightning does. I suggest these poems of hers for the volume:

> *Success is counted sweetest*
> *A wounded deer leaps highest*
> *The heart asks pleasure first*
> *The soul selects her own society*
> *To fight aloud is very brave*
> *I taste a liquor never brewed*
> *I like to see it lap the miles*
> *Hope is a subtle glutton*
> *I felt a cleavage in my mind*
> *At half-past three a single bird*
> *A bird came down the walk*
> *Presentiment*
> *A narrow fellow in the grass*
> *I'll tell you how the sun rose*
> *Elysium is as far as to*
> *If you were coming in the fall*
> *She rose to his requirement*
> *The way I read a letter's this*
> *I died for beauty*
> *I've seen a dying eye*
> *Because I could not stop for Death*
> *After a hundred years*
> *I felt a funeral in my brain*
> *I heard a fly buzz when I died*
> *The difference between despair*
> *She dealt her pretty words like blades*
> *I should not dare to be so sad*
> *I had not minded walls*
> *After great pain a formal feeling comes*
> *I got so I could hear his name*
> *Summer has two beginnings*

Thomas Hardy.—He left behind him in his *Collected Poems* a body of work which in my view far outshines his novels and even his vast drama *The Dynasts.* Hardy (1840–1928) is one of the great English poets, though it takes patience to find him at his best in the huge bulk of the *Collected Poems.* His theory of life was bleak, but his account of it in song and story —he is rich in examples of both—is warm and wonderful. He is most at home in mist and gloom, and then, lo, in brilliant sun. His verse is crabbed and peculiar; but once we are accustomed to his voice it is something we want to keep on hearing. For this volume I nominate the following poems:

> *Hap*
> *Nature's Questioning*
> *Drummer Hodge*
> *On an Invitation to the United States*
> *God-forgotten*
> *The Darkling Thrush*
> *Let Me Enjoy*
> *The Homecoming*
> *The Roman Road*
> *The Pine Planters*
> *The Convergence of the Twain*
> *The Discovery*
> *The Moth-Signal*
> *Near Lanivet, 1872*
> *The Blinded Bird*
> *The Oxen*
> *Old Furniture*
> *Logs on the Hearth*
> *The Head Above the Fog*
> *Weathers*
> *The Garden Seat*
> *"A man was Drawing near to Me"*
> *"If it's ever Spring again"*
> *The Fallow Deer at the Lonely House*
> *After a Romantic Day*
> *The Whitewashed Wall*
> *Epitaph*
> *An Ancient to Ancients*
> *The Sheep Fair*
> *Nobody Comes*
> *The Shiver*
> *Afterwards*

William Butler Yeats.—I can imagine no person who would challenge the right of Yeats (1865–1939) to a high place in this volume. Perhaps the highest; yet, who knows? It is sufficient to say that from his early years in Ireland to his death at 74 he was a poet of commanding importance in the mind of the world. He began with song, he went on in middle life to matters more metaphysical, and then in his old age he returned to song—not with a lilt as in the old days but with a dagger: the dagger of wit. He was a superbly accomplished craftsman at the same time that he reached deeply into the mysteries of existence. He is the most quoted of modern poets in English, and with good reason: he thought priceless thoughts, and for each one of them he found the proper dress. Here are the poems of his that belong, I think, without question:

To an Isle in the Water
Down by the Salley Gardens
The Lake Isle of Innisfree
When You are Old
The Lamentation of the Old Pensioner
The Ballad of Father Gilligan
The Everlasting Voices
The Lover tells of the Rose in his Heart
The Song of Wandering Ængus
To his Heart, bidding it have no Fear
He wishes for the Cloths of Heaven
The Fiddler of Dooney
The Folly of Being Comforted
Never Give all the Heart
O Do Not Love Too Long
His Dream
A Woman Homer Sung
Brown Penny
To a Friend whose Work has come to Nothing
The Cold Heaven
That the Night Come
A Coat
The Wild Swans at Coole
The Cat and the Moon
Easter 1916
The Second Coming
A Prayer for my Daughter
Sailing to Byzantium
Leda and the Swan
Among School Children
For Anne Gregory
Byzantium
Crazy Jane talks with the Bishop
Under Ben Bulben

Edwin Arlington Robinson.—Time has not tarnished the reputation of E. A. Robinson (1869–1935). It was a reputation for wisdom, wit, and singularly delicate feeling which nevertheless delivered its discoveries coolly, with impeccable phrasing. My list of his poems is not long, partly because two of them are longer themselves than might seem to justify my calling them lyrics. Yet "Ben Jonson Entertains a Man from Stratford," possibly Robinson's most famous poem, is one protracted note of extraordinary music; and "Isaac and Archibald" sings likewise to itself. I am certain that this poet will live.

Miniver Cheevy

Mark Van Doren

Old King Cole
Luke Havergal
John Evereldown
The House on the Hill
Mr. Flood's Party
Isaac and Archibald
The Sheaves
New England
The Dark Hills
Variations of Greek Themes
Ben Jonson Entertains a Man from Stratford

Robert Frost.—He wanted his epitaph to be: "I had a lover's quarrel with the world." When Frost (1874–1963) died at 89 he was a man who still puzzled a country that knew him as a familiar figure and thought it loved him as a sage. It did love him, but he was always surprising and disturbing it, or at any rate being quizzical when it thought he should be sober. Robert Frost was never to be caught out or pinned down. New England to the bone, though he was New England only by adoption, he insisted to the end on saying his own say, singing his own song. He had in abundance that most priceless gift for a poet, humor; nor did this mean that he wasn't serious; only, when was he more serious and when was he less? Meanwhile he had published poems which no one has been able to forget; and that is the main thing. They will outlast any of the numerous legends about the man. He remains a poet of world importance, a man speaking with a distinctive voice and saying things of the profoundest kind.

Into My own
Mowing
Revelation
The Tuft of Flowers
Mending Wall
The Death of the Hired Man
The Mountain
Home Burial
After Apple-Picking
The Wood-pile
The Road Not Taken
An Old Man's Winter Night
The Telephone
Hyla Brook
The Oven Bird
Birches
The Cow in Apple-Time
The Hill Wife
Two Witches

Fire and Ice
Nothing Gold can Stay
The Runaway
Stopping by Woods on a Snowy Evening
To Earthward
The Lockless Door
Spring Pools
Once by the Pacific
Bereft
The Flood
Acquainted with the Night
A Drumlin Woodchuck
Desert Places
Neither Out Far nor in Deep
The Silken Tent
The Gift Outright
A Cabin in the Clearing
One More Brevity

T. S. Eliot.—Here is a modern poet in the special and restricted sense which we have in mind when we say "modern art," and mean by that a kind of art that self-consciously breaks with the past. Eliot (1888–1965) was so respectful of the past, so drenched in tradition, that he felt free to continue it in his own brilliant fashion; he never thought of himself, nor should we think of him, as one who ran wild without knowledge of where he was running. His attempt in fact was to restore the greatest tradition of all, the tradition that forces poetry in any age to face the spirit of that age and reflect it without loss or blur. That he succeeded with our age is attested by his great fame; for his vogue, if vogue it was, has never diminished. If at first he sounded strange, and seemed to be in love with disorder, the reason was the view he took of a fragmented culture, a wasteland of poorly remembered things. As soon as this was understood, he ceased to be altogether strange; though the uncanny perfection of his verse will remain strange in the way that perfection always does. His subject matter, satirical in the beginning, slowly moved toward a high seriousness; he became a powerful religious poet. Yet his mind never ceased to play, nor do his final poems truly contradict the poems by which he originally got to be known. He is a haunting figure, destined to last.

The Love Song of J. Alfred Prufrock
Rhapsody on a Windy Night
Morning at the Window
Mr. Appollinax
The Hippopotamus
Sweeney Among the Nightingales

Mark Van Doren

The Waste Land
The Hollow Men
Ash-Wednesday
Journey of the Magi
A Song for Simeon
Marina
Eyes that last I saw in tears
The wind sprang up at four o'clock
Choruses from "The Rock"
Four Quartets

IV. THE SHORT STORY

If *Great Books of the Western World* did not represent what we now call the short story—or the tale, for we use that term for longer stories that are still not novels—the reason clearly was that no corpus of such things existed. It is the nineteenth and twentieth centuries that have supplied the corpus, brilliantly and in abundance. Scattered back over previous periods we encounter tales, to be sure, by Cervantes for example, but these do not bulk significantly, for the form had not been found. The form of the short story or tale may be difficult to describe, but no modern reader is without knowledge that it exists. The product is lyric, not epic; there is no sweep of action, but rather an intense concentration upon one moment, or a series of moments, during which illumination comes. More action may be implied—much action in some cases—but it is not stated. The body of stories that has resulted within the past century is beautiful and important, and it is inconceivable that it should go unrepresented here. The choice has been the problem—of stories, and of authors. I have chosen eleven authors.

Guy de Maupassant.—From the publication of his famous story "Boule de suif" on to the end of a blazing career in France, Maupassant (1850–1893) enjoyed an eminence that has never since been questioned. His people are of many kinds: peasants, priests, soldiers, merchants, clerks, prostitutes—every kind, it would seem. But all of them are driven, as their creator also is while he works out the ironies of their lives; for irony is his matter, as intensity is his manner. The following stories will at least suggest his range:

Boule de suif
Martin's Girl
The Necklace
Yvette
A Piece of String
The Story of a Farm Girl
Hautot Senior and Hautot Junior
The Farmer's Wife

The Olive Grove
A Country Excursion
The Legacy
Miss Harriet

Anton Chekhov.—At about the same time in Russia another master was making himself known. The plays of Chekhov (1860–1904) are few, but his short stories are all but innumerable. Himself a physician by training, he probed the souls of people, many of them frustrated and harassed but some of them happy, with a skill that has few parallels anywhere. Like Maupassant, he worked with lightning speed: no word is wasted, just as no soul is spared his merciless yet merciful scrutiny. I have selected these stories:

Easter Eve
Agafya
The Witch
Volodya
A Father
The Name-Day Party
Gusev
In Exile
The Grasshopper
A Woman's Kingdom
The Man in a Case
The Darling

Henry James.—This man's massive output preponderantly takes the form of novels, but his so-called tales—longer than most short stories, yet shorter at any rate than his own extended narratives—are in my opinion his finest work. Their settings are usually English or European, though James (1843–1916) was American by birth; he lived in England from 1876 until his death. I have selected the following tales:

Daisy Miller
The Turn of the Screw
The Beast in the Jungle

The first of these has for its heroine an American girl, beautiful, innocent, and willful, who goes through Europe without any other thought than that she should behave there as she had behaved at home in Schenectady: her own mistress, free to see whom she pleases and to say whatever is in her mind. Her death from Roman fever is no punishment for this; rather, it is the accidental consequence of a rash visit one night to the Colosseum with a beautiful young man of Rome against whom she has been warned. "Daisy Miller" (1878) lingers in our minds for the lightness of her step and the freedom of her spirit; she was one of James's first

Americans whom he showed against the background of an older world. Not that this is history; it is poetry, or it would not be here.

"The Turn of the Screw" (1898) is James's most famous tale, and one of the best tales in the world. It is a study of evil in the form of a ghost story—a ghost story unless the governess who tells it has imagined it all. Opinions differ as to this; but the evil, whether outside the governess's mind or in it, is real enough for horror of immense dimensions. The pupils of the governess, Miles and Flora, have undoubtedly been corrupted, but by whom? Peter Quint and the former governess, Miss Jessel? The present governess? James does not say, nor would he ever say when asked, just as he refused to name the evil. The great distinction of the tale lies in the very fact that definition is absent; though the thing to be defined is weirdly and profoundly there.

"The Beast in the Jungle" (1903) might seem insubstantial, since nothing happens in it: nothing at any rate of the sort that John Marcher, the protagonist, has spent his life expecting. Something vivid, something terrible, certainly. But at the end he realizes that "he had been the man of his time, *the* man, to whom nothing on earth was to have happened." That is the fate, as it is the sorrow of Mary Bartram whose love he might have returned instead of wasting his days in a jungle of his own mind's making.

Rudyard Kipling.—Kipling (1865–1936) was universally beloved in his time, and the passage of more time has not diminished the force of his best tales, which might be these:

> *The Phantom Rickshaw*
> *The Strange Ride of Morrowbie Jukes*
> *The Man Who Would Be King*
> *"They"*
> *Without Benefit of Clergy*
> *The Mark of the Beast*
> *Rikki-Tikki-Tavi*

All of these except "They" take place in India, where Kipling's imagination was most at home. In "They" there are some children—or are they imaginary?—who may remind us of James's Miles and Flora, but only insofar as their existence is debatable, or rather, the nature of their existence. The Indian stories, now cruel, now tender, reveal a mastery of detail such as only Kipling could achieve. Not that detail is everything in art; understanding is essential too; but Kipling had that, as he had humor and sympathy.

Sir Arthur Conan Doyle.—The character created by this man has no equal for fame in any other character created during the century now past. Sherlock Holmes is familiar around the world: his face, his cap, his pipe, his self-assurance, his apparently unlimited knowledge, and his genius at what he called "deduction." Doyle's success with him, sensational in its time, remains sensational; what we call the detective story, though it had practitioners before Doyle (1859–1930), truly came into being when Holmes and Dr. Watson started talking in the rooms on Baker Street where anything could happen, did happen, and went on happening through endless adventures. England was a web of which this was the twitching center; word traveled here of distant trouble, and in an instant, or at any rate by the next express, Holmes was off to solve and rectify it. With difficulty I have made the following selection; with difficulty, for I like them all:

The Red-headed League
The Boscombe Valley Mystery
The Five Orange Pips
The Adventure of the Speckled Band
The Adventure of the Copper Beeches
The Yellow Face
The Musgrave Ritual
The Adventure of the Empty House
The Adventure of the Dancing Men
The Adventure of the Solitary Cyclist

H. G. Wells.—Before he became a novelist, a historian, and a critic of society, Wells (1866–1946) wrote what has come to be known as science fiction; and in this mode he has never been surpassed. Of his scientific years—but they are more than that, for the imagination in them is serious and civil—"The Time Machine" (1895) may well be the best, though other readers will have other favorites. A machine has been invented which will move backward and forward through time, and in it we travel forward until we are in the year 802, 701. The world then is both different and the same: the same to the extent that it has two sets of inhabitants, the Eloi and the Morlocks, who correspond to the consumers and producers of today; but different to the extent that both sets have degenerated in ways that any reader may see. How prophetic "The Time Machine" may be it will take millennia to tell; yet all of Wells's scientific romances have been prophetic, and this one may be so too.

Joseph Conrad.—Born Józef Teodor Konrad Korzeniowski, Conrad, much of whose life (1857–1924) was spent at sea, became a British subject in 1886 and put the Polish language behind him. His novels are celebrated, but his shorter narratives are no less so. I have chosen among them:

Youth
The Secret Sharer
To-morrow
Typhoon

The first of these has for its chief character an ill-fated but indomitable ship; the second has two chief characters, a young merchant captain and a refugee officer whom he hides in his cabin; the third takes place on land, but a whiff of sea air still blows through it; and the fourth—in my opinion Conrad's masterpiece—takes a ship and its Captain MacWhirr through the terrors of a storm such as never, I think, has had its peer in the pages of any book. The steadfastness of MacWhirr, his incapacity to admit defeat, is rendered with a perfection such as manifests itself in all of Conrad's novels and tales. Steadfastness, fidelity, inarticulate courage—these were the virtues Conrad most admired, and he has no equal in their subtle delineation.

Isak Dinesen.—She was a Danish aristocrat—the Baroness Karen Blixen of Rungstedlund (1885–1962)—who loved Shakespeare and learned to write English; under her pseudonym she became famous in 1934 as the author of *Seven Gothic Tales.* Other volumes followed, all of which had the same quality: stories in her hands became myths, even when the setting was contemporary. She had a magic way of endowing people with powers —beauty, clairvoyance, passion—undreamed of by the realists who surrounded her. Her world is cool, strangely lighted, and somehow perfect. It is a world that time will be helpless to alter. Her position is secure. I have chosen these tales:

> *The Deluge at Norderney*
> *The Supper at Elsinore*
> *The Young Man with the Carnation*
> *Sorrow-Acre*
> *The Sailor-boy's Tale*
> *Peter and Rosa*

Ernest Hemingway.—His world was about as far away from Isak Dinesen's as the imagination can stretch. Not only his world, but the voice in which he reported it. Hemingway (1899–1961) was tight-lipped by comparison, and so were his characters. They implied more than they ever said; and the difference made him famous; younger writers imitated his laconic vein, though most of them failed to put the depth into silence that he did. He was committed to death as a subject, and suffering, and blood; with interludes in which his people, still laconic, nevertheless alluded to such a world—flowing, bright-colored, and beautiful—as Isak Dinesen had always at her command. On the whole, however, bullfights, prizefights, deep-sea fishing, big-animal slaughter, and murder were his meat, served with the sauce of understatement. Of the following stories the last is the best, and indeed it is his masterpiece, partly because the old man in it has a richer mixture of feelings than anyone else in all of Hemingway's work.

> *Indian Camp*

The Undefeated
The Killers
Fifty Grand
An Alpine Idyll
The Short Happy Life of Francis Macomber
The Snows of Kilimanjaro
The Old Man and the Sea

Ring W. Lardner.—When asked what his middle initial stood for, he said "Worm." Lardner (1885–1933) was sardonic to the limit, and diabolically skillful in the art of making stupid or brutal people reveal themselves in speech. It was not that he thought there were only people like that in the world; clearly he believed in wisdom and goodness; but his genius was satire, and he worked at it full time. His gallery of mean and shallow persons has no modern parallel that I know. Readers will visit it for a long time in search of mankind, so to speak, in reverse. He is Swift without parable, he is Timon of Athens without glory. And he is funny as often as he is terrible.

The Maysville Minstrel
I Can't Breathe
Haircut
Champion
A Day With Conrad Green
Old Folks' Christmas
Alibi Ike
The Golden Honeymoon
Some Like Them Cold

James Thurber.—In "The Secret Life of Walter Mitty," he may have made one of the few modern contributions to the world's folklore; for this little man who has daydreams of being big has become famous everywhere that words go, and countless people know his name without ever having heard of Thurber (1894–1961)—the kind of consummation that any author devoutly (and perhaps secretly) wishes. Thurber for two generations of readers has represented modern humor at its highest and best, and his output before he died was so copious that many volumes were needed to contain it. But the three following stories are a sufficient indication of his quality, which was pure and fine, and very funny.

The Night the Bed Fell
The Secret Life of Walter Mitty
The Catbird Seat

It might be objected that the first of these, which is hardly less famous than "Walter Mitty," is autobiography rather than fiction. Certainly it is both; but in any case I could not leave it out.

V. JAMES JOYCE

Joyce (1882–1941) is a literature in himself, and all of his books would belong here were there space enough in a single volume. His genius is such, and his reputation is such, that students of him spend their lives inside his work alone, as if there were no other work in the modern world, no other author worthy of attention. Their devotion is excessive, and yet it is comprehensible. Once he fixes your attention, it is hard to look away. I must be content, however, with the following selection, and even that is long:

> *The Dead*, from *Dubliners*
> *A Portrait of the Artist as a Young Man*
> *Ulysses*

One of the fascinating things about Joyce is his own fascination with language. I do not mean by this merely that he studied many languages other than English and used them more and more steadily from book to book. In college in Dublin he is known to have studied Latin, French, and Italian, and even Norwegian so that he might read Ibsen in the original, for Ibsen was one of his literary heroes. I mean rather, and especially, that language as such—English as such—was the very medium of his imagination, which loved words inordinately, obsessively, and played with them as if they alone were the substance of literature. They are not the substance of literature, nor is it true that Joyce thought so, since his own books have much to say—or, since they are narratives, tell. But his final work, *Finnegans Wake* (1939), is so tortuous with its puns and double meanings, so imbedded in what seems a quagmire, a quicksand, of reference and cross-reference, that only scholars in Joyce have a right to say that they can read it at all. It was the end product of an evolution that conceivably could be called tragic, since it culminated in a book from which most readers are shut out. *Ulysses* (1922) before it had seemed difficult, and it still is difficult for all the familiarity we now have with its contents; but the difficulty of *Ulysses* is less in its language, though that is there too, than in its arrangement, than in the order of its parts. *Dubliners* (1914), at the commencement of this fabulous career, was lucid as any finely written book can be lucid. Yet even *Dubliners* took ten years to get published, and then not in Dublin; for it was considered an insult to Joyce's native city, concerning whose people its stories maintain a detachment so icy as to seem cruel, though the cruelty is now no longer apparent—certainly not in the great short story "The Dead," the last in the book. Indeed there is warmth and depth in "The Dead," though there is no sentiment, a thing foreign to Joyce. The discovery that Gabriel Conroy accidentally makes of a young man in his wife's past, a young man who had died for her in a distant part of Ireland, is deeply touching as Joyce discloses it and immediately after muffles the pain of it in a superb passage describing the snow that begins "falling faintly through the universe and faintly falling, like the descent of their last end, upon all the living and the dead."

The absence of sentiment in Joyce has much to do with another fascinating fact about him, namely, that although Dublin is the scene of all his fiction, and the center of all his thought, he was unable to live there after 1904; the rest of his life was spent in Switzerland, Italy, and France; he was self-exiled as Ibsen was, and possibly for the same reason—a sense of confinement, a fear of being smothered by what each of them felt to be a national sentiment, an organized conspiracy against candor and right judgment. However that was, Joyce at any rate devoted the whole of his art in absentia to the streets and pubs of Dublin, no inch or corner of which he seems to have been able to forget. It was not nostalgia; it was simply that his imagination had all it needed in the region he knew best. And if the tissue of language in which he wrapped this region became ever thicker and richer—well, distance may have had something to do with that, and a consequent sense of Dublin as existing both in and out of place and time: eternally there, a city abstract as well as concrete.

A Portrait of the Artist as a Young Man (1916) is generally understood to have Joyce's own youth in Dublin as its moving subject. Its hero, Stephen Dedalus, in other words, is Joyce himself, with whatever differences art may account for, and doubtless there are many of those. One important difference is that Dedalus was not about to leave Ireland; he is still there in *Ulysses*, where he is one of the two leading characters, the other being Leopold Bloom, who was to have appeared in *Dubliners* except that the story Joyce planned for him was not written then; it was saved for his masterpiece. The story of Dedalus in the *Portrait* is the story of a gifted young man who learns what it is that he no longer believes, and what it is therefore that he must cast out of his mind if he should ever be the artist he hopes to be. The story, then, is the story of how the author became an author: a familiar theme in modern fiction, and one that we shall find again in Proust. What Dedalus rejects is the religion that has been taught him, and the national sentiment. "Look here," he says at the end, "I will not serve that in which I no longer believe, whether it call itself my home, my fatherland, or my church: and I will try to express myself in some mode of life or art as freely as I can and as wholly as I can, using for my defense the only arms I allow myself to use, silence, exile, and cunning." This was Joyce's own program, as the sequel showed; nor was the final entry in Stephen's diary irrelevant to that program: "So be it. Welcome, O life! I go to encounter for the millionth time the reality of experience and to forge in the smithy of my soul the uncreated conscience of my race."

"The uncreated conscience of my race"—a deeply interesting phrase in view of the Dublin, and the Ireland, we find laid open to our gaze in *Ulysses,* whose world is as far removed from the glory of Homer as the world of T. S. Eliot's *Waste Land* was removed from the time when Shakespeare wrote the beautiful unearthly lines that now and then drift into the text as if to underscore the fall from grace that twentieth-century man has committed. The point in either case, if the word "conscience" be remembered, was that the modern world was degenerate without knowing it was; was even, in fact, proud of its ignorance of all that it once had been. The title *Ulysses* is of crucial importance; the parallel with Homer* is always present. Stephen Dedalus, still an unformed youth, stumbling through Dublin with no sense of direction, is searching for his spiritual father, and finds him, more or less, in Leopold Bloom, the central character of the novel. Bloom, a Dublin Jew, has come to little or nothing in his own life, and Molly his wife is about as far from Penelope as a woman could be—her reverie at the close, a single sentence forty-six pages long, is quite as obscene as the censors thought, who for decades prevented the book from being sold above the counter—but Bloom has a rich inner life which he keeps wholly to himself, so that only the reader knows it. He has a scientific imagination; he remembers all the things he has ever read, and he is well-read; he is decent and sensitive; he would be a hero if he could. The scene in which he takes Stephen home with him at the end of the twenty-four hours which the entire action of the book covers is in some sense an unsatisfactory scene, and intentionally so; there is nothing like the recognition of Odysseus by Telemachus;† the climax is anticlimax at the best. Yet it is a kind of climax; the one, Joyce seems to be suggesting, that Dublin now deserves, just as Molly's reverie is all that Bloom, poor good fellow, has the potency to inspire.

Of course I have mentioned only three persons in a book that seems to contain thousands, so rich it is in character and event, so noisy with talk, so overlaid with meanings new and old. A behemoth among modern novels, it rages with energy throughout, and is brilliant everywhere. To read it is a discipline, but the discipline is something that any successful reader must consider to have been worth acquiring. Most of the world's fiction since its day has been formed or influenced by it. It is a monument that time will not overturn; or so I guess.

VI. MARCEL PROUST

Remembrance of Things Past, that endless novel—but endlessly absorbing, too—in which Proust (1871–1922) recaptured his life, appeared between 1913 and 1927 in seven parts:

---

* *The Odyssey; GBWW,* Vol. 4.
† *Ibid.,* Book 16; *GBWW,* Vol. 4, p. 274a.

Doubtless not all of its thousands of pages can be crammed into the present volume, but it would be wonderful if they could, for the work, however long drawn out, is still one piece, and I can merely recommend that as much of it as possible, beginning with the beginning, be included. If it has to be cut off after *The Guermantes Way*, so be it. But what a pity to lose *Cities of the Plain*, and the next two parts dealing with Albertine, and the final part that draws so many threads together.

I shall discuss it all, for I do not know how to separate its themes that are one theme, any more than Proust knew how to hurry his novel toward its end. Asthmatic since childhood, he sealed himself at last into a cork-lined room and did nothing but write in a race with death; the last three parts appeared posthumously in France, when the fame of the work was already firmly established; yet he never skimped his task, he continued at the leisurely, looping pace he had started with. The pace is leisurely without ever seeming slow, or, at any rate, dull. The analysis of action and motive, the description of landscapes and rooms, the carrying out of every impression and thought to the finest end—these ought to make for tedium, but strangely they do not, in spite too of sentences so long that sometimes they run for pages. The reason is the author's saturation with his subject, which infects us so that we are with him wherever he is, wanting to know what he wants to know; for the story is of how he gradually learns the truth about a number of things—the truth from other points of view in the beginning, then finally, or more or less finally, from his own. More or less, because the relativity of truth is constantly announcing itself in this novel that seems to occupy all space, all time.

I remarked of Joyce's *Ulysses* and indeed of all the works of Joyce that their central subject was the preparation of the author for becoming the author he was; and I said that this would also be true of *Remembrance of Things Past*. It is still more true. The narrator of *Remembrance of Things Past*, a boy named Marcel who grows older with every volume, and who writes the entire work in the first person, has ambitions to be a writer; it is assumed by his family and friends that that is what he will become; and he does, he tells us, from the moment when as a man he tastes a little cake, a madeleine soaked in tea, such as he had loved when he was a child—tastes the cake, and there by some miracle his own past lies around him like a living thing. So he starts to put it down in words; goes on; branches out into further landscapes that are folded within these like Chinese boxes; remembers persons, places, things; peers at them passionately in order to make sure that he understands their relations to one another; thence on and on to what of course could never be an end, except that one is satisfactorily present in a final sentence which shows him still wanting to live long enough—naturally he did not—to understand absolutely everything.

The narrator is named Marcel, and much of what he remembers is what Marcel Proust remembered. Yet the novel is so much more than this that it lives in its own right as a work of the imagination. It finally makes no difference which Marcel is telling us these things, the author himself or a person he has invented. I for one, notwithstanding the parallels that scholars in the subject keep finding between persons inside and outside *Remembrance of Things Past*—so-and-so is identified as so-and-so—prefer to take the whole thing as a glorious fiction, illuminated by laws of its own making and true as poetry is true. In other words, I insist on believing that it is the Marcel of the book, not the Marcel whose last name was Proust, who tells what he remembers. And what he remembers! The list of persons whom *we* shall remember is long and long, beginning with Marcel's mother and grandmother in the country house at Combray, and Françoise, the old servant whom Marcel will never be able to do without, either at Combray or later on in Paris, when he will live in a house connected with the great house of the Duc de Guermantes and the Duchess—live there with Albertine as his prisoner. But this is to anticipate, as it also is to make any mention of the fabulous Guermantes, although they are neighbors of Marcel's family in the country too, and never indeed are out of Marcel's mind; as M. Charles Swann is not, a friend of his parents who made a disastrous marriage with the courtesan Odette—disastrous, yet he survived it, and in fact their daughter, Gilberte, was the first girl whom Marcel loved, long before he met Albertine at Balbec, the seaside resort on the coast of Normandy where she and the girls who were her friends came and went from sight like little waves from the deep, and she herself was to obsess Marcel through most of the years of his life, though he was finally to banish her from his bed and she was to die of an accident in Balbec.

I realize suddenly how hopeless it is to attempt a synopsis of this book, whose component parts weave in and out of our attention, entangled from beginning to end in a tissue which holds them all and never lets any one of them fly off by itself. I know I am suggesting confusion; but there is no confusion. Every detail, of person or of place, is clear as dreams are clear, even though, as is true in dreams, emphasis and meaning are constantly in process of change: of change into still greater clarity, for many things that Marcel begins by thinking of as fixed are by no means fixed, and characters will shift and recombine as the bits of colored glass do in a kaleidoscope, or as details in a magic-lantern picture are clarified when

301

the focus is perfected. The focus here is always being altered as Marcel learns more and more; as for instance in the case of the Baron de Charlus, another friend of Marcel's family who never disappears out of the work, though he grows more and more monstrous as the work proceeds. He is the arch-homosexual of a book that contains many of his tribe, not only in the section called *Cities of the Plain* (the French title is *Sodome et Gomorrhe*) but everywhere else as well. The jealousy that devours Swann is not only of the men who may be Odette's lovers but of the women who perhaps have been, or for that matter still are. And the jealousy that consumes Marcel—for the novel is among other things a study of this universal passion in all of its phases—has the same base: a suspicion, which time makes a certainty, that Albertine's girl friends are Lesbian friends.

But I still have only begun to name the persons who throng this book. Bloch, Marcel's friend. Bergotte, the novelist. The Marquis de Norpois. The Marquise de Villeparisis. The composer Vinteuil and his daughter (also a Lesbian). The Verdurins, who maintain a salon which they think is the last word in elegance, but they are absurdly ignorant of who anyone is. Robert de Saint-Loup, who deserves a paragraph to himself. Elstir, the painter. The Prince and Princesse des Laumes. The Princesse de Parme. The actress Berma. And there are hundreds more, for all of France seems to be here; not only the Faubourg Saint-Germain where the nobility have fabulous parties in fabulous houses, but seaside inns as well, and apartments of the middle class, and at the bottom of the scale the terrible room where Charlus, far gone in his vice, hires young men to flog him with a cat-o'-nine-tails studded with nails. These young men have no idea who the Baron is; and neither in the last analysis does Marcel think *he* does; for he refrains from judging his old friend, as indeed he exercises a similar restraint throughout his unending memoir. It is as if he thought of himself as a historian merely; such and such things happened, and he slowly became aware of what they meant.

Remembrance of Things Past is not the history of France between 1880 and 1920, though the Dreyfus case is at one point much in evidence, and World War I is important in the closing part. Nor is it sociology, though the wealthy and functionless nobility of the Faubourg might seem at moments to be the object of a student's scrutiny. No, it is fiction; which is to say that it is poetry. Seldom has any poem contained so much, or been so memorable. If portions of it seem evanescent and trivial, if the dukes and duchesses have their preposterous side as well as their overwhelming reality in Marcel's dream, then we can say, as I have said in another place, that *Remembrance of Things Past* lacks the solidity of Homer's and Tolstoy's poetry, where the whole world is somehow present and looks exactly like what it is. This world is a special one, even a decayed one, and doubtless that is a limitation. Nothing like it, nevertheless, has come to view in modern literature, and it would be as wrong to leave it out of the present set as it would be to leave out *Ulysses,* or certain other large works still to come; or as it would have been to leave out *Huckleberry Finn,* the stories of Sholom Aleichem, and the plays of Ibsen and Shaw.

VII. THOMAS MANN

Mann's *Joseph and His Brothers* (1933–44) is not as long as *Remembrance of Things Past,* but it is long, and Proust's title would be a perfect fit for it if its own title were not the simple one it doubtless ought to bear. It is concerned with time—centuries of it in this case—and it has a comic overcast comparable with that which I might have noted, and did not, in *Remembrance of Things Past.* The events in it are serious events, but the view taken of them is so long a view that any suggestion of tragedy dissipates in the perspective Mann (1875–1955) establishes. The end of course is happy—Joseph is reunited with his father, Jacob— but that is not what I mean. I have in mind rather the great stretch of time that takes the edge of crisis off things and renders them equal, so that no one thing is more crucial than any other. The comic spirit— man's profoundest invention—has never been more at home than it has been in the modern novel, as the masterpieces of Joyce, Proust, and Mann alone would attest. The emphasis in those masterpieces is upon perspectives that shift even as we watch them, so that judgments we have been tempted to pass have to be reconsidered; the truth is richer than at first it seemed to be, and its outlines more multiple. The spirit of comedy likes to view things from all angles, and insists upon suspended judgment. That is why it takes its time; why it is willing to be long; and why on the way it delights in the kind of conversation that dissolves barriers even while it illuminates the field of vision.

Joseph and His Brothers is forty-five times as long as the portion of *Genesis* where we first find the story.* *Genesis,* we may be inclined to suppose, did its job perfectly; and so it did, for the story of Joseph there is one of the finest in the world. Why then did Mann retell it as he did? The answer is that he wanted to write a novel, not a fable or a tale, and that he hoped to exhaust all of the possible meanings the Bible left unexplored. The Bible was interested, there as elsewhere, only in what Mann calls "the facts," and it knew how to put those down so that they would stay put, as certainly they have. Mann, respecting his original so much that he never departed from it in any essential, went on to fill in the interstices between the doings, the gaps where there was no psychology; for in the Bible there is no psychology, no discussion of reasons why things are done; the people do them and that is that. It is possible that

---

* *Genesis,* 37:39–50.

in the very longest run this is still the best way to proceed, since there are fashions in psychology, and what is said about motives in one age may be unintelligible in another. In the case of the Joseph story, however, we may congratulate ourselves upon having both things: the tale and the novel. For *Joseph and His Brothers* was not intended as a substitute for the biblical narrative which its author constantly refers to. It was intended as an elaboration of it in terms, among other things, of time. It was intended as a celebration of the immemorial quality, the ageless truth, that, if we only know how to look for it, we can find in any ancient tale that has come down to us.

Mann commences not with Joseph but with the deep well of time down which we can peer and see his forefathers, all of whom look like him and like one another, though there are differences too, since men are both the same and other: the same in that they are men, and other in that they are individuals, are unique. Yet comedy is less interested in the uniqueness than in the sameness. The same things happen over and over in human time; the actors in tales are barely distinguishable from one another, given enough of that human time; and comedy rubs its hands over this, because the last thing it cherishes is novelty. It rejoices because there is nothing new under the sun; because fathers and sons have forever been what they are today; and because, when a father has a favorite son, and says so, he is committing an error so ancient that nobody can remember when the consequences were not thus and so. Error is possibly the wrong word here; the partiality of Jacob for his brilliant and beautiful boy Joseph was something we might have felt had we been he. Which is precisely the point, and which has nothing to do with the consequences of whatever it was if it wasn't error. Comedy passes no judgments in such cases; it simply remembers and nods its head.

Abraham, Isaac, and Jacob in his early days are figures, then, in the deep well of time at the edge of which Mann stands at the beginning of his epic, looking down and down. Soon enough, however, Joseph rises out of the well and takes over: Joseph, and his brothers who hate him because their common father so obviously adores him and favors him. Joseph even adores himself; he takes it for granted that any boy as bright as he must be lovable, as indeed he is. His vanity is something that Mann handles with great delicacy and skill. It is not a vice, not a sin; it is entirely natural. But so is the hatred of the brothers, and soon enough there is the selling of Joseph into captivity, and his disappearance from the family view for all the years that it takes him to get to Egypt and to become indispensable there; for his brightness and his beauty never fail him, and though he begins by being Potiphar's Hebrew slave he ends by being in effect his master, whom neither Potiphar nor his wife can live without.

It is this section that Mann most lavishly embroiders. The court of

Pharaoh, the household of Potiphar, the whole splendor of Egypt unroll before us in a profusion that we cannot help finding wonderful. To old Jacob back in Israel, grieving for his son whom he considers dead, all this would not be beautiful; or if it were, the beauty would have about it the terrible aspect that things Egyptian had for every Jew, and that they would continue to have after Moses in later times. Egypt for Israel was a corrupt place, worshiping death and defiling life; it was incapable of simplicity, it was unable to conceive the mightiness of an altogether invisible God. But Joseph enjoyed himself there, rose in rank and privilege, learned the secrets of the place, and one day found himself beloved by the wife of Potiphar. He did not return this love, yet it somehow pleased him. As for Potiphar's wife, it meant nothing but agony until she could revenge herself by getting Joseph thrown into jail—where, ironically, his fortunes really began to rise. Before long he is for all practical purposes a prince of Egypt, who eventually marries an Egyptian girl and so seems to cast off all ties to his own race. Yet not so; for there is the famine, and there is the coming of his brothers by whom he is recognized and with whom he is reconciled, and at last there is the swift journey to the Land of Goshen in a magnificent chariot from which Joseph alights to greet his father, come all the way from Israel in a wagon with his family and herds about him. It was a great meeting, and of course Mann makes the most of it, though he does not neglect to have Jacob before he dies predict that Joseph will never have a prime place among the patriarchs of his race. His contribution to that race has been the saving of it, yet the salvation was not spiritual; and so he will not be mentioned in times to come in the same breath with Abraham and Isaac; Jacob does not add his own name, but the Bible does. Abraham, Isaac, and Jacob: those were the First Fathers, and Joseph was never of their company.

If Mann's Joseph did not fully understand this, though in filial piety he accepted it, the reason had something to do with the fact of his being the hero of a comedy. All heroes, whether of comedy or of tragedy, lack self-knowledge at some point. However brilliant they may be, they still cannot see themselves as others see them, or as God does. So Joseph, for all his cleverness, cannot see that there is something much greater than cleverness: simplicity of soul and grandeur of heart. Mann's recognition of this in the case of Joseph is by no means inconsistent with his adoration of Joseph, an adoration we also feel. Nevertheless, Joseph has his limits; and it is Mann's comedy that reveals them. The achievement is classic in our time. Mann left other novels of true distinction behind him, and there may be those who would prefer to find one of them here. But *Joseph and His Brothers*, if only because it is a masterpiece of comedy— I hope it is clear how seriously I take the term—belongs, I think, where I have placed it.

VIII. WILLIAM FAULKNER

Once again the question of poetry and history raises its head. Does Faulkner's distinction lie in the report his novels made of life in northern Mississippi, or does it lie in the use he made—as a poet—of that life as he knew it, remembered it, and understood it? Certainly he knew it; he lived there; and he did unquestionably make use of it, for it supplies his landscape and his atmosphere, not to speak of his people, who may or may not be portraits of particular persons but who have the air of belonging in a world outside his fiction to which he can go whenever he pleases for individuals as well as types. Once again, however, it is the inside world that finally matters: the created world which has a consistency, a hue, that only imagination can explain. The world of William Faulkner (1897–1962), one of the richest worlds in modern fiction, is a world transformed; it is not copied, it is not drawn from what we are in the habit of calling life. It has its own life, and the source of it is Faulkner's genius. Otherwise he would not be here.

Of his many books I have chosen these:

Sartoris
The Sound and the Fury
As I Lay Dying
"Barn Burning"
"A Rose for Emily"

Sartoris (1929), the opening novel in the long series dealing with life in and around the fictitious town of Jefferson, Mississippi—Faulkner lived in Oxford—introduces the two families that always will figure in the series: the Sartorises and the Snopeses, who represent respectively the top and the bottom of Jefferson society. The Sartorises are the aristocracy, the Snopeses the scum. Colonel Sartoris, who had a career in the Confederate Army and who subsequently built a fine house for himself outside of town, is the progenitor of the clan as we encounter it, though in *Sartoris* it is only the ghost of his importance that makes itself felt; he had been murdered, as Faulkner's own great-grandfather, Colonel William C. Falkner, had been. Now Bayard Sartoris, an old banker who will die in this book, represents the family, along with young Bayard who has just returned from being an aviator in World War I, and along with Miss Jenny, the ancient sister of Colonel Sartoris, whose tart tongue has much to tell us about the wildness of the tribe—the wildness yet the beauty too, for this is the only family, except for the de Spains, the Sutpens, the Compsons, the Benbows, and the Griersons, that holds on to the decent, gracious traditions of a past now threatened by the Snopeses. A Snopes, who has worked his way out of Frenchman's Bend, a filthy, degenerate village not far out from Jefferson, is working in the bank, of all places; and he is writing anonymous letters to Narcissa Benbow which disgust and terrify her. Narcissa is to fall in love with young Bayard Sartoris and marry him; but wildness in him, after his return to find his first wife dead, has taken the form of racing a car madly about the neighborhood in the hope that he may kill himself: a consummation he achieves at the end, not in his car but in a plane, and this is a fitting death because another thing that haunts him is the death of his twin brother John in France, an aerial death he fancies he might have prevented. There is much more than this in the book. There is the love, for instance, of Horace Benbow for his sister Narcissa, a love that hovers on the edge of incest, like the love of Quentin Compson for his sister Candace in *The Sound and the Fury*.

The Sound and the Fury, also published in 1929—Faulkner, once he conceived the series, rushed to realize it—is perhaps more powerful than *Sartoris* because it is more concentrated; but the concentration is so intense, and the torment of its people so terrible, that Faulkner scrambled his time-scheme in an effort to make all the events seem simultaneous. The result has puzzled and confused many readers, though the passion in these people is authentic passion, and the book has found an audience that justly admires it. The invention of Faulkner is most impressive, as is the capacity to identify himself, then us, with the suffering of the Compsons. His plot is rich with complications that remind us of Dostoevsky; his eloquence is likewise comparable with that of the Russian master. If it is true, as has been said, that he caught fire midway of *Sartoris* and burned steadily thereafter with a purpose that did not rest until the entire series was finished—if indeed it was finished by anything other than his death—then we have the spectacle of an artist profoundly involved with his material, and an artist, furthermore, who gave it the kind of devotion for which there is no other word than love. By which I do not mean sentiment, for a certain humor in him kept sentiment down. In *The Sound and the Fury*, for instance, Jason Compson reveals himself as more a Snopes than a Compson, let alone a Sartoris. He is one of the meanest characters in fiction and as such stands in cold contrast to the Compsons around him: people with hearts and minds, people with the power, whatever their weaknesses and errors, to touch us deeply, to speak with voices that have music in them, as of course Jason's voice has not.

Within a year (1930) Faulkner had published *As I Lay Dying*, which some students of him consider his masterpiece, though if it is a masterpiece it is a minor one, since the subject matter is slight. Perhaps that very slightness is what recommends it to readers who feel that other novels by Faulkner are thickets of conversation and event through which they must fight in order to reach open air once more. Read with the care he deserves, Faulkner does not justify such a feeling any more than Dostoevsky does, though it is true that his fare can be at moments all but unbearably rich. In *As I Lay Dying*, however, we have nothing but a backcountry family on its way to bury Addie Bundren, wife and mother, in Jefferson where she had always wanted to lie. The father and the children—grown sons and daughters—are of an irreducible simplicity. One of them is making a coffin even before the poor woman who is to occupy it has drawn her last breath. The others, including Dewey Dell, who is pregnant out of wedlock and looks forward to finding some medicine in Jefferson that will make all well again, manifest their simplicity in monologues which give Faulkner full rein with the humor he has in ripe abundance. The story is of the trip to Jefferson in a mule wagon with Addie and her coffin properly displayed. The only trouble is that there has been a heavy rain, so that as they ford a swollen river the mules are drowned and the wagon turns over; but it is righted, coffin and all, and at last the burial takes place—in good time, too, for days have passed since the little procession started, and people along the way are offended by what they smell. It is an idyll for all of this, a perfect rendering—wry, ridiculous, charming, moving—of one far-off moment in Faulkner time.

Faulkner's short stories fill in the crevices between the novels; it is as if he could not bear the thought of incompletion. "Barn Burning," one of the best, brings a Snopes and a de Spain together. This Snopes, certainly one of the worst, a savage, cold, terrible man, is given to burning the barns, or threatening to burn them, of landowners to whom he is bound as a sharecropper; any insult from the landowner, real or imagined, brings swift retribution by night. In the present case Snopes is angered by the de Spains: by the lady because she is outraged over his defilement of her house—he has walked through cow dung and he grinds the residue into her finest rug; and by de Spain himself who gets a judgment against him in court. The story is told from the point of view of Snopes's young son, a boy who cannot bear to accompany his father any longer with kerosene and kindling. He is forced to do so this night, but afterward, when his father has been shot, he walks away as if he were going on forever out of a world whose ugliness he has ceased to be able to tolerate. "A Rose for Emily" deals with a Grierson, Miss Emily, who poisons the man she loves and shuts herself up in her house for forty years with his skeleton on her bed. A grim tale, yet even then a grace note to Faulkner's incomparable saga.

IX. KAFKA, CAMUS, AND ORWELL

I put these three together because of one thing they did in common: they wrote parables. Not Utopias, not satires, though sometimes they are credited with that intention, but parables—stories with something abstract in them, something of the universal under the guise of here and now. Our age has produced many such works, for it is an age even more nervous about the future than appalled by the present; it is an unhappy age, as perhaps all ages have been, but with the difference that commentary grows ever sharper and sharper, and the reference to conceivable perfection—only, alas, conceivable—grows more and more pointed. These three men are not alike, either in subject matter or in power; yet neither are they absolutely unlike, for each of them in his way is writing fairy tales of the mind: a valuable thing to do, now or at any time. And all of them have done it with a distinction that will not be forgotten.

The chief of them for me is Franz Kafka (1883–1924), whose two posthumous novels, *The Trial* and *The Castle*, were to have been burned by his friend Max Brod, as Emily Dickinson's poems were to have been burned by her sister Lavinia; but Brod, to our good fortune, saved them and published them. They are among the most brilliant and fascinating works of the present century, and commentary upon them has been various as well as endless. They are often taken to be satires on contemporary society, but I take them to be something deeper and higher than that. For me they are theological in their bearing: *The Trial*, I think, deals with damnation and *The Castle* with election; or, if you prefer, one is a parable of guilt and the other is a parable of grace. This may sound strange in view of the fact that Kafka was a Jew of Prague (he wrote in German), but it is relevant to know that he had read the Danish philosopher Kierkegaard, and almost knew by heart his *Fear and Trembling*. In any case he penetrated to the center of Calvinist dogma, where he discovered things that most people today are ignorant of—and that, incidentally, is one of the things his books mean.

The hero of *The Trial*, called Joseph K., is arrested one morning for reasons he does not know and never will find out. He is not only arrested; he is interrogated; he himself interrogates the court that has condemned him; and finally he is executed, still ignorant of the cause. There is no cause except that he has been picked out of thousands to be damned—something that is plain to us but is not so plain to him. The women of the novel find him attractive, as they find any condemned man attractive, and in our minds too he takes on a certain distinction because of the mystery that attends his fate. Mystery is the word. Why does God hate this man and love that other? Naturally there is no answer, any more than there is an answer to the famous question, as old as the world, What does he see in her, or she in him? Love, like the absence of love, is not to be explained, though the heroes of these two novels break their very brains in search of reasons why they should be treated as they are. For the hero of *The Castle* has been offered grace, again without discernible cause, but he does not know how to accept the gift, and eventually it seems to be withdrawn, though of this we cannot be sure because the novel does not end.

The courts that condemn Joseph K. are unimaginably complex and impenetrable, so that some commentators have assumed that Kafka intended satire upon the law's delays. Not so, I believe. The parallel is inevitable; and hence the parable. But the gist of the matter is unearthly, not earthly. Joseph K. is damned for all eternity, not because he has broken any law, but simply because it suits the universe to damn him. So with K. in *The Castle*, who comes to a snowbound village at the foot of a hill on which a mysterious building stands, expecting to be admitted because he bears a letter inviting him there to be a land surveyor. But he never finds anybody who knows about the letter, and every attempt he makes to communicate with the Castle ends in frustration—the telephone does nothing but buzz, and the offices up there are too busy with documents to consider his case. The only official whose name he ever hears, Klamm, is so far from being available that K. can imagine he doesn't even exist, in spite of evidence—Frieda, Klamm's former mistress—that he does. The people down in the village cannot understand the aggressive eagerness of K. to gain admittance and be recognized. They belong to the Castle even though they live downhill from it, as Piccarda in the *Divine Comedy* says she belongs in Paradise even though she does not inhabit its inmost circle.* The villagers suggest that if K. could relax he might eventually understand that he is already in and of the Castle, but this is something he cannot do. He remains bewildered by the barriers between him and Klamm, somewhat as visitors to modern business offices are thwarted by telephone operators who say their bosses are in conference, or by receptionists whose desks cannot be passed. So *The Castle* has often been taken to be a satire on bureaucracy and paper work, but again it is vastly more than that. Our paper work provides its symbol, but its essence is something more ethereal altogether, just as its moral, supposing it has one, is simpler than a child could say: When grace is given us we should know how to accept it and should not ask for proof that as a gift it is genuine.

In one sense I am misleading about Kafka: my exegesis of him sounds too solemn. His nimble style—short, plain words that run on and on till the reader, enchanted, is out of breath—and his charming invention—delicious details, always so logical and at the same time so surprising—these are primary virtues in one who would write, as I am certain he did, of supernatural things. Then add to all this that he is often amusing; he is said to have laughed uncontrollably when he read the manuscripts aloud. Amusing, yet, under the aspect of eternity, terrible. Eternity is real in these parables, even though we are not permitted to inhabit it. We merely note that those who stray from it into time—into the ordinary world where we ourselves live—soon become weary, and find it hard to breathe. They are God's fish out of water. And who could suggest this

---

* *Paradise* III; *GBWW*, Vol. 21, p. 109d.

but Kafka? It is my way at last of saying that in his two priceless narratives he came as near as mortal man can come to stating the truth about the moral universe. At any rate, we have from him a pair of classics of the highest and purest order.

The Plague, to which some readers may prefer *The Stranger* or *The Fall*, also by Albert Camus (1913–1960), is a parable in a special and perhaps a limited sense. Published in France in 1947, it is ostensibly an account of something that happened in the African city of Oran, namely, the coming of the plague and the long quarantine of the city in consequence, but who has ever doubted that it is really about the German occupation of France, and particularly of Paris, during the painful years between 1940 and 1945? The model for it is surely Defoe's masterpiece of reporting, *A Journal of the Plague Year*, which seems for all the world to be the account of an eyewitness, though Defoe was only five years old when the plague devastated London. This was a good model for Camus to take, because he must have wished to be as plain, and to sound as unimpassioned, as it was possible for him to be, considering how hard he had taken the occupation of his own beloved city. The parallel is all the deadlier for this calm in the narrator's voice. The details of the plague at Oran are wonderfully conceived and placed. It is a permanent work, and its final paragraph, speculating about the possible return of the plague at some future time, cannot be lost on any reader.

Animal Farm, by George Orwell (1903–1950), which preceded *The Plague* by two years (1945), is of a different order altogether. It reads like a children's story, which certainly it is not; or if it is, it is for children much older than their years. I might have chosen his *Nineteen Eighty-Four*, a savage Utopia in reverse, a Swiftian prophecy so bitter that it is all but unbearable, but the year 1984 will soon be here, and what of the prophecy then? True even now, one might declare, but I prefer to represent this mordant critic of the modern world by a book that so far as I can see need never seem out of date. It is a tale of some pigs who suddenly were seized with the desire to form a perfect society. They did so, and then the society, perhaps like all such things, let corruption in. The corruption in this case consisted of letting human beings in, with the result that before too long the men could not be told from the pigs, nor the pigs from the men. A summary all too brief, but it may suffice to show Orwell's intention. His fable, or if you please his parable, continues to the end to read like a children's story: a bedtime one, perhaps, to be read in the last evening of the world.

X. ALEXANDR SOLZHENITSYN

Russian fiction since 1917 has not been notable for any qualities that would remind us of the great novelists—Gogol, Turgenev, Goncharov, Dostoevsky, Tolstoy—of the nineteenth century. Not, that is, until now, when Solzhenitsyn's *The First Circle* has stolen its way out of Russia and been recognized as the masterpiece of horror—and of beauty, too—which I agree with others that it is. I know I am taking a risk when I select for this hypothetical set of great modern works so recent a one as *The First Circle*, but it is a risk I do not hesitate to take, for two readings of it have convinced me that Solzhenitsyn belongs with the masters who preceded him so long ago, when literature in Russia, whatever difficulties beset it, still was not forced to consider itself an arm of government, a celebration of things as they are. No reader of him will doubt that he deals with things as they are, but neither will any reader be surprised to learn that what he has written could not be published in his own country. The wonder is that he could write it at all, and then get it somehow into the hands of the rest of the world.

Once again, and for the last time, I have to remind myself of the difference between poetry and history. *The First Circle* is history to the extent that it satisfies our curiosity concerning one phase of life in Russia under Stalin. The time it covers is four days in 1949, and the scene is a prison on the edge of Moscow where several hundred scientists are confined while they work on projects assigned to them by the authorities above. They are all political prisoners, and most of them—like Solzhenitsyn himself as it happens—had served terms in Siberian labor camps before they were sent here to work in relative comfort; but only relative, since they still were prisoners of an absolutist government and scarcely needed reminding that they had not escaped from hell; they had merely been moved up to its first circle, as the pagan philosophers in Dante had been sent to spend eternity in Limbo*; and they could always be sent down again, as in fact the hero of the novel, Nerzhin, finally is, for no other reason than that he refuses a new assignment. He will never see the bright world again, nor be again with his wife, Nadya, its chief ornament for him as he is for her.

To speak thus of Nerzhin and Nadya, whom we see only once together during a thirty-minute visit she is permitted to pay him—they may not touch each other, nor say what they really mean except with their eyes— is all at once to make it clear that *The First Circle* is poetry: is story, with a hero and a heroine. Before Nerzhin was told that the visit would be paid, he had been tempted to make an assignation with a girl, Simochka, in the Acoustics Laboratory where he works, but now the sight of Nadya sweeps all such desire away, and when the time comes he tells Simochka so. Were there nothing else in the book, this love story would distinguish *The First Circle* among the novels of the world.

But there is much else—so much more that the range of it can merely

---

* *Hell* IV; *GBWW*, Vol. 21, p. 5d.

be suggested here. There is the prison itself, with dozens of men in it whom we come to know intimately as we hear them talk and watch them work. And the central man among them is Nerzhin, whose integrity—of which he never boasts, for it is something he scarcely knows—provides one of the most moving spectacles I have ever encountered. It is this that I had in mind when I spoke of beauty: the human spirit of Nerzhin, doomed though he may be, is a star in the gloom of a prison so dreadful that the mind reels considering it, a star whose light no cruelty or stupidity can extinguish. The specific nature of this cruelty we discover from what happens to a man on the outside, Volodin, whose story begins and ends the book; and his story has a crucial relation to the story of the prisoners, notably Rubin, who will identify in the Acoustics Laboratory the voice of Volodin as that of the man who had tried to telephone a warning to Professor Dobroumov not to put himself in danger from the secret police. The telephone call had been taped, and it is Rubin—Nerzhin's friend—who makes the identification. The consequences for Volodin are too terrible to print, but that is not my present point, which is rather that Solzhenitsyn's art has thus placed the prison itself in a perspective where we shall always see it. Volodin, a hitherto happy denizen of the bright world, is the focus through which we suddenly peer into the grim interior of a circle, a cavern, a pit, where excellent men who cannot be aware of what they are doing do inhuman things.

Even then I have not exhausted the contents of this long and powerful work. To do so might require as much space as the work itself occupies. But that is true of any masterpiece. I am content to call it that, and to put it last, if only in point of time, among its peers.

BIBLIOGRAPHY

CAMUS, ALBERT. *The Plague.* Translated by STUART GILBERT. New York: Random House, Inc., 1966 (paperback).

CHEKHOV, ANTON. *The Major Plays.* Translated by ANN DUNNIGAN. New York: New American Library, Inc., 1964 (paperback).

———. *Selected Tales of Chekhov.* Translated by CONSTANCE GARNETT. 2 vols. New York: Barnes & Noble, Inc., 1963.

CONRAD, JOSEPH [JÓZEF TEODOR KONRAD KORZENIOWSKI]. *The Shorter Tales of Joseph Conrad.* New York: Doubleday, Doran & Co., Inc., 1924.

DICKINSON, EMILY. *The Complete Poems of Emily Dickinson,* ed. THOMAS H. JOHNSON. Boston: Little, Brown & Co., 1960.

DOYLE, ARTHUR CONAN. *The Complete Sherlock Holmes,* ed. CHRISTOPHER MORLEY. New York: Doubleday & Co., Inc., 1953.

ELIOT, T. S. *The Complete Poems and Plays, 1909–1950.* New York: Harcourt, Brace & Co., Inc., 1952.

FAULKNER, WILLIAM. *As I Lay Dying.* New York: The Modern Library, Inc., 1967.

———. *The Collected Stories of William Faulkner.* New York: Random House, Inc., 1950.

———. *The Faulkner Reader.* New York: The Modern Library, Inc., 1959.

———. *Sartoris.* New York: New American Library, Inc., 1957.

———. *The Sound and the Fury.* New York: The Modern Library, Inc., 1967.

FROST, ROBERT. *Complete Poems of Robert Frost, 1949.* New York: Henry Holt & Co., Inc., 1949.

———. *In the Clearing.* New York: Holt, Rinehart & Winston, Inc., 1962.

HARDY, THOMAS. *Collected Poems of Thomas Hardy.* New York: The Macmillan Co., 1926.

HEMINGWAY, ERNEST. *The Old Man and the Sea.* New York: Charles Scribner's Sons, 1954.

———. *The Short Stories of Ernest Hemingway.* New York: Charles Scribner's Sons, 1956.

IBSEN, HENRIK. *Last Plays of Henrik Ibsen.* Translated by WILLIAM ARCHER. New York: Hill & Wang, Inc., 1959 (paperback).

———. *Three Plays of Ibsen.* New York: Dell Publishing Co., 1960 (paperback).

ISAK DINESEN [KAREN BLIXEN]. *Seven Gothic Tales.* New York: The Modern Library, Inc., 1961.

———. *Winter's Tales.* New York: Vintage Books, Inc., 1961.

JAMES, HENRY. *The Turn of the Screw and Other Short Novels.* New American Library, Inc., 1962 (paperback).

JOYCE, JAMES. *Dubliners,* ed. ROBERT SCHOLE and RICHARD ELLMANN. New York: The Viking Press, Inc., 1967.

———. *A Portrait of the Artist as a Young Man.* New York: The Viking Press, Inc., 1967.

———. *Ulysses.* New York: Vintage Books, Inc., 1961 (paperback).

KAFKA, FRANZ. *The Castle.* New York: Alfred A. Knopf, Inc., 1954.

———. *The Trial.* New York: Alfred A. Knopf, Inc., 1957.

KIPLING, RUDYARD. *Kipling: A Selection of His Stories and Poems.* Vol. 2. New York: Doubleday & Co., 1956.

LARDNER, RING. *The Collected Short Stories of Ring Lardner.* New York: The Modern Library, Inc., 1941.

MANN, THOMAS. *Joseph and His Brothers.* New York: Alfred A. Knopf, Inc., 1948.

MARK TWAIN [SAMUEL LANGHORNE CLEMENS]. *The Adventures of Huckleberry Finn.* Indianapolis: Bobbs-Merrill Co., Inc., 1967.

———. *Life on the Mississippi.* New York: Harper & Row, Inc., 1965.

MAUPASSANT, GUY DE. *Complete Short Stories.* New York: Garden City Books, Inc., 1955.

ORWELL, GEORGE. *Animal Farm.* New York: New American Library, Inc., 1956.

PROUST, MARCEL. *Remembrance of Things Past.* New York: Random House, Inc., 1941. (Also available in seven volumes from The Modern Library, Inc.)

ROBINSON, EDWIN ARLINGTON. *Collected Poems.* New York: The Macmillan Co., 1948.

SHAW, GEORGE BERNARD. *Caesar and Cleopatra.* Baltimore: Penguin Books, Inc., 1964.

———. *Heartbreak House.* Baltimore: Penguin Books, Inc., 1964.

———. *Major Barbara.* Baltimore: Penguin Books, Inc., 1965.

———. *Man and Superman.* Baltimore: Penguin Books, Inc., 1957.

———. *Saint Joan.* Baltimore: Penguin Books, Inc., 1962.

SHOLOM ALEICHEM [SOLOMON RABINOWITZ]. *Selected Stories of Sholom Aleichem,* ed. ALFRED KAZIN. New York: The Modern Library, Inc., 1956.

SOLZHENITSYN, ALEXANDR I. *The First Circle.* New York: Harper & Row, Inc., 1968.

THURBER, JAMES. *The Thurber Carnival.* New York: Dell Publishing Co., 1964 (paperback).

WELLS, H. G. *The Time Machine and The War of the Worlds.* New York: Heritage Press, 1964.

YEATS, WILLIAM BUTLER. *The Collected Poems of W. B. Yeats.* New York: The Macmillan Co., 1956.

ADDITIONS

TO THE

GREAT BOOKS LIBRARY

...iue meditationes que subscripte sunt. que ad ex
citandam legentis mentem addei amorem uel
timorem. seu adsumec discussionem edite sunt.
non sunt legende intumultu. sed inquiete
nec uelociter. sed paulatim cum intenta et morosa medi
tatione. Nec debet intendere lector ut quamlibet earum to
tam plegat: sed quantum sentit sibi deo adiuuante ualere
ad accendendum affectum orandi. uel quantum illum de
lectat. Nec necesse habet aliquam semp a principio incipere
sed ubi magis illi placuerit. Ad hoc enim ipsum paragraphis
sunt distincte ppartes. ut ubi elegerit incipiat aut desinat.
ne plixitas aut frequens eiusdem loci repeticio generet fasti
dium. sed potius aliquem inde colligat lector. ppter quod
facte sunt pietatis affectus.

NE tibi xpe re
demptio mea.
salus mea. mise
ricordia mea te
laudo. tibi gras
ago. Quam uis
ualde impares tuis beneficiis qm
uis multum excptis digne deuotionis
quamuis nihil macias a desiderata pinguedine dulcissimi
tui affectus tam qlescunq laudes. qlescunq gras. noqles scio
me debere. sicut potest conari tibi psoluit anima mea. Spes
cordis mei. uirtus anime mee. auxilium infirmitatis mee.

ANSELM OF CANTERBURY

PROSLOGION

with

A REPLY ON BEHALF OF THE FOOL

by Gaunilo

and

THE AUTHOR'S REPLY

INTRODUCTION

The remarkable and extraordinary character of the idea of God has already been emphasized and commented upon by Professor Gilson (above, p. 238). In all the vast literature devoted to it, one of the most remarkable works is a little book written by a Benedictine monk who was later to become Archbishop of Canterbury. In the *Proslogion* (literally an allocution or address), Anselm argues in what since Kant has been called the "ontological proof for the existence of God" in a way that has provided a touchstone for indicating fundamental philosophical affiliation. Accepting it as valid at once puts one in the group that includes Bonaventure, Descartes, Leibniz, and Hegel and that reaches back, one may say, to Plato. Repudiating it puts one in the group with Aquinas, Locke, and Kant that goes back to Aristotle.

The *Proslogion* has always been a vital text in philosophy and theology, but in recent years it has attracted new and special attention. Professor Charles Hartshorne has devoted a book to an analysis and defense of "Anselm's discovery." Two collections have been published—one edited by J. H. Hick and A. G. McGill, the other by Alvin Plantinga—that contain twenty-two recent papers on the subject.* The logic of Anselm has been studied by Professor D. P. Henry (Oxford, 1967), and the *Proslogion* has been newly translated with a long introduction by Professor M. J. Charlesworth (Oxford, 1965). Three problems, in particular, have been discussed: (1) whether the argument in Chapter Three is only a restatement of that in Chapter Two or a completely new one, (2) whether the proof (or proofs) presuppose faith in God or rely on reason alone, and (3) whether the notion of necessity that is involved is logical, ontological, or both.

Little is known of Anselm's early years. He was born about 1033 near Aosta, now in Italy but then an important border town between Lombardy and Burgundy. Both his parents were probably of noble birth and well-to-do. At the age of twenty-three, after the death of his mother, and apparently as a result of a quarrel with his father about the career he should follow, Anselm left home. For three years he wandered through Burgundy and France, and may have studied at the schools in Fleury-sur-Loire and Chartres. In 1059 he arrived at the monastery of Bec in Normandy, attracted perhaps by the fame of its abbot, Lanfranc, and his celebrated school.

In 1060 Anselm became a Benedictine novice at the monastery of Bec and advanced rapidly to offices of authority. Lanfranc left in 1063 to head a new monastery at Caen, and Anselm became his successor as prior and then in 1078 became the abbot, a post he held until 1093. During his

---

* Bibliographical data is given in the list of books at the end of the Gilson essay.

thirty-three years at Bec, Anselm made its monastic school one of the most celebrated in all Europe, and he himself far surpassed in learning the fame of his master, Lanfranc. Anselm won great reputation as a teacher and during these years wrote most of his books that now interest philosophers. In addition to the *Proslogion*, these included the *Monologion, On Truth, On Freedom of the Will*, and the *De Grammatico*, a logical analysis of the way in which substantives and adjectives signify.

As abbot of a wealthy monastery, Anselm could not avoid being drawn into political affairs. The monastery at Bec was favored by William the Conqueror with grants of land in England, and Anselm made several visitations of them. He was summoned to Rouen in 1087 to hear the last confession of the dying William. Anselm entered fully into the world of ecclesiastical politics in 1093 when he agreed to become Lanfranc's successor as Archbishop of Canterbury. At once he became involved in the long and involved struggle between church and state over investiture. Against the desire and efforts of King William Rufus to assert the primacy of the state, Anselm sided with the pope in maintaining the independence and liberty of the church. Refusing to accept his investiture as archbishop from the hands of the king, Anselm went to Rome and, in effect, into exile in 1097. On his accession in 1100, Henry I invited him to return, but in 1103 Anselm again went into exile. A compromise was finally worked out between the monarch and the archbishop, and in 1107 Anselm returned to resume his office at Canterbury. He spent his last two years in peace there, dying April 21, 1109.

Despite these years of turmoil, Anselm was able to write a number of books, including his most famous and important theological works, *On Why God Became Man, On The Sacraments*, and *On the Incarnation*. He also left unfinished a tract dealing with the logic of modality, that is with the logical behavior of such notions as necessity, possibility, and impossibility—thus marking a return to the kind of logical interest that is found in the *Proslogion*.

In 1163 Archbishop Thomas Becket argued his cause for canonization, and it was probably in that same year that Anselm was declared a saint of the church.

The translation of the *Proslogion* and its related documents printed here is taken from that by S. N. Deane (Open Court Publishing Co., 1903), revised in accord with the critical text of the original by F. S. Schmitt (Edinburgh: Thomas Nelson and Sons, 1946).

CONTENTS

PROSLOGION

After I had published, at the solicitous entreaties of certain brethren, a brief work (the *Monologion*) as an example of meditation on the grounds of faith, by one who is investigating, in a course of silent reasoning with himself, matters of which he is ignorant —considering that this book was knit together by the linking of many arguments, I began to ask whether perhaps a single argument could be found, which would require no other for its proof than itself alone; and alone would suffice to demonstrate that God truly exists, that he is the supreme good requiring nothing else, which all other things require for their existence and well-being; and whatever we believe regarding the divine Being.

Although I often and earnestly directed my thought to this end, and at times that which I sought seemed to be just within my reach, while again it wholly evaded my mental vision, at last in despair I was about to cease, as if from the search for a thing that it was impossible to find. But when I wished to exclude this thought altogether, lest, by busying my mind to no purpose, it should keep me from other thoughts, in which I might be successful, then more and more, though I was unwilling and shunned it, it began to force itself upon me, with a kind of importunity. So, one day, when I was exceedingly wearied with resisting its importunity, in the very conflict of my thoughts, the proof which I had despaired of finding offered itself, so that I eagerly embraced the thoughts which I was strenuously repelling.

Thinking, therefore, that what I rejoiced to have found, would, if put in writing, be welcome to readers, I have written the following treatise, dealing with this question and some others, from the point of view of one who strives to lift his mind to the contemplation of God and seeks to understand what he believes. In my judgment, neither this work nor the other, mentioned above deserved to be called a book, or to bear the name of an author; and yet I thought they ought not to be sent forth without some title by which they might, in some sort, invite one into whose hands they fell to their perusal. I accordingly gave each a title, that the first might be known as, An Example of Meditation on the Grounds of Faith, and its sequel as, Faith Seeking Understanding. But, after both had been copied by many under these titles, many urged me, and especially Hugo the reverend Archbishop of Lyons, the apostolic delegate in Gaul, who instructed me to this effect on his apostolic authority—to prefix my name to these writings. And that this might be done more fitly, I named the first *Monologion*, that is, A Soliloquy; but the second, *Proslogion*, that is, An Allocution.

CHAPTER I

Exhortation of the mind to the contemplation of God

Come now, insignificant man! flee, for a little, your occupations; hide yourself, for a time, from your disturbing thoughts. Cast aside, now, your burdensome cares, and put away your toilsome distractions. Yield room for some little time to God; and rest for a little time in him. Enter the inner chamber of your mind; shut out all thoughts save that of God, and such as can aid you in seeking him; close the door and seek him. Speak now, my whole heart! speak now to God, saying, I seek thy face; thy face, Lord, will I seek (*Psalms*, 27:8). And come thou now, O Lord my God, teach my heart where and how it may seek thee, where and how it may find thee.

Lord, if thou art not here, where shall

eek thee, being absent? But if thou art everywhere, why do I not see thee present? Truly thou dwellest in unapproachable light. But where is unapproachable light, or how shall I come to it? Or who shall lead me to that light and into it, that I may see thee in it? Again, by what marks, under what form, shall I seek thee? I have never seen thee, O Lord, my God; I do not know thy form. What, O most high Lord, shall this man do, in exile far from thee? What shall thy servant do, anxious in his love of thee, and cast out afar from thy face? He pants to see thee, and thy face is too far from him. He yearns to come to thee, and thy dwelling-place is inaccessible. He is eager to find thee, and knows not thy place. He desires to seek thee, and does not know thy face. Lord, thou art my God, and thou art my Lord, and never have I seen thee. It is thou that hast made me, and hast made me anew, and hast bestowed upon me all the blessings I enjoy; and not yet do I know thee. I was created to see thee, and not yet have I done that for which I was made.

O wretched lot of man, when he has lost that for which he was made! O hard and terrible was that Fall! Alas, what has he lost, and what has he found? What has departed, and what remains? He has lost the blessedness for which he was made, and has found the misery for which he was not made. That has departed without which nothing is happy, and that remains which, in itself, is only miserable. Man once did eat the bread of angels, for which he hungers now; he eats now the bread of sorrows, which he knew not then. Alas! for the mourning of all mankind, for the universal lamentation of the sons of Hades! He choked with satiety, we sigh with hunger. He abounded, we beg. He possessed in happiness, and miserably forsook his possession; we suffer want in unhappiness, and feel a miserable longing, and alas! we remain empty.

Why did he not keep for us, when he could so easily, that whose lack we should feel so heavily? Why did he shut us away from the light, and cover us over with darkness? With what purpose did he rob us of life, and inflict death upon us? Wretches that we are, whence have we been driven out; whither are we driven on? Whence hurled? Whither consigned to ruin? From our native country into exile, from the vision of God into our present blindness, from the joy of immortality into the bitterness and horror of death. Miserable exchange of how great a good, for how great an evil! Heavy loss, heavy grief, heavy all our fate!

But alas! wretched that I am, one of the sons of Eve, far removed from God! What have I undertaken? What have I accomplished? Where was I going? How far have I come? To what did I aspire? Amid what thoughts am I sighing? I sought blessings, and lo! confusion. I strove toward God, and I stumbled on myself. I sought calm in privacy, and I found tribulation and grief, in my inmost thoughts. I wished to laugh from the joy of my mind, and I am compelled to groan from the sorrow in my heart. Gladness was hoped for, and lo! sighs come thick and fast.

And thou too, O Lord, how long? How long, O Lord, dost thou forget us; how long dost thou turn thy face from us? When wilt thou look upon us, and hear us? When wilt thou enlighten our eyes, and show us thy face? When wilt thou restore thyself to us? Look upon us, Lord; hear us, enlighten us, reveal thyself to us. Restore thyself to us, that it may be well with us—thyself, without whom it is so ill with us. Pity our toilings and strivings toward thee, since we can do nothing without thee. Thou dost invite us; do thou help us. I beseech thee, O Lord, that I may not lose hope in sighs, but may breathe anew in hope. Lord, my heart is made bitter by its desolation; sweeten thou it, I beseech thee, with thy consolation. Lord, in hunger I began to seek thee; I beseech thee that I may not cease to hunger for thee. In hunger I have come to thee; let me not go unfed. I have come in poverty to the Rich, in misery to the Compassionate; let me not return empty and despised. And if, before I eat, I sigh, grant, even after sighs, that which I may eat. Lord, I am bowed down and can only look downward; raise me up that I may look upward. My iniquities have gone over my head; they overwhelm me; and, like a heavy load, they weigh me down. Free me from them; unburden me, that the pit of iniquities may not close over me. Allow me to look up to thy light, even from afar, even from the depths. Teach me to seek thee, and reveal thyself to me, when I seek thee, for I cannot seek thee, except thou teach me, nor find thee, except thou reveal thyself. Let me seek thee in longing, let me long for thee in seeking; let me find thee in love, and love thee in finding.

Lord, I acknowledge and I thank thee that thou hast created in me this thine image, in order that I may remember thee, think of thee, and love thee; but that image has been so consumed and wasted away by vices, and obscured by the smoke of wrong-doing, that it cannot achieve that for which it was made, except thou renew it, and create it anew. I do not endeavor, O Lord, to penetrate thy sublimity, for in no wise do I compare my understanding with that; but I long to understand in some degree thy truth, which my heart believes and loves. For I do not seek to understand that I may believe, but I believe so that I may understand [*credo ut intelligam*]. For this also I believe—that unless I believed, I should not understand.

CHAPTER II

That truly there is a God

And so, Lord, do thou, who dost give understanding to faith, give me, so far as thou knowest it to be suitable, to understand that thou art as we believe; and that thou art that which we believe. And, indeed, we believe that thou art a being than which nothing greater can be conceived. Or is there no such nature, since the Fool hath said in his

heart, there is no God? (*Psalms*, 14:1). But at any rate, this same Fool, when he hear of this of which I speak—a being than-which nothing-greater-can-be-conceived — understands what he hears, and what he under stands is in his understanding; although h does not understand it to exist.

For, it is one thing for an object to be i the understanding, and another to under stand that the object exists. When a painte conceives beforehand what he will make, h has it in his understanding, but he does no yet understand it to be, because he has no yet made it. But when he has actually painte it, he both has it in his understanding, an he understands that it exists, because he ha made it.

Hence, even the Fool is convinced tha something exists in the understanding, a least, than-which-nothing-greater-can-be-con ceived. For, when he hears of this, he unde stands it. And whatever is understood, exist in the understanding. And assuredly tha than-which-a-greater-cannot-be-conceive cannot exist in the understanding alone. Fo suppose it exists in the understanding alone then it can be conceived to exist in reality which is greater.

Therefore, if that-than-which-a-greate cannot-be-conceived exists in the unde standing alone, the very being, than-whicl a-greater-*cannot*-be-conceived, is one, tha which-a-greater-*can*-be-conceived. But obv ously this is impossible. Hence, there is n doubt that there exists a being, than-whicl a-greater-cannot-be-conceived, and it exis both in the understanding and in reality.

CHAPTER III

That God cannot be conceived not to exi

And it assuredly exists so truly, that it ca not be conceived not to exist. For, it is po sible to conceive of a being which cannot b conceived not to exist; and this is greate than one which can be conceived not t exist. Hence, if that, than-which-a-greate

annot-be-conceived, can be conceived not
o exist, it is not that, than-which-a-greater-
annot-be-conceived. But this cannot be.
Something than-which-a-greater-cannot-be-
onceived exists so truly, then, that it cannot
 even be conceived not to exist; and this be-
ng thou art, O Lord, our God.

So truly, therefore, dost thou exist, O
Lord, my God, that thou canst not be conceived not to exist; and rightly so. For, if a
mind could conceive of a being better than
hee, the creature would rise above the Creator and would judge its Creator; and this
s most absurd. And, indeed, whatever else
here is, except thee alone, can be conceived
not to exist. Thou alone, then, of all things
most truly exists and hast being to the highest degree. For, whatever else exists does
not exist so truly, and hence has less being.
Why, then, has the Fool said in his heart,
there is no God (*Psalms*, 14:1), since it is so
manifest, to a rational mind, that thou dost
exist in the highest degree of all? Why, except that he is dull and a fool?

CHAPTER IV

*How the Fool has said in his heart what
cannot be conceived*

But how has the Fool said in his heart
what he could not conceive; or how could he
not conceive what he said in his heart? since
to say in the heart and to conceive are the
same?

But, if really (nay, since really) he both
conceived, because he said in his heart; and
did not say in his heart, because he could
not conceive; there is more than one way
in which a thing is said in the heart or conceived. For, in one sense, a thing is conceived, when the word signifying it is conceived; and in another, when that which is
the thing itself is understood.

In the former sense, then, God can be
conceived not to exist; but in the latter, not
at all. No one who understands what God
is can conceive that God does not exist;

although he says these words in his heart,
either without any, or with some strange,
signification. For, God is that-than-which-a-
greater-cannot-be-conceived. And he who
thoroughly understands this, assuredly understands that this being so truly exists, that
not even in concept can it be non-existent.
Therefore, he who understands that God
so exists, cannot conceive that he does not
exist.

I thank thee, gracious Lord, I thank thee;
because what I formerly believed by thy
bounty, I now so understand by thine illumination, that even if I did not want to
believe that thou dost exist, still I could
understand this to be true.

CHAPTER V

*That God is whatever it is better to be
than not to be, and, existing through himself alone, makes all other things from
nothing*

What art thou, then, Lord God, than
whom nothing greater can be conceived?
But what art thou, except that which, as the
highest of all beings, alone exists through
itself, and makes all other things from nothing? For, whatever is not this is less than a
thing which can be conceived of. But this
cannot be conceived of thee. What good,
therefore, does the supreme Good lack,
through which every good is? Therefore,
thou art just, truthful, blessed, and whatever
it is better to be than not to be. For it is
better to be just than not just; better to be
blessed than not blessed.

CHAPTER VI

*How God is perceptive although he is not
a body*

But, since it is better to be perceptive,
omnipotent, compassionate, impassible, than
not to be these things, how art thou perceptive, if thou art not a body; or omnipotent,

if thou hast not all powers; or at once compassionate and impassible? For, if only corporeal things are capable of perception, since the senses encompass a body and are in a body, how art thou perceptive, although thou art not a body, but a supreme Spirit, who is superior to body? But, if to perceive is only to know, or for the sake of knowledge —for he who perceives obtains knowledge in accordance with the proper functions of his senses; as through sight, of colors; through taste, of flavors—whatever in any way knows is not inappropriately said, in some sort, to perceive.

Therefore, O Lord, although thou art not a body, yet thou art truly perceptive in the highest degree in respect of this, that thou dost know all things in the highest degree; and not as an animal knows, through a corporeal sense.

CHAPTER VII

How he is omnipotent, although there are many things he cannot do

But how art thou omnipotent, if thou canst not do all things? Or, if thou canst not be corrupted, and canst not lie, nor make what is true, false—as, for example, if thou shouldst make what has been done not to have been done, and the like—how canst thou do all things? Or is the ability to do these things not power, but impotence? For, he who can do these things can do what is not for his good, and what he ought not to do; and the more he can do them, the more power have adversity and perversity against him; and the less has he himself against these.

He, then, who can do these things does so not by power, but by impotence. For, he is not said to be able because he is able of himself, but because his impotence gives something else power over him. Or, by a figure of speech, just as many words are improperly applied, as when we use "to be" for "not to be," and "to do" for what is really "not to do," or "to do nothing." For, often we say to a man who denies the existence of something: "It is as you say it is," though it might seem more proper to say, "It is not as you say it is not." In the same way, we say: "This man sits just as that man does," or, "This man rests just as that man does" although to sit is not to do anything, and to rest is to do nothing.

So, then, when one is said to have the power of doing or experiencing what is not for his good, or what he ought not to do impotence is understood in the word "power." For, the more he possesses this power, the more powerful are adversity and perversity against him, and the more powerless is he against them.

Therefore, O Lord, our God, the more truly art thou omnipotent, since thou canst do nothing through impotence, and nothing has power against thee.

CHAPTER VIII

How he is compassionate and impassible

But how art thou merciful, and, at the same time, impassible? For, if thou art impassible, thou dost not feel sympathy; and if thou dost not feel sympathy, thy heart is not wretched from sympathy for the wretched; but this it is to be compassionate But if thou art not compassionate, whence cometh so great consolation to the wretched How, then, art thou compassionate and not compassionate, O Lord, unless because thou art compassionate in terms of our experience and not compassionate in terms of thy being

Truly, thou art so in terms of our experience, but thou art not so in terms of thine own. For, when thou beholdest us in our wretchedness, we experience the effect of compassion, but thou dost not experience the feeling. Therefore, thou art both compassionate, because thou dost save the wretched, and spare those who sin against thee; and not compassionate, because thou art affected by no sympathy for wretchedness

CHAPTER IX

How the all-just and supremely just God spares the wicked and justly pities them

But how dost thou spare the wicked, if thou art all just and supremely just? For how, being all just and supremely just, dost thou aught that is not just? Or, what justice is that to give him who merits eternal death everlasting life? How, then, gracious Lord, good to the righteous and the wicked, canst thou save the wicked, if this is not just, and thou dost not aught that is not just? Or, since thy goodness is incomprehensible, is this hidden in the unapproachable light wherein thou dwellest? Truly, in the deepest and most secret parts of thy goodness is hidden the fountain whence the stream of thy compassion flows.

For thou art all just and supremely just, yet thou art kind even to the wicked, even because thou art all supremely good. For thou wouldst be less good if thou wert not kind to any wicked being. For, he who is good, both to the righteous and the wicked, is better than he who is good to the wicked alone; and he who is good to the wicked, both by punishing and sparing them, is better than he who is good by punishing them · alone. Therefore, thou art compassionate, because thou art all supremely good. And, although it appears why thou dost reward the good with goods and the evil with evils; yet this, at least, is most wonderful, why thou, the all and supremely just, who lackest nothing, bestowest goods on the wicked and on those who are guilty toward thee.

O the depth of thy goodness, God! The source of thy compassion appears, and yet is not clearly seen! We see whence the river flows, but the spring whence it arises is not seen. For, it is from the abundance of thy goodness that thou art good to those who sin against thee; and in the depth of thy goodness is hidden the reason for this kindness.

For, although thou dost reward the good with goods and the evil with evils, out of goodness, yet this the concept of justice seems to demand. But, when thou dost bestow goods on the evil, and it is known that the supremely Good hath willed to do this, we wonder why the supremely Just has been able to will this.

O compassion, from what abundant sweetness and what sweet abundance dost thou well forth to us! O boundless goodness of God, how passionately should sinners love thee! For thou savest the just, because justice goeth with them; but sinners thou dost free by the authority of justice. Those by the help of their deserts; these, although their deserts oppose. Those by acknowledging the goods thou hast granted; these by pardoning the evils thou hatest. O boundless goodness, which dost so exceed all understanding, let that compassion come upon me, which proceeds from thy so great abundance! Let it flow upon me, for it wells forth from thee. Spare, in mercy; avenge not, in justice.

For, though it is hard to understand how thy compassion is not inconsistent with thy justice; yet we must believe that it does not oppose justice at all, because it flows from goodness, which is no goodness without justice; nay, that it is in true harmony with justice. For, if thou art compassionate only because thou art supremely good, and supremely good only because thou art supremely just, truly thou art compassionate even because thou art supremely just. Help me, just and compassionate God, whose light I seek; help me to understand what I say.

Truly, then, thou art compassionate even because thou art just. Is, then, thy compassion born of thy justice? And dost thou spare the wicked, therefore, out of justice? If this is so, my Lord, if this is so, teach me how it is so. Is it because it is just that thou shouldst be so good that thou canst not be conceived better; and that thou shouldst work so powerfully that thou canst not be conceived more powerful? For what can be more just than this? Assuredly it could not be that thou shouldst be good only by way of retribution and not by way of forgiveness, and that thou shouldst make good only those who are not good, and not the wicked also. In this way, therefore, it is just that thou shouldst spare the wicked, and make good men from bad.

Finally, what is not done justly ought not to be done; and what ought not to be done is done unjustly. If, then, thou dost not justly pity the wicked, thou oughtest not to pity them. And, if thou oughtest not to pity them, thou pityest them unjustly. And if it is wrong to say this, it is right to believe that thou justly pityest the wicked.

CHAPTER X

How he justly punishes and justly spares the wicked

But it is also just that thou shouldst punish the wicked. For what is more just than that the good should receive goods, and the evil, evils? How, then, is it just that thou shouldst punish the wicked, and, at the same time, spare the wicked? Or, in one way, dost thou justly punish, and, in another, justly spare them? For, when thou punishest the wicked, it is just, because it is consistent with their deserts; and when, on the other hand, thou sparest the wicked, it is just, not because it is compatible with their deserts, but because it is compatible with thy goodness.

For, in sparing the wicked, thou art as just, according to thy nature, but not according to ours, as thou art compassionate, according to our nature, and not according to thine; seeing that, as in saving us, whom it would be just for thee to destroy, thou art compassionate, not because thou feelest an affection (*affectum*), but because we feel the effect (*effectum*); so thou art just, not because thou requitest us as we deserve, but because thou dost that which becomes thee as the supremely good Being. In this way,

therefore, without contradiction thou dost justly punish and justly spare.

CHAPTER XI

How all the ways of the Lord are mercy and truth; and yet God is just in all his ways

But, is there any reason why it is not also just, according to thy nature, O Lord, that thou shouldst punish the wicked? Surely it is just that thou shouldst be so just that thou canst not be conceived more just; and this thou wouldst in no wise be if thou didst only render goods to the good, and not evil to the evil. For, he who requiteth both good and evil according to their deserts is more just than he who so requites the good alone. It is, therefore, just, according to thy nature, O just and gracious God, both when thou dost punish and when thou sparest.

Truly, then, all the ways of the Lord are mercy and truth (*Psalms*, 25:10); and yet the Lord is righteous in all his ways (*Psalms* 145:17). And assuredly without inconsistency: For, it is not just that those whom thou dost will to punish should be saved and that those whom thou dost will to spare should be condemned. For that alone is just which thou dost will; and that alone unjust which thou dost not will. So, then, thy mercy is born of thy justice.

For it is just that thou shouldst be so good that thou art good in sparing also; and this may be the reason why the supremely Just can will goods for the wicked. But if it can be comprehended in any way why thou canst will to save the wicked, yet by no consideration can we comprehend why of those who are alike wicked, thou savest some rather than others, through supreme goodness; and why thou dost condemn the latter rather than the former, through supreme justice.

So, then, thou art truly perceptive, omnipotent, compassionate, and impassible, as thou art living, wise, good, blessed, eternal: and whatever it is better to be than not to be.

CHAPTER XII

That God is the very life whereby he lives; and so of other like attributes

But certainly, whatever thou art, thou art through nothing else than thyself. Therefore, thou art the very life whereby thou livest; and the wisdom wherewith thou art wise; and the very goodness whereby thou art good to the righteous and the wicked; and so of other like attributes.

CHAPTER XIII

How he alone is uncircumscribed and eternal, although other spirits are uncircumscribed and eternal

But everything that is in any way enclosed by place or time is less than that which no law of place or time confines. Since, then, nothing is greater than thou, no place or time contains thee; but thou art everywhere and always. And since this can be said of thee alone, thou alone art uncircumscribed and eternal. How is it, then, that other spirits also are said to be uncircumscribed and eternal?

Assuredly thou alone art eternal; for thou alone among all beings not only dost not cease to be, but also dost not begin to be.

But how art thou alone uncircumscribed? Is it that a created spirit, when compared with thee, is circumscribed, but when compared with matter, uncircumscribed? For altogether circumscribed is that which, when it is wholly in one place, cannot at the same time be in another. And this is seen to be true of corporeal things alone. But uncircumscribed is that which is, as a whole, at the same time everywhere. And this is understood to be true of thee alone. But circumscribed, and, at the same time, uncircumscribed is that which, when it is any-where as a whole, can at the same time be somewhere else as a whole, and yet not everywhere. And this is recognised as true of created spirits. For, if the soul were not as a whole in the separate members of the body, it would not feel as a whole in the separate members.

Therefore, thou, Lord, art peculiarly uncircumscribed and eternal; and yet other spirits also are uncircumscribed and eternal.

CHAPTER XIV

How and why God is seen and yet not seen by those who seek him

Hast thou found what thou didst seek, my soul? Thou didst seek God. Thou hast found him to be that which is the highest of all beings, that than which nothing better can be conceived; and to be life itself, light, wisdom, goodness, eternal blessedness and blessed eternity, and to be everywhere and always.

For, if thou hast not found thy God, how is he this being which thou hast found, and which thou hast conceived him to be, with so certain truth and so true certainty? But, if thou hast found him, why is it that thou dost not feel thou hast found him? Why, O Lord, our God, does not my soul feel thee, if it hath found thee? Or, has it not found him whom it found to be light and truth? For how did it understand this, except by seeing light and truth? Or, could it understand anything at all of thee, except through thy light and thy truth?

Hence, if it has seen light and truth, it has seen thee; if it has not seen thee, it has not seen light and truth. Or, is what it has seen both light and truth; and still it has not yet seen thee, because it has seen thee only in part, but has not seen thee as thou art? Lord my God, my creator and renewer, speak to the desire of my soul, what thou art other than it hath seen, that it may clearly see what it desires. It strains to see thee more; and sees nothing beyond this which it hath seen, except darkness. Nay, it does not see darkness, of which there is none in thee; but it sees that it cannot see farther, because of its own darkness.

Why is this, Lord, why is this? Is the eye of the soul darkened by its infirmity, or dazzled by thy glory? Surely it is both darkened in itself, and dazzled by thee. Doubtless it is both obscured by its own insignificance, and overwhelmed by thy infinity. Truly, it is both contracted by its own narrowness and overcome by thy greatness.

For how great is that light from which shines every truth that gives light to the rational mind? How ample is that truth in which is everything that is true, and outside which is only nothingness and the false? How boundless is the truth which sees at one glance whatsoever has been made, and by whom, and through whom, and how it has been made from nothing? What purity, what simplicity, what certainty, what splendor is there? Assuredly more than a creature can conceive.

CHAPTER XV

That he is greater than can be conceived

Therefore, O Lord, thou art not only that than which a greater cannot be conceived, but thou art a being greater than can be conceived. For, since it can be conceived that there is such a being, if thou art not this very being, a greater than thou can be conceived. But this cannot be.

CHAPTER XVI

That this is the inaccessible light wherein he dwells

Truly, O Lord, this is the inaccessible light in which thou dwellest; for truly there is nothing else which can penetrate this light, that it may see thee there. Truly, I see it not, because it is too much for me. And yet, whatsoever I see, I see through it, as the weak eye sees what it sees through the light

of the sun, which it cannot look at in the sun itself. My understanding cannot reach that light, for it shines too bright. It does not comprehend it, nor can the eye of my soul bear to gaze upon it long. It is dazzled by the brightness, it is overcome by the greatness, it is overwhelmed by the fullness, dazed by its extent.

O supreme and unapproachable light! O whole and blessed truth, how far art thou from me, who am so near to thee! How far removed art thou from my vision, though I am so near to thine! Everywhere thou art wholly present, and I see thee not. In thee I move, and in thee I have my being; and I cannot come to thee. Thou art within me, and about me, and I feel thee not.

CHAPTER XVII

That in God are harmony, fragrance, sweetness, softness, and beauty, after his ineffable manner

Still thou art hidden, O Lord, from my soul in thy light and thy blessedness; and therefore my soul still walks in its darkness and wretchedness. For it looks, and does not see thy beauty. It hearkens, and does not hear thy harmony. It smells, and does not perceive thy fragrance. It tastes, and does not recognise thy sweetness. It touches, and does not feel thy softness. For thou hast these attributes in thyself, Lord God, after thine ineffable manner, who hast given them to objects created by thee, after their sensible manner; but the senses of my soul have grown rigid, dull, and obstructed from the old disease of sin.

CHAPTER XVIII

That there are no parts in God

And lo, again confusion; again grief and mourning meet him who seeks for joy and gladness. My soul now hoped for satisfaction; and lo, again it is overwhelmed with

eed. I desired now to feast, and lo, I hunger
more. I tried to rise to the light of God,
and I have fallen back into my darkness.
Nay, not only have I fallen into it, but I
feel that I am enveloped in it. I fell before
my mother conceived me. Truly, in darkness
I was conceived, and in the cover of darkness
I was born. Truly, in him we all fell, in
whom we all sinned. In him we all lost, who
kept easily, and wickedly lost to himself
and to us that which when we wish to seek
it, we do not know; when we seek it, we do
not find; when we find, it is not that which
we seek.

Do thou help me for thy goodness' sake!
Lord, I sought thy face; thy face, Lord, will
I seek; hide not thy face far from me (*Psalms,*
27:8). Free me from myself toward thee.
Cleanse, heal, sharpen, enlighten the eye of
my mind, that it may behold thee. Let my
soul recover its strength, and with all its
understanding let it strive toward thee, O
Lord. What art thou, Lord, what art thou?
What shall my heart conceive thee to be?

Assuredly thou art life, thou art wisdom,
thou art truth, thou art goodness, thou art
blessedness, thou art eternity, and thou art
very true good. Many are these attributes:
my straitened understanding cannot see so
many at one view, that it may be gladdened
by all at once. How, then, O Lord, art
thou all these things? Are they parts of thee,
or is each one of these rather the whole,
which thou art? For, whatever is composed
of parts is not altogether one, but is in some
sort plural, and diverse from itself; and
either in fact or in concept is capable of
dissolution.

But these things are alien to thee, than
whom nothing better can be conceived.
Hence, there are no parts in thee, Lord,
nor art thou more than one. But thou art
so truly one and the same with thyself, that
in no respect art thou unlike thyself;
rather thou art unity itself, not divisible by
any intellect. Therefore, life and wisdom
and the rest are not parts of thee, but all
are one; and each of these is the whole,
which thou art, and which all the rest are.

In this way, then, it appears that thou
hast no parts, and that thy eternity, which
thou art, is nowhere and never a part of
thee or of thy eternity. But everywhere thou
art as a whole, and thy eternity exists as a
whole forever.

CHAPTER XIX

*That he is not in place or time, but all
things are in him*

But if through thine eternity thou hast
been, and art, and wilt be; and to have
been is not to be destined to be; and to
be is not to have been, or to be destined
to be, how does thine eternity exist as a
whole forever? Or is it true that nothing of
thy eternity passes away, so that it is not
now; and that nothing of it is destined to
be, as if it were not yet?

Thou wast not, then, yesterday, nor wilt
thou be to-morrow; but yesterday and today and to-morrow thou art; or, rather,
neither yesterday nor to-day nor to-morrow
thou art; but simply, thou art, outside all
time. For yesterday and to-day and to-
morrow have no existence, except in time;
but thou, although nothing exists without
thee, nevertheless dost not exist in space or
time, but all things exist in thee. For nothing
contains thee, but thou containest all.

CHAPTER XX

*That he is before and beyond even all
eternal things*

Hence, thou dost fill and surround all
things. Thou art before all, and beyond all.
And, of a surety, thou art before all; for
before they were made, thou art. But how
art thou beyond all? In what way art thou
beyond those beings which will have no end?
Is it because they cannot exist at all without
thee; while thou art in no wise less, if they
should return to nothingness? For so, in a

certain sense, art thou beyond them. Or, is it also because they can be conceived to have an end; but thou by no means? For so they actually have an end, in a certain sense; but thou, in no sense. And certainly, what in no sense has an end is beyond what is ended in any sense. Or, in this way also art thou beyond all things, even the eternal, because thy eternity and theirs is present as a whole with thee; while they have not yet that part of their eternity which is to come, just as they no longer have that part which is past? For so art thou ever beyond them, since thou art ever present with thyself, and since that to which they have not yet come is ever present with thee.

CHAPTER XXI

Is this the age of the age, or the ages of ages?

Is this, then, the age of the age, or the ages of ages? For, as an age of time contains all temporal things, so thy eternity contains even the ages of time themselves. And these are indeed an age, because of their indivisible unity; but ages, because of their endless immeasurability. And, although thou art so great, O Lord, that all things are full of thee, and exist in thee; yet thou art so without all space, that neither midst, nor half, nor any part, is in thee.

CHAPTER XXII

That he alone is what he is and who he is

Therefore, thou alone, O Lord, art what thou art: and thou art he who thou art. For, what is one thing in the whole and another in the parts, and in which there is something mutable, is not altogether what it is. And what begins from non-existence, and can be conceived not to exist, and unless it subsists through something else, returns to non-existence; and what has a past existence, which is no longer, or a future existence, which is not yet—such a

thing does not properly and absolutely exis But thou art what thou art, because, wha ever thou art at any time, or in any wa thou art as a whole and forever.

And thou art he who thou art, proper and simply; for thou hast neither a pa existence nor a future, but only a preser existence; nor canst thou be conceived as any time not existing. But thou art life, an light, and wisdom, and blessedness, an many goods of this nature. And yet thou a the one and supreme good; thou art a sufficient to thyself, and needest none; an thou art he whom all things need for thei existence and well-being.

CHAPTER XXIII

That this good is equally Father, an Son, and Holy Spirit; and that this is th one, necessary Being, which is altogether wholly, and solely good

This good thou art, thou, God the Father this is thy Word, that is, thy Son. Fo nothing, other than what thou art, o greater or less than thou, can be in th Word by which thou dost express thyself for thy Word is true, as thou art truthful And hence it is truth itself, just as thou art no other truth than thou; and thou art o so simple a nature, that of thee nothing ca be born other than what thou art. Thi very good is the one love common to the and to thy Son, that is, the Holy Spiri proceeding from both. For this love is no unequal to thee or to thy Son; seeing tha thou dost love thyself and him, and he, thee and himself, to the whole extent of thy being and his. Nor is there aught else pro ceeding from thee and from him, which i not unequal to thee and to him. Nor car anything proceed from the supreme sim plicity, other than what this, from which i proceeds, is.

But what each is, separately, this is al the Trinity at once, Father, Son, and Holy Spirit; seeing that each separately is non other than the supremely simple unity, and he supremely unitary simplicity, which can neither be multiplied nor varied.

"Only one thing is necessary" (*Luke*, 10: 42). Now, this is that one thing, necessary, in which is every good; nay, which is wholly, uniquely, altogether, and solely good.

CHAPTER XXIV

Conjecture as to the character and the magnitude of this good

And now, my soul, arouse and lift up all thy understanding, and conceive, so far as thou canst, of what character and how great is that good. For, if individual goods are delectable, conceive in earnestness how delectable is that good which contains the pleasantness of all goods; and not such as we have experienced in created objects, but as different as the Creator from the creature. For, if the created life is good, how good is the creative life! If the salvation given is delightful, how delightful is the salvation which has given all salvation! If wisdom in the knowledge of the created world is lovely, how lovely is the wisdom which has created all things from nothing! Finally, if there are many great delights in delectable things, what and how great is the delight in him who has made these delectable things.

CHAPTER XXV

What goods, and how great, belong to those who enjoy this good

Who shall enjoy this good? And what shall belong to him, and what shall not belong to him? At any rate, whatever he shall wish shall be his, and whatever he shall not wish shall not be his. For, these goods of body and soul will be such as eye hath not seen nor ear heard, neither has the heart of man conceived (*Isaiah*, 64:4; *I Corinthians*, 2:9).

Why, then, do you wander abroad, insignificant man, in search for the goods of your soul and body? Love the one good in which are all goods, and it sufficeth. Desire the simple good which is every good, and it is enough. For, what do you love, my flesh? What do you desire, my soul? There, there is whatever you love, whatever you desire.

If beauty delights you, there shall the righteous shine forth as the sun (*Matthew*, 13:43). If swiftness or endurance, or freedom of body, which naught can withstand, delight you, they shall be as angels of God—because it is sown a natural body; it is raised a spiritual body (*I Corinthians*, 15: 44)—in power certainly, though not in nature. If it is a long and sound life that pleases you, there a healthful eternity is, and an eternal health. For the righteous shall live forever (*Wisdom*, 5:15), and the salvation of the righteous is of the Lord (*Psalms*, 37:39). If it is satisfaction of hunger, they shall be satisfied when the glory of the Lord hath appeared (*Psalms*, 17:15). If it is quenching of thirst, they shall be abundantly satisfied with the fatness of thy house (*Psalms*, 36:8). If it is melody, there the choirs of angels sing forever, before God. If it is any not impure, but pure, pleasure, thou shalt make them drink of the river of thy pleasures, O God (*Psalms*, 36:8).

If it is wisdom that delights you, the very wisdom of God will reveal itself to them. If friendship, they shall love God more than themselves, and one another as themselves. And God shall love them more than they themselves; for they love him, and themselves, and one another, through him, and he, himself and them, through himself. If concord, they shall all have a single will.

If power, they shall have all power to fulfil their will, as God to fulfil his. For, as God will have power to do what he wills, through himself, so they will have power, through him, to do what they will. For, as they will not will aught else than he, he shall will whatever they will; and what he shall will cannot fail to be. If honor and riches, God shall make his good and faithful servants rulers over many things (*Luke*, 12:42); nay, they shall be called sons of God, and gods; and where his Son shall be, there they shall be also, heirs indeed of God, and joint-heirs with Christ (*Romans*, 8:17).

If true security delights you, undoubtedly they shall be as sure that those goods, or rather that good, will never and in no wise fail them; as they shall be sure that they will not lose it of their own accord; and that God, who loves them, will not take it away from those who love him against their will; and that nothing more powerful than God will separate him from them against his will and theirs.

But what, or how great, is the joy, where such and so great is the good! Heart of man, needy heart, heart acquainted with sorrows, nay, overwhelmed with sorrows, how greatly would you rejoice, if you did abound in all these things! Ask your inmost mind whether it could contain its joy over so great a blessedness of its own.

Yet assuredly, if any other whom you loved altogether as yourself possessed the same blessedness, your joy would be doubled, because you would rejoice not less for him than for yourself. But, if two, or three, or many more, had the same joy, you would rejoice as much for each one as for yourself, if you loved each as yourself. Hence, in that perfect love of innumerable blessed angels and sainted men, where none shall love another less than himself, every one shall rejoice for each of the others as for himself.

If, then, the heart of man will scarce contain his joy over his own so great good, how shall it contain so many and so great joys? And doubtless, seeing that every one loves another so far as he rejoices in the other's good, and as, in that perfect felicity, each one should love God beyond compare, more than himself and all the others with him; so he will rejoice beyond reckoning in the felicity of God, more than in his own and that of all the others with him.

But if they shall so love God with all their heart, and all their mind, and all their soul, that still all the heart, and all the mind, and all the soul shall not suffice for the worthiness of this love; doubtless they will so rejoice with all their heart, and all their mind, and all their soul, that all the heart, and all the mind, and all the soul shall not suffice for the fulness of their joy.

CHAPTER XXVI

Whether this is the joy made full which the Lord promises

My God and my Lord, my hope and the joy of my heart, speak unto my soul and tell me whether this is the joy of which thou tellest us through thy Son: Ask and ye shall receive, that your joy may be full (*John*, 16:24). For I have found a joy that is full, and more than full. For when heart, and mind, and soul, and all the man, are full of that joy, joy beyond measure will still remain. Hence, not all of that joy shall enter into those who rejoice; but they who rejoice shall wholly enter into that joy.

Show me, O Lord, show thy servant in his heart whether this is the joy into which thy servants shall enter, who shall enter into the joy of their Lord. But that joy, surely, with which thy chosen ones shall rejoice, eye hath not seen nor ear heard, neither has it entered into the heart of man (*Isaiah*, 64:4; *I Corinthians*, 2:9). Not yet, then, have I told or conceived, O Lord, how greatly those blessed ones of thine shall rejoice. Doubtless they shall rejoice according as they shall love; and they shall love according as they shall know. How far they will know thee, Lord, then! and how much they will love thee! Truly, eye hath not seen, nor ear heard, neither has it entered into the heart of man in this life, how far they shall know thee, and how much they shall love thee in that life.

I pray, O God, to know thee, to love thee, that I may rejoice in thee. And if I cannot attain to full joy in this life, may I at least advance from day to day, until that joy shall come to the full. Let the knowledge of thee advance in me here, and there be made full. Let the love of thee increase, and there et it be full, that here my joy may be great in hope, and there full in truth. Lord, through thy Son thou dost command, nay, thou dost counsel us to ask; and thou dost promise that we shall receive, that our joy may be full. I ask, O Lord, as thou dost counsel through our wonderful Counsellor. will receive what thou dost promise by virtue of thy truth, that my joy may be full.

Faithful God, I ask. I will receive, that my joy may be full. Meanwhile, let my mind meditate upon it; let my tongue speak of it. Let my heart love it; let my mouth talk of it. Let my soul hunger for it; let my flesh thirst for it; let my whole being desire it, until I enter into thy joy, O Lord, who art the Three and the One God, blessed for ever and ever. Amen.

A REPLY ON BEHALF OF THE FOOL BY GAUNILO, A MONK OF MARMOUTIER

1. If one doubts or denies the existence of a being of such a nature that nothing greater than it can be conceived, he receives this answer:

The existence of this being is proved, in the first place, by the fact that he himself, in his doubt or denial regarding this being, already has it in his understanding; for in hearing it spoken of he understands what is spoken of; and further, by the fact that what he understands must exist not only in his understanding, but in reality also.

And the proof of this is as follows—It is a greater thing to exist both in the understanding and in reality than to be in the understanding alone. And if this being is in the understanding alone, whatever existed also in reality would be greater than this being. And so that which was greater than all beings will be less than some being, and would not be greater than all: which is a manifest contradiction.

And hence, that which is greater than all, already proved to be in the understanding, must exist not only in the understanding, but also in reality: for otherwise it could not be greater than all other beings.

2. The Fool might make this reply:

This being is said to be in my understanding already, only because I understand what is said. Now could it not be said that

I similarly have in my understanding all manner of unreal objects, having absolutely no existence in themselves, since I understand these things if one speaks of them, whatever they may be?

Unless indeed it is certain that this being is such that it cannot be held in thought like all unreal objects, or objects whose existence is uncertain: and hence I am not able to conceive of it when I hear of it, or to hold it in thought; but I must understand it and have it in my understanding; because, it seems, I cannot conceive of it in any other way than by understanding it, that is, by comprehending in my knowledge its existence in reality.

But if this is the case, in the first place there will be no distinction between what has precedence in time—namely, the having of an object in the understanding—and what is subsequent in time—namely, the understanding that an object exists; as in the example of the picture, which exists first in the mind of the painter, and afterwards in his work.

Moreover, it could hardly be credible that this being, when it is spoken of and heard of, cannot be conceived not to exist in the way in which even God can be conceived not to exist. For if this is impossible, what was the object of this argument against one who doubts or denies the existence of such a being?

Finally, that it is such that, once it is thought of, it cannot but be certainly perceived by the understanding as undoubtedly existing—this should be proved to me by an indisputable argument, but not by that which you have advanced: namely, that what I understand, when I hear it, already is in my understanding. For thus in my understanding, as I still think, could be all sorts of things whose existence is uncertain, or which do not exist at all, if some one whose words I should understand mentioned them. And so much the more if I should be deceived, as often happens, and believe in them—which argument I still do not believe.

3. Hence, your example of the painter who already has in his understanding what he is to paint does not fit this argument. For the picture, before it is made, is contained in the very art of the painter; and any such thing, existing in the art of any artist, is nothing but a part of his understanding itself. A joiner, St. Augustine says, when he is about to make a box in fact, first has it in his art. The box which is made in fact is not life; but the box which exists in his art is life. For the artificer's soul lives, in which all these things are, before they are produced. Why, then, are these things life in the living soul of the artificer, unless because they are nothing else than the knowledge or understanding of the soul itself?

With the exception, however, of those things which are known to pertain to the nature of the mind, whatever, on being heard and thought by the understanding, is perceived to be true, undoubtedly the truth is one thing, and the understanding itself, by which it is grasped, is another. Hence, even if it were true that there is a being than which a greater is inconceivable: yet to this being, when heard of and understood, the not yet created picture in the mind of the painter is not analogous.

4. Let us notice also the point touched on above, that with regard to this being

which is greater than all which can be conceived, and which, it is said, can be none other than God himself. I, so far as actual knowledge of the object, either by species or genus, is concerned, am as little able to conceive of this being when I hear of it, or to have it in my understanding, as I am to conceive of or understand God himself: whom, indeed, for this very reason I can conceive not to exist. For I do not know that reality itself, nor can I form a conjecture of that reality from other things like it, for you yourself assert that that reality is such that there can be nothing else like it.

For, suppose that I should hear something said of a man absolutely unknown to me, of whose very existence I was unaware. Through that specific or generic knowledge by which I know what man is, or what men are, I could conceive of him also, according to the reality itself, which man is. And yet it would be possible, if the person who told me of him deceived me, that the man himself, of whom I conceived, did not exist; since that reality according to which I conceived of him, though a no less indisputable fact, was not that man, but any man.

Hence, I am not able, in the way in which I should have this unreal being in concept or in understanding, to have that being of which you speak in concept or in understanding, when I hear the word *God* or the words, *a being greater than all other beings*. For I can conceive of the man as a truly existing thing, but of God, or a being greater than all others, I could not conceive at all, except merely according to the word. And according to this alone, one can hardly or never conceive of any truth.

For when one so conceives, it is not so much the word itself (which is, indeed, a real thing—that is, the sound of the letters and syllables) as the signification of the word, when heard, that is conceived. But it [that than which nothing is greater] is not conceived of as by one who knows what is signified by the word—that is, conceived according to a reality and in true conception lone. It is conceived as by a man who does not know the object, and conceives of it only in accordance with the movement of his mind produced by hearing the word, the mind attempting to imagine the signification of the word that is heard. And it would be surprising if he could ever attain to the truth of the thing.

In this and in no other way is this being in my understanding, when I hear and understand a person who says that there is a being greater than anything that can be conceived. So much for the assertion that this supreme nature already is in my understanding.

5. But that this being must exist, not only in the understanding but also in reality, is thus proved to me:

If it did not so exist, whatever exists in reality would be greater than it. And so the being which has been already proved to exist in my understanding, will not be greater than all other beings.

To this I answer: if it must be said that a being which cannot be even conceived in any true sense of a thing, is in the understanding, I do not deny that this being is, in this way, in my understanding. But since from this one can in no wise conclude that it really exists, I do not yet concede to it existence at all, until some certain proof of it shall be given.

For he who says that this being exists, because otherwise the being which is greater than all will not be greater than all, does not attend strictly enough to whom he is speaking. For I do not yet say, no, I even deny or doubt, that this greater is a truly existing thing. Nor do I concede to it any other existence than this (if it should be called existence) which it has when the mind, according to a word merely heard, tries to form the image of an object absolutely unknown to it.

How, then, is the veritable existence of that being proved to me from the assumption, by hypothesis, that it is greater than all other beings? For I should still deny this,

or doubt your demonstration of it, to this extent, that I should not admit that this being is in my understanding and thought even in the way in which many uncertain and doubtful objects are. For it should be proved first that this greater itself really exists somewhere; and then, from the fact that it is greater than all, it will be clear that it also subsists in itself.

6. For example: it is said that somewhere in the ocean is an island, which, because of the difficulty, or rather the impossibility, of discovering what does not exist, is called the lost island. And they say that this island has an inestimable wealth of all manner of riches and delicacies in greater abundance than is told of the Islands of the Blest; and that having no owner or inhabitant, it is more excellent than all other countries, which are inhabited by mankind, in the abundance with which it is stored.

Now if some one should tell me that there is such an island, I should easily understand his words, in which there is no difficulty. But suppose that he went on to say, as if by a logical inference: "You can no more doubt that this island which is more excellent than all lands exists somewhere in reality, than you can doubt that it is in your understanding. And since it is more excellent not to be in the understanding alone, but to exist both in the understanding and in reality, for this reason it must exist. For if it does not exist, any land which really exists will be more excellent than it; and so the island already understood by you to be more excellent will not be more excellent."

If a man should try to prove to me by such reasoning that this island truly exists, and that its existence should no longer be doubted, either I should believe that he was jesting, or I know not which I ought to regard as the greater fool: myself, supposing that I should agree with him, or him, if he should suppose that he had established with any certainty the existence of this island. For he ought to show first that its very excellence exists in my understanding as a real and indubitable thing, and in no wise as any unreal object, or one whose existence is uncertain.

7. This, in the meantime, is the answer the Fool could make to the arguments urged against him. If then one should assert that this being is so great that its non-existence is not even conceivable, and that this in turn is proved on no other ground than the fact that otherwise it will not be greater than all things, the Fool may make the same answer, and say:

When did I say that any such being exists in reality, that is, a being greater than all others?—that on this ground it should be proved to me that it also exists in reality to such a degree that it cannot even be conceived not to exist? That is why in the first place it must be proved that a nature which is higher, that is, greater and better, than all other natures, exists, in order that from this we may then be able to prove all attributes which necessarily cannot be lacking to the being that is greater and better than everything.

When, however, it is said that this supreme being cannot be *conceived* [*cogitari*] not to exist, it might perhaps be better to say that it cannot be *understood* [*intelligi*] not to exist or even to have the possibility of not exist, or even to have the possibility of not existing. For, strictly speaking, unreal objects are unintelligible. Yet their existence is conceivable in the way in which the Fool conceived of the non-existence of God. I most certainly know that I exist, but I know, nevertheless, that it is also possible for me not to exist. As to that supreme being, moreover, which God is, I understand without any doubt both that he exists and cannot not exist. Whether, however, so long as I know most certainly that I exist, I can conceive of my non-existence, I am not sure. But if I can, why can I not conceive of the non-existence of whatever else I know with the same certainty? If, however, I cannot, God will not be the only being of which it can be said, it is impossible to conceive of his non-existence.

8. The other parts of this book are argued with such truth, such brilliancy, such grandeur; and are so replete with usefulness, so fragrant with a certain perfume of devout and holy feeling, that though there are matters in the beginning which, however rightly sensed, are less firmly argued, the rest of the work should not be rejected on this account. Rather these earlier matters ought to be reasoned more cogently, and the whole to be received with great respect and honor.

THE AUTHOR'S REPLY
TO GAUNILO

Since the Fool against whom the argument of my little work was directed is not the author of these objections, who is by no means a fool, but a Catholic speaking on behalf of the Fool, I think it sufficient that I answer the Catholic.

I. You say—whosoever you may be, who say that the Fool is capable of making these statements—that a being-than-which-a-greater-cannot-be-conceived is not in the understanding in any other sense than that in which a being that is altogether inconceivable in terms of reality is in the understanding. You say that the inference that this being exists in reality, from the fact that it is in the understanding, is no more just than the inference that a lost island most certainly exists, from the fact that when it is described the hearer does not doubt that it is in his understanding.

But I say: if a being-than-which-a-greater-cannot-be-conceived is not understood or conceived, and is not in the understanding or in concept, certainly either God s not a being-than-which-a-greater-cannot-be-onceived, or else he is not understood or onceived, and is not in the understanding or in concept. But your faith and conscience are my strongest argument that this s false. Hence, that-than-which-a-greater-cannot-be-conceived is truly understood and onceived, and is in the understanding and n concept. Therefore either the grounds on which you try to controvert me are not true, or else the conclusion which you think to base on those grounds does not follow.

You hold, moreover, that supposing that a being-than-which-a-greater-cannot-be-onceived is understood, it does not follow that this being is in the understanding; nor, f it is in the understanding, does it therefore exist in reality.

In answer to this, I maintain positively: if that being can be even conceived to be, it s necessary that it exist. For that-than-which-a-greater-cannot-be-conceived cannot be conceived except as without beginning. But whatever can be conceived to exist, and does not exist, can be conceived as beginning to exist. Hence what can be conceived to exist, but does not exist, is not the being-than-which-a-greater-cannot-be-conceived. Therefore, if such a being can be conceived to exist, it exists of necessity.

Furthermore: if it can be conceived at all, it must exist. For no one who denies or doubts the existence of a being-than-which-a-greater-cannot-be-conceived, denies or doubts that if it did exist, its non-existence, either in reality or in the understanding, would be impossible. For otherwise it would not be a being-than-which-a-greater-cannot-be-conceived. But as to whatever can be conceived, but does not exist—if there were such a being, its non-existence, either in reality or in the understanding, would be possible. Therefore, if a being-than-which-a-greater-cannot-be-conceived can be even conceived, it cannot not exist.

But let us suppose that it does not exist, even if it can be conceived. Whatever can be conceived, but does not exist, if it existed, would not be a being-than-which-a-greater-cannot-be-conceived. If, then, there were a being-than-which-a-greater-cannot-be-conceived, it would not be a being-than-which-a-greater-cannot-be-conceived, which is most absurd. Hence, it is false to deny that a being-than-which-a-greater-cannot-be-conceived exists, if it can be even conceived; much the more, therefore, if it can be understood or can be in the understanding.

Moreover, I will venture to make this assertion: without doubt, whatever at any place or at any time does not exist—even if it does exist at some place or at some time—can be conceived to exist nowhere and never, as at some place and at some time it does not exist. For what did not exist yesterday, and exists to-day, as it is understood not to have existed yesterday, so it can be apprehended by the intelligence that it never exists. And what is not here, and is elsewhere, can be conceived to be nowhere, just as it is not here. So with regard to an object of which the individual parts do not exist at the same places or times: all its parts and therefore its very whole can be conceived to exist nowhere or never.

For, even if time is said to exist always, and the world everywhere, yet time does not as a whole exist always, nor the world as a whole everywhere. And as individual parts of time do not exist when others exist, so they can be conceived never to exist. And so it can be apprehended by the intelligence that individual parts of the world exist nowhere, as they do not exist where other parts exist. Moreover, what is composed of parts can be dissolved in thought, and can possibly not exist. Therefore, whatever at any place or at any time does not exist as a whole, even if it is existent, can be conceived not to exist.

But that-than-which-a-greater-cannot-be-conceived, if it exists, cannot be conceived not to exist. Otherwise, it is not a being-than-which-a-greater-cannot-be-conceived: which is inconsistent. By no means, then, does it at any place or at any time fail to exist as a whole: but it exists as a whole everywhere and always.

Do you not then believe that this being with regard to which these things are understood can in some way be conceived or understood and be in concept or in the understanding? For if it cannot, these things cannot be understood with reference to it. But if you say that it is not understood and that it is not in the understanding, because it is not thoroughly understood; you should say that a man who cannot face the direct rays of the sun does not see the light of day, which is none other than the sunlight. Assuredly a being-than-which-a-greater-cannot-be-conceived exists, and is in the understanding, at least to this extent—that these statements regarding it are understood.

II. I have said, then, in the argument which you dispute, that when the Fool hears mentioned a being-than-which-a-greater-cannot-be-conceived, he understands what he hears. Certainly a man who does not understand it when spoken in a familiar language, has no understanding at all, or a very dull one. Then I said that if this being is understood, it is in the understanding. Or does that which has been shown necessarily to exist in actual reality exist in no understanding at all?

But you will say that although it is in the understanding, it does not follow that it is understood. But from the fact of its being understood it does follow that it is in the understanding. For as what is conceived, is conceived by conception, and what is conceived by conception, is thus, as conceived, in conception; so what is understood, is understood by understanding, and what is understood by understanding, is thus, as understood, in the understanding. What can be more clear than this?

After this, I have said that if it is even in the understanding alone, it can be conceived also to exist in reality, which is greater. If, then, it is in the understanding alone, obviously the very being-than-which-a-greater-cannot-be-conceived is one than

which a greater can be conceived. What i more logical? For if it exists even in th understanding alone, can it not be cor ceived also to exist in reality? And if it ca be so conceived, does not he who conceive of this conceive of a thing greater than tha being, if it exists in the understandin alone? What could follow more logicall than this: that if a being-than-which-a greater-*cannot*-be-conceived is in the unde standing alone, it is the same as that-than which-a-greater-*can*-be-conceived?

But, assuredly, in no understanding is a be ing-than-which-a-greater-*can*-be-conceived th same as a being-than-which-a-greater-*canno* be-conceived. Does it not follow, then, tha if a being-than-which-a-greater-cannot-be conceived is in any understanding, it doe not exist in the understanding alone? For i it is in the understanding alone, it is a being than-which-a-greater-*can-be-conceived*, whicl is absurd.

III. But, you say, it is as if one shoul suppose an island in the ocean, whicl surpasses all lands in its fertility, and which because of the difficulty, or rather the impos sibility, of discovering what does not exist is called a lost island; and should say tha there can be no doubt that this island trul exists in reality, for this reason, that on who hears it described in words easily under stands what he hears.

Now I promise confidently that if an man shall devise anything existing either i reality or in concept alone (except that-than which-a-greater-cannot-be-conceived) to whicl the sequence of my reasoning applies, I wi discover that thing, and will give him hi lost island, not to be lost again.

But it has been clearly seen that this being than-which-a-greater-cannot-be-conceived can not be conceived not to exist, because i exists on so assured a ground of truth; fo otherwise it would not exist at all.

Hence, if any one says that he conceive this being not to exist, I say that at th time when he conceives of this either h conceives of a being-than-which-a-greater annot-be-conceived, or he does not conceive t all. If he does not conceive of it, he does not conceive of the non-existence of that of which he does not conceive. But if he does conceive of it, he certainly conceives of a being which cannot be even conceived not to exist. For if it could be conceived not to exist, it could be conceived to have a beginning and an end. But this is impossible.

He, then, who conceives of this being conceives of a being which cannot be even conceived not to exist; but he who conceives of this being does not conceive that it does not exist; else he conceives what cannot be conceived. Therefore, that-than-which-a-greater-cannot-be-conceived cannot be conceived not to exist.

IV. You say, moreover, that whereas I assert that this supreme being cannot be *conceived* not to exist, it might better be said that it cannot be *understood* not to exist or even to have the possibility of not existing.

However, it is more proper to say that it cannot be conceived. For if I had said that the object itself cannot be understood not to exist, possibly you yourself, who say that in accordance with the strict meaning of the term what is unreal cannot be understood, would object that nothing which is can be understood not to be, for it is false that what exists does not exist: hence God would not be the only being of which it could be said, it is impossible to understand its non-existence. For thus one of those beings that most certainly exist can be understood not to exist in the same way that other things that certainly exist can be understood not to exist.

But this objection, assuredly, cannot be urged against the term *conception* [*cogitatio*], if one considers the matter well. For although no objects which exist can be *understood* not to exist, yet all objects, except that which exists in the highest degree, can be *conceived* not to exist. For all those objects, and those alone, can be conceived not to exist, which have a beginning or end or

composition of parts: also, as I have already said, whatever at any place or at any time does not exist as a whole.

That being alone, on the other hand, cannot be conceived not to exist, in which any conception discovers neither beginning nor end nor composition of parts, and which any conception finds always and everywhere as a whole.

Be assured, then, that you can conceive of yourself as not existing, although you are most certain that you exist. I am surprised that you have said that you are ignorant of this. For we conceive of many objects which we know to exist as not existing, and of many which we know not to exist as existing; not by judging that they so exist, but by imagining that they exist as we conceive of them.

And indeed, we can conceive of something as not existing, although we know it to exist, because at the same time we can conceive of the former and know the latter. And we cannot conceive of something not existing, so long as we know it to exist, because we cannot conceive of it as existing and not existing at the same time.

If, then, one will thus distinguish these two senses of this statement, he will understand that nothing, so long as it is known to exist, can be conceived not to exist; and that whatever exists, except that being-than-which-a-greater-cannot-be-conceived, can be conceived not to exist, even when it is known to exist.

So, then, of God alone it can be said that it is impossible to conceive of him as not existing; and yet many objects, so long as they exist, in one sense cannot be conceived not to exist. But in what sense it can be said that God can be conceived not to exist, I think has been shown clearly enough in my book.

V. The nature of the other objections which you, in behalf of the Fool, urge against me it is easy, even for a man of small wisdom, to detect; and I had therefore thought it unnecessary to show this. But since

I hear that some readers of these objections think they have some weight against me, I will discuss them briefly.

In the first place, you often repeat that I assert that what is greater than all other beings is in the understanding; and if it is in the understanding, it exists also in reality, for otherwise the being which is greater than all would not be greater than all.

Nowhere in all my writings is such a demonstration found. For *that which is greater than everything* is not the same as *that-than-which-nothing-greater-can-be-conceived*, when it comes to proving the existence of the thing spoken of.

If it should be said that a being-than-which-a-greater-cannot-be-conceived has no real existence, or that it is possible that it does not exist, or even that it can be conceived not to exist, such an assertion can be easily refuted. For what does not exist can possibly not exist, and what can not exist can be conceived not to exist. But whatever can be conceived not to exist, if it exists, is not a being-than-which-a-greater-cannot-be-conceived; but if it does not exist, it would not, even if it existed, be a being-than-which-a-greater-cannot-be-conceived. But it cannot be said that a being-than-which-a-greater-cannot-be-conceived, if it exists, is not a being-than-which-a-greater-cannot-be-conceived; or that if it existed, it would not be a being-than-which-a-greater-cannot-be-conceived.

It is evident, then, that neither does it not exist, nor is it possible that it does not exist, nor can it be conceived not to exist. For otherwise, if it exists, it is not that which it is said to be, and if it existed, it would not be what it is said to be.

But this, it appears, cannot be so easily proved of a being which is said to be *greater than all other beings*. For it is not so evident that what can be conceived not to exist is not greater than all existing beings, as it is evident that it is not a being-than-which-a-greater-cannot-be-conceived. Nor is it so indubitable that if a being greater than all other beings exists, it is no other than the being-than-which-a-greater-cannot-be-conceived; c that if there were such a being, that ther might not be another like it, as it is certai with regard to what is said to be that-thar which-a-greater-cannot-be-conceived.

For consider: if one should say that ther is a being greater than all other beings, an that this being can nevertheless be conceive not to exist; and that a being greater tha this, although it does not exist, can be cor ceived to exist: can it be so clearly inferre in this case that this being is therefore nc a being greater than all other existin beings, as it would be most positively affirme in the other case, that the being under di cussion is not, therefore, a being-than-whicl a-greater-cannot-be-conceived?

For the former conclusion requires anothe premise besides the said *greater than a other beings*. In my argument, on the othe hand, there is no need of any other than th expression, *that-than-which-a-greater-canno be-conceived*.

If what *that-than-which-a-greater-canno be-conceived* by itself proves with respect t itself cannot be similarly proved of what i said to be greater than all others, you hav unjustly censured me for saying what I di not say; since it differs so greatly from wha I actually said. If, on the other hand, th other argument is valid, you ought not t blame me so for having said what can b proved.

Whether this can be proved, howeve he will easily decide who recognises tha this being-than-which-a-greater-cannot-be-cor ceived is demonstrable. For by no mear can this being-than-which-a-greater-cannot-b conceived be understood as any other tha that which alone is greater than all. Henc just as that-than-which-a-greater-cannot-b conceived is understood, and is in the unde standing, and for that reason is asserted exist in true reality, so what is said to b greater than all other beings is understoo and is in the understanding, and therefor it is necessarily inferred that it exists i reality.

You see, then, with how much justice you ave compared me with that stupid person, rho, on the sole ground that he understands what is described to him, would affirm hat a lost island exists.

VI. Another of your objections is that any nreal beings, or beings whose existence is ncertain, can be understood and be in the nderstanding in the same way with that eing which I discussed. I am surprised that ou should make this objection, for I was ttempting to prove what was still uncertain, nd contented myself at first with showing hat this being, understood in any way, is n the understanding. It was my intention hereafter to consider whether this being is n the understanding alone, like an unreal bject, or whether it also exists in fact, as a eal being. For if unreal objects, or objects rhose existence is uncertain, in this way are nderstood and are in the understanding, ecause, when they are spoken of, the hearer nderstands what the speaker means, there s no reason why that being of which I poke should not be understood and be in he understanding.

How, moreover, can these two statements f yours be reconciled: (1) the assertion that f a man should speak of any unreal objects, vhatever they might be, you would understand what he says, and (2) the assertion hat on hearing of that being which does xist, and not in that way in which even nreal objects are held in concept, you vould not say that you conceive of it or ave it in concept; since, as you say, you annot conceive of it in any other way than y understanding it, that is, by comprehending in your knowledge its real existence? How, I ask, can these two things be econciled: that unreal objects are undertood, and that understanding an object is omprehending in knowledge that it really xists? That none of this applies to me you hould have seen. But if unreal objects are lso in some sort understood, and your defi-ition is applicable, not to every under-tanding, but to a certain sort of under-

standing, I ought not to be blamed for saying that a being-than-which-a-greater-cannot-be-conceived is understood and is in the understanding, even before I reached the certain conclusion that this being exists in reality.

VII. Again, you say that it can hardly be believed that this being, when it is spoken of and heard of, cannot be conceived not to exist in the same way in which even God may be conceived not to exist.

Such an objection could be answered by those who have attained but little skill in disputation and argument. For is it reasonable for a man to deny what he understands, because it is said to be that which he denies because he does not understand it? Or, if at some times it is denied, because only to a certain extent is it understood, and is the same as that which is not at all understood: is not what is in doubt more easily proved of a being which exists in some understanding than of one which exists in no understanding?

Hence it cannot be credible that any man denies the existence of a being-than-which-a-greater-cannot-be-conceived, which, when he hears of it, he understands in a certain degree: it is incredible, I say, that any man denies the existence of this being because he denies the existence of God, the meaning of whom he in no way conceives of.

On the other hand, if it is denied because it is not completely understood, yet is not that which is understood in some degree more easily proved than that which is in no way understood?

Not without reason then, has that-than-which-a-greater-cannot-be-conceived been employed in controverting the Fool, for the proof of the existence of God: since in some degree he would understand such a being, but in no wise could he understand God.

VIII. Moreover, your painstaking proof that the being-than-which-a-greater-cannot-be-conceived is not analogous to the not yet executed picture in the understanding of the painter, is quite unnecessary. It was not for this purpose that I suggested the preconceived picture. I had no thought of asserting that the being which I was discussing is of such a nature; but I wished to show that what is not understood to exist can be in the understanding.

Again, you say that when you hear of a being-than-which-a-greater-cannot-be-conceived, you cannot conceive of it as a real object known to you either specifically or generally, nor have it in your understanding. For, you say, you neither know the thing itself, nor can you form an idea of it from anything like it.

But obviously this is not true. For everything that is less good, insofar as it is good, is like the greater good. It is therefore evident to any rational mind, that by ascending from the lesser good to the greater, we can from those things than which something greater *can* be conceived form a considerable notion of a being-than-which-a-greater-cannot-be-conceived.

For instance, who (even if he does not believe that what he conceives of exists in reality) supposing that there is some good which has a beginning and an end, does not conceive that a good is much better, which, if it begins, does not cease to be? And that as the second good is better than the first, so that good which has neither beginning nor end, though it is ever passing from the past through the present to the future, is better than the second? And that far better than this is a being—whether any being of such a nature exists or not—which in no way requires change or motion, nor is compelled to undergo change or motion?

Is this inconceivable, or is some being greater than this conceivable? Or is not this to form a notion from objects than which a greater is conceivable, of the being-than-which-a-greater-cannot-be-conceived? There is, then, a way of forming a notion of a being-than-which-a-greater-cannot-be-conceived.

So easily, then, can the Fool who does not accept sacred authority be refuted, if he denies that a notion may be formed from other objects of a being-than-which-a-greater-

cannot-be-conceived. But if any Catholic would deny this, let him remember that the invisible things of God, from the creation of the world, are clearly seen, being understood by the things that are made, even his eternal power and Godhead (*Romans* 1:20).

IX. But even if it were true that a being-than-which-a-greater-cannot-be-conceived cannot be conceived or understood, yet it would not be false that "that-than-which-a-greater-cannot-be-conceived" is conceivable and intelligible. There is nothing to prevent one's saying *ineffable*, although what is said to be ineffable cannot be spoken of. *Inconceivable* is conceivable, although that to which the word *inconceivable* can be applied is not conceivable. So, when one says, *that-than-which-nothing-greater-is-conceivable*, undoubtedly what is heard is conceivable and intelligible, although that being itself, than-which-a-greater-cannot-be-conceived, cannot be conceived or understood.

Or, though there is a man so foolish as to say that there is no being-than-which-a-greater-cannot-be-conceived, he will not be so shameless as to say that he cannot understand or conceive of what he says. Or, if such a man is found, not only ought his words to be rejected, but he himself should be contemned.

Whoever, then, denies the existence of a being-than-which-a-greater-cannot-be-conceived, at least understands and conceives of the denial which he makes. But this denial he cannot understand or conceive of without its component parts; and one part of this statement is *a-being-than-which-a-greater-cannot-be-conceived*. Whoever, then, makes this denial, understands and conceives of that than-which-a-greater-cannot-be-conceived.

Moreover, it is evident that in the same way one can conceive of and understand that which cannot not exist; but he who conceives of this conceives of a greater being than one which can not exist. Hence, when a being-than-which-a-greater-cannot-be-conceived is conceived, if it is a being that can not exist that is conceived, it is not a being than-which-a-greater-cannot-be-conceived. But an object cannot be at once conceived and not conceived. Hence he who conceives of being-than-which-a-greater-cannot-be-conceived, does not conceive of something that can not exist, but of something that cannot not exist. Therefore, what he conceives of must exist; for anything that can not exist is not that of which he conceives.

X. I believe that I have shown by an argument which is not weak, but sufficiently cogent, that in my former book I proved the real existence of a being-than-which-a-greater-cannot-be-conceived; and that this proof has not been weakened by any strong objection. For so great force does the signification of this reasoning contain in itself, that what is spoken of is of necessity, from the very fact that it is understood or conceived, proved also to exist in reality, and to be whatever we should believe of the divine substance.

For we attribute to the divine substance anything of which it can be conceived that it is better to be than not to be that thing. For example: it is better to be eternal than not eternal; good, than not good; nay, goodness itself, than not goodness itself. But it cannot be that anything of this nature is not a property of the being-than-which-a-greater-cannot-be-conceived. Hence, the being-than-which-a-greater-cannot-be-conceived must be whatever should be attributed to the divine essence.

I thank you for your kindness both in your blame and in your praise for my book. For since you have commended so generously those parts of it which seem to you worthy of acceptance, it is quite evident that you have criticised in no unkind spirit those parts of it which seemed to you weak.

NOTE TO THE READER

The chapter devoted to GOD is the largest chapter in the whole Syntopicon. Of the one hundred and two Great Ideas, the references to discussions about God far exceed all others. KNOWLEDGE is second largest, followed by MAN, and then STATE. As indicated in the essay on "syntopical construction," this fact indicates that among the ideas, at least among those represented in our set of Great Books, GOD has "maximum range, pervading all the major periods and also all the divisions of learning or kinds of literature" (*GBWW*, Vol. 3, p. 1222). Thus the reader may locate a wealth of material dealing with the idea of God by consulting Chapter 29. The topics most directly concerned with the discussion in the *Proslogion*, as well as in Professor Gilson's essay, are Topic 2: The existence of one God; and Topic 10: The denial of God: the position of the atheist.

For discussions of the modal logic that underlies the argument in the third chapter of the *Proslogion*, the reader should consult NECESSITY 4e(1): The modality of propositions or judgments: modal opposition.

The Idea
of the University
in the 19th Century

Humboldt
Newman
Mill

INTRODUCTION

Two ideals of the university came to fruition in the nineteenth century. One of these is the ideal of the university as a center of liberal education, the other that of the university as a center of research. Both ideals, as Dr. Kerr has pointed out in his essay (p. 4), are still present today and still exerting strong attraction.

Wilhelm Freiherr von Humboldt (1767–1835) may be considered the father of the idea of the university as a center of research. Humboldt was appointed to the Prussian ministry of the interior in 1809 with special charge for education. Under the impact of the Napoleonic invasions and wars, the ancient universities of Germany had become moribund if not actually extinct. Thus in effect Humboldt was given the task of rebuilding the education system of Prussia. He laid the foundations for the University of Berlin, and established a policy for it which led to its becoming the foremost university of Germany if not of all Europe. Before the nineteenth century was over, the number of its students exceeded that of every other university except Vienna. More important, the autonomy granted to its professors, many of them the foremost scholars and scientists of their day, with freedom of inquiry and responsibility only to learning and science, established a pattern for the university that was widely imitated elsewhere. The German universities, under the leadership of Berlin, became the most influential in the world. The rise and development of the graduate school in the United States was consciously fashioned according to the German model. In fact, Johns Hopkins, the first predominantly graduate university in America, at the time of its foundation in 1876, had so many German-trained professors that it was referred to as "Göttingen-in-Baltimore."

What might be called the founding document of the University of Berlin is the memoir on the organization of institutions of higher learning that Humboldt wrote for his ministry. It is presented here in a new translation by Clifton Fadiman from the original, "Über die innere und äussere Organisation der höheren wissenschaftlichen Anstalten in Berlin," contained in *Gesammelte Schriften*, Vol. 10, pp. 250–260.

The idea of the university as a center of liberal education received its foremost expression in the writings of Cardinal Newman and of John Stuart Mill. The writings of both men on university education are occasional in origin, but that of Newman is also polemical in a way that Mill's is not. This character resulted from the conditions under which Newman became in 1851 the first Rector of the newly established Catholic

University in Ireland and wrote the series of discourses that were later published as *The Idea of a University*. These lectures were conceived as a way of winning support for the new university by overcoming the opposition of those Irish Catholics who favored a non-denominational university under government control rather than an exclusively Catholic institution; the issue was both delicate and thorny because it aroused the political passions underlying English-Irish relations. Thus the political and ecclesiastical situation in Ireland dictated the main structure of Newman's lectures: (1) an argument for the inclusion of theology in any university curriculum, and (2) an exposition and defense of the nature and function of a university.

Newman's lectures took the form of ten discourses, five of which were delivered in Dublin in the spring of 1852, and the last five written, although never actually given, in the fall of that year. They were published first in pamphlet form and then gathered together in a book in 1852 under the title of *Discourses on the Scope and Nature of University Education, Addressed to the Catholics of Dublin*. Newman reorganized these discourses in 1873 and published them under the title by which they have since been known.

The lectures were scarcely a rhetorical and political success. The divisions among the various parties continued, and the university limped along, until in 1858 Newman resigned and returned to England.* But although the discourses may have failed of their immediate practical purpose, they have since become known for the classical expression they have given to the ideal of liberal education.

In the abridgment of the work offered here, we have concentrated attention exclusively upon the exposition and analysis of this ideal, and anything at all secondary to this concern has been omitted.

John Stuart Mill† was led to give definitive form to his theory of university education by being elected Rector of St. Andrews University in Scotland. This office was purely honorary, and its duties were little more than the presentation of an inaugural address. Mill himself was not a university man, his education being achieved under the personal tutelage of his father. Yet as he declared in his *Autobiography*, he had long considered its problems, and in his discourse at St. Andrews "gave expression to many thoughts and opinions which had been accumulating in me through life, respecting the various studies which belong to a liberal education, their uses and influences, and the mode in which they should be pursued to render their influences most beneficial." The address was delivered February 1, 1867.

---

* For a biography of Cardinal Newman, see *GIT* 1966, p. 409.

† For his biography see *GIT* 1966, p. 456, as well as *GBWW*, Vol. 43, p. 263, and *GGB*, Vol. 6, p. 5.

ON THE ORGANIZATION
OF INSTITUTIONS
OF HIGHER LEARNING
IN BERLIN

Wilhelm Von Humbolt

The moral culture of the nation is crowned by its institutions of higher learning. This statement rests on the idea that the function of such institutions lies in the development of learning (*Wissenschaft*) in its deepest and broadest sense. Such a function is not imposed upon them; instead it grows out of their natural affinity for the basic stuff of spiritual and moral culture.

What is their essence? The core of it is the linkage of objective learning and personal development. Externally it reveals itself by connecting the completed course of preparatory study with the beginnings of independent research—or rather by implementing the transition from one to the other. Learning itself must remain the central point of reference. Though individual variations may occur, the concept of learning, properly apprehended, must be preserved in all its purity.

Our institutions can achieve their end only by continually confronting, as far as possible, this pure idea. Consequently, independence and freedom must be their governing principles.

Yet it is no less true that men's spiritual energies flourish best in a climate of community. It is not merely that one man may compensate for another's deficiency. It is rather that the successful activity of one individual inspires his neighbor. Thus all may be invigorated by that primal, common energy which, in isolation, might be diverted or drained away. Hence our institutions must be so organized as to evoke and maintain a spirit of cooperation—unremitting, self-animating, spontaneous.

Another characteristic of institutions of higher learning is that they always treat learning as an incompletely solved problem continually calling for further investigation. Here they differ from the schools for whom knowledge is complete, settled, defined. Con-sequently the relation between teacher and student alters basically. The teacher no longer merely serves the purposes of the student. Instead both serve learning itself. The teacher's occupation depends on the presence of the student. Lacking this presence, it would prosper less well. If students did not of their own accord gather round him, he would be impelled to seek them out. Thus his goals are more nearly approached through combining his own powers (experi but for that very reason somewhat narrow and lacking in vivacity) with those of the student (weaker and exerted energetically in all directions at once).

What we call institutions of higher learning, therefore, are—when divorced from all political restrictions—simply the spiritual life of those men drawn, by external necessity to inner *élan*, toward learning and research. One man will organize his thoughts in iso lation. Another may ally himself with men of his own generation. Still a third will gather round him a circle of young disciples. The state, in its desire to impose a more rigorous form on such ill-defined and ever fortuitous activity, must respect the loose patterns. It must see to it that:

1. It maintains this activity at its highest pitch of energy.

2. It resists any lowering of the level by preserving, clearly and firmly, the distinction between the higher institutions and the schools—not merely the general theoretical schools but more particularly the various technical ones.

Yet the state must constantly keep in mind that it is not, and cannot really be, the agent of these effects. Indeed it should realize that its interference will prove a hindrance, that things go infinitely better without it.

What then are the state's proper functions?

1. Within the social structure there mus

exist forms and means for the expression of any extensive activity. Hence the state is duty-bound to provide such forms and means for the cultivation of learning.

2. Yet its method of providing them can be harmful to the inner nature of the enterprise. Indeed these external forms and means are alien and generally detrimental in their effect. They degrade to a low material level what should be elevated and spiritual. Therefore the state must, as a first requirement, keep in mind the inner nature of our enterprise. Only in this way can it make good what (even if through no fault of its own) it has impeded or corrupted.

Though this is but another aspect of the same procedure, it has its advantage in actual results. For the state, led to view the matter in this light, will intervene ever more cautiously. Let us remember that, despite common opinion, in politics no theoretically incorrect view remains unpunished, for no political activity is purely automatic.

So much granted, it is easy to see that, with regard to the inner structure of institutions of higher learning, everything rests on a single principle: learning is something not now, nor ever to be, completely discovered; and in this spirit is to be unremittingly pursued.

The moment one abandons the pure pursuit of learning or presumes that it need not be drawn up from the spirit's deepest levels, but instead can be achieved by the collection and arrangement of facts, at that very moment all is forever and irretrievably lost. It is lost to learning itself which, if one persists along this path, escapes, leaving behind an empty husk of words. And it is no less lost to the state. Just as the individual character is transformed only by learning rooted and planted in one's inmost recesses, so the state, like humanity, is more concerned with character and action than with words and information.

If one wishes steadfastly to avoid straying into error, one must exert a vigorous, animated threefold effort.

1. To begin with, everything must be derived from a single, original principle. In this way the interpretation of natural phenomena is, for example, raised from the mechanistic plane to the dynamic, the organic, and at last the psychic, thus assuring the broadest possible understanding.

2. Then everything must be formed and directed toward an ideal.

3. Finally, the principle and the ideal must be combined into a single idea.

To be sure, these efforts cannot be promoted directly. But it will hardly occur to anyone that, among Germans, they need any direct promotion. They form by nature part of the German intellectual character. We need merely see to it that they are not suppressed, whether by force or by those countervailing tendencies which, agreed, also exist.

All narrow-mindedness must be banned from our institutions of higher learning. This catholic attitude will doubtless flush out many scholars to whom it will be alien, as well as a few to whom it will be actually repugnant. In general it can be held, in all its purity and power, only by a minority. However, it need merely appear here and there at intervals to make its influence felt widely and protractedly. But two attitudes must dominate: respect in those aware of it, fear in those who would destroy it.

Though it is in philosophy and art that such an endeavor most fully and distinctly expresses itself, we must keep in mind that by themselves they may easily degenerate. Furthermore we may place little hope in them when their spirit is transfused into the other branches of knowledge and research in an unsuitable or formal logico-mathematical manner.

To sum up: in our institution of higher learning this must be the ruling principle: Seek learning for its own sake, having no regard for anything else. Thus neither unity nor completeness will be lacking. One automatically seeking out the other, both will settle into that proper mutual relationship which is the secret of any sound scientific method.

And so every demand of the inner spirit of the institution is met.

As to the external relationship, the state need merely be responsible for assuring, by its choice of the men to be brought together, a strong and diverse current of spiritual energy. Beyond this, it must guarantee their freedom of action. It is not the state alone that may present a threat to freedom. The institutions themselves may jeopardize it by clinging to some particular program and resisting the introduction of any other. It is the duty of the state to avert any damage such an attitude might cause.

The nub of the matter lies in the choice of men. We will suggest a remedy for faculty selection when we come to consider the division of the whole institution into its separate parts.

In general this depends upon a few simple yet intricately interdependent principles of organization. These too we will discuss under the topic of the separate parts.

Finally we must consider certain auxiliary aids provided by institutions of higher learning. By and large we should not attach overweening importance to the mere accumulation of devitalized collections. On the contrary let us remember that this may very easily conduce to a dulling, a degradation of the spirit. It is by no means always in the richest academies and universities that the arts and sciences enjoy their profoundest, most ingenious development. The state's view of the proper sphere of our institutions of advanced study, considered as a whole, involves their relations, as higher institutions, to the schools, and, as organs of learning, to practical life.

The state must treat its universities neither as secondary nor as specialized schools. Nor must it exploit the academy as a technical or scientific cabinet. In general the state must demand nothing from them directly issuing from its own needs. Rather it should cherish the inner conviction that when their

goal is achieved, its goals are also achieved. Indeed they are achieved on a far loftier and more comprehensive plane, setting in motion powers and instruments of an order higher than the state can itself command.

On the other hand, it is a primary duty of the state to regulate its schools so that they work harmoniously along with our institutions of higher learning. This depends essentially upon a correct insight into the relationship between the two. It rests upon the increasingly fruitful conviction that the schools are not called upon to anticipate the teaching of the university. Nor are the universities a mere complement to them, a kind of higher school. Properly viewed, the transition from school to university represents a stage of youthful experience in which the school, if successful, has so prepared the pupil that he is ready physically, morally, and mentally for freedom and self-reliant activity. Freed from restraint, he will commit himself neither to an idle nor a practical life, but instead will cherish a longing to embrace that career of learning which had previously been but a remote vision.

The path to this goal is simple and sure. The school should stimulate in its pupils the harmonious cultivation of all their faculties. Exercising its powers upon the smallest possible number of objects, it should reveal them from every angle. It should so implant knowledge in the mind that the pupil's understanding, learning, and spiritual productions acquire charm, not through external circumstances, but through their inner precision, harmony, and beauty. To this end and for the preliminary exercise of the mind in the direction of pure learning, mathematics must preferably be studied, as soon as the power of reflection announces itself.

An intelligence so prepared will seize upon learning of his own accord. Another of equal diligence and talent but not so prepared will forthwith or before completing his education, bury himself in practical pursuits. He may spoil himself even for these or, deprived of the inspiration of the higher learning, di sipate his energies among unrelated branches of knowledge.

By institutions of higher learning one usually means the universities and academies of the arts and sciences. It is not difficult to derive these institutions, whose origin is actually fortuitous, from some grand prime conception. But this derivation, so popular since Kant, is partly rather distorted, and partly quite useless.

The important question remains: Is it still worth the trouble to set up or maintain an academy along with a university? What sphere of influence shall be assigned to them separately and together so that each may best express its own genius?

If the university is restricted to the teaching and dissemination of knowledge, while to the academy is assigned its advancement, one obviously does the university an injustice. The fact is that the arts and sciences have universally been as much promoted by university professors as by members of the academy—and in Germany even more so. And it is precisely their function as teachers that has enabled them to make these advances in their disciplines. Talking freely to an audience, which always includes a significant number of sympathetic intelligences, doubtless stimulates a man, once used to this kind of study, just as much as does the solitary leisure of the writer or the loose association of the academic community.

The pace of learning is obviously more animated, more accelerated, at a university crowded with more energetic and robust young minds. In general learning *qua* learning cannot be truly expounded without carrying with it spontaneous comprehension. It is inconceivable that these circumstances should not stimulate discoveries, and with some frequency. Furthermore university teach-

ing is not so irksome that it need interrupt—indeed it may rather benefit—scholarly leisure. Besides every large university contains some men who lecture little or not at all, devoting themselves to solitary study and research. Surely one can entrust the advancement of the arts and sciences exclusively to the universities (provided they are properly organized) and dispense with the academies.

The cooperative association found in academies is, true enough, not always found among university professors. Still this is hardly a sufficient reason for founding such expensive institutions. For one thing, even in the academies this association is rather a loose one. For another, it serves effectively only those observational and experimental sciences that require the rapid communication of isolated facts. Finally, private associations to serve these disciplines form readily without state assistance.

Going into the matter more closely, one notes that academies have flourished more markedly outside Germany, in countries where up to now they have dispensed, hardly even recognizing it, with the benefit of German universities. In our country, academies have flourished, preferably in places without universities or during periods when these universities were deficient in a more liberal and catholic attitude. In recent times no academy has been particularly distinguished, and they have played little or no part in the ascendancy of German scholarship.

Therefore, to keep both institutions vitally active, it is necessary to link them so that, while their activities remain distinct, their individual members are not always and exclusively parts of one or the other. With such a linkage the separate status allows both to be utilized in a new and admirable manner.

These advantages, however, depend much less on the characteristic activities of both institutions than upon their individual structures and their relation to the state; for, in fact, without the establishment of a special academy, its purposes can be wholly achieved through university teachers, especially since they can form, as they have in Göttingen, their own association of scholars (which remains quite distinct from a proper academy).

The university, of course, has a closer relation to practical life and the needs of the state, for it assumes a practical responsibility, the guidance of young people. The academy, however, is concerned purely with learning as such. With respect to the external and internal organization of their discipline, university professors are bound in a general mutual association. But they share their private projects only if so inclined. Otherwise each goes his own way. In contrast, the academy is a community expressly charged with submitting the work of any one to the judgment of all.

Thus we must firmly adhere to the idea of the academy as the highest and final sanctuary of learning, a corporation completely independent of the state. One must take one's chances: for such a corporation, through activities too limited or too one-sided, may or may not assure the triumph of what is right, even under the most favorable external conditions. We must risk it, I repeat, because the idea of the academy is intrinsically beautiful and beneficial, and because at any moment it may worthily fulfill itself.

Rivalry and antagonism currently exist between university and academy, a reciprocal action tending to bring into balance any excess or any deficiency.

In the first place this antagonism is connected with the selection of members for both corporations. Every academician, to be sure, must have the right to give lectures without further qualification (*Habilitation*), relieved of the necessity to become a member of the university. Some scholars should properly be both academicians and university professors; but in both institutions there should be others who are single in their affiliation.

The appointment of university professors must remain exclusively the prerogative of the state. It is certainly not a good arrangement to allow the faculties to have more

influence over the choice than would be accorded by any sensible and fair-minded board of trustees. For, though within the university antagonism and friction may be salutary and necessary, conflict between professors, arising from their specialty as such, may involuntarily distort their viewpoint. Also the quality of the universities is too closely tied in with the immediate interests of the state.

The academy, however, must be allowed to select its own members, subject only to the confirmation—a mere matter of form—of the King. For the academy is a community in which the principle of unity is far more important, and whose pure-research activities do not so closely concern the state as such.

From this situation arises the corrective or remedy, previously mentioned in connection with higher university appointments. For, as state and academy participate almost equally in them, it will soon be clear in what spirit they act. Thus, should they be in error, public opinion itself will forthwith and impartially set both right. But as they are not apt to err simultaneously, or at least not in the same manner, not all appointments run the same risk, and the institution as a whole is safe from one-sidedness.

The salutary diversity of forces here involved is underscored by the circumstance that, in addition to those members appointed by the state and those chosen by the academy, there are also the privatdocents who, at least at the start, are created and sustained merely by the applause of their listeners.

The academy, in addition to its academic labors, can engage in one of its most characteristic activities: systematic observation and experimentations. Of these activities some would be voluntarily undertaken, others commissioned. On those commissioned the university in turn would exercise its influence, thus assuring a fresh and beneficial interchange.

Besides the academy and the university there are certain other institutions devoted to higher learning. These must remain distinct from the other two and be under the immediate supervision of the state. However, both academy and university must be able not only to make use of them (with certain qualifications) but also to exercise control. This control, however, is indirect: they must submit to the state apparatus any memoranda or proposals for improvement.

Through the university the academy may avail itself of such institutions as the anatomical amphitheater and zoological museum. Formerly the academy had no connection with them because they were regarded from a restricted medical viewpoint rather than the broader perspective of the natural sciences.

Academy, university, auxiliary institutes: the three parts, at once independent and integral, of the collective institution. All— the latter two more so, the first less so— remain under the direction and superintendence of the state. Academy and university are alike independent. They are connected by whatever membership they share; by the university's granting to all academicians the right to lecture; and by the academy's role in organizing the observations and experiments initiated by the university. Both use and inspect the auxiliary institutes, the latter function being exercised in practice through the instrumentality of the state.

[Here the manuscript breaks off.]

THE IDEA

OF A UNIVERSITY

John Henry Newman

The view taken of a University in these Discourses is the following: That it is a place of *teaching* universal *knowledge*. This implies that its object is, on the one hand, intellectual, not moral; and, on the other, that it is the diffusion and extension of knowledge rather than the advancement. If its object were scientific and philosophical discovery, I do not see why a University should have students; if religious training, I do not see how it can be the seat of literature and science.

Such is a University in its *essence*, and independently of its relation to the Church. But, practically speaking, it cannot fulfil its object duly, such as I have described it, without the Church's assistance; or, to use the theological term, the Church is necessary for its *integrity*. Not that its main characters are changed by this incorporation: it still has the office of intellectual education; but the Church steadies it in the performance of that office.

. . . .

For instance, some persons may be tempted to complain, that I have servilely followed the English idea of a University, to the disparagement of that Knowledge which I profess to be so strenuously upholding; and they may anticipate that an academical system, formed upon my model, will result in nothing better or higher than in the production of that antiquated variety of human nature and remnant of feudalism, as they consider it, called "a gentleman."

. . . .

Our desideratum is, not the manners and habits of gentlemen—these can be, and are, acquired in various other ways, by good society, by foreign travel, by the innate grace and dignity of the Catholic mind—but the force, the steadiness, the comprehensiveness and the versatility of intellect, the command over our own powers, the instinctive just estimate of things as they pass before us which sometimes indeed is a natural gift, but commonly is not gained without much effort and the exercise of years.

This is real cultivation of mind; and I do not deny that the characteristic excellence of a gentleman are included in it. Nor need we be ashamed that they should be, since the poet long ago wrote, that "Ingenuas didicisse fideliter artes Emollit mores." Certainly a liberal education does manifest itself in a courtesy, propriety, and polish of word and action, which is beautiful in itself, and acceptable to others; but it does much more. It brings the mind into form—for the mind is like the body. Boys outgrow their shape and their strength; their limbs have to be knit together, and their constitution needs tone. Mistaking animal spirits for vigour and overconfident in their health, ignorant what they can bear and how to manage themselves, they are immoderate and extravagant; and fall into sharp sicknesses. This is an emblem of their minds; at first they have no principles laid down within them as a foundation for the intellect to build upon; they have no discriminating convictions, and no grasp of consequences. And therefore they talk at random, if they talk much, and cannot help being flippant, or what is emphatically called "young." They are merely dazzled by phenomena, instead of perceiving things as they are.

It were well if none remained boys all their lives; but what is more common than the sight of grown men, talking on political or moral or religious subjects, in that offhand, idle way, which we signify by the word *unreal?* "That they simply do not know what they are talking about" is the spontaneous silent remark of any man of sense who hears them. Hence such persons have no difficulty in contradicting themselves in successive sentences, without being conscious of it. Hence others, whose defect in intellectual training is more latent, have their most unfortunate crotchets, as they are called, or hobbies, which deprive them of the influence which their estimable qualities would otherwise secure. Hence others can never look straight before them, never see the point, and have no difficulties in the most difficult subjects. Others are hopelessly obstinate and prejudiced, and, after they have been driven from their opinions, return to them the next moment without even an attempt to explain why. Others are so intemperate and intractable that there is no greater calamity for a good cause than that they should get hold of it. It is very plain from the very particulars I have mentioned that, in this delineation of intellectual infirmities, I am drawing, not from Catholics, but from the world at large; I am referring to an evil which is forced upon us in every railway carriage, in every coffee-room or *table-d'hôte*, in every mixed company, an evil, however, to which Catholics are not less exposed than the rest of mankind.

When the intellect has once been properly trained and formed to have a connected view or grasp of things, it will display its powers with more or less effect according to its particular quality and capacity in the individual. In the case of most men it makes itself felt in the good sense, sobriety of thought, reasonableness, candour, self-command, and steadiness of view, which characterize it. In some it will have developed habits of business, power of influencing others, and sagacity. In others it will elicit the talent of philosophical speculation, and lead the mind forward to eminence in this or that intellectual department. In all it will be a faculty of entering with comparative ease into any subject of thought, and of taking up with aptitude any science or profession. All this it will be and will do in a measure, even when the mental formation be made after a model but partially true; for, as far

as effectiveness goes, even false views of things have more influence and inspire more respect than no views at all. Men who fancy they see what is not are more energetic, and make their way better, than those who see nothing; and so the undoubting infidel, the fanatic, the heresiarch, are able to do much, while the mere hereditary Christian, who has never realized the truths which he holds, is unable to do any thing. But, if consistency of view can add so much strength even to error, what may it not be expected to furnish to the dignity, the energy, and the influence of Truth!

[*from the* Preface]

THE RANGE AND UNITY OF KNOWLEDGE

As to the range of University teaching, certainly the very name of University is inconsistent with restrictions of any kind. Whatever was the original reason of the adoption of that term, which is unknown, I am only putting on it its popular, its recognized sense, when I say that a University should teach universal knowledge. That there is a real necessity for this universal teaching in the highest schools of intellect, I will show by-and-by; here it is sufficient to say that such universality is considered by writers on the subject to be the very characteristic of a University, as contrasted with other seats of learning. Thus Johnson, in his Dictionary, defines it to be "a school where all arts and faculties are taught;" and Mosheim, writing as an historian, says that, before the rise of the University of Paris—for instance, at Padua, or Salamanca, or Cologne —"the whole circle of sciences then known was not taught;" but that the school of Paris, "which exceeded all others in various respects, as well as in the number of teachers and students, was the first to embrace all the arts and sciences, and therefore first became a University."

If, with other authors, we consider the word to be derived from the invitation which is held out by a University to students of every kind, the result is the same; for, if certain branches of knowledge were excluded, those students of course would be excluded also, who desired to pursue them.

[*from* Discourse II]

Truth is the object of Knowledge of whatever kind; and when we inquire what is meant by Truth, I suppose it is right to answer that Truth means facts and their relations, which stand towards each other pretty much as subjects and predicates in logic. All that exists, as contemplated by the human mind, forms one large system or complex fact, and this of course resolves itself into an indefinite number of particular facts, which, as being portions of a whole, have countless relations of every kind, one towards another. Knowledge is the apprehension of these facts, whether in themselves, or in their mutual positions and bearings. And, as all taken together form one integral subject for contemplation, so there are no natural or real limits between part and part; one is ever running into another; all, as viewed by the mind, are combined together, and possess a correlative character one with another, from the internal mysteries of the Divine Essence down to our own sensations and consciousness, from the most solemn appointments of the Lord of all down to what may be called the accident of the hour, from the most glorious seraph down to the vilest and most noxious of reptiles.

Now, it is not wonderful that, with all its capabilities, the human mind cannot take in this whole vast fact at a single glance, or gain possession of it at once. Like a shortsighted reader, its eye pores closely, and travels slowly, over the awful volume which lies open for its inspection. Or again, as we deal with some huge structure of many parts and sides, the mind goes round about it, noting down, first one thing, then another, as it best may, and viewing it under different aspects, by way of making progress towards mastering the whole. So by degrees and by

circuitous advances does it rise aloft and subject to itself a knowledge of that univers into which it has been born.

These various partial views or abstractions by means of which the mind looks out upon its object, are called sciences, and embrac respectively larger or smaller portions of the field of knowledge; sometimes extending fa and wide, but superficially, sometimes with exactness over particular departments, some times occupied together on one and the same portion, sometimes holding one part in common, and then ranging on this side or tha in absolute divergence one from the other Thus Optics has for its subject the whole visible creation, so far forth as it is simply visible; Mental Philosophy has a narrower province, but a richer one. Astronomy, plane and physical, each has the same subject matter, but views it or treats it differently lastly, Geology and Comparative Anatomy have subject-matters partly the same, partly distinct. Now these views or sciences, as being abstractions, have far more to do with the relations of things than with things themselves. They tell us what things are, only or principally by telling us their relations, or assigning predicates to subjects; and therefore they never tell us all that can be said about a thing, even when they tell something, nor do they bring it before us, as the senses do. They arrange and classify facts; they reduce separate phenomena under a common law; they trace effects to a cause. Thus they serve to transfer our knowledge from the custody of memory to the surer and more abiding protection of philosophy, thereby providing both for its spread and its advance—for, inasmuch as sciences are forms of knowledge, they enable the intellect to master and increase it; and, inasmuch as they are instruments, to communicate it readily to others. Still, after all, they proceed on the principle of a division of labour, even though that division is an abstraction, not a literal separation into parts; and, as the maker of a bridle or an epaulet has not, on that account, any idea of the science of tactics or strategy, so in a parallel way, it is not every science which equally, nor any one which fully, enlightens the mind in the knowledge of things, as they are, or brings home to it the external object on which it wishes to gaze. Thus they differ in importance; and according to their importance will be their influence, not only on the mass of knowledge to which they all converge and contribute, but on each other.

Since then sciences are the results of mental processes about one and the same subject-matter, viewed under its various aspects, and are true results, as far as they go, yet at the same time separate and partial, it follows that on the one hand they need external assistance, one by one, by reason of their incompleteness, and on the other that they are able to afford it to each other, by reason, first, of their independence in themselves, and then of their connexion in their subject-matter. Viewed altogether, they approximate to a representation or subjective reflection of the objective truth, as nearly as is possible to the human mind, which advances towards the accurate apprehension of that object, in proportion to the number of sciences which it has mastered; and which, when certain sciences are away, in such a case has but a defective apprehension, in proportion to the value of the sciences which are thus wanting, and the importance of the field on which they are employed.

Let us take, for instance, man himself as our object of contemplation; then at once we shall find we can view him in a variety of relations; and according to those relations are the sciences of which he is the subject-matter, and according to our acquaintance with them is our possession of a true knowledge of him. We may view him in relation to the material elements of his body, or to his mental constitution, or to his household and family, or to the community in which he lives, or to the Being who made him; and in consequence we treat of him respectively as physiologists, or as moral philosophers, or as writers of economics, or of politics, or as theologians. When we think of him in all these relations together, or as the subject at once of all the sciences I have named, then we may be said to reach unto and rest in the idea of man as an object or external fact, similar to that which the eye takes of his outward form. On the other hand, according as we are only physiologists, or only politicians, or only moralists, so is our idea of man more or less unreal; we do not take in the whole of him, and the defect is greater or less, in proportion as the relation is, or is not, important, which is omitted, whether his relation to God or to his king, or to his children, or to his own component parts. And if there be one relation, about which we know nothing at all except that it exists, then is our knowledge of him, confessedly and to our own consciousness, deficient and partial, and that, I repeat, in proportion to the importance of the relation.

That therefore is true of sciences in general which we are apt to think applies only to pure mathematics, though to pure mathematics it applies especially, viz., that they cannot be considered as simple representations or informants of things as they are. We are accustomed to say, and say truly, that the conclusions of pure mathematics are applied, corrected, and adapted, by mixed; but so too the conclusions of Anatomy, Chemistry, Dynamics, and other sciences, are revised and completed by each other. Those several conclusions do not represent whole and substantive things, but views, true, so far as they go; and in order to ascertain how far they do go, that is, how far they correspond to the object to which they belong, we must compare them with the views taken out of that object by other sciences. Did we proceed upon the abstract theory of forces, we should assign a much more ample range to a projectile than in fact the resistance of the air allows it to accomplish. Let, however, that resistance be made the subject of scientific analysis, and then we shall have a new science, assisting, and to a certain point completing, for the benefit of questions of fact, the science of projection. On the other hand, the science

361

of projection itself, considered as belonging to the forces it contemplates, is not more perfect, as such, by this supplementary investigation. And in like manner, as regards the whole circle of sciences, one corrects another for purposes of fact, and one without the other cannot dogmatize, except hypothetically and upon its own abstract principles. For instance, the Newtonian philosophy requires the admission of certain metaphysical postulates, if it is to be more than a theory or an hypothesis; as, for instance, that what happened yesterday will happen to-morrow; that there is such a thing as matter, that our senses are trustworthy, that there is a logic of induction, and so on. Now to Newton metaphysicians grant all that he asks; but, if so be, they may not prove equally accommodating to another who asks something else, and then all his most logical conclusions in the science of physics would remain hopelessly on the stocks, though finished, and never could be launched into the sphere of fact.

Again, did I know nothing about the movement of bodies, except what the theory of gravitation supplies, were I simply absorbed in that theory so as to make it measure all motion on earth and in the sky, I should indeed come to many right conclusions, I should hit off many important facts, ascertain many existing relations, and correct many popular errors: I should scout and ridicule with great success the old notion, that light bodies flew up and heavy bodies fell down; but I should go on with equal confidence to deny the phenomenon of capillary attraction. Here I should be wrong, but only because I carried out my science irrespectively of other sciences. In like manner, did I simply give myself to the investigation of the external action of body upon body, I might scoff at the very idea of chemical affinities and combinations, and reject it as simply unintelligible. Were I a mere chemist, I should deny the influence of mind upon bodily health; and so on, as regards the devotees of any science, or family of sciences,

to the exclusion of others; they necessarily become bigots and quacks, scorning all principles and reported facts which do not belong to their own pursuit, and thinking to effect everything without aid from any other quarter. Thus, before now, Chemistry has been substituted for Medicine; and again, Political Economy, or intellectual enlightenment, or the reading of the Scriptures, has been cried up as a panacea against vice, malevolence, and misery.

Summing up, Gentlemen, what I have said, I lay it down that all knowledge forms one whole, because its subject-matter is one; for the universe in its length and breadth is so intimately knit together, that we cannot separate off portion from portion, and operation from operation, except by a mental abstraction; and then again, as to its Creator, though He of course in His own Being is infinitely separate from it, and Theology has its departments towards which human knowledge has no relations, yet He has so implicated Himself with it, and taken it into His very bosom, by His presence in it, His providence over it, His impressions upon it, and His influences through it, that we cannot truly or fully contemplate it without in some main aspects contemplating Him. Next, sciences are the results of that mental abstraction, which I have spoken of, being the logical record of this or that aspect of the whole subject-matter of knowledge. As they all belong to one and the same circle of objects, they are one and all connected together; as they are but aspects of things, they are severally incomplete in their relation to the things themselves, though complete in their own idea and for their own respective purposes; on both accounts they at once need and subserve each other. And further, the comprehension of the bearings of one science on another, and the use of each to each, and the location and limitation and adjustment and due appreciation of them all, one with another, this belongs, I conceive, to a sort of science distinct from all of them, and in some sense a science of

...iences, which is my own conception of what ...meant by Philosophy, in the true sense of ...he word, and of a philosophical habit of ...mind, and which in these Discourses I shall ...all by that name. This is what I have to say ...bout knowledge and philosophical knowl-...dge generally; and now I proceed to apply ...t to the particular science, which has led me ...o draw it out.

I say, then, that the systematic omission of ...ny one science from the catalogue preju-...ices the accuracy and completeness of our ...nowledge altogether, and that, in propor-...ion to its importance.

[*from* Discourse III]

...observe, then, that, if you drop any sci-...ence out of the circle of knowledge, you ...annot keep its place vacant for it; that ...cience is forgotten; the other sciences close ...p, or, in other words, they exceed their ...roper bounds, and intrude where they have ...o right. For instance, I suppose, if Ethics ...vere sent into banishment, its territory ...vould soon disappear, under a treaty of ...partition, as it may be called, between Law, ...political Economy, and Physiology; what, ...gain, would become of the province of Ex-...perimental Science, if made over to the Anti-...quarian Society; or of History, if surrendered ...ut and out to metaphysicians? The case is ...he same with the subject-matter of Theol-...ogy; it would be the prey of a dozen various ...ciences, if Theology were put out of posses-...ion; and not only so, but those sciences ...vould be plainly exceeding their rights and ...heir capacities in seizing upon it. They ...vould be sure to teach wrongly, where they ...had no mission to teach at all. The enemies ...of Catholicism ought to be the last to deny ...his—for they have never been blind to a ...like usurpation, as they have called it, on the ...part of theologians; those who accuse us of ...wishing, in accordance with Scripture lan-...guage, to make the sun go round the earth, ...are not the men to deny that a science which ...exceeds its limits falls into error.

I neither then am able nor care to deny, rather I assert the fact, and to-day I am going on to account for it, that any secular science, cultivated exclusively, may become dangerous to Religion; and I account for it on this broad principle, that no science whatever, however comprehensive it may be, but will fall largely into error, if it be constituted the sole exponent of all things in heaven and earth, and that, for the simple reason that it is encroaching on territory not its own, and undertaking problems which it has no instru-ments to solve. And I set off thus:

One of the first acts of the human mind is to take hold of and appropriate what meets the senses, and herein lies a chief distinction between man's and a brute's use of them. Brutes gaze on sights, they are arrested by sounds; and what they see and what they hear are mainly sights and sounds only. The intellect of man, on the contrary, energizes as well as his eye or ear, and perceives in sights and sounds something beyond them. It seizes and unites what the senses present to it; it grasps and forms what need not have been seen or heard except in its constituent parts. It discerns in lines and colours, or in tones, what is beautiful and what is not. It gives them a meaning, and invests them with an idea. It gathers up a succession of notes into the expression of a whole, and calls it a melody; it has a keen sensibility towards angles and curves, lights and shadows, tints and contours. It distinguishes between rule and exception, between accident and design. It assigns phenomena to a general law, quali-ties to a subject, acts to a principle, and effects to a cause. In a word, it philosophizes; for I suppose Science and Philosophy, in their elementary idea, are nothing else but this habit of *viewing*, as it may be called, the objects which sense conveys to the mind, of throwing them into system, and uniting and stamping them with one form.

This method is so natural to us, as I have said, as to be almost spontaneous; and we are impatient when we cannot exercise it, and in consequence we do not always wait to have the means of exercising it aright, but we often put up with insufficient or absurd views or interpretations of what we meet with, rather than have none at all. We refer the various matters which are brought home to us, material or moral, to causes which we happen to know of, or to such as are simply imaginary, sooner than refer them to nothing; and according to the activity of our intellect do we feel a pain and begin to fret, if we are not able to do so. Here we have an explanation of the multitude of off-hand sayings, flippant judgments, and shallow generalizations, with which the world abounds. Not from self-will only, nor from malevolence, but from the irritation which suspense occasions, is the mind forced on to pronounce, without sufficient data for pronouncing. Who does not form some view or other, for instance, of any public man, or any public event, nay, even so far in some cases as to reach the mental delineation of his appearance or of its scene? yet how few have a right to form any view. Hence the misconceptions of character, hence the false impressions and reports of words or deeds, which are the rule, rather than the exception, in the world at large; hence the extravagances of undisciplined talent, and the narrowness of conceited ignorance; because though it is no easy matter to view things correctly, nevertheless the busy mind will ever be viewing. We cannot do without a view, and we put up with an illusion, when we cannot get a truth.

Now, observe how this impatience acts in matters of research and speculation. What happens to the ignorant and hotheaded, will take place in the case of every person whose education or pursuits are contracted, whether they be merely professional, merely scientific, or of whatever other peculiar complexion. Men, whose life lies in the cultivation of one science, or the exercise of one method of thought, have no more right, though they have often more ambition, to generalize upon the basis of their own pursuit but beyond its range, than the schoolboy or the

ploughman to judge of a Prime Minister. But they must have something to say on every subject; habit, fashion, the public require it of them: and, if so, they can only give sentence according to their knowledge. You might think this ought to make such a person modest in his enunciations; not so: too often it happens that, in proportion to the narrowness of his knowledge, is, not his distrust of it, but the deep hold it has upon him, his absolute conviction of his own conclusions, and his positiveness in maintaining them. He has the obstinacy of the bigot, whom he scorns, without the bigot's apology, that he has been taught, as he thinks, his doctrine from heaven. Thus he becomes, what is commonly called, a man of one idea; which properly means a man of one science, and of the view, partly true, but subordinate, partly false, which is all that can proceed out of any thing so partial. Hence it is that we have the principles of utility, of combination, of progress, of philanthropy, or, in material sciences, comparative anatomy, phrenology, electricity, exalted into leading ideas, and keys, if not of all knowledge, at least of many things more than belong to them—principles, all of them true to a certain point, yet all degenerating into error and quackery, because they are carried to excess, viz. at the point where they require interpretation and restraint from other quarters, and because they are employed to do what is simply too much for them, inasmuch as a little science is not deep philosophy.

Lord Bacon has set down the abuse, of which I am speaking, among the impediments to the Advancement of the Sciences, when he observes that "men have used to infect their meditations, opinions, and doctrines, with some conceits which they have most admired, or *some sciences which they have most applied*; and given all things else a *tincture* according to them *utterly untrue and improper*. . . . So have the alchemists made a philosophy out of a few experiments of the furnace; and Gilbertus our countryman hath made a philosophy out of the obrvations of a loadstone.[1] So Cicero, when, reciting the several opinions of the nature of the soul, he found a musician that held the soul was but a harmony, saith pleasantly, 'ic ab arte suâ non recessit,' 'he was true to is art.' But of these conceits Aristotle speaketh seriously and wisely when he saith, 'Qui espiciunt ad pauca, de facili pronunciant,' 'hey who contemplate a few things have no ifficulty in deciding.' "[2]

[*from* Discourse IV]

KNOWLEDGE ITS OWN END

A University may be considered with reference either to its Students or to its studies; and the principle, that all Knowledge is a whole and the separate Sciences parts of one, which I have hitherto been using in behalf of its studies, is equally important when we direct our attention to its students. Now then I turn to the students, and shall consider the education which, by virtue of this principle, a University will give them; and thus I shall be introduced, Gentlemen, to the second question, which I proposed to discuss, viz., whether and in what sense its teaching, viewed relatively to the taught, carries the attribute of Utility along with it.

I have said that all branches of knowledge are connected together, because the subject-matter of knowledge is intimately united in itself, as being the acts and the work of the Creator. Hence it is that the Sciences, into which our knowledge may be said to be cast, have multiplied bearings one on another, and an internal sympathy, and admit, or rather demand, comparison and adjustment. They complete, correct, balance each other. This consideration, if well-founded, must be taken into account, not only as regards the attainment of truth, which is their common end, but as regards the influence which they exercise upon those whose education consists in

the study of them. I have said already, that to give undue prominence to one is to be unjust to another; to neglect or supersede these is to divert those from their proper object. It is to unsettle the boundary lines between science and science, to disturb their action, to destroy the harmony which binds them together. Such a proceeding will have a corresponding effect when introduced into a place of education. There is no science but tells a different tale, when viewed as a portion of a whole, from what it is likely to suggest when taken by itself, without the safeguard, as I may call it, of others.

. . . .

It is a great point then to enlarge the range of studies which a University professes, even for the sake of the students; and, though they cannot pursue every subject which is open to them, they will be the gainers by living among those and under those who represent the whole circle. This I conceive to be the advantage of a seat of universal learning, considered as a place of education. An assemblage of learned men, zealous for their own sciences, and rivals of each other, are brought, by familiar intercourse and for the sake of intellectual peace, to adjust together the claims and relations of their respective subjects of investigation. They learn to respect, to consult, to aid each other. Thus is created a pure and clear atmosphere of thought, which the student also breathes, though in his own case he only pursues a few sciences out of the multitude. He profits by an intellectual tradition, which is independent of particular teachers, which guides him in his choice of subjects, and duly interprets for him those which he chooses. He apprehends the great outlines of knowledge, the principles on which it rests, the scale of its parts, its lights and its shades, its great points and its little, as he otherwise cannot apprehend them. Hence it is that his education is called "Liberal." A habit of mind is formed which lasts through life, of which the attributes are freedom, equitableness, calmness, moderation, and wisdom; or what in a

---

1 William Gilbert, *On the Loadstone*; GBWW, Vol. 28.

2 Bacon; GBWW, Vol. 30, p. 166.

former Discourse I have ventured to call a philosophical habit. This then I would assign as the special fruit of the education furnished at a University, as contrasted with other places of teaching or modes of teaching. This is the main purpose of a University in its treatment of its students.

And now the question is asked me, What is the *use* of it? and my answer will constitute the main subject of the Discourses which are to follow.

Cautious and practical thinkers, I say, will ask of me, what, after all, is the gain of this Philosophy, of which I make such account, and from which I promise so much. Even supposing it to enable us to exercise the degree of trust exactly due to every science respectively, and to estimate precisely the value of every truth which is anywhere to be found, how are we better for this master view of things, which I have been extolling? Does it not reverse the principle of the division of labour? will practical objects be obtained better or worse by its cultivation? to what then does it lead? where does it end? what does it do? how does it profit? what does it promise? Particular sciences are respectively the basis of definite arts, which carry on to results tangible and beneficial the truths which are the subjects of the knowledge attained; what is the Art of this science of sciences? what is the fruit of such a Philosophy? what are we proposing to effect, what inducements do we hold out to the Catholic community, when we set about the enterprise of founding a University?

I am asked what is the end of University Education, and of the Liberal or Philosophical Knowledge which I conceive it to impart: I answer, that what I have already said has been sufficient to show that it has a very tangible, real, and sufficient end, though the end cannot be divided from that knowledge itself. Knowledge is capable of being its own end. Such is the constitution of the human mind, that any kind of knowledge, if it be really such, is its own reward. And if this is true of all knowledge, it is true also of that

special Philosophy, which I have made t consist in a comprehensive view of truth i all its branches, of the relations of science t science, of their mutual bearings, and the respective values. What the worth of suc an acquirement is, compared with othe objects which we seek—wealth or power o honour or the conveniences and comforts c life—I do not profess here to discuss; but would maintain, and mean to show, that it an object, in its own nature so really and u deniably good, as to be the compensation o a great deal of thought in the compassing and a great deal of trouble in the attaining

Now, when I say that Knowledge is, no merely a means to something beyond it, o the preliminary of certain arts into which naturally resolves, but an end sufficient t rest in and to pursue for its own sake, surel I am uttering no paradox, for I am statin what is both intelligible in itself, and ha ever been the common judgment of philoso phers and the ordinary feeling of mankind I am saying what at least the public opinio of this day ought to be slow to deny, con sidering how much we have heard of lat years, in opposition to Religion, of entertain ing, curious, and various knowledge. I an but saying what whole volumes have bee written to illustrate, viz., by a "selectior from the records of Philosophy, Literature and Art, in all ages and countries, of a body of examples, to show how the most unpropi tious circumstances have been unable t conquer an ardent desire for the acquisitior of knowledge." That further advantage accrue to us and redound to others by it possession, over and above what it is ir itself, I am very far indeed from denying but, independent of these, we are satisfying a direct need of our nature in its very acquisition; and, whereas our nature, unlike that of the inferior creation, does not a once reach its perfection, but depends, in order to it, on a number of external aids and appliances, Knowledge, as one of the princi pal of these, is valuable for what its very presence in us does for us after the manner f a habit, even though it be turned to no urther account, nor subserve any direct end.

Hence it is that Cicero, in enumerating he various heads of mental excellence, lays own the pursuit of Knowledge for its own ake, as the first of them. "This pertains most f all to human nature," he says, "for we are ll of us drawn to the pursuit of Knowledge; n which to excel we consider excellent, vhereas to mistake, to err, to be ignorant, o be deceived, is both an evil and a disrace."[3] And he considers Knowledge the ery first object to which we are attracted, fter the supply of our physical wants. After he calls and duties of our animal existence, s they may be termed, as regards ourselves, ur family, and our neighbours, follows, he ells us, "the search after truth. Accordingly, s soon as we escape from the pressure of ecessary cares, forthwith we desire to see, o hear, and to learn; and consider the nowledge of what is hidden or is wonderful condition of our happiness."

This passage, though it is but one of many imilar passages in a multitude of authors, take for the very reason that it is so familarly known to us; and I wish you to observe, Gentlemen, how distinctly it separates the ursuit of Knowledge from those ulterior bjects to which certainly it can be made to onduce, and which are, I suppose, solely ontemplated by the persons who would ask f me the use of a University or Liberal Eduation. So far from dreaming of the cultivaion of Knowledge directly and mainly in rder to our physical comfort and enjoyment, or the sake of life and person, of health, of he conjugal and family union, of the social ie and civil security, the great Orator implies, that it is only after our physical and political needs are supplied, and when we are 'free from necessary duties and cares," that we are in a condition for "desiring to see, to hear, and to learn." Nor does he contemplate in the least degree the reflex or subsequent action of Knowledge, when acquired,

upon those material goods which we set out by securing before we seek it; on the contrary, he expressly denies its bearing upon social life altogether, strange as such a procedure is to those who live after the rise of the Baconian philosophy, and he cautions us against such a cultivation of it as will interfere with our duties to our fellow-creatures. "All these methods," he says, "are engaged in the investigation of truth; by the pursuit of which to be carried off from public occupations is a transgression of duty. For the praise of virtue lies altogether in action; yet intermissions often occur, and then we recur to such pursuits; not to say that the incessant activity of the mind is vigorous enough to carry us on in the pursuit of knowledge, even without any exertion of our own." The idea of benefiting society by means of "the pursuit of science and knowledge" did not enter at all into the motives which he would assign for their cultivation.

This was the ground of the opposition which the elder Cato made to the introduction of Greek Philosophy among his countrymen, when Carneades and his companions, on occasion of their embassy, were charming the Roman youth with their eloquent expositions of it. The fit representative of a practical people, Cato estimated every thing by what it produced; whereas the Pursuit of Knowledge promised nothing beyond Knowledge itself. He despised that refinement or enlargement of mind of which he had no experience.

Things, which can bear to be cut off from every thing else and yet persist in living, must have life in themselves; pursuits, which issue in nothing, and still maintain their ground for ages, which are regarded as admirable, though they have not as yet proved themselves to be useful, must have their sufficient end in themselves, whatever it turn out to be. And we are brought to the same conclusion by considering the force of the epithet, by which the knowledge under consideration is popularly designated. It is common to speak of *"liberal* knowledge," of the

---

[3] Cicero, *On Duties*, Bk. I, chap. 1.

"*liberal* arts and studies," and of a "*liberal* education," as the especial characteristic or property of a University and of a gentleman; what is really meant by the word? Now, first, in its grammatical sense it is opposed to *servile;* and by "servile work" is understood, as our catechisms inform us, bodily labour, mechanical employment, and the like, in which the mind has little or no part. Parallel to such servile works are those arts, if they deserve the name, of which the poet speaks,[4] which owe their origin and their method to hazard, not to skill; as, for instance, the practice and operations of an empiric. As far as this contrast may be considered as a guide into the meaning of the word, liberal education and liberal pursuits are exercises of mind, of reason, of reflection.

But we want something more for its explanation, for there are bodily exercises which are liberal, and mental exercises which are not so. For instance, in ancient times the practitioners in medicine were commonly slaves; yet it was an art as intellectual in its nature, in spite of the pretence, fraud, and quackery with which it might then, as now, be debased, as it was heavenly in its aim. And so in like manner, we contrast a liberal education with a commercial education or a professional; yet no one can deny that commerce and the professions afford scope for the highest and most diversified powers of mind. There is then a great variety of intellectual exercises, which are not technically called "liberal"; on the other hand, I say, there are exercises of the body which do receive that appellation. Such, for instance, was the palæstra, in ancient times; such the Olympic games, in which strength and dexterity of body as well as of mind gained the prize. In Xenophon we read of the young Persian nobility being taught to ride on horseback and to speak the truth; both being among the accomplishments of a gentleman. War, too,

however rough a profession, has ever been accounted liberal, unless in cases when it becomes heroic, which would introduce us to another subject.

Now comparing these instances together, we shall have no difficulty in determining the principle of this apparent variation in the application of the term which I am examining. Manly games, or games of skill, or military prowess, though bodily, are, it seems, accounted liberal; on the other hand, what is merely professional, though highly intellectual, nay, though liberal in comparison of trade and manual labour, is not simply called liberal, and mercantile occupations are not liberal at all. Why this distinction? because that alone is liberal knowledge, which stands on its own pretensions, which is independent of sequel, expects no complement, refuses to be *informed* (as it is called) by any end, or absorbed into any art, in order duly to present itself to our contemplation. The most ordinary pursuits have this specific character, if they are self-sufficient and complete; the highest lose it, when they minister to something beyond them. It is absurd to balance, in point of worth and importance, a treatise on reducing fractures with a game of cricket or a fox-chase, yet of the two the bodily exercise has that quality which we call "liberal," and the intellectual has it not. And so of the learned professions altogether, considered merely as professions; although one of them be the most popularly beneficial, and another the most politically important, and the third the most intimately divine of all human pursuits, yet the very greatness of their end, the health of the body, or of the commonwealth, or of the soul, diminishes, not increases, their claim to the appellation "liberal," and that still more, if they are cut down to the strict exigencies of that end. If, for instance, Theology, instead of being cultivated as a contemplation, be limited to the purposes of the pulpit or be represented by the catechism, it loses—not its usefulness, not its divine character, not its meritoriousness (rather it gains a claim upon these titles by

---

4 "Art loves chance, and chance loves art" in Aristotle, *Nic. Ethics vi.* 4; *GBWW*, Vol. 9, p. 389a.

ch charitable condescension)—but it does se the particular attribute which I am illustrating; just as a face worn by tears and fasting loses its beauty, or a labourer's hand loses its delicateness—for Theology thus exercised is not simple knowledge, but rather an art or a business making use of Theology. And thus it appears that even what is supernatural need not be liberal, nor need a hero be a gentleman, for the plain reason that one idea is not another idea. And in like manner the Baconian Philosophy, by using its physical sciences in the service of man, does thereby transfer them from the order of liberal Pursuits to, I do not say the inferior, but the distinct class of the Useful. And, to take a different instance, hence again, as is evident, whenever personal gain is the move, still more distinctive an effect has it upon the character of a given pursuit; thus racing, which was a liberal exercise in Greece, forfeits its rank in times like these, so far as it is made the occasion of gambling.

All that I have been now saying is summed up in a few characteristic words of the great philosopher. "Of possessions," he says, "those rather are useful, which bear fruit; those *liberal, which tend to enjoyment.* By fruitful, I mean, which yield revenue; by enjoyable, where *nothing accrues of consequence beyond the using.*"[5]

Do not suppose, that in thus appealing to the ancients, I am throwing back the world two thousand years, and fettering Philosophy with the reasonings of paganism. While the world lasts, will Aristotle's doctrine on these matters last, for he is the oracle of nature and of truth. While we are men, we cannot help, to a great extent, being Aristotelians, for the great Master does but analyze the thoughts, feelings, views, and opinions of human kind. He has told us the meaning of our own words and ideas, before we were born. In many subject-matters, to think correctly, is to think like Aristotle; and we are

his disciples whether we will or no, though we may not know it. Now, as to the particular instance before us, the word "liberal" as applied to Knowledge and Education, expresses a specific idea, which ever has been, and ever will be, while the nature of man is the same, just as the idea of the Beautiful is specific, or of the Sublime, or of the Ridiculous, or of the Sordid. It is in the world now, it was in the world then; and, as in the case of the dogmas of faith, it is illustrated by a continuous historical tradition, and never was out of the world, from the time it came into it. There have indeed been differences of opinion from time to time, as to what pursuits and what arts came under that idea, but such differences are but an additional evidence of its reality. That idea must have a substance in it, which has maintained its ground amid these conflicts and changes, which has ever served as a standard to measure things withal, which has passed from mind to mind unchanged, when there was so much to colour, so much to influence any notion or thought whatever, which was not founded in our very nature. Were it a mere generalization, it would have varied with the subjects from which it was generalized; but though its subjects vary with the age, it varies not itself. The palæstra may seem a liberal exercise to Lycurgus, and illiberal to Seneca; coach-driving and prize-fighting may be recognized in Elis, and be condemned in England; music may be despicable in the eyes of certain moderns, and be in the highest place with Aristotle and Plato—(and the case is the same in the particular application of the idea of Beauty, or of Goodness, or of Moral Virtue, there is a difference of tastes, a difference of judgments) —still these variations imply, instead of discrediting, the archetypal idea, which is but a previous hypothesis or condition, by means of which issue is joined between contending opinions, and without which there would be nothing to dispute about.

I consider, then, that I am chargeable with no paradox, when I speak of a Knowledge

---

Aristotle, *Rhetoric*, I. 5; *GBWW*, Vol. 9, p. 601c.

which is its own end, when I call it liberal knowledge, or a gentleman's knowledge, when I educate for it, and make it the scope of a University. And still less am I incurring such a charge, when I make this acquisition consist, not in Knowledge in a vague and ordinary sense, but in that Knowledge which I have especially called Philosophy or, in an extended sense of the word, Science; for whatever claims Knowledge has to be considered as a good, these it has in a higher degree when it is viewed not vaguely, not popularly, but precisely and transcendently as Philosophy. Knowledge, I say, is then especially liberal, or sufficient for itself, apart from every external and ulterior object, when and so far as it is philosophical, and this I proceed to show.

Now bear with me, Gentlemen, if what I am about to say, has at first sight a fanciful appearance. Philosophy, then, or Science, is related to Knowledge in this way: Knowledge is called by the name of Science or Philosophy, when it is acted upon, informed, or if I may use a strong figure, impregnated by Reason. Reason is the principle of that intrinsic fecundity of Knowledge, which, to those who possess it, is its especial value, and which dispenses with the necessity of their looking abroad for any end to rest upon external to itself. Knowledge, indeed, when thus exalted into a scientific form, is also power; not only is it excellent in itself, but whatever such excellence may be, it is something more, it has a result beyond itself. Doubtless; but that is a further consideration, with which I am not concerned. I only say that, prior to its being a power, it is a good; that it is, not only an instrument, but an end. I know well it may resolve itself into an art, and terminate in a mechanical process, and in tangible fruit; but it also may fall back upon that Reason which informs it, and resolve itself into Philosophy. In one case it is called Useful Knowledge, in the other Liberal. The same person may cultivate it in both ways at once; but this again is a matter foreign to my subject; here I do

but say that there are two ways of using Knowledge, and in matter of fact those who use it in one way are not likely to use it in the other, or at least in a very limited measure. You see, then, here are two methods of Education; the end of the one is to be philosophical, of the other to be mechanical; the one rises towards general ideas, the other is exhausted upon what is particular and external. Let me not be thought to deny the necessity, or to decry the benefit, of such attention to what is particular and practical, as belongs to the useful or mechanical arts; life could not go on without them; we owe our daily welfare to them; their exercise is the duty of the many, and we owe to the many a debt of gratitude for fulfilling that duty. only say that Knowledge, in proportion as it tends more and more to be particular, ceases to be Knowledge. It is a question whether Knowledge can in any proper sense be predicated of the brute creation; without pretending to metaphysical exactness of phraseology, which would be unsuitable to an occasion like this, I say, it seems to me improper to call that passive sensation, or perception of things, which brutes seem to possess, by the name of Knowledge. When speak of Knowledge, I mean something intellectual, something which grasps what it perceives through the senses; something which takes a view of things; which sees more than the senses convey; which reasons upon what it sees, and while it sees; which invests it with an idea. It expresses itself, not in a mere enunciation, but by an enthymeme: it is of the nature of science from the first, and in this consists its dignity. The principle of real dignity in Knowledge, its worth, its desirableness, considered irrespectively of its results, is this germ within it of a scientific or a philosophical process. This is how it comes to be an end in itself; this is why it admits of being called Liberal. Not to know the relative disposition of things is the state of slaves or children; to have mapped out the Universe is the boast, or at least the ambition of Philosophy.

Moreover, such knowledge is not a mere [in]trinsic or accidental advantage, which is [ou]rs to-day and another's to-morrow, which [m]ay be got up from a book, and easily for[go]tten again, which we can command or [co]mmunicate at our pleasure, which we can [bo]rrow for the occasion, carry about in our [ha]nd, and take into the market; it is an ac[qu]ired illumination, it is a habit, a personal [po]ssession, and an inward endowment. And [th]is is the reason, why it is more correct, as [w]ell as more usual, to speak of a University [as] a place of education, than of instruction, [th]ough, when knowledge is concerned, in[st]ruction would at first sight have seemed the [m]ore appropriate word. We are instructed, [fo]r instance, in manual exercises, in the fine [an]d useful arts, in trades, and in ways of busi[n]ess; for these are methods, which have little [or] no effect upon the mind itself, are con[t]ained in rules committed to memory, to [tr]adition, or to use, and bear upon an end [e]ternal to themselves. But education is a [h]igher word; it implies an action upon our [m]ental nature, and the formation of a char[ac]ter; it is something individual and perma[n]ent, and is commonly spoken of in con[n]exion with religion and virtue. When, then, [w]e speak of the communication of Knowl[e]dge as being Education, we thereby really [im]ply that that Knowledge is a state or con[di]tion of mind; and since cultivation of mind [is] surely worth seeking for its own sake, we [ar]e thus brought once more to the conclu[si]on, which the word "Liberal" and the word ["]Philosophy" have already suggested, that [th]ere is a Knowledge, which is desirable, [th]ough nothing come of it, as being of itself [a] treasure, and a sufficient remuneration of [ye]ars of labour.

. . . .

Useful Knowledge then, I grant, has done [it]s work; and Liberal Knowledge as certainly [h]as not done its work—that is, supposing, as [th]e objectors assume, its direct end, like Re[li]gious Knowledge, is to make men better; [b]ut this I will not for an instant allow, and, [u]nless I allow it, those objectors have said

nothing to the purpose. I admit, rather I maintain, what they have been urging, for I consider Knowledge to have its end in itself. For all its friends, or its enemies, may say, I insist upon it, that it is as real a mistake to burden it with virtue or religion as with the mechanical arts. Its direct business is not to steel the soul against temptation or to console it in affliction, any more than to set the loom in motion, or to direct the steam carriage; be it ever so much the means or the condition of both material and moral advancement, still, taken by and in itself, it as little mends our hearts as it improves our temporal circumstances. And if its eulogists claim for it such a power, they commit the very same kind of encroachment on a province not their own as the political economist who should maintain that his science educated him for casuistry or diplomacy. Knowledge is one thing, virtue is another; good sense is not conscience, refinement is not humility, nor is largeness and justness of view faith. Philosophy, however enlightened, however profound, gives no command over the passions, no influential motives, no vivifying principles. Liberal Education makes not the Christian, not the Catholic, but the gentleman. It is well to be a gentleman, it is well to have a cultivated intellect, a delicate taste, a candid, equitable, dispassionate mind, a noble and courteous bearing in the conduct of life; these are the connatural qualities of a large knowledge; they are the objects of a University; I am advocating, I shall illustrate and insist upon them; but still, I repeat, they are no guarantee for sanctity or even for conscientiousness, they may attach to the man of the world, to the profligate, to the heartless—pleasant, alas, and attractive as he shows when decked out in them. Taken by themselves, they do but seem to be what they are not; they look like virtue at a distance, but they are detected by close observers, and on the long run; and hence it is that they are popularly accused of pretence and hypocrisy, not, I repeat, from their own fault, but because their professors and their admirers persist in taking them for what they are not, and are officious in arrogating for them a praise to which they have no claim. Quarry the granite rock with razors, or moor the vessel with a thread of silk; then may you hope with such keen and delicate instruments as human knowledge and human reason to contend against those giants, the passion and the pride of man.

Surely we are not driven to theories of this kind, in order to vindicate the value and dignity of Liberal Knowledge. Surely the real grounds on which its pretensions rest are not so very subtle or abstruse, so very strange or improbable. Surely it is very intelligible to say, and that is what I say here, that Liberal Education, viewed in itself, is simply the cultivation of the intellect, as such, and its object is nothing more or less than intellectual excellence. Every thing has its own perfection, be it higher or lower in the scale of things; and the perfection of one is not the perfection of another. Things animate, inanimate, visible, invisible, all are good in their kind, and have a *best* of themselves, which is an object of pursuit. Why do you take such pains with your garden or your park? You see to your walks and turf and shrubberies; to your trees and drives; not as if you meant to make an orchard of the one, or corn or pasture land of the other, but because there is a special beauty in all that is goodly in wood, water, plain, and slope, brought all together by art into one shape, and grouped into one whole. Your cities are beautiful, your palaces, your public buildings, your territorial mansions, your churches; and their beauty leads to nothing beyond itself. There is a physical beauty and a moral: there is a beauty of person, there is a beauty of our moral being, which is natural virtue; and in like manner there is a beauty, there is a perfection, of the intellect. There is an ideal perfection in these various subject-matters, towards which individual instances are seen to rise, and which are the standards for all instances whatever. The Greek divinities and demigods, as the statu-

ary has moulded them, with their symmetry of figure, and their high forehead and their regular features, are the perfection of physical beauty. The heroes, of whom history tells, Alexander, or Cæsar, or Scipio, or Saladin, are the representatives of that magnanimity or self-mastery which is the greatness of human nature. Christianity too has its heroes, and in the supernatural order, and we call them Saints. The artist puts before him beauty of feature and form; the poet, beauty of mind; the preacher, the beauty of grace: then intellect too, I repeat, has its beauty, and it has those who aim at it. To open the mind, to correct it, to refine it, to enable it to know, and to digest, master, rule, and use its knowledge, to give it power over its own faculties, application, flexibility, method, critical exactness, sagacity, resource, address, eloquent expression, is an object as intelligible (for here we are inquiring, not what the object of a Liberal Education is worth, nor what use the Church makes of it, but what it is in itself), I say, an object as intelligible as the cultivation of virtue, while at the same time, it is absolutely distinct from it.

This indeed is but a temporal object, and a transitory possession; but so are other things in themselves which we make much of and pursue. The moralist will tell us that man, in all his functions, is but a flower which blossoms and fades, except so far as a higher principle breathes upon him, and makes him and what he is immortal. Body and mind are carried on into an eternal state of being by the gifts of Divine Munificence; but at first they do but fail in a failing world, and if the powers of intellect decay, the powers of the body have decayed before them; and, as an Hospital or an Almshouse, though its end be ephemeral, may be sanctified to the service of religion, so surely may a University, even were it nothing more than I have as yet described it. We attain to heaven by using this world well, though it is to pass away; we perfect our nature, not by undoing it, but by adding to it what is more than

372

ature, and directing it towards aims higher
than its own.

[from Discourse V]

KNOWLEDGE VIEWED
IN RELATION
TO LEARNING

It were well if the English, like the Greek language, possessed some definite word to express, simply and generally, intellectual proficiency or perfection, such as "health," is used with reference to the animal frame, and "virtue," with reference to our moral nature. I am not able to find such a term; talent, ability, genius, belong distinctly to the raw material, which is the subject-matter, not to that excellence which is the result of exercise and training. When we turn, indeed, to the particular kinds of intellectual perfection, words are forthcoming for our purpose, as, for instance, judgment, taste, and skill; yet even these belong, for the most part, to powers or habits bearing upon practice or upon art, and not to any perfect condition of the intellect, considered in itself. Wisdom, again, is certainly a more comprehensive word than any other, but it has a direct relation to conduct, and to human life. Knowledge, indeed, and Science express purely intellectual ideas, but still not a state or quality of the intellect; for knowledge, in its ordinary sense, is but one of its circumstances, denoting a possession or a habit; and science has been appropriated to the subject-matter of the intellect, instead of belonging in English, as it ought to do, to the intellect itself. The consequence is that, on an occasion like this, many words are necessary, in order, first, to bring out and convey what surely is no difficult idea in itself—that of the cultivation of the intellect as an end; next, in order to recommend what surely is no unreasonable object; and lastly, to describe and make the mind realize the particular perfection in which that object consists. Every one knows practically what are the constituents of health or of virtue; and every one recognizes health

and virtue as ends to be pursued; it is otherwise with intellectual excellence, and this must be my excuse, if I seem to any one to be bestowing a good deal of labour on a preliminary matter.

In default of a recognized term, I have called the perfection or virtue of the intellect by the name of philosophy, philosophical knowledge, enlargement of mind, or illumination; terms which are not uncommonly given to it by writers of this day: but, whatever name we bestow on it, it is, I believe, as a matter of history, the business of a University to make this intellectual culture its direct scope, or to employ itself in the education of the intellect, just as the work of a Hospital lies in healing the sick or wounded, of a Riding or Fencing School, or of a Gymnasium, in exercising the limbs, of an Almshouse, in aiding and solacing the old, of an Orphanage, in protecting innocence, of a Penitentiary, in restoring the guilty. I say, a University, taken in its bare idea, and before we view it as an instrument of the Church, has this object and this mission; it contemplates neither moral impression nor mechanical production; it professes to exercise the mind neither in art nor in duty; its function is intellectual culture; here it may leave its scholars, and it has done its work when it has done as much as this. It educates the intellect to reason well in all matters, to reach out towards truth, and to grasp it.

This, I said in my foregoing Discourse, was the object of a University, viewed in itself, and apart from the Catholic Church, or from the State, or from any other power which may use it; and I illustrated this in various ways. I said that the intellect must have an excellence of its own, for there was nothing which had not its specific good; that the word "educate" would not be used of intellectual culture, as it is used, had not the intellect had an end of its own; that, had it not such an end, there would be no meaning in calling certain intellectual exercises "liberal," in contrast with "useful," as is commonly done; that the very notion of a philosophical temper implied it, for it threw us back upon research and system as ends in themselves, distinct from effects and works of any kind; that a philosophical scheme of knowledge, or system of sciences, could not, from the nature of the case, issue in any one definite art or pursuit, as its end; and that, on the other hand, the discovery and contemplation of truth, to which research and systematizing led, were surely sufficient ends, though nothing beyond them were added, and that they had ever been accounted sufficient by mankind.

Here then I take up the subject; and, having determined that the cultivation of the intellect is an end distinct and sufficient in itself, and that, so far as words go it is an enlargement or illumination, I proceed to inquire what this mental breadth, or power, or light, or philosophy consists in. A Hospital heals a broken limb or cures a fever: what does an Institution effect, which professes the health, not of the body, not of the soul, but of the intellect? What is this good, which in former times, as well as our own, has been found worth the notice, the appropriation, of the Catholic Church?

I have then to investigate, in the Discourses which follow, those qualities and characteristics of the intellect in which its cultivation issues or rather consists; and, with a view of assisting myself in this undertaking, I shall recur to certain questions which have already been touched upon. These questions are three: viz. the relation of intellectual culture, first, to *mere* knowledge; secondly, to *professional* knowledge; and thirdly, to *religious* knowledge. In other words, are *acquirements* and *attainments* the scope of a University Education? or *expertness in particular arts and pursuits?* or *moral and religious proficiency?* or something besides these three? These questions I shall examine in succession, with the purpose I have mentioned; and I hope to be excused, if, in this anxious undertaking, I am led to repeat what, either in these Discourses or elsewhere, I have already put upon paper. And first, of

Mere Knowledge, or Learning, and its connexion with intellectual illumination of Philosophy.

I suppose the *primâ-facie* view which the public at large would take of a University considering it as a place of Education, nothing more or less than a place for acquiring a great deal of knowledge on a great many subjects. Memory is one of the first developed of the mental faculties; a boy's business when he goes to school is to learn, that is, to store up things in his memory. For some years his intellect is little more than an instrument for taking in facts, or a receptacle for storing them; he welcomes them as fast as they come to him; he lives on what is without; he has his eyes ever about him; he has a lively susceptibility of impressions; he imbibes information of every kind; and little does he make his own in a true sense of the word, living rather upon his neighbours all around him. He has opinions, religious, political, and literary, and, for a boy, is very positive in them and sure about them; but he gets them from his schoolfellows, or his masters, or his parents, as the case may be. Such as he is in his other relations, such also is he in his school exercises; his mind is of servant, sharp, ready, retentive; he is almost passive in the acquisition of knowledge. I say this in no disparagement of the idea of a clever boy. Geography, chronology, history, language, natural history, he heaps up the matter of these studies as treasures for a future day. It is the seven years of plenty with him: he gathers in by handfuls, like the Egyptians, without counting; and though, as time goes on, there is exercise for his argumentative powers in the Elements of Mathematics, and for his taste in the Poets and Orators, still, while at school, or at least, till quite the last years of his time, he acquires and little more; and when he is leaving for the University, he is mainly the creature of foreign influences and circumstances, and made up of accidents, homogeneous or not as the case may be. Moreover, the moral habits, which are a boy's praise, encourage

nd assist this result; that is, diligence, as-
duity, regularity, despatch, persevering ap-
lication; for these are the direct conditions
f acquisition, and naturally lead to it. Ac-
uirements, again, are emphatically produc-
le, and at a moment; they are a something
 show, both for master and scholar; an
udience, even though ignorant themselves
f the subjects of an examination, can com-
rehend when questions are answered and
hen they are not. Here again is a reason
hy mental culture is in the minds of men
lentified with the acquisition of knowledge.

The same notion possesses the public
ind, when it passes on from the thought of
school to that of a University: and with the
est of reasons so far as this, that there is no
rue culture without acquirements, and that
hilosophy presupposes knowledge. It re-
uires a great deal of reading, or a wide
ange of information, to warrant us in put-
ing forth our opinions on any serious sub-
ct; and without such learning the most
riginal mind may be able indeed to dazzle,
 amuse, to refute, to perplex, but not to
ome to any useful result or any trustworthy
nclusion. There are indeed persons who
rofess a different view of the matter, and
ven act upon it. Every now and then you
ill find a person of vigorous or fertile mind,
ho relies upon his own resources, despises
ll former authors, and gives the world, with
he utmost fearlessness, his views upon region, or history, or any other popular sub-
ct. And his works may sell for a while; he
ay get a name in his day; but this will be
ll. His readers are sure to find on the long
un that his doctrines are mere theories, and
ot the expression of facts, that they are chaff
nstead of bread, and then his popularity
rops as suddenly as it rose.

Knowledge then is the indispensable con-
ition of expansion of mind, and the instru-
ent of attaining to it; this cannot be de-
ied, it is ever to be insisted on; I begin with
 as a first principle; however, the very truth
f it carries men too far, and confirms to
hem the notion that it is the whole of the
matter. A narrow mind is thought to be that
which contains little knowledge; and an enlarged mind, that which holds a great deal;
and what seems to put the matter beyond
dispute is, the fact of the great number of
studies which are pursued in a University, by
its very profession. Lectures are given on
every kind of subject; examinations are held;
prizes awarded. There are moral, metaphysical, physical Professors; Professors of
languages, of history, of mathematics, of experimental science. Lists of questions are published, wonderful for their range and depth,
variety and difficulty; treatises are written,
which carry upon their very face the evidence
of extensive reading or multifarious information; what then is wanting for mental
culture to a person of large reading and scientific attainments? what is grasp of mind
but acquirement? where shall philosophical
repose be found, but in the consciousness and
enjoyment of large intellectual possessions?

And yet this notion is, I conceive, a mistake, and my present business is to show that
it is one, and that the end of a Liberal Education is not mere knowledge, or knowledge
considered in its *matter;* and I shall best attain my object, by actually setting down some
cases, which will be generally granted to be
instances of the process of enlightenment or
enlargement of mind, and others which are
not, and thus, by the comparison, you will be
able to judge for yourselves, Gentlemen,
whether Knowledge, that is, acquirement, is
after all the real principle of the enlargement, or whether that principle is not rather
something beyond it.

For instance, let a person, whose experience has hitherto been confined to the more
calm and unpretending scenery of these islands, whether here or in England, go for the
first time into parts where physical nature
puts on her wilder and more awful forms,
whether at home or abroad, as into moun-
tainous districts; or let one, who has ever
lived in a quiet village, go for the first time
to a great metropolis—then I suppose he will
have a sensation which perhaps he never had

before. He has a feeling not in addition or increase of former feelings, but of something different in its nature. He will perhaps be borne forward, and find for a time that he has lost his bearings. He has made a certain progress, and he has a consciousness of mental enlargement; he does not stand where he did, he has a new centre, and a range of thoughts to which he was before a stranger.

Again, the view of the heavens which the telescope opens upon us, if allowed to fill and possess the mind, may almost whirl it round and make it dizzy. It brings in a flood of ideas, and is rightly called an intellectual enlargement, whatever is meant by the term.

And so again, the sight of beasts of prey and other foreign animals, their strangeness, the originality (if I may use the term) of their forms and gestures and habits and their variety and independence of each other, throw us out of ourselves into another creation, and as if under another Creator, if I may so express the temptation which may come on the mind. We seem to have new faculties, or a new exercise for our faculties, by this addition to our knowledge; like a prisoner, who, having been accustomed to wear manacles or fetters, suddenly finds his arms and legs free.

Hence Physical Science generally, in all its departments, as bringing before us the exuberant riches and resources, yet the orderly course, of the Universe, elevates and excites the student, and at first, I may say, almost takes away his breath, while in time it exercises a tranquilizing influence upon him.

Again, the study of history is said to enlarge and enlighten the mind, and why? because, as I conceive, it gives it a power of judging of passing events, and of all events, and a conscious superiority over them, which before it did not possess.

And in like manner, what is called seeing the world, entering into active life, going into society, travelling, gaining acquaintance with the various classes of the community, coming into contact with the principles and modes of thought of various parties, interests,

and races, their views, aims, habits and manners, their religious creeds and forms of worship, gaining experience how various ye how alike men are, how low-minded, how bad, how opposed, yet how confident in their opinions; all this exerts a perceptible influence upon the mind, which it is impossible to mistake, be it good or be it bad, and is popularly called its enlargement.

And then again, the first time the mind comes across the arguments and speculations of unbelievers, and feels what a novel light they cast upon what he has hitherto accounted sacred; and still more, if it gives in to them and embraces them, and throws off as so much prejudice what it has hitherto held, and, as if waking from a dream, begins to realize to its imagination that there is now no such thing as law and the transgression of law, that sin is a phantom, and punishment a bugbear, that it is free to sin, free to enjoy the world and the flesh; and still further, when it does enjoy them, and reflects that it may think and hold just what it will, that "the world is all before it where to choose," and what system to build up as its own private persuasion; when this torrent of wilful thoughts rushes over and inundates it, who will deny that the fruit of the tree of knowledge, or what the mind takes for knowledge, has made it one of the gods, with a sense of expansion and elevation—an intoxication in reality, still, so far as the subjective state of the mind goes, an illumination? Hence the fanaticism of individuals or nations, who suddenly cast off their Maker. Their eyes are opened; and, like the judgment-stricken king in the Tragedy, they see two suns, and a magic universe, out of which they look back upon their former state of faith and innocence with a sort of contempt and indignation, as if they were then but fools, and the dupes of imposture.

On the other hand, Religion has its own enlargement, and an enlargement, not of tumult, but of peace. It is often remarked of uneducated persons, who have hitherto thought little of the unseen world, that, on heir turning to God, looking into themselves, regulating their hearts, reforming heir conduct, and meditating on death and judgment, heaven and hell, they seem to become, in point of intellect, different beings from what they were. Before, they took things as they came, and thought no more of one thing than another. But now every event has a meaning; they have their own estimate of whatever happens to them; they are mindful of times and seasons, and compare the present with the past; and the world, no longer dull, monotonous, unprofitable, and hopeless, is a various and complicated drama, with parts and an object, and an awful moral.

Now from these instances, to which many more might be added, it is plain, first, that the communication of knowledge certainly is either a condition or the means of that sense of enlargement or enlightenment, of which at this day we hear so much in certain quarters: this cannot be denied; but next, it is equally plain, that such communication is not the whole of the process. The enlargement consists, not merely in the passive reception into the mind of a number of ideas hitherto unknown to it, but in the mind's energetic and simultaneous action upon and towards and among those new ideas, which are rushing in upon it. It is the action of a formative power, reducing to order and meaning the matter of our acquirements; it is a making the objects of our knowledge subjectively our own, or, to use a familiar word, it is a digestion of what we receive, into the substance of our previous state of thought; and without this no enlargement is said to follow. There is no enlargement, unless there be a comparison of ideas one with another, as they come before the mind, and a systematizing of them. We feel our minds to be growing and expanding *then*, when we not only learn, but refer what we learn to what we know already. It is not the mere addition to our knowledge that is the illumination; but the locomotion, the movement onwards, of that mental centre, to which both what we know, and what we are learning, the accumulating mass of our acquirements, gravitates. And therefore a truly great intellect, and recognized to be such by the common opinion of mankind, such as the intellect of Aristotle, or of St. Thomas, or of Newton, or of Goethe (I purposely take instances within and without the Catholic pale, when I would speak of the intellect as such), is one which takes a connected view of old and new, past and present, far and near, and which has an insight into the influence of all these one on another; without which there is no whole, and no centre. It possesses the knowledge, not only of things, but also of their mutual and true relations; knowledge, not merely considered as acquirement, but as philosophy.

Accordingly, when this analytical, distributive, harmonizing process is away, the mind experiences no enlargement, and is not reckoned as enlightened or comprehensive, whatever it may add to its knowledge. For instance, a great memory, as I have already said, does not make a philosopher, any more than a dictionary can be called a grammar. There are men who embrace in their minds a vast multitude of ideas, but with little sensibility about their real relations towards each other. These may be antiquarians, annalists, naturalists; they may be learned in the law; they may be versed in statistics; they are most useful in their own place; I should shrink from speaking disrespectfully of them; still, there is nothing in such attainments to guarantee the absence of narrowness of mind. If they are nothing more than well-read men, or men of information, they have not what specially deserves the name of culture of mind, or fulfils the type of Liberal Education.

In like manner, we sometimes fall in with persons who have seen much of the world, and of the men who, in their day, have played a conspicuous part in it, but who generalize nothing, and have no observation, in the true sense of the word. They abound in information in detail, curious and entertaining, about men and things; and, having lived under the influence of no very clear or settled principles, religious or political, they speak of every one and every thing, only as so many phenomena, which are complete in themselves, and lead to nothing, not discussing them, or teaching any truth, or instructing the hearer, but simply talking. No one would say that these persons, well informed as they are, had attained to any great culture of intellect or to philosophy.

The case is the same still more strikingly where the persons in question are beyond dispute men of inferior powers and deficient education. Perhaps they have been much in foreign countries, and they receive, in a passive, otiose, unfruitful way, the various facts which are forced upon them there. Seafaring men, for example, range from one end of the earth to the other; but the multiplicity of external objects, which they have encountered, forms no symmetrical and consistent picture upon their imagination; they see the tapestry of human life, as it were on the wrong side, and it tells no story. They sleep, and they rise up, and they find themselves, now in Europe, now in Asia; they see visions of great cities and wild regions; they are in the marts of commerce, or amid the islands of the South; they gaze on Pompey's Pillar, or on the Andes; and nothing which meets them carries them forward or backward, to any idea beyond itself. Nothing has a drift or relation; nothing has a history or a promise. Every thing stands by itself, and comes and goes in its turn, like the shifting scenes of a show, which leave the spectator where he was. Perhaps you are near such a man on a particular occasion, and expect him to be shocked or perplexed at something which occurs; but one thing is much the same to him as another, or, if he is perplexed, it is as not knowing what to say, whether it is right to admire, or to ridicule, or to disapprove, while conscious that some expression of opinion is expected from him; for in fact he has no standard of judgment at all, and no landmarks to guide him to a

conclusion. Such is mere acquisition, and, I repeat, no one would dream of calling it philosophy.

Instances, such as these, confirm, by the contrast, the conclusion I have already drawn from those which preceded them. That only is true enlargement of mind which is the power of viewing many things at once as one whole, of referring them severally to their true place in the universal system, of understanding their respective values, and determining their mutual dependence. Thus is that form of Universal Knowledge, of which I have on a former occasion spoken, set up in the individual intellect, and constitutes its perfection. Possessed of this real illumination, the mind never views any part of the extended subject-matter of Knowledge, without recollecting that it is but a part, or without the associations which spring from this recollection. It makes every thing in some sort lead to every thing else; it would communicate the image of the whole to every separate portion, till that whole becomes in imagination like a spirit, every where pervading and penetrating its component parts, and giving them one definite meaning. Just as our bodily organs, when mentioned, recall their function in the body, as the word "creation" suggests the Creator, and "subjects" a sovereign, so, in the mind of the Philosopher, as we are abstractedly conceiving of him, the elements of the physical and moral world, sciences, arts, pursuits, ranks, offices, events, opinions, individualities, are all viewed as one, with correlative functions, and as gradually by successive combinations converging, one and all, to the true centre.

To have even a portion of this illuminative reason and true philosophy is the highest state to which nature can aspire, in the way of intellect; it puts the mind above the influences of chance and necessity, above anxiety, suspense, unsettlement, and superstition, which is the lot of the many. Men whose minds are possessed with some one object, take exaggerated views of its imporince, are feverish in the pursuit of it, make the measure of things which are utterly oreign to it, and are startled and despond : it happens to fail them. They are ever in larm or in transport. Those on the other and who have no object or principle whatver to hold by, lose their way, every step hey take. They are thrown out, and do not now what to think or say, at every fresh uncture; they have no view of persons, or ccurrences, or facts, which come suddenly pon them, and they hang upon the opinion f others, for want of internal resources. But he intellect, which has been disciplined to he perfection of its powers, which knows, nd thinks while it knows, which has learned o leaven the dense mass of facts and events ith the elastic force of reason, such an ntellect cannot be partial, cannot be exclu- ve, cannot be impetuous, cannot be at a ∍ss, cannot but be patient, collected, and najestically calm, because it discerns the nd in every beginning, the origin in every nd, the law in every interruption, the limit ι each delay; because it ever knows where it ands, and how its path lies from one point ɔ another. It is the *Tetragonos*[6] of the Peri- atetic, and has the "nil admirari"[7] of the toic,—

Felix qui potuit rerum cognoscere causas,
Atque metus omnes, et inexorabile fatum
Subjecit pedibus, strepitumque
    Acherontis avari.[8]

here are men who, when in difficulties, riginate at the moment vast ideas or azzling projects; who, under the influence f excitement, are able to cast a light, almost s if from inspiration, on a subject or course

---

Cf. Aristotle, *Nic. Ethics*, 1.10; *GBWW*, Vol. 9, p. 346a: The happy man is "foursquare (*tetragonos*) beyond reproach."

Cf. Horace, *Epistles*, 1.6.1: "To be surprised at nothing (*nil admirari*) is perhaps the one and only thing, Numicius, that can make and keep a man happy."

Virgil, *Georgics II*, 490–93; *GBWW*, Vol. 13, p. 65b.

of action which comes before them; who have a sudden presence of mind equal to any emergency, rising with the occasion, and an undaunted magnanimous bearing, and an energy and keenness which is but made in- tense by opposition. This is genius, this is heroism; it is the exhibition of a natural gift, which no culture can teach, at which no Institution can aim; here, on the contrary, we are concerned, not with mere nature, but with training and teaching. That perfection of the Intellect, which is the result of Educa- tion, and its *beau ideal*, to be imparted to individuals in their respective measures, is the clear, calm, accurate vision and compre- hension of all things, as far as the finite mind can embrace them, each in its place, and with its own characteristics upon it. It is almost prophetic from its knowledge of his- tory; it is almost heart-searching from its knowledge of human nature; it has almost supernatural charity from its freedom from littleness and prejudice; it has almost the repose of faith, because nothing can startle it; it has almost the beauty and harmony of heavenly contemplation, so intimate is it with the eternal order of things and the music of the spheres.

[*from* Discourse VI]

KNOWLEDGE, UTILITY, AND PROFESSIONAL SKILL

I have been insisting, in my two preceding Discourses, first, on the cultivation of the intellect, as an end which may reasonably be pursued for its own sake; and next, on the nature of that cultivation, or what that cul- tivation consists in. Truth of whatever kind is the proper object of the intellect; its culti- vation then lies in fitting it to apprehend and contemplate truth. Now the intellect in its present state, with exceptions which need not here be specified, does not discern truth intuitively, or as a whole. We know, not by a direct and simple vision, not at a glance, but, as it were, by piecemeal and accumulation, by a mental process, by going round an object, by the comparison, the combination, the mutual correction, the continual adaptation, of many partial notions, by the employment, concentration, and joint action of many faculties and exercises of mind. Such a union and concert of the intellectual powers, such an enlargement and development, such a comprehensiveness, is necessarily a matter of training. And again, such a training is a matter of rule; it is not mere application, however exemplary, which introduces the mind to truth, nor the reading many books, nor the getting up many subjects, nor the witnessing many experiments, nor the attending many lectures. All this is short of enough; a man may have done it all, yet be lingering in the vestibule of knowledge: he may not realize what his mouth utters; he may not see with his mental eye what confronts him; he may have no grasp of things as they are; or at least he may have no power at all of advancing one step forward of himself, in consequence of what he has already acquired, no power of discriminating between truth and falsehood, of sifting out the grains of truth from the mass, of arranging things according to their real value, and, if I may use the phrase, of building up ideas. Such a power is the result of a scientific formation of mind; it is an acquired faculty of judgment, of clear-sightedness, of sagacity, of wisdom, of philosophical reach of mind, and of intellectual self-possession and repose—qualities which do not come of mere acquirement. The bodily eye, the organ for apprehending material objects, is provided by nature; the eye of the mind, of which the object is truth, is the work of discipline and habit.

This process of training, by which the intellect, instead of being formed or sacrificed to some particular or accidental purpose, some specific trade or profession, or study or science, is disciplined for its own sake, for the perception of its own proper object, and for its own highest culture, is called Liberal Education; and though there is no one in whom it is carried as far as is

conceivable, or whose intellect would be a pattern of what intellects should be made, yet there is scarcely any one but may gain an idea of what real training is, and at least look towards it, and make its true scope and result, not something else, his standard of excellence; and numbers there are who may submit themselves to it, and secure it to themselves in good measure. And to set forth the right standard, and to train according to it, and to help forward all students toward it according to their various capacities, this I conceive to be the business of a University.

Now this is what some great men are very slow to allow; they insist that Education should be confined to some particular and narrow end, and should issue in some definite work, which can be weighed and measured. They argue as if every thing, as well as every person, had its price; and that where there has been a great outlay, they have a right to expect a return in kind. This they call making Education and Instruction "useful," and "Utility" becomes their watchword. With a fundamental principle of this nature they very naturally go on to ask, what there is to show for the expense of a University; what is the real worth in the market of the article called "a Liberal Education," on the supposition that it does not teach us definitely how to advance our manufactures, or to improve our lands, or to better our civil economy; or again, if it does not at once make this man a lawyer, that an engineer, and that a surgeon; or at least if it does not lead to discoveries in chemistry, astronomy, geology, magnetism, and science of every kind.

. . . .

Let us take "useful," as Locke takes it, in its proper and popular sense, and then we enter upon a large field of thought, to which I cannot do justice in one Discourse, though to-day's is all the space that I can give to it. I say, let us take "useful" to mean, not what is simply good, but what *tends* to good, or is the *instrument* of good; and in this sense also, Gentlemen, I will show you how beral education is truly and fully a useful, though it be not a professional, education. "Good" indeed means one thing, and "useful" means another; but I lay it down as a principle, which will save us a great deal of anxiety, that, though the useful is not always good, the good is always useful. Good is not only good, but reproductive of good; this is one of its attributes; nothing is excellent, beautiful, perfect, desirable for its own sake, but it overflows, and spreads the likeness of itself all around it. Good is prolific; it is not only good to the eye, but to the taste; it not only attracts us, but it communicates itself; it excites first our admiration and love, then our desire and our gratitude, and that, in proportion to its intenseness and fulness in particular instances. A great good will impart great good. If then the intellect is so excellent a portion of us, and its cultivation so excellent, it is not only beautiful, perfect, admirable, and noble in itself, but in a true and high sense it must be useful to the possessor and to all around him; not useful in any low, mechanical, mercantile sense, but as diffusing good, or as a blessing, or a gift, or power, or a treasure, first to the owner, then through him to the world. I say then, if a liberal education be good, it must necessarily be useful too.

You will see what I mean by the parallel of bodily health. Health is a good in itself, though nothing came of it, and is especially worth seeking and cherishing; yet, after all, the blessings which attend its presence are so great, while they are so close to it and so redound back upon it and encircle it, that we never think of it except as useful as well as good, and praise and prize it for what it does, as well as for what it is, though at the same time we cannot point out any definite and distinct work or production which it can be said to effect. And so as regards intellectual culture, I am far from denying utility in this large sense as the end of Education, when I lay it down, that the culture of the intellect is a good in itself and its own end; I do not exclude from the idea of intellectual culture

what it cannot but be, from the very nature of things; I only deny that we must be able to point out, before we have any right to call it useful, some art, or business, or profession, or trade, or work, as resulting from it, and as its real and complete end. The parallel is exact: As the body may be sacrificed to some manual or other toil, whether moderate or oppressive, so may the intellect be devoted to some specific profession; and I do not call *this* the culture of the intellect. Again, as some member or organ of the body may be inordinately used and developed, so may memory, or imagination, or the reasoning faculty; and *this* again is not intellectual culture. On the other hand, as the body may be tended, cherished, and exercised with a simple view to its general health, so may the intellect also be generally exercised in order to its perfect state; and this *is* its cultivation.

Again, as health ought to precede labour of the body, and as a man in health can do what an unhealthy man cannot do, and as of this health the properties are strength, energy, agility, graceful carriage and action, manual dexterity, and endurance of fatigue, so in like manner general culture of mind is the best aid to professional and scientific study, and educated men can do what illiterate cannot; and the man who has learned to think and to reason and to compare and to discriminate and to analyze, who has refined his taste, and formed his judgment, and sharpened his mental vision, will not indeed at once be a lawyer, or a pleader, or an orator, or a statesman, or a physician, or a good landlord, or a man of business, or a soldier, or an engineer, or a chemist, or a geologist, or an antiquarian, but he will be placed in that state of intellect in which he can take up any one of the sciences or callings I have referred to, or any other for which he has a taste or special talent, with an ease, a grace, a versatility, and a success, to which another is a stranger. In this sense then, and as yet I have said but a very few words on a large subject, mental culture is emphatically *useful*.

If then I am arguing, and shall argue, against Professional or Scientific knowledge as the sufficient end of a University Education, let me not be supposed, Gentlemen, to be disrespectful towards particular studies, or arts, or vocations, and those who are engaged in them. In saying that Law or Medicine is not the end of a University course, I do not mean to imply that the University does not teach Law or Medicine. What indeed can it teach at all, if it does not teach something particular? It teaches *all* knowledge by teaching all *branches* of knowledge, and in no other way. I do but say that there will be this distinction as regards a Professor of Law, or of Medicine, or of Geology, or of Political Economy, in a University and out of it, that out of a University he is in danger of being absorbed and narrowed by his pursuit, and of giving Lectures which are the Lectures of nothing more than a lawyer, physician, geologist, or political economist; whereas in a University he will just know where he and his science stand, he has come to it, as it were, from a height, he has taken a survey of all knowledge, he is kept from extravagance by the very rivalry of other studies, he has gained from them a special illumination and largeness of mind and freedom and self-possession, and he treats his own in consequence with a philosophy and a resource, which belongs not to the study itself, but to his liberal education.

This then is how I should solve the fallacy, for so I must call it, by which Locke and his disciples would frighten us from cultivating the intellect, under the notion that no education is useful which does not teach us some temporal calling, or some mechanical art, or some physical secret. I say that a cultivated intellect, because it is a good in itself, brings with it a power and a grace to every work and occupation which it undertakes, and enables us to be more useful, and to a greater number. There is a duty we owe to human society as such, to the state to which we belong, to the sphere in which we move, to the individuals towards whom we are vari-

ously related, and whom we successively en counter in life; and that philosophical o liberal education, as I have called it, whic is the proper function of a University, if refuses the foremost place to profession interests, does but postpone them to th formation of the citizen, and, while it sul serves the larger interests of philanthrop prepares also for the successful prosecutio of those merely personal objects, which first sight it seems to disparage.

. . . .

But I must bring these extracts to an en To-day I have confined myself to saying th that training of the intellect, which is best f the individual himself, best enables him t discharge his duties to society. The Philoso pher, indeed, and the man of the world diffe in their very notion, but the methods, b which they are respectively formed, are prett much the same. The Philosopher has th same command of matters of thought, whic the true citizen and gentleman has of matte of business and conduct. If then a practic end must be assigned to a University cours I say it is that of training good members o society. Its art is the art of social life, and i end is fitness for the world. It neither con fines its views to particular professions o the one hand, nor creates heroes or inspire genius on the other. Works indeed of geni fall under no art; heroic minds come unde no rule; a University is not a birthplace o poets or of immortal authors, of founders o schools, leaders of colonies, or conquero of nations. It does not promise a generatio of Aristotles or Newtons, of Napoleons o Washingtons, of Raphaels or Shakespeare though such miracles of nature it has befo now contained within its precincts. Nor is content on the other hand with forming th critic or the experimentalist, the economi or the engineer, though such too it includ within its scope. But a University training the great ordinary means to a great bi ordinary end; it aims at raising the intelle tual tone of society, at cultivating the publ mind, at purifying the national taste, applying true principles to popular enthusiasm and fixed aims to popular aspiration, at giving enlargement and sobriety to the ideas of the age, at facilitating the exercise of political power, and refining the intercourse of private life. It is the education which gives a man a clear conscious view of his own opinions and judgments, a truth in developing them, an eloquence in expressing them, and a force in urging them. It teaches him to see things as they are, to go right to the point, to disentangle a skein of thought, to detect what is sophistical, and to discard what is irrelevant. It prepares him to fill any post with credit, and to master any subject with facility. It shows him how to accommodate himself to others, how to throw himself into their state of mind, how to bring before them his own, how to influence them, how to come to an understanding with them, how to bear with them. He is at home in any society, he has common ground with every class; he knows when to speak and when to be silent; he is able to converse, he is able to listen; he can ask a question pertinently, and gain a lesson seasonably, when he has nothing to impart himself; he is ever ready, yet never in the way; he is a pleasant companion, and a comrade you can depend upon; he knows when to be serious and when to trifle, and he has a sure tact which enables him to trifle with gracefulness and to be serious with effect. He has the repose of a mind which lives in itself, while it lives in the world, and which has resources for its happiness at home when it cannot go abroad. He has a gift which serves him in public,

and supports him in retirement, without which good fortune is but vulgar, and with which failure and disappointment have a charm. The art which tends to make a man all this, is in the object which it pursues as useful as the art of wealth or the art of health, though it is less susceptible of method, and less tangible, less certain, less complete in its result.

[*from* Discourse VII]

[I have been] inquiring what a University is, what is its aim, what its nature, what its bearings. I have accordingly laid down first, that all branches of knowledge are, at least implicitly, the subject-matter of its teaching; that these branches are not isolated and independent one of another, but form together a whole or system; that they run into each other, and complete each other, and that, in proportion to our view of them as a whole, is the exactness and trustworthiness of the knowledge which they separately convey; that the process of imparting knowledge to the intellect in this philosophical way is its true culture; that such culture is a good in itself; that the knowledge which is both its instrument and result is called Liberal Knowledge; that such culture, together with the knowledge which effects it, may fitly be sought for its own sake; that it is, however, in addition, of great secular utility, as constituting the best and highest formation of the intellect for social and political life.

[*from* Discourse IX]

INAUGURAL ADDRESS

AT ST. ANDREWS

John Stuart Mill

In complying with the custom which pre-
scribes that the person whom you have
called by your suffrages to the honorary
presidency of your University should em-
body in an Address a few thoughts on the
subjects which most nearly concern a seat of
liberal education; let me begin by saying,
that this usage appears to me highly com-
mendable. Education, in its larger sense, is
one of the most inexhaustible of all topics.
Though there is hardly any subject on which
so much has been written, by so many of the
wisest men, it is as fresh to those who come
to it with a fresh mind, a mind not hopelessly
filled full with other people's conclusions, as
it was to the first explorers of it: and notwithstanding the great mass of excellent
things which have been said respecting it, no
thoughtful person finds any lack of things
both great and small still waiting to be said,
or waiting to be developed and followed out
to their consequences.

Education, moreover, is one of the subjects
which most essentially require to be considered by various minds, and from a variety
of points of view. For, of all many-sided subjects, it is the one which has the greatest
number of sides. Not only does it include
whatever we do for ourselves, and whatever
is done for us by others, for the express purpose of bringing us somewhat nearer to the
perfection of our nature; it does more: in its
largest acceptation, it comprehends even the
indirect effects produced on character and
on the human faculties, by things of which
the direct purposes are quite different; by
laws, by forms of government, by the industrial arts, by modes of social life; nay even
by physical facts not dependent on human
will; by climate, soil, and local position.
Whatever helps to shape the human being;
to make the individual what he is, or hinder
him from being what he is not—is part of
his education. And a very bad education it

often is; requiring all that can be done b
cultivated intelligence and will, to counter
act its tendencies. To take an obvious ir
stance; the niggardliness of Nature in som
places, by engrossing the whole energies c
the human being in the mere preservation c
life, and her over-bounty in others, affordin
a sort of brutish subsistence on too eas
terms, with hardly any exertion of the huma
faculties, are both hostile to the spontaneou
growth and development of the mind; and i
is at those two extremes of the scale that w
find human societies in the state of mos
unmitigated savagery.

I shall confine myself, however, to educa
tion in the narrower sense; the culture which
each generation purposely gives to those wh
are to be its successors, in order to qualif
them for at least keeping up, and if possibl
for raising, the level of improvement which
has been attained. Nearly all here presen
are daily occupied either in receiving or i
giving this sort of education: and the part c
it which most concerns you at present is tha
in which you are yourselves engaged—th
stage of education which is the appointe
business of a national University.

The proper function of an University i
national education is tolerably well under
stood. At least there is a tolerably genera
agreement about what an University is no
It is not a place of professional educatior
Universities are not intended to teach th
knowledge required to fit men for some spe
cial mode of gaining their livelihood. Thei
object is not to make skilful lawyers, o
physicians, or engineers, but capable an
cultivated human beings. It is very right tha
there should be public facilities for the stud
of professions. It is well that there shoul
be Schools of Law, and of Medicine, and i
would be well if there were schools of eng
neering, and the industrial arts. The coun
tries which have such institutions are greatl

better for them; and there is something to be said for having them in the same localities, and under the same general superintendence, as the establishments devoted to education properly so called. But these things are no part of what every generation owes to the next, as that on which its civilization and worth will principally depend. They are needed only by a comparatively few, who are under the strongest private inducements to acquire them by their own efforts; and even those few do not require them until after their education, in the ordinary sense, has been completed. Whether those whose speciality they are, will learn them as a branch of intelligence or as a mere trade, and whether, having learnt them, they will make a wise and conscientious use of them or the reverse, depends less on the manner in which they are taught their profession, than upon what sort of minds they bring to it—what kind of intelligence, and of conscience, the general system of education has developed in them.

Men are men before they are lawyers, or physicians, or merchants, or manufacturers; and if you make them capable and sensible men, they will make themselves capable and sensible lawyers or physicians. What professional men should carry away with them from an University, is not professional knowledge, but that which should direct the use of their professional knowledge, and bring the light of general culture to illuminate the technicalities of a special pursuit. Men may be competent lawyers without general education, but it depends on general education to make them philosophic lawyers—who demand, and are capable of apprehending, principles, instead of merely cramming their memory with details. And so of all other useful pursuits, mechanical included. Education makes a man a more intelligent shoemaker, if that be his occupation, but not by teaching him how to make shoes; it does so by the mental exercise it gives, and the habits it impresses.

This, then, is what a mathematician would call the higher limit of University education: its province ends where education, ceasing to be general, branches off into departments adapted to the individual's destination in life. The lower limit is more difficult to define. An University is not concerned with elementary instruction: the pupil is supposed to have acquired that before coming here. But where does elementary instruction end, and the higher studies begin? Some have given a very wide extension to the idea of elementary instruction. According to them, it is not the office of an University to give instruction in single branches of knowledge from the commencement. What the pupil should be taught here (they think), is to methodize his knowledge: to look at every separate part of it in its relation to the other parts, and to the whole; combining the partial glimpses which he has obtained of the field of human knowledge at different points, into a general map, if I may so speak, of the entire region; observing how all knowledge is connected, how we ascend to one branch by means of another, how the higher modifies the lower, and the lower helps us to understand the higher; how every existing reality is a compound of many properties, of which each science or distinct mode of study reveals but a small part, but the whole of which must be included to enable us to know it truly as a fact in Nature, and not as a mere abstraction.

This last stage of general education destined to give the pupil a comprehensive and connected view of the things which he has already learnt separately, includes a philosophic study of the Methods of the sciences; the modes in which the human intellect proceeds from the known to the unknown. We must be taught to generalize our conception of the resources which the human mind possesses for the exploration of nature; to understand how man discovers the real facts of the world, and by what tests he can judge whether he has really found them. And doubtless this is the crown and consummation of a liberal education: but before we restrict an University to this highest department of instruction—before we confine it to teaching, not knowledge, but the philosophy of knowledge—we must be assured that the knowledge itself has been acquired elsewhere. Those who take this view of the function of an University are not wrong in thinking that the schools, as distinguished from the universities, ought to be adequate to teaching every branch of general instruction required by youth, so far as it can be studied apart from the rest. But where are such schools to be found? Since science assumed its modern character, nowhere: and in these islands less even than elsewhere.

This ancient kingdom, thanks to its great religious reformers, had the inestimable advantage, denied to its southern sister, of excellent parish schools, which gave, really and not in pretence, a considerable amount of valuable literary instruction to the bulk of the population, two centuries earlier than in any other country. But schools of a still higher description have been, even in Scotland, so few and inadequate, that the Universities have had to perform largely the functions which ought to be performed by schools; receiving students at an early age, and undertaking not only the work for which the schools should have prepared them, but much of the preparation itself. Every Scottish University is not an University only, but a High School, to supply the deficiency of other schools. And if the English Universities do not do the same, it is not because the same need does not exist, but because it is disregarded. Youths come to the Scottish Universities ignorant, and are there taught. The majority of those who come to the English Universities come still more ignorant, and ignorant they go away.

In point of fact, therefore, the office of a Scottish University comprises the whole of a liberal education, from the foundations upwards. And the scheme of your Universities has, almost from the beginning, really aimed at including the whole, both in depth and in breadth. You have not, as the English Universities so long did, confined all the stress of your teaching, all your real effort to teach, within the limits of two subjects, the classical languages and mathematics. You did not wait till the last few years to establish a Natural Science and a Moral Science Tripos. Instruction in both those departments was organized long ago: and your teachers of those subjects have not been nominal professors, who did not lecture: some of the greatest names in physical and in moral science have taught in your Universities, and by their teaching contributed to form some of the most distinguished intellects of the last and present centuries.

To comment upon the course of education at the Scottish Universities is to pass in review every essential department of general culture. The best use, then, which I am able to make of the present occasion, is to offer a few remarks on each of those departments considered in its relation to human cultivation at large: adverting to the nature of the claims which each has to a place in liberal education; in what special manner they each conduce to the improvement of the individual mind and the benefit of the race; and how they all conspire to the common end, the strengthening, exalting, purifying, and beautifying of our common nature, and the fitting out of mankind with the necessary mental implements for the work they have to perform through life.

Let me first say a few words on the great controversy of the present day with regard to the higher education, the difference which most broadly divides educational reformers and conservatives; the vexed question between the ancient languages and the modern sciences and arts; whether general education should be classical—let me use a wider expression, and say literary—or scientific. A dispute as endlessly, and often as fruitlessly agitated as that old controversy which it resembles, made memorable by the names of Swift and Sir William Temple in England and Fontenelle in France—the contest for superiority between the ancients and the moderns. This question, whether we should be taught the classics or the sciences, seems to me, I confess, very like a dispute whether painters should cultivate drawing or colouring, or, to use a more homely illustration, whether a tailor should make coats or trousers. I can only reply by the question, why not both? Can anything deserve the name of a good education which does not include literature and science too? If there were no more to be said than that scientific education teaches us to think, and literary education to express our thoughts, do we not require both? and is not any one a poor, maimed, lopsided fragment of humanity who is deficient in either?

We are not obliged to ask ourselves whether it is more important to know the languages or the sciences. Short as life is, and shorter still as we make it by the time we waste on things which are neither business, nor meditation, nor pleasure, we are not so badly off that our scholars need be ignorant of the laws and properties of the world they live in, or our scientific men destitute of poetic feeling and artistic cultivation. I am amazed at the limited conception which many educational reformers have formed to themselves of a human being's power of acquisition. The study of science, they truly say, is indispensable: our present education neglects it: there is truth in this too, though it is not all truth: and they think it impossible to find room for the studies which they desire to encourage, but by turning out, at least from general education, those which are now chiefly cultivated. How absurd, they say, that the whole of boyhood should be taken up in acquiring an imperfect knowledge of two dead languages. Absurd indeed: but is the human mind's capacity to learn measured by that of Eton and Westminster to teach? I should prefer to see these reformers pointing their attacks against the shameful inefficiency of the schools, public and private, which pretend to teach these two languages and do not. I should like to hear

them denounce the wretched methods of teaching, and the criminal idleness and supineness, which waste the entire boyhood of the pupils without really giving to most of them more than a smattering, if even that, of the only kind of knowledge which is even pretended to be cared for. Let us try what conscientious and intelligent teaching can do, before we presume to decide what cannot be done.

Scotland has on the whole, in this respect, been considerably more fortunate than England. Scotch youths have never found it impossible to leave school or the University having learnt somewhat of other things besides Greek and Latin; and why? Because Greek and Latin have been better taught. A beginning of classical instruction has all along been made in the common schools: and the common schools of Scotland, like her Universities, have never been the mere shams that the English Universities were during the last century, and the greater part of the English classical schools still are. The only tolerable Latin grammars for school purposes that I know of, which had been produced in these islands until very lately, were written by Scotchmen. Reason, indeed, is beginning to find its way by gradual infiltration even into English schools, and to maintain a contest, though as yet a very unequal one, against routine.

A few practical reformers of school tuition, of whom Arnold was the most eminent, have made a beginning of amendment in many things: but reforms, worthy of the name, are always slow, and reform even of governments and churches is not so slow as that of schools, for there is the great preliminary difficulty of fashioning the instruments: of teaching the teachers. If all the improvements in the mode of teaching languages which are already sanctioned by experience, were adopted into our classical schools, we should soon cease to hear of Latin and Greek as studies which must engross the school years, and render impossible any other acquirements. If a boy learnt Greek and Latin on the same principle on which a mere child learns with such ease and rapidity any modern language, namely, by acquiring some familiarity with the vocabulary by practice and repetition, before being troubled with grammatical rules—those rules being acquired with tenfold greater facility when the cases to which they apply are already familiar to the mind; an average schoolboy, long before the age at which schooling terminates, would be able to read fluently and with intelligent interest any ordinary Latin or Greek author in prose or verse, would have a competent knowledge of the grammatical structure of both languages, and have had time besides for an ample amount of scientific instruction.

I might go much further; but I am as unwilling to speak out all that I think practicable in this matter, as George Stephenson was about railways, when he calculated the average speed of a train at ten miles an hour, because if he had estimated it higher, the practical men would have turned a deaf ear to him, as that most unsafe character in their estimation, an enthusiast and a visionary. The results have shewn, in that case, who was the real practical man. What the results would shew in the other case, I will not attempt to anticipate. But I will say confidently, that if the two classical languages were properly taught, there would be no need whatever for ejecting them from the school course, in order to have sufficient time for everything else that need be included therein.

Let me say a few words more on this strangely limited estimate of what it is possible for human beings to learn, resting on a tacit assumption that they are already as efficiently taught as they ever can be. So narrow a conception not only vitiates our idea of education, but actually, if we receive it, darkens our anticipations as to the future progress of mankind. For if the inexorable conditions of human life make it useless for one man to attempt to know more than one thing, what is to become of the human intellect as facts accumulate? In every genera-

tion, and now more rapidly than ever, the things which it is necessary that somebody should know are more and more multiplied. Every department of knowledge becomes so loaded with details, that one who endeavours to know it with minute accuracy, must confine himself to a smaller and smaller portion of the whole extent: every science and art must be cut up into subdivisions, until each man's portion, the district which he thoroughly knows, bears about the same ratio to the whole range of useful knowledge that the art of putting on a pin's head does to the field of human industry.

Now, if in order to know that little completely, it is necessary to remain wholly ignorant of all the rest, what will soon be the worth of a man, for any human purpose except his own infinitesimal fraction of human wants and requirements? His state will be even worse than that of simple ignorance. Experience proves that there is no one study or pursuit, which, practised to the exclusion of all others, does not narrow and pervert the mind; breeding in it a class of prejudices special to that pursuit, besides a general prejudice, common to all narrow specialities, against large views, from an incapacity to take in and appreciate the grounds of them. We should have to expect that human nature would be more and more dwarfed, and unfitted for great things, by its very proficiency in small ones. But matters are not so bad with us: there is no ground for so dreary an anticipation. It is not the utmost limit of human acquirement to know only one thing, but to combine a minute knowledge of one or a few things with a general knowledge of many things. By a general knowledge I do not mean a few vague impressions.

An eminent man, one of whose writings is part of the course of this University, Archbishop Whately, has well discriminated between a general knowledge and a superficial knowledge. To have a general knowledge of a subject is to know only its leading truths, but to know these not superficially but thoroughly, so as to have a true conception of the bject in its great features; leaving the inor details to those who require them for e purposes of their special pursuit. There no incompatibility between knowing a ide range of subjects up to this point, and me one subject with the completeness re uired by those who make it their principal ccupation. It is this combination which gives a enlightened public: a body of cultivated intellects, each taught by its attainments i its own province what real knowledge , and knowing enough of other subjects be able to discern who are those that now them better. The amount of knowl dge is not to be lightly estimated, which ualifies us for judging to whom we may ave recourse for more. The elements of the ore important studies being widely diffused, hose who have reached the higher summits nd a public capable of appreciating their periority, and prepared to follow their ad.

It is thus too that minds are formed ca able of guiding and improving public opin in on the greater concerns of practical life. overnment and civil society are the most omplicated of all subjects accessible to the uman mind: and he who would deal com etently with them as a thinker, and not s a blind follower of a party, requires not nly a general knowledge of the leading facts f life, both moral and material, but an un erstanding exercised and disciplined in the rinciples and rules of sound thinking, up a point which neither the experience of fe, nor any one science or branch of knowl dge, affords. Let us understand, then, that should be our aim in learning, not merely know the one thing which is to be our rincipal occupation, as well as it can be nown, but to do this and also to know omething of all the great subjects of human nterest: taking care to know that something ccurately; marking well the dividing line etween what we know accurately and what e do not: and remembering that our object hould be to obtain a true view of nature nd life in their broad outline, and that it

is idle to throw away time upon the details of anything which is to form no part of the occupation of our practical energies.

It by no means follows, however, that every useful branch of general, as distinct from professional, knowledge, should be included in the curriculum of school or university studies. There are things which are better learnt out of school, or when the school years, and even those usually passed in a Scottish University, are over. I do not agree with those reformers who would give a reg ular and prominent place in the school or University course to modern languages. This is not because I attach small importance to the knowledge of them. No one can in our age be esteemed a well-instructed person who is not familiar with at least the French language, so as to read French books with ease; and there is great use in cultivating a familiarity with German. But living lan guages are so much more easily acquired by intercourse with those who use them in daily life; a few months in the country itself, if properly employed, go so much farther than as many years of school lessons; that it is really waste of time for those to whom that easier mode is attainable, to labour at them with no help but that of books and masters: and it will in time be made attainable, through international schools and colleges, to many more than at present. Universities do enough to facilitate the study of modern languages, if they give a mastery over that ancient language which is the foundation of most of them, and the possession of which makes it easier to learn four or five of the continental languages than it is to learn one of them without it.

Again, it has always seemed to me a great absurdity that history and geography should be taught in schools; except in elementary schools for the children of the labouring classes, whose subsequent access to books is limited. Who ever really learnt history and geography except by private reading? and what an utter failure a system of education must be, if it has not given the pupil a sufficient taste for reading to seek for himself those most attractive and easily intelligible of all kinds of knowledge? Besides, such history and geography as can be taught in schools exercise none of the faculties of the intelligence except the memory. An University is indeed the place where the student should be introduced to the Philosophy of History; where Professors who not merely know the facts but have exercised their minds on them, should initiate him into the causes and explanation, so far as within our reach, of the past life of mankind in its principal features. Historical criticism also— the tests of historical truth—are a subject to which his attention may well be drawn in this stage of his education. But of the mere facts of history, as commonly accepted, what educated youth of any mental activity does not learn as much as is necessary, if he is simply turned loose into an historical library? What he needs on this, and on most other matters of common information, is not that he should be taught it in boyhood, but that abundance of books should be accessible to him.

The only languages, then, and the only literature, to which I would allow a place in the ordinary curriculum, are those of the Greeks and Romans; and to these I would preserve the position in it which they at present occupy. That position is justified, by the great value, in education, of knowing well some other cultivated language and literature than one's own, and by the peculiar value of those particular languages and literatures.

There is one purely intellectual benefit from a knowledge of languages, which I am specially desirous to dwell on. Those who have seriously reflected on the causes of human error, have been deeply impressed with the tendency of mankind to mistake words for things. Without entering into the metaphysics of the subject, we know how common it is to use words glibly and with apparent propriety, and to accept them confidently when used by others, without ever

having had any distinct conception of th[e] things denoted by them. To quote aga[in] from Archbishop Whately, it is the habit [of] mankind to mistake familiarity for accura[te] knowledge. As we seldom think of asking th[e] meaning of what we see every day, so whe[n] our ears are used to the sound of a wor[d] or a phrase, we do not suspect that it conve[ys] no clear idea to our minds, and that w[e] should have the utmost difficulty in definin[g] it, or expressing, in any other words, wha[t] we think we understand by it. Now it [is] obvious in what manner this bad habit tend[s] to be corrected by the practice of translatin[g] with accuracy from one language to anothe[r] and hunting out the meanings expressed i[n] a vocabulary with which we have not grow[n] familiar by early and constant use.

I hardly know any greater proof of th[e] extraordinary genius of the Greeks, tha[n] that they were able to make such brillia[nt] achievements in abstract thought, knowin[g] as they generally did, no language but the[ir] own. But the Greeks did not escape the e[f]fects of this deficiency. Their greatest i[n]tellects, those who laid the foundation [of] philosophy and of all our intellectual cu[l]ture, Plato and Aristotle, are continually le[d] away by words; mistaking the accidents [of] language for real relations in nature, an[d] supposing that things which have the sam[e] name in the Greek tongue must be the sam[e] in their own essence. There is a well-know[n] saying of Hobbes, the far-reaching signi[f]icance of which you will more and mor[e] appreciate in proportion to the growth [of] your own intellect: "Words are the counte[rs] of wise men, but the money of fools. [*GBWW*, Vol. 23, p. 56d.] With the wise ma[n] a word stands for the fact which it represent[s] to the fool it is itself the fact.

To carry on Hobbes' metaphor, the counte[r] is far more likely to be taken for mere[ly] what it is, by those who are in the habit [of] using many different kinds of counters. Bu[t] besides the advantage of possessing anothe[r] cultivated language, there is a further co[n]sideration equally important. Withou[t] nowing the language of a people, we never really know their thoughts, their feelings, and their type of character: and unless we do possess this knowledge, of some other people than ourselves, we remain, to the hour of our death, with our intellects only half expanded. Look at a youth who has never been out of his family circle: he never dreams of any other opinions or ways of thinking than those he has been bred up in; or, if he has heard of any such, attributes them to some moral defect, or inferiority of nature or education. If his family are Tory, he cannot conceive the possibility of being a Liberal; if Liberal, of being a Tory. What the notions and habits of a single family are to a boy who has had no intercourse beyond it, the notions and habits of his own country are to him who is ignorant of every other. Those notions and habits are to him human nature itself; whatever varies from them is an unaccountable aberration which he cannot mentally realize: the idea that any other ways can be right, or as near an approach to right as some of his own, is inconceivable to him. This does not merely close his eyes to the many things which every country still has to learn from others: it hinders every country from reaching the improvement which it could otherwise attain by itself.

We are not likely to correct any of our opinions or mend any of our ways, unless we begin by conceiving that they are capable of amendment: but merely to know that foreigners think differently from ourselves, without understanding why they do so, or what they really do think, does but confirm us in our self-conceit, and connect our national vanity with the preservation of our own peculiarities. Improvement consists in bringing our opinions into nearer agreement with facts; and we shall not be likely to do this while we look at facts only through glasses coloured by those very opinions. But since we cannot divest ourselves of preconceived notions, there is no known means of eliminating their influence but by frequently using the differently coloured glasses of other

people: and those of other nations, as the most different, are the best.

But if it is so useful, on this account, to know the language and literature of any other cultivated and civilized people, the most valuable of all to us in this respect are the languages and literature of the ancients. No nations of modern and civilized Europe are so unlike one another, as the Greeks and Romans are unlike all of us; yet without being, as some remote Orientals are, so totally dissimilar, that the labour of a life is required to enable us to understand them. Were this the only gain to be derived from a knowledge of the ancients, it would already place the study of them in a high rank among enlightening and liberalizing pursuits. It is of no use saying that we may know them through modern writings. We may know something of them in that way; which is much better than knowing nothing. But modern books do not teach us ancient thought; they teach us some modern writer's notion of ancient thought. Modern books do not shew us the Greeks and Romans; they tell us some modern writer's opinions about the Greeks and Romans. Translations are scarcely better. When we want really to know what a person thinks or says, we seek it at first hand from himself. We do not trust to another person's impression of his meaning, given in another person's words; we refer to his own. Much more is it necessary to do so when his words are in one language, and those of his reporter in another. Modern phraseology never conveys the exact meaning of a Greek writer; it cannot do so, except by a diffuse explanatory circumlocution which no translator dares use. We must be able, in a certain degree, to think in Greek, if we would represent to ourselves how a Greek thought; and this not only in the abstruse region of metaphysics, but about the political, religious, and even domestic concerns of life.

I will mention a further aspect of this question, which, though I have not the merit of originating it, I do not remember to have seen noticed in any book. There is no part of our knowledge which it is more useful to obtain at first hand—to go to the fountain head for—than our knowledge of history. Yet this, in most cases, we hardly ever do. Our conception of the past is not drawn from its own records, but from books written about it, containing not the facts, but a view of the facts which has shaped itself in the mind of somebody of our own or a very recent time. Such books are very instructive and valuable; they help us to understand history, to interpret history, to draw just conclusions from it; at the worst, they set us the example of trying to do all this; but they are not themselves history. The knowledge they give is upon trust, and even when they have done their best, it is not only incomplete but partial, because confined to what a few modern writers have seen in the materials, and have thought worth picking out from among them.

How little we learn of our own ancestors from Hume, or Hallam, or Macaulay, compared with what we know if we add to what these tell us, even a little reading of contemporary authors and documents! The most recent historians are so well aware of this, that they fill their pages with extracts from the original materials, feeling that these extracts are the real history, and their comments and thread of narrative are only helps towards understanding it. Now it is part of the great worth to us of our Greek and Latin studies, that in them we do read history in the original sources. We are in actual contact with contemporary minds; we are not dependent on hearsay; we have something by which we can test and check the representations and theories of modern historians.

It may be asked, why then not study the original materials of modern history? I answer, it is highly desirable to do so; and let me remark by the way, that even this requires a dead language; nearly all the documents prior to the Reformation, and many subsequent to it, being written in Latin. But the

exploration of these documents, though most useful pursuit, cannot be a branch of education. Not to speak of their vast extent and the fragmentary nature of each, the strongest reason is, that in learning the spirit of our own past ages, until a comparatively recent period, from contemporary writers, we learn hardly anything else. Those authors, with a few exceptions, are little worth reading on their own account. While, in studying the great writers of antiquity, we are not only learning to understand the ancient mind, but laying in a stock of wise thought and observation, still valuable to ourselves; and at the same time making ourselves familiar with a number of the most perfect and finished literary compositions which the human mind has produced—compositions which, from the altered conditions of human life, are likely to be seldom paralleled, in their sustained excellence, by the times to come.

Even as mere languages, no modern European language is so valuable a discipline to the intellect as those of Greece and Rome, on account of their regular and complicated structure. Consider for a moment what grammar is. It is the most elementary part of logic. It is the beginning of the analysis of the thinking process. The principles and rules of grammar are the means by which the forms of language are made to correspond with the universal forms of thought. The distinctions between the various parts of speech, between the cases of nouns, the moods and tenses of verbs, the functions of particles, are distinctions in thought, not merely in words. Single nouns and verbs express objects and events, many of which can be cognized by the senses; but the modes of putting nouns and verbs together express the relations of objects and events, which can be cognized only by the intellect; and each different mode corresponds to a different relation. The structure of every sentence is a lesson in logic. The various rules of syntax oblige us to distinguish between the subject and predicate of a proposition, between the agent, the action, and the thing acted upon; to mark when an idea is intended to modify or qualify, or merely to unite with, some other idea; what assertions are categorical, what only conditional; whether the intention is to express similarity or contrast, to make a plurality of assertions conjunctively or disjunctively; what portions of a sentence, though grammatically complete within themselves, are mere members or subordinate parts of the assertion made by the entire sentence. Such things form the subject-matter of universal grammar; and the languages which teach it best are those which have the most definite rules, and which provide distinct forms for the greatest number of distinctions in thought, so that if we fail to attend precisely and accurately to any of these, we cannot avoid committing a solecism in language. In these qualities the classical languages have an incomparable superiority over every modern language, and over all languages, dead or living, which have a literature worth being generally studied.

But the superiority of the literature itself, for purposes of education, is still more marked and decisive. Even in the substantial value of the matter of which it is the vehicle, it is very far from having been superseded. The discoveries of the ancients in science have been greatly surpassed, and as much of them as is still valuable loses nothing by being incorporated in modern treatises: but what does not so well admit of being transferred bodily, and has been very imperfectly carried off even piecemeal, is the treasure which they accumulated of what may be called the wisdom of life: the rich store of experience of human nature and conduct, which the acute and observing minds of those ages, aided in their observations by the greater simplicity of manners and life, consigned to their writings, and most of which retains all its value.

The speeches in Thucydides, the *Rhetoric*, *Ethics*, and *Politics* of Aristotle; the *Dialogues* of Plato; the *Orations* of Demosthenes; the *Satires*, and especially the *Epistles* of Horace; all the writings of Tacitus; the great

work of Quintilian, a repertory of the best thoughts of the ancient world on all subjects connected with education; and, in a less formal manner, all that is left to us of the ancient historians, orators, philosophers, and even dramatists, are replete with remarks and maxims of singular good sense and penetration, applicable both to political and to private life: and the actual truths we find in them are even surpassed in value by the encouragement and help they give us in the pursuit of truth. Human invention has never produced anything so valuable, in the way both of stimulation and of discipline to the inquiring intellect, as the dialectics of the ancients, of which many of the works of Aristotle illustrate the theory, and those of Plato exhibit the practice. No modern writings come near to these, in teaching, both by precept and example, the way to investigate truth, on those subjects, so vastly important to us, which remain matters of controversy, from the difficulty or impossibility of bringing them to a directly experimental test.

To question all things; never to turn away from any difficulty; to accept no doctrine either from ourselves or from other people without a rigid scrutiny by negative criticism, letting no fallacy, or incoherence, or confusion of thought, slip by unperceived; above all, to insist upon having the meaning of a word clearly understood before using it, and the meaning of a proposition before assenting to it; these are the lessons we learn from the ancient dialecticians. With all this vigorous management of the negative element, they inspire no scepticism about the reality of truth, or indifference to its pursuit. The noblest enthusiasm, both for the search after truth and for applying it to its highest uses, pervades these writers, Aristotle no less than Plato, though Plato has incomparably the greater power of imparting those feelings to others. In cultivating, therefore, the ancient languages as our best literary education, we are all the while laying an admirable foundation for ethical and philosophical culture.

In purely literary excellence—in perfection

of form—the pre-eminence of the ancients is not disputed. In every department which they attempted, and they attempted almost all, their composition, like their sculpture, has been to the greatest modern artists an example, to be looked up to with hopeless admiration, but of inappreciable value as a light on high, guiding their own endeavours. In prose and in poetry, in epic, lyric, or dramatic, as in historical, philosophical, and oratorical art, the pinnacle on which they stand is equally eminent. I am now speaking of the form, the artistic perfection of treatment: for, as regards substance, I consider modern poetry to be superior to ancient, in the same manner, though in a less degree, as modern science: it enters deeper into nature.

The feelings of the modern mind are more various, more complex and manifold, than those of the ancients ever were. The modern mind is, what the ancient mind was not, brooding and self-conscious; and its meditative self-consciousness has discovered depths in the human soul which the Greeks and Romans did not dream of, and would not have understood. But what they had got to express, they expressed in a manner which few even of the greatest moderns have seriously attempted to rival. It must be remembered that they had more time, and that they wrote chiefly for a select class, possessed of leisure. To us who write in a hurry for people who read in a hurry, the attempt to give an equal degree of finish would be loss of time. But to be familiar with perfect models is not the less important to us because the element in which we work precludes even the effort to equal them. They shew us at least what excellence is, and make us desire it, and strive to get as near to it as is within our reach. And this is the value to us of the ancient writers, all the more emphatically, because their excellence does not admit of being copied, or directly imitated. It does not consist in a trick which can be learnt, but in the perfect adaptation of means to ends.

The secret of the style of the great Greek and Roman authors, is that it is the perfection of good sense. In the first place, they never use a word without a meaning, or a word which adds nothing to the meaning. They always (to begin with) had a meaning, they knew what they wanted to say; and their whole purpose was to say it with the highest degree of exactness and completeness, and bring it home to the mind with the greatest possible clearness and vividness. It never entered into their thoughts to conceive of a piece of writing as beautiful in itself, abstractedly from what it had to express: its beauty must all be subservient to the most perfect expression of the sense. The *curiosa felicitas* which their critics ascribed in a pre-eminent degree to Horace, expresses the standard at which they all aimed. Their style is exactly described by Swift's definition, "the right words in the right places."

Look at an oration of Demosthenes; there is nothing in it which calls attention to itself as style at all: it is only after a close examination we perceive that every word is what it should be, and where it should be, to lead the hearer smoothly and imperceptibly into the state of mind which the orator wishes to produce. The perfection of the workmanship is only visible in the total absence of any blemish or fault, and of anything which checks the flow of thought and feeling, anything which even momentarily distracts the mind from the main purpose. But then (as has been well said) it was not the object of Demosthenes to make the Athenians cry out "What a splendid speaker!" but to make them say "Let us march against Philip!"

It was only in the decline of ancient literature that ornament began to be cultivated merely as ornament. In the time of its maturity, not the merest epithet was put in because it was thought beautiful in itself; nor even for a merely descriptive purpose, for epithets purely descriptive were one of the corruptions of style which abound in Lucan, for example: the word had no business there unless it brought out some feature which was wanted, and helped to place the object in the light which the purpose of the composition required. These conditions being complied with, then indeed the intrinsic beauty of the means used was a source of additional effect, of which it behoved them to avail themselves, like rhythm and melody of versification. But these great writers knew that ornament for the sake of ornament, ornament which attracts attention to itself, and shines by its own beauties, only does so by calling off the mind from the main object, and thus not only interferes with the higher purpose of human discourse, which ought, and generally professes, to have some matter to communicate, apart from the mere excitement of the moment, but also spoils the perfection of the composition as a piece of fine art, by destroying the unity of effect.

This, then, is the first great lesson in composition to be learnt from the classical authors. The second is, not to be prolix. In a single paragraph, Thucydides can give a clear and vivid representation of a battle, such as a reader who has once taken it into his mind can seldom forget. The most powerful and affecting piece of narrative perhaps in all historical literature, is the account of the Sicilian catastrophe in his seventh book, yet how few pages does it fill! The ancients were concise, because of the extreme pains they took with their compositions; almost all moderns are prolix, because they do not. The great ancients could express a thought so perfectly in a few words or sentences, that they did not need to add any more: the moderns, because they cannot bring it out clearly and completely at once, return again and again, heaping sentence upon sentence, each adding a little more elucidation, in hopes that though no single sentence expresses the full meaning, the whole together may give a sufficient notion of it.

In this respect I am afraid we are growing worse instead of better, for want of time and patience, and from the necessity we are in of addressing almost all writings to a busy and imperfectly prepared public. The de-

mands of modern life are such—the work to be done, the mass to be worked upon, are so vast—that those who have anything particular to say—who have, as the phrase goes, any message to deliver—cannot afford to devote their time to the production of masterpieces. But they would do far worse than they do, if there had never been masterpieces, or if they had never known them. Early familiarity with the perfect, makes our most imperfect production far less bad than it otherwise would be. To have a high standard of excellence often makes the whole difference of rendering our work good when it would otherwise be mediocre.

For all these reasons I think it important to retain these two languages and literatures in the place they occupy, as a part of liberal education, that is, of the education of all who are not obliged by their circumstances to discontinue their scholastic studies at a very early age. But the same reasons which vindicate the place of classical studies in general education, shew also the proper limitation of them. They should be carried as far as is sufficient to enable the pupil, in after life, to read the great works of ancient literature with ease. Those who have leisure and inclination to make scholarship, or ancient history, or general philology, their pursuit, of course require much more, but there is no room for more in general education.

The laborious idleness in which the school-time is wasted away in the English classical schools deserves the severest reprehension. To what purpose should the most precious years of early life be irreparably squandered in learning to write bad Latin and Greek verses? I do not see that we are much the better even for those who end by writing good ones. I am often tempted to ask the favourites of nature and fortune, whether all the serious and important work of the world is done, that their time and energy can be spared for these *nugæ difficiles*? I am not blind to the utility of composing in a language, as a means of learning it accurately. I hardly know any other means equally effectual. But why should not prose composition suffice? What need is there of original composition at all? if that can be called original which unfortunate schoolboys, without any thoughts to express, hammer out on compulsion from mere memory, acquiring the pernicious habit which a teacher should consider it one of his first duties to repress, that of merely stringing together borrowed phrases? The exercise in composition, most suitable to the requirements of learners, is that most valuable one, of retranslating from translated passages of a good author: and to this might be added, what still exists in many Continental places of education, occasional practice in talking Latin.

There would be something to be said for the time spent in the manufacture of verses, if such practice were necessary for the enjoyment of ancient poetry; though it would be better to lose that enjoyment than to purchase it at so extravagant a price. But the beauties of a great poet would be a far poorer thing than they are, if they only impressed us through a knowledge of the technicalities of his art. The poet needed those technicalities: they are not necessary to us. They are essential for criticizing a poem, but not for enjoying it. All that is wanted is sufficient familiarity with the language, for its meaning to reach us without any sense of effort, and clothed with the associations on which the poet counted for producing his effect. Whoever has this familiarity, and a practised ear, can have as keen a relish of the music of Virgil and Horace, as of Gray, or Burns, or Shelley, though he know not the metrical rules of a common Sapphic or Alcaic. I do not say that these rules ought not to be taught, but I would have a class apart for them, and would make the appropriate exercises an optional, not a compulsory part of the school teaching.

Much more might be said respecting classical instruction, and literary cultivation in general, as a part of liberal education. But it is time to speak of the uses of scientific instruction: or rather its indispensable necessity, for it is recommended by every consideration which pleads for any high order of intellectual education at all.

The most obvious part of the value of scientific instruction, the mere information that it gives, speaks for itself. We are born into a world which we have not made; a world whose phenomena take place according to fixed laws, of which we do not bring any knowledge into the world with us. In such a world we are appointed to live, and in it all our work is to be done. Our whole working power depends on knowing the laws of the world—in other words, the properties of the things which we have to work with, and to work among, and to work upon. We may and do rely, for the greater part of this knowledge, on the few who in each department make its acquisition their main business in life. But unless an elementary knowledge of scientific truths is diffused among the public, they never know what is certain and what is not, or who are entitled to speak with authority and who are not: and they either have no faith at all in the testimony of science, or are the ready dupes of charlatans and impostors. They alternate between ignorant distrust, and blind, often misplaced, confidence. Besides, who is there who would not wish to understand the meaning of the common physical facts that take place under his eye? Who would not wish to know why a pump raises water, why a lever moves heavy weights, why it is hot at the tropics and cold at the poles, why the moon is sometimes dark and sometimes bright, what is the cause of the tides? Do we not feel that he who is totally ignorant of these things, let him be ever so skilled in a special profession, is not an educated man but an ignoramus?

It is surely no small part of education to put us in intelligent possession of the most important and most universally interesting facts of the universe, so that the world which surrounds us may not be a sealed book to us, uninteresting because unintelligible. This, however, is but the simplest and most obvious art of the utility of science, and the part which, if neglected in youth, may be the most easily made up for afterwards. It is more important to understand the value of scientific instruction as a training and disciplining process, to fit the intellect for the proper work of a human being. Facts are the materials of our knowledge, but the mind itself is the instrument: and it is easier to acquire facts, than to judge what they prove, and how, through the facts which we know, to get to those which we want to know.

The most incessant occupation of the human intellect throughout life is the ascertainment of truth. We are always needing to know what is actually true about something or other. It is not given to us all to discover great general truths that are a light to all men and to future generations; though with better general education the number of those who could do so would be far greater than it is. But we all require the ability to judge between the conflicting opinions which are offered to us as vital truths; to choose what doctrines we will receive in the matter of religion, for example; to judge whether we ought to be Tories, Whigs, or Radicals, or to what length it is our duty to go with each; to form a rational conviction on great questions of legislation and internal policy, and on the manner in which our country should behave to dependencies and to foreign nations. And the need we have of knowing how to discriminate truth, is not confined to the larger truths. All through life it is our most pressing interest to find out the truth about all the matters we are concerned with. If we are farmers we want to find what will truly improve our soil; if merchants, what will truly influence the markets of our commodities; if judges, or jurymen, or advocates, who it was that truly did an unlawful act, or to whom a disputed right truly belongs. Every time we have to make a new resolution or alter an old one, in any situation in life, we shall go wrong unless we know the truth about the facts on which our resolution depends. Now, however different these searches

for truth may look, and however unlike they really are in their subject-matter, the methods of getting at truth, and the tests of truth, are in all cases much the same.

There are but two roads by which truth can be discovered; observation, and reasoning: observation, of course, including experiment. We all observe, and we all reason, and therefore, more or less successfully, we all ascertain truths: but most of us do it very ill, and could not get on at all were we not able to fall back on others who do it better. If we could not do it in any degree, we should be mere instruments in the hands of those who could: they would be able to reduce us to slavery. Then how shall we best learn to do this? By being shewn the way in which it has already been successfully done. The processes by which truth is attained, reasoning and observation, have been carried to their greatest known perfection in the physical sciences. As classical literature furnishes the most perfect types of the art of expression, so do the physical sciences those of the art of thinking. Mathematics, and its application to astronomy and natural philosophy, are the most complete example of the discovery of truths by reasoning; experimental science, of their discovery by direct observation. In all these cases we know that we can trust the operation, because the conclusions to which it has led have been found true by subsequent trial. It is by the study of these, then, that we may hope to qualify ourselves for distinguishing truth, in cases where there do not exist the same ready means of verification.

In what consists the principal and most characteristic difference between one human intellect and another? In their ability to judge correctly of evidence. Our direct perceptions of truth are so limited; we know so few things by immediate intuition, or, as it used to be called, by simple apprehension—that we depend for almost all our valuable knowledge, on evidence external to itself; and most of us are very unsafe hands at estimating evidence, where an appeal cannot be made to actual eyesight. The intellectual part of our education has nothing more important to do, than to correct or mitigate this almost universal infirmity—this summary and substance of nearly all purely intellectual weakness. To do this with effect needs all the resources which the most perfect system of intellectual training can command. Those resources, as every teacher knows, are but of three kinds: first, models, secondly, rules, thirdly, appropriate practice. The models of the art of estimating evidence are furnished by science; the rules are suggested by science; and the study of science is the most fundamental portion of the practice.

Take in the first instance mathematics. It is chiefly from mathematics we realize the fact that there actually is a road to truth by means of reasoning; that anything real, and which will be found true when tried, can be arrived at by a mere operation of the mind. The flagrant abuse of mere reasoning in the days of the schoolmen, when men argued confidently to supposed facts of outward nature without properly establishing their premises, or checking the conclusions by observation, created a prejudice in the modern, and especially in the English mind, against deductive reasoning altogether, as a mode of investigation. The prejudice lasted long, and was upheld by the misunderstood authority of Lord Bacon; until the prodigious applications of mathematics to physical science—to the discovery of the laws of external nature—slowly and tardily restored the reasoning process to the place which belongs to it as a source of real knowledge.

Mathematics, pure and applied, are still the great conclusive example of what can be done by reasoning. Mathematics also habituate us to several of the principal precautions for the safety of the process. Our first studies in geometry teach us two invaluable lessons. One is, to lay down at the beginning, in express and clear terms, all the premises from which we intend to reason. The other is, to keep every step in the reasoning distinct and separate from all the other steps, and to make each step safe before proceeding to another; expressly stating to ourselves, at every joint in the reasoning, what new premise we there introduce. It is not necessary that we should do this at all times, in all our reasonings. But we must be always able and ready to do it. If the validity of our argument is denied, or if we doubt it ourselves, that is the way to check it. In this way we are often enabled to detect at once the exact place where paralogism or confusion get in, and after sufficient practice we may be able to keep them out from the beginning.

It is to mathematics, again, that we owe our first notion of a connected body of truth; truths which grow out of one another, and hang together so that each implies all the rest; that no one of them can be questioned without contradicting another or others, until in the end it appears that no part of the system can be false unless the whole is so. Pure mathematics first gave us this conception; applied mathematics extends it to the realm of physical nature. Applied mathematics shews us that not only the truths of abstract number and extension, but the external facts of the universe, which we apprehend by our senses, form, at least in a large part of all nature, a web similarly held together. We are able, by reasoning from a few fundamental truths, to explain and predict the phenomena of material objects: and what is still more remarkable, the fundamental truths were themselves found out by reasoning; for they are not such as are obvious to the senses, but had to be inferred by a mathematical process from a mass of minute details, which alone came within the direct reach of human observation.

When Newton, in this manner, discovered the laws of the solar system, he created, for all posterity, the true idea of science. He gave the most perfect example we are ever likely to have, of that union of reasoning and observation, which by means of facts that can be directly observed, ascends to laws which govern multitudes of other facts—laws which not only explain and account for what we see, but give us assurance beforehand of much that we do not see, much that we never could have found out by observation, though, having been found out, it is always verified by the result.

While mathematics, and the mathematical sciences, supply us with a typical example of the ascertainment of truth by reasoning; those physical sciences which are not mathematical, such as chemistry, and purely experimental physics, shew us in equal perfection the other mode of arriving at certain truth, by observation, in its most accurate form, that of experiment. The value of mathematics in a logical point of view is an old topic with mathematicians, and has even been insisted on so exclusively as to provoke a counter-exaggeration, of which a well-known essay by Sir William Hamilton is an example: but the logical value of experimental science is comparatively a new subject, yet there is no intellectual discipline more important than that which the experimental sciences afford. Their whole occupation consists in doing well, what all of us, during the whole of life, are engaged in doing, for the most part badly.

All men do not affect to be reasoners, but all profess, and really attempt, to draw inferences from experience: yet hardly any one, who has not been a student of the physical sciences, sets out with any just idea of what the process of interpreting experience really is. If a fact has occurred once or oftener, and another fact has followed it, people think they have got an experiment, and are well on the road towards shewing that the one fact is the cause of the other. If they did but know the immense amount of precaution necessary to a scientific experiment; with what sedulous care the accompanying circumstances are contrived and varied, so as to exclude every agency but that which is the subject of the experiment—or, when disturbing agencies cannot be excluded, the minute accuracy with which their influence is calculated and allowed for, in order that the residue may contain nothing but what is due to the one agency under examination; if these things were attended to, people would be much less easily satisfied that their opinions have the evidence of experience; many popular notions and generalizations which are in all mouths, would be thought a great deal less certain than they are supposed to be; but we should begin to lay the foundation of really experimental knowledge, on things which are now the subjects of mere vague discussion, where one side finds as much to say and says it as confidently as another, and each person's opinion is less determined by evidence than by his accidental interest or prepossession.

In politics, for instance, it is evident to whoever comes to the study from that of the experimental sciences, that no political conclusions of any value for practice can be arrived at by direct experience. Such specific experience as we can have, serves only to verify, and even that insufficiently, the conclusions of reasoning. Take any active force you please in politics, take the liberties of England, or free trade: how should we know that either of these things conduced to prosperity, if we could discern no tendency in the things themselves to produce it? If we had only the evidence of what is called our experience, such prosperity as we enjoy might be owing to a hundred other causes, and might have been obstructed, not promoted, by these. All true political science is, in one sense of the phrase, *a priori,* being deduced from the tendencies of things, tendencies known either through our general experience of human nature, or as the result of an analysis of the course of history, considered as a progressive evolution. It requires, therefore, the union of induction and deduction, and the mind that is equal to it must have been well disciplined in both. But familiarity with scientific experiment at least does the useful service of inspiring a wholesome scepticism about the conclusions which the mere surface of experience suggests.

The study, on the one hand, of mathematics and its applications, on the other, of experimental science, prepares us for the prin-

Great Books Library

cipal business of the intellect, by the practice of it in the most characteristic cases, and by familiarity with the most perfect and successful models of it. But in great things as in small, examples and models are not sufficient: we want rules as well. Familiarity with the correct use of a language in conversation and writing does not make rules of grammar unnecessary; nor does the amplest knowledge of sciences of reasoning and experiment dispense with rules of logic. We may have heard correct reasonings· and seen skilful experiments all our lives—we shall not learn by mere imitation to do the like, unless we pay careful attention to how it is done. It is much easier in these abstract matters, than in purely mechanical ones, to mistake bad work for good. To mark out the difference between them is the province of logic. Logic lays down the general principles and laws of the search after truth; the conditions which, whether recognised or not, must actually have been observed if the mind has done its work rightly. Logic is the intellectual complement of mathematics and physics. Those sciences give the practice, of which Logic is the theory. It declares the principles, rules, and precepts, of which they exemplify the observance.

The science of Logic has two parts; ratiocinative and inductive logic. The one helps to keep us right in reasoning from premises, the other in concluding from observation. Ratiocinative logic is much older than inductive, because reasoning in the narrower sense of the word is an easier process than induction, and the science which works by mere reasoning, pure mathematics, had been carried to a considerable height while the sciences of observation were still in the purely empirical period. The principles of ratiocination, therefore, were the earliest understood and systematized, and the logic of ratiocination is even now suitable to an earlier stage in education than that of induction. The principles of induction cannot be properly understood without some previous study of the inductive sciences: but

the logic of reasoning, which was already carried to a high degree of perfection by Aristotle, does not absolutely require even a knowledge of mathematics, but can be sufficiently exemplified and illustrated from the practice of daily life.

Of Logic I venture to say, even if limited to that of mere ratiocination, the theory of names, propositions, and the syllogism, that there is no part of intellectual education which is of greater value, or whose place can so ill be supplied by anything else. Its uses, it is true, are chiefly negative; its function is, not so much to teach us to go right as to keep us from going wrong. But in the operations of the intellect it is so much easier to go wrong than right; it is so utterly impossible for even the most vigorous mind to keep itself in the path but by maintaining a vigilant watch against all deviations, and noting all the byways by which it is possible to go astray—that the chief difference between one reasoner and another consists in their less or greater liability to be misled. Logic points out all the possible ways in which, starting from true premises, we may draw false conclusions. By its analysis of the reasoning process, and the forms it supplies for stating and setting forth our reasonings, it enables us to guard the points at which a fallacy is in danger of slipping in, or to lay our fingers upon the place where it has slipped in.

When I consider how very simple the theory of reasoning is, and how short a time is sufficient for acquiring a thorough knowledge of its principles and rules, and even considerable expertness in applying them, I can find no excuse for omission to study it on the part of any one who aspires to succeed in any intellectual pursuit. Logic is the great disperser of hazy and confused thinking: it clears up the fogs which hide from us our own ignorance, and make us believe that we understand a subject when we do not. We must not be led away by talk about inarticulate giants who do great deeds without knowing how, and see into the most recondite truths without any of the ordinary helps, and without being able to explain to other people how they reach their conclusions, nor consequently to convince any other people of the truth of them. There may be such men, as there are deaf and dumb persons who do clever things, but for all that, speech and hearing are faculties by no means to be dispensed with.

If you want to know whether you are thinking rightly, put your thoughts into words. In the very attempt to do this you will find yourselves, consciously or unconsciously, using logical forms. Logic compels us to throw our meaning into distinct propositions, and our reasonings into distinct steps. It makes us conscious of all the implied assumptions on which we are proceeding, and which, if not true, vitiate the entire process. It makes us aware what extent of doctrine we commit ourselves to by any course of reasoning, and obliges us to look the implied premises in the face, and make up our minds whether we can stand to them. It makes our opinions consistent with themselves and with one another, and forces us to think clearly, even when it cannot make us think correctly. It is true that error may be consistent and systematic as well as truth; but this is not the common case. It is no small advantage to see clearly the principles and consequences involved in our opinions, and which we must either accept, or else abandon those opinions. We are much nearer to finding truth when we search for it in broad daylight. Error, pursued rigorously to all that is implied in it, seldom fails to get detected by coming into collision with some known and admitted fact.

You will find abundance of people to tell you that logic is no help to thought, and that people cannot be taught to think by rules. Undoubtedly rules by themselves, without practice, go but a little way in teaching anything. But if the practice of thinking is not improved by rules, I venture to say it is the only difficult thing done by human beings that is not so. A man learns to saw wood principally by practice, but there are rules for doing it, grounded on the nature of the operation, and if he is not taught the rules, he will not saw well until he has discovered them for himself. Wherever there is a right way and a wrong, there must be a difference between them, and it must be possible to find out what the difference is; and when found out and expressed in words, it is a rule for the operation. If any one is inclined to disparage rules, I say to him, try to learn anything which there are rules for, without knowing the rules, and see how you succeed.

To those who think lightly of the school logic, I say, take the trouble to learn it. You will easily do so in a few weeks, and you will see whether it is of no use to you in making your mind clear, and keeping you from stumbling in the dark over the most outrageous fallacies. Nobody, I believe, who has really learnt it, and who goes on using his mind, is insensible to its benefits, unless he started with a prejudice, or, like some eminent English and Scottish thinkers of the past century, is under the influence of a reaction against the exaggerated pretensions made by the schoolmen, not so much in behalf of logic as of the reasoning process itself.

Still more highly must the use of logic be estimated, if we include in it, as we ought to do, the principles and rules of Induction as well as of Ratiocination. As the one logic guards us against bad deduction, so does the other against bad generalization, which is a still more universal error. If men easily err in arguing from one general proposition to another, still more easily do they go wrong in interpreting the observations made by themselves and others. There is nothing in which an untrained mind shows itself more hopelessly incapable, than in drawing the proper general conclusions from its own experience. And even trained minds, when all their training is on a special subject, and does not extend to the general principles of induction, are only kept right when there are ready opportunities of verifying their inferences by facts.

403

Able scientific men, when they venture upon subjects in which they have no facts to check them, are often found drawing conclusions or making generalizations from their experimental knowledge, such as any sound theory of induction would shew to be utterly unwarranted. So true is it that practice alone, even of a good kind, is not sufficient without principles and rules. Lord Bacon had the great merit of seeing that rules were necessary, and conceiving, to a very considerable extent, their true character. The defects of his conception were such as were inevitable while the inductive sciences were only in the earliest stage of their progress, and the highest efforts of the human mind in that direction had not yet been made. Inadequate as the Baconian view of induction was, and rapidly as the practice outgrew it, it is only within a generation or two that any considerable improvement has been made in the theory; very much through the impulse given by two of the many distinguished men who have adorned the Scottish universities, Dugald Stewart and Brown.

I have given a very incomplete and summary view of the educational benefits derived from instruction in the more perfect sciences, and in the rules for the proper use of the intellectual faculties which the practice of those sciences has suggested. There are other sciences, which are in a more backward state, and tax the whole powers of the mind in its mature years, yet a beginning of which may be beneficially made in university studies, while a tincture of them is valuable even to those who are never likely to proceed further.

The first is physiology; the science of the laws of organic and animal life, and especially of the structure and functions of the human body. It would be absurd to pretend that a profound knowledge of this difficult subject can be acquired in youth, or as a part of general education. Yet an acquaintance with its leading truths is one of those acquirements which ought not to be the exclusive property of a particular profession. The value of such knowledge for daily uses has been made familiar to us all by the sanitary discussions of late years. There is hardly one among us who may not, in some position of authority, be required to form an opinion and take part in public action on sanitary subjects. And the importance of understanding the true conditions of health and disease —of knowing how to acquire and preserve that healthy habit of body which the most tedious and costly medical treatment so often fails to restore when once lost, should secure a place in general education for the principal maxims of hygiene, and some of those even of practical medicine.

For those who aim at high intellectual cultivation, the study of physiology has still greater recommendations, and is, in the present state of advancement of the higher studies, a real necessity. The practice which it gives in the study of nature is such as no other physical science affords in the same kind, and is the best introduction to the difficult questions of politics and social life. Scientific education, apart from professional objects, is but a preparation for judging rightly of Man, and of his requirements and interests. But to this final pursuit, which has been called *par excellence* the proper study of mankind, physiology is the most serviceable of the sciences, because it is the nearest. Its subject is already Man: the same complex and manifold being, whose properties are not independent of circumstance, and immovable from age to age, like those of the ellipse and hyperbola, or of sulphur and phosphorus, but are infinitely various, indefinitely modifiable by art or accident, graduating by the nicest shades into one another, and reacting upon one another in a thousand ways, so that they are seldom capable of being isolated and observed separately.

With the difficulties of the study of a being so constituted, the physiologist, and he alone among scientific enquirers, is already familiar. Take what view we will of man as a spiritual being, one part of his nature is far more like another than either of them is like

nything else. In the organic world we study
ature under disadvantages very similar to
nose which affect the study of moral and
olitical phenomena: our means of making
xperiments are almost as limited, while the
xtreme complexity of the facts makes the
onclusions of general reasoning unusually
recarious, on account of the vast number
f circumstances that conspire to determine
very result. Yet in spite of these obstacles,
, is found possible in physiology to arrive
t a considerable number of well-ascertained
nd important truths. This therefore is an
xcellent school in which to study the means
f overcoming similar difficulties elsewhere.
t is in physiology too that we are first in-
roduced to some of the conceptions which
lay the greatest part in the moral and social
iences, but which do not occur at all in
nose of inorganic nature. As, for instance,
ne idea of predisposition, and of predis-
osing causes, as distinguished from exciting
auses. The operation of all moral forces is
nmensely influenced by predisposition:
rithout that element, it is impossible to ex-
lain the commonest facts of history and
ocial life.

Physiology is also the first science in which
e recognise the influence of habit—the tend-
ncy of something to happen again merely
ecause it has happened before. From phys-
ology, too, we get our clearest notion of
rhat is meant by development or evolution.
he growth of a plant or animal from the
rst germ is the typical specimen of a phe-
omenon which rules through the whole
ourse of the history of man and society—
ncrease of function, through expansion and
ifferentiation of structure by internal forces.
cannot enter into the subject at greater
ength; it is enough if I throw out hints
rhich may be germs of further thought in
ourselves. Those who aim at high intellec-
ual achievements may be assured that no
art of their time will be less wasted, than
hat which they employ in becoming familiar
rith the methods and the main conceptions
f the science of organization and life.

Physiology, at its upper extremity, touches
on Psychology, or the Philosophy of Mind:
and without raising any disputed questions
about the limits between Matter and Spirit,
the nerves and brain are admitted to have so
intimate a connexion with the mental operations, that the student of the last cannot dis-
pense with a considerable knowledge of the
first. The value of psychology itself need
hardly be expatiated upon in a Scottish
university; for it has always been there studied with brilliant success. Almost everything
which has been contributed from these islands towards its advancement since Locke
and Berkeley, has until very lately, and
much of it even in the present generation,
proceeded from Scottish authors and Scottish
professors. Psychology, in truth, is simply the
knowledge of the laws of human nature. If
there is anything that deserves to be studied
by man, it is his own nature and that of his
fellow-men: and if it is worth studying at all,
it is worth studying scientifically, so as to
reach the fundamental laws which underlie
and govern all the rest.

With regard to the suitableness of this
subject for general education, a distinction
must be made. There are certain observed
laws of our thoughts and of our feelings
which rest upon experimental evidence, and,
once seized, are a clue to the interpretation
of much that we are conscious of in ourselves,
and observe in one another. Such, for example, are the laws of association. Psychology,
so far as it consists of such laws—I speak of
the laws themselves, not of their disputed
applications—is as positive and certain a
science as chemistry, and fit to be taught as
such. When, however, we pass beyond the
bounds of these admitted truths, to questions
which are still in controversy among the different philosophical schools—how far the
higher operations of the mind can be explained by association, how far we must
admit other primary principles—what faculties of the mind are simple, what complex,
and what is the composition of the latter—
above all, when we embark upon the sea of

metaphysics properly so called, and enquire, for instance, whether time and space are real existences, as is our spontaneous impression, or forms of our sensitive faculty, as is maintained by Kant, or complex ideas generated by association; whether matter and spirit are conceptions merely relative to our faculties, or facts existing *per se*, and in the latter case, what is the nature and limit of our knowledge of them; whether the will of man is free or determined by causes, and what is the real difference between the two doctrines; matters on which the most thinking men, and those who have given most study to the subjects, are still divided; it is neither to be expected nor desired that those who do not specially devote themselves to the higher departments of speculation should employ much of their time in attempting to get to the bottom of these questions.

But it is a part of liberal education to know that such controversies exist, and, in a general way, what has been said on both sides of them. It is instructive to know the failures of the human intellect as well as its successes, its imperfect as well as its perfect attainments; to be aware of the open questions, as well as of those which have been definitively resolved. A very summary view of these disputed matters may suffice for the many; but a system of education is not intended solely for the many: it has to kindle the aspirations and aid the efforts of those who are destined to stand forth as thinkers above the multitude: and for these there is hardly to be found any discipline comparable to that which these metaphysical controversies afford. For they are essentially questions about the estimation of evidence; about the ultimate grounds of belief; the conditions required to justify our most familiar and intimate convictions; and the real meaning and import of words and phrases which we have used from infancy as if we understood all about them, which are even at the foundation of human language, yet of which no one except a metaphysician has rendered to himself a complete account. Whatever philosophical opinions the study of

these questions may lead us to adopt, no on ever came out of the discussion of them wit out increased vigour of understanding, a increased demand for precision of though and language, and a more careful and exa appreciation of the nature of proof.

There never was any sharpener of th intellectual faculties superior to the Berk leian controversy. There is even now no rea ing more profitable to students—confinin myself to writers in our own language, an notwithstanding that so many of their spec lations are already obsolete—than Hobb and Locke, Reid and Stewart, Hume, Har ley, and Brown: on condition that thes great thinkers are not read passively, a masters to be followed, but actively, as su plying materials and incentives to though To come to our own contemporaries, he wh has mastered Sir William Hamilton and you own lamented Ferrier as distinguished repr sentatives of one of the two great schools philosophy, and an eminent Professor in neighbouring University, Professor Bai probably the greatest living authority in th other, has gained a practice in the mo searching methods of philosophic investig tion applied to the most arduous subject which is no inadequate preparation for an intellectual difficulties that he is ever likel to be called on to resolve.

In this brief outline of a complete scientifi education, I have said nothing about d rect instruction in that which it is the chief all the ends of intellectual education t qualify us for—the exercise of thought o the great interests of mankind as mor and social beings—ethics and politics, i the largest sense. These things are not, i the existing state of human knowledge, th subject of a science, generally admitted an accepted. Politics cannot be learnt once fo all, from a text-book, or the instructio of a master. What we require to be taugh on that subject, is to be our own teacher It is a subject on which we have no ma ters to follow; each must explore for hin elf and exercise an independent judgment. scientific politics do not consist in having a et of conclusions ready made, to be applied verywhere indiscriminately, but in setting he mind to work in a scientific spirit to discover in each instance the truths applicable o the given case. And this, at present, carcely any two persons do in the same way. Education is not entitled, on this subject, to ecommend any set of opinions as resting on he authority of established science. But it an supply the student with materials for his own mind, and helps to use them. It can make him acquainted with the best speculations on the subject, taken from different points of view: none of which will be found complete, while each embodies some considerations really relevant, really requiring to be taken into the account.

Education may also introduce us to the principal facts which have a direct bearing on the subject, namely the different modes or stages of civilization that have been found among mankind, and the characteristic properties of each. This is the true purpose of historical studies, as prosecuted in an University. The leading facts of ancient and modern history should be known by the student from his private reading: if that knowledge be wanting, it cannot possibly be supplied here. What a Professor of History has to teach, is the meaning of those facts. His office is to help the student in collecting from history what are the main differences between human beings, and between the institutions of society, at one time or place and at another: in picturing to himself human life and the human conception of life, as they were at the different stages of human development: in distinguishing between what is the same in all ages and what is progressive, and forming some incipient conception of the causes and laws of progress.

All these things are as yet very imperfectly understood even by the most philosophic enquirers, and are quite unfit to be taught dogmatically. The object is to lead the student to attend to them; to make him take interest in history not as a mere narrative, but as a chain of causes and effects still unwinding itself before his eyes, and full of momentous consequences to himself and his descendants; the unfolding of a great epic or dramatic action, to terminate in the happiness or misery, the elevation or degradation, of the human race; an unremitting conflict between good and evil powers, of which every act done by any of us, insignificant as we are, forms one of the incidents; a conflict in which even the smallest of us cannot escape from taking part, in which whoever does not help the right side is helping the wrong, and for our share in which, whether it be greater or smaller, and let its actual consequences be visible or in the main invisible, no one of us can escape the responsibility.

Though education cannot arm and equip its pupils for this fight with any complete philosophy either of politics or of history, there is much positive instruction that it can give them, having a direct bearing on the duties of citizenship. They should be taught the outlines of the civil and political institutions of their own country, and in a more general way, of the more advanced of the other civilized nations. Those branches of politics, or of the laws of social life, in which there exists a collection of facts or thoughts sufficiently sifted and methodized to form the beginning of a science, should be taught *ex professo*.

Among the chief of these is Political Economy; the sources and conditions of wealth and material prosperity for aggregate bodies of human beings. This study approaches nearer to the rank of a science, in the sense in which we apply that name to the physical sciences, than anything else connected with politics yet does. I need not enlarge on the important lessons which it affords for the guidance of life, and for the estimation of laws and institutions, or on the necessity of knowing all that it can teach in order to have true views of the course of human affairs, or form plans for their improvement which will stand actual trial. The same persons who cry down Logic will generally warn you against Political Economy. It is unfeeling, they will tell you. It recognises unpleasant facts. For my part, the most unfeeling thing I know of is the law of gravitation: it breaks the neck of the best and most amiable person without scruple, if he forgets for a single moment to give heed to it. The winds and waves too are very unfeeling. Would you advise those who go to sea to deny the winds and waves—or to make use of them, and find the means of guarding against their dangers? My advice to you is to study the great writers on Political Economy, and hold firmly by whatever in them you find true; and depend upon it that if you are not selfish or hard-hearted already, Political Economy will not make you so.

Of no less importance than Political Economy is the study of what is called Jurisprudence; the general principles of law; the social necessities which laws are required to meet; the features common to all systems of law, and the differences between them; the requisites of good legislation, the proper mode of constructing a legal system, and the best constitution of courts of justice and modes of legal procedure. These things are not only the chief part of the business of government, but the vital concern of every citizen; and their improvement affords a wide scope for the energies of any duly prepared mind, ambitious of contributing towards the better condition of the human race. For this, too, admirable helps have been provided by writers of our own or of a very recent time.

At the head of them stands Bentham; undoubtedly the greatest master who ever devoted the labour of a life to let in light on the subject of law; and who is the more intelligible to non-professional persons, because, as his way is, he builds up the subject from its foundation in the facts of human life, and shows by careful consideration of ends and means, what law might and ought to be, in deplorable contrast with what it is. Other enlightened jurists have followed with

contributions of two kinds, as the type of which I may take two works, equally admirable in their respective times.

Mr. Austin, in his *Lectures on Jurisprudence*, takes for his basis the Roman law, the most elaborately consistent legal system which history has shewn us in actual operation, and that which the greatest number of accomplished minds have employed themselves in harmonizing. From this he singles out the principles and distinctions which are of general applicability, and employs the powers and resources of a most precise and analytic mind to give to those principles and distinctions a philosophic basis, grounded in the universal reason of mankind, and not in mere technical convenience.

Mr. Maine, in his treatise on *Ancient Law in its relations to Modern Thought*, shews from the history of law, and from what is known of the primitive institutions of mankind, the origin of much that has lasted till now, and has a firm footing both in the law and in the ideas of modern times; shewing that many of these things never originated in reason, but are relics of the institutions of barbarous society, modified more or less by civilization, but kept standing by the persistency of ideas which were the offspring of those barbarous institutions, and have survived their parent. The path opened by Mr. Maine has been followed up by others, with additional illustrations of the influence of obsolete ideas on modern institutions, and of obsolete institutions on modern ideas; an action and reaction which perpetuate, in many of the greatest concerns, a mitigated barbarism: things being continually accepted as dictates of nature and necessities of life which, if we knew all, we should see to have originated in artificial arrangements of society, long since abandoned and condemned.

To these studies I would add International Law, which I decidedly think should be taught in all universities, and should form part of all liberal education. The need of it is far from being limited to diplomatists and lawyers; it extends to every citizen. What is alled the Law of Nations is not properly aw, but a part of ethics: a set of moral rules, ccepted as authoritative by civilized states. t is true that these rules neither are nor ught to be of eternal obligation, but do and nust vary more or less from age to age, as the onsciences of nations become more enlight-ned and the exigencies of political society ndergo change. But the rules mostly were at heir origin, and still are, an application of he maxims of honesty and humanity to the ntercourse of states. They were introduced y the moral sentiments of mankind, or by heir sense of the general interest, to mitigate he crimes and sufferings of a state of war, nd to restrain governments and nations rom unjust or dishonest conduct towards ne another in time of peace.

Since every country stands in numerous nd various relations with the other countries f the world, and many, our own among the umber, exercise actual authority over some f these, a knowledge of the established rules f international morality is essential to the luty of every nation, and therefore of every erson in it who helps to make up the na-ion, and whose voice and feeling form a part f what is called public opinion. Let not any ne pacify his conscience by the delusion that e can do no harm if he takes no part, and orms no opinion. Bad men need nothing nore to compass their ends, than that good nen should look on and do nothing. He is ot a good man who, without a protest, llows wrong to be committed in his name, nd with the means which he helps to supply, ecause he will not trouble himself to use his nind on the subject. It depends on the habit f attending to and looking into public ransactions, and on the degree of informa-ion and solid judgment respecting them hat exists in the community, whether the onduct of the nation as a nation, both vithin itself and towards others, shall be elfish, corrupt, and tyrannical, or rational nd enlightened, just and noble.

Of these more advanced studies, only a mall commencement can be made at schools and universities; but even this is of the high-est value, by awakening an interest in the subjects, by conquering the first difficulties, and inuring the mind to the kind of exertion which the studies require, by implanting a desire to make further progress, and direct-ing the student to the best tracks and the best helps. So far as these branches of knowl-edge have been acquired, we have learnt, or been put into the way of learning, our duty, and our work in life. Knowing it, however, is but half the work of education; it still re-mains, that what we know, we shall be will-ing and determined to put in practice. Never-theless, to know the truth is already a great way towards disposing us to act upon it. What we see clearly and apprehend keenly, we have a natural desire to act out. "To see the best, and yet the worst pursue," is a pos-sible but not a common state of mind; those who follow the wrong have generally first taken care to be voluntarily ignorant of the right. They have silenced their conscience, but they are not knowingly disobeying it. If you take an average human mind while still young, before the objects it has chosen in life have given it a turn in any bad direction, you will generally find it desiring what is good, right, and for the benefit of all; and if that season is properly used to implant the knowledge and give the training which shall render rectitude of judgment more habitual than sophistry, a serious barrier will have been erected against the inroads of selfish-ness and falsehood. Still, it is a very im-perfect education which trains the intelli-gence only, but not the will. No one can dis-pense with an education directed expressly to the moral as well as the intellectual part of his being. Such education, so far as it is direct, is either moral or religious; and these may either be treated as distinct, or as differ-ent aspects of the same thing.

The subject we are now considering is not education as a whole, but scholastic educa-tion, and we must keep in view the inevitable limitations of what schools and universities can do. It is beyond their power to educate morally or religiously. Moral and religious education consist in training the feelings and the daily habits; and these are, in the main, beyond the sphere and inaccessible to the control of public education. It is the home, the family, which gives us the moral or religious education we really receive: and this is completed, and modified, sometimes for the better, often for the worse, by society, and the opinions and feelings with which we are there surrounded. The moral or religious influence which an University can exercise, consists less in any express teaching, than in the pervading tone of the place. Whatever it teaches, it should teach as penetrated by a sense of duty; it should present all knowledge as chiefly a means to worthiness of life, given for the double purpose of making each of us practically useful to his fellow-creatures, and of elevating the character of the species itself; exalting and dignifying our nature.

There is nothing which spreads more contagiously from teacher to pupil than elevation of sentiment: often and often have students caught from the living influence of a professor, a contempt for mean and selfish objects, and a noble ambition to leave the world better than they found it, which they have carried with them throughout life. In these respects, teachers of every kind have natural and peculiar means of doing with effect, what every one who mixes with his fellow-beings, or addresses himself to them in any character, should feel bound to do to the extent of his capacity and opportunities. What is special to an University on these subjects belongs chiefly, like the rest of its work, to the intellectual department. An University exists for the purpose of laying open to each succeeding generation, as far as the conditions of the case admit, the accumulated treasure of the thoughts of mankind.

As an indispensable part of this, it has to make known to them what mankind at large, their own country, and the best and wisest individual men, have thought on the great subjects of morals and religion. There should be, and there is in most universities professorial instruction in moral philosophy but I could wish that this instruction were of a somewhat different type from what is ordinarily met with. I could wish that it were more expository, less polemical, and above all less dogmatic. The learner should be made acquainted with the principal systems of moral philosophy which have existed and been practically operative among mankind and should hear what there is to be said for each: the Aristotelian, the Epicurean, the Stoic, the Judaic, the Christian in the various modes of its interpretation, which differ almost as much from one another as the teachings of those earlier schools. He should be made familiar with the different standard of right and wrong which have been taken as the basis of ethics: general utility, natural justice, natural rights, a moral sense, principles of practical reason, and the rest.

Among all these, it is not so much the teacher's business to take a side, and fight stoutly for some one against the rest, as it is to direct them all towards the establishment and preservation of the rules of conduct most advantageous to mankind. There is no one of these systems which has not its good side; not one from which there is not something to be learnt by the votaries of the others; not one which is not suggested by a keen, though it may not always be a clear perception of some important truths, which are the prop of the system, and the neglect or undervaluing of which in other systems is their characteristic infirmity. A system which may be as a whole erroneous, is still valuable, until it has forced upon mankind a sufficient attention to the portion of truth which suggested it.

The ethical teacher does his part best when he points out how each system may be strengthened even on its own basis, by taking into more complete account the truths which other systems have realized more fully and made more prominent. I do not mean that he should encourage an essentially scepical eclecticism. While placing every system in the best aspect it admits of, and endeavouring to draw from all of them the most salutary consequences compatible with their nature, I would by no means debar him from enforcing by his best arguments his own preference for some one of the number. They cannot be all true; though those which are false as theories may contain particular truths, indispensable to the completeness of the true theory. But on this subject, even more than on any of those I have previously mentioned, it is not the teacher's business to impose his own judgment, but to inform and discipline that of his pupil.

And this same clue, if we keep hold of it, will guide us through the labyrinth of conflicting thought into which we enter when we touch the great question of the relation of education to religion. As I have already said, the only really effective religious education is the parental—that of home and childhood. All that social and public education has in its power to do, further than by a general pervading tone of reverence and duty, amounts to little more than the information which it can give; but this is extremely valuable. I shall not enter into the question which has been debated with so much vehemence in the last and present generation, whether religion ought to be taught at all in universities and public schools, seeing that religion is the subject of all others on which men's opinions are most widely at variance. On neither side of this controversy do the disputants seem to me to have sufficiently freed their minds from the old notion of education, that it consists in the dogmatic inculcation from authority, of what the teacher deems true.

Why should it be impossible, that information of the greatest value, on subjects connected with religion, should be brought before the student's mind; that he should be made acquainted with so important a part of the national thought, and of the intellectual labours of past generations, as those relating to religion, without being taught dogmatically the doctrines of any church or sect? Christianity being a historical religion, the sort of religious instruction which seems to me most appropriate to an University is the study of ecclesiastical history. If teaching, even on matters of scientific certainty, should aim quite as much at showing how the results are arrived at, as at teaching the results themselves, far more, then, should this be the case on subjects where there is the widest diversity of opinion among men of equal ability, and who have taken equal pains to arrive at the truth. This diversity should of itself be a warning to a conscientious teacher that he has no right to impose his opinion authoritatively upon a youthful mind. His teaching should not be in the spirit of dogmatism, but in that of enquiry. The pupil should not be addressed as if his religion had been chosen for him, but as one who will have to choose it for himself. The various Churches, established and unestablished, are quite competent to the task which is peculiarly theirs, that of teaching each its own doctrines, as far as necessary, to its own rising generation.

The proper business of an University is different: not to tell us from authority what we ought to believe, and make us accept the belief as a duty, but to give us information and training, and help us to form our own belief in a manner worthy of intelligent beings, who seek for truth at all hazards, and demand to know all the difficulties, in order that they may be better qualified to find, or recognise, the most satisfactory mode of resolving them. The vast importance of these questions—the great results as regards the conduct of our lives, which depend upon our choosing one belief or another—are the strongest reasons why we should not trust our judgment when it has been formed in ignorance of the evidence, and why we should not consent to be restricted to a one-sided teaching, which informs us of what a particular teacher or association of teachers receive as true doctrine and sound argument, but of nothing more.

I do not affirm that an University, if it

represses free thought and enquiry, must be altogether a failure, for the freest thinkers have often been trained in the most slavish seminaries of learning. The great Christian reformers were taught in Roman Catholic Universities; the sceptical philosophers of France were mostly educated by the Jesuits. The human mind is sometimes impelled all the more violently in one direction, by an over-zealous and demonstrative attempt to drag it in the opposite. But this is not what Universities are appointed for—to drive men from them, even into good, by excess of evil. An University ought to be a place of free speculation. The more diligently it does its duty in all other respects, the more certain it is to be that. The old English Universities, in the present generation, are doing better work than they have done within human memory in teaching the ordinary studies of their curriculum; and one of the consequences has been, that whereas they formerly seemed to exist mainly for the repression of independent thought, and the chaining up of the individual intellect and conscience, they are now the great foci of free and manly enquiry, to the higher and professional classes, south of the Tweed. The ruling minds of those ancient seminaries have at last remembered that to place themselves in hostility to the free use of the understanding, is to abdicate their own best privilege, that of guiding it. A modest deference, at least provisional, to the united authority of the specially instructed, is becoming in a youthful and imperfectly formed mind; but when there is no united authority—when the specially instructed are so divided and scattered that almost any opinion can boast of some high authority, and no opinion whatever can claim all; when, therefore, it can never be deemed extremely improbable that one who uses his mind freely may see reason to change his first opinion; then, whatever you do, keep, at all risks, your minds open: do not barter away your freedom of thought.

Those of you who are destined for the clerical profession are, no doubt, so far held to a certain number of doctrines, that if they ceased to believe them they would not be justified in remaining in a position in which they would be required to teach insincerely. But use your influence to make those doctrines as few as possible. It is not right that men should be bribed to hold out against conviction—to shut their ears against objections, or, if the objections penetrate, to continue professing full and unfaltering belief when their confidence is already shaken. Neither is it right that if men honestly profess to have changed some of their religious opinions, their honesty should as a matter of course exclude them from taking a part for which they may be admirably qualified, in the spiritual instruction of the nation. The tendency of the age, on both sides of the ancient Border, is towards the relaxation of formularies, and a less rigid construction of articles.

This very circumstance, by making the limits of orthodoxy less definite, and obliging every one to draw the line for himself, is an embarrassment to consciences. But I hold entirely with those clergymen who elect to remain in the national church, so long as they are able to accept its articles and confessions in any sense or with any interpretation consistent with common honesty, whether it be the generally received interpretation or not. If all were to desert the church who put a large and liberal construction on its terms of communion, or who would wish to see those terms widened, the national provision for religious teaching and worship would be left utterly to those who take the narrowest, the most literal, and purely textual view of the formularies; who, though by no means necessarily bigots, are under the great disadvantage of having the bigots for their allies, and who, however great their merits may be, and they are often very great, yet if the church is improvable, are not the most likely persons to improve it.

Therefore, if it were not an impertinence in me to tender advice in such a matter, should say, let all who conscientiously can, remain in the church. A church is far more easily improved from within than from without. Almost all the illustrious reformers of religion began by being clergymen: but they did not think that their profession as clergymen was inconsistent with being reformers. They mostly indeed ended their days outside the churches in which they were born; but it was because the churches, in an evil hour for themselves, cast them out. They did not think it any business of theirs to withdraw. They thought they had a better right to remain in the fold, than those had who expelled them.

I have now said what I had to say on the two kinds of education which the system of schools and universities is intended to promote—intellectual education, and moral education: knowledge and the training of the knowing faculty, conscience and that of the moral faculty. These are the two main ingredients of human culture; but they do not exhaust the whole of it. There is a third division, which, if subordinate, and owing allegiance to the two others, is barely inferior to them, and not less needful to the completeness of the human being; I mean the esthetic branch; the culture which comes through poetry and art, and may be described as the education of the feelings, and the cultivation of the beautiful.

This department of things deserves to be regarded in a far more serious light than is the custom of these countries. It is only of late, and chiefly by a superficial imitation of foreigners, that we have begun to use the word Art by itself, and to speak of Art as we speak of Science, or Government, or Religion: we used to talk of the Arts, and more specifically of the Fine Arts: and even by them were vulgarly meant only two forms of Art, Painting and Sculpture, the two which as a people we cared least about—which were regarded even by the more cultivated among us as little more than branches of domestic ornamentation, a kind of elegant upholstery.

The very words "Fine Arts" called up a notion of frivolity, of great pains expended on a rather trifling object—on something which differed from the cheaper and commoner arts of producing pretty things, mainly by being more difficult, and by giving fops an opportunity of pluming themselves on caring for it and on being able to talk about it. This estimate extended in no small degree, though not altogether, even to poetry; the queen of arts, but, in Great Britain, hardly included under the name. It cannot exactly be said that poetry was little thought of; we were proud of our Shakespeare and Milton, and in one period at least of our history, that of Queen Anne, it was a high literary distinction to be a poet; but poetry was hardly looked upon in any serious light, or as having much value except as an amusement or excitement, the superiority of which over others principally consisted in being that of a more refined order of minds. Yet the celebrated saying of Fletcher of Saltoun, "Let who will make the laws of a people if I write their songs," might have taught us how great an instrument for acting on the human mind we were under-valuing. It would be difficult for anybody to imagine that "Rule Britannia," for example, or "Scots wha hae," had no permanent influence on the higher region of human character; some of Moore's songs have done more for Ireland than all Grattan's speeches: and songs are far from being the highest or most impressive form of poetry.

On these subjects, the mode of thinking and feeling of other countries was not only not intelligible, but not credible, to an average Englishman. To find Art ranking on a complete equality, in theory at least, with Philosophy, Learning, and Science—as holding an equally important place among the agents of civilization and among the elements of the worth of humanity; to find even painting and sculpture treated as great social powers, and the art of a country as a feature in its character and condition, little inferior in importance to either its religion or its government; all this only did not amaze and puzzle Englishmen, because it was too strange for them to be able to realize it, or, in truth, to believe it possible: and the radical difference of feeling on this matter between the British people and those of France, Germany, and the Continent generally, is one among the causes of that extraordinary inability to understand one another, which exists between England and the rest of Europe, while it does not exist to anything like the same degree between one nation of Continental Europe and another. It may be traced to the two influences which have chiefly shaped the British character since the days of the Stuarts: commercial money-getting business, and religious Puritanism. Business, demanding the whole of the faculties, and whether pursued from duty or the love of gain, regarding as a loss of time whatever does not conduce directly to the end; Puritanism, which looking upon every feeling of human nature, except fear and reverence for God, as a snare, if not as partaking of sin, looked coldly, if not disapprovingly, on the cultivation of the sentiments.

Different causes have produced different effects in the Continental nations; among whom it is even now observable that virtue and goodness are generally for the most part an affair of the sentiments, while with us they are almost exclusively an affair of duty. Accordingly, the kind of advantage which we have had over many other countries in point of morals—I am not sure that we are not losing it—has consisted in greater tenderness of conscience. In this we have had on the whole a real superiority, though one principally negative; for conscience is with most men a power chiefly in the way of restraint—a power which acts rather in staying our hands from any great wickedness, than by the direction it gives to the general course of our desires and sentiments. One of the commonest types of character among us is that of a man all whose ambition is self-regarding; who has no higher purpose in life than to enrich or raise in the world himself and his family; who never dreams of making the good of his fellow-creatures or of his country an habitual object, further than giving away, annually or from time to time certain sums in charity; but who has a conscience sincerely alive to whatever is generally considered wrong, and would scruple to use any very illegitimate means for attaining his self-interested objects.

While it will often happen in other countries that men whose feelings and whose active energies point strongly in an unselfish direction, who have the love of their country, of human improvement, of human freedom, even of virtue, in great strength, and of whose thoughts and activity a large share is devoted to disinterested objects, will yet, in the pursuit of these or of any other objects that they strongly desire, permit themselves to do wrong things which the other man, though intrinsically, and taking the whole of his character, farther removed from what a human being ought to be, could not bring himself to commit. It is of no use to debate which of these two states of mind is the best, or rather the least bad. It is quite possible to cultivate the conscience and the sentiments too. Nothing hinders us from so training a man that he will not, even for a disinterested purpose, violate the moral law, and also feeding and encouraging those high feelings, on which we mainly rely for lifting men above low and sordid objects, and giving them a higher conception of what constitutes success in life. If we wish men to practise virtue, it is worth while trying to make them love virtue, and feel it an object in itself, and not a tax paid for leave to pursue other objects. It is worth training them to feel, not only actual wrong or actual meanness, but the absence of noble aims and endeavours, as not merely blameable but also degrading: to have a feeling of the miserable smallness of mere self in the face of this great universe, of the collective mass of our fellow creatures, in the face of past history and of the indefinite future—the poorness and insignificance of human life if t is to be all spent in making things comfortable for ourselves and our kin, and raising ourselves and them a step or two on the social ladder. Thus feeling, we learn to respect ourselves only so far as we feel capable of nobler objects: and if unfortunately those by whom we are surrounded do not share our aspirations, perhaps disapprove the conduct to which we are prompted by them—to sustain ourselves by the ideal sympathy of the great characters in history, or even in fiction, and by the contemplation of an idealized posterity: shall I add, of ideal perfection embodied in a Divine Being?

Now, of this elevated tone of mind the great source of inspiration is poetry, and all literature so far as it is poetical and artistic. We may imbibe exalted feelings from Plato, or Demosthenes, or Tacitus, but it is in so far as those great men are not solely philosophers or orators or historians, but poets and artists. Nor is it only loftiness, only the heroic feelings, that are bred by poetic cultivation. Its power is as great in calming the soul as in elevating it—in fostering the milder emotions, as the more exalted. It brings home to us all those aspects of life which take hold of our nature on its unselfish side, and lead us to identify our joy and grief with the good or ill of the system of which we form a part; and all those solemn or pensive feelings, which, without having any direct application to conduct, incline us to take life seriously, and predispose us to the reception of anything which comes before us in the shape of duty.

Who does not feel a better man after a course of Dante, or of Wordsworth, or, I will add, of Lucretius or the *Georgics*, or after brooding over Gray's *Elegy*, or Shelley's *Hymn to Intellectual Beauty?* I have spoken of poetry, but all the other modes of art produce similar effects in their degree. The races and nations whose senses are naturally finer and their sensuous perceptions more exercised than ours, receive the same kind of impressions from painting and sculpture: and many of the more delicately organized

among ourselves do the same. All the arts of expression tend to keep alive and in activity the feelings they express. Do you think that the great Italian painters would have filled the place they did in the European mind, would have been universally ranked among the greatest men of their time, if their productions had done nothing for it but to serve as the decoration of a public hall or a private *salon?* Their Nativities and Crucifixions, their glorious Madonnas and Saints, were to their susceptible Southern countrymen the great school not only of devotional, but of all the elevated and all the imaginative feelings. We colder Northerns may approach to a conception of this function of art when we listen to an oratorio of Handel, or give ourselves up to the emotions excited by a Gothic cathedral.

Even apart from any specific emotional expression, the mere contemplation of beauty of a high order produces in no small degree this elevating effect on the character. The power of natural scenery addresses itself to the same region of human nature which corresponds to Art. There are few capable of feeling the sublimer order of natural beauty, such as your own Highlands and other mountain regions afford, who are not, at least temporarily, raised by it above the littlenesses of humanity, and made to feel the puerility of the petty objects which set men's interests at variance, contrasted with the nobler pleasures which all might share.

To whatever avocations we may be called in life, let us never quash these susceptibilities within us, but carefully seek the opportunities of maintaining them in exercise. The more prosaic our ordinary duties, the more necessary it is to keep up the tone of our minds by frequent visits to that higher region of thought and feeling, in which every work seems dignified in proportion to the ends for which, and the spirit in which, it is done; where we learn, while eagerly seizing every opportunity of exercising higher faculties and performing higher duties, to regard all useful and honest work as a public function, which may be ennobled by the mode of performing it—which has not properly any other nobility than what that gives—and which, if ever so humble, is never mean but when it is meanly done, and when the motives from which it is done are mean motives.

There is, besides, a natural affinity between goodness and the cultivation of the Beautiful, when it is real cultivation, and not a mere unguided instinct. He who has learnt what beauty is, if he be of a virtuous character, will desire to realize it in his own life—will keep before himself a type of perfect beauty in human character, to light his attempts at self-culture. There is a true meaning in the saying of Goethe, though liable to be misunderstood and perverted, that the Beautiful is greater than the Good; for it includes the Good, and adds something to it: it is the Good made perfect, and fitted with all the collateral perfections which make it a finished and completed thing. Now, this sense of perfection, which would make us demand from every creation of man the very utmost that it ought to give, and render us intolerant of the smallest fault in ourselves or in anything we do, is one of the results of Art cultivation. No other human productions come so near to perfection as works of pure Art. In all other things, we are, and may reasonably be, satisfied if the degree of excellence is as great as the object immediately in view seems to us to be worth: but in Art, the perfection is itself the object.

If I were to define Art, I should be inclined to call it, the endeavour after perfection in execution. If we meet with even a piece of mechanical work which bears the marks of being done in this spirit—which is done as if the workman loved it, and tried to make it as good as possible, though something less good would have answered the purpose for which it was ostensibly made— we say that he has worked like an artist. Art, when really cultivated, and not merely practised empirically, maintains, what it first gave the conception of, an ideal Beauty,

to be eternally aimed at, though surpassing what can be actually attained; and by this idea it trains us never to be completely satisfied with imperfection in what we ourselves do and are: to idealize, as much as possible, every work we do, and most of all, our own characters and lives.

And now, having travelled with you over the whole range of the materials and training which an University supplies as a preparation for the higher uses of life, it is almost needless to add any exhortation to you to profit by the gift. Now is your opportunity for gaining a degree of insight into subjects larger and far more ennobling than the minutiæ of a business or a profession, and for acquiring a facility of using your minds on all that concerns the higher interests of man, which you will carry with you into the occupations of active life, and which will prevent even the short intervals of time which that may leave you, from being altogether lost for noble purposes. Having once conquered the first difficulties, the only ones of which the irksomeness surpasses the interest; having turned the point beyond which what was once a task becomes a pleasure; in even the busiest after-life, the higher powers of your mind will make progress imperceptibly, by the spontaneous exercise of your thoughts, and by the lessons you will know how to learn from daily experience. So, at least, it will be if in your early studies you have fixed your eyes upon the ultimate end from which those studies take their chief value—that of making you more effective combatants in the great fight which never ceases to rage between Good and Evil, and more equal to coping with the ever new problems which the changing course of human nature and human society present to be resolved.

Aims like these commonly retain the footing which they have once established in the mind; and their presence in our thoughts keeps our higher faculties in exercise, and makes us consider the acquirements and powers which we store up at any time of our

ives, as a mental capital, to be freely expended in helping forward any mode which
presents itself of making mankind in any
respect wiser or better, or placing any portion of human affairs on a more sensible and
rational footing than its existing one. There
is not one of us who may not qualify himself so to improve the average amount of
opportunities, as to leave his fellow-creatures
some little the better for the use he has
known how to make of his intellect. To
make this little greater, let us strive to keep
ourselves acquainted with the best thoughts
that are brought forth by the original minds
of the age; that we may know what movements stand most in need of our aid, and
that, as far as depends on us, the good seed
may not fall on a rock, and perish without
reaching the soil in which it might have
terminated and flourished.

You are to be a part of the public who are
to welcome, encourage, and help forward
the future intellectual benefactors of humanity; and you are, if possible, to furnish your
contingent to the number of those benefactors. Nor let any one be discouraged by
what may seem, in moments of despon-
dency, the lack of time and of opportunity.

Those who know how to employ opportunities will often find that they can create
them: and what we achieve depends less on
the amount of time we possess, than on the
use we make of our time. You and your like
are the hope and resource of your country
in the coming generation.

All great things which that generation is
destined to do, have to be done by some
like you; several will assuredly be done by
persons for whom society has done much
less, to whom it has given far less preparation, than those whom I am now addressing.
I do not attempt to instigate you by the
prospect of direct rewards, either earthly or
heavenly; the less we think about being rewarded in either way, the better for us. But
there is one reward which will not fail you,
and which may be called disinterested, because it is not a consequence, but is inherent
in the very fact of deserving it; the deeper
and more varied interest you will feel in
life: which will give it tenfold its value,
and a value which will last to the end. All
merely personal objects grow less valuable
as we advance in life: this not only endures
but increases.

Albrecht von Wallenstein

THE PICCOLOMINI

PART ONE OF

WALLENSTEIN

A DRAMA IN TWO PARTS

Translated from the German of

Friedrich Schiller

by

Samuel Taylor Coleridge

Schiller

Coleridge

INTRODUCTION

In 1772, the Duke of Württemberg appointed 13-year-old Friedrich Schiller to study at the military academy founded and personally supervised by the Duke. In the small German towns where his father was stationed as an Army surgeon, Friedrich had been given a sound grammar school education in the hopes of his preparing for the ministry, but now he was to study law. Medicine was later included in the curriculum and Friedrich was allowed to switch to his father's profession, but he was virtually cut off from his family and the outside world for eight years. Forbidden books were smuggled in by the boys and Friedrich read Rousseau, Shakespeare translated by Wieland, and the early Goethe. His enthusiasm for poetry, always encouraged by his mother, now produced his first verses and the beginning of a drama in prose, *The Robbers*, which the demands of his studies did not allow him to finish. Quotations from Shakespeare, however, were included in "The Connection Between the Animal and Spiritual in Man," the dissertation he wrote to meet the medical requirements in 1780. With this, the Duke appointed 21-year-old Schiller to serve as assistant medical officer to a Stuttgart regiment.

The Robbers was completed in Stuttgart and Schiller borrowed the money to have it printed. The play was performed on January 13, 1782 at the National Theatre in Mannheim. The theatrical skill with which his band of outlaws exposed conventionalism and official corruption made the work a sensation. The Duke heard of the absences to Mannheim without leave, and the 22-year-old surgeon was confined to quarters for two weeks and forbidden to write any more plays or books or to communicate with anyone outside of Württemberg. Armed with the manuscript of another play, *Fiesco*, Schiller fled to Mannheim, but the theatre director was not interested. Destitute, Schiller appealed to the family of an academy classmate in the country, and their hospitality for seven months enabled him to write his third play, *Intrigue and Love*. The Mannheim director appointed him dramatic poet to the theatre. *Fiesco* was staged but not well received and *Intrigue and Love*, though its performance excited admiration for his continuing stage mastery, did not lead to the renewal of his annual contract with the theatre.

His debts and an entanglement with a married woman prompted Schiller to accept the hospitality of admirers in Saxony. In two years he completed *Don Carlos*, his first verse drama, which showed two young idealists in Hapsburg Spain attempting to subvert Church and State in order to liberate the Netherlands. With the play printed in 1787, he went to Weimar, Germany's literary capital. Schiller turned to the Dutch rebellion itself in his *History of the Decline of the Netherlands* (1788). On its strength, Goethe secured for Schiller the post of professor of history at the University of Jena in 1789.

He then wrote of the conflict fought on the German front by the Austrian Hapsburgs in his *History of the Thirty Years' War* (1791–1793). Although he finished it in 1793, the Macbeth-like figure of the war's great general, Wallenstein, continued to haunt his creative imagination. Schiller spent the 1790's, his decade at Jena, searching for the format to deal with this minor noble who amassed as a businessman a fortune so great that he could bail out the Hapsburg treasury, whose administrative ability made him the only undefeated commander in the bloodiest modern war (before the 20th century), and who, seeing himself in the stars, was murdered in bed by his own men.

Stimulated by the philosophy of Kant, Schiller wrote a series of essays on the nature of art and literature. Man's need for play, as well as his instincts for the sensuous and the formal, accounted for art, which Schiller concluded is the indispensable instrument for developing the harmonious personality. With his *Letters on the Aesthetic Education of Man*, Goethe declared, Schiller laid the foundation of modern criticism.

He was now a close friend of Goethe, who was having his own writing problems with *Faust*. The two poets engaged in a ballad competition and Goethe conceded defeat. He finally advised Schiller to handle the Wallenstein material as a trilogy. Schiller already had a descriptive prelude of 500 lines, *Wallenstein's Camp*, and this vignette of the common soldier was doubled in length to form the first part. For the drama proper, Schiller compressed the last events of the generalissimo's life into four days that culminated in his murder. This work, *The Piccolomini* and *The Death of Wallenstein*, was completed in six months, and the whole was performed at Weimar twice to acclamation during the winter of 1798 and spring of 1799.

Schiller's publisher contacted the London firm of Longmans and Rees to arrange for the publication of an English translation of *Wallenstein* simultaneous with the German. Longmans hired a 27-year-old poet, Samuel Taylor Coleridge, who had just returned from eleven months of study in Germany. Coleridge had already published a number of books of verse, including *The Fall of Robespierre: An Historic Drama*. With a manuscript from Schiller, Coleridge left his family for the quiet of Charles and Mary Lamb's, and then of Wordsworth's, and completed the translation in six weeks. "There was nothing more astonishing," Wordsworth said later, "than the ease and rapidity with which it was done." In his *Life of Schiller*, Thomas Carlyle pronounced it "the best, indeed the only sufferable translation from the German, with which our literature has been enriched," a judgment that still stands for many critics.

With *Wallenstein*'s success, Schiller resolved to devote himself to writing for the theatre. Critics assured him that his youthful dream had indeed come true, and that he now could, as he had written in an early poem, meet "Shakespeare's shade" as an equal. To be near a theatre and his friend Goethe, Schiller resigned his university post and moved his family—he had married in 1790 and had four children—to Weimar. In the next five years, despite his continually failing health, Schiller turned out nine works for the Weimar theatre. Along with *Mary Stuart* (1800), *The Maid of Orleans* (1801), *The Bride of Messina* (1803), *William Tell* (1804), he wrote versions of *Macbeth*, *Turandot*, *Phèdre*, and two comedies of Picard. *Demetrius*, a tragedy on the Boris Godunov theme, was unfinished when he died on May 9, 1805, aged 45.

The text, based on the *Wallenstein* in the Chandos Classics edition of *The Poetical Works of S. T. Coleridge*, has been edited in the light of the first edition (London, 1800). Coleridge did not translate the 1,000-line prelude, *Wallenstein's Camp*, because to duplicate its rhymes and lilting meter "would have been incompatible with a faithful adherence to the sense of the German. Schiller's intention," Coleridge said, "seems to have been merely to have prepared his reader for the Tragedies by a lively picture of the laxity of discipline, and the mutinous dispositions of Wallenstein's soldiery. It is not necessary as a preliminary explanation." *The Death of Wallenstein*, the second of the drama's two parts, will appear in *The Great Ideas Today, 1970*.

DRAMATIS PERSONÆ

WALLENSTEIN, Duke of Friedland, Generalissimo of the Imperial Forces in the
 Thirty Years' War

OCTAVIO PICCOLOMINI, Lieutenant-General

MAX PICCOLOMINI, his Son, Colonel of a Regiment of Cuirassiers

COUNT TERTSKY, the Commander of several regiments, and Brother-in-law of
 Wallenstein

ILLO, Field-Marshal, Wallenstein's Confidant

ISOLANI, General of the Croats

BUTLER, an Irishman, Commander of a regiment of Dragoons

TIEFENBACH,

DON MARADAS,
} Generals under Wallenstein

GOETZ,

KOLATTO,

NEUMANN, Captain of Cavalry, Aide-de-camp to Tertsky

VON QUESTENBERG, the War Commissioner, Imperial Envoy

GENERAL WRANGEL, Swedish Envoy

BAPTISTA SENI, Astrologer

DUCHESS OF FRIEDLAND, Wife of Wallenstein

THEKLA, her Daughter, Princess of Friedland

THE COUNTESS TERTSKY, Sister of the Duchess

A CORNET

COLONELS and GENERALS (several)

PAGES and ATTENDANTS belonging to Wallenstein

ATTENDANTS and HOBOISTS belonging to Tertsky

MASTER OF THE CELLAR to Count Tertsky

VALET DE CHAMBRE of Count Piccolomini

ACT I

SCENE I: *An old Gothic chamber in the Council-house at Pilsen, decorated*
 with colours and other war insignia. ILLO, *with* BUTLER *and*
 ISOLANI.

ILLO: Ye have come late—but ye are come! The distance,
  Count Isolan, excuses your delay.

ISOLANI: Add this too, that we come not empty-handed.
  At Donauwert it was reported to us,
  A Swedish caravan was on its way,
  Transporting a rich cargo of provision,
  Almost six hundred waggons. This my Croats
  Plunged down upon and seized, this weighty prize!
  We bring it hither—

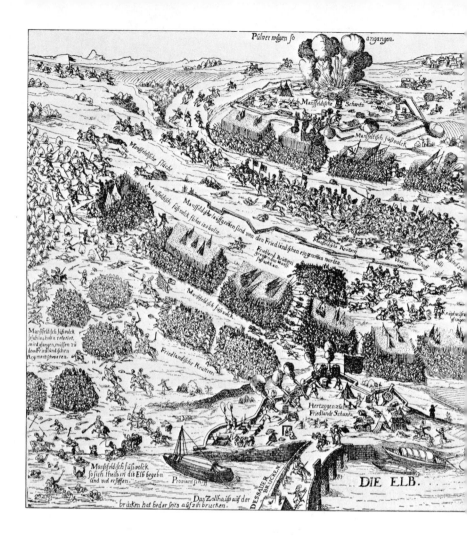

Pülver mögen so angangen.

DIE ELB.

ILLO:	Just in time to banquet
	The illustrious company assembled here.
BUTLER:	'Tis all alive! a stirring scene here!
ISOLANI:	Ay!
	The very churches are full of soldiers. [*Casts his eye round.*
	And in the Council-house too, I observe,
	You're settled, quite at home! Well, well! we soldiers
	Must shift and suit us in what way we can.
ILLO:	We have the Colonels here of thirty regiments,
	You'll find Count Tertsky here, and Tiefenbach,
	Kolatto, Goetz, Maradas, Hinnersam,
	The Piccolomini, both son and father—
	You'll meet with many an unexpected greeting
	From many an old friend and acquaintance. Only
	Galas is wanting still, and Altringer.
BUTLER:	Expect not Galas!

424

In 1625, forces of Christian IV, the Protestant king of Denmark, invaded the Holy Roman Empire and menaced the throne of the Catholic emperor Ferdinand II. To withstand the attack, the emperor appointed Albrecht von Wallenstein commander of his army. An ambitious soldier of fortune from Bohemia, Wallenstein converted to Catholicism, amassed a large fortune through marriage and astute business enterprize, and gained the emperor's confidence through successful service in the Venetian and Bohemian wars. Made duke of Friedland and governor of Bohemia by his grateful sovereign, Wallenstein soon became one of the wealthiest men in Europe and was able to raise and supply the imperial army from his own purse and to turn his duchy into a vast arms and supply center. The new army won its first great victory near Dessau (shown here in a contemporary engraving) on April 25, 1626. This battle was followed by a series of hard-won triumphs that forced Denmark to sue for peace and earned more of the emperor's lavish gratitude: Wallenstein was made duke of Mecklenburg

We were engaged with Mansfield hard by Dessau,
I see the youth, in my mind's eye I see him,
Leap his black war-horse from the bridge adown
And t'ward his father, then in extreme peril,
Beat up against the strong tide of the Elbe.

Act I, scene 1

ILLO	*(hesitating):* How so? Do you know—
ISOLANI	*(interrupting him):*
	Max Piccolomini here? O bring me to him.
	I see him yet ('tis now ten years ago,
	We were engaged with Mansfield hard by Dessau),
	I see the youth, in my mind's eye I see him,
	Leap his black war-horse from the bridge adown
	And t'ward his father, then in extreme peril,
	Beat up against the strong tide of the Elbe.
	The down was scarce upon his chin! I hear
	He has made good the promise of his youth,
	And the full hero now is finishèd in him.
ILLO:	You'll see him yet ere evening. He conducts
	The Duchess Friedland hither, and the Princess
	From Carnthen. We expect them here at noon.
BUTLER:	Both wife and daughter does the Duke call hither?

425

| | He crowds in visitants from all sides. |
| ISOLANI: | Hm! |

So much the better! I had framed my mind
To hear of nought but warlike circumstance,
Of marches, and attacks, and batteries:
And lo! the Duke provides, that something too
Of greater sort, and lovely, should be present
To feast our eyes.

ILLO *(who has been standing in the attitude of meditation, to* BUTLER, *whom he leads a little on one side)*:

And how came you to know
That the Count Galas joins us not?

BUTLER: Because
He importuned me to remain behind.

ILLO *(with warmth)*:
And you? You hold out firmly? [*Grasping his hand with affection.*
Noble Butler!

BUTLER: After the obligation which the Duke
Had laid so newly on me—

ILLO: I had forgotten
A pleasant duty—Major-General,
I wish you joy!

ISOLANI: What, you mean, of his regiment?
I hear, too, that, to make the gift still sweeter,
The Duke has given him the very same
In which he first saw service, and since then,
Worked himself, step by step, thro' each preferment,
From the ranks upwards. And verily, it gives
A precedent of hope, a spur of action
To the whole corps, if once in their remembrance
An old deserving soldier makes his way.

BUTLER: I am perplexed and doubtful, whether or no
I dare accept this your congratulation.
The Emperor has not yet confirmed th' appointment.

ISOLANI: Seize it, friend! Seize it! The hand which in that post
Placed you, is strong enough to keep you there,
Spite of the Emperor and his Ministers!

ILLO: Ay, if we would but so consider it!
If we would *all* of us consider it so!
The Emperor gives us nothing; from the Duke
Comes all—whate'er we hope, whate'er we have.

ISOLANI *(to* ILLO):
My noble brother! did I tell you how
The Duke will satisfy my creditors?
Will be himself my banker for the future,
Make me once more a creditable man!
And this is now the third time, think of that!
This kingly-minded man has rescued me

426

OCTAVIVS PICCOLOMINI DE ARAGONA

At Wallenstein's side through many battles was Octavio
Piccolomini, a tough soldier and wily diplomat. His son
Max, who plays an important role in Schiller's tragedy, is a
fiction, created by the playwright for dramatic purposes

ILLO: From absolute ruin, and restored my honour.
O that his power but kept pace with his wishes!
Why, friend! he'd give the whole world to his soldiers
But at Vienna, brother! here's the grievance!
What politic schemes do they not lay to shorten
His arm, and, where they can, to clip his pinions.
Then these new dainty requisitions! these,
Which this same Questenberg brings hither!

BUTLER: Ay,
These requisitions of the Emperor—
I too have heard about them; but I hope
The Duke will not draw back a single inch!

ILLO: Not from his right most surely, unless first
—From office!

BUTLER (*shocked and confused*):
                            Know you aught then?
You alarm me.

ISOLANI (*at the same time with* BUTLER, *and in a hurrying voice*):
We should be ruined, every one of us!

ILLO: No more!
Yonder I see our worthy friend approaching
With the Lieutenant-General, Piccolomini.

BUTLER (*shaking his head significantly*):
I fear we shall not go hence as we came.

SCENE II: *Enter* OCTAVIO PICCOLOMINI *and* QUESTENBERG.

OCTAVIO (*still in the distance*):
Ay, ay! more still! still more new visitors!
Acknowledge, friend! that never was a camp,
Which held at once so many heads of heroes.
                                    [*Approaching nearer.*
Welcome, Count Isolani!

ISOLANI: My noble brother,
Even now am I arrived; it had been else my duty—

OCTAVIO: And Colonel Butler—trust me, I rejoice
Thus to renew acquaintance with a man
Whose worth and services I know and honour.
See, see, my friend!
There might we place at once before our eyes
The sum of war's whole trade and mystery—
        [*To* QUESTENBERG, *presenting* BUTLER *and* ISOLANI *at the same
        time to him.*
These two the total sum—Strength and Dispatch.

QUESTENBERG (*to* OCTAVIO):
And lo! betwixt them both experienced Prudence!

OCTAVIO (*presenting* QUESTENBERG *to* BUTLER *and* ISOLANI):
The Chamberlain and War-commissioner Questenberg,

	The bearer of the Emperor's behests,
	The long-tried friend and patron of all soldiers,
	We honour in this noble visitor. *[Universal silence.*
ILLO	*(moving towards* QUESTENBERG*):*
	'Tis not the first time, noble Minister,
	You have shown our camp this honour.
QUESTENBERG:	Once before
	I stood before these colours.
ILLO:	Perchance, too, you remember *where* that was.
	It was at Znäim in Moravia, where
	You did present yourself upon the part
	Of the Emperor, to supplicate our Duke
	That he would straight assume the chief command.
QUESTENBERG:	To *supplicate?* Nay, noble General!
	So far extended neither my commission
	(At least to my own knowledge) nor my zeal.
ILLO:	Well, well, then—to *compel* him, if you choose,
	I can remember me right well, Count Tilly
	Had suffered total rout upon the Lech.
	Bavaria lay all open to the enemy,
	Whom there was nothing to delay from pressing
	Onwards into the very heart of Austria.
	At that time you and Werdenberg appeared
	Before our General, storming him with prayers,
	And menacing the Emperor's displeasure,
	Unless he took compassion on this wretchedness.
ISOLANI	*(steps up to them):*
	Yes, yes, 'tis comprehensible enough,
	Wherefore with your commission of to-day
	You were not all too willing to remember
	Your former one.
QUESTENBERG:	Why not, Count Isolan?
	No contradiction sure exists between them.
	It was the urgent business of that time
	To snatch Bavaria from her enemy's hand;
	And my commission of to-day instructs me
	To free her from her good friends and protectors.
ILLO:	A worthy office! After with our blood
	We have wrested this Bohemia from the Saxon,
	To be swept *out* of it is all our thanks,
	The sole reward of all our hard won victories.
QUESTENBERG:	Unless that wretched land be doom'd to suffer
	Only a change of evils, it must be
	Freed from the scourge alike of friend and foe.
ILLO:	What? 'Twas a favourable year; the Boors
	Can answer fresh demands already.
QUESTENBERG:	Nay,
	If *you* discourse of herds and meadow-grounds—

ISOLANI: The war maintains the war. Are the Boors ruined,
The Emperor gains so many more new soldiers.

QUESTENBERG: And is the poorer by even so many subjects.

ISOLANI: Poh! We are all his subjects.

QUESTENBERG: Yet with a difference, General! the one fill
With profitable industry the purse,
The others are well skilled to empty it.
The sword has made the Emperor poor; the plough
Must reinvigorate his resources.

ISOLANI: Sure!
Times are not yet so bad. Methinks I see
              [*He eyes the dress and ornaments of* QUESTENBERG.
Good store of gold that still remains uncoined.

QUESTENBERG: Thank Heaven! that means have been found out to hide
Some little from the fingers of the Croats.

ILLO: There! The Stawata and the Martinitz,
On whom the Emperor heaps his gifts and graces,
To the heart-burning of all good Bohemians—
Those minions of court favour, those court harpies,
Who fatten on the wrecks of citizens
Driven from their house and home—who reap no harvests
Save in the general calamity—
Who now, with kingly pomp, insult and mock
The desolation of their country—*these*,
Let *these*, and such as these, support the war,
The fatal war, which they alone enkindled!

BUTLER: And those state-parasites, who have their feet
So constantly beneath the Emperor's table,
Who cannot let a benefice fall, but they
Snap at it with dog's hunger—they, forsooth,
Would *pare* the soldier's bread, and cross his reckoning.

ISOLANI: My life long will it anger me to think,
How when I went to court seven years ago,
To see about new horses for our regiment,
How from one antechamber to another
They dragged me on, and left me by the hour
To kick my heels among a crowd of simpering,
Feast-fattened slaves, as if I had come thither
A mendicant suitor for the crumbs of favour
That fall beneath their tables. And, at last,
Whom should they send me but a Capuchin!
Straight I began to muster up my sins
For absolution—but no such luck for *me!*
This was the man, this Capuchin, with whom
I was to treat concerning the army horses:
And I was forced at last to quit the field,
The business unaccomplished. Afterwards
The Duke procured me in three days, what I

	Could not obtain in thirty at Vienna.
QUESTENBERG:	Yes, yes! your travelling bills soon found their way to us:
	Too well I know we have still accounts to settle.
ILLO:	War is a violent trade; one cannot always
	Finish one's work by soft means; every trifle
	Must not be blackened into sacrilege.
	If we should wait till you, in solemn council,
	With due deliberation had selected
	The smallest out of four-and-twenty evils,
	I' faith we should wait long.
	'Dash! and through with it!' That's the better watchword.
	Then after come what may come. 'Tis man's nature
	To make the best of a bad thing once past.
	A bitter and perplexed 'What shall I do?'
	Is worse to man than worst necessity.
QUESTENBERG:	Ay, doubtless, it is true; the Duke *does* spare us
	The troublesome task of choosing.
BUTLER:	Yes, the Duke
	Cares with a father's feelings for his troops;
	But how the Emperor feels for us, we see.
QUESTENBERG:	*His* cares and feelings all ranks share alike,
	Nor will he offer one up to another.
ISOLANI:	And therefore thrusts he us into the deserts,
	As beasts of prey, that so he may preserve
	His dear sheep fattening in his fields at home.
QUESTENBERG *(with a sneer)*:	
	Count, this comparison you make, not I.
BUTLER:	Why, were we all the court supposes us,
	'Twere dangerous, sure, to give us liberty.
QUESTENBERG:	You have taken liberty—it was not given you.
	And therefore it becomes an urgent duty
	To rein it in with curbs.
OCTAVIO	*(interposing and addressing* QUESTENBERG):
	My noble friend,
	This is no more than a remembrancing
	That you are now in camp, and among warriors.
	The soldier's boldness constitutes his freedom.
	Could he act daringly, unless he dared
	Talk even so? One runs into the other.
	The boldness of this worthy officer [*pointing to* BUTLER.
	Which now has but mistaken in its mark,
	Preserved, when nought but boldness could preserve it,
	To the Emperor his capital city, Prague,
	In a most formidable mutiny
	Of the whole garrison. [*Military music at a distance.*
	Hah! here they come!
ILLO:	The sentries are saluting them: this signal
	Announces the arrival of the Duchess.

431

OCTAVIO   (*to* QUESTENBERG):
> Then my son Max too has returned. 'Twas he
> Fetched and attended them from Carnthen hither.

ISOLANI   (*to* ILLO): Shall we not go in company to greet them?

ILLO: Well, let us go. Ho! Colonel Butler, come.
> (*to* OCTAVIO)
> You'll not forget that yet ere noon we meet
> The noble Envoy at the General's palace.

> > [*Exeunt all but* QUESTENBERG *and* OCTAVIO.

SCENE III: QUESTENBERG *and* OCTAVIO.

QUESTENBERG   (*with signs of aversion and astonishment*):
> What have I not been forced to hear, Octavio!
> What sentiments! what fierce, uncurbed defiance!
> And were this spirit universal—

OCTAVIO: Hm!
> You are now acquainted with three-fourths of the army.

QUESTENBERG: Where must we seek then for a second host
> To have the custody of this? That Illo
> Thinks worse, I fear me, than he speaks. And then
> This Butler too—he cannot even conceal
> The passionate workings of his ill intentions.

OCTAVIO: Quickness of temper—irritated pride;
> 'Twas nothing more. I cannot give up Butler.
> I know a spell that will soon dispossess
> The evil spirit in him.

QUESTENBERG   (*walking up and down in evident disquiet*):
> > Friend, friend!
> O! this is worse, far worse, than we had suffered
> Ourselves to dream of at Vienna. There
> We saw it only with a courtier's eyes,
> Eyes dazzled by the splendour of the throne.
> We had not seen the War-chief, the Commander,
> The man all-powerful in his camp. Here, here,
> 'Tis quite another thing.
> Here is no Emperor more—the Duke is Emperor.
> Alas, my friend! alas, my noble friend!
> This walk which you have ta'en me through the camp
> Strikes my hopes prostrate.

OCTAVIO: Now you see yourself
> Of what a perilous kind the office is,
> Which you deliver to me from the Court.
> The least suspicion of the General
> Costs me my freedom and my life, and would
> But hasten his most desperate enterprise.

QUESTENBERG: Where was our reason sleeping when we trusted
> This madman with the sword, and placed such power

In such a hand? I tell you, he'll refuse,
Flatly refuse, t'obey the Imperial orders.
Friend, he *can* do't, and what he can, he will.
And then th' impunity of his defiance—
O! What a proclamation of our weakness!

OCTAVIO: D'ye think, too, he has brought his wife and daughter
Without a purpose hither! Here in camp!
And at the very point of time, in which
We're arming for the war? That he has taken
These, the last pledges of his loyalty,
Away from out the Emperor's domains—
This is no doubtful token of the nearness
Of some eruption!

QUESTENBERG: How shall we hold footing
Beneath this tempest, which collects itself
And threats us from all quarters? Th' enemy
Of th' empire on our Borders, now already
The master of the Danube, and still farther,
And farther still, extending every hour!
In our interior, the alarum-bells
Of insurrection—peasantry in arms—
All orders discontented—and the army,
Just in the moment of our expectation
Of aidance from it—lo! this very army
Seduced, run wild, lost to all discipline,
Loosened, and rent asunder from the state
And from their sov'reign, the blind instrument
Of the most daring of mankind, a weapon
Of fearful power, which at his will he wields!

OCTAVIO: Nay, nay, friend! let us not despair too soon.
Men's words are ever bolder than their deeds:
And many a resolute, who now appears
Made up to all extremes, will, on a sudden,
Find in his breast a heart he wot not of,
Let but a single honest man speak out
The true name of his crime! Remember, too,
We stand not yet so wholly unprotected.
Counts Altringer and Galas have maintained
Their little army faithful to its duty,
And daily it becomes more numerous.
Nor can he take us by surprise; you know,
I hold him all encompassed by my list'ners.
Whate'er he does, is mine, even while 'tis doing—
No step so small, but instantly I hear it;
Yea, his own mouth discloses it.

QUESTENBERG: 'Tis quite
Incomprehensible, that he detects not
The foe so near!

OCTAVIO: Beware, you do not think
That I by lying arts, and complaisant
Hypocrisy, have skulked into his graces;
Or with the sustenance of smooth professions
Nourish his all-confiding friendship! No—
Compelled alike by prudence, and that duty
Which we all owe our country, and our sovereign,
To hide my genuine feelings from him, yet
Never have I duped him with base counterfeits!

QUESTENBERG: It is the visible ordinance of heaven.

OCTAVIO: I know not what it is that so attracts
And links him both to me and to my son.
Comrades and friends we always were—long habit,
Adventurous deeds performed in company,
And all those many and various incidents
Which store a soldier's memory with affections,
Had bound us long and early to each other—
Yet I can name the day when all at once
His heart rose on me, and his confidence
Shot out in sudden growth. It was the morning
Before the memorable fight at Lützner.
Urged by an ugly dream, I sought him out,
To press him to accept another charger.
At distance from the tents, beneath a tree,
I found him in a sleep. When I had waked him,
And had related all my bodings to him,
Long time he stared upon me, like a man
Astounded; thereon fell upon my neck,
And manifested to me an emotion
That far outstripped the worth of that small service.
Since then his confidence has followed me
With the same pace that mine has fled from him.

QUESTENBERG: You lead your son into the secret?

OCTAVIO: No!

QUESTENBERG: What! and not warn him either what bad hands
His lot has placed him in?

OCTAVIO: I must perforce
Leave him in wardship to his innocence.
His young and open soul—dissimulation
Is foreign to its habits! Ignorance
Alone can keep alive the cheerful air,
The unembarrassed sense and light free spirit,
That make the Duke secure.

QUESTENBERG (*anxiously*): My honoured friend! most highly do I deem
Of Colonel Piccolomini—yet—if—
Reflect a little—

OCTAVIO: I must venture it.
Hush! There he comes!

SCENE IV: MAX PICCOLOMINI, OCTAVIO PICCOLOMINI, QUESTENBERG.

MAX: Ha! there he is himself. Welcome, my father!
> [*He embraces his father. As he turns round, he observes*
> QUESTENBERG, *and draws back with a cold and*
> *reserved air.*

You are engaged, I see. I'll not disturb you.

OCTAVIO: How, Max? Look closer at this visitor,
Attention, Max, an old friend merits—Reverence
Belongs of right to the envoy of your sovereign.

MAX   (*drily*):
Von Questenberg! Welcome—if you bring with you
Aught good to our head-quarters.

QUESTENBERG   (*seizing his hand*):   Nay, draw not
Your hand away, Count Piccolomini!
Not on mine own account alone I seized it,
And nothing common will I say therewith.
> [*taking the hands of both.*

Octavio—Max Piccolomini!
O saviour names, and full of happy omen!
Ne'er will her prosperous Genius turn from Austria,
While two such stars, with blessed influences
Beaming protection, shine above her hosts.

MAX: Heh! Noble minister! You miss your part.
You came not here to act a panegyric.
You're sent, I know, to find fault, and to scold us—
I must not be beforehand with my comrades.

OCTAVIO   (*to* MAX):
He comes from court, where people are not quite
So well contented with the duke, as here.

MAX: What now have they contrived to find out in him?
That he alone determines for himself
What he himself alone doth understand?
Well, therein he does right, and will persist in't.
Heaven never meant him for that passive thing
That can be struck and hammered out to suit
Another's taste and fancy. He'll not dance
To every tune of every minister.
It goes against his nature—he can't do it.
He is possessed by a commanding spirit,
And his too is the station of command.
And well for us it is so! There exist
Few fit to rule themselves, but few that use
Their intellects intelligently. Then
Well for the whole, if there be found a man,
Who makes himself what nature destined him,
The pause, the central point of thousand thousands—
Stands fixed and stately, like a firm-built column,

Where all may press with joy and confidence.
Now such a man is Wallenstein; and if
Another better suits the court—no other
But such a one as he can serve the army.

QUESTENBERG: The army? Doubtless!

OCTAVIO (*to* QUESTENBERG): Hush! suppress it, friend!
Unless *some* end were answered by the utterance.
Of *him* there you'll make nothing.

MAX (*continuing*): In their distress
They call a spirit up, and when he comes,
Straight their flesh creeps and quivers, and they dread him
More than the ills for which they called him up.
The uncommon, the sublime, must seem and be
Like things of every day. But in the field,
Ay, *there* the *Present Being* makes itself felt.
The personal must command, the actual eye
Examine. If to be the chieftain asks
All that is great in nature, let it be
Likewise his privilege to move and act
In all the correspondencies of greatness.
The oracle within him, that which *lives*,
He must invoke and question—not dead books,
Not ordinances, not mould-rotted papers.

OCTAVIO: My son! of those old narrow ordinances
Let us not hold too lightly. They are weights
Of priceless value, which oppressed mankind
Tied to the volatile will of their oppressors.
For always formidable was the league
And partnership of free power with free will.
The way of ancient ordinance, tho' it winds,
Is yet no devious way. Straight forward goes
The lightning's path, and straight the fearful path
Of the cannon-ball. Direct it flies and rapid,
Shatt'ring that it *may* reach, and shatt'ring what it reaches.
My son! the road the human being travels,
That, on which Blessing comes and goes, doth follow
The river's course, the valley's playful windings,
Curves round the corn-field and the hill of vines,
Honouring the holy bounds of property!
And thus secure, tho' late, leads to its end.

QUESTENBERG: O hear your father, noble youth! hear *him*,
Who is at once the hero and the man.

OCTAVIO: My son, the nursling of the camp spoke in thee!
A war of fifteen years
Hath been thy education and thy school.
Peace hast thou never witnessed! There exists
A higher than the warrior's excellence.
In war itself war is no ultimate purpose.

The vast and sudden deeds of violence,
Adventures wild, and wonders of the moment,
These are not they, my son, that generate
The Calm, the Blissful, and th' enduring Mighty!
Lo there! the soldier, rapid architect!
Builds his light town of canvas, and at once
The whole scene moves and bustles momently,
With arms, and neighing steeds, and mirth, and quarrel!
The motley market fills; the roads, the streams
Are crowded with new freights; trade stirs and hurries!
But on some morrow morn, all suddenly,
The tents drop down, the horde renews its march.
Dreary, and solitary as a church-yard,
The meadow and down-trodden seed-plot lie,
And the year's harvest is gone utterly.

MAX: O let the Emperor make peace, my father!
Most gladly would I give the blood-stained laurel
For the first violet of the leafless spring,
Plucked in those quiet fields where I have journeyed!

OCTAVIO: What ails thee? What so moves thee all at once?

MAX: Peace have I ne'er beheld? I *have* beheld it.
From thence am I come hither: O! that sight,
It glimmers still before me, like some landscape
Left in the distance—some delicious landscape!
My road conducted me thro' countries where
The war has not yet reached. Life, life, my father—
My venerable father, life has charms
Which *we* have ne'er experienced. We have been
But voyaging along its barren coasts,
Like some poor ever-roaming horde of pirates,
That, crowded in the rank and narrow ship,
House on the wild sea with wild usages,
Nor know aught of the main land, but the bays
Where safeliest they may venture a thieves' landing.
Whate'er in the inland dales the land conceals
Of fair and exquisite, O! nothing, nothing,
Do we behold of that in our rude voyage.

OCTAVIO (*attentive, with an appearance of uneasiness*):
And so your journey has revealed this to you?

MAX: 'Twas the first leisure of my life. O tell me,
What is the meed and purpose of the toil,
The painful toil, which robbed me of my youth,
Left me a heart unsouled and solitary,
A spirit uninformed, unornamented.
For the camp's stir and crowd and ceaseless larum,
The neighing war-horse, the air-shattering trumpet,
Th' unvaried, still-returning hour of duty,
Word of command, and exercise of arms—

The Thirty Years' War, of which the Danish war was only a part, was marked by great cruelty on both the Protestant and Catholic sides. Ruthless pillaging and brutal repression were common military practice of the period, and religious hatred fanned the flames. These etchings, made by the French artist Jacques Callot in 1633, show some of the horrors to which Piccolomini wished to call a halt

Dreary, and solitary as a church-yard,
The meadow and down-trodden seed-plot lie,
And the year's harvest is gone utterly.
                    Act I, scene 4

There's nothing here, there's nothing in all this
To satisfy the heart, the gasping heart!
Mere bustling nothingness, where the soul is not—
This cannot be the sole felicity,
These cannot be man's best and only pleasures!

OCTAVIO: Much hast thou learnt, my son, in this short journey.

MAX: O! day thrice lovely! when at length the soldier
Returns home into life; when he becomes
A fellow-man among his fellow-men.
The colours are unfurled, the cavalcade
Marshals, and now the buzz is hushed, and hark!
Now the soft peace-march beats, home, brothers, home!
The caps and helmets are all garlanded
With green boughs, the last plundering of the fields.
The city gates fly open of themselves,
They need no longer the petard to tear them.
The ramparts are all filled with men and women,
With peaceful men and women, that send onwards
Kisses and welcomings upon the air,
Which they make breezy with affectionate gestures.
From all the towers rings out the merry peal,
The joyous vespers of a bloody day.
O happy man, O fortunate! for whom
The well-known door, the faithful arms are open,
The faithful tender arms with mute embracing.

QUESTENBERG   (*apparently much affected*): O! that you should speak
Of such a distant, distant time, and not
Of the to-morrow, not of this to-day.

MAX   (*turning round to him quick and vehement*):
Where lies the fault but on you in Vienna?
I will deal openly with you, Questenberg.
Just now, as first I saw you standing here,
(I'll own it to you freely) indignation
Crowded and pressed my inmost soul together.
'Tis ye that hinder peace, ye! and the warrior,
It is the warrior that must force it from you.
Ye fret the General's life out, blacken him,
Hold him up as a rebel, and Heaven knows
What else still worse, because he spares the Saxons,
And tries to awaken confidence in the enemy;
Which yet's the only way to peace; for if
War intermits not during war, *how* then
And *whence* can peace come? Your own plagues fall on you.
Even as I love what's virtuous, hate I you.
And here make I this vow, here pledge myself;
My blood shall spurt out for this Wallenstein,
And my heart drain off, drop by drop, ere ye
Shall revel and dance jubilee o'er his ruin.   [*Exit.*

SCENE V: QUESTENBERG, OCTAVIO PICCOLOMINI.

QUESTENBERG: Alas, alas! and stands it so?

> [*then in pressing and impatient tone.*

What, friend! and do we let him go away
In this delusion—let him go away?
Not call him back immediately, not open
His eyes upon the spot?

OCTAVIO   (*recovering himself out of a deep study*):

> He has now opened mine,

And I see more than pleases me.

QUESTENBERG: What is it?

OCTAVIO: Curse on this journey!

QUESTENBERG: But why so? What is it?

OCTAVIO: Come, come along, friend! I must follow up
The ominous track immediately. Mine eyes
Are opened now, and I must use them. Come!

> [*Draws* QUESTENBERG *on with him.*

QUESTENBERG: What now? *Where* go you then?

OCTAVIO: To her herself.

QUESTENBERG: To—

OCTAVIO   (*interrupting him, and correcting himself*):
To the Duke. Come, let us go. 'Tis done, 'tis done!
I see the net that is thrown over him.
O! he returns not to me as he went.

QUESTENBERG: Nay, but explain yourself.

OCTAVIO: And that I should not
Foresee it, not prevent this journey. Wherefore
Did I keep it from him? You were in the right.
I should have warned him! Now it is too late.

QUESTENBERG: But *what's* too late? Bethink yourself, my friend,
That you are talking absolute riddles to me.

OCTAVIO   (*more collected*):
Come! to the Duke's. 'Tis close upon the hour
Which he appointed you for audience. Come!
A curse, a threefold curse, upon this journey!

> [*He leads* QUESTENBERG *off.*

SCENE VI: *Changes to a spacious chamber in the house of the Duke of*
Friedland. SERVANTS *employed in putting the tables and chairs*
in order. During this enters SENI, *like an old Italian doctor in*
black, and clothed somewhat fantastically. He carries a white
staff, with which he marks out the quarters of the heaven.

1ST SERVANT: Come—to it lads, to it! Make an end of it. I hear the sentry call
out, 'Stand to your arms!' They will be there in a minute.

2ND SERVANT: Why were we not told before that the audience would be held
here? Nothing prepared—no orders—no instructions—

3RD SERVANT: Ay, and why was the balcony-chamber countermanded; that with
the great worked carpet? there one can look about one.

1ST SERVANT: Nay, that you must ask the mathematician there. He says it is an
unlucky chamber.

2ND SERVANT: Poh! stuff and nonsense! That's what I call a *hum*. A chamber is
a chamber; what much can the place signify in the affair?

SENI (*with gravity*):
My son, there's *nothing* insignificant,
Nothing! But yet in every earthly thing
First and most principal is place and time.

1ST SERVANT (*to the* SECOND): Say nothing to him, Nat. The Duke must let him
have his own will.

SENI (*counts the chairs, half in a loud, half in a low voice, till he
comes to eleven, which he repeats*):
Eleven! an evil number! Set twelve chairs.
Twelve! twelve signs hath the zodiac: five and seven,
The holy numbers, include themselves in twelve.

2ND SERVANT: And what may you have to object against eleven? I should like
to know that, now.

SENI: Eleven is—transgression: eleven oversteps
The ten commandments.

2ND SERVANT: That's good! and why do you call five a holy number?

SENI: Five is the soul of man: for even as man
Is mingled up of good and evil, so
The five is the first number that's made up
Of even and odd.

2ND SERVANT: The foolish old coxcomb!

1ST SERVANT: Ay! let him alone though. I like to hear him; there is more in his
words than can be seen at first sight.

3RD SERVANT: Off! They come.

2ND SERVANT: There! Out at the side door.

[*They hurry off,* SENI *follows slowly. A* PAGE *brings the staff of
command on a red cushion, and places it on the table near
the Duke's chair. They are announced from without, and
the wings of the door fly open.*

SCENE VII: WALLENSTEIN, DUCHESS.

WALLENSTEIN: You went then through Vienna, were presented
To the Queen of Hungary?

DUCHESS: Yes; and to the Empress too;
And by both Majesties were we admitted
To kiss the hand.

WALLENSTEIN: And how was it received,
That I had sent for wife and daughter hither
To the camp, in winter time?

DUCHESS: I did even that
Which you commissioned me to do. I told them,

	You had determined on our daughter's ma_riage,
	And wished, ere yet you went into the field,
	To show th' elected husband his betrothed.
WALLENSTEIN:	And did they guess the choice which I had made?
DUCHESS:	They only hoped and wished it may have fallen
	Upon no foreign nor yet Lutheran noble.
WALLENSTEIN:	And you—what do you wish, Elizabeth?
DUCHESS:	Your will, you know, was always mine.
WALLENSTEIN	(*after a pause*): Well then!
	And in all else, of what kind and complexion
	Was your reception at the court?

[*The* DUCHESS *casts her eyes on the ground and remains silent.*
Hide nothing from me. How were you received?

DUCHESS: O! my dear Lord, all is not what it was.
A cankerworm, my lord, a cankerworm
Has stolen into the bud.

WALLENSTEIN: Ay! is it so?
What, they were lax? they failed of th' old respect?

DUCHESS: Not of respect. No honours were omitted,
No outward courtesy; but in the place
Of condescending, confidential kindness,
Familiar and endearing, there were given me
Only these honours and that solemn courtesy.
Ah! and the tenderness which was put on,
It was the guise of pity, not of favour.
No! Albrecht's wife, Duke Albrecht's princely wife,
Count Harrach's noble daughter, should not so—
Not wholly so should she have been received.

WALLENSTEIN: Yes, yes; they have ta'en offence. My latest conduct,
They railed at it, no doubt.

DUCHESS: O that they had!
I have been long accustomed to defend you,
To heal and pacify distempered spirits.
No; no one railed at you. They wrapped them up,
O Heaven! in such oppressive, solemn silence!
Here is no every-day misunderstanding,
No transient pique, no cloud that passes over;
Something most luckless, most unhealable,
Has taken place. The Queen of Hungary
Used formerly to call me her dear aunt,
And ever at departure to embrace me—

WALLENSTEIN: Now she omitted it?

DUCHESS (*wiping away her tears, after a pause*):
She *did* embrace me,
But then first when I had already taken
My formal leave, and when the door already
Had closed upon me, then did she come out
In haste, as she had suddenly bethought herself,

And pressed me to her bosom, more with anguish
Than with tenderness.

WALLENSTEIN (*seizes her hand soothingly*):
                         Nay now, collect yourself.
And what of Eggenberg and Lichtenstein,
And of our other friends there?

DUCHESS (*shaking her head*):   I saw none.

WALLENSTEIN: Th' Ambassador from Spain, who once was wont
To plead so warmly for me?

DUCHESS: Silent, silent!

WALLENSTEIN: These suns then are eclipsed for us. Henceforward
Must we roll on, our own fire, our own light.

DUCHESS: And were it—were it, my dear Lord, in that
Which moved about the Court in buzz and whisper,
But in the country let itself be heard
Aloud—in that which Father Lamormain
In sundry hints and—

WALLENSTEIN (*eagerly*):   Lamormain! what said he?

DUCHESS: That you're accused of having daringly
O'erstepped the power entrusted to you, charged
With traitorous contempt of th' Emperor
And his supreme behests. The proud Bavarian,
He and the Spaniards stand up your accusers.
That there's a storm collecting over you,
Of far more fearful menace than that former one
Which whirled you headlong down at Regensburg.
And people talk, said he, of—Ah!
                      [*stifling extreme emotion.*

WALLENSTEIN: Proceed!

DUCHESS: I cannot utter it!

WALLENSTEIN: Proceed!

DUCHESS: They talk—

WALLENSTEIN: Well!

DUCHESS: Of a second—   [*Catches her voice and hesitates.*

WALLENSTEIN: Second—

DUCHESS: More disgraceful
—Dismission.

WALLENSTEIN: Talk they?
        [*Strides across the chamber in vehement agitation.*
           O! they force, they thrust me
With violence, against my own will, onward!

DUCHESS (*presses near to him, in entreaty*):
O! if there yet be time, my husband! If
By giving way and by submission, this
Can be averted—my dear Lord, give way!
Win down your proud heart to it! Tell that heart,
It is your sovereign lord, your Emperor,
Before whom you retreat. O let no longer

That you're accused of having daringly
O'erstepped the power entrusted to you, charged
With traitorous contempt of th' Emperor
And his supreme behests.

Act I, scene 7

Low trickling malice blacken your good meaning
With abhorred venomous glosses. Stand you up,
Shielded and helmed and weaponed with the truth,
And drive before you into uttermost shame
These slanderous liars! Few firm friends have we.
You know it! The swift growth of our good fortune
It hath but set us up, a mark for hatred.
What are we, if the sovereign's grace and favour
Stand not before us!

SCENE VIII: *Enter the* COUNTESS TERTSKY, *leading in her hand the* PRINCESS
THEKLA, *richly adorned with brilliants.* COUNTESS, THEKLA,
WALLENSTEIN, DUCHESS.

COUNTESS: How, sister? What already upon business,
        [observing the countenance of the DUCHESS.
And business of no pleasing kind I see,
Ere he has gladdened at his child. The first
Moment belongs to joy. Here, Friedland! father!
This is thy daughter.
  *[*THEKLA *approaches with a shy and timid air, and bends herself*
  as about to kiss his hand, he receives her in his arms, and
  remains standing for some time lost in the feeling of her
  presence.

WALLENSTEIN: Yes; pure and lovely hath hope risen on me;
I take her as the pledge of greater fortune.

DUCHESS: 'Twas but a little child when you departed
To raise up that great army for the Emperor:
And after at the close of the campaign,
When you returned home out of Pomerania,

---

*Ferdinand II was the ruler of a patchwork empire of quarrelsome princely states.
Deeply divided by history and religious conflict, the German princes were united
only in their determination to maintain their own independence and thwart the
emperor's dream of imperial supremacy. The triumph of Wallenstein's army
disturbed them because they feared its very existence as a threat to their
freedom. They lost little time in plotting to remove the threat. The ambitious
Wallenstein lost little time in playing into their hands. He began to act as an
independent power, undermining the emperor's hard line at the Danish peace
talks, negotiating with Protestant princes, opposing the emperor's Edict of
Restitution that would have restored Catholic suzerainty throughout the empire,
and planning a grandiose international trading company. Although the emperor's
new-found power rested on Wallenstein's military brilliance (despite the martial
air of this contemporary portrait Ferdinand rarely ventured near the battlefield),
he too soon grew suspicious of his commander's power and independence and
three times fell prey to pressures from the princes—twice dismissing
Wallenstein and finally ordering his murder*

Your daughter was already in the convent,
Wherein she has remained till now.

WALLENSTEIN: The while
We in the field here gave our cares and toils
To make her great, and fight her a free way
To the loftiest of earthly good; lo! mother Nature
Within the peaceful silent convent walls
Has done her part, and out of her free grace
Hath she bestowed on the beloved child
The godlike; and now leads her thus adorned
To meet her splendid fortune, and my hope.

DUCHESS   (*to* THEKLA):
Thou wouldst not have recognized thy father,
Wouldst thou, my child? She counted scarce eight years,
When last she saw your face.

THEKLA: O yes, yes, mother!
At the first glance! my father is not altered.
The form, that stands before me, falsifies
No feature of the image that hath lived
So long within me!

WALLENSTEIN: The voice of my child!

                                        [*then after a pause.*

I was indignant at my destiny
That it denied me a man-child to be
Heir of my name and of my prosperous fortune,
And re-illume my soon extinguished being
In a proud line of princes.
I wronged my destiny. Here upon this head,
So lovely in its maiden bloom, will I
Let fall the garland of a life of war;
Nor deem it lost, if only I can wreathe it,
Transmitted to a regal ornament,
Around these beauteous brows.

                    [*He clasps her in his arms as* PICCOLOMINI *enters.*

SCENE IX: *Enter* MAX PICCOLOMINI, *and some time after* COUNT TERTSKY,
the others remaining as before.

COUNTESS: There comes the Palladin who protected us.
WALLENSTEIN: Max! Welcome, ever welcome! Always wert thou
The morning star of my best joys!
MAX: My General—
WALLENSTEIN: Till now it was the Emperor who rewarded thee,
I but the instrument. This day thou hast bound
The father to thee, Max! the fortunate father,
And this debt Friedland's self must pay.
MAX: My prince!
You made no common hurry to transfer it.

I come with shame. Yea, not without a pang!
For scarce have I arrived here, scarce delivered
The mother and the daughter to your arms,
But there is brought to me from your equerry
A splendid richly plated hunting dress,
So to remunerate me for my trouble—
Yes, yes, remunerate me! Since a trouble
It must be, a mere office, not a favour
Which I leapt forward to receive, and which
I came already with full heart to thank you for.
No! 'twas not so intended, that my business
Should be my highest, best good fortune!

> [TERTSKY *enters and delivers letters to the* DUKE *which he
> breaks open hurryingly.*

COUNTESS (*to* MAX):
Remunerate your trouble! For his joy
He makes you recompense. 'Tis not unfitting
For you, Count Piccolomini, to feel
So tenderly—my brother it beseems
To show himself for ever great and princely.

THEKLA: Then I too must have scruples of his love:
For his munificent hands did ornament me
Ere yet the father's heart had spoken to me.

MAX: Yes: 'tis his nature ever to be giving,
And making happy.

> [*He grasps the hand of the* DUCHESS *with still increasing
> warmth.*

How my heart pours out
Its all of thanks to him: O! how I seem
To utter all things in the dear name Friedland.
While I shall live, so long will I remain
The captive of this name: in it shall bloom
My every fortune, every lovely hope.
Inextricably as in some magic ring
In this name hath my destiny charm-bound me!

COUNTESS (*who during this time has been anxiously watching the* DUKE, *and
remarks that he is lost in thought over the letters*):
My brother wishes us to leave him. Come.

WALLENSTEIN (*turns himself round quickly, collects himself, and speaks with
cheerfulness to the* DUCHESS):
Once more I bid thee welcome to the camp.
Thou art the hostess of this court. You, Max,
Will now again administer your old office,
While we perform the sovereign's business here.

> [MAX PICCOLOMINI *offers the* DUCHESS *his arm, the* COUNTESS
> *accompanies the* PRINCESS.

TERTSKY (*calling after him*):
Max, we depend on seeing you at the meeting.

The youthful object of
Wallenstein's scorn was the young
Ferdinand III, shown here in an
engraving made in 1637, the year
he became emperor at his father's
death. Despite Wallenstein's words
and his own unprepossessing
appearance, the young Ferdinand
was to become a shrewd, pragmatic
ruler. Crowned king of Hungary
at seventeen and king of Bohemia
two years later, Ferdinand aided in
the overthrow of Wallenstein, led
the imperial armies to final victory
over the Swedes, helped forge the
peace of Prague, and, after
succeeding to his father's throne,
brought peace to the empire in the
treaty of Westphalia in 1648

It is the king of Hungary, Ferdinand,
The Emperor's delicate son! he's their saviour,
He's the new star that's rising now!
Act I, scene 10

SCENE X: WALLENSTEIN, COUNT TERTSKY.

WALLENSTEIN *(in deep thought to himself)*:
She hath seen all things as they are—It is so,
And squares completely with my other notices.
They have determined finally in Vienna,
Have given me my successor already;
It is the king of Hungary, Ferdinand,
The Emperor's delicate son! he's now their saviour,
He's the new star that's rising now! Of us
They think themselves already fairly rid,
And as we were deceased, the heir already
Is entering on possession—Therefore—despatch!
[*As he turns round he observes* TERTSKY, *and gives him a letter.*
Count Altringer will have himself excused,
And Galas too—I like not this!

TERTSKY: And if
Thou loiterest longer, all will fall away,
One following the other.

WALLENSTEIN: Altringer
Is master of the Tyrole passes. I must forthwith
Send some one to him, that he let not in
The Spaniards on me from the Milanese.
—Well, and the old Sesin, that ancient trader

448

<table>
<tr><td></td><td>In contraband negotiations, he
Has shown himself again of late. What brings he
From the Count Thur?</td></tr>
<tr><td>TERTSKY:</td><td>The Count communicates,
He has found out the Swedish chancellor
At Halberstadt, where the convention's held,
Who says, you've tired him out, and that he'll have
No further dealings with you.</td></tr>
<tr><td>WALLENSTEIN:</td><td>And why so?</td></tr>
<tr><td>TERTSKY:</td><td>He says, you are never in earnest in your speeches;
That you decoy the Swedes—to make fools of them,
Will league yourself with Saxony against them,
And at last make yourself a riddance of them
With a paltry sum of money.</td></tr>
<tr><td>WALLENSTEIN:</td><td>So then, doubtless,
Yes, doubtless, this same modest Swede expects
That I shall yield him some fair German tract
For his prey and booty, that ourselves at last
On our own soil and native territory,
May be no longer our own lords and masters!
An excellent scheme! No, no! They must be off,
Off! off! away! we want no such neighbours.</td></tr>
<tr><td>TERTSKY:</td><td>Nay, yield them up that dot, that speck of land—
It goes not from your portion. If you win
The game, what matters it to you who pays it?</td></tr>
<tr><td>WALLENSTEIN:</td><td>Off with them, off! Thou understand'st not this.
Never shall it be said of me, I parcelled
My native land away, dismembered Germany,
Betrayed it to a foreigner, in order
To come with stealthy tread, and filch away
My own share of the plunder. Never! never!
No foreign power shall strike root in the empire,
And least of all these Goths! these hunger-wolves!
Who send such envious, hot, and greedy glances
T'wards the rich blessings of our German lands!
I'll have their aid to cast and draw my nets,
But not a single fish of all the draught
Shall they come in for.</td></tr>
<tr><td>TERTSKY:</td><td>You will deal, however,
More fairly with the Saxons? They lose patience
While you shift ground and make so many curves.
Say, to what purpose all these masks? Your friends
Are plunged in doubts, baffled, and led astray in you.
There's Oxenstein, there's Arnheim—neither knows
What he should think of your procrastinations.
And in the end I prove the liar; all
Pass through me. I have not even your handwriting.</td></tr>
<tr><td>WALLENSTEIN:</td><td>I never give my hand-writing; thou know'st it.</td></tr>
</table>

TERTSKY: But how can it be known that you're in earnest
If the act follows not upon the word?
You must yourself acknowledge, that in all
Your intercourses hitherto with th' enemy,
You might have done with safety all you have done,
Had you meant nothing further than to gull him
For th' Emperor's service.

WALLENSTEIN (*after a pause, during which he looks narrowly on* TERTSKY):
And from whence dost *thou* know
That I'm *not* gulling him for the Emperor's service?
Whence knowest thou that I'm not gulling all of you?
Dost thou know *me* so well? When made I thee
Th' intendant of my secret purposes?
I am not conscious that I ever opened
My inmost thoughts to thee. Th' Emperor, it is true,
Hath dealt with me amiss; and if I would,
I could repay him with usurious interest
For th' evil he hath done me. It delights me
To know my power; but whether I shall use it,
Of that, I should have thought that thou couldst speak
No wiselier than thy fellows.

TERTSKY: So hast thou always played thy game with us.   [*Enter* ILLO.

SCENE XI: ILLO, WALLENSTEIN, TERTSKY.

WALLENSTEIN: How stand affairs without? Are they prepared?

ILLO: You'll find them in the very mood you wish.
They know about the Emperor's requisitions,
And are tumultuous.

WALLENSTEIN: How hath Isolan
Declared himself?

ILLO: He's yours both soul and body,
Since you built up again his Faro-bank.

WALLENSTEIN: And which way doth Kolatto bend? Hast thou
Made sure of Tiefenbach and Deodate?

ILLO: What Piccolomini does, that they do too.

WALLENSTEIN: You mean, then, I may venture somewhat with them?

ILLO: —If you are assured of the Piccolomini.

WALLENSTEIN: Not more assured of mine own self.

TERTSKY: And yet
I would you trusted not so much to Octavio,
The fox!

WALLENSTEIN: Thou teachest me to know my man?
Sixteen campaigns I have made with that old warrior.
Besides, I have his horoscope,
We both are born beneath like stars—in short
                                        [*with an air of mystery.*
To this belongs its own particular aspect.

450

	If therefore thou canst warrant me the rest—
ILLO:	There is among them all but this one voice
	You *must* not lay down the command. I hear
	They mean to send a deputation to you.
WALLENSTEIN:	If I'm in aught to bind myself to them,
	They too must bind themselves to me.
ILLO:	Of course.
WALLENSTEIN:	Their words of honour they must give, their oaths,
	Give them in writing to me, promising
	Devotion to my service *unconditional*.
ILLO:	Why not?
TERTSKY:	Devotion *unconditional?*
	The exception of their duties towards Austria
	They'll always place among the premises.
	With this reserve—
WALLENSTEIN	(*shaking his head*): All unconditional!
	No premises, no reserves.
ILLO:	A thought has struck me.
	Does not Count Tertsky give us a set banquet
	This evening?
TERTSKY:	Yes; and all the Generals
	Have been invited.
ILLO	(*to* WALLENSTEIN): Say, will you here fully
	Commission me to use my own discretion?
	I'll gain for you the Generals' words of honour,
	Even as you wish.
WALLENSTEIN:	Gain me their signatures!
	How you come by them, that is your concern.
ILLO:	And if I bring it to you, black on white,
	That all the leaders who are present here
	Give themselves up to you, without condition;
	Say, will you then—then will you show yourself
	In earnest, and with some decisive action
	Make trial of your luck?
WALLENSTEIN:	The signatures!
	Gain me the signatures.
ILLO:	Seize, seize the hour
	Ere it slips from you. Seldom comes the moment
	In life, which is indeed sublime and weighty.
	To make a great decision possible,
	O! many things, all transient and all rapid,
	Must meet at once: and, haply, they thus met
	May, by that confluence, be enforced to pause
	Time long enough for wisdom, though too short,
	Far, far too short a time for doubt and scruple!
	This is that moment. See, our army chieftains,
	Our best, our noblest, are assembled round you,
	Their kinglike leader! On your nod they wait.

451

The single threads, which here your prosperous fortune
Hath woven together in one potent web
Instinct with destiny, O! let them not
Unravel of themselves. If you permit
These chiefs to separate, so unanimous
Bring you them not a second time together.
'Tis the high tide that heaves the stranded ship,
And every individual's spirit waxes
In the great stream of multitude. Behold,
They are still here, here still! But soon the war
Bursts them once more asunder, and in small
Particular anxieties and interests
Scatters their spirit, and the sympathy
Of each man with the whole. He, who to-day
Forgets himself, forced onward with the stream,
Will become sober, seeing but himself,
Feel only his own weakness, and with speed
Will face about, and march on in the old
High road of duty, the old broad-trodden road,
And seek but to make shelter in good plight.

WALLENSTEIN: The time is not yet come.

TERTSKY: So you say always.
But when will it be time?

WALLENSTEIN: When I shall say it.

ILLO: You'll wait upon the stars, and on their hours,
Till the earthly hour escapes you. O! believe me,
In your own bosom are your destiny's stars.
Confidence in yourself, prompt resolution,
This is your Venus! and the sole malignant,
The only one that harmeth you, is Doubt.

WALLENSTEIN: Thou speakest as thou understand'st. How oft
And many a time I've told thee, Jupiter,
That lustrous god, was setting at thy birth.
Thy visual power subdues no mysteries;
Mole-eyed, thou mayst but burrow in the earth,
Blind as that subterrestrial, who, with wan,
Lead-coloured shine, lighted thee into life.
The common, the terrestrial, thou mayst see,
With serviceable cunning knit together,
The nearest with the nearest; and therein
I trust thee and believe thee! but whate'er
Full of mysterious import Nature weaves,
And fashions in the depths—the spirit's ladder,
That from this gross and visible world of dust
Even to the starry world, with thousand rounds,
Builds itself up; on which the unseen powers
Move up and down on heavenly ministries—
The circles in the circles, that approach

The central sun with ever-narrowing orbit—
These see the glance alone, the unsealed eye,
Of Jupiter's glad children born in lustre.
> [*He walks across the chamber, then returns, and standing still, proceeds.*

The heavenly constellations make not merely
The day and night, summer and spring; not merely
Signify to the husbandman the seasons
Of sowing and of harvest. Human action,
That is the seed too of contingencies,
Strewed on the dark land of futurity
In hopes to reconcile the powers of fate.
Whence it behoves us to seek out the seed time,
To watch the stars, select their proper hours,
And trace with searching eye the heavenly houses,
Whether the enemy of growth and thriving,
Hide himself not, malignant, in his corner.
Therefore permit me my own time. Meanwhile
Do you your part. As yet I cannot say
What *I* shall do—only, give way I will not.
Depose me too they shall not. On these points
You may rely.

PAGE (*entering*): My Lords the Generals.

WALLENSTEIN: Let them come in.

SCENE XII: WALLENSTEIN, TERTSKY, ILLO. *To them enter* QUESTENBERG, OCTAVIO, *and* MAX PICCOLOMINI, BUTLER, ISOLANI, MARADAS, *and three other* GENERALS. WALLENSTEIN *motions* QUESTENBERG, *who, in consequence, takes the chair directly opposite to him; the others follow, arranging themselves according to their rank. There reigns a momentary silence.*

WALLENSTEIN: I have understood, 'tis true, the sum and import
Of your instructions, Questenberg, have weighed them,
And formed my final, absolute resolve;
Yet it seems fitting, that the Generals
Should hear the will of th' Emperor from your mouth.
May't please you then to open your commission
Before these noble Chieftains.

QUESTENBERG: I am ready
To obey you; but will first entreat your Highness,
And all these noble Chieftains, to consider,
Th' Imperial dignity and sov'reign right
Speaks from my mouth, and not my own presumption.

WALLENSTEIN: We excuse all preface.

QUESTENBERG: When his Majesty
The Emperor to his courageous armies
Presented in the person of Duke Friedland

453

A most experienced and renowned commander,
He did it in glad hope and confidence,
To give thereby to the fortune of war
A rapid and auspicious change. The onset
Was favourable to his royal wishes.
Bohemia was delivered from the Saxons,
The Swede's career of conquest checked! These lands
Began to draw breath freely, as Duke Friedland
From all the streams of Germany forced hither
The scattered armies of the enemy,
Hither invoked, as round one magic circle,
The Rhinegrave, Bernhard, Banner, Oxenstirn,
Yea, and that never-conquered king himself;
Here finally, before the eye of Nürnberg,
The fearful game of battle to decide.

WALLENSTEIN: May't please you, to the point.

QUESTENBERG: In Nürnberg's camp the Swedish monarch left
His fame—in Lützen's plains his life. But who
Stood not astounded, when victorious Friedland
After this day of triumph, this proud day,
Marched towards Bohemia with the speed of flight,
And vanished from the theatre of war;
While the young Weimar hero forced his way
Into Franconia, to the Danube, like
Some delving winter stream, which, where it rushes,
Makes its own channel; with such sudden speed
He marched, and now at once 'fore Regensburg
Stood to th' affright of all good Catholic Christians.
Then did Bavaria's well-deserving Prince
Entreat swift aidance in his extreme need;
The Emperor sends seven horsemen to Duke Friedland,
Seven horsemen couriers sends he with th' entreaty:
He superadds his own, and supplicates,
Where as the sovereign lord he can command.
In vain his supplication! At this moment
The Duke hears only his old hate and grudge,
Barters the general good to gratify
Private revenge—and so falls Regensburg.

WALLENSTEIN: Max, to what period of the war alludes he?
My recollection fails me here.

MAX: He means
When we were in Silesia.

WALLENSTEIN: Ay! Is it so?
But what had we to do there?

MAX: To beat out
The Swedes and Saxons from the province.

WALLENSTEIN: True.
In that description which the minister gave
I seemed to have forgotten the whole war.

Well, but proceed a little.   [*To* QUESTENBERG.

QUESTENBERG: Yes! at length
Beside the river Oder did the Duke
Assert his ancient fame. Upon the fields
Of Steinau did the Swedes lay down their arms,
Subdued without a blow. And here, with others,
The righteousness of Heaven to his avenger
Delivered that long practised stirrer-up
Of insurrection, that curse-laden torch
And kindler of this war, Matthias Thur.
But he had fallen into magnanimous hands!
Instead of punishment he found reward,
And with rich presents did the Duke dismiss
The arch-foe of his Emperor.

WALLENSTEIN *(laughs)*:   I know,
I know you had already in Vienna,
Your windows and balconies all forestalled
To see him on the executioner's cart.
I might have lost the battle, lost it too
With infamy, and still retained your graces—
But, to have cheated them of a spectacle,
Oh! *that* the good folks of Vienna never,
No, never can forgive me.

QUESTENBERG: So Silesia
Was freed, and all things loudly called the Duke
Into Bavaria, now pressed hard on all sides.
And he *did* put his troops in motion; slowly,
Quite at his ease, and by the longest road
He traverses Bohemia; but ere ever
He hath once seen the enemy, faces round,
Breaks up the march, and takes to winter quarters.

WALLENSTEIN: The troops were pitiably destitute
Of every necessary, every comfort.
The winter came. What thinks his Majesty
His troops are made of? A'n't we men? subjected
Like other men to wet, and cold, and all
The circumstances of necessity?
O miserable lot of the poor soldier!
Wherever he comes in, all flee before him,
And when he goes away the general curse
Follows him on his rout. All must be seized,
Nothing is given him. And compelled to seize
From every man, he's every man's abhorrence.
Behold, here stand my Generals. Karaffa!
Count Deodate! Butler! Tell this man
How long the soldier's pay is in arrears.

BUTLER: Already a full year.

WALLENSTEIN: And 'tis the hire
That constitutes the hireling's name and duties,

In July of 1630, Gustavus Adolphus, the Protestant king of Sweden, invaded southern Germany and, joining forces with the elector of Saxony, swept toward Austria. His throne threatened, Ferdinand was forced to beg Wallenstein to resume command of the imperial armies. The bitter ex-commander made him pay dearly for his earlier insult: the exact terms under which Wallenstein agreed to go to war again are not known but they probably included full treaty-making powers and a promise of the electorships of Bohemia and Brandenburg. Once in charge, Wallenstein slowed the Swedish onslaught and drove the invaders from southern Germany. Encamped near Lützen on November 16, 1632, Wallenstein's men were surprised by a massive Swedish attack, shown here in a contemporary engraving. Although Gustavus' forces almost overwhelmed the imperial lines, Wallenstein's hastily built defenses held. At nightfall the body of Gustavus Adolphus was found among the Swedish dead. With the death of Ferdinand's archenemy, the house of Hapsburg could breathe a bit more easily—and Wallenstein once again became indispensable. Apparently hoping to impose his own peace, Wallenstein now began to flirt with the enemy and plot to maintain his hold over the army. Ferdinand viewed his independent intrigues as treason and quickly moved to punish him

In Nürnberg's camp the Swedish monarch left
His fame—in Lützen's plains his life.

Act I, scene 12

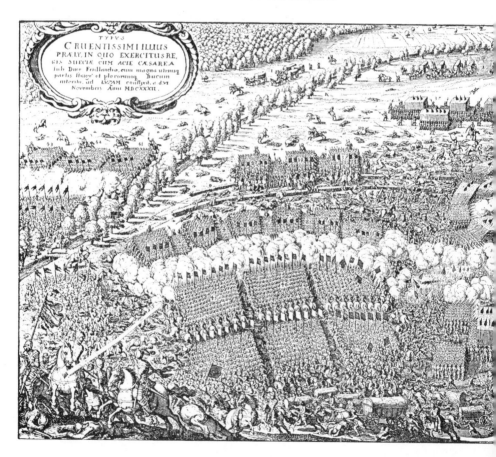

TYPUS
CRUENTISSIMI ILLIUS
PRÆLY, IN QUO EXERCITUS RE,
GIS SUECIÆ CUM ACIE CÆSAREA
Sub Duce Fridlandiæ, cum magna utriusq
partis Slage' et plerorumq Ducum
interitu, ad LUZAM conflixit, e dVI
Novembris Anni MDCXXXII.

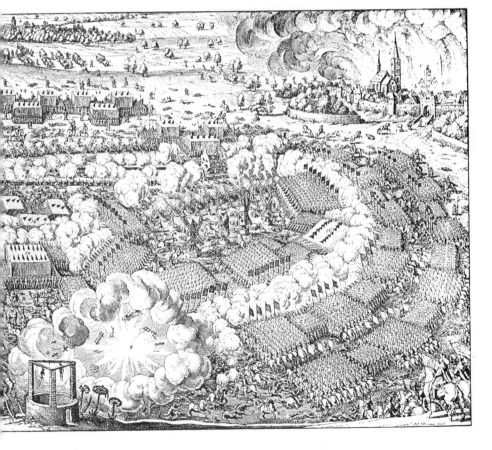

The soldier's pay is the soldier's covenant.

QUESTENBERG: Ah! this is a far other tone from that
In which the Duke spoke eight, nine years ago.

WALLENSTEIN: Yes! 'tis my fault, I know it: I myself
Have spoilt the Emperor by indulging him.
Nine years ago, during the Danish war,
I raised up a force, a mighty force,
Forty or fifty thousand men, that cost him
Of his own purse no doit. Through Saxony
The fury goddess of the war marched on,
E'en to the surf-rocks of the Baltic, bearing
The terrors of his name. That was a time!
In the whole Imperial realm no name like mine
Honoured with festival and celebration—
And Albrecht Wallenstein, it was the title
Of the third jewel in his crown!
But at the Diet, when the Princes met
At Regensburg, there, there the whole broke out,
There 'twas laid open, there it was made known,
Out of what money-bag I had paid the host.
And what was now my thanks, what had I now,
That I, a faithful servant of the Sovereign,
Had loaded on myself the people's curses,
And let the Princes of the empire pay
The expenses of this war, that aggrandizes
The Emperor alone—What thanks had I!
What? I was offered up to their complaints,
Dismissed, degraded!

QUESTENBERG: But your Highness knows
What little freedom he possessed of action
In that disastrous Diet.

WALLENSTEIN: Death and hell!
I had that which could have procured him freedom.
No! Since 'twas proved so inauspicious to me
To serve the Emperor at the empire's cost,
I have been taught far other trains of thinking
Of th' empire, and the Diet of the empire.
From th' Emperor, doubtless, I received this staff.
But now I hold it as the empire's General—
For the common weal, the universal interest,
And no more for that one man's aggrandizement!
But to the point. What is it that's desired of me?

QUESTENBERG: First, His Imperial Majesty hath willed,
That without pretexts of delay the army
Evacuate Bohemia.

WALLENSTEIN: In this season?
And to what quarter, wills the Emperor
That we direct our course?

REGENSPURG.

In July and August of 1630, the German princes met with the
emperor at Regensburg (shown here in an engraving made three
years later). Determined to destroy Ferdinand's hope of imperial
ascendancy, the princes sought to weaken imperial power by
removing Wallenstein and disbanding most of his army. Their
position was strengthened by the general's embarrassing inability
to take the Danish-occupied port of Stralsund (shown below in a
1632 diagram) and by the emperor's desire to have his son
elected king of the Romans. They refused to elect the young
Ferdinand unless Wallenstein was dismissed. Reluctantly,
Ferdinand agreed

But at the Diet, when the Princes met
At Regensburg, there, the whole broke out. . . .
                        Act I, scene 12

QUESTENBERG: To the enemy.
His majesty resolves, that Regensburg
Be purified from the enemy ere Easter,
That Luth'ranism may be no longer preached
In that cathedral, nor heretical
Defilement desecrate the celebration
Of that pure festival.

WALLENSTEIN: My Generals,
Can this be realized?

ILLO: 'Tis not possible.

BUTLER: It can't be realized.

QUESTENBERG: The Emperor
Hath already commanded Colonel Suys
To advance toward Bavaria.

WALLENSTEIN: What did Suys?

QUESTENBERG: That which his duty prompted. He advanced!

WALLENSTEIN: What? he advanced! And I, his General,
Had given him orders, peremptory orders,
Not to desert his station! Stands it thus
With my authority? Is this th' obedience
Due to my office, which being thrown aside
No war can be conducted? Chieftains, speak!
You be the judges, Generals! What deserves
That officer, who, of his oath neglectful,
Is guilty of contempt of orders?

ILLO: Death.

WALLENSTEIN (*raising his voice, as all but* ILLO *had remained silent, and
seemingly scrupulous*):
Count Piccolomini, what has he deserved?

MAX   (*after a long pause*):
According to the letter of the law,
Death.

ISOLANI: Death.

BUTLER: Death, by the laws of war.
[QUESTENBERG *rises from his seat,* WALLENSTEIN *follows, all the
rest rise.*

WALLENSTEIN: To this the law condemns him, and not I.
And if I show him favour, 'twill arise
From the rev'rence that I owe my Emperor.

QUESTENBERG: If so, I can say nothing further—*here!*

WALLENSTEIN: I accepted the command but on conditions!
And this the first, that to the diminution
Of my authority, no human being,
Not even the Emperor's self, should be entitled
To do aught, or to say aught, with the army.
If I stand warranter of the event,
Placing my honour and my head in pledge,
Needs must I have full mastery in all

The means thereto. What rendered this Gustavus
Resistless, and unconquered upon earth?
This: that he was the monarch in his army;
A monarch, one who is indeed a monarch,
Was never yet subdued but by his equal.
But to the point! The best is yet to come.
Attend now, generals!

QUESTENBERG: The Prince Cardinal
Begins his route at the approach of spring
From the Milanese; and leads a Spanish army
Thro' Germany into the Netherlands.
That he may march secure and unimpeded,
'Tis th' Emperor's will, you grant him a detachment
Of eight horse-regiments from the army here.

WALLENSTEIN: Yes, yes! I understand! Eight regiments! Well,
Right well concerted, father Lamormain!
Eight thousand horse! Yes, yes! 'Tis as it should be!
I see it coming.

QUESTENBERG: There is nothing coming;
All stands in front: the counsel of state-prudence,
The dictate of necessity!

WALLENSTEIN: What then?
What, my Lord Envoy? May I not be suffered
To understand that folks are tired of seeing
The sword's hilt in *my* grasp: and that your court
Snatch eagerly at this pretence, and use
The Spanish title, to drain off my forces,
To lead into the empire a new army
Unsubjected to my control. To throw me
Plumply aside—I am still too powerful for you
To venture that. My stipulation runs,
That all the Imperial forces shall obey me
Where'er the German is the native language.
Of Spanish troops, and of Prince Cardinals,
That take their route, as visitors, thro' the empire,
There stands no syllable in my stipulation.
No syllable! And so the politic court
Steals in a tiptoe, and creeps round behind it;
First makes me weaker, then to be dispensed with,
Till it dares strike at length a bolder blow
And make short work with me.
What need of all these crooked ways, Lord Envoy?
Straight-forward, man! His compact with me pinches
The Emperor. He would that I moved off!
Well! I will gratify him!
  [*Here there commences an agitation among the generals which
    increases continually.*
It grieves me for my noble officers' sake!

461

I see not yet, by what means they will come at
The moneys they have advanced, or how obtain
The recompense their services demand.
Still a new leader brings new claimants forward,
And prior merit superannuates quickly.
There serve here many foreigners in the army,
And were the man in all else brave and gallant,
I was not wont to make nice scrutiny
After his pedigree or catechism.
This will be otherwise i' the time to come.
Well—me no longer it concerns.   [*He seats himself.*

MAX: Forbid it, Heaven, that it should come to this!
Our troops will swell in dreadful fermentation—
The Emperor is abused—it cannot be.

ISOLANI: It cannot be; all goes to instant wreck.

WALLENSTEIN: Thou has said truly, faithful Isolani!
What *we* with toil and foresight have built up,
Will go to wreck—all go to instant wreck.
What then? another chieftain is soon found,
Another army likewise (who dares doubt it?)
Will flock from all sides to the Emperor
At the first beat of his recruiting drum.

          [*During this speech,* ISOLANI, TERTSKY, ILLO, *and* MARADAS *talk
          confusedly with great agitation.*

MAX   (*busily and passionately going from one to another, and soothing
them*):
Hear, my commander! hear me, Generals!
Let me conjure you, Duke! Determine nothing,
Till we have met and represented to you
Our joint remonstrances. Nay, calmer! Friends!
I hope all may be yet set right again.

TERTSKY: Away! let us away! in th' antechamber
Find we the others.   [*They go.*

BUTLER   (*to* QUESTENBERG):   If good counsel gain
Due audience from your wisdom, my Lord Envoy!
You will be cautious how you show yourself
In public for some hours to come—or hardly
Will that gold key protect you from mal-treatment.

          [*Commotions heard from without.*

WALLENSTEIN: A salutary counsel—Thou, Octavio!
Wilt answer for the safety of our guest.
Farewell, Von Questenberg!   [QUESTENBERG *is about to speak.*
                    Nay, not a word.
Not one word more of that detested subject!
You have performed your duty—We know how
To separate the office from the man.

          [*As* QUESTENBERG *is going off with* OCTAVIO, GOETZ, TIEFENBACH,
          KOLATTO, *press in, several other generals following them.*

GOETZ:	Where's he, who means to rob us of our General?
TIEFENBACH	(*at the same time*):
	What are we forced to hear? That thou wilt leave us?
KOLATTO	(*at the same time*):
	We will live with thee, we will die with thee.
WALLENSTEIN	(*with stateliness, and pointing to* ILLO):
	There! the Field-Marshal knows our will. [*Exit.*

[*While all are going off the stage, the curtain drops.*

ACT II

SCENE I: *A small Chamber.* ILLO *and* TERTSKY.

TERTSKY:	Now for this evening's business! How intend you
	To manage with the generals at the banquet?
ILLO:	Attend! We frame a formal declaration,
	Wherein we to the Duke consign ourselves
	Collectively, to be and to remain
	His both with life and limb, and not to spare
	The last drop of our blood for *him*, provided
	So doing we infringe no oath or duty
	We may be under to the Emp'ror. Mark!
	This reservation we expressly make
	In a particular clause, and save the conscience.
	Now hear! This formula so framed and worded
	Will be presented to them for perusal
	Before the banquet. No one will find in it
	Cause of offence or scruple. Hear now further!
	After the feast, when now the vap'ring wine
	Opens the heart, and shuts the eyes, we let
	A counterfeited paper, in the which
	This one particular clause has been left out,
	Go round for signatures.
TERTSKY:	How? think you then
	That they'll believe themselves bound by an oath,
	Which we had tricked them into by a juggle?
ILLO:	We shall have caught and caged them! Let them then
	Beat their wings bare against the wires, and rave
	Loud as they may against our treachery,
	At court their signatures will be believed
	Far more than their most holy affirmations.
	Traitors they are, and must be; therefore wisely
	Will make a virtue of necessity.
TERTSKY:	Well, well, it shall content me; let but something

	Be *done*, let only some decisive blow
	Set us in motion.
ILLO:	Besides, 'tis of subordinate importance
	How, or how far, we may thereby propel
	The generals. 'Tis enough that we persuade
	The Duke, that they are his—Let him but act
	In his determined mood, as if he had them,
	And he *will* have them. Where he plunges in,
	He makes a whirlpool, and all stream down to it.
TERTSKY:	His policy is such a labyrinth,
	That many a time when *I* have thought myself
	Close at his side, he's gone at once, and left me
	Ignorant of the ground where I was standing.
	He lends the enemy his ear, permits me
	To write to them, to Arnheim, to Sesina;
	Himself comes forward blank and undisguised,
	Talks with us by the hour about his plans,
	And when I think I have him—off at once—
	He has slipped from me, and appears as if
	He had no scheme, but to retain his place.
ILLO:	He give up his old plans! I'll tell you, friend!
	His soul is occupied with nothing else,
	Even in his sleep—they are his thoughts, his dreams—
	That day by day he questions for this purpose
	The motions of the planets—
TERTSKY:	Ay! you know
	This night, that is now coming, he with Seni
	Shuts himself up in the astrological tower
	To make joint observations—for I hear,
	It is to be a night of weight and crisis,
	And something great, and of long expectation,
	Is to make its procession in the heaven.
ILLO:	Come! be we bold and make despatch. The work
	In this next day or two must thrive and grow
	More than it has for years. And let but only
	Things first turn up auspicious here below—
	Mark what I say—the right stars too will show themselves.
	Come to the generals. All is in the glow,
	And must be beaten while 'tis malleable.
TERTSKY:	Do you go thither, Illo. I must stay
	And *wait* here for the Countess Tertsky. Know,
	That we too are not idle. Break one string,
	A second is in readiness.
ILLO:	Yes! Yes!
	I saw your Lady smile with such sly meaning.
	What's in the wind?
TERTSKY:	A secret. Hush! she comes.

[*Exit* ILLO.

464

SCENE II: (*The* COUNTESS *steps out from a closet.*) COUNT *and* COUNTESS TERTSKY.

TERTSKY: Well—is she coming? I can keep him back
No longer.

COUNTESS: She will be there instantly;
You only send him.

TERTSKY: I am not quite certain,
I must confess it, Countess, whether or no
We are earning the Duke's thanks hereby. You know
No ray has broke out from him on this point.
You have o'erruled me, and yourself knows best
How far you dare proceed.

COUNTESS: I take it on me.
[*talking to herself, while she is advancing.*
Here's no need of full powers, and commissions—
My cloudy Duke! we understand each other—
And without words. What, could I not unriddle,
Wherefore the daughter should be sent for hither,
Why first *he*, and no other, should be chosen
To fetch her hither! This sham of betrothing her
To a bridegroom, whom no one knows—No! no!
This may blind others! I see thro' thee, Brother!
But it beseems thee not, to draw a card
At such a game. Not yet! It all remains
Mutely delivered up to my finessing—
Well—thou shalt not have been deceived, Duke Friedland!
In her who is thy sister.

SERVANT (*enters*): The commanders!

TERTSKY (*to the* COUNTESS):
Take care you heat his fancy and affections—
Possess him with a reverie, and send him
Absent and dreaming to the banquet; that
He may not boggle at the signature.

COUNTESS: Take you care of your guests! Go, send him hither.

TERTSKY: All rests upon his undersigning.

COUNTESS (*interrupting him*):
Go to your guests! Go—

ILLO (*comes back*):
Where art staying, Tertsky?
The house is full, and all expecting you.

TERTSKY: Instantly! instantly! [*To the* COUNTESS.
And let him not
Stay here too long. It might awake suspicion
In the old man—

COUNTESS: A truce with your precautions!
[*Exeunt* TERTSKY *and* ILLO.

SCENE III: COUNTESS, MAX PICCOLOMINI.

MAX   (*peeping in on the stage shily*):
Aunt Tertsky! may I venture!
> [*Advances to the middle of the stage, and looks around him with uneasiness.*

                She's not here!
Where is she?

COUNTESS: Look but somewhat narrowly
In yonder corner, lest perhaps she lie
Concealed behind that screen.

MAX: There lie her gloves!
> [*Snatches at them, but the* COUNTESS *takes them herself.*

You unkind Lady! You refuse me this—
You make it an amusement to torment me.

COUNTESS: And this the thanks you give me for my trouble?

MAX: O, if you felt the oppression at *my* heart!
Since we've been here, so to constrain myself—
With such poor stealth to hazard words and glances—
These, these are not my habits!

COUNTESS: You have still
Many new habits to acquire, young friend!
But on this proof of your obedient temper
I must continue to insist; and only
On this condition can I play the agent
For your concerns.

MAX: But wherefore comes she not?
Where is she?

COUNTESS: Into *my* hands you must place it
Whole and entire. Whom could you find, indeed,
More zealously affected to your interest?
No soul on earth must know it—not your father.
He must not above all.

MAX: Alas! what danger?
Here is no face on which I might concentre
All, the enraptured soul stirs up within me.
O Lady! tell me. Is all changed around me;
Or is it only I?
          I find myself
As among strangers! Not a trace is left
Of all my former wishes, former joys.
Where has it vanished to? There was a time
When even, methought, with such a world as this
I was not discontented. Now, how flat!
How stale! No life, no bloom, no flavour in it!
My comrades are intolerable to me.
My father—Even to him I can say nothing.
My arms, my military duties—O!

| | They are such wearying toys! |
| COUNTESS: | But, gentle friend! |

I must entreat it of your condescension,
You would be pleased to sink your eye, and favour
With one short glance or two this poor stale world,
Where even now much, and of much moment,
Is on the eve of its completion.

MAX: Something,
I can't but know, is going forward round me.
I see it gathering, crowding, driving on,
In wild uncustomary movements. Well,
In due time, doubtless, it will reach even me.
Where think you I have been, dear Lady? Nay,
No raillery. The turmoil of the camp,
The spring-tide of acquaintance rolling in,
The pointless jest, the empty conversation,
Oppressed and stifled me. I gasped for air—
I could not breathe—I was constrained to fly,
To seek a silence out for my full heart;
And a pure spot wherein to feel my happiness.
No smiling, Countess! In the church was I.
There is a cloister here to the heaven's gate,
Thither I went, there found myself alone.
Over the altar hung a holy mother;
A wretched painting 'twas, yet 'twas the friend
That I was seeking in this moment. Ah,
How oft have I beheld that glorious form
In splendour, 'mid extatic worshippers,
Yet still it moved me not! and now at once
Was my devotion cloudless as my love.

COUNTESS: Enjoy your fortune and felicity!
Forget the world around you. Meantime, friendship
Shall keep strict vigils for you, anxious, active.
Only be manageable when that friendship
Points you the road to full accomplishment.
How long may it be since you declared your passion?

MAX: This morning did I hazard the first word.

COUNTESS: This morning the first time in twenty days?

MAX: 'Twas at that hunting-castle, betwixt here
And Nepomuck, where *you* had joined us, and—
That was the last relay of the whole journey!
In a balcony we were standing mute,
And gazing out upon the dreary field:
Before us the dragoons were riding onward,
The safe-guard which the Duke had sent us—heavy
The inquietude of parting lay upon me,
And trembling ventured I at length these words:
This all reminds me, noble maiden, that

467

To-day I must take leave of my good fortune.
A few hours more, and you will find a father,
Will see yourself surrounded by new friends,
And I henceforth shall be but as a stranger,
Lost in the many—'Speak with my aunt Tertsky!'
With hurrying voice she interrupted me.
She faltered. I beheld a glowing red
Possess her beautiful cheeks, and from the ground
Raised slowly up, her eye met mine—no longer
Did I control myself.

      [*The* PRINCESS THEKLA *appears at the door, and remains*
        standing, observed by the COUNTESS, *but not by*
        PICCOLOMINI.

            With instant boldness
I caught her in my arms, my mouth touched hers;
There was a rustling in the room close by;
It parted us—'Twas you. What since has happened,
You know.

COUNTESS   (*after a pause, with a stolen glance at* THEKLA):
        And is it your excess of modesty;
Or are you so incurious, that you do not
Ask me too of my secret?

MAX: Of *your* secret?

COUNTESS: Why, yes! When in the instant after you
I stepped into the room, and found my niece there,
What she in this first moment of the heart,
Ta'en with surprise—

MAX   (*with eagerness*):   Well!

SCENE IV: THEKLA (*hurries forward*), COUNTESS, MAX PICCOLOMINI.

THEKLA   (*to the* COUNTESS):
   Spare yourself the trouble.
   That hears he better from myself.

MAX   (*stepping backward*):   My Princess!
What have you let her hear me say, aunt Tertsky!

THEKLA   (*to the* COUNTESS):
   Has he been here long?

COUNTESS: Yes; and soon must go.
Where have *you* stayed so long?

THEKLA: Alas! my mother
Wept so again! and I—I see her suffer,
Yet cannot keep myself from being happy.

MAX: Now once again I have courage to look on you,
To-day at noon I could not.
The dazzle of the jewels that played round you
Hid the beloved from me.

THEKLA: Then you saw me
With your eye only—and not with your heart?

MAX: This morning, when I found you in the circle
Of all your kindred, in your father's arms,
Beheld myself an alien in this circle,
O! what an impulse felt I in that moment
To fall upon his neck, to call him *father!*
But his stern eye o'erpowered the swelling passion—
It dared not but be silent. And those brilliants,
That like a crown of stars enwreathed your brows,
They scared me too! O wherefore, wherefore should he
At the first meeting spread as 'twere the bann
Of excommunication round you, wherefore
Dress up the angel as for sacrifice,
And cast upon the light and joyous heart
The mournful burthen of *his* station? Fitly
May love dare woo for love; but such a splendour
Might none but monarchs venture to approach.

THEKLA: Hush! not a word more of this mummery,
You see how soon the burthen is thrown off.
He is not in spirits. Wherefore is he not?   [*to the* COUNTESS.
'Tis you, aunt, that have made him all so gloomy!
He had quite another nature on the journey—
So calm, so bright, so joyous, eloquent.
It was my wish to see you always so,   [*to* MAX.
And never otherwise!

MAX: You find yourself
In your great father's arms, beloved lady!
All in a new world, which does homage to you,
And which, were't only by its novelty,
Delights your eye.

THEKLA: Yes; I confess to you
That many things delight me here: this camp,
This motley stage of warriors which renews
So manifold the image of my fancy,
And binds to life, binds to reality,
What hitherto had but been present to me
As a sweet dream!

MAX: Alas! not so to me.
It makes a dream of my reality.
Upon some island in the ethereal heights
I've lived for these last days. This mass of men
Forces me down to earth. It is a bridge
That, reconducting to my former life,
Divides me and my heaven.

THEKLA: The game of life
Looks cheerful, when one carries in one's heart
The unalienable treasure. 'Tis a game,

469

Which having once reviewed, I turn more joyous
Back to my deeper and appropriate bliss.
                    [breaking off and in a sportive tone.
In this short time that I've been present here,
What new unheard of things have I not seen?
And yet they all must give place to the wonder
Which this mysterious castle guards.

COUNTESS   (*recollecting*):   And what
Can this be then? Methought I was acquainted
With all the dusky corners of this house.

THEKLA   (*smiling*):
Ay, but the road thereto is watched by spirits,
Two griffins still stand sentry at the door.

COUNTESS   (*laughs*):
The astrological tower! How happens it
That this same sanctuary, whose access,
Is to all others so impracticable,
Opens before you e'en at your approach?

THEKLA: A dwarfish old man with a friendly face
And snow-white hairs, whose gracious services
Were mine at first sight, opened me the doors.

MAX: That is the Duke's astrologer, old Seni.

THEKLA: He questioned me on many points; for instance,
When I was born, what month, and on what day,
Whether by day or in the night.

COUNTESS: He wished
To erect a figure for your horoscope.

THEKLA: My hand too he examined, shook his head
With much sad meaning, and the lines, methought,
Did not square over truly with his wishes.

COUNTESS: Well, Princess, and what found you in this tower?
My highest privilege has been to snatch
A side glance, and away!

THEKLA: It was a strange
Sensation that came o'er me, when at first
From the broad sunshine I stepped in; and now
The narrowing line of day-light, that ran after
The closing door, was gone; and all about me
'Twas pale and dusky night, with many shadows
Fantastically cast. Here six or seven
Colossal statues, and all kings, stood round me
In a half circle. Each one in his hand
A sceptre bore, and on his head a star,
And in the tower no other light was there
But from these stars: all seemed to come from them.
'These are the planets,' said that low old man,
'They govern wordly fates, and for that cause
Are imaged here as kings. That farthest from you,

Spiteful and cold, an old man melancholy,
With bent and yellow forehead, he is Saturn.
He opposite, the king with the red light,
An armed man for the battle, that is Mars:
And both these bring but little luck to man.'
But at his side a lovely lady stood,
The star upon her head was soft and bright,
And that was Venus, the bright star of joy.
On the left hand, lo! Mercury, with wings.
Quite in the middle glittered silver-bright
A cheerful man, and with a monarch's mien;
And this was Jupiter, my father's star:
And at his side I saw the Sun and Moon.

MAX: O never rudely will I blame his faith
In the might of stars and angels! 'Tis not merely
The human being's pride that peoples space
With life and mystical predominance;
Since likewise for the stricken heart of Love
This visible nature, and this common world,
Is all too narrow: yea, a deeper import
Lurks in the legend told my infant years
Than lies upon that truth, we live to learn.
For fable is Love's world, his home, his birthplace:
Delightedly dwells he 'mong fays, and talismans,
And spirits; and delightedly believes
Divinities, being himself divine.
The intelligible forms of ancient poets,
The fair humanities of old religion,
The power, the beauty, and the majesty,
That had their haunts in dale, or piny mountain,
Or forest by slow stream, or pebbly spring,
Or chasms and wat'ry depths; all these have vanished;
They live no longer in the faith of reason!
But still the heart doth need a language, still
Doth the old instinct bring back the old names.
And to yon starry world they now are gone,
Spirits or gods, that used to share this earth
With man as with their friend; and to the lover
Yonder they move, from yonder visible sky
Shoot influence down: and even at this day
'Tis Jupiter who brings whate'er is great,
And Venus who brings every thing that's fair!

THEKLA: And if this be the science of the stars,
I too, with glad and zealous industry,
Will learn acquaintance with this cheerful faith
It is a gentle and affectionate thought,
That in immeasurable height above us,
At our first birth, the wreath of love was woven,

471

With sparkling stars for flowers.

COUNTESS: Not only roses,
But thorns too hath the heaven; and well for you
Leave they your wreath of love inviolate.
What Venus twined, the bearer of glad fortune,
The sullen orb of Mars soon tears to pieces.

MAX: Soon will its gloomy empire reach its close,
Blest be the General's zeal: into the laurel
Will he inweave the olive-branch, presenting
Peace to the shouting nations. Then no wish
Will have remained for his great heart! Enough
Has he performed for glory, and can now
Live for himself and his. To his domains
Will he retire; he has a stately seat
Of fairest view at Gitschin; Reichenberg,
And Friedland Castle, both lie pleasantly—
Even to the foot of the huge mountains here
Stretches the chase and covers of his forests;
His ruling passion, to create the splendid,
He can indulge without restraint; can give
A princely patronage to every art,
And to all worth a sovereign's protection.
Can build, can plant, can watch the starry courses—

COUNTESS: Yet I would have you look, and look again,
Before you lay aside your arms, young friend!
A gentle bride, as she is, is well worth it
That you should woo and win her with the sword.

MAX: O, that the sword could win her!

COUNTESS: What was that?
Did you hear nothing? Seemed as if I heard
Tumult and larum in the banquet-room.   [*Exit* COUNTESS.

SCENE V: THEKLA *and* MAX PICCOLOMINI.

THEKLA   (*as soon as the* COUNTESS *is out of sight, in a quick low voice to*
PICCOLOMINI):
Don't trust them! They are false!

MAX: Impossible!

THEKLA: Trust no one here but me. I saw at once,
They had a *purpose*.

MAX: Purpose! but what purpose?
And how can we be instrumental to it?

THEKLA: I know no more than you; but yet, believe me,
There's some design in this! To make us happy,
To realize our union—trust me, love!
They but pretend to wish it.

MAX: But these Tertskies—
Why use we them at all? Why not your mother?
Excellent creature! she deserves from us

A full and filial confidence.

THEKLA: She doth love you,
Doth rate you high before all others—but—
But such a secret—she would never have
The courage to conceal it from my father.
For her own peace of mind we must preserve it
A secret from her too.

MAX: Why any secret?
I love not secrets. Mark what I will do.
I'll throw me at your father's feet—let *him*
Decide upon my fortunes! He is true,
He wears no mask—he hates all crooked ways—
He is so good, so noble!

THEKLA *(falls on his neck):*   *That* are you!

MAX: You knew him only since this morn; but I
Have lived ten years already in his presence,
And who knows whether in this very moment
He is not merely waiting for us both
To own our loves, in order to unite us.
You are silent?
You look at me with such a hopelessness!
What have you to object against your father?

THEKLA: I? Nothing. Only he's so occupied—
He has no leisure time to think about
The happiness of us two.   [*Taking his hand tenderly.*
                    Follow me!
Let us not place too great a faith in men.
These Tertskies—we will still be grateful to them
For every kindness, but not trust them further
Than they deserve; and in all else rely—
On our own hearts!

MAX: O! shall we *e'er* be happy?

THEKLA: Are we not happy now? Art thou not mine?
Am I not thine? There lives within my soul
A lofty courage—'tis love gives it me!
I ought to be less open—ought to hide
My heart more from thee—so decorum dictates.
But where in this place could'st thou seek for truth,
If in my mouth thou did'st not find it?

SCENE VI: *To them enters the* COUNTESS TERTSKY.

COUNTESS *(in a pressing manner):*   Come!
My husband sends me for you—It is now
The latest moment.
            [*They not appearing to attend to what she says, she steps
                between them.*
                    Part you!

THEKLA: O, not yet!

473

It has been scarce a moment.

COUNTESS: Ay! Then time
Flies swiftly with your Highness, Princess niece!

MAX: There is no hurry, aunt.

COUNTESS: Away! away!
The folk begin to miss you. Twice already
His father has asked for him.

THEKLA: Ha! his father?

COUNTESS: You understand *that*, niece.

THEKLA: Why needs he
To go at all to that society?
'Tis not his proper company. They may
Be worthy men, but he's too young for them.
In brief, he suits not such society.

COUNTESS: You mean, you'd rather keep him wholly here?

THEKLA: (*with energy*):
Yes! you have hit it, aunt! That is my meaning.
Leave him here wholly! Tell the company—

COUNTESS: What? Have you lost your senses, niece?
Count, you remember the conditions. Come!

MAX   (*to* THEKLA):
Lady, I must obey. Farewell, dear lady!
        [THEKLA *turns away from him with a quick motion.*
What say you then, dear lady?

THEKLA   (*without looking at him*):   Nothing. Go!

MAX: Can I, when you are angry—
        [*He draws up to her, their eyes meet, she stands silent a*
            moment then throws herself into his arms; he
            presses her fast to his heart.

COUNTESS: Off! Heavens! if any one should come!
Hark! What's that noise? It comes this way. Off!
        [MAX *tears himself away out of her arms, and goes. The*
           COUNTESS *accompanies him.* THEKLA *follows him with*
           her eyes at first, walks restlessly across the room, then
           stops, and remains standing, lost in thought. A guitar
           lies on the table, she seizes it as by a sudden emotion,
           and after she has played awhile an irregular and
           melancholy symphony, she falls gradually into the
           music and sings.

THEKLA   (*plays and sings*):
    The cloud doth gather, the greenwood roar,
    The damsel paces along the shore;
    The billows they tumble with might, with might;
    And she flings out her voice to the darksome night;
        Her bosom is swelling with sorrow:
    The world it is empty, the heart will die,
    There's nothing to wish for beneath the sky:
    Thou Holy One, call thy child away!

I've lived and loved, and that was to-day—
Make ready my grave-clothes to-morrow.

SCENE VII: COUNTESS (*returns*), THEKLA.

COUNTESS: Fie, lady niece! to throw yourself upon him,
Like a poor gift to one who cares not for it,
And so must be flung after him! For you,
Duke Friedland's only child, I should have thought
It had been more beseeming to have shown yourself
More chary of your person.

THEKLA (*rising*): And what mean you?

COUNTESS: I mean, niece, that you should not have forgotten
Who *you* are, and who he is. But perchance
That never once occurred to you.

THEKLA: What then?

COUNTESS: That you're the daughter of the Prince-duke Friedland.

THEKLA: Well—and what further?

COUNTESS: What? a pretty question!

THEKLA: He was *born* that which we have but *become*.
He's of an ancient Lombard family,
Son of a reigning princess.

COUNTESS: Are you dreaming?
Talking in sleep? An excellent jest, forsooth!
We shall, no doubt, right courteously *entreat* him
To honour with his hand the richest heiress
In Europe.

THEKLA: That will not be necessary.

COUNTESS: Methinks 'twere well tho' not to run the hazard.

THEKLA: His father loves him, Count Octavio
Will interpose no difficulty—

COUNTESS: *His!*
His father! *his!* But yours, niece, what of yours?

THEKLA: Why I begin to think you fear his father,
So anxiously you hide it from the man;
His father, *his*, I mean.

COUNTESS (*looks at her, as scrutinizing*):
Niece, you are *false*.

THEKLA: Are you then wounded? O, be friends with me!

COUNTESS: You hold your game for won already. Do not
Triumph too soon!

THEKLA (*interrupting her, and attempting to soothe her*):
Nay now, be friends with me.

COUNTESS: It is not yet so far gone.

THEKLA: I believe you.

COUNTESS: Did you suppose your father had laid out
His most important life in toils of war,
Denied himself each quiet earthly bliss,

	Had banished slumber from his tent, devoted
	His noble head to care, and for this only,
	To make a happy pair of you? At length
	To draw you from your convent, and conduct
	In easy triumph to your arms the man
	That chanced to please your eyes! All this, methinks,
	He might have purchased at a cheaper rate.

THEKLA: That which he did not plant for me, might yet
Bear me fair fruitage of its own accord.
And if my friendly and affectionate fate,
Out of his fearful and enormous being,
Will but prepare the joys of life for me—

COUNTESS: Thou seest it with a lovelorn maiden's eyes.
Cast thine eye round, bethink thee who thou art.
Into no house of joyance hast thou stepped,
For no espousals dost thou find the walls
Decked out, no guests the nuptial garland wearing.
Here is no splendour but of arms. Or think'st thou
That all these thousands are here congregated
To lead up the long dances at thy wedding?
Thou seest thy father's forehead full of thought,
Thy mother's eyes in tears: upon the balance
Lies the great destiny of all our house.
Leave now the puny wish, the girlish feeling,
O thrust it far behind thee! Give thou proof,
That thou'rt the daughter of the Mighty—*his*
Who where he moves creates the wonderful.
Not to herself the woman must belong,
Annexed and bound to alien destinies.
But she performs the best part, she the wisest,
Who can transmute the alien into self,
Meet and disarm necessity by choice:
And what must be, take freely to her heart,
And bear and foster it with mother's love.

THEKLA: Such ever was my lesson in the convent.
I had no loves, no wishes, knew myself
Only as his—his daughter—his, the Mighty!
His fame, the echo of whose blast drove to me
From the far distance, wakened in my soul
No other thought than this—I am appointed
To offer up myself in passiveness to him.

COUNTESS: That *is* thy fate. Mould thou thy wishes to it.
I and thy mother gave thee the example.

THEKLA: My fate hath shown me *him*, to whom behoves it
That I should offer up myself. In gladness
Him will I follow.

COUNTESS: Not thy fate hath shown him;
Thy heart, say rather—'twas thy heart, my child!

THEKLA: Fate hath no voice but the heart's impulses.
I am all his! *His* present—*his* alone
Is this new life, which lives in me. He hath
A right to his own creature. What was I
Ere his fair love infused a soul into me?

COUNTESS: Thou would'st oppose thy father then, should he
Have otherwise determined with thy person?

            [THEKLA *remains silent. The* COUNTESS *continues.*
Thou mean'st to force him to thy liking? Child,
His name is Friedland.

THEKLA: *My* name too is Friedland.
He shall have found a genuine daughter in me.

COUNTESS: What? he has vanquished all impediment,
And in the wilful mood of his own daughter
Shall a new struggle rise for him? Child! child!
As yet thou hast seen thy father's smiles alone;
The eye of his rage thou hast not seen. Dear child,
I will not frighten thee. To that extreme,
I trust, it ne'er shall come. His will is yet
Unknown to me: 'tis possible, his aims
May have the same direction as thy wish.
But this can never, never be his will,
That thou, the daughter of his haughty fortunes,
Should'st e'er demean thee as a love-sick maiden;
And like some poor cost-nothing, fling thyself
Toward the man, who, if that high prize ever
Be destined to await him, yet, with sacrifices
The highest love can bring, must pay for it.   [*Exit* COUNTESS.

THEKLA   (*who during the last speech had been standing evidently lost in
her reflections*):
I thank thee for the hint. It turns
My sad presentiment to certainty.
And it is so! Not one friend have we here,
Not one true heart! we've nothing but ourselves!
O she said rightly—no auspicious signs
Beam on this covenant of our affections.
This is no theatre, where hope abides.
The dull thick noise of war alone stirs here.
And Love himself, as he were armed in steel,
Steps forth, and girds him for the strife of death.

                 [*Music from the banquet-room is heard.*
There's a dark spirit walking in our house,
And swiftly will the destiny close on us.
It drove me hither from my calm asylum,
It mocks my soul with charming witchery,
It lures me forward in a seraph's shape,
I see it near, I see it nearer floating,
It draws, it pulls me with a god-like power—

And lo! the abyss—and thither am I moving—
I have no power within me not to move!
        [*The music from the banquet-room becomes louder.*
O when a house is doomed in fire to perish,
Many and dark heaven drives his clouds together,
Yea, shoots his lightnings down from sunny heights,
Flames burst from out the subterraneous chasms,
And fiends and angels, mingling in their fury,
Fling fire-brands at the burning edifice.   [*Exit* THEKLA.

SCENE VIII: *A large saloon lighted up with festal splendour; in the midst of it, and in the centre of the stage, a table richly set out, at which eight generals are sitting, among whom are* OCTAVIO PICCOLOMINI, TERTSKY, *and* MARADAS. *Right and left of this, but farther back, two other tables, at each of which six persons are placed. The middle door, which is standing open, gives to the prospect a fourth table, with the same number of persons. More forward stands the sideboard. The whole front of the stage is kept open for the pages and servants in waiting. All is in motion. The band of music belonging to Tertsky's regiment march across the stage, and draw up round the tables. Before they are quite off from the front of the stage,* MAX PICCOLOMINI *appears;* TERTSKY *advances towards him with a paper,* ISOLANI *comes up to him with a beaker or service-cup.* TERTSKY, ISOLANI, MAX PICCOLOMINI.*

ISOLANI: Here, brother, what we love! Why, where hast been?
Off, to thy place—quick! Tertsky here has given
The mother's holiday wine up to free booty.
Here it goes on as at the Heidelberg castle.
Already hast thou lost the best. They're giving
At yonder table ducal crowns in shares;
There's Sternberg's lands and chattels are put up,
With Eggenberg's, Stawata's, Lichtenstein's,
And all the great Bohemian feudalities.
Be nimble, lad! and something may turn up
For thee—who knows? Off—to thy place! quick! march!

TIEFENBACH
and GOETZ   (*call out from the second and third tables*):
                Count Piccolomini!

TERTSKY: Stop, ye shall have him in an instant. Read
This oath here, whether as 'tis here set forth,
The wording satisfies you. They've all read it,
Each in his turn, and each one will subscribe
His individual signature.

MAX   (*reads*):   'Ingratis servire nefas.'

ISOLANI: That sounds to my ears very much like Latin,
And being interpreted, pray what may't mean?

TERTSKY: No honest man will serve a thankless master.

MAX: 'Inasmuch as our supreme commander, the illustrious Duke of Friedland, in consequence of the manifold affronts and grievances which he has received, had expressed his determination to quit the Emperor, but on our unanimous entreaty has graciously consented to remain still with the army, and not to part from us without our approbation thereof, so we, collectively and *each in particular*, in the stead of an oath personally taken, do hereby oblige ourselves—likewise by him honourably and faithfully to hold, and in no wise whatsoever from him to part, and to be ready to shed for his interests the last drop of our blood, so far, namely, as *our oath to the Emperor will permit it. (These last words are repeated by* ISOLANI.) In testimony of which we subscribe our names.'

TERTSKY: Now! are you willing to subscribe this paper?

ISOLANI: Why should he not? All officers of honour
Can do it, ay, must do it. Pen and ink here!

TERTSKY: Nay, let it rest till after meal.

ISOLANI *(drawing* MAX *along)*:
Come, Max. [*Both seat themselves at their table.*

SCENE IX: TERTSKY, NEUMANN.

TERTSKY *(beckons to* NEUMANN *who is waiting at the side table, and steps forward with him to the edge of the stage)*:
Have you the copy with you, Neumann? Give it.
It may be changed for the other?

NEUMANN: I have copied it
Letter by letter, line by line; no eye
Would e'er discover other difference,
Save only the omission of that clause,
According to your Excellency's order.

TERTSKY: Right! Lay it yonder, and away with this—
It has performed its business—to the fire with it—
[NEUMANN *lays the copy on the table, and steps back again to the side table.*

SCENE X: ILLO *(comes out from the second chamber)*, TERTSKY.

ILLO: How goes it with young Piccolomini?

TERTSKY: All right, I think. He has started no objection.

ILLO: He is the only one I fear about—
He and his father. Have an eye on both!

TERTSKY: How looks it at your table? You forget not
To keep them warm and stirring?

ILLO: O, quite cordial,
They are quite cordial in the scheme. We have them.
And 'tis as I predicted too. Already
It is the talk, not merely to maintain

479

The Duke in station. 'Since we're once for all
Together and unanimous, why not,'
Says Montecuculi, 'ay, why not onward,
And make conditions with the Emperor
There in his own Vienna?' Trust me, Count,
Were it not for these said Piccolomini,
We might have spared ourselves the cheat.

TERTSKY: And Butler?
How goes it there? Hush!

SCENE XI: *To them enters* BUTLER *from the second table.*

BUTLER: Don't disturb yourselves.
Field-Marshal, I have understood you perfectly,
Good luck be to the scheme; and as to me,
                                        [*with an air of mystery.*
You may depend upon me.

ILLO *(with vivacity):*   May we, Butler?

BUTLER: With or without the clause, all one to me!
You understand me? My fidelity
The Duke may put to any proof—I'm with him!
Tell him so! I'm the Emperor's officer,
As long as 'tis his pleasure to remain
The Emperor's general; and Friedland's servant,
As soon as it shall please him to become
His own lord.

TERTSKY: You would make a good exchange;
No stern economist, no Ferdinand,
Is he to whom you plight your services.

BUTLER *(with a haughty look):*
I do not put up my fidelity
To sale, Count Tertsky! Half a year ago
I would not have advised you to have made me
An overture to that, to which I now
Offer myself of my own free accord.
But that is past! and to the Duke, Field-Marshal,
I bring myself together with my regiment.
And mark you, 'tis my humour to believe,
The example which I give will not remain
Without an influence.

ILLO: Who is ignorant,
That the whole army look to Colonel Butler,
As to a light that moves before them?

BUTLER: Ey?
Then I repent me not of that fidelity
Which for the length of forty years I held,
If in my sixtieth year my good old name
Can purchase for me a revenge so full.
Start not at what I say, sir generals!

My real motives—they concern not you.
And you yourselves, I trust, could not expect
That this your game had crooked *my* judgment—or
That fickleness, quick blood, or such like cause,
Has driven the old man from the track of honour,
Which he so long had trodden. Come, my friends!
I'm not thereto determined with less firmness,
Because I know and have looked steadily
At that on which I have determined.

ILLO: Say,
And speak roundly, what are we to deem you?

BUTLER: A friend! I give you here my hand! I'm yours
With all I have. Not only men, but money
Will the Duke want. Go, tell him, sirs!
I've earned and laid up somewhat in his service,
I lend it him! and is he my survivor,
It has been already long ago bequeathed him.
He is my heir. For me, I stand alone
Here in the world; nought know I of the feelings
That bind the husband to a wife and children,
My name dies with me, my existence ends.

ILLO: 'Tis not your money that he needs—a heart
Like yours weighs tons of gold down, weighs down millions!

BUTLER: I came a simple soldier's boy from Ireland
To Prague—and with a master, whom I buried.
From lowest stable duty I climbed up,
Such was the fate of war, to this high rank,
The plaything of a whimsical good fortune.
And Wallenstein too is a child of luck,
I love a fortune that is like my own.

ILLO: All powerful souls have kindred with each other.

BUTLER: This is an awful moment! to the brave,
To the determined, an auspicious moment.
The Prince of Weimer arms, upon the Maine
To found a mighty dukedom. He of Halberstadt,
That Mansfield wanted but a longer life
To have marked out with his good sword a lordship
That should reward his courage. Who of these
Equals our Friedland? There is nothing, nothing
So high, but he may set the ladder to it!

TERTSKY: That's spoken like a man!

BUTLER: Do you secure the Spaniard and Italian—
I'll be your warrant for the Scotchman Lesly.
Come! to the company!

TERTSKY: Where is the master of the cellar? Ho!
Let the best wines come up. Ho! cheerly, boy!
Luck comes to-day, so give her hearty welcome.

                    [*Exeunt each to his tables.*

481

SCENE XII: *The* MASTER OF THE CELLAR *advancing with* NEUMANN, SERVANTS *passing backwards and forwards.*

MASTER: The best wines! O! if my old mistress, his lady mother, could but see these wild goings on, she would turn herself round in her grave. Yes, yes, sir officer! 'tis all down the hill with this noble house! no end, no moderation! And this marriage with the Duke's sister, a splendid connection, a very splendid connection! but I tell you, sir officer, it bodes no good.

NEUMANN: Heaven forbid! Why, at this very moment the whole prospect is in bud and blossom!

MASTER: You think so? Well, well, much may be said on that head.

1ST SERVANT *(comes):* Burgundy for the fourth table.

MASTER: Now, sir lieutenant, if this isn't the seventieth flask—

1ST SERVANT: Why, the reason is, that German lord, Tiefenbach, sits at that table.

MASTER   *(continuing his discourse to* NEUMANN*):*
They are soaring too high. They would rival kings and electors in their pomp and splendour; and wherever the Duke leaps, not a minute does my gracious master, the Count, loiter on the brink. *(To the* SERVANTS.*)* What do you stand there listening for? I will let you know you have legs presently. Off! see to the tables, see to the flasks! Look there! Count Palfi has an empty glass before him!

RUNNER   *(comes):* The great service-cup is wanted, sir; that rich gold cup with the Bohemian arms on it. The Count says you know which it is.

MASTER: Ay! that was made for Frederick's coronation, by the artist William—there was not such another prize in the whole booty at Prague.

RUNNER: The same! a health is to go round in him.

MASTER   *(shaking his head while he fetches and rinses the cup):*
This will be something for the tale-bearers—this goes to Vienna.

NEUMANN: Permit me to look at it. Well, this is a cup indeed! How heavy! as well it may be, being all gold. And what neat things are embossed on it! how natural and elegant they look! There, on the first quarter, let me see. That proud Amazon there on horseback, she that is taking a leap over the crosiers and mitres, and carries on a wand, a hat, together with a banner, on which there's a goblet represented. Can you tell me what all this signifies?

MASTER: The woman whom you see there on horseback, is the Free Election of the Bohemian crown. That is signified by the round hat, and by that fiery steed on which she is riding. The hat is the pride of man; for he who cannot keep his hat on before kings and emperors is no free man.

NEUMANN: But what is the cup there on the banner?

MASTER: The cup signifies the freedom of the Bohemian Church, as it was in our forefathers' times. Our forefathers, in the wars of the Hussites, forced from the pope this noble privilege; for the pope, you know, will not grant the cup to any layman. Your true Moravian values nothing beyond the cup; it is his costly jewel, and has cost the Bohemians their precious blood in many and many a battle.

NEUMANN: And what says that chart that hangs in the air there, over it all?

MASTER: That signifies the Bohemian letter royal, which we forced from the Emperor Rodolph—a precious, never to be enough valued parchment, that secures to the new Church the old privileges of free singing and open psalmody. But since he of Steiermärk has ruled over us, that is at an end; and after the battle at Prague, in which Count Palatine Frederick lost his crown and empire, our faith hangs upon the pulpit and altar—and our brethren look at their homes over their shoulders; but the letter royal the Emperor himself cut to pieces with his scissors.

NEUMANN: Why, my good Master of the Cellar! you are deep read in the chronicles of your country?

MASTER: So were my forefathers, and for that reason were they minstrels, and served under Procopius and Ziska. Peace be with their ashes. Well, Well! they fought for a good cause tho'—There! carry it up!

NEUMANN: Stay! let me but look at this second quarter. Look *there!* That is, when at Prague Castle the Imperial Counsellors, Martinitz and Stawata, were hurled down head over heels. 'Tis even so! there stands Count Thur who commands it.

[RUNNER *takes the service-cup and goes off with it.*

MASTER: O let me never more hear of that day. It was the three and twentieth of May, in the year of our Lord one thousand, six hundred, and eighteen. It seems to me as it were but yesterday—from that unlucky day it all began, all the heart-aches of the country. Since that day it is now sixteen years, and there has never once been peace on the earth.

[*Health drank aloud at the second table.*

The Prince of Weimar! Hurra!

[*At the third and fourth tables.*

Long live Prince William! Long live Duke Bernard! Hurra!

[*Music strikes up.*

1ST SERVANT: Hear'em! Hear'em! What an uproar!

2ND SERVANT (*comes in running*): Did you hear? They have drunk the Prince of Weimar's health.

3RD SERVANT: The Swedish Chief Commander!

1ST SERVANT (*speaking at the same time*): The Lutheran!

2ND SERVANT: Just before, when Count Deodate gave out the Emperor's health, they were all as mum as a nibbling mouse.

MASTER: Poh, poh! When the wine goes in strange things come out. A good servant hears and hears not! You should be nothing but eyes and feet, except when you're called to.

2ND SERVANT	(*to the* RUNNER, *to whom he gives secretly a flask of wine, keeping his eye upon the* MASTER OF THE CELLAR, *standing between him and the* RUNNER):
	Quick, Thomas, before the Master of the Cellar looks this way— 'tis a flask of Frontignac! Snapped it up at the third table. Can'st go off with it?
RUNNER	(*hides it in his pocket*): All right! [*Exit the* 2ND SERVANT.
3RD SERVANT	(*aside, to the first*): Be on the hark, Jack! that we may have right plenty to tell to Father Quivoga—He will give us right plenty of absolution in return for it.
1ST SERVANT:	For that very purpose I am always having something to do behind Illo's chair! He is the man for speeches to make you stare with.
MASTER	(*to* NEUMANN): Who, pray, may that swarthy man be, he with the cross, that is chatting so confidentially with Esterhats?
NEUMANN:	Ay, he too is one of those to whom they confide too much. He calls himself Maradas, a Spaniard is he.
MASTER	(*impatiently*): Spaniard! Spaniard! I tell you, friend, nothing good comes of these Spaniards. All these outlandish fellows are little better than rogues.
NEUMANN:	Fie, fie! you should not say so, friend. There are among them

In Prague on May 23 a group of rebellious members of the estates, led by Count Heinrich Matthias Thurn, hurled two imperial governors from the casement windows of the Hradcany palace. They landed unhurt but the "defenestration of Prague," shown here in a contemporary engraving, signaled a bloody war between Frederick V, Protestant elector of the Palatinate, whom the rebels elected king, and the emperor and his allies. The rebellion was crushed at the titanic battle of the White Mountain. Now Ferdinand ruled a greater area than any emperor since Charles V some sixty years before

Look there! That is, when at Prague castle the Imperial counsellors, Martinitz and Stawata, were hurled down head over heels. 'Tis even so! There stands Count Thur who commanded it. . . .

    Act II, scene 12

our very best generals, and those on whom the Duke at this
moment relies the most.

MASTER (*taking the flask out of the* RUNNER's *pocket*):
My son, it will be broken to pieces in your pocket.

> [TERTSKY *hurries in, fetches away the paper, and calls to a
> servant for pen and ink, and goes to the back of the
> stage.*

MASTER (*to the* SERVANTS): The Lieutenant-General stands up. Be on the
watch. Now! They break up. Off, and move back the forms!

> [*They rise at all the tables, the* SERVANTS *hurry off the front of
> the stage to the tables; part of the guests come forward.*

SCENE XIII: OCTAVIO PICCOLOMINI *enters in conversation with* MARADAS,
*and both place themselves quite on the edge of the stage on one
side of the proscenium. On the side directly opposite,* MAX
PICCOLOMINI, *by himself, lost in thought, and taking no part in
anything that is going forward. The middle space between both,
but rather more distant from the edge of the stage, is filled up
by* BUTLER, ISOLANI, GOETZ, TIEFENBACH, *and* KOLATTO.

ISOLANI (*while the company is coming forward*): Good night, good night,
Kolatto! Good night, Lieutenant-General! I should rather say
good morning.

GOETZ (*to* TIEFENBACH): Noble brother!

> [*making the usual compliment after meals.*

TIEFENBACH: Ay! 'twas a royal feast indeed.

GOETZ: Yes, my Lady Countess understands these matters. Her
mother-in-law, heaven rest her soul, taught her! Ah! that was
a housewife for you.

TIEFENBACH: There was not her like in all Bohemia for setting out a table.

OCTAVIO (*aside to* MARADAS): Do me the favour to talk to me—talk of what
you will—or of nothing. Only preserve the appearance at least of
talking. I would not wish to stand up myself, and yet I
conjecture that there will be goings on here worthy of our
attentive observation.

> [*He continues to fix his eye on the whole following scene.*

ISOLANI (*on the point of going*): Lights, lights!

TERTSKY (*advances with the paper to* ISOLANI): Noble brother! two minutes
longer! here is something to subscribe.

ISOLANI: Subscribe as much as you like—but you must excuse me from
reading it.

TERTSKY: There is no need. It is the oath which you have already read.
Only a few marks of your pen!

> [ISOLANI *hands over the paper to* OCTAVIO *respectfully.*

TERTSKY: Nay, nay, first come first served. There is no precedence here.

> [OCTAVIO *runs over the paper with apparent indifference;
> TERTSKY watches him at some distance.*

... den Zwölften Januarÿ Anno 1634

Only a few marks of your pen. . . .
Act II, scene 13

This document contains the signatures of forty-nine of Wallenstein's officers, with which they pledged their loyalty to their chief in the Pilsen declaration of Jan. 12, 1634. Within two months all but Tertsky and Illo were to betray their pledge

GOETZ	(*to* TERTSKY): Noble Count! with your permission—Good night.
TERTSKY:	Where's the hurry? Come, one other composing draught—(*To the* SERVANTS)—Ho!
GOETZ:	Excuse me—an't able.
TERTSKY:	A thimble-full!
GOETZ:	Excuse me.
TIEFENBACH	(*sits down*): Pardon me, nobles. This standing does not agree with me.
TERTSKY:	Consult only your own convenience, General.
TIEFENBACH:	Clear at head, sound in stomach—only my legs won't carry me any longer.
ISOLANI	(*pointing at his corpulence*): Poor legs! how should they? Such an unmerciful load!

> [OCTAVIO *subscribes his name, and reaches over the paper to* TERTSKY, *who gives it to* ISOLANI; *and he goes to the table to sign his name.*

TIEFENBACH:	'Twas that war in Pomerania that first brought it on. Out in all weathers—ice and snow—no help for it. I shall never get the better of it all the days of my life.
GOETZ:	Why, in simple verity, your Swede makes no nice enquiries about the season.
TERTSKY	(*observing* ISOLANI, *whose hand trembles excessively, so that he can scarcely direct his pen*): Have you had that ugly complaint long, noble brother? Despatch it.
ISOLANI:	The sins of youth! I have already tried the Chalybeate waters. Well—I must bear it.

> [TERTSKY *gives the paper to* MARADAS; *he steps to the table to subscribe.*

OCTAVIO	(*advancing to* BUTLER): You are not over-fond of the orgies of Bacchus, Colonel! I have observed it. You would, I think, find yourself more to your liking in the uproar of a battle, than of a feast.
BUTLER:	I must confess, 'tis not in my way.
OCTAVIO	(*stepping nearer to him friendlily*): Nor in mine either, I can assure you; and I'm not a little glad, my much-honoured Colonel Butler, that we agree so well in our opinions. A half-dozen good friends at most, at a small round table, a glass of genuine Tokay, open hearts, and a rational conversation—that's my taste!
BUTLER:	And mine too, when it can be had.

> [*The paper comes to* TIEFENBACH, *who glances over it at the same time with* GOETZ *and* KOLATTO. MARADAS *in the mean time returns to* OCTAVIO. *All this takes place, the conversation with* BUTLER *proceeding uninterrupted.*

OCTAVIO	(*introducing* MARADAS *to* BUTLER): Don Balthasar Maradas! likewise a man of our stamp, and long ago your admirer. [BUTLER *bows.*

OCTAVIO	(*continuing*): You are a stranger here—'twas but yesterday you arrived; you are ignorant of the ways and means here. 'Tis a wretched place—I know, at our age, one loves to be snug and quiet—What if you moved your lodgings? Come, be my visitor. (BUTLER *makes a low bow.*) Nay, without compliment! For a friend like you, I have still a corner remaining.
BUTLER	(*coldly*): Your obliged humble servant, my Lord Lieutenant-General.

[*The paper comes to* BUTLER, *who goes to the table to subscribe it. The front of the stage is vacant, so that both the* PICCOLOMINIS, *each on the side where he had been from the commencement of the scene, remain alone.*

OCTAVIO	(*after having some time watched his son in silence, advances somewhat nearer to him*): You were long absent from us, friend!
MAX:	I—urgent business detained me.
OCTAVIO:	And, I observe, you are still absent!
MAX:	You know this crowd and bustle always make me silent.
OCTAVIO	(*advancing still nearer*): May I be permitted to ask what the business was that detained you? Tertsky knows it without asking!
MAX:	What does Tertsky know?
OCTAVIO:	He was the only one who did not miss you.
ISOLANI	(*who has been attending to them from some distance, steps up*): Well done, father! Rout out his baggage! Beat up his quarters! There is something there that should not be.
TERTSKY	(*with the paper*): Is there none wanting? Have the whole subscribed?
OCTAVIO:	All.
TERTSKY	(*calling aloud*): Ho! who subscribes?
BUTLER	(*to* TERTSKY): Count the names. There ought to be just thirty.
TERTSKY:	Here is a cross.
TIEFENBACH:	That's my mark.
ISOLANI:	He cannot write; but his cross is a good cross, and is honoured by Jews as well as Christians.
OCTAVIO	(*presses on to* MAX): Come, General; let us go. It is late.
TERTSKY:	*One* Piccolomini only has signed.
ISOLANI	(*pointing to* MAX): Look! that is your man, that statue there, who has had neither eye, ear, nor tongue for us the whole evening.

[MAX *receives the paper from* TERTSKY, *which he looks upon vacantly.*

SCENE XIV: *To these enter* ILLO *from the inner room. He has in his hand the golden service-cup, and is extremely distempered with drinking.* GOETZ *and* BUTLER *follow him, endeavouring to keep him back.*

ILLO:	What do you want? Let me go.

GOETZ *and* BUTLER:	Drink no more, Illo! For heaven's sake, drink no more.
ILLO	(*goes up to* OCTAVIO, *and shakes him cordially by the hand, and then drinks*):
	Octavio! I bring this to you! Let all grudge be drowned in this friendly bowl! I know well enough, ye never loved me—Devil take me! and I never loved you! I am always even with people in that way! Let what's past be past—that is, you understand—forgotten! I esteem you infinitely. (*Embracing him repeatedly.*) You have not a dearer friend on earth than I—but that you know. The fellow that cries rogue to you, calls me villain—and I'll strangle him! my *dear* friend!
TERTSKY	(*whispering to him*):
	Art in thy senses? For heaven's sake, Illo! think where you are.
ILLO	(*aloud*): What do you mean? There are none but friends here, are there? (*Looks round the whole circle with a jolly and triumphant air.*) Not a sneaker among us, thank heaven!
TERTSKY	(*to* BUTLER, *eagerly*): Take him off with you, force him off, I entreat you, Butler!
BUTLER	(*to* ILLO): Field-Marshal! a word with you.
	[*Leads him to the side-board.*
ILLO	(*cordially*): A thousand for one! Fill—Fill it once more up to the brim. To this gallant man's health!
ISOLANI	(*to* MAX, *who all the while has been staring on the paper with fixed but vacant eyes*):
	Slow and sure, my noble brother! Hast *parsed* it all yet? Some words yet to go thro'? Ha?
MAX	(*waking as from a dream*): What am I to do?
TERTSKY	(*and at the same time* ISOLANI): Sign your name.
	[OCTAVIO *directs his eyes on him with intense anxiety.*
MAX	(*returns the paper*): Let it stay till to-morrow. It is *business*— to-day I am not sufficiently collected. Send it to me to-morrow.
TERTSKY:	Nay, collect yourself a little.
ISOLANI:	Awake, man! awake! Come, thy signature, and have done with it! What? Thou art the youngest in the whole company, and would'st be wiser than all of us together? Look there! thy father has signed—we have all signed.
TERTSKY	(*to* OCTAVIO): Use your influence. Instruct him.
OCTAVIO:	My son is at the age of discretion.
ILLO	(*leaves the service-cup on the sideboard*): What's the dispute?
TERTSKY:	He declines subscribing the paper.
MAX:	I say, it may as well stay till to-morrow.
ILLO:	It cannot stay. We have all subscribed to it—and so must you. You must subscribe.
MAX:	Illo, good night.
ILLO:	No! You come not off so. The Duke shall learn who are his friends.
	[*All collect round* ILLO *and* MAX.

490

MAX:	What my sentiments are towards the Duke, the Duke knows, every one knows—what need of this wild stuff?
ILLO:	This is the thanks the Duke gets for his partiality to Italians and foreigners. Us Bohemians he holds for little better than dullards—nothing pleases him but what's outlandish.
TERTSKY	(*in extreme embarrassment, to the commanders, who at Illo's words gave a sudden start, as preparing to resent them*): It is the wine that speaks and not his reason. Attend not to him, I entreat you.
ISOLANI	(*with a bitter laugh*): Wine invents nothing: it only *tattles*.
ILLO:	He who is not with me is against me. Your tender consciences! Unless they can slip out by a back-door, by a puny proviso!
TERTSKY	(*interrupting him*): He is stark mad—don't listen to him.
ILLO	(*raising his voice to the highest pitch*): Unless they can slip out by a *proviso*. What of the proviso? The devil take this proviso!
MAX	(*has his attention roused, and looks again into the paper*): What is there here then of such perilous import? You make me curious—I must look closer at it.
TERTSKY	(*in a low voice to* ILLO): What are you doing, Illo? You are ruining us.
TIEFENBACH	(*to* KOLATTO): Ay, ay! I observed, that before we sat down to supper, it was read differently.
GOETZ:	Why, I seemed to think so too.
ISOLANI:	What do I care for that? Where there stand other names, mine can stand too.
TIEFENBACH:	Before supper there *was* a certain proviso therein, or short clause concerning our duties to the Emperor.
BUTLER	(*to one of the commanders*): For shame, for shame! Bethink you. What is the main business here? The question now is, whether we shall keep our General, or let him retire. One must not take these things too nicely and over-scrupulously.
ISOLANI	(*to one of the generals*): Did the Duke make any of these provisos when he gave you your regiment?
TERTSKY	(*to* GOETZ): Or when he gave you the office of army-purveyancer, which brings you in yearly a thousand pistoles.
ILLO:	He is a rascal who makes us out to be rogues. If there be any one that wants satisfaction, let him say so. I am his man.
TIEFENBACH:	Softly, softly! 'Twas but a word or two.
MAX	(*having read the paper gives it back*): Till to-morrow, therefore!
ILLO	(*stammering with rage and fury, loses all command over himself, and presents the paper to* MAX *with one hand, and his sword in the other*): Subscribe—Judas!
ISOLANI:	Out upon you, Illo!
OCTAVIO, TERTSKY, BUTLER	(*all together*): Down with the sword.

491

MAX   (*rushes on him suddenly and disarms him, then to* COUNT
             TERTSKY):
             Take him off to bed.
                [MAX *leaves the stage.* ILLO *cursing and raving is held back by*
                   some of the officers, and amidst a universal confusion the
                   curtain drops.

ACT III

SCENE I: *Scene, a chamber in Piccolomini's Mansion. It is Night.*
             OCTAVIO PICCOLOMINI. *A* VALET DE CHAMBRE, *with Lights.*

OCTAVIO: —And when my son comes in, conduct him hither. What is
             the hour?
VALET: 'Tis on the point of morning.
OCTAVIO: Set down the light. We mean not to undress.
             You may retire to sleep.
                [*Exit* VALET. OCTAVIO *paces, musing, across the chamber.* MAX
                   PICCOLOMINI *enters unobserved, and looks at his father for*
                   some moments in silence.

MAX: Art thou offended with me? Heaven knows
             That odious business was no fault of mine.
             'Tis true, indeed, I saw thy signature.
             What *thou* hadst sanctioned should not, it might seem,
             Have come amiss to me. But—'tis my nature—
             Thou know'st, that in such matters I must follow
             My own light, not another's.
OCTAVIO   (*goes up to him, and embraces him*):
                       Follow it,
             O follow it still further, my best son!
             To-night, dear boy! it hath more faithfully
             Guided thee than th' example of thy father.
MAX: Declare thyself less darkly.
OCTAVIO: I will do so.
             For after what has taken place this night,
             There must remain no secrets 'twixt us two.
                          [*Both seat themselves.*
             Max Piccolomini; what think'st thou of
             The oath that was sent round for signatures?
MAX: I hold it for a thing of harmless import,
             Altho' I like not these set declarations.
OCTAVIO: And on no other ground hast thou refused
             The signature they fain had wrested from thee?
MAX: It was a serious business—I was absent—
             The affair itself seemed not so urgent to me.
OCTAVIO: Be open, Max. Thou hadst then no suspicion?

MAX: Suspicion! what suspicion? Not the least.

OCTAVIO: Thank thy good angel, Piccolomini;
He drew thee back unconscious from the abyss.

MAX: I know not what thou meanest.

OCTAVIO: I will tell thee.
Fain would they have extorted from thee, son,
The sanction of thy name to villany;
Yea, with a single flourish of thy pen,
Made thee renounce thy duty and thy honour!

MAX *(rises)*:
Octavio!

OCTAVIO: Patience! Seat yourself. Much yet
Hast thou to learn from me, friend! hast for years
Lived in incomprehensible illusion.
Before thine eyes is treason drawing out
As black a web as e'er was spun from venom:
A power of hell o'erclouds thy understanding.
I dare no longer stand in silence—dare
No longer see thee wandering on in darkness,
Nor pluck the bandage from thine eyes.

MAX: My father!
Yet, ere thou speak'st, a moment's pause of thought.
If your disclosures should appear to be
Conjectures only—and almost I fear
They will be nothing further—spare them! I
Am not in that collected mood at present,
That I could listen to them quietly.

OCTAVIO: The deeper cause thou hast to hate this light,
The more impatient cause have I, my son,
To force it on thee. To the innocence
And wisdom of thy heart I could have trusted thee
With calm assurance—but I see the net
Preparing—and it is thy heart itself
Alarms me for thine innocence—that secret,
                [fixing his eyes steadfastly on his son's face.
Which thou concealest, forces *mine* from me.
      *[*MAX *attempts to answer, but hesitates, and casts his eyes to
          the ground embarrassed.*

OCTAVIO *(after a pause)*:
Know, then, they are duping thee; a most foul game
With thee and with us all—nay, hear me calmly—
The Duke even now is playing. He assumes
The mask, as if he would forsake the army;
And in this moment makes he preparations
That army from the Emperor—to *steal*,
And carry it over to the enemy!

MAX: That low priest's legend I know well, but did not
Expect to hear it from thy mouth.

OCTAVIO: That mouth,
From which thou hear'st it at this present moment
Doth warrant thee that it is no priest's legend.

MAX: How mere a maniac they suppose the Duke.
What, he can meditate? the Duke? can dream
That he can lure away full thirty thousand
Tried troops and true, all honourable soldiers,
More than a thousand noblemen among them,
From oaths, from duty, from their honour lure them,
And make them all unanimous to do
A deed that brands them scoundrels?

OCTAVIO: Such a deed,
With such a front of infamy, the Duke
No way desires—what he requires of us
Bears a far gentler appellation. Nothing
He wishes, but to give the empire peace.
And so, because the Emperor hates *this* peace,
Therefore the Duke—the Duke will *force* him to it.
All parts of the empire will he pacify.
And for his trouble will retain in payment
(What he has already in his gripe)—Bohemia!

MAX: Has he, Octavio, merited of us,
That we—that we should think so vilely of him?

OCTAVIO: What *we would* think is not the question here.
The affair speaks for itself—and clearest proofs!
Hear me, my son—'tis not unknown to thee,
In what ill credit with the Court we stand.
But little dost thou know or guess what tricks,
What base intrigues, what lying artifices,
Have been employed—for this sole end—to sow
Mutiny in the camp! All bands are loosed—
Loosed all the bands that link the officer
To his liege Emperor, all that bind the soldier
Affectionately to the citizen.
Lawless he stands, and threat'ningly beleaguers
The state he's bound to guard. To such a height
'Tis swoln, that at this hour the Emperor
Before his armies—his own armies—trembles;
Yea, in his capital, his palace, fears
The traitors' poniards, and is meditating
To hurry off and hide his tender offspring—
Not from the Swedes, not from the Lutherans—
No! from his own troops hide and hurry them!

MAX: Cease, cease! thou tortur'st, shatter'st me. I know
That oft we tremble at an empty terror;
But the false phantasm brings a real misery.

OCTAVIO: It is no phantasm. An intestine war,
Of all the most unnatural and cruel,

Will burst out into flames, if instantly
We do not fly and stifle it. The Generals
Are many of them long ago won over;
The subalterns are vacillating—whole
Regiments and garrisons are vacillating.
To foreigners our strong-holds are entrusted;
To that suspected Schafgotch is the whole
Force of Silesia given up; to Tertsky
Five regiments, foot and horse—to Isolani,
To Illo, Kinsky, Butler, the best troops.

MAX:
Likewise to both of us.

OCTAVIO:
                 Because the Duke
Believes he has secured us—means to lure us
Still further on by splendid promises.
To me he portions forth the princedoms Glatz
And Sagan; and too plain I see the angel
With which he doubts not to catch *thee.*

MAX:
                            No! no!
I tell thee—no!

OCTAVIO:
               O open yet thine eyes!
And to what purpose think'st thou he has called us
Hither to Pilsen? To avail himself
Of our advice? O when did Friedland ever
Need our advice? Be calm, and listen to me.
To sell ourselves are we called hither, and
Decline we that—to be his hostages.
Therefore doth noble Galas stand aloof;
Thy father, too, thou would'st not have seen here,
If higher duties had not held him fettered.

MAX:
He makes no secret of it—needs make none—
That we're called hither for his sake—he owns it.
He needs our aidance to maintain himself—
He did so much for us; and 'tis but fair
That we, too, should do somewhat now for him.

OCTAVIO:
And know'st thou what it is which we must do?
That Illo's drunken mood betrayed it to thee.
Bethink thyself—what hast thou heard, what seen?
The counterfeited paper—the omission
Of that particular clause, so full of meaning,
Does it not prove that they would bind us down
To nothing good?

MAX:
               That counterfeited paper
Appears to me no other than a trick
Of Illo's own device. These underhand
Traders in great men's interests, ever use
To urge and hurry all things to the extreme.
They see the Duke at variance with the Court,
And fondly think to serve him, when they widen

The breach irreparably. Trust me, father,
The Duke knows nothing of all this.

OCTAVIO: It grieves me
That I must dash to earth, that I must shatter
A faith so specious; but I may not spare thee!
For this is not a time for tenderness.
Thou must take measures, speedy ones—must act.
I therefore will confess to thee, that all
Which I've intrusted to thee now—that all
Which seems to thee so unbelievable,
That—yes, I will tell thee—(*a pause*)—Max, I had it all
From his own mouth—from the Duke's mouth I had it.

MAX   (*in excessive agitation*):
No! no! never!

OCTAVIO: Himself confided to me
What I, 'tis true, had long before discovered
By other means—himself confided to me,
That 'twas his settled plan to join the Swedes!
And, at the head of the united armies,
Compel the Emperor—

MAX: He is passionate.
The Court has stung him—he is sore all over
With injuries and affronts; and in a moment
Of irritation, what if he, for once,
Forgot himself? He's an impetuous man.

OCTAVIO: Nay, in cold blood, he did confess this to me;
And having construed my astonishment
Into a scruple of his power, he showed me
His written evidences—showed me letters,
Both from the Saxon and the Swede, that gave
Promises of aidance, and defined th' amount.

MAX: It cannot be! can *not* be! *can* not be!
Dost thou not see, it cannot!
Thou wouldest of necessity have shown him
Such horror, such deep loathing—that or he
Had taken thee for his better genius, or
Thou stood'st not now a living man before me—

OCTAVIO: I have laid open my objections to him,
Dissuaded him with pressing earnestness;
But my *abhorrence,* the full sentiment
Of my *whole* heart—that I have still kept sacred
To my own consciousness.

MAX: And *thou* hast been
So treacherous? That looks not like my father!
I trusted not thy words, when thou didst tell me
Evil of him; much less can I *now* do it,
That thou calumniatest thy own self.

OCTAVIO: I did not thrust myself into his secrecy.

496

MAX: Uprightness merited his confidence.

OCTAVIO: He was no longer worthy of sincerity.

MAX: Dissimulation, sure, was still less worthy
            Of thee, Octavio!

OCTAVIO: Gave I him a cause
            To entertain a scruple of my honour?

MAX: That he did not, evinced his confidence.

OCTAVIO: Dear son, it is not always possible
            Still to preserve that infant purity
            Which the voice teaches in our inmost heart.
            Still in alarm, for ever on the watch
            Against the wiles of wicked men, e'en Virtue
            Will sometimes bear away her outward robes
            Soiled in the wrestle with Iniquity.
            This is the curse of every evil deed,
            That, propagating still, it brings forth evil.
            I do not cheat my better soul with sophisms;
            I but perform my orders; the Emperor
            Prescribes my conduct to me. Dearest boy,
            Far better were it, doubtless, if we all
            Obeyed the heart at all times; but so doing,
            In this our present sojourn with bad men,
            We must abandon many an honest object.
            'Tis now our call to serve the Emperor,
            By what means he can best be served—the heart
            May whisper what it will—this is our call!

MAX: It seems a thing appointed that to-day
            I should not comprehend, not understand thee.
            The Duke, thou say'st, did honestly pour out
            His heart to thee, but for an evil purpose;
            And thou dishonestly hast cheated him
            For a good purpose! Silence, I entreat thee—
            My friend thou stealest not from me—
            Let me not lose my father?

OCTAVIO   (suppressing resentment):
            As yet thou know'st not all, my son. I have
            Yet somewhat to disclose to thee.   [After a pause.
                            Duke Friedland
            Hath made his preparations. He relies
            Upon his stars. He deems us unprovided,
            And thinks to fall upon us by surprise.
            Yea, in his dream of hope, he grasps already
            The golden circle in his hand. He errs.
            We too have been in action—he but grasps
            His evil fate, most evil, most mysterious!

MAX: O nothing rash, my sire. By all that's good
            Let me invoke thee—no precipitation!

OCTAVIO: With light tread stole he on his evil way,

497

And light of tread hath Vengeance stole on after him.
Unseen she stands already, dark behind him—
But one step more—he shudders in her grasp!
Thou hast seen Questenberg with me. As yet
Thou know'st but his ostensible commission—
He brought with him a *private* one, my son,
And that was for me only.

MAX: May I know it?

OCTAVIO   (*seizes the patent*):   Max!   [*A pause.*
—In this disclosure place I in thy hands
The Empire's welfare and thy father's life.
Dear to thy inmost heart is Wallenstein:
A powerful tie of love, of veneration,
Hath knit thee to him from thy earliest youth.
Thou nourishest the *wish*—O let me still
Anticipate thy loitering confidence!
The *hope* thou nourishest to knit thyself
Yet closer to him—

MAX: Father—

OCTAVIO: O my son!
I trust thy heart undoubtingly. But am I
Equally sure of thy collectedness?
Wilt thou be able, with calm countenance,
To enter this man's presence, when that I
Have trusted to thee his whole fate?

MAX: According
As thou dost trust me, father, with his crime.
            [OCTAVIO *takes a paper out of his escritoire, and gives it*
                to him.

MAX: What? how? a full imperial patent!

OCTAVIO: Read it.

MAX   (*just glances on it*):
Duke Friedland sentenced and condemned!

OCTAVIO: Even so.

MAX   (*throws down the paper*):
O this is too much! O unhappy error!

OCTAVIO: Read on. Collect thyself.

MAX   (*after he has read further with a look of affright and
           astonishment on his father*):
How! what! Thou! thou!

OCTAVIO: But for the present moment, till the King
Of Hungary may safely join the army,
Is the command assigned to me

MAX: And think'st thou,
Dost thou believe, that thou wilt tear it from him?
O never hope it! Father! father! father!
An inauspicious office is enjoined thee.
This paper here—this! and wilt thou enforce it?

	The mighty, in the middle of his host,
	Surrounded by his thousands, him would'st thou
	Disarm—degrade! Thou'rt lost, both thou and all of us.
OCTAVIO:	What hazard I incur thereby, I know.

In the great hand of God I stand. The Almighty
Will cover with his shield the imperial house,
And shatter, in his wrath, the work of darkness.
The Emperor hath true servants still; and, even
Here in the camp, there are enough brave men,
Who for the good cause will fight gallantly.
The faithful have been warned—the dangerous
Are closely watched. I wait but the first step,
And then immediately—

MAX: What! on suspicion?
Immediately?

OCTAVIO: The Emperor is no tyrant.
The deed alone he'll punish, not the wish.
The Duke hath yet his destiny in his power.
Let him but leave the treason uncompleted,
He will be silently displaced from office,
And make way to his Emperor's royal son.
An honourable exile to his castles
Will be a benefaction to him rather
Than punishment. But the first open step—

MAX: What call'st thou such a step? A wicked step
Ne'er will he take: but thou might'st easily,
Yea, thou hast done it, misinterpret him.

OCTAVIO: Nay, howsoever punishable were
Duke Friedland's purposes, yet still the steps
Which he hath taken openly, permit
A mild construction. It is my intention
To leave this paper wholly unenforced
Till some act is committed which convicts him
Of a high-treason, without doubt or plea,
And that shall sentence him.

MAX: But who the judge?

OCTAVIO: Thyself.

MAX: For ever, then, this paper will lie idle.

OCTAVIO: Too soon, I fear, its powers must all be proved.
After the counter-promise of this evening,
It cannot be but he must deem himself
Secure of the majority with *us;*
And of the army's general sentiment
He hath a pleasing proof in that petition
Which thou deliver'st to him from the regiments.
Add this too—I have letters that the Rhinegrave
Hath changed his route, and travels by forced marches
To the Bohemian Forest. What this purports,

	Remains unknown; and, to confirm suspicion,
	This night a Swedish nobleman arrived here.
MAX:	I have thy word. Thou'lt not proceed to action
	Before thou hast convinced me—me myself.
OCTAVIO:	Is it possible? Still, after all thou know'st,
	Canst thou believe still in his innocence?
MAX	(*with enthusiasm*):
	Thy judgment may mistake; my heart cannot.

[*moderates his voice and manner.*

These reasons might expound thy spirit or mine,
But they expound not Friedland—I have faith:
For as he knits his fortunes to the stars,
Even so doth he resemble them in secret,
Wonderful, still inexplicable courses!
Trust me, they do him wrong. All will be solved.
These smokes, at once, will kindle into flame—
The edges of this black and stormy cloud
Will brighten suddenly, and we shall view
The Unapproachable glide out in splendour.

OCTAVIO: I will await it.

SCENE II: OCTAVIO *and* MAX *as before. To them the* VALET OF THE
CHAMBER.

OCTAVIO:	How now, then?
VALET:	A despatch is at the door.
OCTAVIO:	So early? From whom comes he then? Who is it?
VALET:	That he refused to tell me.
OCTAVIO:	Lead him in:
	And, hark you—let it not transpire.

[*Exit* VALET—*the* CORNET *steps in.*

Ha! Cornet—is it you? and from Count Galas?
Give me your letters.

CORNET:	The Lieutenant-General
	Trusted it not to letters.
OCTAVIO:	And what is it?
CORNET:	He bade me tell you—Dare I speak openly here?
OCTAVIO:	My son knows all.
CORNET:	We have him.
OCTAVIO:	Whom?
CORNET:	*Sesina.*
	The old negociator.
OCTAVIO	(*eagerly*): And you have him?
CORNET:	In the Bohemian forest, Captain Mohrbrand
	Found and secured him yester-morning early:
	He was proceeding then to Regensburg,
	And on him were despatches for the Swede.
OCTAVIO:	And the despatches—

CORNET: The Lieutenant-General
Sent them that instant to Vienna, and
The prisoner with them.

OCTAVIO: This is, indeed, a tiding!
That fellow is a precious casket to us,
Enclosing weighty things. Was much found on him?

CORNET: I think, six packets, with Count Tertsky's arms.

OCTAVIO: None in the Duke's own hand?

CORNET: Not that I know.

OCTAVIO: And old Sesina?

CORNET: He was sorely frightened,
When it was told him he must to Vienna.
But the Count Altringer bade him take heart,
Would he but make a full and free confession.

OCTAVIO: Is Altringer then with your lord? I heard
That he lay sick at Linz.

CORNET: These three days past
He's with my master, the Lieutenant-General,
At Frauemburg. Already have they sixty
Small companies together, chosen men:
Respectfully they greet you with assurances,
That they are only waiting your commands.

OCTAVIO: In a few days may great events take place.
And when must you return?

CORNET: I wait your orders.

OCTAVIO: Remain till evening.
           [CORNET *signifies his assent and obeisance, and is going.*

OCTAVIO: No one saw you—ha?

CORNET: No living creature. Thro' the cloister wicket
The Capuchins, as usual, let me in.

OCTAVIO: Go, rest your limbs, and keep yourself concealed.
I hold it probable, that yet ere evening
I shall despatch you. The development
Of this affair approaches: ere the day,
That even now is dawning in the heaven,
Ere this eventful day hath set, the lot
That must decide our fortunes will be drawn.   [*Exit* CORNET.

SCENE III: OCTAVIO *and* MAX PICCOLOMINI.

OCTAVIO: Well—and what now, son? All will soon be clear,
For all, I'm certain, went thro' that Sesina.

MAX   *(who through the whole of the foregoing scene has been in a*
violent and visible struggle of feelings, at length starts as one
resolved):
I will procure me light a shorter way.
Farewell.

OCTAVIO: Where now? Remain here.

MAX:	To the Duke.
OCTAVIO	(*alarmed*):
	What—
MAX	(*returning*): If thou hast believed that I shall act
	A part in this thy play—
	Thou hast miscalculated on me grievously.
	My way must be straight on. True with the tongue,
	False with the heart—I may not, cannot be:
	Nor can I suffer that a man should trust me—
	As his friend trust me—and then lull my conscience
	With such low pleas as these: 'I asked him not—
	He did it all at his own hazard—and
	My *mouth* has never lied to him.' No, no!
	What a friend takes me for, that I must be.
	—I'll to the Duke; ere yet this day is ended
	Will I demand of him that he do save
	His good name from the world, and with one stride
	Break through and rend this fine-spun web of yours.
	He can, he will! *I* still am his believer.
	Yet I'll not pledge myself, but that those letters
	May furnish you, perchance, with proofs against him.
	How far may not this Tertsky have proceeded—
	What may not he himself, too, have permitted
	Himself to do, to snare the enemy,
	The laws of war excusing? Nothing save
	His own mouth shall convict him—nothing less!
	And face to face will I go question him.
OCTAVIO:	Thou wilt?
MAX:	I will, as sure as this heart beats.
OCTAVIO:	I have, indeed, miscalculated on thee.
	I calculated on a prudent son,
	Who would have blest the hand beneficent
	That plucked him back from the abyss—and lo!
	A fascinated being I discover,
	Whom his two eyes befool, whom passion wilders,
	Whom not the broadest light of noon can heal.
	Go, question him! Be mad enough, I pray thee.
	The purpose of thy father, of thy Emperor,
	Go, give it up free booty! Force me, drive me
	To an open breach before the time. And now,
	Now that a miracle of heaven had guarded
	My secret purpose even to this hour,
	And laid to sleep Suspicion's piercing eyes,
	Let me have lived to see that mine own son,
	With frantic enterprise, annihilates
	My toilsome labours and state-policy.
MAX:	Ay—this state-policy! O how I curse it!
	You will some time, with your state-policy,

Compel him to the measure: it may happen,
Because ye are *determined* that he's guilty,
Guilty ye'll *make* him. All retreat cut off,
You close up every outlet, hem him in
Narrower and narrower, till at length ye force him—
Yes, ye—ye *force* him, in his desperation,
To set fire to his prison. Father! father!
That never can end well—it cannot—will not!
And let it be decided as it may,
I see with boding heart the near approach
Of an ill-starred unblest catastrophe.
For this great Monarch-spirit, if he fall,
Will drag a world into the ruin with him.
And as a ship, that midway on the ocean
Takes fire, at once, and with a thunder-burst,
Explodes, and with itself shoots out its crew
In smoke and ruin betwixt sea and heaven;
So will he, falling, draw down in his fall
All us, who're fixed and mortised to his fortune.
Deem of it what thou wilt; but pardon me,
That I must bear me on in my own way.
All must remain pure betwixt him and me;
And, ere the day-light dawns, it must be known
Which I must lose—my father, or my friend.

[*During his exit the curtain drops.*

ACT IV

SCENE I: *Scene—a room fitted up for astrological labours, and provided with celestial charts, with globes, telescopes, quadrants, and other mathematical instruments. Seven colossal figures, representing the planets, each with a transparent star of a different colour on its head, stand in a semi-circle in the back-ground, so that Mars and Saturn are nearest the eye. The remainder of the scene, and its disposition, is given in the fourth scene of the second act. There must be a curtain over the figures, which may be dropped, and conceal them on occasions. [In the fifth scene of this act it must be dropped: but, in the seventh scene, it must be again drawn up wholly or in part.] WALLENSTEIN at a black table, on which a speculum astrologicum is described with chalk. SENI is taking observations through a window.*

WALLENSTEIN: All well—and now let it be ended, Seni. Come,
The dawn commences, and Mars rules the hour.
We must give o'er the operation. Come,
We know enough.

SENI: Your Highness must permit me

Just to contemplate Venus. She's now rising:
Like as a sun, so shines she in the east.

WALLENSTEIN: She is at present in her perigee,
And shoots down now her strongest influences.

[*Contemplating the figure on the table.*

Auspicious aspect—fateful in conjunction,
At length the mighty three corradiate;
And the two stars of blessing, Jupiter
And Venus, take between them the malignant
Slily-malicious Mars, and thus compel
Into *my* service that old mischief-founder:
For long he viewed me hostilely, and ever
With beam oblique, or perpendicular,
Now in the quartile, now in the secundan,
Shot his red lightnings at my stars, disturbing
Their blessed influences and sweet aspects.
Now they have conquered the old enemy,
And bring him in the heavens a prisoner to me.

SENI *(who has come down from the window)*:
And in a corner house, your Highness—think of that!
That makes each influence of double strength.

WALLENSTEIN: And sun and moon, too, in the sextile aspect,
The soft light with the veh'ment—so I love it.
Sol is the heart, Luna the head of heaven.
Bold be the plan, fiery the execution.

SENI: And both the mighty lumina by no
Maleficus affronted. Lo! Saturnus,
Innocuous, powerless, in cadente domo.

WALLENSTEIN: The empire of Saturnus is gone by:
Lord of the secret birth of things is he;
Within the lap of earth, and in the depths
Of the imagination dominates;
And his are all things that eschew the light.
The time is o'er of brooding and contrivance;
For Jupiter, the lustrous, lordeth now,
And the dark work, complete of preparation,
He draws by force into the realm of light.
Now must we hasten on to action, ere
The scheme and most auspicious positure
Parts o'er my head, and takes once more its flight;
For the heavens journey still, and sojourn not.

[*There are knocks at the door.*

There's some one knocking there. See who it is.

TERTSKY *(from without)*:
Open, and let me in.

WALLENSTEIN: Ay—'tis Tertsky.
What is there of such urgence? We are busy.

TERTSKY   (*from without*):
               Lay all aside at present, I entreat you.
               It suffers no delaying.
WALLENSTEIN: Open, Seni!
               [*While* SENI *opens the door for* TERTSKY, WALLENSTEIN *draws
                        the curtain over the figures.*
TERTSKY   (*enters*):
               Hast thou already heard it? He is taken.
               Galas has given him up to the Emperor.
                               [SENI *draws off the black table, and exit.*

SCENE II: WALLENSTEIN, COUNT TERTSKY.

WALLENSTEIN   (*to* TERTSKY):
               Who has been taken? Who is given up?
TERTSKY: The man who knows our secrets, who knows every
               Negotiation with the Swede and Saxon,
               Thro' whose hands all and everything has passed—
WALLENSTEIN   (*drawing back*):
               Nay, not Sesina? Say, No! I entreat thee.
TERTSKY: All on his road for Regensburg to the Swede
               He was plunged down upon by Galas' agent,
               Who had been long in ambush, lurking for him.
               There must have been found on him my whole packet
               To Thur, to Kinsky, to Oxenstirn, to Arnheim:
               All this is in their hands; they have now an insight
               Into the whole—our measures, and our motives.

SCENE III: *To them enters* ILLO.

ILLO   (*to* TERTSKY):
               Has he heard it?
TERTSKY: He has heard it.
ILLO   (*to* WALLENSTEIN):   Think'st thou still
               To make thy peace with the Emp'ror, to regain
               His confidence? E'en were it now thy wish
               To abandon all thy plans, yet still they know
               What thou hast wished; then forward thou must press;
               Retreat is now no longer in thy power.
TERTSKY: They have documents against us, and in hands,
               Which show beyond all power of contradiction—
WALLENSTEIN: Of my hand-writing—no iota. Thee
               I punish for thy lies.
ILLO: And thou believ'st
               That what this man, that what thy sister's husband
               Did in thy name, will not stand on thy reckoning?
               His word must pass for thy word with the Swede,

505

	And not with those that hate thee at Vienna.
TERTSKY:	In writing thou gav'st nothing—But bethink thee,
	How far thou ventured'st by word of mouth
	With this Sesina? And will he be silent?
	If he can save himself by yielding up
	Thy secret purposes, will he retain them?
ILLO:	Thyself dost not conceive it possible;
	And since they now have evidence authentic
	How far thou hast already gone, speak! tell us,
	What art thou waiting for? Thou canst no longer
	Keep thy command; and beyond hope of rescue
	Thou'rt lost, if thou resign'st it.

WALLENSTEIN: In the army
Lies my security. The army will not
Abandon me. Whatever they may know,
The power is mine, and they must gulp it down—
And substitute I caution for my fealty;
They must be satisfied, at least appear so.

ILLO:	The army, Duke, *is* thine now—for this moment—
	'Tis thine: but think with terror on the slow,
	The quiet power of time. From open vi'lence
	The attachment of thy soldiery secures thee
	To-day—to-morrow; but grant'st thou them a respite,
	Unheard, unseen, they'll undermine that love
	On which thou now dost feel so firm a footing,
	With wily theft will draw away from thee
	One after th' other—

WALLENSTEIN: 'Tis a cursed accident!

ILLO:	O I will call it a most blessed one
	If it work on thee as it ought to do,
	Hurry thee on to action—to decision—
	The Swedish General—

WALLENSTEIN: He's arrived! Know'st thou
What his commission is—

ILLO: To thee alone
Will he intrust the purpose of his coming.

WALLENSTEIN:	A cursed, cursed accident! Yes, yes,
	Sesina knows too much, and won't be silent.
TERTSKY:	He's a Bohemian fugitive and rebel,
	His neck is forfeit. Can he save himself
	At thy cost, think you he will scruple it?
	And if they put him to the torture, will he,
	Will *he*, that dastardling, have strength enough—
WALLENSTEIN	(*lost in thought*):
	Their confidence is lost—irreparable!
	And I may act what way I will, I shall
	Be and remain for ever in their thought
	A traitor to my country. How sincerely

	Soever I return back to my duty,
	It will no longer help me—
ILLO:	Ruin thee,
	That it will do! Not thy fidelity,
	Thy weakness will be deemed the sole occasion—
WALLENSTEIN	(*pacing up and down in extreme agitation*):
	What! I must realize it now in earnest,
	Because I toyed too freely with the thought?
	Accursed he who dallies with a devil!
	And must I—I *must* realize it now—
	Now, while I have the power, it *must* take place?
ILLO:	Now—now—ere they can ward and parry it!
WALLENSTEIN	(*looking at the paper of signatures*):
	I have the Generals' words—a written promise!
	Max Piccolomini stands not here—how's that?
TERTSKY:	It was—he fancied—
ILLO:	Mere self-willedness.
	There needed no such thing 'twixt him and you.
WALLENSTEIN:	He is quite right—there needeth no such thing.
	The regiments, too, deny to march for Flanders—
	Have sent me in a paper of remonstrance,
	And openly resist the imperial orders.
	The first step to revolt's already taken.
ILLO:	Believe me, thou wilt find it far more easy
	To lead them over to the enemy
	Than to the Spaniard.
WALLENSTEIN:	I will hear, however,
	What the Swede has to say to me.
ILLO	(*eagerly to* TERTSKY): Go, call him!
	He stands without the door in waiting.
WALLENSTEIN:	Stay!
	Stay yet a little. It hath taken me
	All by surprise—it came too quick upon me;
	'Tis wholly novel that an accident,
	With its dark lordship, and blind agency,
	Shall force me on with it.
ILLO:	First hear him only,
	And after weigh it. [*Exeunt* TERTSKY *and* ILLO.

SCENE IV:

WALLENSTEIN	(*in soliloquy*): Is it possible?
	Is't so? I can no longer what I *would?*
	No longer draw back at my liking? I
	Must *do* the deed because I *thought* of it.
	And fed this heart here with a dream? Because
	I did not scowl temptation from my presence,

Dallied with thoughts of possible fulfilment,
Commenced no movement, left all time uncertain,
And only kept the road, the access open?
By the great God of Heaven! it was not
My serious meaning, it was ne'er resolve.
I but amused myself with thinking of it.
The free-will tempted me, the power to do
Or not to do it. Was it criminal
To make the fancy minister to hope,
To fill the air with pretty toys of air,
And clutch fantastic sceptres moving toward me?
Was not the will kept free? Beheld I not
The road of duty close beside me—but
One little step, and once more I was in it!
Where am I? Whither have I been transported?
No road, no track behind me, but a wall,
Impenetrable, insurmountable,
Rises obedient to the spells I muttered
And meant not—my own doings tower behind me.
                    [*Pauses and remains in deep thought.*
A punishable man I seem, the guilt,
Try what I will, I cannot roll off from me;
The equivocal demeanour of my life
Bears witness on my prosecutor's party;
And even my purest acts from purest motives
Suspicion poisons with malicious gloss.
Were I that thing for which I pass, that traitor,
A goodly outside I had sure reserved,
Had drawn the covering thick and double round me,
Been calm and chary of my utterance.
But being conscious of the innocence
Of my intent, my uncorrupted will,
I gave way to my humours, to my passion:
Bold were my words, because my deeds were *not*.
Now every planless measure, chance event,
The threat of rage, the vaunt of joy and triumph,
And all the May-games of a heart o'erflowing,
Will they connect, and weave them all together
Into one web of treason: all will be plain,
My eye ne'er absent from the far-off mark,
Step tracing step, each step a politic progress;
And out of all they'll fabricate a charge
So specious, that I must myself stand *dumb*.
I'm caught in my own net, and only force,
Nought but a sudden *rent*, can liberate me.   [*Pauses again.*
How else! since that the heart's unbiassed instinct
Impelled me to the daring deed, which now
Necessity, self-preservation, *orders*.

Stern is the on-look of necessity,
Not without shudder may a human hand
Grasp the mysterious urn of destiny.
My deed was mine, remaining in my bosom.
Once suffered to escape from its safe corner
Within the heart, its nursery and birth-place,
Sent forth into the foreign, it belongs
For ever to those sly malicious powers
Whom never art of man conciliated.

    [*Paces in agitation through the chamber, then pauses, and after
       the pause, breaks out again into audible soliloquy.*

What is thy enterprise? thy aim? thy object?
Hast honestly confessed it to thyself?
Power seated on a quiet throne thou'dst shake,
Power on an ancient consecrated throne,
Strong in possession, founded in old custom;
Power by a thousand tough and stringy roots
Fixed to the people's pious nursery-faith.
This, this will be no strife of strength with strength.
That feared I not. I brave each combatant,
Whom I can look on, fixing eye to eye,
Who full himself of courage kindles courage
In me too. 'Tis a foe invisible
The which I fear—a fearful enemy,
Which in the human heart opposes me,
By its coward fear alone made fearful to me.
Not that, which full of life, instinct with power,
Makes known its present being, that is not
The true, the perilously formidable.
O no! it is the common, the quite common,
The thing of an eternal yesterday.
What ever was, and ever more returns,
Sterling to-morrow, for to-day 'twas sterling!
For of the wholly common is man made,
And custom is his nurse! Woe then to them,
Who lay irreverent hands upon his old
House furniture, the dear inheritance
From his forefathers. For time consecrates;
And what is grey with age becomes religion.
Be in possession, and thou hast the right,
And sacred will the many guard it for thee!

                    [*To the* PAGE *who here enters.*

The Swedish officer? Well, let him enter.

    [*The* PAGE *exit,* WALLENSTEIN *fixes his eye in deep thought on
       the door.*

Yet is it pure—as yet! the crime has come
Not o'er this threshold yet—so slender is
The boundary that divideth life's two paths.

SCENE V: WALLENSTEIN *and* WRANGEL.

WALLENSTEIN   (*after having fixed a searching look on him*):
Your name is Wrangel?

WRANGEL: Gustavus Wrangel, General
Of the Sudermanian blues.

WALLENSTEIN: It was a Wrangel
Who injured me materially at Stralsund,
And by his brave resistance was the cause
Of th' opposition which that sea-port made.

WRANGEL: It was the doing of the element
With which you fought, my Lord! and not my merit.
The Baltic Neptune did assert his freedom;
The sea and land, it seemed, were not to serve
One and the same.

WALLENSTEIN   (*makes a motion for him to take a seat, and seats himself*):
And where are your credentials?
Come you provided with full powers, Sir General?

WRANGEL: There are so many scruples yet to solve—

WALLENSTEIN   (*having read the credentials*):
An able letter! Ay—he is a prudent,
Intelligent master, whom you serve, Sir General!
The Chancellor writes me, that he but fulfils
His late departed Sovereign's own idea
In helping me to the Bohemian crown

WRANGEL: He says the truth. Our great King, now in heaven,
Did ever deem most highly of your Grace's
Pre-eminent sense and military genius;
And always the commanding intellect,
He said, should have command, and be the King.

WALLENSTEIN: Yes, he *might* say it safely. General Wrangel,
[*taking his hand affectionately.*
Come, fair and open. Trust me, I was always
A Swede at heart. Ey! that did you experience
Both in Silesia and at Nuremburg;
I had you often in my power, and let you
Always slip out by some back door or other.
'Tis this for which the court can ne'er forgive me,
Which drives me to this present step: and since
Our interests so run in one direction,
E'en let us have a thorough confidence
Each in the other.

WRANGEL: Confidence will come,
Has each but only first security.

WALLENSTEIN: The Chancellor still, I see, does not quite trust me,
And I confess—the game does not lie wholly
To my advantage—Without doubt he thinks
If I can play false with the Emperor,

Who is my Sov'reign, I can do the like
With the enemy, and that *the one*, too, were
Sooner to be forgiven me than the *other*.
Is not this your opinion too, Sir General?

WRANGEL: I have here an office merely, no opinion.

WALLENSTEIN: The Emperor hath urged me to the uttermost.
I can no longer honourably serve him.
For my security in self-defence,
I take this hard step which my conscience blames.

WRANGEL: That I believe. So far would no one go
Who was not forced to it.   [*After a pause.*
                What may have impelled
Your princely Highness in this wise to act
Toward your Sovereign Lord and Emperor,
Beseems not us to expound or criticize.
The Swede is fighting for his good old cause,
With his good sword and conscience. This concurrence,
This opportunity, is in our favour,
And all advantages in war are lawful.
We take what offers without questioning;
And if all have its due and just proportions—

WALLENSTEIN: Of what then are ye doubting? Of my will?
Or of my power? I pledged me to the Chancellor,
Would he trust *me* with sixteen thousand men,
That I would instantly go over to them
With eighteen thousand of the Emperor's troops.

WRANGEL: Your Grace is known to be a mighty war-chief,
To be a second Attila and Pyrrhus.
'Tis talked of still with fresh astonishment,
How some years past, beyond all human faith,
You called an army forth, like a creation:
But yet—

WALLENSTEIN: But yet?

WRANGEL: But still the Chancellor thinks,
It might yet be an easier thing from nothing
To call forth sixty-thousand men of battle,
Than to persuade one sixtieth part of them—

WALLENSTEIN: What now? Out with it, friend!

WRANGEL: To break their oaths.

WALLENSTEIN: And he thinks so? He judges like a Swede,
And like a Protestant. You Lutherans
Fight for your Bible. You are int'rested
About the cause; and with your *hearts* you follow
Your banners. Among *you*, whoe'er deserts
To the enemy, hath broken covenant
With two Lords at one time. We've no such fancies.

WRANGEL: Great God in Heaven! Have then the people here
No house and home, no fire-side, no altar?

511

WALLENSTEIN: I will explain that to you, how it stands—
The Austrian *has* a country, ay, and loves it,
And has good cause to love it—but this army
That calls itself th' Imperial, this that houses
Here in Bohemia, this has none—no country;
This is an outcast of all foreign lands,
Unclaimed by town or tribe, to whom belongs
Nothing, except the universal sun.

WRANGEL: But then the nobles and the officers?
Such a desertion, such a felony,
It is without example, my Lord Duke,
In the world's history.

WALLENSTEIN: They all are mine—
Mine unconditionally—mine on all terms.
Not me, your own eyes you may trust.
[*He gives him the paper containing the written oath.* WRANGEL
*reads it through, and having read it, lays it on the table
remaining silent.*
So then?
Now comprehend you?

WRANGEL: Comprehend, who can?
My Lord Duke! I will let the mask drop—yes!
I've full powers for a final settlement.
The Rhinegrave stands but four days' march from here
With fifteen thousand men, and only waits
For orders to proceed and join your army.
These orders *I* give out, immediately
We're compromised.

WALLENSTEIN: What asks the Chancellor?

WRANGEL (*considerately*):
Twelve regiments, every man a Swede—my head
The warranty—and all might prove at last
Only false play—

WALLENSTEIN (*starting*): Sir Swede!

WRANGEL (*calmly proceeding*): Am therefore forced
T' insist thereon, that he do formally,
Irrevocably break with th' Emperor,
Else not a Swede is trusted to Duke Friedland.

WALLENSTEIN: Come, brief and open! what is the demand?

WRANGEL: That he forthwith disarm the Spanish reg'ments
Attached to th' Emperor, that he seize Prague,
And to the Swedes give up that city, with
The strong pass Egra.

WALLENSTEIN: That is much indeed!
Prague! Egra's granted—But—but Prague! 'Twon't do.
I give you every security
Which you may ask of me in common reason—
But Prague—Bohemia—these, Sir General,

I can myself protect.

WRANGEL: We doubt it not.

But 'tis not the protection that is now
Our sole concern. We want security,
That we shall not expend our men and money
All to no purpose.

WALLENSTEIN: 'Tis but reasonable.

WRANGEL: And till we are indemnified, so long
Stays Prague in pledge.

WALLENSTEIN: Then trust you us so little?

WRANGEL *(rising)*:
The Swede, if he would treat well with the German,
Must keep a sharp look-out. We have been called
Over the Baltic, we have saved the empire
From ruin—with our best blood have we sealed
The liberty of faith, and gospel truth.
But now already is the benefaction
No longer felt, the load alone is felt—
Ye look askance with evil eye upon us,
As foreigners, intruders in the empire,
And would fain send us, with some paltry sum
Of money, home again to our old forests.
No, no! my Lord Duke! no! it never was
For Judas' pay, for chinking gold and silver,
That we did leave our King by the Great Stone.*
No, not for gold and silver have there bled
So many of our Swedish nobles—neither
Will we, with empty laurels for our payment,
Hoist sail for our own country. *Citizens*
Will we remain upon the soil, the which
Our monarch conquered for himself, and died.

WALLENSTEIN: Help to keep down the common enemy,
And the fair border land must needs be yours.

WRANGEL: But when the common enemy lies vanquished,
Who knits together our new friendship then!
We know, Duke Friedland! though perhaps the Swede
Ought not t' have known it, that you carry on
Secret negotiations with the Saxons.
Who is our warranty, that *we* are not
The sacrifices in those articles
Which 'tis thought needful to conceal from us?

WALLENSTEIN *(rises)*:
Think you of something better, Gustave Wrangel!
Of Prague no more.

WRANGEL: Here my commission ends.

---

* A great stone near Lützen, since called the Swede's Stone, the body of their great king
having been found at the foot of it, after the battle in which he lost his life.

WALLENSTEIN: Surrender up to you my capital!
　　　　　Far liever would I face about, and step
　　　　　Back to my Emperor.
WRANGEL: 　　　　　　　　　　If time yet permits—
WALLENSTEIN: That lies with me, even now, at any hour.
WRANGEL: Some days ago, perhaps. To-day, no longer;
　　　　　No longer since Sesina's been a prisoner.
　　　　　　　　　[WALLENSTEIN *is struck, and silenced.*
　　　　　My Lord Duke, hear me—We believe that you
　　　　　At present do mean honourably by us.
　　　　　Since *yesterday* we're sure of that—and now
　　　　　This paper warrants for the troops, there's nothing
　　　　　Stands in the way of our full confidence.
　　　　　Prague shall not part us. Hear! The Chancellor
　　　　　Contents himself with Albstadt; to your Grace
　　　　　He gives up Ratschin and the narrow side,
　　　　　But Egra, above all, must open to us,
　　　　　Ere we can think of any junction.
WALLENSTEIN: 　　　　　　　　　　　　　You,
　　　　　You therefore must I trust, and you not me?
　　　　　I will consider of your proposition.
WRANGEL: I must entreat that your consideration
　　　　　Occupy not too long a time. Already
　　　　　Has this negotiation, my Lord Duke!
　　　　　Crept on into the second year. If nothing
　　　　　Is settled this time, will the Chancellor
　　　　　Consider it as broken off for ever.
WALLENSTEIN: Ye press me hard. A measure, such as this,
　　　　　Ought to be *thought* of.
WRANGEL: 　　　　　　　　　　Ay! but think of this too,
　　　　　That sudden action only can procure it
　　　　　Success—think first of this, your Highness.　　　[*Exit* WRANGEL.

SCENE VI: WALLENSTEIN, TERTSKY *and* ILLO (*re-enter*).

ILLO: Is't all right?
TERTSKY: 　　　　　　Are you compromised?
ILLO: 　　　　　　　　　　　　　　This Swede
　　　　Went smiling from you. Yes! you're compromised.
WALLENSTEIN: As yet is nothing settled: and (well weighed)
　　　　I feel myself inclined to leave it so.
TERTSKY: How? What is that?
WALLENSTEIN: 　　　　　　　　Come on me what will come,
　　　　The doing evil to avoid an evil
　　　　Cannot be good!
TERTSKY: 　　　　　　　Nay, but bethink you, Duke?
WALLENSTEIN: To live upon the mercy of these Swedes!
　　　　Of these proud-hearted Swedes! I could not bear it.

ILLO: Goest thou as fugitive, as mendicant?
                    Bring'st thou not more to them than thou receiv'st?

SCENE VII: *To these enter the* COUNTESS TERTSKY.

WALLENSTEIN: Who sent for you? There is no business here
                    For women.
COUNTESS: I am come to bid you joy.
WALLENSTEIN: Use thy authority, Tertsky, bid her go.
COUNTESS: Come I perhaps too early? I hope not.
WALLENSTEIN: Set not this tongue upon me, I entreat you,
                    You know it is the weapon that destroys me.
                    I am routed, if a woman but attack me.
                    I cannot traffic in the trade of words
                    With that unreasoning sex.
COUNTESS: I had already
                    Given the Bohemians a king.
WALLENSTEIN (*sarcastically*):   They have one,
                    In consequence, no doubt.
COUNTESS (*to the others*):   Ha! what new scruple?
TERTSKY: The Duke will not.
COUNTESS: He *will not* what he *must!*
ILLO: It lies with you now. Try. For I am silenced,
              When folks begin to talk to me of conscience,
              And of fidelity.
COUNTESS: How? then, when all
              Lay in the far-off distance, when the road
              Stretched out before thine eyes interminably,
              Then hadst thou courage and resolve; and now,
              Now that the dream is being realized,
              The purpose ripe, the issue ascertained,
              Dost thou begin to play the dastard now?
              Planned merely, 'tis a common felony;
              Accomplished, an immortal undertaking;
              And with success comes pardon hand in hand;
              For all event is God's arbitrement.
SERVANT (*enters*):
              The Colonel Piccolomini.
COUNTESS (*hastily*):   Must wait.
WALLENSTEIN: I cannot see him now. Another time.
SERVANT: But for two minutes he entreats an audience;
              Of the most urgent nature is his business.
WALLENSTEIN: Who knows what he may bring us? I will hear him.
COUNTESS (*laughs*):
              Urgent for him, no doubt; but thou may'st wait.
WALLENSTEIN: What is it?
COUNTESS: Thou shalt be informed hereafter.
              First let the Swede and thee be compromised.   [*Exit* SERVANT.

WALLENSTEIN: If there were yet a choice; if yet some milder
Way of escape were possible—I still
Will choose it, and avoid the last extreme.

COUNTESS: Desirest thou nothing further? Such a way
Lies still before thee. Send this Wrangel off.
Forget thou thy old hopes, cast far away
All thy past life; determine to commence
A new one. Virtue hath her heroes too,
As well as Fame and Fortune. To Vienna—
Hence—to the Emperor—kneel before the throne;
Take a full coffer with thee—say aloud,
Thou didst but wish to prove thy fealty;
Thy whole intention but to dupe the Swede.

ILLO: For that, too, 'tis too late. They know too much.
He would but bear his own head to the block.

COUNTESS: I fear not that. They have not evidence
To attaint him legally, and they avoid
The avowal of an arbitrary power.
They'll let the Duke resign without disturbance.
I see how all will end. The king of Hungary
Makes his appearance, and 'twill of itself
Be understood, that then the Duke retires.
There will not want a formal declaration.
The young King will administer the oath
To the whole army; and so all returns
To the old position. On some morrow morning
The Duke departs; and now 'tis stir and bustle
Within his castles. He will hunt, and build,
Superintend his horses' pedigrees,
Creates himself a court, gives golden keys,
And introduceth strictest ceremony
In fine proportions, and nice etiquette;
Keeps open table with high cheer; in brief
Commenceth mighty king—in miniature.
And while he prudently demeans himself,
And gives himself no actual importance,
He will be let appear whate'er he likes;
And who dares doubt, the Friedland will appear
A mighty Prince to his last dying hour?
Well now, what then? Duke Friedland is as others,
A fire-new Noble, whom the war hath raised
To price and currency, a Jonah's gourd,
An over-night creation of court-favour,
Which with an undistinguishable ease
Makes Baron or makes Prince.

WALLENSTEIN (*in extreme agitation*): Take her away.
Let in the young Count Piccolomini.

COUNTESS: Art thou in earnest? I entreat thee! Canst thou

Consent to bear thyself to thy own grave,
So ignominiously to be dried up?
Thy life, that arrogated such a height,
To end in such a nothing! To be nothing,
When one was always nothing, is an evil
That asks no stretch of patience, a light evil;
But to become a nothing, having been—

WALLENSTEIN (*starts up in violent agitation*):
Show me a way out of this stifling crowd,
Ye Powers of aidance? Show me such a way
As *I* am capable of going. I
Am no tongue-hero, no fine virtue-prattler;
I cannot warm by thinking! cannot say
To the good luck that turns her back upon me,
Magnanimously: 'Go! I need thee not.'
Cease I to work, I am annihilated.
Dangers nor sacrifices will I shun,
If so I may avoid the last extreme;
But ere I sink down into nothingness,
Leave off so little, who begun so great,
Ere that the world confuses me with those
Poor wretches, whom a day creates and crumbles,
This age and after-ages speak my name
With hate and dread; and Friedland be redemption
For each accursed deed!

COUNTESS: What is there here, then,
So against nature? Help me to perceive it!
O let not Superstition's nightly goblins
Subdue thy clear bright spirit! Art thou bid
To murder? with abhorred, accursed poniard,
To violate the breasts that nourished thee?
That *were* against our nature, that might aptly
Make thy flesh shudder, and thy whole heart sicken;
Yet not a few, and for a meaner object,
Have ventured even this, ay, and performed it.
What is there in thy case so black and monstrous?
Thou art accused of treason—whether with
Or without justice, is not now the question—
Thou'rt lost if thou dost not avail thee quickly
Of the power which thou possessest. Friedland! *Duke!*
Tell me, where lives that thing so meek and tame,
That doth not all his living faculties
Put forth in preservation of his life?
What deed so daring, which necessity
And desperation will not sanctify?

WALLENSTEIN: Once was this Ferdinand so gracious to me:
He loved me; he esteemed me; I was placed
The nearest to his heart. Full many a time

517

We, like familiar friends, both at one table,
Have banquetted together. He and I—
And the young kings themselves held me the basin
Wherewith to wash me—and is't come to this?

COUNTESS: So faithfully preserv'st thou each small favour,
And hast no memory for contumelies?
Must I remind thee how at Regensburg
This man repaid thy faithful services?
All ranks and all conditions in the empire
Thou hadst wronged, to make him great, hadst loaded on thee,
On *thee*, the hate, the curse of the whole world
No friend existed for thee in all Germany,
And why? because thou hadst existed only
For th' Emperor. To th' Emperor alone
Clung Friedland in that storm which gathered round him.
At Regensburg in the Diet—and he dropped thee!
He let thee fall! He let thee fall! a victim
To the Bavarian, to that insolent!
Deposed, stript bare of all thy dignity
And power, amid the taunting of thy foes,
Thou wert let drop into obscurity.
Say not, the restoration of thy honour
Has made atonement for that first injustice.
No honest good-will was it that replaced thee,
The law of hard necessity replaced thee,
Which they had fain opposed, but that they could not.

WALLENSTEIN: Not to their good wishes, that is certain,
Nor yet to his affection I'm indebted
For this high office; and if I abuse it,
I shall therein abuse no confidence.

COUNTESS: Affection! confidence! They *needed* thee.
Necessity, impetuous remonstrant!
Who not with empty names, or shows of proxy,
Is served, who'll have the thing and not the symbol,
Ever seeks out the greatest and the best,
And at the rudder places *him*, e'en though
She had been forced to take him from the rabble,
She, this Necessity, it was that placed thee
In this high office, it was she that gave thee
Thy letters patent of inauguration.
For, to the uttermost moment that they can,
This race still help themselves at cheapest rate
With slavish souls, with puppets! At the approach
Of extreme peril, when a hollow image
Is found a hollow image and no more,
Then falls the power into the mighty hands
Of nature, of the spirit giant-born,
Who listens only to himself, knows nothing

Of stipulation, duties, reverences;
And, like th' emancipated force of fire,
Unmastered scorches, ere it reaches them,
Their fine-spun webs, their artificial policy.

WALLENSTEIN: 'Tis true! they saw me always as I am—
Always! I did not cheat them in the bargain.
I never held it worth my pains to hide
The bold, all-grasping habit of my soul.

COUNTESS: Nay rather—thou hast ever shown thyself
A formidable man, without restraint;
Hast exercised the full prerogatives
Of thy impetuous nature, which had been
Once granted to thee. Therefore, Duke, not *thou*,
Who hast still remained consistent with thyself,
But *they* are in the wrong, who fearing thee,
Intrusted such a power in hands they feared.
For, by the laws of spirit, in the right
Is every individual character
That acts in strict consistence with itself.
Self-contradiction is the only wrong.
Wert thou another being, then, when thou
Eight years ago pursued'st thy march with fire
And sword, and desolation, through the circles
Of Germany, the universal scourge,
Didst mock all ordinances of the Empire,
The fearful rights of strength alone exerted'st,
Trampled'st to earth each rank, each magistracy,
All to extend thy Sultan's domination?
Then was the time to break thee in, to curb
Thy haughty will, to teach thee ordinance.
But no! the Emperor felt no touch of conscience,
What served him pleased him, and without a murmur
He stamped his broad seal on these lawless deeds.
What at that time was right, because thou didst it
For him, to-day is all at once become
Opprobrious, foul, because it is directed
Against him. O most flimsy superstition!

WALLENSTEIN (*rising*):
I never saw it in this light before.
'Tis even so. The Emperor perpetrated
Deeds through my arm, deeds most unorderly.
And even this prince's mantle, which I wear,
I owe to what were services to him,
But most high misdemeanours 'gainst the Empire.

COUNTESS: Then betwixt thee and him (confess it, Friedland!)
The point can be no more of right and duty,
Only of power and th' opportunity.
That opportunity, lo! it comes yonder,

519

Approaching with swift steeds; then with a swing
Throw thyself up into the chariot-seat,
Seize with firm hand the reins, ere thy opponent
Anticipate thee, and himself make conquest
Of the now empty seat. The moment comes,
It is already here, when thou must write
The absolute total of thy life's vast sum.
The constellations stand victorious o'er thee,
The planets shoot good fortune in fair junctions,
And tell thee, 'Now's the time!' The starry courses
Hast thou thy life long measured to no purpose?
The quadrant and the circle, were they playthings?
                              [*pointing to the different objects in the room.*
The zodiacs, the rolling orbs of heaven,
Hast pictured on these walls, and all around thee,
In dumb, foreboding symbols hast thou placed
These seven presiding lords of destiny—
For toys? Is all this preparation nothing?
Is there no marrow in this hollow art,
That even to thyself it doth avail
Nothing, and has no influence over thee
In the great moment of decision?

WALLENSTEIN   (*during this last speech walks up and down with inward struggles,
labouring with passions; stops suddenly, stands still, then
interrupting the* COUNTESS):
Send Wrangel to me—I will instantly
Despatch three couriers—

ILLO   (*hurrying out*):   God in heaven be praised!

WALLENSTEIN: It is *his* evil genius and *mine*.
Our evil genius! It chastises *him*
Through me, the instrument of his ambition;
And I expect no less than that revenge
E'en now is whetting for *my* breast the poniard.
Who sows the serpent's teeth, let him not hope
To reap a joyous harvest. Every crime
Has, in the moment of its perpetration,
Its own avenging angel—dark misgiving,
An ominous sinking at the inmost heart.
He can no longer trust me. Then no longer
Can I retreat—so come that which must come,
Still destiny preserves its due relations;
The heart within us is its absolute
Vicegerent.   [*to* TERTSKY.
      Go, conduct your Gustave Wrangel
To my state-cabinet. Myself will speak to
The couriers. And despatch immediately
A servant for Octavio Piccolomini.
            [*to the* COUNTESS, *who cannot conceal her triumph.*

No exultation! woman, triumph not!
For jealous are the powers of destiny
Joy premature, and shouts ere victory,
Encroach upon their rights and privileges.
We sow the seed, and they the growth determine.
                        [*While he is making his exit, the curtain drops.*

ACT V

SCENE I: *Scene as in the preceding Act.* WALLENSTEIN, OCTAVIO
            PICCOLOMINI.

WALLENSTEIN   (*coming forward in conversation*):
               He sends me word from Linz, that he lies sick;
               But I have sure intelligence, that he
               Secretes himself at Frauenberg with Galas.
               Secure them both, and send them to me hither.
               Remember, thou tak'st on thee the command
               Of those same Spanish regiments, constantly
               Make preparation, and be never ready;
               And if they urge thee to draw out against me,
               Still answer *yes,* and stand as thou wert fettered.
               I know, that it is doing thee a service
               To keep thee out of action in this business.
               Thou lov'st to linger on in fair appearances;
               Steps of extremity are not thy province,
               Therefore have I sought out this part for thee
               Thou wilt this time be of most service to me
               By thy inertness. The mean time, if fortune
               Declare itself on my side, thou wilt know
               What is to do.   [*Enter* MAX PICCOLOMINI.
                        Now go, Octavio.
               This night must thou be off, take my own horses:
               Him here I keep with me—make short farewell—
               Trust me. I think we all shall meet again
               In joy and thriving fortunes.
OCTAVIO   (*to his son*):   I shall see you
               Yet ere I go.

SCENE II: WALLENSTEIN, MAX PICCOLOMINI.

MAX   (*advances to him*):
               My General!
WALLENSTEIN: That am I no longer, if
               Thou styl'st thyself the Emperor's officer.
MAX: Then thou wilt leave the army, General?
WALLENSTEIN: I have renounced the service of the Emperor.

MAX:	And thou wilt leave the army?
WALLENSTEIN:	Rather hope I

To bind it nearer still and faster to me.   [*He seats himself.*
Yes, Max, I have delayed to open it to thee,
Even till the hour of acting 'gins to strike.
Youth's fortunate feeling doth seize easily
The absolute right, yea, and a joy it is
To exercise the single apprehension
Where the sums square in proof;
But where it happens, that of two sure evils
One must be taken, where the heart not wholly
Brings itself back from out the strife of duties,
There 'tis a blessing to have no election,
And blank necessity is grace and favour.
This is now present: do not look behind thee—
It can no more avail thee. Look thou forwards!
Think not! judge not! prepare thyself to act!
The Court—it hath determined on my ruin,
Therefore I will to be beforehand with them.
We'll join the Swedes—right gallant fellows are they,
And our good friends.

        [*He stops himself, expecting* PICCOLOMINI'S *answer.*
I have ta'en thee by surprise. Answer me not.
I grant thee time to recollect thyself.

        [*He rises, and retires to the back of the stage.* MAX *remains for*
        a long time motionless, in a trance of excessive anguish. At
        his first motion WALLENSTEIN *returns, and places himself*
        before him.

MAX: My General, this day thou makest me
Of age to speak in my own right and person,
For till this day I have been spared the trouble
To find out my own road. Thee have I followed
With most implicit, unconditional faith,
Sure of the right path if I followed thee.
To-day, for the first time, dost thou refer
Me to myself, and forcest me to make
Election between thee and my own heart.

WALLENSTEIN: Soft cradled thee thy fortune till to-day:
Thy duties thou could'st exercise in sport,
Indulge all lovely instincts, act for ever
With undivided heart. It can remain
No longer thus. Like enemies, the roads
Start from each other. Duties strive with duties.
Thou must needs choose thy party in the war
Which is now kindling 'twixt thy friend and him
Who is thy Emperor.

MAX: War! is that the name?
War is as frightful as heaven's pestilence,

Yet it is good, is it heaven's will as that is.
Is that a good war, which against the Emperor
Thou wagest with the Emperor's own army?
O God of Heaven! what a change is this.
Beseems it me to offer such persuasion
To thee, who, like the fixed star of the pole,
Wert all I gazed at on life's trackless ocean?
O! what a rent thou makest in my heart!
The ingrained instinct of old reverence,
The holy habit of obediency,
Must I pluck life asunder from thy name?
Nay, do not turn thy countenance upon me—
It always was a god looking at me!
Duke Wallenstein, its power is not departed:
The senses still are in thy bonds; although,
Bleeding, the soul hath freed itself.

WALLENSTEIN: Max hear me.

MAX: O! do it not, I pray thee, do it not!
There is a pure and noble soul within thee,
Knows not of this unblest, unlucky doing.
Thy will is chaste, it is thy fancy only
Which hath polluted thee—and innocence,
It will not let itself be driven away
From that world-awing aspect. Thou wilt not,
Thou canst not end in this. It would reduce
All human creatures to disloyalty
Against the nobleness of their own nature.
'Twill justify the vulgar misbelief,
Which holdeth nothing noble in free will,
And trusts itself to impotence alone,
Made powerful only in an unknown power.

WALLENSTEIN: The world will judge me sternly; I expect it.
Already have I said to my own self
All thou canst say to me. Who but avoids
Th' extreme—can he by going round avoid it?
But here there is no choice. Yes—I must use
Or suffer violence—so stands the case,
There remains nothing possible but that.

MAX: O that is never possible for thee!
'Tis the last desperate resource of those
Cheap souls, to whom their honour, their good name,
Is their poor *saving*, their last worthless *keep*,
Which having staked and lost, they stake themselves
In the mad rage of gaming. Thou art rich,
And glorious: with an unpolluted heart
Thou canst make conquest of whate'er seems highest!
But he, who once hath acted infamy,
Does nothing more in this world.

WALLENSTEIN (*grasps his hand*):   Calmly, Max!
Much that is great and excellent will we
Perform together yet. And if we only
Stand on the height with dignity, 'tis soon
Forgotten, Max, by what road we ascended.
Believe me, many a crown shines spotless now,
That yet was deeply sullied in the winning.
To the evil spirit doth the earth belong,
Not to the good. All that the powers divine
Send from above, are universal blessings:
Their light rejoices us, their air refreshes,
But never yet was man enriched by them:
In their eternal realm no *property*
Is to be struggled for—all there is general.
The jewel, the all-valued gold we win
From the deceiving powers, depraved in nature,
That dwell beneath the day and blessed sun-light.
Not without sacrifices are they rendered
Propitious, and there lives no soul on earth
That e'er retired unsullied from their service.

MAX: Whate'er is human, to the human being
Do I allow—and to the vehement
And striving spirit readily I pardon
Th' excess of action; but to thee, my General!
Above *all* others make I large concession,
For thou must move a world, and be the master—
He kills thee, who condemns thee to inaction.
So be it then! maintain thee in thy post
By violence. Resist the Emperor,
And if it must be, force with force repel:
I will not praise it, yet I can forgive it.
But not—not to the *traitor*—yes! the word
Is spoken out—
Not to the traitor can I yield a pardon.
That is no mere excess! that is no error
Of human nature—that is wholly different,
O that is black, black as the pit of hell!
                    [WALLENSTEIN *betrays a sudden agitation.*
Thou canst not hear it *named*, and wilt thou *do* it?
O turn back to thy duty. That thou canst
I hold it certain. Send me to Vienna.
I'll make thy peace for thee with th' Emperor.
He knows thee not. But I do know thee. He
Shall see thee, Duke! with my unclouded eye,
And I bring back his confidence to thee.

WALLENSTEIN: It is too late. Thou know'st not what has happened.

MAX: Were it too late, and were it gone so far,
That a crime only could prevent thy fall,

Then—fall! fall honourably, even as thou stood'st.
Lose the command. Go from the stage of war.
Thou canst with splendour do it—do it too
With innocence. Thou hast lived much for others,
At length live thou for thy own self. I follow thee.
My destiny I never part from thine.

WALLENSTEIN: It is too late! Even now, while thou art losing
Thy words, one after the other are the mile-stones
Left fast behind by my post couriers,
Who bear the order on to Prague and Egra.

> [MAX *stands as convulsed, with a gesture and countenance*
> *expressing the most intense anguish.*

Yield thyself to it. We act as we are forced.
I cannot give assent to my own shame
And ruin. *Thou*—no—thou canst not forsake me!
So let us do, what must be done, with dignity,
With a firm step. What am I doing worse
Than did famed Cæsar at the Rubicon,
When he the legions led against his country,
The which his country had delivered to him?
Had he thrown down the sword he had been lost,
As I were, if I but disarmed myself.
I trace out something in me of his spirit.
Give me his luck, *that other thing* I'll bear.

> [MAX *quits him abruptly.* WALLENSTEIN, *startled and*
> *overpowered, continues looking after him, and*
> *is still in this posture when* TERTSKY *enters.*

SCENE III: WALLENSTEIN, TERTSKY.

TERTSKY: Max Piccolomini just left you?
WALLENSTEIN: Where is Wrangel?
TERTSKY: He is already gone.
WALLENSTEIN;   In such a hurry?
TERTSKY: It is as if the earth had swallowed him.
He had scarce left thee when I went to seek him.
I wished some words with him—but he was gone.
How, when, and where, could no one tell me. Nay,
I half believe it was the devil himself;
A human creature could not so at once
Have vanished.
ILLO *(enters):*   Is it true that thou wilt send Octavio?
TERTSKY: How, Octavio! Whither send him?
WALLENSTEIN: He goes to Frauenberg, and will lead hither
The Spanish and Italian regiments.
ILLO: No!
Nay, Heaven forbid!

WALLENSTEIN:	And why should Heaven forbid?
ILLO:	Him! that deceiver! Would'st thou trust to him
	The soldiery? Him wilt thou let slip from thee,
	Now, in the very instant that decides us—
TERTSKY:	Thou wilt not do this! No! I pray thee, no!
WALLENSTEIN:	Ye are whimsical.
ILLO:	O but for this time, Duke,
	Yield to our warning! Let him not depart.
WALLENSTEIN:	And why should I not trust him only this time,
	Who have always trusted him? What, then, has happened
	That I should lose my good opinion of him?
	In complaisance to your whims, not my own,
	I must, forsooth, give up a rooted judgment.
	Think not I am a woman. Having trusted him
	E'en till to-day, to-day too will I trust him.
TERTSKY:	Must it be he—he only? Send another.
WALLENSTEIN:	It must be he, whom I myself have chosen!
	He is well fitted for the business. Therefore
	I gave it him.
ILLO:	Because he's an Italian—
	Therefore is he well fitted for the business.
WALLENSTEIN:	I know you love them not—nor sire nor son—
	Because that I esteem them, love them—visibly
	Esteem them, love them more than you and others,
	E'en as they merit. Therefore are they eye-blights,
	Thorns in your footpath. But your jealousies,
	In what affect they me or my concerns?
	Are they the worse to *me,* because you hate them?
	Love or hate one another as you will,
	I leave to each man his own moods and likings;
	Yet know the worth of each of you to me.
ILLO:	Von Questenberg, while he was here, was always
	Lurking about with this Octavio.
WALLENSTEIN:	It happened with my knowledge and permission.
ILLO:	I know that secret messengers came to him
	From Galas—
WALLENSTEIN:	That's not true.
ILLO:	O thou art blind,
	With thy deep-seeing eyes.
WALLENSTEIN:	Thou wilt not shake
	My faith for me—my faith which founds itself
	On the profoundest science. If 'tis false,
	Then the whole science of the stars is false.
	For know, I have a pledge from fate itself,
	That he is the most faithful of my friends.
ILLO:	Hast thou a pledge, that this pledge is not false?
WALLENSTEIN:	There exist moments in the life of man,
	When he is nearer the great Soul of the world

Than is man's custom, and possesses freely
The power of questioning his destiny:
And such a moment 'twas, when in the night
Before the action in the plains of Lützen,
Leaning against a tree, thoughts crowding thoughts,
I looked out far upon the ominous plain.
My whole life, past and future, in this moment
Before my mind's eye glided in procession,
And to the destiny of the next morning
The spirit, filled with anxious presentiment,
Did knit the most removed futurity.
Then said I also to myself, 'So many
Dost thou command. They follow all thy stars,
And as on some great number set their all
Upon thy single head, and only man
The vessel of thy fortune. Yet a day
Will come, when Destiny shall once more scatter
All these in many a several direction:
Few be they who will stand out faithful to thee.'
I yearned to know which one was faithfullest
Of all this camp included. Great Destiny,
Give me a sign! And he shall be the man,
Who, on th' approaching morning, comes the first
To meet me with some token of his love:
And thinking this, I fell into a slumber.
Then midmost in the battle was I led
In spirit. Great the pressure and the tumult!
Then was my horse killed under me: I sank;
And over me away, all unconcernedly,
Drove horse and rider—and thus trod to pieces
I lay, and panted like a dying man.
Then seized me suddenly a saviour arm.
It was Octavio's—I awoke at once.
'Twas broad day, and *Octavio* stood before me.
'My brother,' said he, 'do not ride to-day
The dapple, as you're wont; but mount the horse
Which I have chosen for thee. Do it, brother!
In love to me. A strong dream warned me so.'
It was the swiftness of this horse that snatched me
From the hot pursuit of Bannier's dragoons.
My cousin rode the dapple on that day,
And never more saw I or horse or rider.

ILLO: That was a chance.

WALLENSTEIN (*significantly*): There's no such thing as chance.
In brief, 'tis signed and sealed that this Octavio
Is my good angel—and now no word more. [*He is retiring.*

TERTSKY: This is my comfort—Max remains our hostage.

ILLO: And he shall never stir from here alive.

WALLENSTEIN (*stops, and turns himself round*):
Are ye not like the women, who for ever
Only recur to their first word, altho'
One had been talking reason by the hour?
Know, that the human being's thoughts and deeds
Are not, like ocean billows, blindly moved.
The inner world, his microcosmus, is
The deep shaft, out of which they spring eternally,
They grow by certain laws, like the tree's fruit—
No juggling chance can metamorphose them.
Have I the human *kernel* first examined?
Then I know, too, the future will and action.

SCENE IV: *Scene—a chamber in Piccolomini's dwelling-house.* OCTAVIO
PICCOLOMINI, ISOLANI, (*entering*).

ISOLANI: Here am I—Well! who comes yet of the others?
OCTAVIO (*with an air of mystery*):
But, first, a word with you, Count Isolani.
ISOLANI (*assuming the same air of mystery*):
Will it explode, ha? Is the Duke about
To make th' attempt? In me, friend, you may place
Full confidence. Nay, put me to the proof.
OCTAVIO: That may happen.
ISOLANI: Noble brother, I am
Not one of those men who in words are valiant,
And when it comes to action skulk away.
The Duke has acted towards me as a friend.
God knows it is so; and I owe him all—
He may rely on my fidelity.
OCTAVIO: That will be seen hereafter.
ISOLANI: Be on your guard.
All think not as I think; and there are many
Who still hold with the Court—yes, and they say
That those stolen signatures bind them to nothing.
OCTAVIO: I am rejoiced to hear it.
ISOLANI: You rejoice!
OCTAVIO: That the Emperor hath yet such gallant servants
And loving friends.
ISOLANI: Nay, jeer not, I entreat you.
They are no such worthless fellows, I assure you.
OCTAVIO: I am assured already. God forbid
That I should jest! In very serious earnest
I am rejoiced to see an honest cause
So strong.
ISOLANI: The devil! what! why, what means this?
Are you not, then—For what, then, am I here?
OCTAVIO: That you may make full declaration, whether

You will be called the friend or enemy
Of th' Emperor.

ISOLANI *(with an air of defiance):*

                That declaration, friend,
I'll make to him in whom a right is placed
To put that question to me.

OCTAVIO:

                        Whether, Count,
That right is mine, this paper may instruct you.

ISOLANI *(stammering):*

Why—why—what! this is the Emperor's hand and seal?

                                                [*Reads.*

'Whereas the officers collectively
Throughout our army will obey the orders
Of the Lieutenant-General Piccolomini,
As from ourselves.' *Hem!* Yes! so! Yes! yes!
I—I give you joy, Lieutenant-General!

OCTAVIO: And you, submit you to the order?

ISOLANI: I—
But you have taken me so by surprise—
Time for reflection one *must* have—

OCTAVIO: Two minutes.

ISOLANI: My God! But then the case is—

OCTAVIO: Plain and simple.
You must declare you, whether you determine
To act a treason 'gainst your Lord and Sovereign,
Or whether you will serve him faithfully.

ISOLANI: Treason! My God! But who talks then of treason?

OCTAVIO: That is the case. The Prince-duke is a traitor—
Means to lead over to the enemy
The Emperor's army. Now, Count! brief and full—
Say will you break your oath to th' Emperor?
Sell yourself to the enemy? Say, will you?

ISOLANI: What mean you? I—I break my oath, d'ye say,
To his Imperial Majesty.
Did I say so? When, when have I said that?

OCTAVIO: You have not said it yet—not yet. This instant
I wait to hear, Count, whether you *will* say it.

ISOLANI: Ay! that delights me now, that you yourself
Bear witness for me that I never said so.

OCTAVIO: And you renounce the Duke then?

ISOLANI: If he's planning
Treason—why, treason breaks all bonds asunder.

OCTAVIO: And are determined, too, to fight against him?

ISOLANI: He has done me service—but if he's a villain,
Perdition seize him! All scores are rubbed off.

OCTAVIO: I am rejoiced that you're so well disposed.
This night break off in th' utmost secrecy
With all the light-armed troops—it must appear

As came the order from the Duke himself.
At Frauenberg's the place of rendezvous;
There will Count Galas give you further orders.

ISOLANI: It shall be done. But you'll remember me
With th' Emperor—how well-disposed you found me.

OCTAVIO: I will not fail to mention it honourably.

[*Exit* ISOLANI. *A* SERVANT *enters.*

What, Colonel Butler! Show him up.

ISOLANI (*returning*):
Forgive me, too, my bearish ways, old father!
Lord God! how should I know, then, what a great
Person I had before me.

OCTAVIO: No excuses.

ISOLANI: I am a merry lad, and if at times
A rash word might escape me 'gainst the court
Amidst my wine—you know no harm was meant. [*Exit.*

OCTAVIO: You need not be uneasy on that score.
That has succeeded. Fortune favour us
With all the others only but as much!

SCENE V: OCTAVIO PICCOLOMINI, BUTLER.

BUTLER: At your command, Lieutenant-General.

OCTAVIO: Welcome, as honoured friend and visitor.

BUTLER: You do me too much honour.

OCTAVIO (*after both have seated themselves*):
You have not
Returned the advances which I made you yesterday—
Misunderstood them, as mere empty forms.
That wish proceeded from my heart—I was
In earnest with you—for 'tis now a time
In which the honest should unite most closely.

BUTLER: 'Tis only the like-minded can unite.

OCTAVIO: True! and I name all honest men like-minded.
I never charge a man but with those acts
To which his character deliberately
Impels him; for alas! the violence
Of blind misunderstandings often thrusts
The very best of us from the right track.
You came thro' Frauenberg. Did the Count Galas
Say nothing to you? Tell me. He's my friend.

BUTLER: His words were lost on *me*.

OCTAVIO: It grieves me sorely
To hear it, for his counsel was most wise.
I had myself the like to offer.

BUTLER: Spare
Yourself the trouble—me th' embarrassment,
To have deserved so ill your good opinion.

OCTAVIO: The time is precious—let us talk openly.
You know how matters stand here. Wallenstein
Meditates treason—I can tell you further—
He has committed treason; but few hours
Have past, since he a covenant concluded
With th' enemy. The messengers are now
Full on their way to Egra and to Prague.
To-morrow he intends to lead us over
To th' enemy. But he deceives himself;
For prudence wakes—the Emperor has still
Many and faithful friends here, and they stand
In closest union, mighty tho' unseen.
This manifesto sentences the Duke—
Recalls the obedience of the army from him,
And summons all the loyal, all the honest,
To join and recognize in me their leader.
Choose—will you share with us an honest cause?
Or with the evil share an evil lot?

BUTLER *(rises)*: His lot is mine.

OCTAVIO: Is that your last resolve?

BUTLER: It is.

OCTAVIO: Nay, but bethink you, Colonel Butler!
As yet you have time. Within my faithful breast
That rashly uttered word remains interred.
Recall it, Butler! choose a better party.
You have not chosen the right one.

BUTLER *(going)*:   Any other
Commands for me, Lieutenant-General?

OCTAVIO: See your white hairs! Recall that word!

BUTLER: Farewell!

OCTAVIO: What would you draw this good and gallant sword
In such a cause? Into a curse would you
Transform the gratitude which you have earned
By forty years' fidelity from Austria?

BUTLER *(laughing with bitterness)*:
Gratitude from the house of Austria.   [*He is going.*

OCTAVIO *(permits him to go as far as the door, then calls after him)*:
Butler!

BUTLER: What wish you?

OCTAVIO: How was't with the Count?

BUTLER: Count? what?

OCTAVIO *(coldly)*:   The title that you wished I mean.

BUTLER *(starts in sudden passion)*:
Hell and damnation!

OCTAVIO *(coldly)*:   You petitioned for it—
And your petition was repelled—Was't so?

BUTLER: Your insolent scoff shall not go by unpunished.
Draw!

OCTAVIO: Nay! your sword to its sheath! and tell me calmly
How all that happened. I will not refuse you
Your satisfaction afterwards. Calmly, Butler.

BUTLER: Be the whole world acquainted with the weakness
For which I never can forgive myself,
Lieutenant-General! Yes, I have ambition.
Ne'er was I able to endure contempt.
It stung me to the quick, that birth and title
Should have more weight than merit has in th' army.
I would fain not be meaner than my equal,
So in an evil hour I let myself
Be tempted to that measure—It was folly!
But yet so hard a penance it deserved not.
It might have been refused; but wherefore barb
And venom the refusal with contempt?
Why dash to earth and crush with heaviest scorn
The grey-haired man, the faithful veteran?
Why to the baseness of his parentage
Refer him with such cruel roughness, only
Because he had a weak hour and forgot himself?
But nature gives a sting e'en to the worm
Which wanton power treads on in sport and insult.

OCTAVIO: You must have been calumniated. Guess you
The enemy, who did you this ill service?

BUTLER: Be't who it will—a most low-hearted scoundrel,
Some vile court-minion must it be, some Spaniard,
Some young squire of some ancient family,
In whose light I may stand, some envious knave,
Stung to his soul by my fair self-earned honours!

OCTAVIO: But tell me! Did the Duke approve that measure?

BUTLER: Himself impelled me to it, used his interest
In my behalf with all the warmth of friendship.

OCTAVIO: Ay? Are you sure of that?

BUTLER: I read the letter.

OCTAVIO: And so did I—but the contents were different.

                                     [BUTLER *is suddenly struck.*
By chance I'm in possession of that letter—
Can leave it to your own eyes to convince you.

                                  [*He gives him the letter.*

BUTLER: Ha! what is this?

OCTAVIO: I fear me, Colonel Butler,
An infamous game have they been playing with you.
The Duke, you say, impelled you to this measure?
Now, in this letter talks he in contempt
Concerning you; counsels the minister
To give sound chastisement to your conceit,
For so he calls it.

[BUTLER *reads through the letter, his knees tremble, he seizes a chair, and sinks down in it.*
You have no enemy, no persecutor;
There's no one wishes ill to you. Ascribe
The insult you received to the Duke only.
His aim is clear and palpable. He wished
To tear you from your Emperor—he hoped
To gain from your revenge what he well knew
(What your long-tried fidelity convinced him)
He ne'er could dare expect from your calm reason.
A blind tool would he make you, in contempt
Use you as means of most abandoned ends.
He has gained his point. Too well has he succeeded
In luring you away from that good path
On which you had been journeying forty years!

BUTLER   (*his voice trembling*):
Can e'er the Emperor's Majesty forgive me?

OCTAVIO: More than forgive you. He would fain compensate
For that affront, and most unmerited grievance
Sustained by a deserving, gallant veteran.
From his free impulse he confirms the present,
Which the Duke made you for a wicked purpose.
The regiment, which you now command, is yours.

[BUTLER *attempts to rise, sinks down again. He labours
inwardly with violent emotions; tries to speak, and
cannot. At length he takes his sword from the belt,
and offers it to* PICCOLOMINI.

OCTAVIO: What wish you? Recollect yourself, friend.

BUTLER: O take it.

OCTAVIO: But to what purpose? Calm yourself.

BUTLER: O take it!
I am no longer worthy of this sword.

OCTAVIO: Receive it then anew from my hands—and
Wear it with honour for the right cause ever.

BUTLER: —Perjure myself to such a gracious Sovereign!

OCTAVIO: You'll make amends. Quick! break off from the Duke!

BUTLER: Break off from him!

OCTAVIO: What now? Bethink thyself.

BUTLER   (*no longer governing his emotion*):
Only break off from him! He dies! he dies!

OCTAVIO: Come after me to Frauenberg, where now
All, who are loyal, are assembling under
Counts Altringer and Galas. Many others
I've brought to a remembrance of their duty.
This night be sure that you escape from Pilsen.

BUTLER   (*strides up and down in excessive agitation, then steps up to*
OCTAVIO *with resolved countenance*):

Count Piccolomini! Dare that man speak
Of honour to you, who once broke his troth.

OCTAVIO: He, who repents so deeply of it, dares.

BUTLER: Then leave me here, upon my word of honour!

OCTAVIO: What's your design?

BUTLER: Leave me and my regiment.

OCTAVIO: I have full confidence in you. But tell me
What are you brooding?

BUTLER: That the deed will tell you
Ask me no more at present. Trust to me
Ye may trust safely. By the living God
Ye give him over, not to his good angel!
Farewell!   [*Exit* BUTLER.

SERVANT (*enters with a billet*):
     A stranger left it, and is gone.
The Prince-Duke's horses wait for you below.   [*Exit* SERVANT.

OCTAVIO (*reads*):
'Be sure, make haste! Your faithful Isolan.'
—O that I had but left this town behind me.
To split upon a rock so near the haven!
Away! This is no longer a safe place for me!
Where can my son be tarrying?

SCENE VI: OCTAVIO *and* MAX PICCOLOMINI.

(MAX *enters almost in a state of derangement from extreme
agitation, his eyes roll wildly, his walk is unsteady, and he appears
not to observe his father, who stands at a distance, and gazes at
him with a countenance expressive of compassion. He paces with
long strides through the chamber, then stands still again, and at
last throws himself into a chair, staring vacantly at the object
directly before him.*)

OCTAVIO (*advances to him*):
I am going off, my son.
        [*Receiving no answer, he takes his hand.*
       My son, farewell.

MAX: Farewell.

OCTAVIO: Thou wilt soon follow me?

MAX: I follow thee?
Thy way is crooked—it is not my way.
       [OCTAVIO *drops his hand, and starts back.*
O, hadst thou been but simple and sincere,
Ne'er had it come to this—all had stood otherwise.
He had not done that foul and horrible deed,
The virtuous had retained their influence o'er him:
He had not fallen into the snares of villains.
Wherefore so like a thief, and thief's accomplice,
Didst creep behind him—lurking for thy prey?

O, unblest falsehood! Mother of all evil!
Thou misery-making demon, it is thou
That sink'st us in perdition. Simple truth,
Sustainer of the world, had saved us all!
Father, I will not, I cannot excuse thee!
Wallenstein has deceived me—O, most foully!
But thou has acted not much better.

OCTAVIO: Son!
My son, ah! I forgive thy agony!

MAX   (*rises and contemplates his father with looks of suspicion*):
Was't possible? hadst thou the heart, my father,
Hadst thou the heart to drive it to such lengths,
With cold premeditated purpose? Thou—
Hadst thou the heart, to wish to see him guilty,
Rather than saved? Thou risest by his fall.
Octavio, 'twill not please me.

OCTAVIO: God in heaven!

MAX: O, woe is me! sure I have changed my nature.
How comes suspicion here—in the free soul?
Hope, confidence, belief, are gone; for all
Lied to me, all that I e'er loved or honoured.
No! No! Not all; She—she yet lives for me,
And she is true, and open as the heavens!
Deceit is everywhere, hypocrisy,
Murder, and poisoning, treason, perjury:
The single holy spot is our love,
The only unprofaned in human nature.

OCTAVIO: Max! we will go together. 'Twill be better.

MAX: What? ere I've taken a last parting leave,
The very last—no, never!

OCTAVIO: Spare thyself
The pang of necessary separation,
Come with me! Come, my son!
                                        [*Attempts to take him with him.*

MAX: No! as sure as God lives, no!

OCTAVIO   (*more urgently*):
Come with me, I command thee! I, thy father.

MAX: Command me what is human. I stay here.

OCTAVIO: Max! in the Emperor's name I bid thee come.

MAX: No Emperor hath power to prescribe
Laws to the heart; and would'st thou wish to rob me
Of the sole blessing which my fate has left me,
Her sympathy. Must then a cruel deed
Be done with cruelty? The unalterable
Shall I perform ignobly—steal away,
With stealthy coward flight forsake her? No!
She shall behold my suffering, my sore anguish,
Hear the complaints of the disparted soul,

	And weep tears o'er me. O! the human race
	Have steely souls—but she is as an angel.
	From the black deadly madness of despair
	Will she redeem my soul, and in soft words
	Of comfort, plaining, loose this pang of death!
OCTAVIO:	Thou wilt not tear thyself away, thou canst not.
	O, come, my son! I bid thee save thy virtue.
MAX:	Squander not thou thy words in vain;
	The heart I follow, for I dare trust to it.
OCTAVIO	*(trembling, and losing all self-command):*
	Max! Max! if that most damned thing could be,
	If thou—my son—my own blood—(dare I *think* it?)
	Do sell thyself to him, the infamous;
	Do stamp this brand upon our noble house;
	Then shall the world behold the horrible deed,
	And in unnatural combat shall the steel
	Of the son trickle with the father's blood.
MAX:	O hadst thou always better thought of men,
	Thou hadst then acted better. Curst suspicion!
	Unholy miserable doubt! To him
	Nothing on earth remains unwrenched and firm,
	Who has no faith.
OCTAVIO:	And if I trust thy heart,
	Will it be always in thy power to follow it?
MAX:	The heart's voice *thou* hast not o'erpowered—as little
	Will Wallenstein be able to o'erpower it.
OCTAVIO:	O Max! I see thee never more again!
MAX:	Unworthy of thee wilt thou never see me.
OCTAVIO:	I go to Frauenberg—the Pappenheimers
	I leave thee here, the Lothrings too; Toskana
	And Tiefenbach remain here to protect thee.
	They love thee, and are faithful to their oath,
	And will far rather fall in gallant contest
	Than leave their rightful leader, and their honour.
MAX:	Rely on this, I either leave my life
	In the struggle, or conduct them out of Pilsen.
OCTAVIO:	Farewell, my son!
MAX:	Farewell!
OCTAVIO:	How? not one look
	Of filial love? No grasp of the hand at parting?
	It is a bloody war, to which we are going,
	And the event uncertain and in darkness.
	So used we not to part—it was not so!
	Is it then true? I have a son no longer.

> [MAX *falls into his arms, they hold each other for a long time
> in a speechless embrace, then go away at different sides.
> The curtain drops.*

Schiller: The Piccolomini

I would say that we should proceed to the perusal of *Wallenstein*," Coleridge suggests, "from *Richard II* or the three parts of *Henry VI*." The Shakespeare play to which *Wallenstein* is most frequently compared is, of course, *Macbeth*. *Great Books of the Western World* provides the texts for the other classic authors who strongly influenced Schiller: Rousseau, Montesquieu, and Kant. His critical essays were a development upon Kant's "Critique of Aesthetic Judgment" (*GBWW*, Vol. 42, pp. 476–549). Two sections of Montesquieu's *Spirit of the Laws* are of special interest: "Of Laws in General" (*GBWW*, Vol. 38, pp. 1–3) and "That the Laws of Education Ought to Be in Relation to the Principles of Government" (*GBWW*, Vol. 38, pp. 13–18).

Discussions of Schiller's twin themes, Liberty and Education, may be found by consulting these ideas in the Syntopicon. The chapters on Art, History, Philosophy, and Poetry discuss the nature of the disciplines in which Schiller worked. His essay "On Simple and Sentimental Poetry" may be consulted in *Gateway to the Great Books*, Vol. 5, pp. 155–211. For a comparison of his views with those of his translator, the reader may look at the prefaces to *The Lyrical Ballads*, which Coleridge wrote with Wordsworth (*GIT*, 1968, pp. 357–380). An eyewitness report on Coleridge on the eve of his translating *Wallenstein* was provided by William Hazlitt, "My First Acquaintance with Poets" (*GGB*, Vol. 5, pp. 264–279). Schiller's biographer, Thomas Carlyle, analyses a problem rooted in *Wallenstein* in his "The Hero as King" (*GGB*, Vol. 6, pp. 110–145).

Picture Credits

—**PAGE 3** (t.) United Press International (b.) The Granger Collection —**4** Ray Moulin of Moulin Studios —**7** George W. Gardner —**9** Elliott Erwitt from Magnum —**11** George W. Gardner —**18-19** Ian Berry from Magnum —**30** © Chicago Tribune —**32** Wide World Photos —**33** Pix —**35** George W. Gardner —**40** Owen Franken —**44** Charles Gatewood —**48** Charles Harbutt from Magnum —**51** Vernon Merritt III from Black Star —**52-53** Bruno Barbey from Magnum —**53** Mark Riboud from Magnum —**56** (t.l.) Gilles Caron from Gamma, Pix —**56-57** (t.) Photo-Graphics, Inc., from Pix (b.) Gamma from Pix —**57** (t.r.) Colin Davey from Camera Press, Pix (b.r.) Orion Press from Pix —**62** Center for the Study of Democratic Institutions, Santa Barbara —**67** Jean Lattes from Gamma, Pix —**69** Elliott Erwitt from Magnum —**72** Joe Molner —**76-77** *The New York Times* —**81** Leonard Freed from Magnum —**86** (t.) Erich Lessing from Magnum (b.) Dennis Stock from Magnum —**86-87** Cornell Capa from Magnum —**87** Burke Uzzle from Magnum —**93** Bruce Davidson from Magnum —**100** Blackstone—Shelburne, N.Y. —**111** Joe Molner —**114-115** Educational Facilities Laboratories, photo: Rondal Partridge° —**115** Educational Facilities Laboratories, photo: George Zimbel —**119** Charles Gatewood —**122** George W. Gardner —**128-129** Charles Gatewood —**138-139** George W. Gardner —**146** University of Minnesota —**155** © Warburg Institute, photo: Helmut Gernsheim —**179** Culver Pictures —**186-187** Ray Atkeson —**196** (t.), (b.) Culver Pictures —**209** The Granger Collection —**217, 218-219** Arthur Leipzig —**220-221, 222-223, 224-225** George W. Gardner —**238** Etienne Gilson° —**276** Mark Van Doren° —**316** © Anselm Filmstrip, Bodleian Library, Oxford —**344** Erich Hartmann from Magnum —**348** The Bettmann Archive —**356** Culver Pictures —**384** National Portrait Gallery, London —**418, 420** (l.) The Granger Collection —**420** (r.) The Bettmann Archive —**424, 427** The Granger Collection —**438** (t.), (c.) The Victoria and Albert Museum° (b.) The British Museum —**444, 448, 456-457, 457, 484, 486-487** The Granger Collection.

The type for this book was set primarily by SSPA Typesetting, Inc., Carmel, Indiana, and the book was printed and bound by Kingsport Press, Inc., Kingsport, Tennessee.

GB

Authors

in Great Books of the Western World

Homer

Aeschylus

Sophocles

Herodotus

Euripides

Thucydides

Hippocrates

Aristophanes

Plato

Aristotle

Euclid

Archimedes

Apollonius

Lucretius

Virgil

Plutarch

Tacitus

Epictetus

Nicomachus

Ptolemy

Marcus Aurelius

Galen

Plotinus

Augustine

Thomas Aquinas

Dante

Chaucer

Machiavelli

Copernicus

Rabelais

Montaigne

Gilbert

Cervantes

Francis Bacon

Galileo

Shakespeare

Kepler